Sir Walter Besant

Ready-money Mortiboy

A matter-of-fact story

Sir Walter Besant

Ready-money Mortiboy

A matter-of-fact story

ISBN/EAN: 9783744723183

Printed in Europe, USA, Canada, Australia, Japan

Cover: Foto ©Suzi / pixelio.de

More available books at **www.hansebooks.com**

READY-MONEY MORTIBOY

A MATTER-OF-FACT STORY

—BY

WALTER BESANT AND JAMES RICE

AUTHORS OF
"THE GOLDEN BUTTERFLY" "WITH HARP AND CROWN" "MY LITTLE GIRL"
"THE CASE OF MR LUCRAFT" "THIS SON OF VULCAN"
"THE MONKS OF THELEMA" ETC.

A NEW EDITION

London
CHATTO & WINDUS, PICCADILLY

LONDON: PRINTED BY
SPOTTISWOODE AND CO., NEW-STREET SQUARE
AND PARLIAMENT STREET

READY-MONEY MORTIBOY.

A Matter-of-Fact Story.

CHAPTER THE FIRST.

MARKET BASING, in Holmshire, there are five or six good houses that were built, some of them eighty, some of them a hundred years ago—in a word, before the town was what it is. They stood there when the linendrapers, grocers, and silversmiths lived over their shops in the main streets, and not in pretentious villas of unenduring stucco scattered along the Hunslope road, as they do now. For in those honest days, strange to say, a shopkeeper kept his shop, and wasn't a bit ashamed of it. And these old houses are tenanted now by persons of the same class as those who occupied them when their bricks were new and red. The one by the church is Lawyer Battiscombe's. It was his grandfather's before him. That house a hundred yards nearer the middle of the town is Mr. Francis Melliship's ; and a mile in Oxford Street and twenty perches in Market Basing mean about the same thing—for in these small towns, a house five steps from your door is in an out-of-the-way place it requires an effort to reach. Read the legend in dingy, gilt relief letters over the door— they were much stared at when first put up, being a novelty from London—MELLISHIP, MORTIBOY, & CO. Melliship's Bank,

B

for there is no Mortiboy in it now. Mortiboy's Bank is at the other end of the street, by the post-office. In many ways, the two banks are wide as the poles apart. At the other end of the town, in Derngate, is another of these old houses. Here lives Mr. Richard Matthew Mortiboy, by the courtesy of Market Basing—when addressing him in writing—styled Esquire, but commonly spoken of as Ready-money Mortiboy.

The reason why, I will tell you presently.

The blinds of two of these houses, from garret to kitchen, are drawn down, and the shutters farthest from the door pushed to.

But at the house in Derngate, the shutters next the door on either side are closed, and two mutes, with vulgar faces and silk covered broomsticks, stand on the steps.

Susan Mortiboy is dead, and is about to be buried in St. Giles's Church; and the mutes stand at her brother's door— one on the right hand, and one on the left, arrayed in funeral trappings, bearing the insignia of their order.

Sentinels of honour, to tell us that the Commander-in-Chief, Death, has himself entered the house, and receives the homage of Respectability, his humble servant, in this wise.

Outside, it is cold January frost: inside, in the parlour, are the mourners. They have a good fire, and are as comfortable as decency on such occasions will allow. Ready-money Mortiboy's parlour is a gaunt, cold room, with long, narrow windows, wire blinds, horsehair chairs, a horsehair sofa, red moreen curtains, and a round table with a red cover reaching to the floor. A decanter of sherry and eight glasses are on it.

The company assembled have not had any of the sherry, but sit looking at it. If one catches another's eye, the one instantly pretends to be intensely occupied with the ceiling, the pictures, the fire, the street view, anything but the sherry. Till, as by a spell, the one's eyes dwell again on the decanter, are caught in the act, and revert with guilty speed to the street view, pictures, fire, ceiling, anything but the sherry.

Mr. Richard Matthew Mortiboy, the chief mourner, stands with his back to the fireplace. He sighs occasionally with creditable emphasis. He intends his ejaculations to be taken for expressions of grief: they really tell of weariness, and a heartfelt wish that it was all over.

He is sixty-three years old, tall, bald-headed, and of spare frame. His black clothes—he was married in the coat—fit him so tightly that, until you were very well used to his appearance your mind would wander into useless speculation as to the ways and means by which he can get into his suits, and once in, can ever get out again.

But those who know old Ready-money well, have discovered that he is one of those human eels who can wriggle out of anything they can wriggle into.

Lydia Heathcote, his niece, sits with the Bible open at the Book of Leviticus, looking at her uncle.

She is his next-of-kin now Susan, his sister, is dead, and old Mortiboy is a millionaire.

Honest John Heathcote, her husband, sits next her. The farmer is the only personage in the company who does not take his eyes off the decanter of wine when he is caught looking at it. He does not think it exactly, but he feels that it is the only pleasant object in the room, and stares straight at it accordingly.

The family lawyer, Benjamin Battiscombe, fills the easy chair.

The family doctor, Mr Kerby, is expected every minute.

Mr. Hopgood, mayor of Market Basing, and linendraper, is present in person, out of respect for the family, in his official capacity of undertaker. His face wears an aspect of melancholy solemnity only one shade less deep than he puts on for a county magnate, deceased—undertaken by Hopgood, Son & Pywell.

George Ghrimes, as Mr. Mortiboy's confidential and managing clerk, and the friend and adviser of Susan Mortiboy, deceased, is present.

And in this goodly company there is one real mourner, Mrs. Heathcote's daughter, Lucy, whose gentle hand smoothed the last pillow of Susan Mortiboy, her aunt.

"Put out to be drunk, I suppose," grunted John Heathcote, with his brown hand on the decanter, to his wife in an undertone. Then aloud, "Shall I give you a glass of sherry, Lydia?"

Mrs. Heathcote objected, but took it.

The ice thus broken, a glass was filled for everybody but the chief mourner.

Up to this time there was no conversation, but its place was to some extent supplied by the tolling of St. Giles's bass bell.

B-ong!—B-ong!—B-ong!—at intervals of half a minute.

Mr. Mortiboy broke the silence.

"What *are* we waiting for?" he asked, with the impatience of weariness.

"We are waiting for Mr. Francis Melliship and Mr. Kerby," said the Mayor.

"Oh-h-h!" sighed the chief mourner, with a look of resignation.

"Francis Melliship all over—eh, Uncle Richard?" said Mrs. Heathcote, feeling her way. "He always is behind at everything. I have often heard my poor mother say that, when you married his sister Emily, he kept you all waiting a quarter of an hour before he came to church to give her away. Ha! ha! ha!"—quickly suppressed: it was a funeral.

But her uncle looked angry at this mention of his marriage to Miss Melliship, and Lydia Heathcote saw her mistake before he growled out in reply—

"Mr. Melliship's cavalier proceedings in private life have not come under my notice for years."

"How long is it since he has been in your house?" asked John Heathcote, bluntly.

"A dozen years, I suppose," said Lydia.

"I'll tell you," said Mr. Mortiboy. "He hasn't been here since my poor wife was buried—sixteen years ago last April."

Omnes. "Ah!"

Lucy Heathcote. "Poor dear aunt—I remember her very well, though I was but a little child. She always brought something over to Hunslope for Grace and me whenever she came to see us. I recollect her little boxes of sweets, and I have got two of her dolls now. Poor Aunt Emily!"

Mrs. Heathcote. "Ah, poor thing!"

Mr. Mortiboy. "She was like all the Melliships since the days of Methuselah—always giving something to somebody that was none the better for being made a fool of, Lu, my girl."

In this particular way Lucy's grand-uncle Mortiboy had never made a fool of his niece.

"We are all older since then," said John Heathcote, who was a slow thinker.

"Mr. Melliship affronted me in a way I shall never forget —though I hope I have forgiven him," said Mr. Mortiboy. He was one of that numerous class of homuncules that think ill, yet speak well.

"Why not be friends, then? I like to see a family all friendly. for my part."

"That is a worthy sentiment, sir," said the lawyer. It was the first opportunity he had had of creeping into the conversation.

"Nobody would ever quarrel with you, John," said his wife, half reproachfully.

"And I quarrel with nobody."

"If they let you alone," said Mr. Mortiboy; "but I was slighted, John. Good—dear me, here is the hearse!" He pulled out his watch. "Ah! I thought as much—we are due at the church now."

"Shall we send round for Francis Melliship, uncle?"

"No, Lydia," said her uncle, with severe irony. "We all of us dance attendance on Mr. Francis Melliship: everybody in Market Basing always has done, since I've known it."

"Don't be hard on a man behind his back," began the farmer.

Mrs. Heathcote shot a glance at him from her dark eyes that meant—"How dare you oppose Uncle Mortiboy?"—but her husband did not choose to see it. He went on, regardless of consequences.

"I have always respected Mr. Melliship. I hope I always shall. And I wish he came to Hunslope oftener than he does."

His wife pinched him viciously. Hers was a difficult part to play. She was very friendly, in her way, with the family at the other bank; but she was Ready-money Mortiboy's nearest of kin.

"My brother-in-law," said Mr. Mortiboy, in tones of satire, "is dressing himself with more than his usual care"—then, in one gruff blast—"and Francis Melliship is the greatest Peacock in Market Basing! I—hate—Peacockery in man or woman!"

Mrs. Heathcote smoothed her crape demurely. She loved it: I don't mean the crape—Dress.

"Farmer-like—eh, John?—for you and me. We are not going to begin Peacocking, I think."

The Mayor's chief assistant now entered with a mournful bow, and proceeded to decorate the chief mourner with a long crape scarf. The chief mourner resented this.

Holding up the scarf, he said, looking at the man—

"What is the meaning of this gewgaw?"

"A scarf, sir—quite usual—at all respectable funerals."

"Always worn, sir," said the Mayor.

"*I* never wore one before," said Mr. Mortiboy, testily. "I

should have stopped the affair at hatbands and gloves, I think. Plain, but respectable. I hate show. Poor Susan, too, never cared for ostentation. Mr. Ghrimes—"

"I left the matter to Mr. Hopgood, sir. He knows better than I do what to do."

"Always our practice, sir," said the Mayor.

"Well, well. Come, put it on then. As they're made, we must have them, I suppose. Poor Susan!"

The old man looked mournfully askant at the great crape rosette at his hip, and at the ends of the scarf dangling about his knees.

He shook his head, and taking from his pocket a sad-coloured silk handkerchief full of holes, he wiped his eyes, but not of tears. There was only one loss Mr Mortiboy would have shed tears over—the loss of money. At sight of his grief, all the company were affected likewise in different degrees. Lucy Heathcote was by his side in an instant. She kissed the old man. At this he wiped his eyes again.

"I have lost all—all—that—were near to me—now," he said.

"Not all, Uncle Richard," put in Mrs. Heathcote, meekly, and hiding her face in turn in her handkerchief.

But the old man never noticed her interruption. He went on—

"There was Emily—gone—taken from me just—as—we knew each—other—well—"

"Oh!—oh!—oh!" sobbed Lydia Heathcote. She had despised poor Mrs. Mortiboy all her life, said every sharp thing she could think of about her behind her back, and would not have called her back again to Market Basing for worlds.

"And Dick—my son—my son! I loved that boy—if—ever—I loved anything—"

His father had turned him out of the house one night—years ago, neck and crop.

"—Goes and runs away from me—and—I'm left alone—now—Susan's—"

He looked up towards the bedroom above.

"Not alone, uncle dear," said Lucy, in a sweet voice. This young thing loved the old hunks himself, and not his money.

The others hung on his words, for he was the greatest man in the town.

Market Basing, town and people, belonged to him—almost. "Wife dead and gone from me." He wiped the unsubstantial tears from his eyes again. "Son dead—and—buried—who knows where? Susan—Susan—gone! I'm an old man. We spent three hundred—at least, Susan did—trying to—find Dick."

"He was a great trouble to you, sir," said the lawyer, who had got Dick Mortiboy out of some nasty scrapes.

"The pocket-money that—boy—had"—here he nearly cried in earnest—"that his aunt Susan gave him. If it was not speaking ill of the dead," said Mr. Mortiboy, "I should say—Susan—spoilt him. She always sided with him against his father. Ah! I've said hundreds of times, 'My boy, Lightly come, lightly go.' He thought nothing of the money he spent. I did not want him to be a spoilt Peacock. She gave him a gold watch and chain the day he was ten years old. I never had one till my father died. I wanted him to be like me. But—it—wasn't to be. People said, 'what you've been all your life getting 'll soon be spent after you're—gone, M-o-rtiboy—'"

Mrs. Heathcote groaned at this picture, and looked hard at her uncle.

"'—After you are—gone—M-o-o-rtiboy.' I used to hope he'd grow up, and alter his ways, and be fond of business, and —all that. But no! Dick's dead—my boy's dead—and—and —I never recollect being separated from Susan before."

"Poor thing! she was such an invalid," said Mrs. Heathcote soothingly.

The old man stared at his niece, but went on without noticing her interruption.

"Ah-h, I—couldn't have said it then, I dare say I couldn't, but I could say it now if I only had—my—boy—Dick—again, 'Let him spend it if he likes.' I could say—when people said to me, 'Mr. Mortiboy, your money will all be spent'—I could say, 'From—all—my—heart.'"

It was quite a physiological curiosity, this heart of his, that he spoke of so feelingly. It was such a very little one.

"'—I could say from all my heart, 'Well, if those that have the spending of it have as much pleasure in spending it as I have had in getting it'"—(here Mrs. Heathcote smoothed her dress, and solemnly shook her head, as if there could be no pleasure to her in spending old Ready-money's hoards; at the same time, she listened with all her ears),—"'I'm a satisfied man.'"

"You can't take yours out of the world with you, any more than anybody else can, I suppose," said Mr. Heathcote.

"John!!" whispered his wife, in a key of the strongest remonstrance.

"No, Heathcote—no," said the old man; "and I don't know that I want. Money's a trouble and an anxiety—and that's all."

A quick step outside; a gentle knock at the hall door.

One second after, Mr. Melliship was in the parlour in the midst of them.

He took his stand close to the table: a fine, handsome man of middle age, whose coat and gloves fitted him perfectly. They bore in their cut the indelible mark of a West-end tailor's skill.

Now, Mr. Melliship was a gentleman, and moved in the best county circles. The others did not, and were afraid of him accordingly. He bowed to them all, but without looking at anybody. His eyes looked straight before him at the wall.

They bowed in return.

Mrs. Heathcote addressed him.

"We began to fear something had kept you, Mr. Melliship, —on this melancholy—"

"Occasion" died away on her voluble tongue.

There was something very strange about the fixed gaze of Mortiboy's brother-in-law.

They all stared where he stared, and found themselves looking at the picture of Susan Mortiboy, painted when she was a comely young woman.

Mrs. Heathcote—irrepressible—recovered herself at once, and translated, in an audible whisper, for the company the thoughts that were passing in Mr. Melliship's mind.

"It is a long time since he was here. He is thinking of Susan, or of his sister Emily. It is a melancholy occasion—"

"I beg your pardon, Mr. Mortiboy," he began. Then pressed his thumb-nail hard against his teeth, and looked at the red cloth.

He gulped down some rising in his throat, made an effort to recover his self-possession, and continued—thrusting his hand into his coat-pocket—

"I—I'm rather absent, I fear. To tell you all the truth, I hardly feel well this morning. I found this to-day. It—it—rather shook me. You will know the writing. I wish it were true."

He handed a yellow scrap of antique letter paper to Mr. Mortiboy.

The old man took it. It was his wife's writing—a voice from the dead—though that was nothing to him. He opened the note; then bursting with anger, turned purple in the face, for he read—

"*THE LATE MR. GASH'S RECIPE FOR REMOVING BALD PATCHES ON THE HEAD:—USE CAYENNE PEPPER AND COD-LIVER OIL, WELL RUBBED IN, NIGHT AND MORNING.*"

Old Ready-money boiled with rage, and gasped for breath.

The top of his own head was as bald as a billiard ball. Trembling violently, he handed the paper in silence to Mrs. Heathcote. She read it with amazement, and stared in expectation, first at her uncle, then at Mr. Melliship.

"Cod-liver oil and cayenne pepper! Good God, man! Years ago—your insult—to me! With my dead sister lying upstairs, have you come here to insult me over her coffin?" roared Mr. Mortiboy, clutching his cravat with his lank fingers.

"I beg your pardon—there must be some mistake here. I am innocent of any intention to insult you."

He took the paper from Mrs. Heathcote, folded it mechanically, and replaced it in his pocket, and stared again at the portrait.

On the others the late Mr. Gash's recipe had fallen like a bombshell.

As a matter of course for a moment there was a slight titter. Old Ready-money was so angry—so bald—and altogether it was so funny, they forgot where they were.

A titter, instantly suppressed.

They looked at Mr. Melliship for an explanation.

And he looked so strange that morning, not one of them dared ask him for it.

So they sat mute.

Meanwhile Mrs. Heathcote and Lucy, with well-meant but unsuccessful endeavours, tried to soothe the old man.

"He's d-r-u-n-k, I firmly believe," her uncle hissed in Mrs. Heathcote's ear; and he cast an angry glance at the man he had for twenty good years treated as a foe.

But there was yet one more outrage on propriety for them to bear.

Francis Melliship advanced—his head up, his chest thrust forward.

Old Ready-money involuntarily shrank from him. He was a coward, and afraid.

Mr. Melliship took another step in advance. Hitherto they had looked at his face, for the table cover had hidden his legs. Now they looked at them.

"Good heavens! Mr. Melliship. Sir——" cried the chief assistant, who had been about to endue the banker with a scarf like the others.

"Mr. Melliship!" exclaimed the lawyer and the mayor in a breath, opening their eyes to their widest.

The old man looked. Lucy looked.

"Merciful goodness!" her mother shrieked; "why, you've got light—ahem!—trousers on!"

The astonishment and confusion you can imagine. if you doubt it, try the effect yourself on a like occasion.

Another knock; slightly louder than Mr. Melliship's had been.

Dr. Kerby entered the room—suave, polite. He began to stammer an apology for being a few minutes late; in fact, "he had been—a—attending Lady——"

"Mr. Mortiboy—Mr. Battiscombe—what is the matter?"

A pause. He looked round, and met Francis Melliship's eyes full.

And he read their meaning.

"Oh-h-h! we are very old friends, and very good friends," he said, linking his arm in Mr. Melliship's; "and, my dear sir, as one of the most amiable and polite men I ever met—a man who never refused me a request—"

"No; my purse is always at the service of the—poor. You mean—the cheque—for the Hospital I said I would—"

"I must ask you for five minutes of your valuable time; and, as a great favour, now—at once."

They walked out arm-in-arm in the direction of Mr. Melliship's house.

As the two left the room, the doctor had looked behind him very significantly.

Then they forgot everything in the strange scene they had just witnessed. The old man all angry—Lucy sorry—the others curious.

"I say he's disgracefully tipsy, at one o'clock in the day,

and the doctor knew it. But, Mr. Francis Melliship, I shall be even with you"—then, in a lower tone, "some day—soon."

The politic lawyer was inclined to assent. True, he did not number among his clients Francis Melliship.

John Heathcote spoke out his mind.

"I think, Mr. Mortiboy, you do Melliship an injustice. Before to-day I have heard of his drinking more than is good for him; but I never believed it. I think he is ill!"

"John?" exclaimed his wife.

"He never meant to insult you or anybody else. He is too much the gentleman to do it."

The old man was getting purple again.

"John!!"—and Lydia pinched him as hard as she could.

Various suggestions were made as to the cause and meaning of this strange conduct of Mr. Melliship's.

All the while, the solution lay neatly folded on the floor.

Lucy's eye caught it. She picked up a crumpled letter in the same handwriting as the recipe for bald spots.

She just glanced at the contents—lest, perchance, she should add fuel to the fire—and handed her uncle a letter in which his wife, Francis Melliship's sister, had tried to heal a family dispute between her husband and her brother with true woman's tact; and hoped and foretold, and prayed too, that they might live in brotherly love for the future.

The old man read it, and frowned over it.

"This is what Mr. Melliship meant to give you, Uncle Richard, I feel sure. He gave you the other by mistake."

Old Ready-money shook his head slowly and incredulously.

"Why did he give me the other, then? He is not sober, that's why."

Everybody else believed Lucy's surmise was true. But this did not explain Mr. Melliship's extraordinary conduct in coming to a funeral without being dressed for one.

The whole thing was a riddle, and they were dying to solve it, but could not.

"Will he come back? Are we to wait?" they whispered.

Now all this had wasted half an hour or more; and the men standing at the door were frozen.

No stress of weather must shake a mute's decorum. So their teeth chattered, and their hands and feet were numbed dead.

A decent servant maid came in, and whispered something in the ear of Mrs. Heathcote. She referred her to her uncle.

But the chief mourner was deaf, and the message had to be

repeated aloud. When he heard it, he exclaimed, with much irritation—

"Hester! Brandy! Who for? The mutes? Now what do mutes want with brandy?"

"They are starved, sir, with the cold," said the chief assistant, "and I thought you might be pleased to send them a little drop before we start. Very sorry to trouble you, but the maid said you had the key."

"Certainly not. They can't require it at such a time. They're paid, I suppose."

"Their teeth, sir, they quite chatter; and Mr. Mopes, he's snivelling with the cold, and can't help himself, poor man. I beg your pardon, sir; but a day like this, mutes will get chilled; and when one's teeth get chattering, it looks like a snivel, hold your silk how you may."

"Then tell him not to snivel, from me. He was before me the other day—he snivelled then. It's a way he's got, I think. God bless my heart—can't they jump about, and keep 'emselves warm? I'd do it."

The revolutionary boldness of Mr. Mortiboy's proposition so utterly staggered the undertaker, that he stood full thirty seconds before he spoke in reply.

"Not well, sir. You see, it isn't usual, sir—with the profession. But I'll tell them what you say."

A grunt.

Enter Hester, the maid, again.

"Dr. Kerby's compliments, sir, and he's very sorry, and neither he nor Mr. Melliship will be able to be present at the funeral. Mr. Melliship's taken ill."

The others wondered very much, and went without them.

Mrs. Heathcote and Lucy spent the time that they were away in settling the nature of Mr. Francis Melliship's complaint.

But they were a long way out in their guesses.

CHAPTER THE SECOND.

FTER the coaches had set the mourners down again at Mr. Mortiboy's house, the funeral party had still two pieces of business to perform.

They had to eat the luncheon provided for them, and to hear the will read.

The question they silently debated was whether Susan Mortiboy—who all her life had spent half her income in works of charity, and the other half on keeping up a house for her brother to live in—had ventured to leave any of her money to anything or anybody but Ready-money Mortiboy by her will. She possessed a sum of twenty-five thousand pounds, left her by her father. This sum her brother at once took out of the Three per Cent Consols for her, and reinvested it at two per cent—grudgingly paid—with himself. As her life was for years considered a bad one—physically—her brother paid the interest over to her for two very good reasons. First, because he thought he should not have to pay it very long; secondly, because she had the absolute power of disposing of the principal by her will.

This led him to regard charitable institutions of all kinds as his natural enemies—though, for decency's sake, he subscribed five guineas a-year to the County Infirmary, and two to the Albert Dispensary. For he felt sure that, if he did not inherit his sister's money, the charities would get it among them.

So, twelve years and two months before our story opens, he availed himself of a fit of indisposition more severe than usual to help his sister Susan to make her will. Now, he had in his library a mischievous octavo volume called "Every Man his own Lawyer," published for one Grantham, in the Strand, and several other worthies of the trade, in the year of our Lord 1826. Out of this he took a form of a testamentary instrument, in which Richard Roe bequeathed to John Doe certain personal property, under certain conditions, set out with all the old-fashioned piety and verbosity common in the wills and testaments of half a century ago. For this will in the book fitted his sister Susan's intentions to a T. Mr. Mortiboy had struggled hard to make her bequeath her property to him absolutely, but she would not consent; so he gave in with a good grace, made her will himself, and saved three or four guineas Lawyer Battiscombe ought to have pocketed. He read it over to her, and she signed it in the presence of Hester Noble, domestic servant, and George Smith, gardener; and Mr. Mortiboy locked it up in his safe till it should be wanted: through having taken effect. And this was it: fairly written out, in old Ready-money's clerkly autograph—

"In the name of God Amen I Susan Mortiboy of Derngate

in the town of Market Basing in the county of Holm spinster being of sound and disposing mind memory and understanding but mindful of my mortality do this second day of December in the year of our Lord eighteen hundred and forty-nine make and publish this my last Will and testament in manner and form following that is to say First I desire to be decently and privately buried in the churchyard of the parish in which I shall happen to die without any funeral pomp and with as little expense as may be—"

"Now, that I perfectly agree with," her brother had said, as he was making a rough draft of the will. "The author? Mr. Gifford. Well, Mr. Gifford, you're a very sensible man. You're just of my mind in the matter. No useless pomp and expense."

At this point in the proceedings, however, the old gentleman's feelings had been grossly outraged, for his sister had put him to the pain of writing the words that gave away four hundred pounds sterling, and made certain little specific bequests of personal effects. Reluctantly, too, he had added—

"And as to all the rest residue and remainder of my estate whatsoever and wheresoever and of what nature kind and quality soever the same may be and not hereinbefore given and disposed of after payment of my just debts legacies funeral expenses and the expense of proving this my Will I do hereby give and bequeath the same to and unto John Heathcote of Hunslope in the county of Holm gentleman and to and unto George Heathcote of Launton Grange in the same county gentleman nevertheless in trust for and to the use of—"

And the trust was this.

The trustees were to hold the twenty-five thousand pounds for twelve years, and then pay it, with the interest accruing thereon, to Richard Matthew Mortiboy, testatrix's brother—if her nephew, Richard Melliship Mortiboy, should not during that time be heard of, or his death be satisfactorily proved. In the event of his coming back, he was to have the money absolutely.

The twelve years had gone. Dick had not turned up, and it was two months over the limit put down in the will.

The money was Mr. Mortiboy's.

So after a little preliminary humming and hawing, he went to the safe, and fetched the will.

"I did not draw that instrument," said Mr. Battiscombe.

"I made it myself," said Mr. Mortiboy.

"The lawyer's best friend is the man that makes his own will—or, for the matter of that, anybody else's."

"Anybody who can read and write, and add two and two together, can make a will, Mr. Ghrimes? I've heard you say so, often enough."

"We shall see," said the lawyer, telegraphing privately under the table to Ghrimes, by treading on his only corn.

"You *will* see, Mr. Battiscombe," replied the old gentleman, proudly. He loved law, and delighted to dabble in high-sounding phraseology, of the technical meaning of which he knew nothing at all.

"I think you might have let me have a finger in the pie, sir."

As he spoke the lawyer telegraphed again to Ghrimes; but the tender toe was gone this time. Mr. Battiscombe's boot only crushed the carpet.

"The Court always carries out a man's clear and obvious intentions. I've known this ever since I could read about a probate case."

"Subject to certain rules, more or less clearly defined, sir. No doubt Mr. Mortiboy has made no mistake—" signalling to Ghrimes again. "At least, I'm sure I hope so."

"The thing's as plain as a pikestaff. Your boy—that sweeps your office—might have put down my poor dear sister Susan's wishes in black and white as well as you could, Mr. Battiscombe."

"Permit me to doubt it, Mr. Mortiboy: as I found out, one day last week, that he can read, but can't write."

"Then it's a scandal to Market Basing; for there—are—no—less—than four charity schools!"

"He came from Hunslope."

"I asked Battiscombe to take him," said Mr. Heathcote. "He's my wife's gardener's boy."

"We can't be expected to teach all Hunslope the three Rs, Uncle Richard," said his niece, apologetically.

"Certainly not, Lydia. Now, I think I may read the—subject of discussion. It is very simple, and ver-y clear—hem!—to my mind."

Old Mortiboy took up his stand near the window. The rest faced round. Ghrimes and Battiscombe exchanged signals again. Having cleared his throat several times, the old gentleman threw himself heart and soul into the business on hand.

He read the will through, from end to end, and nobody made a remark.

"There," said he, looking triumphantly at the lawyer. "I think that is clear enough, even for you, Mr. Battiscombe; and I will say, I have always found you a clear-headed man. The effect is plain, except for those conf—ahem!—legacies. She left her money to Dick—though she knew he was dead when she did it: that was like a woman's obstinacy. And Dick has not come within the twelve years—it's two months over now. And the money's mine—eh, John Heathcote? You see it? You're a trustee?"

Mr. Heathcote made a motion with his hand towards Mr. Battiscombe.

They all looked at the lawyer. He said—

"So far as regards the effect you intended it to produce, Mr. Mortiboy, the will is waste paper, and—"

"Now, Battiscombe, you're a pleasant man, and like your joke, and all that; but I put it to you—is this a time for fun?"

"And I answer—no time for fun. Sir, I will stake my reputation, as your legal adviser, on what I say. The trust takes effect from the death of Miss Mortiboy, not from the making of her will. I should have told you that if you had honoured me with your instructions."

The folios of blue paper dropped from Mr. Mortiboy's hand. He gasped for breath, turned very yellow, and looked faint as a spent stag.

Lydia—quick-witted—recovered herself first: she saw through the matter in a moment.

"Well, uncle," she said, trying to put the best face on the affair, "you'll have the interest for twelve years, and then have the money. It won't matter to you much, I dare say."

She said this quite cheerfully to her uncle.

The old man pointed his trembling finger towards Ghrimes, and shook his head.

The managing clerk had risen from his seat.

"Mr. Mortiboy," he said, "I feel it is time I should speak. Perhaps you will think I have done wrong. My excuse must be that Miss Mortiboy—to whose kindness I owed much all my life—made me do what I did. I—I——There is a codicil to the will you have read."

And as he said this he pulled a folded sheet of paper from his pocket.

Except the lawyer, everybody was alive with interest.

"Go on, Ghrimes," said the old man, hoarsely. "You never deceived me before."

" Miss Susan made us—Mr. Battiscombe and me—promise sacredly we would never mention this to—"
" You never deceived me before—that I know of—young man. But no promise ought to have kept you from coming straight to me. When did—my sister—make a fool of herself, eh ?—eh ? Go on ! "
" The week before she died, Miss Susan called in—"
" You and Battiscombe. Go on! What has she done ? For God's sake, out with it ! "
Briefly told, she had done this. Revoked her bequest to her nephew, Richard Melliship Mortiboy ; given the twenty-five thousand pounds to her brother ; made him sole executor and residuary legatee, and directed him to put a stained window to her memory in St. Giles's Church ; ratified and confirmed the other legacies contained in her will.

The executor's face brightened for one moment when Ghrimes got to the important clause of the codicil.

It clouded again when he heard of the window he was to pay for out of his money.

This subject of complaint lasted him for the rest of the short afternoon, as they sat gloomily over the port and sherry, and the remnants of the funeral collation.

But if he forgot his trouble about the window, it was to recollect his grievance against his sister for not trusting him, and against the lawyer and his confidential clerk for not telling him what was being done.

" She knew I never would have let her have any window or nonsense ; that was it," he said, over and over again.

The truth was, his sister had loved her church, had loved her work at the schools and among the poor, and she did want her memory to dwell among them.

At last—and it seemed a long time in coming—the old man was left alone.

Now, as we know that Mr. Richard Matthew Mortiboy—commonly called Ready-money Mortiboy—is the principal legatee under this codicil to his sister's will ; and as he is a very rich man, and gives the title to this matter-of-fact story, let us here trace his pedigree, and say a word or two about him.

The Mortiboy pedigree is not a long one. There are four generations in it: old Ready-money, his father, his grandfather, and his great-grandfather. Who his great-great-grandfather was, nobody knows.

c

Of the four personages who constitute the trunk and chief branches of the heraldic tree, three lived, thrived, and died at Market Basing; and, at the time our story opens, the last is alive and more thriving than any of his ancestors were: for money gets money. If you have but much, you must, in spite of yourself, have more.

The town of Market Basing is on the high road to the North, at such a distance between two more important places that, in the old days, all the coaches stopped there time enough for the passengers to get down, and eat a meal. So, before railways upset everything on the coach roads, there was no traveller between London and the Land o' Cakes who did not know Market Basing a great deal better than people nowadays know Rugby Junction on the great iron road from London to Liverpool.

The principal inn was the Horse and Jockey; and at this substantial hostelry, the gentleman we will designate Mortiboy the First filled the important though subordinate post of ostler.

Like many other ostlers on the road, Mat Mortiboy had the right of supplying the beasts under his care with his own hay and corn and his master's water. The profit arising from such sale was his perquisite—and a very handsome one it was: and close indeed Mat always was about the savings—which he kept in an old stocking in his hayloft, and in a leathern pocket-book under his coarse shirt.

On the other hand, the proprietor of the Horse and Jockey was proverbially easy as an old shoe: while the servants got fat, the master starved.

In tavern business this is not unfrequently the case

In 1746, times were bad at Market Basing; and when nobody else would lend mine host of the Horse and Jockey the money he stood in sore need of, his ostler, Mat Mortiboy, tumbled two thousand guineas into his lap—at his lawyer's, and took a mortgage deed and covenant for interest at six per centum per annum in return. This + was his signature to the parchment, for he could not write.

Mat was master of the situation now. The innkeeper, old and ruined, died, and Mr. Mortiboy and his fat wife became host and hostess of the principal inn at Market Basing. This worthy couple were sharp as needles, and saving as magpies. They died rich—the widow two days after her husband—leaving every sixpence of their fortune to their only child, Matthew. And here begins the reign of Mortiboy the Second. He married, started a brewery on a good scale, and brought up the only child who lived out of a family of five, what he called a "scholard." In his turn, he died, and was buried; and all he had inherited from his father, with all he had gained and saved added to it, he left to his son. Not one groat's worth to church, charity, or his wife's poor relations.

Then begins the long reign of Mortiboy the Third—"the Scholard." This man was a genius—of the lowest order: your pounds, shillings, and pence, and two and two make four, genius. He cut the Horse and Jockey—taking in his successor smartly; kept the brewery on; sent out travellers all over three or four adjacent counties with his beer, and put half his fortune into Melliship's bank. He became banker, alderman, oracle, and esquire. His union with Miss Ann Ghrimes was blessed with happiness and three children :—

Ann, his firstborn, who married her cousin, Mr. Ghrimes, and became Lydia Heathcote's mother.

Susan, d.s.p.

And Richard Matthew—the first of his race that ever had a two-barrelled Christian name before the patronymic Mortiboy.

The "scholard" smoked his pipe, and drank fourpennyworth of gin and water cold, at the rival house—for he dared not face the poor man at his old inn—and took the best company away with him. One-third of a shilling's worth of liquor lasted him a whole evening. If it did not, he smoked a dry pipe, or helped himself from the blue jug that was at everybody's service, pretended it was gin and water and was just as happy. But he learned a great deal in the parlour of the Angel : who was safe and who was queer; which were the warm men, and which the poor devils out in the cold. And he turned his information to good account—letting Brown overdraw to his heart's content, but pulling his neighbour Smith up short at half a crown.

This man was wise in his generation. He saw that Market Basing would spread itself: so bought every acre of land close to the town that came into the market, and lent money on the rest.

Living in a time that saw what are called "manias," Mr. Mortiboy bought—good value—when all the world about him were red-hot for selling; and sold—bad value—when all bought. He carried out the great Tory statesman's maxim—like many another trader—long before it was put into epigrammatic form. All his life he bought in the cheapest market and sold in the dearest; and he never slept out of his native town a single night, nor wasted a single farthing piece in his life. He lived before tourists were born.

Ann, his daughter, got a thousand pounds down on her wedding day, and all the world grasped Alfred Ghrimes's hand and congratulated him. But his wife died soon after Lydia, their daughter, was born, and he never got another penny from his father-in-law. Indeed, the banker hinted that, after what had happened, he ought to refund the thousand pounds. But Ghrimes was a farmer, and farmers are a good deal "cuter" than the men of cities give them credit for being. He did not hand over the money, and thence arose a mortal feud. He and his father-in-law never spoke again.

So, when the third Mortiboy died, he had two children to leave his fortune to.

He left his daughter Susan twenty-five thousand pounds in hard cash; and the rest, residue, and remainder of his estate, of whatsoever kind and wheresoever situate, to Richard Matthew, his only son.

Ready-money reigned in his father's stead.

The fourth Mortiboy had not a scrap of his father's talent. But he was cautious as the typical Scotchman, greedy as the typical Jew, and cunning as any old fox in a Holmshire cover.

He carried on his bunch one at least of the keys of wealth.

He never spent anything.

He came of three sires who had money and worshipped it as a god, as the only good thing: father, grandfather, great-grandfather. He sucked in the *auri sacra fames* with his mother's milk. He never heard anything talked about in the old house he was reared in, but money,—how to get it, how to keep it, how to put it out to use, and make it breed like Jacob's ewes.

As a baby, his mother checked him when he shook his silver and coral rattle, for fear he should wear out the bells that jingled on it.

He wore calico drawers till his father's trousers fitted him in everything but length.

At school, he was always the boy who regarded a penn'orth of marbles as an investment to be turned into three-half-pence —not played with.

And this, his father told him, if kept up the year round (Sundays left out), was fifteen thousand six hundred and fifty per cent. per annum. And the boy entered into this great fact, and understood it; worked it out on his slate, and kept it up in apples, pegtops, tennis balls, and other commodities, when marbles were out and these things in.

So he grew up, and was initiated early in life into the mysteries of keeping a country bank. And when you once are on the inside of the counter, you find there is no mystery in it at all.

It consists in getting hold of as much of other people's money as ever they will leave with you, and putting it out, by way of earning interest for your own benefit. In lending an apple or two where you know there is an orchard; but not so much as a seedling pip where there isn't one.

In his father's time, Melliship, Mortiboy & Co. had split. The Melliship of the day started a new bank; and Ready-money's father kept the old one to himself, continuing to trade under the old style and title. Then, besides the bank, he had the brewery—a sound, prosperous concern, that only troubled him twice a year : to take the profits.

The Holmshire iron is not bad stuff for working up when mixed with Staffordshire pig. A clever man, named Hardinge, found this out and mortgaged his estate for thirty thousand pounds to work the ore in the stone that lay under nearly every field.

But it was not enough. He applied to Mr. Mortiboy, and mortgaged his foundry and his plant, and further encumbered his estate. More money was wanted, and Mortiboy would lend no more. A few thousands would have made the works a fortune to him. But the banker pulled up short, and nobody dared "stand against Mr. Mortiboy," though a dozen would have formed a company and found the money. Mr. Mortiboy foreclosed. Mr. Hardinge died of a broken heart; and works, plant and estate, were the mortgagee's.

Ghrimes, a man of hard and sound judgement, managed everything. He was Ready-money Mortiboy's factotum, and was incorruptibly honest. Even his master could trust George

Ghrimes, and he did. He would have let him dip his hands in treacle, and put them into a bag of Koh-i-noors in the dark and never felt a qualm. But for this weakness he conceived it his duty to distrust everybody else. He made this vice—in his own eyes—a virtue. He did not believe in any honesty but the honesty of paying what perforce you must pay. And by himself and his standard he gauged all other men, and thus suspected everybody—his sister, his niece, his clerks, his servants, his customers.

So in Market Basing the charitable called him eccentric— the malicious a miser. Small towns develop character.

You can see in a tumbler what you fail to observe in a vat.

Mr. Mortiboy was usually called "Old Ready-money." There were half a dozen anecdotes about the origin of the so- briquet. Who wouldn't like to have it? This was the commonly received version :—There had come to Market Basing parish church a new parson, and his wife had come with him. Proverbially, new brooms sweep clean, and the parish was in an awful state of heathenism; so she, poor thing, bent on all sorts of good works, called first—subscription-book in hand—on Mr. Mortiboy, their richest parishioner. She did not know he went to chapel. She encountered a shabby man in the bank—on the doorstep, indeed.

" Is Mr. Mortiboy in ? "

" My name, ma'am—at your service."

They stood on the pavement outside.

The rector's wife opened her eyes, and took him in from top to toe in a glance—as a quick woman can.

" Are you Mr. R. M. Mortiboy, sir ?—Mr. Rob—"

" Ready-money Mortiboy, ma'am."

So the tale is told. I don't know if this is the true version; but the old man carried his nickname to his grave, and never was called anything else—behind his back.

He was the last man in the world to be asked for alms. Polite enough, but hard as nails. He had a formula of his own invention, applicable to all occasions.

If anything was wanted for Market Basing—he was the greatest victim of the poor rates.

If flannels and New Testaments were to be given to the starved niggers of Quashiboo, he thought the stream of charity should be turned on the hungry and houseless ones at home.

But if anybody made a call on him for these, he was in- stantly impressed with the importance of foreign missions.

For both—he was a little deaf, and times were bad, and his interest in changes of the weather absorbing.

Now when his guests were gone, and he was alone, his sister's charge concerning the stained glass window preyed on Mr. Mortiboy's mind. It was all very well for a bishop, in a cathedral—where there are plenty of windows, and plenty of money—to have a memorial window put up to his memory; but, in his sister Susan, such an injunction was an outrage of propriety. Old Ready-money had very clear notions on his own station in life. And, after all, a parish church had no business with coloured windows. At chapel, they did without them. And then, his sister's station was not high enough for memorial windows.

"I'll take Battiscombe's advice about it if it's down in the bill, 'thirteen and fourpence—engaged a long time.' If I can get out of such an absurd direction, I will. What will people say? Very likely, think *I* did it—and think I'm mad into the bargain. It's just the sort of thing Francis Melliship would go and do, now. Put up a stained glass window! She should have left it—poor thing!—to her Sunday-school teachers and parsons, that have had her money for years, to do that for her! They would have done it, no doubt!"

Mr. Mortiboy quite chuckled at this humorous idea. His face suddenly changed, however, from gay to very grave.

The four candles lighted for his guests were burning on the table!

He quickly blew out three, quenching the last spark of fire at the wick ends with a wet forefinger and thumb—avoiding smell, and possible waste.

Then he held up the decanters to the solitary candle, and measured their cubic contents of port and sherry with his greedy eye.

Next, he took the candle up in his shaky old hand, walked slowly round the table, and collected the glasses.

"Ghrimes has left half his last glass. Well, George Ghrimes never did drink anything, so I'm not surprised."

He poured the half-glass of port back into the bottle.

"Lydia, my girl, you'll"—holding the glass Mrs. Heathcote had used upside down—"get—red—in the—face—like your mother was, if you don't take care."

At last he got to Lawyer Battiscombe's seat.

"Ah! I thought so. Trust a lawyer. Not a drop, if you squeezed the glass for a week."

Then he sat down by the fire, took a lump or two of coal off, and put his feet on the fender. He sat in his easy chair, in thought. Wondering what they would have thought if they had seen him pouring the wine back into the decanters; —thinking he should not have cared a rush if they had. Wondering whether Lydia Heathcote counted on his death; —thinking she was not quite sure of his money yet. Wondering why his sister Susan could not have left him all her money; —thinking he would do his best to defeat her intentions, and secure the odd hundreds he had neither a legal nor moral right to. Wondering why he felt so drowsy;—thinking—

He was fast asleep.

He slept an hour, and the candle burnt down two inches and a half before he was awakened.

His sister's maid had brought in the tea-tray at the usual hour, and her entrance roused her master.

He woke with a start: counted the biscuits on the dish, and questioned the girl in a breath.

"Was I asleep? Ah!—four—I didn't take—six—my nap —eight—to-day: that's it. Never get into—I'm sure, I thought I made nine of 'em before—bad habits, Mary."

"No, sir,"—and exit.

"The minx had had time to have one, I believe. They think they'll take advantage of me; but they're mistaken. They won't."

He got up, fumbled for his keys, and put away the wine and biscuits in the cupboard by the fireplace.

Then he walked to the window, and looked out into the night. It was dark—the moon had not risen; but the street lamp opposite his door threw a good deal of light into the room.

He blew out his last candle.

"If I'm only thinking—and, goodness knows, I've plenty to think of—I can think quite as well without a candle. Besides, this room is always light."

He never touched his tea, but sat musing till he dozed off again.

When he woke, his fire was out, his legs were cramped, and it was a quarter to nine by his watch. He pulled the bell.

"What a thing habit is! Because I don't happen to have twenty minutes' sleep in the afternoon, I waste the whole of a precious evening."

"Shall I lay the cloth here, sir?"

"No. Certainly not. I shall take my supper in the kitchen when you're gone to bed. Tell Hester and the cook to come to me."

Dressed in black gowns, and with their aprons ready for their eyes, the servants waited his commands. They found him sitting with a little housekeeping book of his sister's in his hands. They thought Mr. Mortiboy was about to improve the occasion. But they had misjudged him. He was going to discharge them.

"Habit is a curious thing," he began, pouring out a cup of the cold tea, and sipping it appreciatively. "I missed my usual little nap on the stairs to-day, and I have wasted a precious evening—a pr-e-ci-ous evening through it."

The corners of the white aprons dropped. The three domestics waited for him while he took another sip of his tea.

"I ought to have done this earlier; but thoughts of her who is gone"—he looked upwards—"kept me from it."

The aprons up again, ready for use. Hester, a very old retainer, in real tears.

"You've heard me called eccentric?"

"Oh! no, sir!"—mumbled.

"You've heard 'em call me old Ready-money?"

"Oh! no, sir!"—very loud.

"Yes, you have. You were—Susan's—servants, not mine. You've heard me called rich, now?"

"Yes, sir."

"Well, I should not have been called rich if I had spent all my money like my poor sister did. One servant will be quite as many as I shall want." Aprons dropped again.

"Hester, you can do all I shall require. So, cook and Mary, my girl, I really must give you notice, for I can't keep you. But I can give you excellent characters, both of you."

"Thank you, Mr. Mortiboy," said the cook—facing him, with arms a-kimbo—"thank you, Mr. Mortiboy; but my mistress, as I lived with four year and three-quarters—come Michaelmas was five years—would do that for me any day. And I've only been here four months, which—"

"I have given you notice," Mr. Mortiboy interposed. "I shall not keep you your month. I shall pay your wages instead."

He was getting angry.

"Thank you, sir. Which is the law, and rich and pore must both abide by it"—dropping a most irritating curtsey.

"I'll pay you now!" cried Mr. Mortiboy.

"If you please, sir; and I'll pack up my boxes this very night, and go. For I couldn't abear—"

Poor little Mary, frightened out of her wits, tugged at cook's gown.

"Don't pull me, Mary. Mr. Mortiboy never was my master —and never shall be."

"I'll take your black dress away from you if you say another word."

"No, sir—'xcuse me, that'll go with me to my next place; and I shan't trouble you for a character. And I *have* heard you called old Ready-money, and called you so mysel—"

Before she could finish her sentence, the ruler of the roast was dragged out of the room by Hester and Mary.

An hour and a half later, Mr. Mortiboy had recovered from his discomfiture, paid the cook, and seen her and her baggage off the premises, and sent Mary and Hester to bed.

He sat before the kitchen fire, eating a slice of cold boiled beef laid on a crust of bread. He dispensed with a plate and fork, but had a very sharp knife in his hand.

He cut his mouthfuls into equal parallelograms, with mathematical precision, and slowly got through his frugal supper.

He rose from his chair, unfastened the door, and looked out into his garden.

The moon was up, but heavy clouds obscured it every moment, drifting swiftly past.

An idea had for half an hour held possession of his mind. He was going out.

To pay a visit to the churchyard.

To find out for himself really which was the smallest window. The will said nothing about the size.

He found his great-coat hanging in the passage, without a light.

He fumbled at the latch and bolts of the front door, and let himself out.

The moon shone brightly on it and him; and he saw in chalk characters,

"*OLD REDDY-MUNNY IS A MIZER*"

scrawled on it.

"Now this is too bad—to-day," he exclaimed, producing from his inner coat pocket the sad-coloured handkerchief full of holes. "I must wipe it off. What is the good of a policeman? I'd give—I'd give—a—a shilling to know who does it, and hang the little devils for it too."

He rubbed the writing off his door, and went on his way. His house opened on the street. Across the street was a paddock. The field belonged to him. He had a key, and let himself in.

This close was a little gold mine to him. It was the arena on which all flower-shows, agricultural and horse shows, wild-beast shows, and riders' circuses were held.

A few sheep started as he crossed the wet grass at the side by the church.

In the churchyard, the clouds hid the moon, and hid the ponderous figure that had dogged him there—from his house door, over the paddock wall, into the grave-yard.

The old man went on.

"The moon gone in? But I'm not superstitious. I'd as soon sleep in a churchyard as anywhere else," he said to himself as he groped his way round the south wall of the church. "Ha! light again!"

The man behind him dropped three or four paces back.

Not a sound was heard in the deep wet grass.

"Now we shall see what we are at. There is a smaller window than this though, I know—and this is not a big one. I should have made a first-rate window-peeper in the old tax days.

"Ha! this is the window I had in my eye. Now could it cost ten pounds to put in a beau—u—tiful window there?"

The moon was clouded again, and his attendant gained on him. There was a corner between them that was all.

"Be whipped if I think it could cost ten pounds. Eight ought to do it."

The man came nearer. His arm was raised.

"No mention of which window you meant to have, Susan, my poor dear sister. Ha! ha! Ghrimes was taken into your confidence, not your own flesh and blood."

Nearer still the arm came. It almost touched him.

"Well, now, I've been all round the church, I think. I'll go back, or I shall go and catch cold in this grass. It's like a little river. D—n! What's this?"

He had stumbled over some hard substance in his path.

The moon shone out brightly, and showed him the footstone of his wife's grave. He had not been near it for years.

He read the inscription on the headstone in the bright moonlight.

"Want's doing up a bit," he muttered.

The man who was dogging him was close at his back.

"There's room for Dick's name now, if we had heard about him. But no, poor fellow—no!—I think I'll go in again now. I feel chilly—I—".

As he spoke, a hand like a blacksmith's fell on his shoulder, and held him in a vice!

CHAPTER THE THIRD.

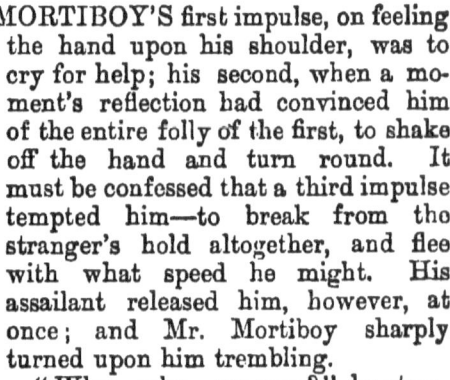

MORTIBOY'S first impulse, on feeling the hand upon his shoulder, was to cry for help; his second, when a moment's reflection had convinced him of the entire folly of the first, to shake off the hand and turn round. It must be confessed that a third impulse tempted him—to break from the stranger's hold altogether, and flee with what speed he might. His assailant released him, however, at once; and Mr. Mortiboy sharply turned upon him trembling.

"Who—who—are you?" he stammered.

It was a figure he did not know; that of a tall strong man, warmly wrapped in a thick pilot jacket, with a stout stick in his hand, and a round felt hat upon his head. As the moon came out by fits and starts between the flying clouds, Mr. Mortiboy made out, besides these details, a thick black beard, which covered all the face from the eyes downwards, and hid a foot or so of throat and chest.

"Old Mr. Mortiboy, I think you are?" said the stranger, in a rough harsh voice

"Mr. Mortiboy certainly—and perhaps old. Pray, who are you, and what do you want?"

"I want to speak to you. Come out of this mouldy old churchyard, and go home. I will walk with you."

"You can come to-morrow to the bank. That is where I receive strangers."

"I shall do nothing of the kind. I shall go home with you now. So as soon as you've done your business—whatever that may be—in this convivial gathering-place, we'll go on together to Derngate."

"Is it business you want to see me about?"

"I suppose you don't have many evening callers for pleasure —do you, Mr. Mortiboy?"

"I do not. I am not one who wastes his time in gossiping with people."

"Not had many parties since your son went away, I suppose?"

Mr. Mortiboy laid his hand upon the stranger's arm.

"My son! Did you know my son Dick? Can you tell me anything about him?"

"Go on home, and I will tell you all I know."

"It's twelve years and two months," growled Mr. Mortiboy to himself—"twelve years and two months, yesterday. I wonder if he'll tell me what became of the boy."

He led the way home: not by the paddock, through the streets—a way the stranger seemed to know pretty well, as he swung along the street by the side of him, great-shouldered and burly, looking up at the names over the shops, as if he was trying to read them; nodding his head, too, with a certain air of recognition, as they passed the public-houses.

But it does not take long to exhaust the streets at Market Basing; and the pair found themselves in a very few minutes on the steps of Mr. Mortiboy's house.

"Still live here, eh?" asked the stranger.

Mr. Mortiboy, not without a certain feeling of uneasiness, opened the door, and admitted his guest. The hall was perfectly dark, and he bade him wait while he struck a light. To his terror and amazement, the stranger, who evidently knew where things stood, deposited his hat on the hat-stand and his stick in the umbrella-stand. Now this familiarity with places in a perfect stranger, and in the dark, savoured of the supernatural; and though Mr. Mortiboy was not a superstitious or a nervous man, he trembled slightly, and looked over his shoulder at his visitor, as he led the way to the parlour.

As he peered curiously at him, he could not help thinking of the devil.

It was the room which had been the scene of the will-reading. There was no fire; and only the one bed-room candle which Mr. Mortiboy carried in his hand.

The stranger—he was visible now—was a man who seemed about thirty-two or three years of age. His black curling hair was crisp and short; his figure was tall and muscular; his forehead was broad and square; and his eyes had a sort of fierce light about them which might mean many things.

Mr. Mortiboy raised the candle, and coolly held it before his face while he scrutinised him. He put it down after his inspection, which the stranger bore without flinching.

"I don't know you. What do you want with me? And what have you got to tell me?"

"You do not know me?" asked the other.

"I do not, sir. And, to tell the truth, I hardly want to know you; for I mistrust the look of you."

His visitor reached out his hand, and seized a decanter with a glass of wine left in it.

"It's a cold night, and with your leave—" he smelt it, and put it down with a shudder of disgust. "Sherry. No, thank you. But haven't you got a fire anywhere? Isn't there one in the kitchen?"

Mr. Mortiboy stared at him with amazement. What had this familiar stranger to do with his kitchen? It was a lonely house, and he began to think of violence and midnight marauders.

"If we have business, it will be short, I suppose, and you can transact it in this room, cold or not, just as well as in the kitchen. Sit down, and say what you have to say, and go."

"We have business; but it is so long that I shall probably stay here all night. Take the candle, Mr. Mortiboy, and we will go to the kitchen, where you generally sit when Hester goes to bed. Follow me. I know the way."

He took the candle; and, going into the hall, turned to the left.

The old man went after him as he strode out of the room, and clanked in his great boots along the passages—which he seemed to know well enough—in great wonderment and not a little terror. But how was he to disobey a man so big and so masterful—a man too, who knew the house as well as he did himself?

There was a bright fire in the kitchen, and the strange visitor sat down, and warmed himself.

"It is twelve years," said the stranger in a deep bass voice, "since your son Dick ran away;—since, rather, you turned him out of the house."

"Twelve years and two months. Twelve years and two months, yesterday."

"Hang your two months. You have never heard from him since he left you?"

"Never."

"Would you like to hear from him again?"

"If I knew he had been doing well. If it was to hear that the promise of his youth had been broken, I should like to hear of him."

"Would you like, then, to hear that your son Dick, very early in his history after leaving you, saw the many errors of his ways, and reformed; that he became steady, industrious and respectable; that, in short, he got money, and is, consequently, much revered and respected by all good men?"

"I should. Good heavens, man, if this is what you have to tell me, be quick about it!"

"First, Mr. Mortiboy "—he had spoken throughout in a rough, constrained voice—" I have had a longish journey, and have caught a cold. Give me a glass of brandy."

"Brandy—brandy! It's what the confounded undertakers asked for this morning. I am sorry that I have no brandy at hand, sir. Would you like some gin?"

The stranger nodded. Mr. Mortiboy went to a cupboard which he unlocked, and took out a bottle and a wine glass. Before handing it to his guest, he held it up to the light, and then measured the contents by the length of his finger. It was two joints over the length of the middle finger. He shook his head; and muttering, "I'm half afraid she's found the way to the cupboard," poured out a glass cautiously, as if it had been the finest Chartreuse. His visitor tossed it off quickly; and, taking the bottle from his hands, filled a second glass, and tossed that off. Then he sat down, and meditated for a few moments: Mr. Mortiboy watching him with his hands on his knees. The old man's nature was stirred up by the mention of his son's name. Old hopes, old affections, old

memories rose again in his heart, where they had been silent
and buried for more than half a score of years.

"Tell me about Dick," he said impatiently, drumming his
heels upon the floor.

The stranger stood up and half bent over him.

"I am Dick," he said softly and in his natural voice.

Mr. Mortiboy leapt up as if he had been shot. He seized
the candle again, and held it to his face. He peered in his
eyes. He looked again. Then he put down the candle, and
answered in a quavering voice, almost in the words of Scripture—

"The eyes are the eyes of my son Dick, and the voice is
his voice. But I do not know him—I do not know him.
Dick was not so tall; Dick was smooth-faced; Dick was
afraid of me. You are not Dick, sir. You are some impudent
impostor, trying to cheat me out of a few pounds because you
know that I want my son Dick to come back again. That I
want him," he repeated, piteously. "I want him."

"Dick was nineteen when you turned him out of your
house, and bade him darken your doors no more. It is no
great wonder if his face *was* smooth; and I think you will
remember, if you reflect, that you gave him ample cause to be
afraid of you."

"Prove to me—prove to me—that you are my son; my
own son!"

The old man's spare, thin form—almost as tall as his son's
—shook with emotion and excitement, and he stretched out
his arms in a sort of wild yearning.

"Shake hands, father, and sit down, and I will tell you
everything."

He held out both hands frankly.

Mr. Mortiboy took one hand timidly, and kept it in his,
patting it coaxingly.

"Tell me something," he said—"the smallest thing—to
prove that you are really Dick."

The stranger put his hand into his breast pocket, and took
out a little roll.

"When your son left your house, did you tell any one the
reason why you turned him out in disgrace?"

"No one to this day knows the reason but Dick and myself. Whisper it."

"Then—is no one listening?—I will tell you. He was not
extravagant, but he wanted money from time to time—as all

young men will. His aunt Susan gave him a little. You gave him none. He forged a cheque: it was only for five pounds. But—he forged it! Have you got that cheque?"

"It has never left my pocket-book."

"Take it out, then. I am going to have it back again. You paid the money, and you told him that you would never forgive him—that you would never see his face again."

"I did—God forgive me!—I did."

"You did. You wrote him a letter to London, in answer to his. Here is the letter. I will read it. You remember that it was very short?

"'Your father sends you the enclosed ten pound note. Go, and retrieve your character.'

"Is not this the letter?"

The old man took it with trembling hands

"It is," he cried—"it is. And you are really Dick?"

"Stay. Let me finish. The ten pounds and the five pounds make fifteen. Suppose we say that this sum had accumulated at compound interest for twelve years: it would by this time have amounted to twenty-six pounds, eighteen shillings, and perhaps a penny or so over. Here are twenty-six pounds, eighteen shillings, and sixpence, which I propose to give you, in return for the cheque."

He took the money out of a small bag, into which it had been counted, and poured it on the table.

Mr. Mortiboy counted it over again carefully; but this was habit. Then he took out from a pocket-book—one of those flat leather books, bursting with papers, which suggest all sorts of things to do with investments—an envelope.

It was labelled, grimly enough, "The last of Dick." In it was an old cheque, stamped and initialled by the clerks of the bank. He handed it across, and waited in silence.

His visitor read it, put it in the fire, and went on.

"So far we are quits. You have your money back. But our quarrel has yet to be made up. By the way, do you remember my falling into the fire when I was a boy, and burning my arm? See here!" He drew up his sleeve, and showed a small, deep scar in the left arm. "One does not imitate these things."

"*You are Dick,*" cried his father. "I know you now. I knew you, really, directly you spoke in your old voice. But everything else has changed in you. And you are so big."

D

"Will you shake hands?"

His father shook hands with him—but not, as yet, quite cordially. In his mind—the moment he found it was his son, and no other who had come back to him—arose a feeling which jarred upon and was discordant with the natural joy of his heart: a suspicion that perhaps he had only come to borrow money—or, worse still, to live upon him. Parental affection was nipped in the very bud by the prospect of fresh expense, like the apple blossoms by an east wind.

"Go on Dick—tell me about yourself."

"No. Tell me first about yourself."

"I am well—I am well. Not much better off it's true; but bodily, well."

"And my aunt?"

"Dead, Dick—dead. She died last week, and was buried to-day. And oh, Dick, Dick—what a pity you did not come home a week sooner!"

"Why?"

"Because, if you had, you would have come in for all her money. As it is, I have it—I have it. Not much it is true; and saddled with all sorts of vexatious bequests. A hundred here, and a hundred there, and a memorial window to put up. Dear, dear; what a waste—what a waste!"

"A memorial window?—ho, ho! In the church?—ha, ha! But we'll have a cheap one, father—we'll have a cheap one. I know the way to set about getting painted glass at cost price."

"Do you?" asked his father, eagerly. "Tell me how."

"Matter of business, my dear sir," answered the son, with an air of importance. "We must see our way in other things first. And so the poor old lady's dead! Well, I'm sorry."

"And what have you been doing with yourself?"

"Do you want me to give you the history of twelve years? That will take more than one evening's talk. As many evenings, perhaps, as I shall be with you."

"Why, Dick—why? You are not going away directly you come home, are you?"

"Business may take me. I've got my affairs to look after."

Mr. Mortiboy brightened up; and his fatherly affection, relieved of the cold wind of doubt, glowed and flamed in his heart, till he was fain to rise from his chair, and seize his son's hand, which he shook for several moments with every sign of lively emotion. Then he poked the fire, and took up the gin bottle.

"Dick, on such a night as this, we must drink our own healths. Shall it be port—they did not drink it all—or shall it be brandy?"

"Brandy, father, for me."

Mr. Mortiboy retired with the one candle, and presently returned, bearing a bottle of brandy, which he opened with great care and ceremony.

His son had lit a short wooden pipe, and was smoking as quietly as if he had never left his native land.

"I always have one pipe, and a glass of something," said his father. "And since poor Susan was taken, I mean to get rid of everybody but old Hester, and she goes to bed at eight. I send 'em to bed early. So that we are quiet and to ourselves down here. Now, talk to me, Dick."

Dick took a long pull at the brandy and water.

"Where am I to begin? Let me see. Well, when I left England, which was not very long after I left you, I went first to the Cape, where I tried my hand up country at sheep and sheep-farming. But it was poor work. No money to be got, be as careful as you please. Got tired of that. Went to America. Went to the Californian diggings, and did pretty well. Went prospecting to Mexico—"

"What's 'prospecting,' Dick?"

"Looking for silver. Found plenty, of which I will tell you another time. Then the American war broke out, and then I had a grand stroke of luck; for I took up blockade-running."

"No—did you really, though, Dick?—did you really?" The old man's eyes sparkled with satisfaction "There was money to be got there."

"There was, and we got it. But that came to grief at last. We ran the good little craft ashore—here's to her memory—and lost her. Then—to make a long story short—we realized our investments, bought a cotton estate of three thousand acres, and have been doing well enough ever since."

"And you're really worth money, my boy?"

"Worth—well, I don't know how many thousands, that's a fact; because we haven't reckoned up for the best part of two years. But we've got money; and here I am—ready to invest some of it by your advice, if you like to help me in that way."

"Then you're welcome, Dick"—Mr. Mortiboy held out his hand this time with real cordiality—"you're welcome, my boy; and I will help you to invest it."

"So you shall, sir."

"And—and—you haven't taken to drinking, Dick, and are quiet, I hope? Because I have a very quiet house here—very quiet and retired—and could not change my habits."

"As for my habits, a mouse couldn't be quieter. You'll let me smoke, I suppose?"

"Yes."

"And as for drink—let me have a glass or so of grog, of an evening—gin and water—anything—and, as long as I stay with you, I shall be contented. Let us save money, at any rate."

"Well said—well said. Now, look here, Dick. I allow myself a bottle of gin a-week. We will have two bottles between us. Is it a bargain?"

"It is."

"And we could share the expense—extra expense, I mean —between us, Dick."

Richard Melliship Mortiboy—*i.e.* Mr. Mortiboy, junior— looked at the author of his being with an amused twinkle in his eye.

"We shall not quarrel about that. And so long as I am here, I shall be able to help you about the bank, and all the rest of it. Not for nothing, you know."

"Assuredly not for nothing. And you can tell me about the blockade-running, and how the money was got. Any of it come home with you, Dick?"

"Some of it—a little—is in London. The rest is in Mexico ; safely invested."

"Oh! in Mexico. But that's a long way off."

"Only four weeks. That's where the estate is. You can't bring the land away, you know."

"Ah! no. Dick, I am glad you've come back. Be a credit to me, and—and—there's no saying what may not turn up. But, oh! Dick, what a pity you did not turn up seven days ago, in time to get your poor aunt's money."

"And so you went to the churchyard to-night."

"I was passing, by the merest accident in the world; and it just occurred to me that I would turn in, and see what would be the properest window—the best, you know, for the memorial of your aunt."

"Not quite by accident, father. I followed you," said his son. "I'd pick out the smallest."

"No! Would you, though? Would you really, Dick? Don't you think people would talk? I did think of it, it's true."

"Let 'em talk! And now, governor, that we're all friends again, let us have one more go of brandy and water, and I'll light another pipe; and we'll have a talk about old times."

They talked till a very late hour for Mr. Mortiboy. And then Dick asked where he was to sleep.

"Lord!" replied his father, "I never thought of that. There's only my bed and your poor aunt's. The spare beds are not made up and ready."

"Well, she's gone, you know. So I suppose I can have that?"

"If you don't mind."

"Mind? Not I indeed. Put me anywhere. I once slept in the bed of a man who had been bowie-knifed in it the night before, and was none the worse for it. Mind? Not I. It's the old room, I suppose?"

"His father led him to the room. Dick gave a look of approval round it, and proceeded to undress. Round his waist was a heavy belt, which he threw on the table with a crash.

"What's that?"

"Some of the 'ready,'" he said. "Some of the stuff that we're all so fond of. Gold, father—gold!"

"Dick," said Mr. Mortiboy, solemnly, "I'm *very* glad you've come back. And more glad still, that you've come back with so much right principle."

He went away, and his son went on with his toilette

Mr. Mortiboy came back, and put his head in at the door.

"Don't waste the light, Dick. You're burning one of your poor aunt's waxes. I like to see all the lights out before I get into bed myself."

"All right, governor," said his son, blowing it out. "The old chap's the same as ever," he muttered. "Damn his bottle of gin a week. I think the compound interest showed true repentance, though."

In three minutes he was sleeping the sleep of the virtuous. And this is how Dick Mortiboy came home again.

CHAPTER THE FOURTH.

R. MELLISHIP and Dr. Kerby after they left Mr. Mortiboy's house on the morning of the funeral, walked to the bank—the doctor leading the other gently by the arm. They entered at the private door, and the banker led the way to his study, where he sat down and leaned his head on his hand.

"Still the same symptoms?" asked the doctor.

"Still the same. I forget what I am doing. You see how I have offended everybody this morning. My mind is dwelling perpetually on one subject."

"What is that?"

"Money, my friend, money. My brain seems troubled at times, and I hardly know whether the thing I am thinking of is real, or only the vision of a disordered fancy. Can your medicine do nothing to relieve me?"

"Have you been trying no medicine of your own?"

The banker sighed.

"I have not been able to keep my hands from the brandy."

The doctor shook his head gravely, and said nothing for a while.

"You must go away, you know. I told you so months ago. You must have complete rest and change for three months at least."

"As well talk of rest and change for three years."

"My dear old friend—the human brain is not like an iron machine. You can't work it for the whole period of your natural life without rest. You must take a holiday."

"I cannot—yet, doctor."

"If I speak as your doctor, I must say professionally—then get some other advice than mine. But let me speak as a friend, and say, for God's sake take a holiday, or something evil will happen to you."

"What, doctor—what?" asked Mr. Melliship, eagerly.

But his adviser put the question by.

"There are all sorts of mischief—to brain, to stomach, to heart—wrought by long and continuous work. Let us avoid them all by taking a holiday."

Mr. Melliship hesitated. Then he took up an almanack, dotted with memoranda.

"If I cannot trust my memory, I can trust these," he murmured. "I shall be comparatively free in a fortnight, doctor. I promise you that, if I possibly can, I will take a holiday then."

" And until then, no more stimulant than is absolutely necessary?"

" I promise that, too."

When this conversation was over, it was too late to go to the funeral.

The doctor went his way. And the banker rang the bell, and summoned his chief clerk, to whom he explained that a sudden indisposition had prevented him from attending the funeral, and would keep him in his own study. And then he wheeled up his sofa to the table, and fell into a long reverie.

Half an hour before six he rose, and went up to dress for dinner.

Dinner at Mr. Melliship's was a solemn and sacred institution, hedged round by the triple armour of an absolute punctuality, evening dress, and a certain stately courtesy, with which the master of the house treated his guests.

To-night there were no visitors, and Mr. Melliship, descending to his drawing-room at five minutes before six, found that the only occupants were his wife and daughter. His son Frank had still to come. But the banker, taking no notice of his absence, sat thoughtfully in an easy chair, and resting his head on his hand contemplated the coals. His womankind, to whom all his moods were sacred, abstained from interrupting him; and to the astonishment of the servants, six o'clock struck without the familiar accompaniment of the bell by which Mr. Melliship was wont to intimate to his *famuli* that he waited for no one.

It was a quarter past six when Frank, who had returned late and dressed hastily, came into the room. Mr. Melliship looked at his watch abstractedly, and rang the bell without saying a word.

The banker was a man who loved to have finished with the day before the dinner hour. The evening was his time of enjoyment and recreation. Unlike Mr. Mortiboy, he took little pleasure in work, and none in the daily details over which he exercised a compulsory rule. Naturally indolent, and finding his chief pleasure in literary and artistic pursuits, he yet worked conscientiously every day in his office behind the bank, where his clients found him when they came to deposit their money with him or to ask his advice. He had no confidential manager, such as Mr. Ghrimes—probably because he had not had the good fortune to find among his clerks a man of ability and integrity enough to gain his entire confidence. He was well served, however—better than Mr. Mortiboy was—because his people liked him; but his staff were all of inferior capacity, and there was not one among them whom he could trust with aught beyond the routine business of the bank. The work, consequently, was sufficiently difficult at all times, and of late had been—owing to the issue of certain transactions—more arduous than ever. It was in the evening, when the desks were locked and the papers put by, that Mr. Melliship was able to breathe freely, and might fairly be said to live.

For many years he had looked forward to the time when his son Frank should be able to take his place, and carry on the business of the bank. That time had now come. Frank's education at Harrow and Cambridge was finished, and young Melliship had returned home—though with no great amount of distinction—and was ready, as soon as his father should propose it, to begin the preliminary course of bank training which was to fit him for the work of his life. But, strangely enough, his father as yet had made no sign; and though all the world knew that Frank was to become a partner, his days were idle, and, against his will, spent chiefly in shooting and hunting.

Nor was this all. Of late, a singular change had come over his father. Mr. Melliship, once the most genial and even-tempered of men, was now uncertain in his moods, fitful and capricious. The old expansiveness of his character seemed to be gone; and he had ceased to take his old interest in those things which had been formerly his chief topic of conversation.

Frank felt—what both he and his sister were somehow afraid of saying openly—that his father's character had undergone some sort of deterioration. How and why, he was unable to guess. Only Dr. Kerby knew, what we know, that in his overworked head were the seeds of that most subtle and dangerous disease—paralysis of the brain.

The change showed itself in many ways. Mr. Melliship had been a great giver of dinners. To sit at the head of his own table, feeling himself in culture, intellect, and—it must not be forgotten—in personal appearance, the superior of his usual guests, was an infinite pleasure to this handsome and stately man. He had some acquaintance—such acquaintance as men in the country reckon no small distinction—among literary men, and could invite a lion of lesser repute to stay with him. The lion would roar at his dinners. And he had friends on the Continent who sent him visitors. So that Mr. Melliship had opportunities of calling together his friends to meet distinguished foreigners, and to hear him converse with them—which he could do fluently—in French and Italian. And he used to patronise artists, and invite them to stay with him. Moreover, it was whispered that he had written papers for what were vaguely called "the Quarterlies"—though to this he never confessed. He was a special friend of the rector by reason chiefly of this culture he had acquired, which sat so gracefully upon him. The squirearchy of the neighbourhood regarded him as an ornament to their society; and by all men, in all classes, Mr. Melliship was spoken well of: by all men but one—his brother-in-law, the man who had married his sister. Ready-money Mortiboy had called him hard names for twenty years.

But now the hospitalities at the bank were contracted; fewer visitors came from town, and no dinners were given: To all Frank's inquiries of his sister, he could get no satisfactory answer, save that things were really changed, and that his father's old serenity was gone, to give way to fits of taciturnity and a habit of retreating to the study, sacred to his own privacy since the birth of his children.

This night, at dinner, he was more silent than ever. The talk, however, such as it was, was chiefly carried on by Mr. Melliship himself, in a jerky manner, and with an evident effort.

He sent away his plate almost untouched, but swallowed bumper after bumper of Madeira—a new thing for him to do. Frank and Kate observed it with silent consternation. Then he broke upon the little chatter of his wife with a sudden and disagreeable laugh.

"The most absurd thing," he said, "really the most laughable thing—I actually went to the funeral to-day in coloured trousers!"

"Why, my dear," exclaimed the wife, "it will be town talk!"

"I can't help it. I forgot entirely that I was not dressed. It was certainly the most absurd mistake I ever made."

Then he lapsed again into silence; while Frank—on whom a very uneasy feeling had fallen—hastened to relate stories of absent-minded men, and how they put themselves into ridiculous positions. But his father took no notice.

Frank noticed, with relief, that he drank very little wine

after dinner; and he proposed, almost immediately after his mother and sister had retired, that they should go upstairs for tea.

Mr. Melliship rose at once, and led the way; but turning back, as if he recollected something, he sat down again.

"There was something I wanted to say, Frank—what was it? Yes—yes; I have not been altogether well for some little time."

"So I have observed, sir. Can I not do something to help you at the bank—assist you in some way?"

"No, my dear boy—no—not just yet. But in a few days I hope to get everything settled—everything arranged for your joining me. And my own—Yes, if things turn out so. But suppose they do not?"

Then he relapsed into silence again.

"Come, father, we will hope they will turn out all right. Why should they not? Let us go and have some tea, and a little music."

Mr. Melliship laughed.

"Yes; tea, and a little music. So we wind up the day, and ease our cares. 'Gratior it dies.' Which of them was it —I think there was one—who had soft music played while his veins were opened in a bath?"

"Good heavens! I don't know," said Frank, looking at his father anxiously. "But come upstairs."

Mr. Melliship took his tea-cup, and sat in his chair, and began to talk—for the first time for many weeks—of the little ordinary matters of the day to his wife.

"Play me *my* sonata, Kate," he said to his daughter, "while I tell you all the particulars of to-day's gloomy business."

Frank watched him through the evening with a growing intensity of anxiety. These singular transitions from a gloomy taciturnity to an almost incoherent utterance, and from this back to the old easy, pleasant manner, alarmed him. And then his reference to affairs of business. What affairs? He had never inquired into them; he knew nothing about his father's pecuniary position. He had always been accustomed to the appearance of wealth in the domestic arrangements, to an ample allowance, to the gratification of all reasonable wishes, and he had asked no more. It occurred to him now, for the first time, that these gloomy fits of his father's might have some solid cause in the affairs of the bank; and a shudder passed through him when he reflected—also for the first time

—that banks in other places got into difficulties, and why not the bank of Melliship & Co.

But Kate played on, and her mother, with her work in her hands, chattered, while the two men trembled. Are not women happy in this, that they seldom feel the blow before it falls? To men belong the long agony of anticipation, the despairing efforts at warding off the stroke of fate, the piquancy of remorse, the bitterness of regret, and the dull, dead pain of foreshadowing—that προσδόκια of which Paul speaks. These they bear in silence mostly; while their women wonder what has come over them, or are only vaguely distressed in mind with the fear that something has disagreed with the stomachs of those they love. For women have this very odd and inexplicable feeling about men, that their first thought of how to please them takes the form of something to eat, and their first thought of uneasiness flies back to something eaten. And on them, so unprepared, comes the blow—heavy and cruel it may be, but not so heavy, not so cruel, not so destitute of comfort and compensation as it has appeared to the men who have suffered from it for so many months already.

About ten Mr. Melliship got up.

"Good night, children," he said. "I am going to my study. Where did I put the book I was reading?"

"What was it, papa?" asked Kate.

"'The Memoirs of Lord Castlereagh.' Thank you, my dear, here it is. Have you read it, Frank? You shall have it, if you like, to-morrow. There is a very singular story about him. One night, as he was lying awake in a long, rambling room in an old house in Ireland, a fire burning at the other end of the room, he saw a child step out from the embers. The child, advancing towards him, grew larger and larger, and at last stood by his bedside, a giant in stature, glaring at him with the wild look of despair, wounded and bloody. He rose, seized his sword, and advanced upon the phantom. As he drew near, the shape retreated, growing smaller and smaller, till it became a child again, and vanished in the fire. You know he afterwards fell by his own hand. Do you think the figure appeared to him again? I have sometimes thought so."

He looked round the room in a strange, wistful way, and went away without saying another word.

"I don't know, I'm sure," said Mrs. Melliship, as her

husband left the room, "why your father should tell us such a dreadful story; and to-day, too, after the funeral, when we wanted cheering up."

"I suppose," said Kate, "that his own thoughts have been turned all day in the direction of death, and that he cannot shake off the impression of the morning. Besides, you know how fond he was of poor Miss Mortiboy."

They did not know he had been closeted with Dr. Kerby while the service was being said at the church.

A ray of hope struck Frank. His father was not well. The funeral of his old friend had, as Kate put it, turned his thoughts in the direction of death.

"I will go," he said, "and see whether I can be of any use to my father. He is certainly not well to-night."

"He ate no dinner at all," said his mother. "See if he will have something sent up."

The study at the bank was a room at the back of the house, approached from the main stairs by a long, dark passage. It was not the custom of any one in the house, save the master, ever to enter the room, except in the morning, when Kate herself superintended the dusting operations, and made it her care that none of the papers should be disturbed.

Mr. Melliship entered his room, and turned up his lamp. Sitting down before the fire, he opened the book he had been reading, and read over again the story of Lord Castlereagh's suicide. As he read, his face grew haggard, and his cheeks pinched.

Then he pushed the book from him with a sigh, and opened a cellaret at his elbow, whence he drew, with a little hesitation of manner, a bottle of brandy and a glass. As he was taking out the cork, he heard Frank's footstep in the passage. He had just time to put back the bottle, and to resume his seat, when Frank's knock at the door was followed by his entrance.

"Come in, my boy," said Mr. Melliship, "come in. You find me very busy."

"I am come to be of use, sir."

"That, Frank, you cannot be to-night. And so, if that is all, and I cannot help you, leave me to silence and work."

"But you are not well, my dear father."

"I am not, Frank," he said, sadly.

"Will you see a doctor to-morrow?"

"I have seen Dr. Kerby to-day; and he prescribes what I

hope you will help me very soon to take—a long holiday. But I cannot begin it just yet. And so, good-night, my dear son."

With that explanation—something, at least—Frank retired. As soon as his footsteps had reached the end of the passage, Mr. Melliship drew out the brandy bottle again, and filled his glass. As he held it to the light, a look of weariness came across his face. He put it down untasted.

"What is the good?" he muttered. "It brings stupefaction; but what is the use of stupefaction? It brings hope; but what is the use of hope? It paints the future bright, when the future is all black and gloomy. Good God! can I not find strength enough to meet my fate? At least, let me do what I can, and write to the accursed man who pulls these strings that are strangling me."

He sat down to the table, and took his pen.

"MY DEAR MORTIBOY,—It is in your power to relieve me of all my embarrassments, or to—"

And here he stopped—because between his eyes and the paper on which he was writing there seemed to fall a cloud, and his brain was turned. His face dropped into his hands, and he groaned aloud. The clock ticked on, but he sat there motionless. Presently, he lifted his head, with a heavy sigh, and looked round furtively. What was it he saw, that on his brow there stood beads of perspiration, that his cheeks were blanched with terror, that his eyes were starting from his head.

The table at which he wrote was in the centre of the room: his back to the fire. He sat on one of those wooden chairs which revolve without the trouble of lifting them. As he turned, and looked straight forwards, there was the fire burning brightly and cheerily; there was the mantelshelf, with all its dainty decorations, and above it the large oil painting of his children at four years and six—of Kate and Frank.

Was there nothing else? To us, had we been there, there was nothing. Thus, as the harmless rustic passed the pool where Diana and her nymphs were bathing, he saw nothing, because nothing was to be seen. Presently, Actæon comes along, and with the glimpse of that other world he loses his perception of the present. So, too, when the Arcadian shepherd piped upon the mountain-side, the gods, Pan and the Dryads and the Fauns sported and revelled about him, and he neither heard nor saw. But to some luckless one—some dweller among cities, some poet whose brain is drunk already with the wine that he finds in the chambers of imagery—great Pan himself appears in all his terrors; and then the brain reels and totters, and the poor poet speaks never more coherent language.

So the banker, leaning forward, was face to face with an apparition from the other world.

"Woman," he cried, stretching out his hands in helpless agony—"dead woman—why do you haunt me?"

It was the woman he had gone to bury that very morning: Susan Mortiboy—his old playmate, his first love. She stood —or seemed to stand—before the portrait of his children, and held out her hands before the canvas, as if to protect them. A tall, thin figure, with a worn and sad face, full of the sweet and passionless tenderness which comes of a life spent wholly for others and ignorant of that human love which makes, at one time in their lives, all women selfish who are loved.

"Why?" cried Mr. Melliship. "Why?"

Her lips, as he thought, moved; and, though no sound came forth, to him she seemed to speak, but only echoed back the terror of his heart.

"The time of success is past—the time of ruin is at hand. Be strong to meet your fate."

"Strong?" he cried, "But how—but how?"

And then the bloodless lips parted again, and the words which were not uttered floated across his brain—

"Be strong to meet your fate!"

"O Susan!" he murmured, "do not mock me. This is now the second time. The first time was on the night you died, and then you told me what you tell me now. Great God of heaven! have you nothing more to say? To be strong—to let the ruin come—to be able to do nothing—to smile and pretend to resignation! Yes; but what is that of avail to help my children? And to save my own honour? Show me a way! show me a way!"

The time for the help of saints has gone. Susan Mortiboy a sainted and holy woman, had, it seemed to him, no advice to give; for the figure before his eyes was silent, still and motionless. It spoke not; but it looked steadily in his face, while he gazed fixedly forwards, as one in a mesmeric trance.

And presently, as it seemed, the figure moved from the front of the fireplace to the side, and turned to the picture of the children, whither followed the eye of their father. All the deep affection of his nature, all the keenness of his anxiety, all the bitterness of his terror, were concentrated in that gaze.

The features of the children faded away, and Mr. Melliship *looked through* the portrait again to see his own drawing-room. By the fire sat his wife, asleep over her work; at the other end of the room his son and his daughter, talking in whispers. O death!—O life!—O joy!—O sorrow!—so far apart and yet together! The father, with his spectral guest, with his breast racked, and tortured, and torn; the son with his sister, but two rooms away, talking lightly of love and hope and pleasure.

"O Kate," whispered Frank, so that his mother should not hear, "if you knew how I love her."

"So do I," said Kate. "Not as you do, silly boy; because I know she is not an angel at all—not a bit more than I am."

"And do you really think she loves me?"

"Why of course she does. I have seen it for months."

"But how—O Kate!—how could you have seen what I have hoped to tell you so long?"

"By ever so many little things—by signs and tokens—by things that men are too stupid to see. It must be a great misfortune to be a man," said Kate, sententiously.

"Not at all," replied her brother; "because if I were not a man I should not have fallen in love with Grace Heathcote, and you would not have had the pleasure of helping me in my difficulties."

"I don't believe you will have any difficulties, only you imagine obstacles that do not really exist. But I am not going to talk this nonsense any longer. Come, let us sing our duet, and then we will go to bed."

Stories are told of men who have heard conversations hundreds of miles away. They may be true or false; but here was Mr. Melliship hearing a whispered talk that took place under his own roof, only two rooms distant from him.

But as he listened and looked, a cloud floated over the picture, and it became once more the picture of two children playing.

The figure that turned its face towards him seemed to be weeping.

"Why," said the banker, "does all that I do or hope for turn to disappointment? You told me years ago, Susan, of my indolence, my vacillation, my love for making things pleasant, and smoothing over difficulties. You alone knew my nature, because you loved me, unworthy as I am. Yes, you loved me; and once I loved you. Would to God that you had been with me always—a protector from my evil genius, the best mother to my children that they or I could have had. And now you come, when the game of life is played, and I have lost, to mock me with words that mean nothing. Susan, is this well done?"

She pointed again at the picture.

He looked, and saw a very shabby, ill-furnished room. It was in a great city, for there was a never-ending rumbling of wheels outside; it was in a crowded part, because you could hear them passing and repassing beneath the window; it was in a poor part, because you could hear the cries of those who vended their wares and hawked their goods about the streets.

In the room, lying on an old horsehair sofa, was his wife. By her sat Kate—his golden-haired Kate, the darling of his heart, his softly nurtured and tenderly cherished daughter, in a worn black dress, in mourning—God of heaven! for whom?—bathing her mother's temples with water. And in the window, catching the last light of a winter day, Frank bending over some work.

"Be strong! But how? O merciful Lord! must it come to this?"

The gray dawn of the February day breaks through the blind of Mr. Melliship's study, where the lamp has long since spent itself, and gone out. The light prowls round the room furtively. There is nothing in the room. It gets stronger, and looks again. There is a sitting figure in a chair. There is a painting over the mantelshelf, wherein two innocent children are laughing upon the white face that looks up on them: and there is nothing else. No figure of a dead woman, moving clay-cold lips, and parting the folds of a shroud to tell of coming danger; no voice from the grave; no phantom of a disordered brain; for the brain has passed through the troubled stage of disorder, and has settled down again into brightness. The brightness of insanity. Mr. Melliship is mad at last; and is waking again, with all this night forgotten, and only one idea left to act upon. On the brink of ruin, which yet might have been averted if his brain were only clear, he has the delusion that he is rich—immeasurably rich!

CHAPTER THE FIFTH.

THURSDAY morning, Dick Mortiboy went up to town to see the "partner" of whom he had told his father. "Meet me," he wrote to him, "at Euston, in time for the two o'clock train." At ten minutes before two there arrived on the platform of the terminus a thin, slightly built man, who began pacing up and down, and irritably glancing every moment at his watch.

He was about forty years of age. His closely shaven cheeks were sallow and pale, save in the part where a beard should have been, and this was of a blue-black. His hair—worn close and short—was black and straight. His features, at first sight, appeared to be delicately and clearly cut; looked at more closely, it seemed as if the lines, skilfully designed, had been roughly executed—much as an engraver spoils a drawing on the block. His eyes were small, bright, and set well in the head. His lips were thin and mobile; and his chin was long, nearly straight, and very sharp. Now persons with long straight chins are not unfrequently remarkable for tenacity and obstinacy. What constitutes a look of cruelty? I cannot define it. But Mr. Richard Mortiboy's partner and friend had it, distinctly and unmistakably.

Looking at him for the first time, a sort of shudder ran through you; and though after-acquaintance might remove the dislike of first thoughts, a secret suspicion was always awakened in men's minds whenever the name of Alcide Lafleur was mentioned. Not in Dick's, it is true, because Dick had not a sensitive nature. He was one of that numerous tribe of mankind who are physically strong, and intellectually self-reliant and clear-sighted. It belongs to a timid nature to take fright at the sight of a stranger—to see intuitively a certain friend in one man, and a certain enemy in another: to open out, like a sensitive plant, in presence of the first; to shut up and shrink, as the plant folds up its leaves and bends back its fibres recoiling, at the contact of the other.

E

M. Alcide Lafleur was irreproachably dressed, in a dark gray suit and black coat. His appearance proclaimed him a foreigner; but when he addressed one of the guards, his accent was perfectly pure, and his English that of a well-educated gentleman—English, say, a little better than that we hear in the drawing-rooms of London: such as an American of the highest class talks.

The train came in true to time, and among the first to step out was Dick Mortiboy. The partners shook hands, and walked out of the station, taking a Hansom which passed along the road.

"Never take a cab from a station," said Dick, with the air of a man who propounds a new maxim in philosophy, "unless you want all the world to know where you are going."

"Where are we going?" asked his companion.

"Anywhere you like, my dear Lafleur, provided we have a quiet place to ourselves, and a talk. I've got a devil of a lot to say."

Lafleur shouted to the cabman through the trap, and in a few minutes they were deposited on the pavement of Greek-street, Soho.

"A quiet house," said Lafleur, leading Richard into it—"a house where donkeys of conspirators meet and devise schemes, which never come to anything, for the upsetting of the world. I use it sometimes."

"Are you turned politician and republican?"

"Yes, to get their secrets, such as they are: poor things, when you know them all. But come in."

The house was externally the modest establishment of a blanchisseuse. Two or three Frenchwomen in clean, white caps, and faces which looked almost as clean and white, were ironing and folding before the window. One looked up as they entered.

"Tiens!—it is you, M. Lafleur. And monsieur is your friend?"

"It is I, madame," returned Lafleur, taking off his hat. "And monsieur is my friend."

"And charmed," said Dick, in French, "to make the acquaintance of madame."

"Let us have a room, madame, and a fire, and a bottle of brandy, and—and—"

"And a beefsteak, and a pot of stout, and a pack of cards," said Dick.

"You shall have them all, messieurs. Follow me, if you please."

She took them upstairs to a back room on the first floor, which looked out cheerfully on an old churchyard: a very pauper among churchyards—so green and grimy were the tombstones that should have been white, so black and bare the ground that should have been grass. Dick looked out and laughed.

"Here," he said, "is a lively and desirable locality to choose for one's own bed-room."

"Eh? What does it matter? I would as soon sleep in a churchyard as in a hotel."

"We have slept in one, my dear friend, not so very long ago, without experiencing any harm."

Lafleur laughed—an uneasy, unpleasant laugh. It was this coarse-minded Englishman's chief fault that he was always making some reference to former unpleasantness.

Madame brought them, with a beaming face, a huge beefsteak from an adjoining eating-house, with the other luxuries they had called for; and, after putting them on the round table in the middle of the room, added, quite as a matter of course, and as if it were as much an accessory to the table as a saltcellar, an inkstand, pens, and a few sheets of paper.

Then she lingered for a moment, gazing admiringly at the stalwart Dick—the handsomest conspirator she had ever entertained in her hotbed of treason.

"Monsieur brings good news?" she asked.

Dick looked at her, somewhat puzzled. But Lafleur answered for him—

"Good, madame, but secret."

"I understand," she said. "I wish you success."

Then she retired, shutting the door carefully, and making as much noise as possible in going downstairs, in order to show that she was not listening outside.

"She thinks you are a messenger from the International somewhere or other," said Lafleur, carelessly. "Let us get to business."

"Let us get to dinner," said Dick. "Good Lord, how hungry I am! Do you remember—"

"No, I do not. I remember nothing of the past. I wish you did not."

Dick laughed, and sat down to the table.

"Have some steak, Lafleur. No place like England for beefsteaks. Eat, my friend—eat: that will refresh your memory of many things"

"Tell me how you are getting on," said his friend, taking a small piece.

"In the first place, I'm nearly starved."

"That I see," returned Lafleur.

"The old man is the same as ever, but shakier than he was. And now, attend carefully, because this will change all our plans. He has not only forgiven and forgotten, as he says, but he believes everything I tell him. And he is going to be guided by all I advise, if only I play the cards well."

"Did you say anything about the mines?"

"He won't listen to the mines."

"Did you tell him about the sunken treasure?"

"I tried it on last night; but he didn't rise as I could have wished. The fact is, Lafleur— Do have some more steak. No? Then I'll finish it."

He finished the steak before he finished his sentence. Then he pushed back his plate, drained the pewter too; and turning his chair to the fire, pulled out a pipe, filled it, and lighted it.

"My father always has his meals in the kitchen," he observed "It is a delightful custom. So do I. We sit opposite to each other; and the old woman cuts the meat. The governor only eats a plateful, if it's hot; or a slice on a piece of bread, if it's cold; I do the same. I tell him it reminds me of my camp life, and that I like it. Queer, isn't it? And he believes me!"

Then he began to smoke his pipe.

"You forget my impatience, my dear Richard," said Lafleur, softly.

"No, I don't. At night we sit opposite to each other, and I smoke my pipe, and tell him of my partner's skill and prudence; how we managed to get money; and how we've been hoarding it, and saving it, and grinding and screwing, to get more."

"Aha!" said Lafleur with a smile.

"Very well, sir. All this is to lay a foundation, and was exactly what we agreed upon. But, you see, the old man believes the tales to such an incredible extent, that we can do better; or, at all events, I can do better."

"What are you going to do? Dick, you're not going to throw me over, are you?" asked Lafleur, leaning forward eagerly.

"I think I am," returned the other, coolly. "Look here.

I come home with you. We've got our little pot. It is agreed that we shall make it out to be a great deal bigger than it is. I am to go down, like the Prodigal Son, to the old man: I am to say to him, 'Father, I'm truly penitent for what I did.'"

"What did you do?" asked Lafleur.

"That's nothing to do with you, my Alcide. I am to repent and weep, and tell him that nothing but filial love brings me home again; that, and a desire to show him with my own hands what I have done. Very well. I am then to put into his hands the documents of partnership, and tell him all about the cotton. Eh? And then I am to propose to him a mortgage of our valuable estates, or a loan, or some means by which we can raise five thousand pounds, of which you are to have half. Is all that correct?"

"It is. Five thousand will do it."

"You are quite sure of your system?"

"Sure, Dick! Am I sure? What made our last pot?"

"Your system."

"What kept us afloat at San Francisco?"

"Your system, still."

"Then you ask if I am sure!" said Lafleur, flushing to the eyes. "Dick, if I only had a dollar in the world, and was certain that I should never make another, I'd lump it all on my system. Give me only five thousand pounds, I'll break any bank in Europe; and then go to America, and break any bank there. And then we'll share the spoil!"

"Very well," said Dick, coolly. "Now, I tell you what I'm going to do. I'll buy, and take to Market Basing to-morrow, all the things we agreed upon, and show them to the governor. But after that, I'm going on another tack. I'm going to see if I can't stay there, and get more than a paltry five thousand. I'm going—don't you perceive?—to be a support to my father's failing age, my friend."

"Ah!" said Lafleur, in a tone which might mean a great deal.

"Yes. And I may possibly make him see that things will be carried on better with me than without me. But give me three months."

"And meantime?"

"I am quite certain, Lafleur—quite certain: you know me? —that I can get you the money, one way or the other."

"One way or the other?"

Lafleur looked meaningly in his friend's face.

"Yes," said Dick, with a firm setting of his eyebrows. "It can be done, and I can do it. In three months' time you shall have your five thousand and I shall either be a rich man, or else—"

"Else what?"

"Still a member of the firm of Lafleur, Roaring Dick & Co., formerly respectable traders in San Francisco, New Orleans, the city of Cairo, and other places in the United States, and elsewhere in this populous and little-witted globe."

"I can live very well for three months," said Lafleur meditatively. "There is not much to be done, it is true. But there is something. I know a place or two already. And I still have a thousand left."

"You mean *we* have a thousand."

"Of course—of course."

"It is just as well, my partner, to be accurate. In this particular juncture it makes a little difference, because I want half of it to take back to Market Basing."

"What are you going to do with it there?"

"Don't you understand? I have seen my partner. He hands me a cheque on account. It is my share of the profits of one venture. Eh? And my partner is going to sail directly, to look after this year's crops."

Lafleur nodded.

"Where's the money?" asked Dick.

"In the bank. You must wait till to-morrow. Very respectable thing to have a banker's account, you know."

"Then let us go and buy the things we want; and, after that, we'll have a pleasant evening. Where am I to sleep?"

"Here, if you like. Madame often makes up beds for her conspirators. You are not suspicious?"

"My dear Lafleur, when was I ever suspicious? Besides, look here."

He half opened his waistcoat. In a pocket on either side, were two handles: one straight—that appertained to a bowie-knife; the other rounded—that belonged to a six-shooter.

"You stick to old friends, then?"

"All old friends. My knife, and my pistol, and my Lafleur. But come, while we have daylight."

It was a singular collection of things that they brought home that night; and Dick spread them out on the table with an air of great triumph.

"Here's the cotton: the raw material out of which we

make our great profits. Here's a photograph of the plantation. Looks devilish like, doesn't it. Here is the dark-skinned but impressionable and intelligent African; free, contented, and happy; hoeing with all the zeal and energy of a British pauper, all for love of Lafleur, Roaring Dick & Company. Here are the feathers presented me by the Queen of Madagascar, and a map of the estate—wants a little touching up with a pen and ink—which her Majesty gave me. Here is my nugget, which I picked up in California—that's no lie, at any rate!—and was so virtuous as to resist the temptation of staying to pick up more, because I preferred a life of steady industry and religion to one of unsettled aims, uncertain prospects, in some wild spot, perhaps far away from any place of worship."

" Is the old man religious ? "

" No," said Dick. " I forgot that. But somebody else is sure to be religious. Only I must be careful not to draw the long bow too much. Well, have I got everything I want? The bowie-knife used by the wicked Yankee."

" Have you got the rough plan showing where the sunken treasure is ? "

" Here it is. The same that the honest old bo's'n gave me, the day I relieved his wants out of my slender stock."

" I say, Dick, be mild. Yours is a very lively imagination."

" And here is a bit of silver ore from that mine which you and I know of, up in the Mexican mountains, which no one else knows of, and which we can get for a mere song. I've got them all. And now, Lafleur, here's the brandy, and here are the cards, and let us have a game. Upon my word, I don't think there's a single soul in all Market Basing that knows the game of euchre. The usual stake, I suppose ? "

Each friend laid a small handful of gold on the table, and began. It was a curious feature about their play, that each kept an eye on his own, and one on the other's hand. Moreover, there was a sort of ostentation of integrity about them, as they sat with their hands well forward upon the table, and their cuffs pulled back, and shuffled, dealt and out in a manner which seemed to say, " You see how honest and simple I am ? "

After playing till twelve, Lafleur rose—he had been winning slightly--and put on his hat. It was characteristic of the man that, though he had drunk nearly half the bottle of brandy to his own share his face was as pale and his manner as quiet as before.

"Must you go? Then I will meet you at the bank tomorrow, and draw the money. Send up that Frenchwoman, will you?"

Madame came up. M. Lafleur had spoken about the room. It was in readiness. Would monsieur step upstairs?

Madame was a bright little body of about five and twenty, not uncomely in features, and clean of appearance. So Dick —who had an eye for beauty—invited her to sit down, compounded her a glass of brandy and water, and entertained her by a few descriptions—drawn from that boundless store-house, his own imagination—of Eastern scenes, and the places he had seen. And after an hour's relaxation, he went to his bedroom.

There was neither lock nor bolt on it, and Dick noticed, with a little suspicion, that it opened outwards. This gave him no means of protection at all, and he carried about with him a largish sum in valuables and money. But he was a man of boundless resource. He drew a piece of string from his pocket, undressed, tied one end to his great toe, and the other to the handle of the door. Then he placed his pistol and knife under the pillow, and got into bed.

"Ho! ho!" he laughed. "If they open the door—"

CHAPTER THE SIXTH.

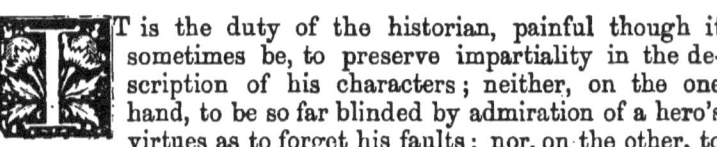T is the duty of the historian, painful though it sometimes be, to preserve impartiality in the description of his characters; neither, on the one hand, to be so far blinded by admiration of a hero's virtues as to forget his faults; nor, on the other, to visit his errors with so heavy a displeasure that any gleams of virtue may be quite overlooked and forgotten. In obedience to this rule, it is incumbent upon me to state plainly, what has already been intimated, that Richard Mortiboy the younger was by no means the manner of man that he wished to appear in the eyes of his confiding father. There was no cotton estate; there were no mines; there was no sunken treasure; there was nothing but a pocketful of money, gotten together by by various shifts and devices more than questionable. And

right in the unsuspecting heart of Market Basing—as innocent a town as any in the guileless realm of England—there had dropped, though not from heaven, one of the most unscrupulous, crafty, and thorough-going rascals that might be found in a long day's march : even by Ariel the rapid.

We, who write history, would fain have all our characters virtuous. How sweet and easy-flowing would be the years; how quiet and gentle the conversations; how empty of pity and terror the lives; and, oh, how bereft of interest would be our books! For when the villain ceases out of the land, and the voice of the tyrant is heard no more, history will cease too; because there will be nothing left to chronicle but the wooing of turtles. "The purpose for which snakes was built," writes an American natural philosopher, "is not yet explored." But here is doubtless one reason why rogues and rascals were constructed, and why villainy and roguery are allowed to prosper: to furnish material wherewith the historian is enabled to point his moral and adorn his tale.

It was now twelve years since a certain cold wild night in November, when, about nine o'clock, Mr. Mortiboy, senior, followed by his son—then a tall stripling of eighteen—walked down that dark passage in the house which we know, and opened the door. The wind blew in, and the rain was pouring down. The father was trembling with passion: the son cold and stolid. Mr. Mortiboy pointed to the darkness, and said, in constrained, hard tones—

"Go. Darken my doors no more. You are no longer my son."

The son said nothing; but looked up and down the street as if inspecting the state of the weather before taking a walk.

"Go," repeated his father.

"One may as well first put on a great coat, on a night like this," returned the boy coolly. "Had you not better shut the door, father, for fear of catching cold, while I delay you for one minute?"

His father took no notice, but stood steadfastly gazing at him. The young man, taking his time to get comfortably into the great coat, selected his umbrella from the stand, and put on his hat. Then he took out his purse and looked at it.

"You must give me some money," he said.

"Write to me from London, and I will tell you what I will do for you. Now, go. Your aunt shall not know why."

Two days later, a letter came from London, containing nothing but young Mortiboy's address. To this the father replied by a ten-pound note, without a word of forgiveness or of blame; and from this time all correspondence had ceased, and Dick Mortiboy's name was no more mentioned in his father's house.

It was understood vaguely that he had " done something."

The young man, with his ten-pound note, and five or six pounds besides, which he got by selling his watch and chain, went to the docks, and looked for a ship about to sail—whither he cared not. What he wanted—for very special and cogent reasons of his own—was to get away at once, and never to come back again at all.

He found one clearing out, with her cargo on board, her papers ready, bound for Palmiste Island, and going to sail the very next day. He took a second-class passage for ten pounds; getting a half-promise from the purser that, if he made himself useful on the voyage, he might have some of the ten pounds returned on their arrival. And a few days afterwards, young Mortiboy was sailing merrily across the Bay of Biscay, his cares all thrown to the winds, delighted at the prospect of seeing the world, and getting away from the difficulties and debts which had driven him to—convey, the wise call it— imitate his father's signature so carefully, with all its dots and flourishes, that not even the bank clerks could tell that it was not the genuine autograph of Ready-money Mortiboy.

He did more than make himself useful to the purser—he did all his work for him; and that so easily, lightly, and well, that the ship's books were never better kept. The purser showed his gratitude. He not only bestowed a daily ration of grog upon him—which was really a delicate attention—but, he persuaded the skipper to enter him on the books as purser's clerk; to give him back his passage money; and when the ship, after her three months' voyage, was tugged into the harbour of Port Dauphin, in the Island of Palmiste, to present him with a trifle besides, by way of acknowledgment. And then, when Dick had refused an offer to be taken back again in the same ship, still as clerk, his patron sent him to a business house in the town, with a recommendation to the effect that Mr. Mellon—as Dick called himself—was a young man of excellent business habits, and respectable connections. The latter clause, being put in as likely to help, was certainly not a greater untruth—although the purser knew nothing whatever about his relatives—than is told a thousand times a-day by people who write testimonials alike for the deserving and the undeserving poor.

The recommendation was accepted as sufficient; and Dick found himself on what seemed to him—he had never before drawn more than a pound a week—a princely salary of one hundred and fifty pounds a year, in one of the best business houses of Port Dauphin. His hours were not long; and he had his day, after four o'clock, entirely to himself. Now, this was the unfortunate part of it. From four o'clock to six— that is to say, in the cool of the evening—one might stroll under the trees; one might climb the hills—though this was hot work—or one might sit and do nothing. At six, just as the sun went down, came the table d'hôte, which brought you well on to seven. And here, Dick—whose income was not much more than enough to find his breakfast and dinner, and pay the rent of the little wooden box he slept in, for which he paid a pound a month—ought to have ended his day, and gone home to bed. Unfortunately, there was a billiard-room in the hotel, and he found it pleasanter to smoke his cigar— cigars, even at a half-penny a-piece, the current price in Palmiste, mount up—than to go home to his dreary room, and go to bed. Added to which, the younger Mortiboy had the eye of a Roberts for billiards. So he used to play, and to make his little pot every night. Then the descent of Avernus, which had been checked by the voyage out, began over again. For to billiards was speedily added brandy and soda; and not unfrequently, as the weeks passed on, a little game at écarté, where his winnings at billiards were generally transferred to his opponents' pockets. Presently, these proceedings coming to the ears of his employers—respectable and, considering all things, even God-fearing merchants—it was not astonishing that Mr. Mellon received one morning a polite, but firm, intimation that his services would not be required after the end of the current month. But Dick again fell on his feet. In Palmisto are coffee and sugar estates. And among the planters who sold their sugar to Dick's employers was an old Englishman, who had been struck by Dick's handsome face and his frank manner. Learning that he was without employment, he offered him a place on his own estate, where his sole business would be to pay the coolies engaged for the canes, look after their rations, and keep the accounts. And he bargained to give him, over and above a house and allowances, fifteen pounds a month in hard cash. Dick accepted the offer with joy, and went down to the Hautbois estate with the delight of a schoolboy. For it was characteristic of this young man, that no sooner was he out of a scrape than all his good spirits returned to him.

For some months all went well. Hautbois was at the other side of the island, some forty miles from the town of Port Dauphin. There was no billiards, no écarté, and no loafers about hotel verandahs ready to propose or to accept a brandy and soda, on the slightest possible pretext. It is true that there was no society; but he had work during the day, and was sufficiently tired at night to go to bed with pleasure at nine o'clock. Hautbois stood ten miles away from any other house: an estate cut out of the virgin forest, which here sloped down to the very sea shore, until it merged into the mangroves, where they grew standing thickly together, with their unwholesome leaves, and their long, slimy roots—the nursing places and cradles of the young sharks, who disported themselves about the tendrils in the shallow water in all the innocence of childhood. Round the estate lay the deep, silent woods, where there were no birds, because the monkeys ate the eggs, or the hurricanes blew the nests away out to sea. Away in the glades, you came upon deer that were only frightened at the sight of man for twelve weeks in the year, during the shooting season—a periodical time of misery, whose approach they yearly expected with terror, and saw themselves safely passed through with a lively gratitude. Wild and fearful beasts there are none in Palmiste. Unlike most of the other West Indian Islands, it has no snakes; and, with the exception of a centipede or so, a big spider of ferocious and bloodthirsty build, and a few scorpions, there is nothing in all Palmiste to scare a girl. To the north rose the mountains, tall and wooded. And over all these lay the bright, soft blue, never hidden by fog, seldom by cloud, with a warmth which got into the bones, and made one lazy and thoughtful, and inclined for rest: an air which makes men good, because it is too much trouble to be anything else. Here for a while Dick was happy. Mr. Oswald, his employer, asked him to dinner; talked about England, and the old days when he was a young man, and George the Third was king; told old stories of his Oxford life, and of the princes and their wild doings; and surrounded the young man with a pure and peaceful atmosphere, which made him for a while look back on his past with shame and regret. And then old Mrs. Oswald took a fancy to him; made him come and talk to her when her husband was up in town; inquired into the condition of his wardrobe. This was scanty: Mr. Oswald made it plentiful; saw that his little house was properly furnished, and made comfortable for him; and instructed him in the best way of dealing with his Indians.

His duties took up about three hours in the day. Then he would go over to the mill, and watch the sugar-making. By degrees he grew expert at this, as in anything which he took up; and Mr. Oswald added another five pounds a month to his salary, and made him one of the mill superintendents. On Saturday he had to overlook the distribution of rations to the men. On these days, there was a great scene round the storehouse over which he presided—as the Indians came, accompanied by their wives and children, to receive the weekly dole of rice, and grain, and salt fish. It was then that Dick—who loved nothing so well as to command and administer—was in all his pride. He learned to talk Hindustani, and achieved a reputation—easy enough, but not entirely without its merits—of being able to swear as hard as any coolie of them all in his own tongue.

Dick ruled them with a rod of iron.

Standing over his stores and his accounts, with his long, thin figure, his flashing eye, his ready hand—which many an Indian remembered as being heavier than most of those he had encountered—and above all, his ready tongue, he was at once the terror and the admiration of the shrinking crowd which gathered round him, and received, in such silence as was compatible with their stage of civilization, the weekly allowances.

So Dick's days passed pleasantly away, and the memory of the past troubled him little. Came presently the hunting season, when Mr. Oswald gave his great parties. To these the young accountant was asked, and discovered other talents. For the eye which had been chiefly trained at a billiard-table was found the truest of any with a rifle, and most of the honours of the hunt fell to young Mellon, of Hautbois estate. He could ride, too, because he belonged to a riding country, and many were the mounts he had got as a boy from his cousin Heathcote or his uncle Mr. Melliship. So it came about that, in spite of his inferior position—one generally held by mulattoes of the island—young Mellon began to be known as a gentleman of a station not contemptible, and manners which belonged to a higher grade. And since no one is satisfied to recognise a man as a friend till a coherent and intelligible story of at least ten years of antecedents has been made out about him, it was whispered abroad that young Mellon was one who had quarrelled with his father, a man of colossal fortune, and had run away. This was spread abroad so industriously that it ended by being received as gospel, and Dick found all doors open to him.

No harm was done so long as he remained at Hautbois, or only went about to the neighbouring estates. In these visits, he made the acquaintance of the young ladies, who led lives as dull as ditchwater in their secluded homes, and were delighted to get some one, if only an employé on an estate, to talk to. And such an employé!—a mysterious stranger with the manners of a nobleman; a tall and graceful youth of twenty, with all the beauty of a hero of romance, all the possible passion which lay undoubtedly hidden under black curls and splendid eyes, and a little dark moustache, and a cheek which had hardly yet forgotten how to blush. And so the fame of him went up even to the great and important city of Port Dauphin; and when the races came, and the Governor gave his ball, and the garrison theirs, and the bachelors theirs, and there were dinners every day, and dances when there were no balls, interest was used to get Mr. Mellon cards of invitation; and he, too, with Mr. and Mrs. Oswald, went up to town to enjoy himself.

We cannot, historians though we are, linger over this most fatal week. Dick had been six months with Mr. Oswald. It is easy, therefore, to calculate how much money he had saved, at the rate of about ten pounds a month. With this in his pocket, he took a chamber at the hotel for the week of the races, and prepared to be happy. Everybody liked him: the young ladies because he was young and handsome, and danced well, and looked like a chevalier; the men because he was never ill-natured, never in the way, never in the least snobbish—a thing which could not always be said of the Palmiste bachelors—and because he would sit up all night, sing a good song, and play a game at cards when the dancing was over. This little game of cards it was that brought him to grief; for Dick went back at the end of his week with a sorrowful heart, and fifty pounds to pay in the course of the next month—a debt of honour. He was profoundly miserable. Among all his acquaintances, he had not one friend; there was not a soul in all Palmiste to whom he could have gone for the loan of a ten-pound note, except old Mrs. Oswald. If only the young man had poured out his troubles to her, all would have been well with him. For the heart of the childless old lady yearned to the bright and handsome lad, who might have been her own son, and who looked so innocent and happy.

But Dick had already plucked the fatal apple which brings man to grief. That is, he had passed the portal which leads from innocence to guilt; and having passed through it once, found little difficulty in going through again. 'Ce n'est que le premier pas qui coute': the bravo who can number his hundred murders has almost forgotten the terrible heart-sickness that came upon him when he committed the first.

In the month the debts were paid, and Dick freed from all his difficulties. He went on with his duties, but he looked pale and harassed. Mrs. Oswald used to ask him if he were ill, and made him dine at the house oftener—thinking, in her kindness, that he wanted society. And her husband offered him a holiday at Port Dauphin for a fortnight, if that would do him good. But Dick shook his head, tried to look pleased, and declined.

Thus two or three months passed away. One day Mr. Oswald received a letter, which he read with perplexity. He had his horses put in at once, and drove away to town. Mr. Oswald did not come back that night. That was nothing unusual. But he came the next day accompanied by two men whom Dick knew, when he saw them, to be inspectors of police. As the carriage drove up, he was crossing the open space between the mill and his own cottage. Why did he stop, and turn as if for flight; and then, trembling in all his limbs, seem to lose in a moment all his pride and manliness, and crouch together as he continued his walk?

Mr. Oswald called him. The old gentleman was perfectly haggard with anxiety and terror. To look at him, you would have thought that he was himself the criminal whom the officers came to look for.

Dick tried to pull himself together. He succeeded to a small extent, and advanced with a conscious swagger to the verandah where his employer was standing.

"Mr. Mellon," said Mr. Oswald, "a very painful thing has happened. Some person has forged an order to a cheque for fifty pounds, and the money has been paid. The forged cheque has been placed by the bank in the hands of the Crown Solicitor, and they—they—say it is you." He cleared his throat. " Of course, I am quite certain it is a mistake."

" Quite, sir," said Dick, with a nervous twitching at the mouth. " These gentlemen—"

He looked at the inspectors.

" We have to arrest you, Mr. Mellon."

" Oh! May I have a word with you, Mr. Oswald?"

The inspectors, in reply to a look of interrogation from the old planter, nodded; and Mr. Oswald led his clerk into the dining-room. As they came in at one door, Mrs. Oswald entered at another. Dick did not see her.

"I do not want to waste your time, sir," he said. "You have been very kind to me—more than kind; but the thing is true."

" What thing?" asked Mrs. Oswald.

" I am arrested for forging a cheque. It is quite true. I did it. You will not tell them in the court what I have told you, I am certain, Mr. Oswald. I gambled during the race week and lost all I had, and fifty pounds besides. How was I to pay it?"

"Why did you not ask me?" cried Mrs. Oswald. "Oh! my boy, why did you not ask me?"

" I wish I had," said Dick, ruefully.

" If you must forge some one's name," said Mr. Oswald, almost weeping, " why, in Heaven's name, why not have forged mine?"

"I wish I had," said Dick, looking at him with real emotion. " I wish to God I had!"

And while Mrs. Oswald cried and lamented, and the worthy old man, her husband, sat mournfully with his head in his hands, the young fellow went off with his captors, to be locked up in the gaol of Port Dauphin. One touch of compunction —the only one for many years—visited his heart when he saw the grief of the good old couple.

CHAPTER THE SEVENTH.

IT IS NOT a pleasant thing, apart from the shame which every one feels, except the true philosopher, to be clapped into prison in any climate; but it must be most unpleasant of all under a tropical sun. The absence of fresh and free air, and the deprivation of those small comforts which alone make life in Palmiste tolerable, are of themselves enough to make a weak man commit suicide, and a strong man go mad. Poor Dick sat, the first night of his confinement, on the stone couch which did duty for a bed in his cell, mournfully thinking over his chances; and speculating—for the case was far too clear to admit of any hope of acquittal—how long a term of imprisonment he would be likely to have. Then, with the elasticity of youth, he went on to speculate, further, what he should do when he got out. And presently, wearied with so much thinking, he lay back upon his grass mat and went to sleep till the sun rose, and shining in at his barred window, awakened him. He started up, and instead of his little room at Hautbois, made neat and comfortable by the care of Mrs. Oswald, he found himself in a white-washed cell, with a stone floor, and iron bars instead of green jalousies. The window looked into the courtyard of the prison, where some miserable Indians, prisoners, were huddled together, waiting for the guards who were to take them to work. Presently his door opened, and a mulatto turnkey appeared—a fat, merry-looking rascal—who gave him the usual instructions as to the rules of the cell, and let him know that he was to be brought before the magistrate that morning.

Perhaps, in Dick Mortiboy's whole life—which was chequered enough, and had its banyan days—there was but one recollection to which he turned as seldom as he could, only one which caused him bitter shame and pain even to think of. It was the recollection of the dismal and degraded procession— of which he formed one—that filed out from the prison doors,

F

and was marched solemnly down the street, *coram populo*, to the magistrate's court. It was headed by a brace of weeping Indians, charged with burglary and attempt to murder—they shed tears as they went, and howled their innocence; then three or four men who had been drunk and disorderly—these were the most shamefaced of the lot; then a negro, who pretended to laugh at the absurdity of the charge against him—he had been stealing ducks; then Dick—the bright, handsome young Englishman—walking along, red with shame and misery, with this crew; then a Chinaman, against whom something unlawful connected with other people's pork was alleged—he wore a surprised countenance, as one who should say, "Dear me! this is very singular—very singular, indeed! What can be the motive of this?" then half a dozen more Indians; and then the procession was closed by two policemen. A long string passed down the file, which every man had to hold with one hand. The Indian is quite contented so long as he keeps his fingers closed on the string, and considers himself laden with fetters. If he is driven along loose, he runs away multivious.

That dreary day! Many of his acquaintances—including the man for whom he had forged the cheque, who was the principal witness—were in the court; and not one—not one of all the men with whom he had lived and drunk and sung—seemed to have a kind or pitying look. Dick tried to steel his heart, ineffectually, against the shame. It was bruised and seared by this day's misery, and it was long before it became again as it had been once—soft, relenting, charitable. Have you not noticed that criminals appear to have no sense at all of moral culpability? It is because circumstances, as well as repetition, deaden the feeling of remorse. Thus, when Dick forged his father's name, in the first place, the consequences were sharp and decisive; secondly, they were not accompanied by any public shame; thirdly, he was in dire straits in the town, and only too glad to get out of Market Basing; and lastly, his father had always restricted his pleasures, and cut down his allowances to the merest pittance; so that he hated his home, and left it with delight. Now it was different: he had a chance in life, and he threw it away. He made friends, and he lost them. He got a certain sort of position, and he put himself out of it by his own act and deed. It is the public consequence of a crime that causes the remorse and agony of the sinner; not those hidden consequences which are unseen, yet, perhaps, more retributive, because they sear the heart, and paralyse the will.

The day came to an end at last, and the procession was reformed to return—Dick being fully committed for trial at the next sessions, now some two months off. They pushed him into his cell, gave him his dinner, and left him to his meditations.

There are only occasionally in Palmiste prisoners of any social grade or rank above that of merchant-sailor, or Indian coolie; but at this moment there was another prisoner also awaiting his trial—a young Frenchman, some few years older than Dick. At stated hours the prisoners were allowed to walk in the courtyard, between which and the main entrance was a strongly locked gate, opening into a sort of barrack-room, where policemen and guards were always about. There was also another entrance, by an iron door, never opened, which led into the chief gaoler's private house, and was designed as a means of getting into the prison without going through the guard-room, in case of a disturbance; and at the back of the court lay a large bare room open to it, which had been built for the prisoners as a place where they might work out of the sun when in-door work had to be done.

In this room, on the second day of his confinement, Dick, being released for his walk, saw a man sitting on the stone bench which ran round the four walls, and formed the only furniture. He started, for a moment changed colour, and half turned to escape; only there was nowhere to go to, and he stopped. For the man he saw there was one of his old friends—a man who used to dine at the same table d'hôte with him in Port Dauphin. He was a young Frenchman of the colony—like himself, a merchant's clerk, and, like himself, a gambler; but Lafleur had already a reputation beyond his years. He was slightly built, and pale, with close black hair and a thick massive beard, like the Frenchmen of the South. Dick knew him chiefly as connected with a card story in which he figured as the principal actor. The quarrel had been made up by a duel, in which Lafleur's opponent gave information to the police, and the combat was stopped on the ground. But men looked shy on him after this affair, and even in Port Dauphin, where public morality runs low, were chary of being seen much in his company.

The man started at the sound of Dick's step, and turned a haggard and careworn face to see who was coming. He rose, with a strange, constrained air, quite unusual to him, and half held out his hand.

"You are come to see me, Mellon? This is kind of you."

"I? No, by gad! You have come to see me. I am"—Dick turned red for a moment—"I am a prisoner."

"So am I," returned the other.

"You, too? What have you been doing?"

"They pretend that I murdered young Deschamps."

Dick involuntarily recoiled. Then he laughed defiantly.

"They pretend I forged a cheque. Damn it!—they will pretend anything. Only, I say, Lafleur, you're in a worse scrape than I am."

"Bah!" said the Frenchman; "it is nothing. In the first place, it was a duel. I am innocent. And in the second—"

"Nonsense," said Dick. "What a fool you must have been."

"Well, there's no evidence."

Dick shrugged his shoulders, and sat down—glad enough to have a talk even with a murderer. It will be understood that prison discipline in Port Dauphin is lax.

The days passed on. Lafleur grew more anxious. Only his lawyer came to see him; none of his own relations entering the prison. Mr. Oswald got a lawyer, too, who came to see Dick from time to time. But his visits did not tend to make the young man more cheerful: his spirits sank every hour.

One day Lafleur looked, for the first time, bright and even hopeful.

"What is it?" asked Dick. He felt particularly low that morning. "Hang it, man, if you were acquitted you couldn't look jollier."

"I see hope, my friend. I have a plan. We may escape yet."

"Don't see how."

"Listen."

He took Dick's arm, curiously, before he began to speak, and felt the biceps. Now Dick was strong-limbed and muscular, besides being tall.

"My faith, my friend, if I had your strength—"

"Go on, man—go on."

Lafleur looked round. No one was in the court-yard except a couple of policemen, whose backs were turned. He drew a key from his pocket, and furtively showed it to Dick.

"It is the governor's own key—the key of the iron door."

Dick nodded, and said nothing.

"The mulatto gaoler got it for me. He is my father's son."

"Your brother?"

"Pardon me—I said my father's son. Now listen. It depends on you. At six, we have to go up to our cells. Who always conducts us?"

"Pierre, your—your friend, and Smith."

"Just so. You will have to floor Smith. Pierre will be managed by me without any trouble. It is all squared with him."

Dick looked thoughtful.

"Smith's a big man; but I think I can tackle him. Are we to wait till six? O Lafleur! why did you tell me so soon?"

The day was interminable.

Slowly the leaden-footed hours crept away.

From two to five they were locked up.

At five they were let out for another breath of fresh air; and Dick's heart beat fast as the hour approached.

The clock struck a quarter to six. The sun was already setting behind the mountains, and in a few minutes it would be dark.

Presently, making a great jingle with his keys, Smith, a ponderous Englishman of sixteen stone, followed by Pierre, came through the large gate. According to custom, he stopped to lock the door behind him, and leisurely crossed the yard to the work-room. Dick held himself at the inside of the door.

"Come," said Smith, standing at the door, "time's up. Where's Mr. Mellon?"

He was looking straight into the room, where Lafleur was standing, motionless and trembling.

"Here," cried Dick, striking him full in the temple with his fist. Smith reeled, and would have cried for help; but another blow, from the left, knocked him with his head against the corner of the stone bench, and he fell, senseless and bleeding.

He was stunned.

Lafleur rushed out, followed by Dick. They had forgotten to knock down poor Pierre, who waited stupidly : standing still, to be despatched with such a blow as had felled the gigantic Smith. To his astonishment, they had opened the little door, and were gone without giving him so much as a tap. Now, he had specially signified a strong desire to receive from his affectionate half-brother exactly the same treatment as that designed for Smith. They had disappointed him.

A single passage led through the governor's house to his garden in the front. There was no one there. They passed across, and stood without—for the moment, free.

Outside the door, in the road, but to the left of them, was a small knot of policeman and gaolers, idly talking and enjoying the cool breeze of the evening. Lafleur touched his companion lightly on the arm, and they stepped to the right. Another turn brought them to a bye-street. It was now quite dark—for there is no twilight in latitude 8°; and fortunately there was no moon.

"Where now?" asked Dick, breathlessly, wondering what was the use of liberty in a place where there was nowhere to hide.

"Follow me. It is all arranged. If only we can find the boat."

Dick began to understand a little; and they walked quickly along the narrow streets of the Indian quarter, where they were little likely to meet Europeans who might know them.

They passed no one, a stray Indian or two excepted, and in ten minutes were out of the town and on the high road.

Here it ran across a bare and rocky plain, which stretched for a mile or so from the sea-shore. Lafleur led the way still, and now began to run. No one was ever on the plain, by day or night. They reached the shore. The sea was calm and smooth, save where, a quarter of a mile out, the breakers of the coral reef shone clear and bright as they rolled in, and formed their long, white crests like a fringe round the shore, or like a bulwark to protect the island they loved so well. But the two were in no mood for similes or sentiment.

"What the devil are we to do next?" said Dick.

"See this white post? It is a landmark. We are to keep in a line with this and the fort—"

"But I can't see the fort."

"I know the direction: it is exactly over there—and they will be off the reef. It is all arranged, I tell you. Can you swim?"

"Can I walk?"

"Then follow me."

It was low tide—the sea, as well as everything else, seeming to favour them. They stepped into the water, keeping as well as they could in the line along which they had started. This was not easy, for it was quite dark. They slipped and fell. Now their feet would catch in a branch of coral. Now they would step upon a large sea slug—a bloated worm, two feet long—into whose miry body their heels would crush and sink, conveying a horrible sense of danger and misery; now a hole in the coral, and they would be up to their armpits. But they struggled on in silence, and at last stood close to the very edge of the reef, and peered eagerly into the darkness. The crash of the waves was all that they could hear. The white breakers rose higher than their heads, and they could see nothing beyond them. Worse, they could hear no sound of oars or oarsmen.

"Where are they?" cried Dick, almost breaking down at last. "Good God! have you brought me to this horrible place to look for a boat in darkness like this?"

"Better to die here than to be hanged. Remember it was you who killed Smith."

Dick said nothing: standing shivering in the water up to his middle.

For nearly half an hour—they thought it half the night—they stood so: silent, washed by the waves. The tide was rising, and they would shortly have to choose between wading back or being drowned. But neither dared speak to the other.

Suddenly Dick caught Lafleur's arm.

"I hear voices!" he cried. "Shout, man, shout!"

Lafleur listened with a sort of sob. Suppose it should not be his boat! But, no—it was impossible that another boat should be off the reef in so desolate a place, and at such a time.

He shouted. There was no reply.

He shouted again; but in vain. Then Dick put his two hands to his mouth, and gave a cry that might have been—and I dare say was—heard on shore.

A hoarse sailor's call was the answer, followed by a shrill whistle. It sounded close at hand; but they could see nothing.

"All right," cried Lafleur. "Let us keep close together. Now!"

He plunged through the breakers and disappeared.

"Lord keep the sharks off!" thought Dick, and followed him.

Outside, a boat lay tossing in the roll of the Atlantic,

the crew resting on their oars; all with their faces turned anxiously towards the shore. There was a cry near them, and they turned a light in its direction. In two minutes they were alongside the escaped prisoners. Dick, who was the first, clambered in over the stern, and sat in the bottom shaking and trembling. Lafleur was more exhausted. He seized an oar, but had not strength enough to climb into the boat. They drew him over the side; and the next moment—for the lantern had been used to facilitate the business—a huge black fin showed for an instant above the water, and then disappeared.

"It's a shark," said the man at the helm.

"I touched him with my foot," said Dick, his voice soft and shaking. "Good God!—give me some brandy."

They gave him brandy, and he revived a little. Then they performed the same kind office for Lafleur.

The Frenchman pointed to Dick.

"He did it all," he gasped. "Without him I should never have succeeded. You must put him on board too."

The men murmured; but the helmsman stopped them.

"One man makes little difference. I will settle it with the captain."

Two miles from the reef, in the roadstead, lay a small schooner. The night was so dark that she could only be reached by her lights, and the men pulled unskilfully. But they got alongside at last; and the moment they touched, a rope was lowered.

"Captain," said the man at the helm, who seemed to be one holding authority, "there are two. You will hear from me at your port."

"Right, sir, right. Now then, gentlemen, quick's the word."

Dick clambered up. He touched the deck, and looked wildly round; for he almost thought it was all a dream.

The captain clapped him on the back.

"Come," said he, "this was bravely done. Where's the other?"

As Lafleur climbed the rope, the men in the boat shouted "Adieu," and pushed off.

The captain whistled, the sails of the schooner fell, and Dick felt her move. In half an hour they were in open sea, bound for the port of Havana.

The captain took them below, and showed them a small

cabin, with a pair of bunks. He had, too, changes of clothing; and, though it was difficult to fit a man of Dick's height, it was something to be dry, even with six inches of leg between boot and trouser.

"No one of the sailors," said the captain, "knows anything. We've only been in port two days, and none of them have been ashore except the cook, and he's deaf. Mr. Lafleur, you're welcome, for your father's sake. And you, young sir, for any sake you like, whatever you have done."

Dick shuddered. "What had he done?" The thought of the big turnkey, whose black blood he had seen oozing out upon the stones, struck cold at his heart.

He held out his hand to Lafleur, and said, with an emotion that had nothing simulated about it—

"You've rescued me from that infernal place, and you stood by me in the boat. I swear to you, Lafleur, by all that I can swear by, that I will stand by you till the last. If I can help you, I will help you. If I can defend you, I will defend you. If I can save you in any trouble, I will save you. If I have any money, you shall have half, and more. If I have any luck, you shall have half, and more. So help me God!"

Lafleur took his hand in his, and pressed it, and said nothing. So was plighted between them the troth that made them partners for life.

Next day they were in the trade winds, bowling merrily along; for the schooner was as fast a vessel as any in those waters.

"Who were the men in the boats?" asked Dick, as they leaned over the taffrail, after breakfast, watching the flying fish and the porpoises.

"The man who held the rudder strings was my father; one of the others was my brother; the rest were my cousins. The whole thing was arranged by the lawyer, my cousin. Pierre got an impression of the key in wax, and made it himself. He's a clever locksmith. You see, it would hardly do to have a man in my position tried for murder—though it was a fair duel—and I knew they would do something for me, sooner or later."

"By Jove," said Dick, "you must be a devilish clever family. And suppose the shark had spoiled our little game! I wish I hadn't hit Smith so hard. He was a good fellow, after all. But it is deuced hard to regulate your stroke so as just to stun, and not to kill. It wants a lighter wrist than mine."

Smith, however, was not dead—he was only stunned; and directly he came to himself, which was three minutes after the birds were flown, he staggered to his feet, and instantly collared Pierre, making a great roaring, because he felt too groggy on his feet to hold on long. Pierre lost his situation; and notwithstanding he made great protestation of his innocence, he was not observed to care very much about his *démission*, and applied his talents subsequently, with great success, to the trade of a locksmith. The last time I heard of Pierre, I was told that he had sent his two sons to England— one to be made a barrister, and the other a doctor. They were smart young fellows; and when they went back to Palmiste, refused to speak to their father because the poor man was coloured. Now this was ungrateful.

It would take me too long to follow the fortunes of Dick for the ten years which intervened between his escape from Palmiste and his return to England. He did, always with Lafleur and the captain, a little trade in black humanity, running in the fast-sailing schooner between Congo and some quiet creek in Cuba. And they never got caught. It was during this period that he grew his beard, and developed his former meagre proportions. Presently came the American war, and the game of blockade-running began. By this time the captain to whom the schooner belonged, was dead; and Dick and Laflour, like the pirates of old, took quiet command of the craft, no questions being asked as to the approval of the skipper's heirs. And then, for a couple of years, a merry time. There is a port, little frequented by English ships, some few hundred miles east of New Orleans. There the adventurers found their market; and many a glorious run they had from Nassau, laden with contraband of war. But the pitcher ofttimes taken to the well, gets smashed at last; and one fine morning, when the day broke, after a thick black night, a Federal cruiser was discovered only a mile away; and the tight little schooner, driven on shore, was broken up and destroyed.

But they had made by this time a pretty little sum between them, which was lying to their credit in Havana; and the catastrophe afflicted them but little. Meanwhile, in these long days and nights at sea, Dick had imbibed from his companion a large share of his gambling spirit. He was now heart and soul a gambler. How far Lafleur played fair or false, no one knows; but I think he never cheated Dick, in his worst moments. Their partnership was true; and though there was neither friendship, respect, nor affection between them, there was the mutual bond of self-interest, and it may have been, a sentiment, an unseen fetter—forged on that day when they braved the terrors of the reef—which both felt, and both were either unwilling or unable to break.

Between '65 and '68—the year of their home-coming—had been an alternation of reverses and victories, chiefly carried on at the gambling-tables of the Southern States and Mexico. They won, they fought; they lost, they fought. And it was Dick who—after a lucky night or two at New Orleans had pulled them out of the mire, and set them up with a handful of money—proposed to go over to England, and see whether anything could be made out of the old man. There was no risk to speak of. Long since, the escape of Mellon and Lafleur had been forgotten, or only remembered as a mysterious disappearance, in Palmiste. It had never been understood. The only ship which sailed from the port that day was a small schooner which had passed out of port at three in the afternoon, and was said to have sailed before nightfall. The woods were searched, but in vain; and the police had finally given up the hopeless task of trying to find them. Moreover, who would now have recognised either of them?

And so they came to England, like the wild beasts of the forest, seeking whom they might devour.

CHAPTER THE EIGHTH.

PARKSIDE, where the Heathcotes lived, was seated on a sunny slope, just outside the straggling village of Hunslope. From the windows you had a view of scattered cottages, a farmhouse or two standing sheltered by their rickyards, the church tower peeping over Lord Hunslope's elms, and in the distance, the white turnpike road to Market Basing. John Heathcote's house was well named: the gravelled drive up to the door skirted one of the parks that surrounded Hunslope Towers. The farmer's garden was six feet lower than the park; so there was a natural fence. The only disadvantage attending this was that, once a year or so, a Southdown of his lordship's tumbled over into Mrs. Heathcote's flower-beds. About which catastrophes, when they occurred, Mrs. Heathcote made more fuss than the sheep did. She was a born grumbler. She grumbled for self and husband; when it was wet, because it was not fine; when the sun shone, because the turnips wanted rain; when beef was dear, because corn was low; when the markets rose, because John had sold too soon; when they fell, because he had held on to his corn or his bullocks.

And she was infallible.

John Heathcote—as honest and sensible a man as ever sowed one grain in the hope of reaping twenty—farmed five hundred and thirty acres of land, good, bad, and indifferent. Three hundred and eighty acres were his own good freehold. The remaining hundred and fifty he rented of his neighbour, Lord Hunslope. Of the lot, but twenty acres came under the category of bad and indifferent. They served their useful purpose, if they did not pay their way; they gave Mrs. Heathcote good cause of complaint.

"What in the world your father wants to go and pay forty-two shillings an acre for Church Marsh for, nobody but John Heathcote knows," she had said to her daughters and at her husband a thousand times.

But her husband puffed his pipe in peace. She had pecked at him so long, he could not have digested his dinner without his usual desert.

At Parkside, they dined at half-past two in the afternoon. Dinner was over, and they were sitting in their pleasant dining-room. The winter's sun was shining brightly in at the windows.

At one, Lucy sat with some tatting on her lap. Mrs. Heathcote, in her violet silk, at the other, lazily peeling a pear. The farmer was smoking his clean clay pipe by the fire-side.

"What did he say, John?" asked Mrs. Heathcote.

She referred to Dick Mortiboy.

"I didn't see him."

"Didn't see him! I thought you said he was coming over to-day?"

"I saw your Uncle Richard."

"You said Dick was coming over this afternoon."

"I know I did. Your uncle said he was."

"Why didn't you ask him to dinner?"

"I did."

"It's a wonder you thought of it, I'm sure."

John Heathcote gave a grunt in acknowledgment.

"The last time that boy was here, he was brought in with a broken collar-bone."

"Broke it at Codgebroke Brook, on my old black mare. How that boy did ride!"

"When you mounted him. Riding your horses to death! I always said he'd come back like a bad shilling, if he only had time to do it."

"Your mother used to say she knew he was dead—didn't she, Lu?"

"Sometimes she said she thought so, papa," said Lucy, softly.

"I never had a lucky legacy in my life," sighed Mrs. Heathcote.

Her cousin Dick's return was a very bitter pill for her to swallow, but she had got it down.

"What did you want the boy dead for? You've got enough, haven't you, Lydia?" said her husband, rather angrily.

"He never was any good to himself or anybody else. I never counted on Uncle Richard's money though, for I felt sure he'd come back. Such scapegraces always do. What did they say about it, John? I suppose all the world and Market Basing know about it by this time!"

"Market Basing people know all about it," said Mr. Heathcote. "They were all talking about it this morning."

"What did they say?"

"Wait till the boy comes, and see him for yourself. Where's Grace gone?"

"She has gone with Frank Melliship down to the church, to practise something or another on the organ for Sunday. They'll catch their deaths of cold in that church a day like this?"

"Who's gone with 'em to blow?" asked Mr. Heathcote.

"Silly Billy, father," replied Lucy.

She said this quite gravely. Silly Billy had been blower ever since she had known the church.

"Then I'll bet a new hat the greenhouse fire's never been lighted. I told him to light it."

Mr. Heathcote put on his hat, and went out to light it himself.

"I'm quite anxious to see Cousin Dick, mamma," said

Lucy. "I wonder what he's like. Of course I don't recollect him a bit."

"You need not want, child."

"What a number of strange places he must have seen, and after living in a quiet little town like Market Basing! What a change for him! I should like to see foreign places, and—"

"Foreign fiddlesticks!" said her mother. "You shall go to Scarborough with us in the summer, if I can only make Dr. Kerby say you must. Then your father must take us."

"I wonder if Cousin Dick is married."

Her mother started.

"Married! of course not. In those outlandish places, who could there be to marry? Cannibal queens?"

"I don't know, mamma. I only wondered if he was married."

"Pare me another pear, Lucy, and don't be ridiculous. They keep very well; and I like a pear better than grapes, I think."

This accomplished general had been surprised by Dick's return. But she had formed her plans. He should be Grace's husband.

That was why he was not married.

"There is somebody on horseback coming across the park, mamma," said Lucy, looking towards Hunslope Towers.

There was an undisputed right of way across the earl's park.

"Where, girl?" cried her mother, hastily, joining her daughter at her window.

In the distance, there was a figure on a horse to be seen.

"It's your Cousin Dick—and Grace is stopping down at that church all this time. I wanted her to be back."

"Is it Cousin Dick, mamma? Whoever it is, he comes very slowly, I think."

"Yes; it's Dick Mortiboy. I know by the horse. It's that chestnut your poor aunt Susan used to drive. I know it by the blaze face."

"I can't see any white, mamma."

"My eyes are better than yours, Lucy. Put another glass on the table, as if we expected him. He's sure to drink some wine. And Lucy—"

"Yes, mamma."

"See if Mary is dressed. She went upstairs an hour ago. Pull the bell."

Lucy Heathcote carried out her mother's instructions, and returned to the window.

"Look at my hair behind, Lucy. It feels as if the braid was loose?"

"It's all right, mamma. Mamma, it is not a chestnut horse," said the daughter. "Look. It is Lord Launton, I'm sure?"

"So it is. What's he coming sawneying over here about I wonder? I thought he was at college. He was not at church on Sunday."

"Perhaps he's going into the village, mamma."

"Let's hope he is," said her mother.

But a minute or two afterwards, the heir of Hunslope Towers and Mr. Heathcote were seen going towards the stables together.

"If Grace and Frank don't come back before your cousin comes, I shall be very angry with her. I suppose your father will bring Lord Launton in."

"I dare say he will, mamma. Lord Launton never comes to ask papa a question without coming in." Then she added, "I think Grace took the cough stuff for Granny Worley in her pocket, and I believe she meant to take it round to her cottage."

"She never will go fooling all up the lane instead of coming straight home."

"Poor old granny's cough is dreadfully bad."

"Dreadfully fiddlestick! Let Silly Billy take it when he goes home. I've no patience with such nonsense!"

They heard steps in the passage. The matron smoothed her ruffled plumage. Her face beamed with smiles as the door opened, and in came Mr. Heathcote with Lord Launton.

He was a lad about twenty-one, light-haired, short-sighted, tall, and thin; shy, and hesitating in his manner, with a little stammer. Mr. Heathcote was a tenant of the earl's; and this young lord, as a boy had been accustomed to run in and out of Parkside, so that a visit from him had not by any means the social significance which Mrs. Heathcote would have wished to see in it.

"It's nothing, Mrs. Heathcote—really nothing at all," he stammered as he dropped his hat in his effort to find a chair. "How do you do, Miss Heathcote?—I was passing, and I—I thought I should like to ask Mr. Heathcote's opinion about—but it is really a trifle—the horse Mr. Heathcote bought for me turns out to have a corn. I was afraid he might prove lame through it."

He was at Oxford, where he had the reputation of being a

scholar and a poet; but he had not yet learned to hide those signals of confusion and distress which modesty and shamefacedness hung out continually upon his cheeks. A lad, for the rest, of high-born and generous tendencies, who read the tales of his ancestors' valour to profit, seeing that the virtues of self-sacrifice and duty are the modern substitutes for those old ones of bravery and strength; and knowing that with these the nineteenth century may be made as fair a battle-field as any chronicled by Villehardouin and Froissart.

A poetic youth, too, and a dweller in that cloud-land of rosy mist and shapeless castles where the future shines before the eyes of dreaming youth like a landscape by Turner—vague, glorious, and golden. In his own home, with a common-place and rather stupid father, and a mother always occupied with her projects and pet societies, there was no one with whom he could exchange ideas; and so he peopled the solitude with creations of his own brain, and wandered about the glorious old park which surrounds Hunslope Towers until every avenue of it was filled with the fanciful beings of his own imagination, and every glade was a scene of romance, exploit, and endurance. A foolish, fond, and silly way of passing the hours: an unproductive, unpractical, and wasted time, quite useless in these days of competitive examinations—detrimental to honour-lists—and only useful in after-life if, haply, when the fallow years are spent, the soil is found richer and stronger; if, haply, strength of will grows out of vague aspiration, and purpose out of hope.

Ronald, Viscount Launton, was twenty-one: the only son of an impoverished peer. He knew well—it was the bitterness of his life—that he was expected to raise the fortunes of the house by a good marriage. He had always understood this, from the day when he began to understand anything. And at first it did not seem to matter. But there came a time—and it comes to all alike—when he found himself a man; when he felt his sex; when his thoughts turned naturally, and by that noble instinct which it is the business of our civilization to divert or repress, to the love of woman. Chateaubriand, during his years of adolescence, constructed for himself an imaginary woman. One lent him her hair, one her eyes, one her figure, one her hands, and one her mind. This was fatal, because the woman of his dreams never came to him, and he spent his life in looking for her. Ronald was wiser. He found one woman lovely enough, graceful enough, refined

enough for a poet's idol, and set her up to be worshipped in
that Holy of Holies—the heart of a pure man. He seldom
spoke to her: he never told her that he loved her. She never
guessed it. Their stations in life were different: for the idol
of Lord Launton was Grace Heathcote, Farmer John's eldest
daughter.

As the mother, so the boys : as the father, so the girls. A
fanciful rule, and often enough proving itself by its exceptions.
But in the Heathcote family, there was a refinement and
delicacy of feeling about the farmer, in spite of his rough down-
rightness, which you might look for in vain in his wife. Mrs.
Heathcote was essentially common-place—vulgar sometimes,
ambitious always. Her daughters, who had been educated in
London with their cousins—other Heathcotes, of a higher
social position than themselves, with whom we have little to
do—owed, doubtless, some of their refinement to culture and
training. But training is only skin deep, and wears off like
veneer. It was the hereditary quality that showed itself in
them : the gentle blood of the Heathcotes, come down to
them through long centuries of varied and chequered fortunes.

Lucy, the younger, now about nineteen, who had been the
especial favourite of Miss Susan Mortiboy, seemed to have
imbibed something of her cousin's deeply religious character.
She was weakly, and often suffering : her face one of those
thin, pale faces whose beauty is chiefly that of expression—
but yet not without a beauty of its own, with its abundant
wealth of rich brown hair, and large and deep brown eyes. A
girl who seemed to have fixed her thoughts on things above
this world : yet one who found none of its duties beneath her.
John Heathcote loved his daughter Grace with a sort of passionate tenderness ; but when he thought of Lucy, it seemed
to him as if his heart melted within him. Grace was the sun
of his life ; Lucy, like the moonshine, not so bright or so
beautiful, but softer, sweeter, more holy. If Farmer John
were to read what I have written, he would declare that it
was all nonsense and romance. But it is true, nevertheless.
Was Grace, then, beautiful really, or only beautiful in the eyes
of her silent lover ? Wait a moment.

Lord Launton has been sitting all this time, answering Yes
and No to Mrs. Heathcote's questions, and nervously wishing
that he had not called. He stays about a quarter of an hour,
and then, grasping his hat, he asks with a tremendous blush—
"How is Miss Grace ?"

And then he retires, stumbling over the door-mat, and walking off with one of Mr. Heathcote's whips instead of his own.

"I like Lord Launton so much, mamma," said Lucy. "What a pity he is so shy!"

"If he asked my girl to have him, I don't know that she should," thought Mrs. Heathcote. "They're so poor."

Lord Launton turned off along the lane which led to his father's park. A pretty, tree-shaded lane in summer, where blackberry bushes across the ditch sent trailing branches over the abyss, pitfalls into which the children fell in the autumn, and scratched themselves; where honeysuckles, too, twined about among sweet wild roses, and long foxgloves shot up in July; but now, in February, a dismal place enough, with its two frozen ruts, each a foot and a half deep, and the unrelieved brown of its hedgerows.

Two persons found, even on this cold afternoon, some pleasure in the scenery. They were walking slowly down the lane, side by side; and one of them, a girl, had her face bent downwards.

Lord Launton's cheeks flushed a deep crimson when he saw them. He half stopped, as if he would turn back—but changed his mind; and making an effort, rode on with head tossed back, and a curious flash in his blue eyes. At the sound of his horse's hoofs, both looked up. He took off his hat, and held out his hand.

"I have just been to the farm, Miss Heathcote."

"Indeed, Lord Launton. Do you not recognise Mr. Melliship?"

His lordship began to stammer again.

"I—I—I—think we were at Eton together, Mr. Melliship, but you were in a higher form, and you can hardly remember me, I suppose."

Frank Melliship laughed.

"In any case, after five years, we can hardly be expected to remember each other. You are spending the vacation at the Towers?"

"Yes—yes—until I go back to Oxford."

Then Lord Launton left them, riding on fast to conceal his own agitation.

"Heavens!" he thought; "he is a man; and what am I, who cannot for five minutes preserve my presence of mind?" And then was miserable the whole evening, with the feeling that he had made a visible fool of himself. Of course, he had done nothing of the kind.

Of the pair whom he left behind, the girl was taller than the average stature of her sex. Her warm winter dress, with its sealskin jacket and furs, was not so thick as to hide altogether the graceful lines of her admirable figure; nor could her thick veil altogether conceal the roses of her cheek and the brightness of her eyes—eyes with the clear brown tinge, the colour of truth and loyalty. Nor could the dank and misty atmosphere of the winter's day take its gloss from the glorious brown hair, as profuse and as abundant as her sister's, which wanted no artificial helps to set forth its wealth. Grace Heathcote is so lovely, that Lord Launton's boyish infatuation is easily understood ; so lovely, that we seem to know what is passing in the breast of the young man who walks beside her. For a beautiful girl is a treasure—more priceless than any work of art—which makes every man long to call it his own; to envy him who has the happiness to dwell for ever in the magic of her eyes, to revel in the sunshine of her love. We love them at random, and all for the sake of their beauty : we know not what may be the soul that lies beneath : we stake our life and its happiness upon the chance that, under so fair a form, God has given the world as fair a heart. We have an instinct—whether true or false, Heaven knows—that goodness and truth, and fidelity and honour, accompany beauty; that where the loveliness which moves our heedless natures is found, there also those things which make life happy when passion is spent, are found also. If they are not there, we believe them to be; and so life goes on, and our love becomes our wife, and remains an angel still. Socrates treated Xantippe kindly, forgetful of the high spirits which had once carried her so far as to pour the basin of water over his head ; the judicious Hooker rocked the cradle, doing his wife's work, while he was writing his "Ecclesiastical Polity," without a murmur; and the illustrious Dr. Johnson never ceased to mourn the loss of the painted old woman whom his fancy had endowed with the virtues of the celestials.

Grace Heathcote being a woman, was, of course, not an angel. But there were more than one who thought her so. Lord Launton, as we have seen; Frank Melliship, as we have to see; and, at a distance, George Ghrimes—the sturdy bachelor of five-and-thirty, who had her in his heart, laid by like a pleasure to be enjoyed stealthily and in secret, and to be worshipped with the hopeless devotion of one who battles for a hopeless cause—like a Communalist of Paris.

"You were at school with Lord Launton, and yet you have forgotten him, Frank?" asked Grace.

"He has been away whenever I was at home, and I have not seen him for five years. Do you often meet him?" This with the faintest tinge of jealousy.

"Oh, yes—very often. And I like him extremely. He used to come to Parkside when he was quite a little boy."

"So did I."

"Yes; and you used to break my dolls, and make me cry."

"But we always kissed and made it up again."

"Oh, of course. Children always do."

"Well, then, I wish we were children again."

Grace laughed.

"That you might destroy my dolls again?"

"No."

Frank Melliship was silent again. It is not always easy to approach a difficult subject.

Grace took up the talk.

"And now you have really left Cambridge, and come to Market Basing for good; do you think you will be happy in such a dull place?"

"That depends on one or two things."

Grace did not ask what they were.

"There is something wrong about my father," said the young man. "Something seems to be worrying him. That will have to disappear first. He seems very well; but he is sometimes distrait, and returns answers showing that he has not been attending to the questions. And—well, we shall see?"

"And what is the next thing to make you happy?"

"A hope, Grace."

"But any man may have a hope. Then what is yours?"

"I hope to realize the dream I was telling you when Lord Launton passed us, and interrupted me. May I tell it you again?"

"Yes," said Grace, softly.

"Then stand still, for we are close to home, and listen again. I dreamed that a childish fancy was to be the settled purpose of a man, and that what I had thought of as a boy was to be the only thing which could give me happiness when I grew up. I dreamed that what might make me happy might make another too. Grace, tell me if my dream was presumptuous. Tell me—my darling—for I love you!"

She put her hand in his, and looked him frankly in the face.
" You may hope, Frank, if it will make you happy."
" And you, Grace—can my love make you happy? My words have not offended you ?"
This time she looked him full, without blushing, for she saw no reason for shame.
" Frank, nothing that you could say is able to offend me. Nothing will ever make me happy but your love."
For an answer, he lifted the veil from her face, and kissed her lips, and cheeks, and eyes, and white brow. No one saw them ; and the last ray of the early setting sun, as it shone out from the clouds for a moment before it sank, lay upon the pair, as if with the blessing of God.
Then Grace broke from her lover, and laying both her hands in his for a moment, she turned the corner by the great yew-hedge, and fled into the house.

CHAPTER THE NINTH.

E left Dick Mortiboy fast asleep at madame's the blanchisseuse, in Greek-street, Soho, at a few minutes past twelve a.m. on Thursday morning—alone with his purse, his pistol, his bowie-knife ; with the great toe of his right foot communicating with the handle of the door. But his ingenious device was thrown away. He was as safe in the second-floor chamber of madame's house as he would have been in the strong-room of the Bank of England. The people were honest; conspirators, not burglars, frequented the place.

Dick got up at half-past ten: breakfasted with Lafleur at eleven, at the Sablonière, on oysters, galantine, watercresses, black coffee, and the little glass of white brandy. Then came the time of business. He completed his cabinet of specimens, and touched up the map of his Madagascar estate. Dinner at seven, at the Café Quatre Frères, just out of Leicester-square, Euchre till bed-time—winning instead of losing. On Friday, having completed his business in town, he took the afternoon train to Market Basing.

Saturday he walked abroad, and found himself famous.

His father had parted reluctantly from his long-lost son, even for a couple of days. Nothing but the urgency of Dick's London business reconciled the old man to his going.

When he came back after his short visit, old Ready-money showed more delight than he had done when his son came back, and first introduced himself after a twelve years' absence.

Then, Richard Melliship Mortiboy was as a shadow.

Now, "My son Richard" was a reality.

The old man showed his pleasure in many odd ways. He believed in Dick: he swallowed as gospel all he told him: his name was for ever on his father's lips—

"Richard come back again to his old father. A credit to me. What things he's seen! Nobody here like him."

These were the things he said. And he would press his lean hands on Dick's stout sides a dozen times an hour.

The sense of touch assured him of his reality.

He walked from Derngate to the bank that morning with his father. It was market day, and the little town showed its wonted busy aspect—an appearance it put on only once a week. Everybody stared at him as a wonder. People they passed on their way turned to look after old Ready-money and his newly found son.

Dick's return was likely to be a wonder in Market Basing for more than nine days.

At the bank, Ghrimes and the old clerks welcomed him as the prince come back to his father's kingdom.

They bowed down their necks before the heir.

And Dick had a pleasure in their friendly recognitions, and greeted all whom he remembered in his most kindly way, graciously acknowledging the homage they paid him.

After an hour's talk with his father, he said—

"It would be just as well if I looked up a few people to-day; and in the afternoon I shall go over to Hunslope, and spend the evening with the Parkside people, I think.'"

"Very well, Dick—very well. It's Grace's birthday to-morrow. Richard, I'm afraid Cousin Lyddy isn't very glad you're come back. She'd booked my money, and she might have had it, perhaps : for blood is blood, my boy. Where else are you going, Richard ? "

" Well, father, I shall look up Uncle Melliship as well. I never had any grudge against him."

" Well—no, no. He is your uncle. But pride's going to have a fall, Dick—pride's going to have a fall; and peacocks' tails are going to lose their feathers."

" What do you mean, father ? "

" Patience, Richard—patience. Not that I could help it if I would."

Dick did not question his father further.

The old man went off to the foundry, and his son spent an hour with Ghrimes. He showed himself so quick-witted, so ready and apt to comprehend, that Mr. Mortiboy's manager was startled.

" What a pity, Mr. Richard—what a pity you did not stay at home, and be your father's right-hand man."

" Perhaps I've done better by going abroad."

" Perhaps you have. You know best. Anyhow, stay now you have come back. Your father's not so strong as he was. At sixty-five, hard work begins to tell upon a man. And I will say this for Mr. Mortiboy—he has worked harder than any man I ever knew. As for pleasure, he doesn't know the meaning of it."

" I beg your pardon, Mr. Ghrimes—he does know the meaning of it. Every man must have pleasures of some kind, or he dies or goes mad. You will do well to remember that when you have to deal with your clerks. My father's pleasure is to watch the money growing. It isn't a bad sort of pleasure, perhaps ; though it isn't mine."

Old Ready-money had had his pleasure—had driven to the foundry and the brewery in Susan's carriage ; hunted up his tenants, harried his mortgagors, and enjoyed himself every day after his own fashion.

" My own life," Dick went on, with a sort of sigh, " has been one chiefly of hard work. But it has had some of the pleasure of success. There are vicissitudes—vicissitudes in business, Mr. Ghrimes. And over there"—he jerked his finger over his left shoulder, in the direction of the Arctic Pole, but Mr. Ghrimes understood him to mean Mexico— "over there the vicissitudes are very frequent."

" So I suppose.

" Yes. Fancy having your estate confiscated once a year by

a new Government, which only lasts till the old one picks up strength enough to overturn it. Fancy riding down to the port with a caravan of silver, and seeing yourself stripped in a day of six months' work—eh? And fancy having the pleasure of winning it back again at a single *coup*, and hanging all the rascals you haven't shot—eh? There's life, Ghrimes, there's pleasure, there's excitement in that."

Dick slapped him on the back, and laughed, showing all his white teeth, like a jolly, good-tempered lion who slaughters the other beasts for mere pleasure and love of sport.

"You must tell me more about your life in the West," said Mr. Ghrimes.

"So I will. You shall come in one evening. We are devilish lively in the evening, the governor and I. You drink gin?"

Mr. Ghrimes smiled. Everybody in Market Basing knew of Mr. Mortiboy's weekly bottle of gin.

"Come and see me," he said, "and I'll get Frank Melliship. By Jove! I have quite forgotten that boy. What sort of fellow is he?"

"A capital fellow," said Ghrimes, with enthusiasm. "Full of life and energy; full of cleverness too—though not bookish like his father. One that will revive the old bank, and double its work as soon as he gets into it."

"They haven't been doing well lately?"

"Not so well"—Ghrimes spoke cautiously. "But they will pull through. Oh, yes, they *must* pull through."

"Do you know anything, Mr. Ghrimes, that goes on?"

"I know everything that has been done. I don't know everything that is going to be done."

Richard talked to Mr. Ghrimes for some time. Then he put on his hat and strolled out. Not many minutes' walking brought him to the old bank. He stopped, read the faded old letters, "Melliship, Mortiboy & Co," and went in.

"Mr. Melliship in?"

"Yes, sir. Engaged at present. What name?"

"Tell him his nephew, Mr. Richard Mortiboy."

The clerk stared. Was this great bearded giant the son of old Ready-money? The news of his home-coming had been noised abroad, but no report was yet about of the manner of man.

Mr. Melliship was in his private room. With him a clergyman. The banker, looking portly, and handsome and well, was standing with his back to the fire, laying down the law.

"In a case of this nature, it is incumbent on the rich to do all they can. It is especially the work of the rich. All rich men ought to contribute."

"I wish all rich men would," said the clergyman, who was the representative of the Society for Sending Additional Missionaries to Cannibal Parts.

"I shall myself."—Here a clerk whispered in his ear. "Show my nephew in. I shall myself," he continued, as Richard entered the room, "have great pleasure in putting down my name for a hundred pounds."

"My dear sir," began the parson in a delighted tone.

"Not a word—not a word, I beg. My dear nephew, I am indeed rejoiced to see you."

He shook hands with his clerical friend! and then, shutting the door, shook hands again with Dick.

"And so you have come home, and are come to see me. I am glad of it—I am glad of it. Do not let any little ill-feeling which may exist on your father's part towards myself be the cause of coolness between us. And where have you been all this time?" Then he said to himself, "I see Emily again in you."

"Looking for fortune."

"Aha! We all look for fortune. How comes it, as Horace asks, that no one is content with the lot which the gods have assigned him?"

"The gods assigned me a pound a week," said Dick, "so I naturally revolted, and made my way without further help from them."

Which was true—his path and that laid down for mortals by the Olympians having been widely different.

"Have the Fates, then—you know we are all under the will of the Fates—been kinder than they promised at first?"

"Yes—that is, I have forced my way."

"Like the old myth of the Titans' war. You know they defeated the gods."

"Indeed, sir, I know nothing of the sort."

"Well—I suppose your reading has been neglected in your travels. You really have done well? You are immensely improved—if you will permit an impertinence—more like your poor mother. You will dine with us this evening?"

"Not to-night, sir. I have another engagement. Next week, I shall be very happy. How is Frank?"

"Well—he is over at Hunslope. And can I do nothing for you, Dick? Do you want any money?"

"None, sir—none, thank you."

"Your father and I are not, unfortunately, on the best terms possible. Between ourselves, the bitter feeling is all on his part. It arises, Dick "—here Mr. Melliship stooped and whispered—"from jealousy at my superior good luck."

Dick stared. What could this mean? He had heard from his father of his uncle's strange conduct on the day of the funeral.

"The years roll on, and bring only successes to me, Richard. I am oppressed—I am encumbered with my wealth. See here "—he opened a drawer in a safe, and showed it full of sovereigns. "But that is nothing—nothing. This is but a trifle. But, my dear nephew, you must not let me waste my time. I have to negotiate with my agents in London about a loan which demands all my energies, and really nearly all my resources. Good-bye, my dear nephew—good-bye. And remember, you are to dine with us next week."

Dick went away in a sort of amazement. What did his father mean by those mysterious hints about impending misfortune? Here was a man subscribing £100 to a missionary society, offering him money, talking of his wonderful success, and mixing himself up with foreign loans.

In the afternoon he walked over to Hunslope, along the well-remembered road. Not a tree seemed changed in all the years he had been away.

For a mile Lord Hunslope's park wall skirted the road.

At a little door Dick had often ridden under in his hunting days, a young man was trying in vain to reach the latch with his whip-handle. His horse was shy and fresh, and would not go within a yard of it. The rider persevered without success. Dick politely opened the door for him.

"You are Lord Hunslope's son, I know," said Dick to himself.

But he was a stranger to Lord Launton, who thanked him, apologised for his horse's shyness, and rode through the gate into the park.

In twenty minutes more, Dick was at Parkside. He arrived there as the short winter's day was closing in. The door was opened by a tall, comely woman of about six and thirty. The lamp was lighted in the hall, and as Dick came into the light —for it was now about four o'clock—it fell full on his face. The woman gave a little cry, and laid her hand on his arm.

Then he looked her full in the face, and started back, muttering in his teeth—

"Damnation!————It's Polly?"

"You, Dick—is it you? I heard you were back again, and I knew it would not be long before you would be coming to look after your poor—"

"Shut the door, Mary," cried a voice from within. "The wind is blowing right through the house. Who is it? Is it Mr. Richard?"

"Meet me on Sunday," Polly had time to whisper, "in the lane behind your father's house. I'm going to Market Basing to see my mother."

"The old place?"

"Ay, the old place. There will be nobody there. Meet me at church time." She gave his hand a wet, slobbering kiss, and opened the door of Mrs. Heathcote's parlour. "Master Dick Mortiboy, ma'am."

"Cousin Dick!" cried Mrs. Heathcote, springing from her chair. "Master Dick, indeed, Mary, to a big man like this!"

Dick bestowed a cousinly kiss alike on mother and daughters, and shook hands with John Heathcote and Frank Melliship; then he sat down by the fire, and they began to make much of him.

Years before, when Dick was a bright young lad of ten, after his mother died, Hunslope Farm was the place where alone he seemed to be able to escape from the harshness of a father with whom everything that he said or did was said or done wrong. At all times of the year it was a happy place. For in the winter there was a meet of the hounds which cousin John always attended, mounted on a serviceable animal that carried him as well as any scarlet coat's hunter; or he borrowed a gun, and went out with the farmer; or there were parties in the evening, when they danced and played games; or there were the children, Grace and Lucy, and Frank and Kate Melliship, to all of whom he was the senior and the hero. And at other times of the year there would be the woods, full of all manner of delight to boys; with animals put there on purpose to be unsuccessfully hunted, nests only built to be plundered, wild fruit to be gathered. Most of his holidays, therefore, had been spent at Hunslope Farm, till he arrived at the age of sixteen, when his father declared he had had enough schooling, and he put him in the bank at no salary at all, no allowance for pocket-money, and no more holidays. Then his life became very dreary. In that dull old house of his aunt's few visitors ever came. There were no parties; there was no pleasure. She herself, a good woman, whose heart was wholly given up to religion, gave no thought to the wants—other than the spiritual and bodily wants—of the lad who was growing up longing for society, for some variation of the monotonous life he led. Presently, he began to creep out at nights—letting himself down from the bed-room on the first floor when he was supposed, after nine o'clock, to be asleep; and young Dick Mortiboy became familiar with whatever form of dissipation Market Basing had to offer long before he was tempted, from want of money, to commit the offence which led to his expulsion from home. But of his dissipation and his nocturnal vigils with the choice spirits of the market-town good Aunt Susan never knew. And she had mourned for her runaway nephew all the days of her life.

It must be confessed that this return was a fatal blow to Mrs. Heathcote's schemes and projects. Dick returned, not like the Prodigal Son, empty, starving, and repentant—in which case there would have been hopes for her, because his father would infallibly have sent him empty away—but rich, fat, well-looking, and independent. Now, in Mr. Mortiboy's judgment, no proverb could be better than that which the Frenchman invented—" Nothing succeeds like success." Success dazzled him. His son, a successful man—as he said himself, and it was most unlikely he should lie on so important a point—was an object of admiration to him. Had he come home like the young fellow in the parable, Mr. Mortiboy might have shown him the forged cheque, given him another ten-pound note, and bidden him go away again, to show his face no more; but left him his money when he died.

However, Mrs. Heathcote was not the woman to show, even to her own daughters, her regret at an accident so unforeseen. She extended to Dick the hand of friendship and the cheek of affection. She made his visit an occasion of rejoicing; ordered an addition of a brace of birds to the supper; and openly thanked Heaven for his safe return.

Farmer John was unfeignedly glad to see him, and they became at once the best of friends—particularly when, after supper, and over a pipe and brandy and water, Dick reeled off a few of his colonial experiences, of which he had a large stock always ready in his inventive brain. It cost him something not to be able to tell more of the truth to the farmer;

but it would not do. It was too important for his own interest to maintain the fiction of the cotton estate.

They had music. Lucy played. Grace sang a duet with Frank. Dick had not spent an evening in the society of ladies for ten long years. He sat mute and softened in their presence—not because he felt any sense of moral degradation, but because there is in youth and purity something of the power, signified in that old legend of "Una and the Lion," of taming for the time every wild beast that is not maddened with pursuit and terror. Dick was a wild beast which had not been hunted for many a long day.

"You used to sing and play, Cousin Dick," said Lydia. "Sing one of your old songs."

She touched the chords of a simple old air that he used to sing when he wanted to please her, years before.

Dick shook his head.

"I've forgotten the words—and the tune, too, for that matter. But I'll sing you something else, if you like."

He sat down to the piano, letting his fingers run carelessly over the keys for a few minutes: and then, playing that sort of simple accompaniment which a man with a musical ear picks up for himself, he sang a Mexican love song. As he sang it—beating a sort of time now and then with his knuckles on the piano, as a Spaniard beats his guitar at intervals—his rich, flexible voice vibrating in the low room, and his fierce eyes turned full upon the girls—for it was indeed a love song, only they did not know its meaning—Lucy shuddered, and grasped tightly the arm of her chair, while Grace stared at him like some poor bird entranced by a rattlesnake.

They both felt relieved when he finished.

"Come," said Farmer John, "that's what I call something like a song. You must learn a few English ones, and then we shall do famously."

"All the Melliships have fine voices," said Mrs. Heathcote. "Yours is a bass; but has not Frank a splendid tenor? You will hear him in church on Sunday."

"You can hear him here better, Dick," said Mr. Heathcote. "Come up often and see us. It must be precious dull work with the old man. Now, say Good-night to the girls, and we will have a quiet pipe together before you and Frank go. Tomorrow's Sunday. He'll drive you back with him."

CHAPTER THE TENTH.

ICK MORTIBOY'S drive home from Parkside with his cousin, Frank Melliship, had not the effect of making him sleep more soundly than usual. Indeed, he spent a wakeful night—up to three or four o'clock in the morning, at all events. Two things were in his mind. First, he was wondering what in the world had kept Polly in the service of the Heathcotes all the years he had been away, and how in the world he should get her out of the neighbourhood of Market Basing. Secondly, he was struck with the notion that the finest girl he had ever seen in his life was his cousin, Grace Heathcote. And the two together, mistress and maid, crossing each other's paths in the tangled web of Dick Mortiboy's mind, served to keep him awake.

It was half an hour later than the usual breakfast hour when he walked into the parlour. Old Ready-money had finished his meal, and was carefully trimming his nails at the fireplace.

The old gentleman was dressed in the same ancient suit he had worn at the funeral.

"Good morning, father," said Dick, cheerfully. "I have overslept myself by half an hour this morning—a thing I don't do once a year."

"I'm glad to hear you say so, my boy. In a man of business, I love to see punctual habits. Take Time by the forelock, Dick. Look at me: up at daylight—up at daylight—winter and summer. 'Awake, my soul,' the poet says, 'and with the sun, thy daily stage of business run!' I began that as a boy, Dick, and I've always consistently acted up to it. Nobody can say I haven't."

"All very well in England, father, but in countries I've been living in you have to be up before the sun."

"The poet meant England, Dick. It is the country of the business man."

"Yes, sir; though it must be admitted that a fine stroke of business is done by Englishmen abroad."

The old man's lips were moving, though there came from them no audible sound.

Dick's impression was that his father was repeating to himself the couplet he had made his rule of life.

There was a silence of a few moments, which Mr. Mortiboy was the first to break.

"Dick!"

"Well, father!"

"We've got to go to church. John and Lydia will be here soon. We're going to sit in your poor aunt's pew together. Shall you come with us?"

"Well, father, I have thought it over, and I think not. I shall go to chapel with you next Sunday, I hope."

"Very well, my boy. Very well. It's thirty years, I know, since I ever went to church. I've always paid for my pew at chapel, though, and I've often gone."

"Well, you've got a fair return for it, I hope?"

Dick alluded not so much to the spiritual benefit his father might have derived from his Ebenezer, as to the Dissenting connection, which was rich in the town.

"I must go to church to-day, Dick, with the Heathcotes—it's expected of me after the funeral. The Rector's going to preach. I hate a fuss and trouble, though. What is in that box, Dick?" said the old gentleman suddenly, pointing to a case his son had brought back from London with him.

"Only a few specimens and things from the estate, which I got from my partner. Would you like to see them?" asked his son, carelessly.

"Ay—ay—plenty of time before church. The bells don't begin till half-past ten. Open it now, Dick—open it now."

Dick lifted his box on to the table, and opened it.

It was a long deal case inscribed in large ink characters with the names of divers ports and stations situate in different parts of the habitable globe, and in it was packed a variety of things which might have gladdened the heart of a collector. Dick turned them all out upon the table. Some were loose, some in small boxes, some wrapped up in brown paper, one or two in many folds of tissue paper.

He threw a pair of curiously worked objects—apparently all beads and feathers—across the table, and began to lie like the proverbial trooper.

"That's a pair of leggings which I took from an Indian in Nicaragua. They were got by the Indian from the King of Mosquito Coast. The small yellow feathers that you see are taken from a very rare bird. They catch him in a trap, pull out the feathers, and let him go again, economically, to grow more. Of course these leggings are extremely valuable all along that coast"

"Dear me?" said Mr. Mortiboy, handling them with curiosity.

"Yes," Dick continued. "We were prospecting for silver. I had to shoot the Indian before I took the leggings, of course. You will observe the mark of his blood on the left leg."

"You didn't kill him, Dick?"

"Dead as a door-nail. But he would have killed me if I had not. That's the arrow which he was fitting into his bow as I brought him down. Take care of the point, because it's poisoned; and if you pricked yourself with it, no doctor in Market Basing could cure you."

The old man took it by the feathered end, and held it gingerly at arm's length.

"What did you shoot him with, Dick?" he asked curiously.

"With this," replied his son, taking a revolver from his breast pocket.

"Give them all to me," said Mr. Mortiboy, reaching out his hands. "Give them all to me. I will hang them up in my bed-room, over my bed, and look at them every night."

"You may have the leggings and welcome, and the arrow; but I can't let you have the pistol, because it was given to me by my friend Senhor de Las Casas, of Cuba, who made me promise never to part with it as long as I lived. See, it's silver-mounted. Ah! take care—it's loaded."

His father gave it back in haste. A loaded revolver was a fearful and inexplicable weapon, not to be handled.

"But take care yourself, Dick. Good heavens!—if it was to go off in your pocket!"

Dick laughed, and proceeded with his budget.

"This ivory-handled dagger I got from the King of Dahomey for killing a gorilla which we met in the woods. His Majesty perhaps overrated my exploit. This"—he went on quickly, for he saw that his father was about to inquire into the nature and habits of the gorilla—"this is some of the silver ore from the Mexican mine I told you of."

"Let me see that—let me see that. Is it real silver?"

"Silver ore, you know. You have to smelt it. There, you see the dark stuff among the mica. That's silver. Put it on your mantelshelf."

"What!—and have it stolen?"

"A beautiful mine that came from. But I told you about it. It's the mine that only my partner and I know of. And it only wants a capital of £10,000 to work it."

"That's a lot of money, Dick."

"It is—it is—I know it. I suppose we shall have to make a company of it," looking curiously at his father.

Mr. Mortiboy said nothing, and Dick went on to describe his collection.

"This," he said, taking a small roll of parchment, "is one of the most interesting things that I ever got hold of. Now you will never guess what this is?"

"It's a chart, I suppose."

"You're quite right. You never heard of Turks' Islands, did you? I thought not. Between Turks' Islands and the Bahamas are a lot of small islets—little heaps of sand, many of them—where no ships can go. I went among them, however, with the aid of this map, which my old friend Captain— never mind his name—gave me. I went among them, father, and I found what he had told me on his death-bed to be all true."

"True! what was true?"

"The position of the wreck indicated in the map. She lies in six to ten fathom water. I went there alone in the ship's yawl, because I would have no eye-witness. She lay to outside the reefs the while. There lies the old wreck, sir, and on board of her is—"

Here Dick stopped, and heaved a mighty sigh.

"What is there, Dick?"

"A hundred thousand pounds, in hard ingots of sterling gold and silver—that's all. And it wants five or six thousand to get it up."

"My de-ar boy, my de-ar son, do you tell me that you can lay your hands on a hundred thou—a hundred thou—sand pounds?" Mr. Mortiboy gasped with emotion.

"I? Am I a professional diver? Can I navigate a ship all by myself? No, sir; but I can pay men to dive, and sailors to man a craft; and I can command her myself, and bring home a hundred thousand pounds."

"It's a deal of money, Dick. Six thousand pounds! It takes a long time to get it."

"So it does, so it does. Never mind. I don't ask you to advance a farthing. But it's right to tell you of these things. I'll start another company."

Dick gazed fixedly at the map, which he folded up, and replaced in the box.

"All the rest are only things from our estate. Here's some

of the cotton. Did you ever see finer? See, it grows in its pod, just so. We've got a thousand acres already under cultivation, and shall have another thousand next year. Profits are enormous ; I shall be able to buy up Market Basing, father, in ten years' time."

"Don't be too sure. You might find me in the way," said the old man, in great good humour. "What's this, Dick?"

"This?—oh, only a little Californian nugget. I picked it up myself in another man's washing, and he gave it me. Pure gold. Now, that is something worth having. You take it, and have a ring made of it, and wear it. I have got a little bracelet, made of nuggets of the same stuff, I'm going to give Grace to-day, for a birthday present."

"Ah!—well, well, my son, if you had not happily come back to your old father, all would have been very different. Give it her. She's a good girl. I've—I've got something for her myself that will make 'em all stare."

Mr. Mortiboy clutched the nugget greedily. Pure gold!— the thing he had spent his life in scraping together. And here was his son picking it up in the open field, without any trouble or exertion, and thinking nothing of it. It seemed strange to him. This, by the way, was the only genuine thing in all Dick's collection.

The old money-grubber leaned back, and looked at all his new-made treasures, and folded them, so to speak in his arms, and devoured them with his eyes. They represented to his imagination—for he had an imagination—boundless possibilities of gain. Sunken treasure, silver mines, cent. per cent. profit on cotton—why should not he have a share in these things? Why should not he, indeed, be the director, manager, owner, and king of all these? But the risk—the risk : and then he would lose his son again.

Already, Dick had acquired an influence over his father's mind which no one else had ever had. It was his strength, his vigour, his keen intellect, his audacity, his success, which captivated the old man. He was indeed his son—but how changed from the lad of his memories? Mr. Mortiboy's life had been lonely, and without affection. Between his sister and himself there were few topics of interest in common. He had lived almost entirely in his own room—sitting, night after night, bending over those books of which some men never tire : morning, noon, and night: books ruled with blue lines horizontally, and red lines vertically. Living this lonely life, he had ceased for years to look for friendship and kindliness. Those who are themselves brooders over fancied injuries are never capable of even receiving affection without suspicion and distrust. He knew people loved his brother-in-law. They did not love him. But they came to do business with him—first, because he did it better than Mr. Melliship; and, secondly —ha! ha!—because they must; because there was no help for them; because they were wrapped in the coils which he had wound round them; because, if they did not come to him, it only depended on his will whether the cord should be tightened, and their miserable necks wrung. It was something to be powerful: something to be feared. But, meantime, there were gleams of light across his darkened and selfish brain which told him that the love of men was, after all, a good thing to have.

Then suddenly on his monotonous and dismal days had burst the sunshine of vigorous life and strength. In that lonely house there was again a creature that made a noise in it, striding about the place, singing, laughing, having a great voice. Within the circle of Mr. Mortiboy's power had chanced a capture, as he thought, more important than any of the rest —the capture of his errant son. And, good heavens! thought the proud father, what a man he was!—decided in action, quick to comprehend, ready to suggest. Strong, too, and comely in face and figure: a man to be proud of: a man before whom Market Basing ought to bow down and do homage. And then, so quiet with all his superiority: always deferring to his father, yet always independent in his judgment. As Mr. Mortiboy went to his bed at this period, he used to murmur to himself a species of thanks for his splendid son—which was addressed to no Deity in particular, but had its own form quite as much as if it were a Collect, and intimated the gratitude of the parent that in his son's breast no Peacockery could be found. And he did now what, when he was ten years' younger, he. would have been incapable of. He believed firmly, absolutely, all that Dick thought fit to tell him: that he was prosperous—not yet rich, but in the way to wealth: that his life had been a long struggle with fortune, and that he had conquered fate. That was to Mr. Mortiboy's mind mere matter of faith, established by an internal conviction not to be shaken. He was, therefore, already inordinately proud of his son; and it wanted but little for the pear which Dick longed to pluck to drop ripe into his hands.

The sound of church bells beginning to chime fell on their ears; and Mr. Mortiboy, with a groan of disgust, rose to put on his overcoat.

"They'll be all here directly," he said. "Let us put these things away before they come, else they'll very likely want to be presented with some. Help me to carry them to my bedroom."

Dick had not been in that room since his mother died. It was unchanged: the same red canopy to the bed; the same hangings, only somewhat faded; the same carpet, but worn into holes; and the same chintz-covered chair by the bedside. The only piece of furniture which had been added was a long oaken press, occupying half one side of the room.

Mr. Mortiboy opened it. Within were sundry boxes, drawers, and shelves, together with an iron safe.

"Let us put the things here," he said. "It's the only place where they will be safe. Here are all your poor mother's things, Dick. See"—he opened a drawer in which lay packages in tissue paper—"her jewels: they were all good, poor thing. This is her watch. Ah! dear me. And here are Susan's trinkets: I put 'em in here. I want to give something to Lucy Heathcote—I promised Susan—but not to-day, not to-day. There's that present for Grace.—I'll promise it —from Susan's things. Susan was very fond of Lucy.

The old man had contracted a habit of talking to himself, and sometimes forgot that a listener was present. Dick noted with curiosity the collection of odds and ends—old plate, old watches, rings, forks and spoons—which lay in the strong press, whose thick doors—iron lined—were able to turn the burglar's tools for many an hour. He looked and coveted. Then he deposited his Mexican and Californian spoils with the rest, and saw his father safely lock all up. Ten minutes after, Mr. Mortiboy was on his way to church; and at the last sound of the parson's bell, Dick lit his pipe, and strolled into the garden which lay at the back of the house.

"It's awkward"—strongly qualified—"that girl turning up again. I must get her out of the way. Anyhow, the governor must not hear anything—not just as we are getting on comfortably, too. It only wants a week or two to make him open his mouth like an oyster, and take up the silver mine, and the sunken ship, and the cotton estates and all.

The long, old-fashioned garden was bounded by a high brick wall. There was a door in one corner, always kept locked— not even Mr. Mortiboy knew where the key was. Dick had forgotten this, and tried to open it. Then he suddenly remembered, and burst into a laugh.

"By Jove! nothing is changed in the old place. And here's the pump on which I used to step; and here's the vine by which I got to the pump. Let us climb over, as I used to do when I crept out at night to meet Polly. It's exactly like the old times, only Polly's gone off: and I wish she was dead—by gad!"

Suiting the action to the word, by the help of the vine and the pump, he gained the top of the wall, and threw his legs over it. Beneath him, in the lane, stood Polly—the first at the trysting-place, as she always had been.

"Aha!" cried Dick, with his careless laugh—"there you are, old girl. Isn't it like twelve years ago?"

He leapt down, and stood at her side.

A narrow path ran along by the side of a deep sluggish river, between twenty and thirty feet wide. The path came from nowhere, and led nowhere, consequently no one ever walked along it; and particularly on Sunday morning, it was as lonely as a track in the prairie. Across the river stood, quite alone, a small, newly built villa, run up by an enterprising builder. He had failed, as the result of his enterprise, and the villa was now the property of Mr. Mortiboy. But no one had yet taken it.

Polly was dressed gaudily, in her Sunday best. A tall, finely shaped woman, with a face whose beauty was now on the wane: a well-developed, healthy creature, with those common-place features—good enough in their way—which you often see in country women. Her expression was bad, however: low, cunning and animal. She held out her red, strong hand to Dick, who took it without any great show of affection, and returned it to its owner immediately.

"Well, Poll?"

"Well, Poll? Is that all you've got to say to your true and faithful wife?"

"Don't you think, Poll, you had better stow that?"

"Don't you think you had better do something for me? A pretty thing, indeed, for the wife of old Ready-money's son to be cleaning knives in the kitchen while her husband is singing songs in the parlour! I heard you last night, and I had half a mind to spoil the sport."

"Did you though? Had you really?" Dick laid his heavy hand on her shoulder. "Do you know, Polly, it's devilish lucky for you that you stopped at half a mind?"

"Now, look here, Dick. Don't let's have no chaff. What are you going to do?"

"I tell you one thing I'm going to do, my girl. If you let out even by a whisper, or if I find you have let out, I'll tell the governor everything, go abroad at once, and never come back again. Now, you know if the governor's the kind of old boy to tip up handsomely to his son's wife—especially if she should turn out to be Polly Tresler. So be sensible, and let us talk things over."

"I'm sure I only want to be friendly"—beginning to whimper. "But it's hard, when one sees her man after twelve years, not to get so much as a kind word."

"If that's all you want," said Dick, "I've got lots of them put by in a box on purpose. I'll give you as many kind words as you like—and kisses, too, when no one's looking."

"No one's looking now, Dick. And oh, how handsome you've got!"

Dick gave a look north, and another south—that is, up and down the lane. After this concession to nuptial modesty, he bestowed a brace of kisses, one on each of his wife's buxom cheeks. She returned them with a warmth that rather embarrassed him.

"And you've never asked about the boy, Dick," she said, reproachfully.

"Oh, damn it! Is there a boy?"

"A beautiful boy, Dick—the picture of his father."

"And the boy's at Hunslope Farm, I suppose?"

"Then you suppose wrong, because he isn't. I went up to London again directly after you went away and deserted me."

"Hang it! I had to go."

"And never a letter, or a message, or a word, or a single sovereign."

"Hadn't got any sovereigns."

"Well, I went up to London, and the boy was born there, and nobody ever knew anything about it, Dick. And there he is now at school, bless his heart! and nobody would ever believe he was twelve years old."

Certainly there were more persons than one in the world who were ready to swear that the boy was no more than ten; but then, Dick could not be expected to know that.

"And I lived in London for eight years in service. Oh! good, Dick—I was always good. You believe that, don't you, my handsome husband?"

"Humph! Don't see any reason for saying 'No' at present." "And then I came back here, and I've been at Hunslope ever since. And oh! Dick, it's many a time I've been tempted to go to old Ready-money—"

"Wouldn't you have a better chance with him if you called him Mr. Mortiboy?"

"And say to him, 'I'm your lawful daughter, and little Dick'—only his name is Bill—' is your true and lawful grandson, and if you're a Christian you'll do something for him.' He'd have ought to have had every farden of the old man's money if you hadn't a come back. I've asked questions. Oh, Dick, I'm glad you're come."

"My father is a Dissenter, Polly. Perhaps his views of the duties of religion are different from ours. You and I are simple Church folk, you know. But I'm glad you didn't."

"No, I didn't. But what are we to do now, Dick? Am I to come and live with you, as in duty bound?"

Here she smiled affectionately at him.

Dick looked at her blankly.

"Things are as they are," he said, repressing a violent inclination to use profane words. "We can't undo what's done. You know, Polly, what an unlicked cub I was when I married you."

"You won't deny that, I hope?"

"That I was a fool?—oh! that I was married! No. I would if I could; but I can't, because there's a register at the church of St. Pancras; and though I was married—"

"That makes no difference, Dick. I found it out from a lawyer."

"Did you? Then you might have spared yourself the pains. No, I'm not going to deny it. And if you hold your tongue, and say nothing to anybody, now I am back—we can meet of an evening, you know, sometimes—I'll do something handsome for you; but if you talk, I'm off again. So there we are, and make no mistake."

Polly said nothing. All her hopes were knocked on the head. She stood twisting a riband in her red, ungloved hands, and looking at the big man, her husband, who enjoined his laws upon her. But she was constrained to obey. There was something in Dick Mortiboy which made most people feel that it would be better for them to do what he told them. And all the time she had been planning a little design to make him pay for silence, or threaten to acknowledge him openly. It did seem hard, too.

"How are you off for money?"

"I've got none; and Bill wants new clothes."

"I'll go and see Bill some day—not yet. Here's a ten-pound note. Get the little devil—"

"What, Dick, your own son?"

"What's the matter with the girl? Get the young cuss a new pair of breeches, and don't bother me about him."

He sat on a rail by the side of the lane—for they had been walking up and down—and put his hands in his pockets.

"Upon my word, Polly, I had almost forgotten you—I had indeed. And when I saw you at Hunslope, you might have knocked me down yourself, big as I am."

"And weren't you glad to see me, Dick?"

"No—devilish sorry," said her husband, truthfully. "I expected to find you married again, of course."

"Well, I *am* your wife."

"You said that before."

"And I mean to be, too."

"If you don't mean to do what I tell you, it'll be a poor look-out for you. So you'd better make no mistake on that point."

"Don't be cruel, Dick—the very first day and all," said Polly, the tears of vexation rising to her eyes.

The last hardening of a man's heart is the incrustation of that place where a woman's tears take effect. Dick relented a little, and re-stated his case—as a woman's lord and master should; but this time more kindly.

"Now, this is the first and last of it. If I'm to do anything for you, don't interfere. Don't come between me and the old man. I'm not going to be a brute. I married you, and we can't get rid of that fact. So shake hands Polly, and go home. I'll write you a letter to meet me again as soon as I see an opportunity. We're all going to Hunslope Farm to dinner when they come home from church. But you must take no notice of me."

"No, I won't—no manner of notice," said Polly. "I'm going to wait at table, and Mrs. Heathcote says I'm to look after you especial."

"I knew a man down away in Frisco, Polly, who was married twenty years to a girl, without a soul knowing anything about it except the parson, and he got shot in a difficulty."

"Did you, Dick? It wasn't yourself, was it?"

"Now, how the devil could it be, when I've only been away twelve years? Well, they had sixteen children, two pairs of 'em twins. And nobody knew it, mind you. And then the man made his pot; and now she rides about in her carriage. And the last time I saw her she had on a blue satin dress, and a red cachemire shawl, and gold chains as thick as rigging ropes. A pretty woman she is still, Polly, and able to enjoy it all. That was the reward of being silent, you see."

"Lor!" said Polly. "Dick, Old Ready-money—I mean, Mr. Mortiboy—is as rich as rich. And they say he can't live long, because he's sold himself to the devil for all his money. Would you give me a carriage and a gold chain?"

"Half a dozen gold chains and a carriage and four. And all Market Basing shall know that you're my wife, Poll. Give me a kiss, old gal."

They parted friends! The man went off in the direction of his father's house: the woman to visit her mother at her little cottage in the town.

Once they turned back to stare after one another.

Their eyes met! Could each have read the other's mind!

CHAPTER THE ELEVENTH.

R. MORTIBOY'S son was spending half an hour, for the first time in twelve years, with the wife he had married, whilst old Ready-money himself was seated in his late sister's pew in St. Giles's Church. He looked round him with some curiosity.

The church of St. Giles at Market Basing is the parish church, and is situate in the middle of the town, where the cross formed by the four principal streets—Bridge-street, Gold-street, Sheep-street, and High-street—starts from. Within a stone's throw of it are all the public buildings.

Originally, the church was a Gothic edifice, the work of some architect whose name has not come down to posterity. The tower looking west bears witness to his skill. The rest of the building was destroyed by fire in the reign of Charles the Second. That Christian prince thought proper to give a thousand tons of timber from a neighbouring royal forest towards the rebuilding of the church. In return, a grotesque statue and a legend detailing the royal munificence were placed over the portico by the corporation of Market Basing. Sir Christopher Wren rebuilt St. Giles's. He drew a square, with a smaller square running out of it—this was the chancel—for his ground plan, and added it on to the old gothic tower. He built four great walls, and pierced them with four ugly oblong windows, and then three small walls, and three small oblong windows to match, for his chancel. He roofed it over with a dwarfed dome and lantern—reminding you of St. Paul's in a toy box—and left it to the people of Market Basing to worship in, in the stead of their old Gothic church.

So everything remained for a century and a half. Then came a change.

We live now in the age of church restoration; but the fever struck the rector of St. Giles's when the nineteenth century was young.

The dome I have mentioned was supported by four great pillars of white stone; up to these on each side of the church, came the front railing of a gallery. In 1806, the rector laid his plans for pulling down these galleries, slicing a few rows of pews off, and putting them up again clear of the pillars. This was only part of his scheme, though what else he wanted to do does not matter now. Of course he called on his richest parishioner—the third of the Mortiboy race—for a subscription. And "the scholar" promised him a hundred pounds on his assurance that a London architect had pronounced the galleries unsafe. To this promise Mr. Mortiboy added a condition. It was that he should not be asked for any more. Unluckily for the parson, Mr. Mortiboy's own seat was in the front row of one of the galleries, and he had forgotten to mention that the new erections would not be precisely similar to the old ones. And the banker owned what he called a faculty pew; a quasi freehold, to be bought and sold with his house, and for which no pew rent was to be paid.

The very day he heard of the arrangement to sacrifice his seat, he was asked by the rector for a second subscription, on the ground that there was so much more being done than was at first intended. This was more than Mr. Mortiboy could stand. His gallery gone, his hundred pounds gone—this was much; but to be asked to give more for further desecration of vested rights and spoliation of property, was more than he could bear.

So, followed by a good many of the parishioners, he seceded to the modest Little Bethel which had hitherto sufficed for the Nonconformist interest. They pensioned off, economically, the wheezy old man who had preached in it for thirty years—ever since he had given up cobbling on having a call—and sent for an eloquent preacher: an awakener. Then came the tug of war; and Market Basing was divided pretty equally, and with more than the usual bitterness, between Church and Dissent.

Such is the history of the celebrated Market Basing schism, as notable in its way as many a better-known division in the Church.

With a display of that old dog in the manger spirit to gratify which a Shropshire nobleman spent untold sums in building round his great park a wall high enough to keep out the hunting-field, Mr. Mortiboy never went to the church again, nor did he suffer any of his family to go there. But the bitterness wore off gradually. And when he died, his son, our Ready-money—though he never went to church—was not seen so often at chapel; while Susan Mortiboy, his sister, went to every church service that was held, and to every meeting, and in all parish affairs was as good as ten deaconnesses to the parson. Mr. Mortiboy revolved all these things as he sat in the church that morning.

During the service—which was an unfamiliar thing to him, and touched him not—his mind ran back to old times, and he saw himself again playing with Francis Melliship, making love to his sister Emily as he grew older, marrying at that very altar. For a moment the bitter feeling against Mr. Melliship died away—to revive again the moment after, when the thought occurred to him that in a few days his enemy would be at his feet, craving his forbearance and assistance.

The hymns affected him little, because Mr. Mortiboy had no ear for music; and, besides, he was thinking how he should behave when Mr. Melliship came for help. Should he remind him of slights offered five-and-twenty years ago? Or should he be content to take that moment as an acquittance in full, and be friends again as of old? He inclined ever so little to the latter course

In that place he was such an unusual sight, that the people all stared at him over their prayer books. They thought him very much affected by the loss of his sister, because he looked neither to the right nor to the left, but gazed straight before him. Presently, looking forward in this way, his eye caught the face of the preacher, and he was constrained, in spite of himself, to hear the text:

Market Basing is one of those places where funeral sermons are still preached. The text chosen by the friend of Susan Mortiboy, as the theme for his tribute to her memory, was the thirty-eighth and thirty-ninth verses of the eighth chapter of Romans.

The preacher spoke out the words in a clear and penetrating voice :—

" For I am persuaded that neither death, nor life, nor angels, nor principalities, nor powers, nor things present, nor things to come, nor height, nor depth, nor any other creature, shall be able to separate us from the love of God which is in Christ Jesus our Lord."

I have given the text. I will not attempt to reproduce the sermon. I should only do injustice to it. But it seemed to Old Ready-money that it was directed personally at him.

It told of the sin of self-seeking, in its various forms. It showed how the good woman whose death had made a gap in their midst lived wholly for others; and though she could not take her wealth with her—here a warmth crept over the brother's heart, because he knew it was all his—she had made it a blessing to the poor, and used it as if it were a trust. Here Mr. Mortiboy felt aggrieved. And the preacher, waxing eloquent with his theme, showed that the worship of self is shown in more ways than in the hoarding up and misuse of money—here Mr. Mortiboy felt uncomfortable, because the clergyman was really looking at him : why could he not look at Heathcote ?—how by disregarding the interests of others, by ignoring their wishes, by pursuing a line which brings misfortune on them, by failing to anticipate their desires, and by countless other ways, the selfish man makes the paths of others hard for them. Mr. Mortiboy thought of his rival, Mr. Melliship, whose path he was about to make very hard, and almost wished, for a moment, that it was not so. And then he drew two pictures—one of him who had no money, but yet had in his heart charity, and sympathy, and thoughtfulness for his neighbour; and one of the rich man who had these virtues in addition to his wealth; and he showed how each in his way was a kind of Providence to the place—preventing more than healing: making men continue in goodness, rather than repent of evil. And then Mr. Mortiboy turned pale, and a chill fell on his heart, because he knew that he had done no good to anybody else—not so much as to one neighbour, and that the only good he had done to himself was to amass money and increase his wealth. Then the preacher generalized; and such is the power of a contented mind, that Mr. Mortiboy forgot a few moments after where he was, and lost himself in thought——about what he should do with Dick.

It was Sacrament Sunday. The plate came round, and caught him unprepared: at another moment, Mr. Mortiboy would have taken no notice of the intrusion. Now he was softened a little, and recollected he meant to give something when he came; so he dropped a coin into it, with a conscious glow of one who does a good action. Mr. Heathcote, who had been asleep, as was his wont during sermon—not from any disinclination to listen, but from sheer force of long habit —woke up, put a crown piece in the plate, and church was over.

Dinner at Parkside. It had a threefold aim. First, as Mrs. Heathcote observed, it would help to divert that melancholy with which she was persuaded her cousin Mr. Mortiboy was afflicted at the loss of his sister; secondly, to welcome Dick back to England; and thirdly, because it was Grace's birthday, and Grace was twenty-one. There was another reason, which she kept to herself, that on Sunday Mr. Melliship always remained at home and dined *en famille*; so that there was no chance of Frank calling in the evening, and a reasonable excuse for not asking him. Mr. Mortiboy's dislike to his brother-in-law extended to his nephew as well.

Dick was the quietest of the guests, partly because he was still unused to the society of ladies, and felt it was desirable to keep a curb upon his tongue—which had a habit, indeed, of dropping pearls of conversation, but roughly set. The girls, too, were quiet: Lucy, because she was still full of grief for her friend, Aunt Susan, as she was always called; and Grace out of sympathy. But Mr. Mortiboy was in high spirits— perhaps from the influence of that glow of virtue of which we have spoken before, and perhaps from the revulsion of feeling which comes after a time of gloom and trouble. He sat with his chair a foot from the table, leaned forward at an unpleasant angle, and said "Beautiful, beautiful!" to everything eatable presented to his notice. When the pudding was brought in by Polly, he remarked that it shook, and he liked to see a pudding shake—it was a good sign: and as he drank half a glass of port, with a bit of blue Stilton, he was pleased to notice that the cheese was the only bad thing about the dinner. His chief topic of conversation was his son, of whom he spoke as admiringly as if he had not been present at the table, and frequently patted his broad back. Mrs. Heathcote encouraged him, put in little ejaculations of "La! now, uncle!" "Is it possible?" and so on; while the old man garrulously prated of the good days he was going to have now Dick was come back. Mr. Mortiboy, in spite of his penurious ways at home, was by no means averse to the good things of life. He had schooled himself to believe that it was waste of money to have a decent dinner cooked for himself every day; but it would have been a waste of opportunity to refuse whatever good things were offered by others. So the dinner passed off very cheerfully. It was not exactly pleasant for Dick to have his own wife waiting on him—she had ridden back on the box of John Heathcote's sociable—nor was he altogether free from alarm when his cousin asked him if he had left his heart behind him, knowing that Polly had a fine high temper of her own, which could not at all times be trusted. Nothing, however, happened to disturb the peace between them. When the table was cleared, Mr. Heathcote, in a tone of much solemnity, called upon all to fill their glasses. Health-drinking was a ceremony which he would not have omitted for worlds on such an occasion. He began a little speech.

"Bygones," he said, "should be bygones. There is no occasion for crying over what can't be helped. We've had to grieve, and we may now rejoice. Let us drink the health of—"

"My—good—gracious! what a dreadful thing!" cried Old Ready-money, falling back in his chair, his face as pale as ashes.

Mr. Heathcote stopped suddenly. They all started.

"What is it, Uncle Richard?" cried Mrs. Heathcote.

"Well, I shan't forget this!" He was looking at something in his hand.

"What is it, uncle?"

"I *have* done it!" he replied, solemnly. "I've put a sovereign into that plate at the church instead of a shilling."

It was true. In the confusion of the moment, his thoughts distracted from what he was doing, he had put his fingers into the right waistcoat-pocket, where were five sovereigns, instead of the left where were as many shillings.

Mr Heathcote repressed an inclination to roar, as at one of the best jokes he had ever heard—before he caught, just in time, a look of admonition from his wife.

"What *is* to be done? I never made such a mistake in my life before," cried Mr. Mortiboy.

"What can be done?" cried Mrs. Heathcote.

"You have done more good than you intended, Uncle Richard," said Lucy. "Some poor persons will have a better dinner next Sunday."

"Better stuff and rubbish!" said Mr. Mortiboy.

"Well then," said Dick, whose ignorance of church customs must be pleaded in excuse for the hardihood of the suggestion, "write to the parson, and make him give back your change."

"Well—why not? It's only right," said his father.

"Oh!—uncle!" Lucy expostulated.

"I'll send John," said Mr. Heathcote, "if you like."

He saw here the materials for as good a thing as had ever come under his notice, and was determined to make the most of it.

They got paper, and Mr. Mortiboy was going to write, explaining that, in the hurry of the moment, he had made a mistake of some importance—viz., the substitution of a sovereign for a shilling—and begging the rector to return to him the balance due.

But Mrs. Heathcote contrived to make her uncle postpone this till he got home. She did not want the letter dated from Parkside.

Then Mr. Heathcote went on with his speech.

"I have forgotten, now, what I intended to say specially. But I was going to propose Dick's health. Dick, my boy, we're glad to see you, and proud of you; and you're always welcome, as you always were, at Parkside."

Mr. Mortiboy's voice shook a little as he raised his glass and said—

"We'll drink, Dick!—we'll drink, Dick!—your health, my son."

The big prodigal had found his way to his heart; and he loved him better now, far better, than he had ever loved him as a boy.

Dick said a few words; and then Mr. Heathcote filled his glass with an air of business, and looked at his wife, who pulled out her handkerchief. They knew what was coming. But Mr. Mortiboy astonished them all.

"Let me," he said, "say a few words." He turned to Grace. "Grace, my dear, we are going to drink your health, and many happy returns of the day. For twenty-one years, I think, I've dined here on every birthday of yours, and drunk a glass of port to you every year. Lydia, your children are good girls. Had things been different with me—had Dick not, happily, come back to us—I should— But there is no telling what might or would have been done."

Here Mrs. Heathcote buried her face in her handkerchief.

"And now, my dear, I wish you a long and happy life, and a careful husband, and"—here he hesitated a little, and pulled out his pocket book—"here, my dear,"—he took out a crisp and new bank note, and looked at it admiringly for a moment; then he put it from him as if the action cost him something—"here, my dear, is a present for you."

It was a hundred-pound bank note. Grace read the amount with a sort of stupefaction, and passed it to her father. Mr. Heathcote took it gravely, and gave it back to his daughter. And then it went round, and there was a simultaneous cry of gratitude and surprise. They were shocked at the old man's unlikeness to himself.

"But what in the world will you do with it Grace?" said her mother. "You will have to put it into Uncle Mortiboy's bank."

"Yes—do, Grace," said the donor; "and I'll see if I can't give you interest for it."

Five minutes after she had received her present, Grace handed it back to her uncle to "take care of" for her; and he received it with a gasp, and returned it to his pocket-book hastily.

It was at once the cheapest and the handsomest present he could give; and he knew he should get it back again "to take care of," when he decided upon what form his present should take.

Poor Grace? It did seem rather hard to her to be tantalized by the sight of such a splendid sum of money, and then to have it suddenly ravished from her sight, and consigned to the dark dungeons of the bank—a prisoner not to be released.

In the evening, Mr. Mortiboy sat in the easiest chair by the fire, and next him Mrs. Heathcote. And he conversed with her about his son Dick, telling her over and over again how great a comfort to him the boy already was: laying out his schemes for an easier life, and planning the happiness that was to be his, now Dick was come home again. Dick, for his part, was listening to the girls as they sang hymns.

"Your nose, my lady," said Mr. Heathcote that night, laying his manly head upon the pillow, "appears to me to be put out of joint."

"Don't be coarse, John," returned his partner.

"Anyhow, old Ready-money has broken out in a new place. That hundred pounds of his is all our girls will get. But the old man is improved by it, and I'm glad Dick has turned up again."

"Poor boy!" said his wife, with feeling. "So am I. John, mark my words—though you must have seen it—Dick's setting his cap at Grace already."

John was coarse enough to laugh at this remark, and to continue silently shaking till slumber smoothed out his limbs, and composed them for rest.

As for Mr. Mortiboy, he went home well satisfied, and not the less pleased because the morrow would bring his brother-in-law, for the first time in his life, for assistance and forbearance. For he knew well enough that it was quite beyond the power of Francis Melliship to meet his liabilities. It would be something like a new pleasure to see his proud brother-in-law open his case, and admit that he wanted time. It would be a real new pleasure to have him, like all the rest of Market Basing, secretly under his own thumb. Mr. Mortiboy rubbed his hands when he thought of it. He would not ruin Melliship: he would even help him. But he would help him at a price, and that price should be his own aggrandizement. To have both the banks at his command would be almost to rule the county as well as the town. To make of Mr. Melliship a superior Ghrimes would be an ample return for those slights he had endured at his hands so long ago. And it fell out so well for Dick, too. He could go back, arrange his affairs abroad, and return in a year or two to leave Market Basing no more, and to succeed him in all his wealth—and even Mr. Mortiboy himself did not know how much that wealth amounted to by this time.

So he, too, went to sleep; and all Market Basing slumbered —except one man.

CHAPTER THE TWELFTH.

HAT man was Francis Melliship!

Old Ready-money's brother-in-law—rival, as he considered him; enemy, that he had tried to make him—spent the Sunday in his usual fashion. In the morning, he went to church with his household, filled his accustomed seat in the family pew, and heard the funeral sermon; dined early, and in the evening went to church again.

Dr. Kerby walked with the Melliships as far as their own door, after the morning service. He begged his old friend, the banker, to take a rest from his work. He took Mrs. Melliship aside, and whispered to her in terms imperative and strong. He told her she must take her husband for a change of air that very week, on some pretext or another.

"If Mr. Melliship won't take you, my dear lady, you must take him."

"Doctor, you alarm us. What—what is the matter with my dear husband?" she asked, unable to conceal the nervous feeling the doctor's words produced, yet unwilling to tell him of the signs of unnatural change in her husband she saw herself.

These were clear enough: but neither the wife, nor the son, nor the daughter could read their meaning,

They saw the change that cast its shadow over their house. Their anxiety for husband and father was intense.

What could they do? Nothing. And this inaction was terrible to them.

Mr. Melliship was in high spirits all day: he had been in high spirits all the week. His face was flushed, his movements quick and nervous. He was very excitable, and talked in a wild, exaggerated way.

His present was the very opposite of his natural state.

His talk all the week had been perpetually of one kind: about money, about his own wealth. For the first time in her life, his daughter Kate began to think her father ostentatious. The thought but suggested itself, to be stifled as unworthy; the fault was in her, she thought, not in her father.

Now, on this day, he was even more demonstrative of his newly-born pride of purse. He spoke of his intention of removing from the old bank where they had lived so many years, of buying an estate, of having a town house, of getting new plate, of spending money on a hundred things which he had hitherto been quite content to do without.

"But, my dear," expostulated his wife, half in doubt, half in earnest, "all these will cost us a great deal of money."

"And if we have the money to spend on them my dear?" replied her husband. "What says the Latin poet, Frank?

'Vitam quæ faciunt beatiorem,
Jucundissime Martialis hæc sunt,
Res non parta labore, sed relicta—'

Eh? Now, I would wager that you cannot finish it."

"I cannot indeed, father. I don't suppose I can read it."

"This degenerate age!" sighed his father. "And here is a man who has only just taken his degree, and cannot cap a quotation from Martial. It was very different in my time, I can tell you, sir. We read Latin, at any rate. But the

'Res non parta labore'

will be yours, my boy, and that is the great thing, after all. Frank," he suddenly added, "I have often thought how enormously rich a family, starting from absolutely nothing, might become by dint of sheer economy, and allowing themselves no luxuries, so that the money might all accumulate. Thus, the Fuggers in the fourteenth century went on splendidly, till there came a fool who threw the family wealth away. My idea is, that the family is to have no fool at all in it."

"If money is everything," said Frank, "it might be worth the while of a man to found a rich family in this way."

"He would inculcate, as a kind of religion," Mr. Melliship went on, "the laws of frugality and industry. He who failed or came short of his duties, should be solemnly cut off from the rest. In six generations, provided the sons were of average brain power, the family would be as rich as the Rothschilds."

Mr. Melliship grew quite excited as he spoke.

"But is it worth while to take all the trouble?"

"Surely yes, Frank. Money, in all ages, means—if you please to use it for that purpose—comfort and luxury; or it means power and authority; or it means ability to advance the world in any way that seems best to you. Surely, therefore, whether you are an Epicurean or a Christian, you must desire money. Whatever your character, you must wish that you had it. And if it were not for the selfishness of men, they would deny themselves in order that their children might have it."

"At all events, Uncle Richard is not a selfish man, then."

Mr. Melliship laughed.

"He has saved money, I believe—only thousands, though; and his son Dick will have them. My dear, let us have Dick to dinner one day this week. Any day; ask the rector—a very capital fellow, full of energy: a man that you must cultivate, Frank, and learn from him all that he can teach you."

This was how he talked all dinner time. After his wife and daughter left them, he stayed behind with Frank, and finished his bottle of wine. They had some sacred music; and at nine o'clock Mr. Melliship read prayers, as was his wont on Sunday evening, and shortly after retired to his own study. This was not unusual, and did not excite any comment.

He sat down before the fire, with the bottle of brandy by his side. And turning his lamp down so as to have little but the firelight, sat with crossed legs, and a pleased, happy expression of countenance. He was thinking of his revenues, of his vast property, and making schemes for the happiness of his children. Hour after hour passed thus, and he had more than once drained the glass. The clock struck eleven, twelve, and one, without his moving from the chair. And the fire, burning lower and lower, at last went out altogether. The cinders were black. All that remained to tell there had been a fire in the grate was the crackling noise the cooling embers made. Still he moved not. The curtains were not drawn; and the moon, bursting suddenly from behind a cloud, shone through the windows, and fell full upon the portrait of his children above the mantelshelf.

The bright light caught his eye, and in a moment Francis Melliship awakened from his reveries. He started up, passed his hand across his brow, and looked wildly round.

Is there anything in all dramatic literature more dramatic than the awakening of Ajax after his night of madness ? The goddess calls him: the proud king and warrior comes at Athênê's call, blood-stained, breathing fury and revenge ;— telling how in the dead of night he has gone secretly forth, and captured his enemies: how they are within, the two sons of Atreus, bound and tied, waiting to receive the stroke of his sword ; and the crafty son of Laertes, Ulysses the fox, for whom is torture before death. So raging, but contented, he returns to his tent. Presently comes the day, and with it a return of his senses. He wakes from his frenzy, and finds himself surrounded by the carcases of the beasts he had slain in place of the Grecian princes. Then his fortitude gives way. "*Ai, Ai!*" he mourns, "Alas! Alas! there is but this one thing left, nobly to die." And so he bids farewell to his wife and his son, and the dear light of the sun, and falls upon his sword, and goes away to those regions of shade where the souls of departed heroes ever wander sadly, lamenting the days of life.

So in a moment the whole horror of his situation burst upon the unfortunate Francis Melliship. The moonlight, pale and bright, fell on his book of memoranda. His eyes caught the words—"*February 10th, Monday, Mr. Mortiboy.*" These five words spoke volumes. The riches he had boasted of did not exist: there were no investments, or only investments that had lost him money : there were no means of meeting the liabilities that fell due on the morrow. For the last three or four weeks, he had been suffering from delusion and madness. But he was not mad now, and he saw his position in all its miserable conditions. How could he explain ? How make people understand that what they would mistake for the dishonest boasting of a broken swindler was only the natural expression of an overpowering delusion ? He could not: no one could : there would be but one opinion possible. And then to walk for the rest of his days ruined in purse and reputation ; the broken banker : the rash speculator : the dishonest bankrupt: mad Melliship! He who had been the first in the town : the proudest, the most prominent, the best bred, and the most highly considered.

He rose with a gesture of despair, stepped into a dressing-room adjoining his study, and came out with a case in his hand, which he held for a few moments as if dreading to open it.

He held it in his hands hesitating.

The moon shone out, and between his eyes and the moonshine there stood once more the figure of the dead woman which he had seen a week before. Again she appeared to him : and this time not pointing to the picture of his children; not stern, reproachful, and threatening: but smiling, pleased, and happy. Her age seemed to have fallen from her, and she appeared as she had been thirty years before, when they were young together.

"Susan!" cried the unhappy man, stretching out his hands, "speak to me. Susan, my first love, why do you come back in the semblance of those old times? Susan, forgive my broken troth, and the promise that you and I alone know of. Speak to me, Susan!"

She did not speak, but beckoned; and when he looked again she had disappeared.

He sat awhile with troubled brow, trying to think. He could think of two things only: the horror and disgrace of the future, which his disturbed state of imagination augmented; and the image of his old friend—young again— radiant, smiling, beckoning to him. Beckoning!—but where? Surely to some land far off, where there would be no more trouble, but only youth, and love, and pleasant fancies.

* * * * * * *

As the moon shifted round to the west, the light left the portrait of the children, and moving slowly round the room, came upon the form of Mr. Melliship lying prone upon the hearthrug. He was not sleeping but dead; and the black pool that shone in the light of the moon was blood that came from his self-inflicted wound. Like Ajax, he could not bear the disgrace. Without a word of farewell to his children, or of explanation or motive, he had left all his troubles and burdens to be borne by shoulders weaker than his own. Selfish? Perhaps. It is the custom to say that suicides are cowards, and selfish. But there is a point of physical or moral suffering at which every man will give way, and prefer immediate death. We cannot endure beyond that point. Heaven keep us from suffering that even comes near it!

CHAPTER THE THIRTEENTH.

IT was Monday morning, February the tenth. The time, three o'clock. The moon had gone down, and the wind, blowing in gusts, soughed and sighed, as it played round the house, making windows and doors rattle. Within all was quiet. No one in that house heard it.

On the hearth-rug of the study lay the corpse of the ill-fated gentleman, Francis Melliship.

Overhead, his son Frank slept dreamlessly.

In their several chambers, wife, daughter, servants were asleep.

And he, husband, father, master, lay dead!

O giant Death, door of life, what lies not within the compass of thy power!

Over the waking horror of those to whom the dead man was dearest, I draw a veil. Let me pass by the misery of that awakening: the first great shock; the widow's cry of anguish; the wail of the orphans.

It was at five minutes past seven that the news left the door of the bank: whispered in the startled ears of the milk boy. At eight Market Basing breakfasts: by that time, everybody was in possession of the news.

"Mr. Melliship at the bank's dead."

They killed him in twenty different ways. But they gave only one reason for it—the true one: that he was a ruined man.

The bank opened its doors every day at ten.

Long before nine, knots of people were gathered about the street: and every minute they increased in numbers.

People in the town sent sons or servants post haste to tell the news to relatives in the country who banked at the old house, and might be supposed to have money lying there.

"Melliship the banker has cut his throat!"

The truth was out and the town was wild with excitement.

It was assize time. The judges were to come in by the first train, and the town was filling with country people.

The street that the old bank stood in was soon like Gaol-lane on the day of an execution. There was a great crowd, a stifled buzz of voices, and one object of attention: the great stone house, with all the blinds drawn down, and iron shutters that might or might not be raised at ten o'clock.

This was the scene outside. But what was the picture within?

The terrified clerks, who had hurried down to the bank as soon as they heard what had happened, were behind the shutters in the half-dark room, discussing in whispers what was to be done. Of course they suspected that there was something wrong, though not one of them had any knowledge of the real state of affairs. Mr. Sanderson, the cashier, who had been in the bank forty years, only knew that Mr. Melliship had recently made very large payments, on what account he was unable to say.

Frank came down pale as death, his dress in disorder: more ignorant and more distracted than any of them.

"Mr. Sanderson," he said, "the people are collecting in the street. Can we open the bank before ten? Is it possible they suspect that my unhappy father put an end to his life because he was not solvent? They can hardly think that—they must know he did it when he was deranged. Oh father—father!" and the young man sobbed in his agony of grief.

"All will be well, sir, I hope," the old retainer said, in a voice choked with emotion.

"We must have the books and money. Where are the keys?"

"The keys were always in your father's possession," said the old clerk solemnly.

Frank shuddered, and buried his face in his hands. His father's body had been laid on his bed. Who was to take them from it?

The clerk saw his hesitation.

"Excuse me, Mr. Frank," he said, the tears running down his cheeks as he spoke, "but some one must get the keys. Let me get them."

Frank assented, and the old servant went alone into the room where the body of his master lay, and presently came back with a blanched cheek, and the bunches of keys in his trembling hands.

They opened the iron door in his presence—for it was evident there would be a run on the bank—and went in.

It was the honour of his father's name Frank wished to protect. No other feeling could have roused him from the shock his father's awful end had given him.

The force of circumstances compelled him to act at once.

The strong room—the place where books, securities, and "safe custodies" of all sorts were kept—was fire and thief proof; but for still greater safety, in its farthest side was a money safe, built into the wall.

In this the cash was kept; and they unlocked it without delay, for time pressed—people were already drumming the street door with their heels.

The next question was, what did it contain? This was soon settled.

The black leather note-case was examined first.

"Open it," said Frank.

More than half the compartments had their own notes in them—some ready for issue, the bulk of them undated and unsigned.

Sanderson gave a ghastly smile.

Frank understood it.

Paper bearing the signature of Melliship, Mortiboy & Company was at a discount that morning; though a few hours before people would have bought the five-pound notes at four pounds nineteen shillings and eleven pence halfpenny apiece as long as you liked to sell them.

The old cashier turned to the Bank of England notes. Their value was £2,550.

Frank wrote it down on a piece of paper.

Next they counted the gold—£1,100, in yellow canvas bags of a hundred pounds each; fifty-three odd sovereigns.

Then they reckoned up their stock of silver.

Two sacks, with one hundred pounds in each. Nineteen pounds ten and sixpence loose.

"The copper we need not consider, sir," said Mr. Sanderson. "What is the total? Three, nine, two, two, ten, six," he added as he read the amount over Frank's shoulder.

"It seems a large sum, but I have no idea of how far it will go."

"It is enough, sir, and more than enough for any ordinary day; but there will be what I never saw before, and, please God, shall never see again—a run on Melliship's. At any rate, Master Frank, we must go on paying as long as we can."

"Yes."

"The bank is all right, sir, never fear. With a head like your poor father's was—till these last weeks—we're not likely to be far wrong when things are looked into."

The clerk's confidence in the master he had always served was so strong, it would not have been shaken if there had been only twopence found in the locker.

"And if," said Frank, rousing himself with an effort from the fearful thoughts that filled his mind—"if the people's confidence is not established when our stock of ready cash is run out?"

"Then," replied Mr. Sanderson, with trembling lip, "we must put the shutters up—unless Mortiboy's will advance us money." Then, slapping Frank's shoulder, he cried, with energy—"Go quickly, sir—go yourself to Mr. Ghrimes, and tell him what a state we are in; and Mr. Mortiboy, your uncle, too. Go, Master Frank, go. Save our credit. We must have more than we've got, or before twelve o'clock the shutters must go up—which God forbid!"

In town or country, a banker's stock of cash is always lowest on Monday. Saturday is the great day for paying out. On Monday morning customers begin to pay money in. On this day the cash at the old bank was lower than usual by at least a third; for two customers had on Saturday drawn £2,000 in notes between them. One had a mortgage to settle, another had bought a house; and as lawyers don't take cheques for such purposes, they had drawn their money out of the bank, and made their payments in notes.

The persons interested in the solvency of Melliship's were the depositors. Clearly, debtors would not care. It was the creditors that were going to make the run.

They were small shopkeepers, who kept balances of fifty pounds and under at the bank. These men were the most afraid. Larger traders had from one hundred to two hundred and fifty pounds lying to their credit.

The largest balance was kept by Hopgood, Pywell & Co., linendrapers; but their bills had been met on the 4th. On the 10th of the month they had not above a couple of hundred pounds in the bank.

None of these classes could be hurt much.

Trade is a very elastic thing.

But the doctor, with all his little savings there ; the retired shopkeeper; poor gentlemen and gentlewomen in town and country, who had placed nearly all they possessed in Mr. Melliship's custody—for them, his failure meant their ruin.

Here I will show briefly how this failure had been brought about.

Mr. Melliship was by nature a gentleman : he never conceived a mean thought, nor did a mean action. When his father died, instead of carrying on the banking business, he ought to have disposed of it to old Mortiboy, and gone into the country to live the life of a village squire.

Unhappily for himself and his family, he carried the business on, though he was wholly unfit for it.

Sanguine : he invested largely in Foreign Stocks, promising a high rate of interest; in Land and Credit Companies; in South American mining speculations. This was gambling; but he learnt the truth too late.

Then, in conducting the legitimate business of a country bank, he behaved in a way exactly opposite to Ready-money Mortiboy's notions of trading.

And Mortiboy was right, and Melliship wrong.

In agricultural districts, bankers make advances to the farmers. The security is their stock and their crops. Mr. Melliship advanced his customers money at five per cent. Old Mortiboy at six or seven per cent., according to his customer.

Mr. Melliship never pressed a man, never turned a deaf ear to a tale of distress.

A sorrowful tale told to a banker by his debtor always has for its end time or money.

Mr. Melliship belonged to the old-fashioned school of country bankers; he never threw a man over; he gave him time, gave him more money, bolstered him up. He went on throwing good money after bad, making new advances to keep his debtor afloat, till the man became involved beyond the power of extrication. Then came the final crash, and the money of the bank was lost. Buried under a mountain of difficulties.

After harvest is the time at which the farmer repays the banker in corn-producing counties.

Stock sells all the year round ; and so a little dribbles back. In the Southern counties the lambs pay the rent. In April and May, the banker gets his money back through Biggerstaff's or Lacy's, who do the banking of the London salesmen.

In Holmshire there is a little of everything; the land is described by agriculturalists as "useful." Stock, corn, and lambs are produced, and on these securities the bankers at Market Basing make advances.

Mr. Melliship took the bad business; old Mortiboy the good—or none.

There had been four bad years, and the farmers had for once good reasons to complain of their bad luck. There were bad harvests and bad lambing seasons; and disease broke out among the cattle to finish matters.

A bad year means this: the bank must go on advancing till next harvest. This had been repeated three times; and it ruined the old bank; for Mr. Melliship had long before dissipated his father's wealth.

He had been compelled to borrow money in large sums on his promissory notes. He had had no difficulty in doing this: his connection was large and rich. And very few people knew of his embarrassments until four months before his death, when a client of old Mortiboy's died. His son deposited promissory notes of Mr. Melliship's to the amount of £11,575 in the old gentleman's hands for safe keeping and presentation at maturity. They fell due on Monday, February 10th.

Mr. Melliship's difficulties had driven him mad, and Mr. Mortiboy was robbed of the pleasure of seeing his brother-in-law at his feet.

Let us follow Frank. He ran off to see Ghrimes.

It was a quarter to ten, and there was no time to be lost. He walked quickly into the street, and through the knots of excited talkers, who made way for him, with no words of salutation, for his hat was drawn over his eyes.

Mr. Ghrimes lived at the other end of Market Basing. When Frank got there it wanted five minutes to ten, and he was gone—just gone—to the other bank. Frank hastened after him.

"Good Heavens! Mr. Frank—what's this?" cried the manager, when he saw him.

"You know it, Mr. Ghrimes. It is all true. Come round, for God's sake, and help us!" Frank gasped, breathless with excitement and haste. "There is going to be a run upon the bank. Hark! there is ten striking. Come, quick, Mr. Ghrimes. I must get back.'

It was scarcely etiquette, but Mr. Mortiboy's manager threw formality to the winds, and went.
Mr. Sanderson would not allow the bank to be opened till Frank returned.
"Open the doors at once," said Frank; "Ghrimes will be here immediately."
As the doors opened, a crowd of men surged in. The younger clerks shrank back frightened; but Mr. Sanderson advanced to the counter with bland and reassuring smile. They all opened at once, like so many hounds at scenting a fox. Mr. Sanderson held up his hand. They were silent directly.
"Hush! gentlemen, hush! Have you not heard the dreadful news? Mr. Frank is in there. Do not let us disturb him.
"I warnt to dra' moy money," roared a bluff old publican—who had about fifty pounds in the bank—from the neighbourhood of the door.
"Pray, gentleman, let that person come and take his money," said Mr. Sanderson. "Oh! it's you, is it, Mr Stubbs? You are to be served before anybody else, because you haven't got the manners to wait."
This created a little laugh. The panic was only just beginning. The man received his fifty pounds and went off, grumbling. When he got outside, he hesitated. Had he turned back, and given his money again to the bank—as was his first impulse, on finding it so promptly paid—all might have been well. For men possess themselves largely the sheep-like propensity of following where one leads. But a moment of indecision was succeeded by the cold breath of doubt; and Stubbs buttoned up his gold, and walked away.
Stubbs was met outside by his friends.
"Got it—is it arl right? Can they pay?"
"Aye, aye—I'm got moin all square. Moin warn't much. I dra'ad it out, though—all goold." And he tapped his pocket.
"Goold, mun—arl goold? That looks 'nation bad, that do!"
"Whoy, Bill?" demanded Stubbs. "They cain't pay'ee in nothint better nor goold, can 'em?"
"Looks 'nation bad, though, neighbour—tell'ee whoy. It's arl over with 'em—now, taak my word furrit. Bank of England won't troost 'em wi' no more notes—that's whoy they pays arl in goold, mun."

And this version was believed in, and helped to smash Melliship's.

Then Mr. Sanderson, telling his assistant to be as slow as possible in paying cheques, but to preserve the appearance of alacrity and readiness began to converse with the crowd—every one of whom he knew personally—who were waiting their turn to be paid. To his dismay, it grew thicker; and those who pressed at the door were more impatient than those who first entered. But as very few of those who got to the front knew the amount of their balances, and as this had in every instance to be ascertained, payment took place slowly.

"What a dreadful thing it is!" said Mr. Sanderson, in a stage whisper. "They say he was affected by the success of his own enterprises."

People inside heard this, and began to wish they had not been so hasty. But the pressure went on increasing from without.

"Yes; and to look at the crowd here, one would think there was reason to doubt Melliship's bank. Really, gentlemen at the door, you must have patience. Every one in his turn. We shall attend to your business as soon as we possibly can. Jones, here is old Mrs. Clarke. Ladies first. Now do not let Mrs. Clarke wait."

Mrs. Clarke was deaf, extremely stupid, and always disputed the accuracy of every account. She had come to draw out all her money, including the odd halfpence, and was likely to keep the clerk Jones occupied for a good quarter of an hour. First, her passbook had to be compared with their ledger. Next, she had to be heard in support of her belief that she had more money than their books showed.

Mr. Sanderson stepped into the manager's room. Frank was standing before the fire, anxious and dejected.

"Mr. Frank, we can't go on—we can't indeed, unless help comes from the other bank. In half an hour we shall be at the end of our resources, unless the tide turns. God grant it may!"

"Ghrimes promised to be here as soon as he could. We can do nothing but hope. Send round a clerk for him."

But as they spoke Mr. Ghrimes appeared in the bank, having entered from the back. A murmur of relief ran through the expectant crowd as they saw him—for "Mortiboy's Ghrimes" was trusted implicitly in Market Basing. And then people began to look at each other, and to feel as if they were doing a very foolish thing.

"What is all this crowd about?" asked Ghrimes of one of the clerks, running his fingers through his stubbly iron-grey hair, and looking right through the people, as if he had never seen one of them before in his life.

"We want our money, sir," said one of them, less sheepish than the rest.

"Oh, do you?" growled Mortiboy's manager. "Then you had better take it; and don't come to our place with it, if that's the way you intend to inconvenience your bankers at a time of domestic calamity. Pay them all their money as quick as you can, Mr. Jones, and let them go."

The applicants—who, as yet, were chiefly the tradespeople of the place—were moved by this rebuke, and two or three declared their intention of letting the money "be." But these were few, and the rest only pressed on to the counter Ghrimes might be right; but after all money was money, and if that wasn't safe, there was no knowing what would happen next. For the popular notion of banking in the Market Basing mind was that the banker kept all the money in gold, in cellars or strong boxes; that to use it, or take it out for any purpose save that of returning it to its rightful owner, would be akin to embezzlement. How bankers lived they never inquired.

Mr. Ghrimes pushed into the back room. Frank gave a sigh of relief.

"It is all right, my dear boy," he said. "Go on paying them, Mr. Sanderson. They are putting up the gold at our place for you. As fast as you pay it out, the people bring it over to us; so that it is all right, and you can meet any number of their demands."

"But not any number of bills," said Mr. Sanderson.

"Do not let us meet trouble half-way," said Mr. Mortiboy's manager. "Our first business is to stop the mouths of those fools outside. Let one of your clerks be ready to receive and weigh when our men come over."

Mr. Sanderson went back to his counter with a lighter heart.

"I've had a terrible time with the old man," said Mr. Ghrimes. "He seems knocked off his head with this dreadful news. I could not get him to consent to anything. At last his son Dick made him give way. He hardly understood, I think."

It was quite true. The shock of Mr. Melliship's death had been almost more than Mr. Mortiboy could bear. He had gone to bed light-hearted and happy. He had got up in the morning still happier: for the day was come at last when his rival—the man he had hated—would be in his power. He desired no more. In his power? The man who had never been as rich as he, but of so much greater weight and influence. The man whom people respected and courted, when he could get no one to do more than fear him.

Remember, he did not seek to ruin Mr. Melliship: it was not his intention to shut up his bank, even if he had the power. But it was his intention to sit alone in that grimy kitchen in the evening, and reflect that the proud man was humble before him. Now the day was come, and the proud man—too proud for humiliation—had escaped by the only gate open to him. So that when Mr. Mortiboy heard the news, his heart felt like lead within him, and a cloud that never lifted again fell upon his brain.

He was sitting pale and speechless when Ghrimes came for authority to stop the run. But he could at first only be got to answer incoherently.

"Eleven thousand five hundred and seventy-five pounds! The bills are due this morning at twelve o'clock. I knew he could not meet it. I told you so, Ghrimes. You can't say I did not tell you so? Well, then—nobody can blame me. Francis Melliship was mad—mad at your Aunt Susan's funeral —was not even dressed like a man in his senses—I see it now, too late! Eleven thousand pounds, Dick. They were lodged with us for safe custody. Eleven thousand pounds! Poor Francis Melliship! We were boys together, Dick; and I married his sister—your mother, poor thing! And Susan always had a kind word for him, though we were not the best of friends. And now it's come to this. He's quite dead, you said, Dick?"

"Dead as a ninepin," said his son.

"Yes. They're all gone—they're all gone."

"Mr. Mortiboy, time presses. There's a run on Melliship's, I tell you. Can't we make him understand, Mr. Richard?"

"Look here, sir," said Dick, shaking him gently by the shoulder, "there's a run upon their bank, and if you don't stop it, the bank will stop; and then there'll be a run upon yours; and if that stops too, there will be the devil to pay, and no mistake. So you had better say 'Yes' to Mr. Ghrimes, I'm witness enough."

The old man muttered a feeble "Yes;" and then went on maundering.

So Ghrimes went away.

Before, however, any help was actually needed at Melliship's, a singular thing happened. For at first those who drew their money from Melliship's took it across the road—it was only beyond the church on the other side—to Mortiboy's in order to deposit it there. There were thus two rivulets of people—the larger going to Melliship's, the smaller to Mortiboy's. But presently Mortiboy's depositors, seeing the double stream, began to imagine that there was a run upon both banks; and a panic set in in both directions.

This was half-past eleven, when the town was filled with people—for it was the first day of the assizes, and the news of Mr. Melliship's death was spreading in all directions. People in gigs quietly jogging into Market Basing from north, south, east, and west, were overtaken by others driving wildly for dear life.

"Haven't you heard? Melliship's bank has smashed, they say."

The main street was blocked with vehicles. My lord judge, riding with the high sheriff and his chaplain in Sir Harbury Nobottle's grand carriage, was nearly upset; and for the first time within the memory of living men, the twelve javelin men, walking in martial array by the sides of the carriage, were of use. They pointed their antiquated weapons at the crowd, and protected his lordship from the indignity of being jostled by the farmers' chaises.

At the judges' lodgings, by the Court House, only three or four ragged urchins were present to hear the imposing fanfare of the liveried trumpeters, and see his lordship get out.

The ceremonious pageant of the Law was neglected. Every man rushed to the bank, whether he had anything there or not.

The consternation was universal. It came home to all. The panic spread like wildfire. Country people swelled the crowd of residents in the town, surging round the doors of the old bank. The game was every man for himself; *sauve qui peut*. So they pushed and shoved one another like mad people.

Let money be at stake to see human nature with the paint off.

As the clock of St. Giles's struck twelve, there were as

K

many people besieging Mortiboy's, at the new bank, as there were trying to gain an entrance at Melliship's.

It was some little time before Mr. Ghrimes could clearly understand that the panic was going to affect their house as well as the other : the thing seemed too absurd.

It was so, however; and, with a heavy heart, he stopped the transfer of the gold to Melliship's, and sent a hasty messenger to Derngate, whither Dick Mortiboy had gone, to beg him to bring his father to the bank without a moment's delay.

At five minutes after twelve, Frank received a note from Mr. Ghrimes. It said—

"*We cannot help you: the panic has attacked us. There is a run on us now: we shall want every sovereign we have got.*"

Frank handed the note over, with a look of despair, to Mr. Sanderson, who read it; then sat down and pulled out his pocket-handkerchief, and wiped his brow.

"It will be over, Mr. Frank," he said, "in a few minutes."

"You mean that we shall have paid out all our money."

"Every farthing. We have just cashed some heavy cheques. After that we must put the shutters up, and then we must examine the books, and find out our liabilities, and —and—please God—go on again."

Then a loud voice was heard from the street, which Frank knew well. It was his cousin's, John Heathcote.

"Now then, let me pass please—let me pass. I am going to pay *my* money in."

"It's no good, Mr. Frank," whispered Sanderson. "What he can bring can do nothing for us. We must stop."

"Stay," said Frank, "I must say a word first."

He went out. At the sight of his tall figure, and his pale and suffering face, a stillness fell upon all who saw him.

"My friends," said Frank, "you must go away. We cannot pay you to-day, because we have no more money in the house; nor can I tell you when you will be paid. But you will be paid, be sure of that."

"You will be paid," echoed Mr. Sanderson.

"I promise you, in the name of my poor father, who lies dead upstairs, that rather than one of you shall lose a farthing by us, if the worst comes to the worst, we will strip ourselves of everything in the world. But go quietly now, because we have no money left."

They were awe-stricken by his solemnity. They could not murmur, because his trouble was so great, at their own probable or possible losses. Some of them went out with streaming eyes—all of them without a word. And then the iron shutters were let down, and the door closed—and Melliship's bank had stopped.

A very different scene went on at the other house. The news of the run on his bank acted on the old man like cold water on a fainting woman. He left off maundering to his son, raised his head erect, and looked in sheer wonder at the messenger who brought him the news. A run on *his* bank? —on Mortiboy's? The [thing was impossible, absurd! As well expect the whole race of sheep to assert their independence, or the infant in arms to demand a separate establishment, as that his customers should dare to distrust him.

He rose, and grasped his stick in a menacing manner, as if the appearance of that weapon alone would restore confidence; and placing his hat firmly on his head, he walked out of the house followed by Dick.

As he marched down the street—his step firm, his bearing confident, his aspect stern—the people fell back right and left, and those who were hurrying to his bank to draw out their deposits, slackened their steps, and allowed him to go on first.

The whole street front was blocked with people.

"You had better go round by the back way, sir," suggested a bystander, in a meek whisper.

Old Mortiboy turned upon him like a wild cat, gnashing and gnawing with her teeth.

"Who the devil asked for your advice?" he gasped out, and passed straight on to the front entrance, blocked up as it was. They fell back to make way as his tall thin figure passed through their midst, followed by his great son, Dick— like Saul, a head taller than anybody else.

"Now," said Mr. Mortiboy, in a loud, shrill voice, "perhaps you will let me get through to my own bank, gentlemen."

There was some hesitation in the crowd.

"If I cannot get through you," said the old man, "by God, I'll have the shutters up in three minutes."

But Dick the stalwart was in front of him—clearing a path by the free use of his elbows. To get into the bank itself was a more difficult matter; for here, with every goodwill, the

K 2

people were so jammed and pressed together, that they could not possibly make room. As Mr. Mortiboy put his foot upon the steps, a little slip of an old man, whose terror was almost comical, fell at his feet crying—
"Oh, Mr. Mortiboy, Mr. Mortiboy, don't rob me of my money! Oh, sir, I'm a small man—I must draw it out! Oh, sir, let me have it. I'm ruined—I'm ruined!"
"What the devil is the matter with the man?" answered Mr. Mortiboy; and then, standing on the step, and turning to the people, he made the shortest and most effective speech they had ever heard—"YOU FOOLS!" was the whole of it.

Dick caught the little man under the arms, and lifted him up high.

"By gad!" he said—"isn't it Pig-faced Barnsby?"

The crowd roared with laughter. The little man, a barber by profession, had enjoyed that appellation from some fancied resemblance between his own and a porker's face, in the memory of all who had been boys in Market Basing in Dick's time.

"Look here, my men," said Dick, "let us give Pig-face his money first. How much is it, old man?"

"Mr. Richard—sir—if you please—twenty-six pounds six and fourpence, sir. I'm only a little man, Oh, this is *serious* —this *is* serious!" he whined.

"All right. Now, make way for my father, please. Come along, Pig-faced Barnsby."

He seized him by his breeches and the collar of his coat, raised him aloft, and carried him tortoise fashion over his head into the bank. Then he deposited him in a corner, and told him to wait patiently till he could be attended to.

Dick Mortiboy was in his father's private room. He drew back the green curtain of the door, and watched the cashiers paying away the money over the counter.

The pressure from without increased.

Melliship's bank had stopped. Men must make themselves safe. So Mr. Mortiboy's customers laid siege to his bank.

"This can't go on for ever," said Dick, after looking on for a few minutes. "We shall be run out too."

"Eh? eh?" said the old man feebly.

The momentary excitement had gone by. He was sitting in his armchair, low and dejected, brooding over the tragedy of the night.

"I must stop the run," said his son.

He had been thinking over old stories he had heard his father tell before he left home: of bankers who had paid in silver, in a fight against time: of an Irish story of sovereigns heated in a shovel, to appear that moment coined, and served hot and hot to the clamorous creditors.

"You will let me act for you, sir?" he said.

For Dick Mortiboy had hit upon a plan.

"Yes, Dick—yes. I leave all to you—I leave all to you. Do anything you like."

His son rushed off to the stable-yard in Derngate, ran up the granary steps, and carried down a pile of empty sacks on his shoulder.

They were barley sacks from the brewery. He called for assistance, and got the gardener and old Hester to help him put the sacks in two large empty boxes. They nailed down the lids. Then they drove them to the back entrance of the bank. There they emptied the boxes of their contents.

The sacks were carried into the strong room: the doors faced the counter. It was on the ground floor of the building behind the large room where the ordinary business of the bank was transacted. Housekeeper, servants, clerks, helped to ransack the house. They stuffed twenty of the sacks with bed-linen, pillows, bolsters, curtains, hangings, saw-dust, sand, paper, anything that would make them look solid, and that they could at the moment lay their hands on. They rammed the stuffing down hard, and set the sacks in double rank opposite the door that opened into the public room—ten before and ten behind.

Then Dick summoned Mr. Ghrimes, and told him what he meant to do. The manager went with him to the money safe, and they took out fifty bags of sovereigns, with £100 in each; and into the mouth of each sack in the front row they poured the golden contents of five bags. The back row of sacks they tied up with strings.

Mr. Richard Mortiboy, the younger, was going to practise on the credulity of Market Basing.

If his sacks had really been full of sovereigns, they must have contained £400,000—for they would have held £20,000 a-piece. And who could have carried the sacks there?

I can carry 4,000 sovereigns.

Dick Mortiboy could manage, at the outside, 7,000—he was almost a giant in strength.

Hercules himself might walk off with 10,000 on his back.
But the people the spectacle was prepared for did not think of these little things.
The originator of the plan knew he might trust to their simplicity for success.
He was right!
They threw open the door, and showed the glittering metal.
The " Open Sesame " had been said; and there before their wondering eyes, was more treasure than Ali Baba's fabled cave had held.
Gold!—Gold!—Gold!—Gold!!
Riches beyond the dreams of avarice! The sight of the dazzling heaps of specie wrought like a magical charm on the panic-stricken crowd.
They gaped, and were satisfied. Their money was all there.
Mortiboy's was saved!
Dick had stayed the run!!

CHAPTER THE FOURTEENTH.

THREE weeks have passed since the suicide of Mr. Melliship and the failure of his bank. The town of Market Basing has in some measure recovered its tranquillity, and those who have lost money are beginning to consider that they are lucky in pulling something out of the wreck. Meantime, official assignees have taken possession of the old bank, books, papers, and assets. The bereaved and ruined family have stripped themselves of their last farthing, save a poor hundred pounds a-year, the slender portion which Mrs. Melliship brought her husband—the large settlements made upon her at her marriage being absolutely surrendered for the benefit of the creditors. For their advantage, too, the books, pictures, and furniture are to be sold.

It is the last day the Melliships have to spend in their old house. For, obeying the usual instinct of broken people, they have decided on going to London, and hiding their poverty and ruin where no one will be likely to see it. The wounded beast seeks the thickest covert, where he can die undisturbed: the stricken Briton looks for the deepest solitude, which is in the streets of infinite London, where he may brood over his sorrows, and meditate fresh enterprises.

Kate Melliship goes sadly from room to room, taking her farewell of all that she has known and loved so long. There are the stately bookcases, the portfolios of prints and drawings, the music, the pianos, the very chairs and sofas which have witnessed their happy hours. Dry-eyed, but with a breaking heart, she turns over the leaves of the books, and takes a last look at the pictures in the portfolios. Nothing is to be taken away. They have decided, Frank and she, because their mother is helpless, that nothing but the barest necessaries of clothing can be retained by them, not even the smallest trinket, not the most precious keepsake, not the most trifling memento. Whatever happens, they will be able to say that, in the wreck of their father's house, they too were wrecked and lost their all. Even the ring upon her finger, with her father's hair, will to-night go into the jewel-box, and in a few days be put up for sale with the rest. Alas for this wrenching up of all the tendrils and spreading roots with which a girl's affection clings to her home! Agony as was that bitter awaking when the shrieks of the maid roused Kate from her sleep in the early morning, it almost seems as if this is worse, when everything has to be left behind, and of the father who cherished and loved her so tenderly, nothing will be left at all but the memory. Surely, it were something to have a few books of his—to preserve some little token, the sight of which would always bring him back to mind. It is not to be; and poor Kate, too wretched for tears, sits silent and sad in the lonely, fireless room, and feels as if there were no more possibility of life, or light, or joy.

Let me try to depict her.

She is, like her brother, fair-haired; and, like him, tall. Not so fascinating as Grace Heathcote, she has a certain dignity of bearing which makes her more striking in appearance. Grace is a maiden fair—Kate is a queen. Grace is a young man's goddess. For Kate, the Knight Bayard himself, when his locks were touched with grey, and his beard grizzled with forty years, might yet have been proud to break a lance. Sweet, good, tender, and true is Grace—strong with a woman's strength, but all womanly. All this Kate is, and more, because she adds resolution, self-reliance, independence. These she has in a greater degree than her brother Frank.

While she sits with her mother in the cold drawing-room,

the door is opened, and Grace Heathcote herself runs in, in her quick and impulsive way, and throws herself upon her neck.

"My Kate—my poor Kate," she cries, with the ready tears of sympathy.

Kate answers coldly—

"We leave to-morrow. I am saying farewell to the old house."

"But you are not going to leave everything behind you?"

"Everything—everything. Until every single debt is paid, Frank says we have no right even to the clothes we wear. All will be sold, Grace, dear. It seems strange. I cannot sometimes understand how a single month can make so great a difference. We were so happy then, and we are so miserable now."

"Kate, dear," whispered Grace, "I have brought a present for you, with a message for Frank."

"Who sends us presents now?"

Grace turned very red.

"It—it is from Uncle Mortiboy—your uncle, Kate. Here it is, with his best love and kind wishes."

Grace held in her hand an envelope, unsealed. In it was a Bank of England note for a hundred pounds. In their poverty and distress, a hundred pounds seemed to her a large sum. It was the very first gift of any kind they had ever received from their uncle.

"Did he send it of his own free will, Grace?"

Grace nodded with pertinacity.

"Did no one suggest it to him, Grace?"

Grace shook her head violently, blushing very red.

"Did you suggest it? No? It seems very kind of him— very kind indeed of him," said Kate. "But you must ask Frank if we could accept it."

"Yes," said her mother. "Frank manages for us now. I am hardly consulted about anything; and poor Frank's ideas are so unworldly and boyish. Oh, my poor dear husband! Oh, Francis, Francis, to think that you should have had such an end!"

The widowed lady sobbed as if her heart would break, and fell back on the ottoman she was sitting on.

"Go," whispered Kate to Grace. "You will find Frank downstairs."

A little while before, Grace would have romped all over the

house after Frank; but since that conversation of theirs in the lane at Hunslope, her feelings were altered very much. Now she was very coy; and her little heart beat fast as she tapped lightly at the door of the room Frank had from boyhood called his own.

His voice said, "Come in."

Grace entered his sanctum blushing, and looking all the more lovely for it.

She gave Frank her hand to shake; with the other, she held the note in her pocket.

Now, though it is hard to do it, the truth must be told, that in this business of the hundred pounds Grace Heathcote had been deceiving Kate grossly. Such was the fact.

She went to call upon her uncle with the secret intention of asking him to do something for the Melliships—what, she did not know. She found the old man in a peevish and irritable frame of mind. He was ailing in body, besides; and had had a stormy interview that morning with Ghrimes, his manager, who had dared to put in a word for the unfortunate Melliships. Mr. Mortiboy softened a little at sight of his favourite niece; but his face grew hard as the nether millstone when she told him on what errand she had come.

"Who sent you?" he cried, angrily. "Who told you that they had any claim upon me?"

"Nobody, my dear uncle. I came by myself."

He began to walk up and down the room, muttering—

"I had nothing to do with his death—nothing. I could not prevent it. I did not foresee it. I shall lose money as it is through it, I dare say. He has upset everything. No, girl —I cannot do anything for them. I must be just—just before I am generous."

Grace knew Mr. Mortiboy well enough to know that when he talked in this way his resolution was final. She sighed, and tried another tack.

"I suppose, dear uncle"—the little deceiver put her lovely arm round him—"you would not object to helping them indirectly? I mean if it were at no expense of—of justice."

"What do you mean?"

"Why, uncle, do you remember the kind and generous gift you made me—of a whole hundred pounds—only three weeks ago, when you dined with us? Now, that is mine—is it not? Well, I want to give that to my cousins."

"The girl's mad!"

"And for them not to know that it comes from me. So, if you don't mind, dear uncle, giving it me back again, we can manage in this way very well. You shall sign a cheque—a piece of paper—for it, which I will give to them, and tell them it comes from you."

Here was an opportunity of being generous, as Grace had put it, without the infringement of those bulwarks of justice with which Mr. Mortiboy loved to surround a mean and selfish action. The girl, of course, was Quixotic, mad, and romantic; but, then, it was always the way of girls; and, of course, if she insisted on it—if she was quite sure it was the only way, and if she was quite sure that Kate would not suspect—he was ready to give way. He wrote the cheque, gave it to Grace, and saw her depart on her errand of mercy and charity with quite a glow at his own heart, as if he had done it himself.

So he had. He had gained a reputation on the first gift to Grace which was now going to be doubled, at no greater expense, by the second—the only drawback being that it had really cost him a hundred pounds. Now, Mr. Mortiboy would have preferred a reputation for generosity which had cost him nothing at all.

But all this was a secret from Frank. To conceal anything from him was very painful to Grace, and she felt awkward and embarrassed. She wanted to get the affair of the present over at once; but when she tried to approach the subject her heart fluttered so that she dared not venture to begin about it.

So she stood there—rooted, it seemed, to the spot on which she had taken her stand when she entered the room. Her eyelashes lay in a black fringe on her cheeks—Frank could not see a bit of her eyes—and her manner was restrained, and not at all like Grace Heathcote's usual demeanour.

"Frank."

"Grace."

And then neither spoke.

The poor boy looked at the carpet, the ceiling, and at his mistress's face, and thought to read his fate there. But Grace stood inscrutable as the Sphinx. They had not met since the day of that walk in the Hunslope lane, when Mr. Frank professed his love. What painful events had happened to both since that afternoon! Yet the memory of it rushed into their hearts at the same moment, and they blushed like children.

They stood for a few moments in silence.

"There have been words between us, Grace," said Frank, "that must be as if they had never been said."
"That cannot be," said Grace, firmly. "We cannot unsay."
"Then we must forget."
"We cannot forget," said the girl. "Tell me, Frank, what you mean, plainly. Tell me all that is in your heart. Do you love me no longer?"
"My love, my darling! I love you better—a thousand times better; but it is because you are so far off from me. Do you know that I am a beggar—that the very clothes I stand in belong properly to our creditors? Grace, I dare not think of love. Yet how hard it is to forget! I have first to pay my father's creditors—how, I do not know. It is my sacred duty. I swore it. I must keep my oath. It will be my life's work. But you, Grace—my dear, dear girl—forget me. Let me go and toil on without nursing an idle hope. Release me; help me to tear away every illusion, so that I may face the reality. I am a pauper indeed, for I am stripped of more than money—I must give you back your love."
As he spoke this, his voice shook with emotion. With the last word he broke down.
Grace looked up in his eyes, bent upon her with his soft, sad gaze. A tear stood in them.
"What, Frank, is a woman's love such a light thing that it can be taken up and given back at any moment? For shame, sir! Do you think it is not till the wedding service that we take each other for better for worse? For shame, Frank! Do you suppose that I love you less because you have no more money? You silly boy! Don't you think I love you more because you are unhappy, and because—oh! Frank—Frank——"
And here she dropped her head upon his shoulder. There was nobody by to see her.
It is five minutes later. The interval has been spent in their mingled tears and kisses. Their lips separate, their arms drop from each other's; but by this, their second sacrament of love, the twain are henceforth one.
"I shall tell them myself," whispered Grace, "and to-night. I shall write to you if I can get permission; but I must not without. And now, Frank—my Frank—we must part. You will trust me, Frank? Kiss me, and tell me again that you love me."
"I love you, Grace, I love you—I love you! Oh, God! when shall I tell you so again?"

Then Grace told Frank the story of the bank note she had brought in her pocket to give him.

When the name of Mr. Mortiboy was mentioned, Frank flushed with agitation, and refused to soil his fingers with any of the money of his uncle.

"My father's enemies are mine," he said, looking, it must be confessed, very manly and noble; for Frank Melliship was a fine fellow.

This forced the truth from Grace.

She told him old Ready-money did not give the hundred pounds. It was her money, and he only had charge of it for her; and if she had a hundred thousand million of hundred-pound notes, all were Frank's; but this was all she had got. She laid it at his feet, and so on.

Pride at last gave way, and Frank pocketed the note.

"I consent to take it, Grace, on trust, to hold it for Kate and my mother. I will never touch a penny of it, nor shall they, unless we want bread. Some day, Grace"—he was enthusiastic, and his eyes flashed—"when I am rich and famous, I shall give you back this note, and claim your hand."

He held out his arm, looked at his clenched fist, and shook it, as one who means to move the world.

Grace tried to pull down his arm. All she said was—

"Silly boy!"

But she liked to see him brave, and ready to fight the world —for her.

They were disturbed by the voice of Kate Melliship. She was calling Grace's name as if she was not sure where she would find her. She had her own womanly instinct to tell her that there was something of a very private nature going on between them.

"Come, Grace, dear," she said, "here is your father come in to see poor mamma, and he has sent me to find you."

Grace kissed Kate, called her sister, looked farewell at Frank, and sailed out of the room with her arm round sister Kate's neck.

Frank had several visitors that day. One was his cousin, Dick Mortiboy.

"When do you go away, all of you?" he asked.

"To-morrow."

"Send me your address, Frank, will you? Promise that, for old times. Dick Mortiboy never forgets old friends, my boy—nor old enemies. It is not always possible to pay back old scores to either; but I do my best. There are not many men between this and the Pacific who have done me a mischief that go about comfortable and easy in their minds. Well, let us have the address, for your father's sake. Many is the tip I have had from him in the days when tips were scarce."

Frank promised; and Dick, shaking hands with him, strode off.

John Heathcote was another visitor.

"But what are you going to do, my boy?" he asked Frank.

"I don't know. I hope something will turn up."

"Something turn up, indeed! Yes: and you may be a clerk in a bank at a hundred a year, with permission to marry when you get a hundred and fifty. No, no—we must find something for you, Frank, my boy."

Mr. Heathcote pressed his hand, and took his leave. Folded in a packet was the farmer's present—the same as his daughter's, a note for a hundred pounds—which he left in Frank's hand like a physician's fee. Frank's heart was full. He had more than half a mind to tell Mr. Heathcote of his relation to his daughter; but he could not. He sat, and buried his face in his hands, in that same chair where his father had sat a month before, with wild eyes gazing upon the imaginary spectre. Presently, when his thoughts were too oppressive for him to bear, he seized his hat, and went out to drive away some of his care and sorrow by dint of physical exertion.

He took a walk up the Hunslope-road. A mile out of Market Basing stands Queen's Cross—one of the monuments erected by King Edward to the memory of Eleanor. From the little hill that the cross stands on there is a fine view of the town. Frank stood contemplating the familiar prospect, when he was aware of somebody standing by his side.

It was Grace. He took her hand, and pressed it tenderly in his.

"I came on first," she said. "The carriage will be here directly. Papa was talking a long time at the Angel to Mr. Mortiboy, and I walked on; and I have walked, and walked, till you see I have got as far as this."

As she spoke, the Heathcotes' sociable drove up, and stopped to take up Grace and set down old Mr. Mortiboy, whose foundry was behind the hill, within a quarter of a mile of the cross.

Frank was to have one more meeting that day.

His uncle sat by the side of John Heathcote, with his long, lean, bending figure; and his outstretched arm looked in the dim twilight like some bird of prey.

"So," said he, in his creaking voice, "you go away to-morrow, young gentleman, I hear—you go to-morrow."

"We do, Mr. Mortiboy."

"Well, I hope that you will prosper and—and get money, and take care of it—not like your poor father."

"If my father did spend money, he knew how to spend it on good and worthy objects, Mr. Mortiboy," retorted Frank, hotly.

"Ay, ay—we all knew Francis Melliship."

"I will have nothing said about my father from you," said Frank. "You were always his enemy. You took a pleasure in going up and down the town saying spiteful things of him. You envied him, Mr. Mortiboy. When he was richest, you had treble his wealth; and though you care more for money than for any other mortal thing, you envied him. You saw how people loved and respected him, and you looked in vain round Market Basing to find a soul that either loved or respected you. Do not dare to speak, sir, of a dead man whom you might have saved. Yes, Mr. Mortiboy, there is a letter lying on the study table now—an unfinished letter—telling me that you might have saved him. Do not dare, sir, to speak of the man whose death you have compassed."

"Upon my word!" said Mr. Mortiboy. "Upon my word! Now this is pretty peacockery!"

Nevertheless, though the old man's words were brave, his cheeks were white, and his fingers trembling. The blow had struck home more deeply than his nephew thought.

Mr. Heathcote caught Frank by the arm.

"Don't, Frank," he cried. "What's the good?"

Mr. Mortiboy raised himself erect. He was taller than Frank, and it always gives a man a moral advantage to be able to point downwards.

He shook his forefinger, solemnly, two inches in front of Frank's nose.

"Young man," he said, "it ill becomes one of your years and inexperience to speak of things of which you know nothing. Some day you will be sorry for what you have said. Go home now, and see your sister. You will be sorry for what you have said this very evening. I wish you well, sir,"

Mr. Mortiboy, it will be seen, alluded to the hundred pound cheque of Grace's. The old man did not know that Frank had been told the truth. It was gracefully done, and conveyed an expression—dim and vague, but vast—of secret generosity, which affected Frank disagreeably. He felt as if he had been speaking too hastily, and, wishing Grace and her father good night, without another word, went home.

CHAPTER THE FIFTEENTH.

O London! Cry of the young and ambitious. Let those who will sit at home grub for money piece by piece, die and be forgotten. To London!—battle-field where glory is to be won, gold-diggings richer than any in California, diamond fields more fertile than any in Natal:—the place to make fortunes, to repair ruin, to hide disgrace, to realize dreams, to bury shame. No fable is it, invented for the delusion of youth —that of the rich man who came to London with a single sixpence in his pocket. It is a reality which happens every day. Nor does it matter whether the beginning be made with a sixpence or a hundred pounds, for the end is certain to him who has brains, and pluck, and patience.

The widow, with her two children, and such small impedimenta as remained from the general wreck, came to London. They had their modest one hundred pounds a year—Mrs. Melliship's dowry at her marriage; they had besides, two hundred pounds in cash. A small stock to start with; but Frank and Kate had youth and hope.

"We will paint pictures, Kate," said Frank, "and sell them. I would give the world to be a great painter. We will get hung in the Royal Academy, and all the world will run to buy."

Kate smiled.

"Find me subjects, Frank, and find me strength and skill."

"You at least have the genius," said her brother.

It was true. Kate Melliship had been taught as carefully as Market Basing professors could teach—though it had not been possible, in a country town, to give her those lessons in painting which are essential to making a finished artist. And she had genius, which her brother had not. While Frank's drawings were sometimes stiff and always weak, hers were vigorous and free. If her conceptions were generally too difficult for her powers of execution, they were always artistic and genuine. Art was her passion. To be an artist for bread would bring no sense of shame with it, but rather of pride, as it ought. The only thing was to find out how to make bread out of it.

They took lodgings in South Kensington, near the Museum, and began to work. Mrs. Melliship, with the view of doing something to help the family, wrote secretly to a certain first cousin—her nearest relation. The first cousin sent her a ten-pound note: throwing the money to them like a bone to a dog. Kate made her mother promise to write no more begging letters, and said nothing to Frank about it.

This was the dreariest period in Kate Melliship's life. Her mother always in tears, or querulously comparing things present with things of old; Frank alternately in enthusiastic hopes of success and sheer despair; and her own work going on all too slowly for her impatience. They were exiles, too, and not yet settled into acquiescence with their lot.

"Nos dulcia linquimus arva,
Nos patriam fugimus,"

they might have cried had any one of the three known so much Latin, or found any consolation in applying it. Some women, if anything goes wrong, find a text in the Bible which fits their case, and are immediately comforted and consoled. It does not help them with any advice, it does not show them that they are punished for their own faults, it does not promise anything for the future:—but then it is a text; and the feminine heart, after receiving it, feels soothed and warmed, like a cold man with a glass of brandy and water. Kate was not one of these women. She had the bravery to look things in the face. Her mother was not one of these women, because she never looked anything in the face.

Frank, too, in spite of his enthusiasm had moments when his courage failed. At night, Kate would hear him walking to and fro far into the small hours. This was when he was haunted with the thought of failure, knowing that on success depended his hopes of Grace—battling with the temptation to ask of silent Heaven, *why*: that *why* which every innocent victim of sin and folly is tempted to ask, so that the Giver of all good is perpetually assailed with the reproach that He has given evil.

"Is it not hard, Kate?"—he would ask sometimes, when his mother had gone to bed—"Is it not hard?"—selfish in his sorrow. "All was in my grasp. Grace loved me; we were rich; we——"

"Don't look back, Frank dear. Look forward. She loves you still. If she is worth having, she will wait."

"Wait? Look here, Kate"—he tore the cover from a picture he had just finished. "This is the kind of daub which is to make me famous, is it?"

"Indeed, Frank, it is not bad. Your colouring is always rather cold." She bent over it, trying to find points for praise, but there were none. "At any rate you can copy."

"And earn about fifty pounds a year."

He was not always in this hopeless mood. Sometimes he was ready to laugh over little privations which had become necessary in their diminished means. It was in the time of that celebrated series of letters in the *Daily Telegraph* which showed how a man can marry, bring up ten children in luxury, be the proud proprietor of a pew, and save sixpence per annum to meet contingencies, all on eighty pounds a year; and he would read out the details, applying them to their own case, till Mrs. Melliship would be astonished by hearing their old laughter almost as loud and bright as before. At twenty-four one can't be always crying, even though things do look hopelessly bad.

"I can't do anything with it, Kate," said Frank, ruefully contemplating his grand classical picture, "The Death of Antigone," which he had begun with such confidence and pride. "I shall never be a painter. What shall I try next? The more I look at that stiff-necked Antigone, the more I hate her. Shall I advertise for a post as light porter? Look at her eyes: she squints. Shall I become a photographer's tout? Aid me, my wise sister, with counsel."

But Kate had none to give.

As the slow, cold spring crept on, Mrs. Melliship's health began to decline. More trouble for poor Kate. She did not dare tell Frank that the London confinement was telling

L

upon their mother. So she waited, hoping and fearing, and working bravely while the weeks crept by. Grace and Lucy Heathcote wrote to her.

Lucy's letters were all about Grace. Grace was becoming more womanly; she thought she was paler than she used to be; she was more thoughtful; she seemed more religious.

Grace wrote about things in general. She did not disguise from Kate the hard battle she always had with her mother. The girls, indeed, had never been greatly influenced by Mrs. Heathcote—inferior as she was to her daughters in point of both education and feeling.

"Tell Frank," she wrote, "that I have promised papa not to write to him. I told him, too, that I was going to send him messages. Tell him, dear Kate, that he is to go on loving me if he can, for I shall always love him. He is not to be worried if he does not succeed at first, because I can wait, and he is not to be impatient.

"My mother and I had a scene yesterday. Poor Lucy only cried. It was about Cousin Dick. You know poor mamma's *insane* idea that Dick wants to marry me.

"'Pray, how long are you going to encourage Dick's attentions?' she asked me.

"'Until I find out he *is* paying me attentions,' I replied.

"Then she said things that made me go out of the room, and I refused to go back until papa came home. Dick, indeed!

"Dick is a real good fellow, though, and I like him tremendously. He is as good-natured as a big man always is, and never in the way like little men. Pray, Kate, how is it that little men take up so much more room than big men? He says wonderful things, too; and invents stories, if you ask him for an anecdote, as if he was a Trollope. I hold up my finger, and say—'Dick, a Mexican story.' And he begins at once quite gravely, 'When I was in Texas,' and then always something new. He confessed to me the other day that he invents. Mamma says that he is a young man of excellent religious principles. If so, my dear, he takes care to keep his light hidden, for he never goes to church, wanted once to play cards on Sunday, smokes cigars all day if he can, and I once heard him swear at Silly Billy till the poor man turned white. But I like Dick. Here he comes, and I am going to be shown the lasso trick—wait till I come back.

"Oh, Kate, my dear, Cousin Dick is an Admirable Crichton. He has been throwing the lasso as they do in his beloved

Texas—Lucy and I looking on. The miserable victim was a colt; its leg is hurt. Colts in this country don't understand the lasso, as I told Dick. He swore in Spanish. It sounded very deep and grand, like a church organ in a rage, not like the ugly and vulgar sounds which issue from the mouth of the rural Briton. Kate, my dear, I'm very miserable, because I can't help being happy sometimes, and I am afraid you and Frank are not. Forgive me, dear. Mamma refuses to recognize our engagement. Of course, that makes no difference. Poor old Uncle Mortiboy looks greatly changed in the last few weeks. His hand shakes, his head shakes, and he shakes all over. Lucy goes to see him oftener than I, because she is a better girl than your wicked Grace—whom you and F—— love so much—and does her duty. He sits and shakes, and talks perpetually about what is going to happen when he is gone.

"' When I am gawn,' he says in such a doleful way that you would think he was going at once. But he is quite happy when Dick is with him. He follows him with his eyes. He cannot bear to spend his evenings without him. Dick, like a good creature, sits and talks with his father every night of his life. . . . I've told you all the gossip I know. Papa wants me to give his love to you, and tell Frank to keep a good heart. The dear old man! I had a walk and a talk with him yesterday all over the ploughed fields, and came back with mud up to my eyes. I told him, what I tell you, that I love Frank, and shall never marry anybody else, even if anybody should ask me. Cousin Dick, indeed!

"Please give my kind remembrances, and Lucy's and mamma's, to Mrs. Melliship and to Mr. Frank Melliship—is that cold enough for you?—and send me a long and happy letter."

Dick was not without his troubles. The old man bored him almost beyond endurance. To make the evenings livelier, he conceived the brilliant idea of keeping his father's weekly bottle of gin always half full. Then the old man, quite unconsciously, took to drinking double and treble allowance, and would go to bed an hour earlier, staggering up the stairs. In the morning, he was tremulous and nervous. He did not like to be left alone. The death of Mr. Melliship seemed to have suddenly aged him. At night he lay awake—unless he had taken more spirit than was good for him—trembling at

L 2

imaginary whispers. Ghrimes, at the bank, found that his capacity for business was gone altogether; and yet he would not give up his attendance at the bank.

With all this, tighter than ever with the money. Nothing to be got out of him for any of Dick's foreign schemes. And all the more hopeless now, because the old man had only one thought—to keep his son at home.

Second trouble—Polly. Once a week or so, she came to see him. Dick went to the trysting-place with as much joy as a boy goes to keep an appointment with the head-master after school. She was always gushing and affectionate; always wanting more money for little Bill; and, which was his only comfort, always afraid of him.

Third trouble—Lafleur. With his usual bad luck, this worthy had got through his share of the thousand, and was wanting more. Before long, his own would be all gone. And his promise to raise five thousand in three months! More than two of them gone. And how to raise the money?

CHAPTER THE SIXTEENTH.

IT WAS about this time Mr. Mortiboy took to sending for his lawyer three or four times a week. After each interview he would be more nervous, more shaken than before. He kept the reason of these visits a secret—even from Ghrimes. But to Lucy Heathcote—with whom he spoke more frankly of himself than to any other human being—the old man told some of his perplexities.

"I am getting old, my dear, and I am getting shaky. I've a deal to trouble and worry me.

"But there is Cousin Dick, uncle."

"Yes, there's Dick. But it is all my property that's on my mind. I always intended to do something for you two, my dear—always."

"Never mind that now, uncle."
"And perhaps I ought for the young Melliships as well; though why for them I don't know. And I'm ill, Lucy. Sometimes I think I am going to die. And—and—I try to read—the—Bible at night, my dear; but it's no use—it's no use. All the property is on my mind, and I can think of nothing else."

"Shall I read to you, uncle?"

"No, child!—nonsense!—certainly not," he replied, angrily. "I'm not a Pauper."

Being "read to," whether you liked it or not, suggested the condition of such helpless impecuniosity, that he turned quite red in the face, and gasped. His breath was getting rather short.

Presently he went on complaining again.

"At night I see coffins, and dream of funerals and suicides. It's a dreadful thing to have a funeral going on all night long. I think, my dear, if I had the property off my mind, I should be better. If it was safe, and in good hands, I should be very much easier. If it was still growing, I should be lighter in my mind. Dick is very good. He sits with me every evening. But he can't be with me when I am asleep, you know, Lucy; and these dreams haunt me."

The old man passed his hand across his brow, and sighed heavily. He could not bear even to think of death; and here was death staring him in the face every night.

"I know I ought to make a will," he went on to his patient listener, Lucy, who did not repeat things—as the old man knew very well. "I ought to; but I can't, my dear. There's such a lot of money, and so many people; and after one is gone, one will be abused for not doing what was right; and—and—I haven't the heart to divide it, my dear. It's such a shame to cut Property up, and split it into pieces."

"Can't you take advice, uncle?"

"I don't trust to anybody, Lucy. They're all thinking of themselves—all of them." This, as if he had been himself the most disinterested of mankind.

"There's Mr. Ghrimes. You trust him, uncle?"

"Well—yes—I trust him. But then he's well paid for it, you see."

Ghrimes got £200 a year for his work, which a London employer would have considered cheap at five times that sum.

"And you trust Cousin Dick."

"Yes," said the old man, brightening up a little. "I do trust Dick. I trust my boy. He is a great comfort to me—a great comfort. He is very clever—Dick is—he has a wonderful head for business. He manages everything well. Look what a window he got from London for your poor Aunt Susan's memorial—and for twenty pounds. Oh, Dick does everything well, and he's a great comfort to me.. But it is not only the division of the Property, Lucy—think of the Awful Probate duty! There's a waste of money—there's a sacrifice; a most iniquitous tax, a tax upon prudence! I'm not so well off as I ought to be, my dear—not so well as my poor father thought I should be, but I've done pretty well. And the probate duty is a terrible thing to think of—it's really appalling. Two per cent. on money left to your son! Thousands will be lost! Dear me! dear me! Thousands!"

These confidences were for Lucy Heathcote alone, with whom the old man felt himself safe. No talk of property to Dick; no confessions to his son; no asking of advice; no offers of money. So far from giving or lending, Mr. Mortiboy received from Dick, every Saturday morning, a sovereign in payment for a week's board, and two shillings and threepence for a bottle of gin. While pocketing the money, the parent never failed to remind his son of the cheapness of his board, and the fact that he was charged nothing at all for bed and lodging. He always added, solemnly, that it gave him great pleasure to entertain his son, even at a loss.

As for their evenings together, they were always alike. A single candle lighted the kitchen where they sat; the father in a Windsor arm-chair, with his bottle of gin at his elbow, and a long pipe in his mouth; the son opposite him, with a short pipe and another bottle. Between them a deal table. As Dick grew tired of telling stories, he used sometimes to beguile the hours by showing his father tricks with the cards. Mr. Mortiboy, senior, did not approve of games of chance. They gave no opening for the prudent employment of capital, and risked Property. Nor did he approve of so-called games of skill, such as whist; because the element of chance entered so largely into them, that, as he argued, not the richest man was safe. But his admiration was excessive when Dick—feigning, for the sake of effect, that his father was a credulous and simple-minded person—showed how thousands might be won by the turning up of a certain card; telling which card had been touched; making cards hide themselves in pockets, and drawers, and so forth. These feats of skill, with the stories which, like a child, he loved to hear over and over again, rekindled and inflamed Mr. Mortiboy's imagination, previously as good as dead, so that his fancy ran riot in dreams of unbounded wealth to be found in distant countries—dreams which Dick could have turned to good use had it not been for the want of nerve which had fallen upon his father after Mr. Melliship's death.

Between eight and nine, the old man, who shows signs of having taken as much gin and water as he can well carry, rises to go to bed. Dick lights his candle, and watches the tall, thin figure of his father—stooping now and bent—climbing the stairs.

He heaves a great sigh of relief, and closes the double doors which connect the kitchen, built out at the back, with the rest of the house.

"What has the old woman got for me?" says Dick, unlocking a cupboard. "Steak again. Well, where's the gridiron?"

The economical principles on which Mr. Mortiboy's household was conducted generally left his son an exceeding hungry man at nine o'clock; and, by private arrangement with old Hester, materials for supper were always secretly left out for him.

Dick deftly cooks the steak, drinks a pint of stout, and producing a bottle of brandy from the recesses of the cupboard, mixes a glass of grog, and smokes a pipe before going to bed.

"It's infernal hard work," he sighs to himself; "and something ought to come of it—or what the devil shall I do with Lafleur?"

Then came a letter from that gentleman. Bad news, of course; had been to Paris; done capitally with his System for a time. Turn of luck; not enough capital; was cleaned out. Would his partner send him more money, or would he run up to town, and bring him some?

He afterwards explained that the System was working itself out like a mathematical problem, but that he had been beguiled by the *beaux yeux* of the Countess de Parabère—in whose house was the play—and weakly allowed her to stand behind his chair. Dick quite understood the significance of this folly, and forbore to make any remark. Bad luck, indeed, affected his spirits but slightly, and he was too well acquainted with his partner to blame him for those indiscretions which the wisest and strongest of men may fall into.

Out of the thousand pounds they brought to England, only one hundred remained. Lafleur, in three months, had had eight hundred; Polly nearly a hundred; and a hundred remained in the bank. Dick, in this crisis, drew out fifty, and went up to town with it.

Lafleur was in his lodgings in Jermyn-street, sitting at work on his System—an infallible method of breaking the banks. He had a pack of cards, and a paper covered with calculations. Occasionally he tested his figures, and always, as it appeared, with satisfactory results. At present he was without a shilling—having lost the last in an attempt to win a little money at pool, at which he had met with provokingly back luck.

"I have brought you something to carry on with for the present," said Dick, "and we must talk about the future."

Lafleur counted the money, and locked it up.

"Permit me to remind my Dick," he said, in his softest accents, "that the three months are nearly up."

"I know," replied Dick, gloomily.

"Let us go and dine. You can sleep here to-night, if you like. There is a spare room. And we can have a little game of cards."

They dined: they came back: they had a little game of cards. At midnight, Lafleur turned his chair to the fire, and lighting a cigarette, looked at his friend with an expression of inquiry.

"Après, my Richard."

Dick stood before the fire in silence for a while.

"Look here, Lafleur. Did I ever break a promise?"

"Never, Dick. Truthful James was a fool to you."

"Very well, then. Now, listen to me."

He told how his father was falling into dotage; how he held tighter than ever to his money; how the old man grew every day more fond of him; and how he must, at all hazards, contrive to hold on.

"The property is worth half a million at least, Lafleur. Think of that, man. Think of five hundred thousand pounds —two and a half million dollars—twelve and a half million francs? The old man keeps such a grip upon it that I can touch nothing. Makes me pay him a pound a week for my grub. But I *must* hold on. It would be madness to cross or anger him now. You must wait, Lafleur."

"I will wait, certainly. Make your three months six, if

you like—or nine, or twelve. Only, how are we to live meantime? Get me some money, Dick—if it is only a few hundreds. Can't you get his signature to a bank cheque? or—or—copy his signature?"

"No—quite impossible. He hardly ever draws a cheque; and Ghrimes would know at once."

"Cannot the respectable Ghrimes be squared. No? Ah! Are there no rents that you can receive?"

"None. Ghrimes has a system, I tell you."

"Is there nothing in the house, Dick?"

Dick started. The man had touched on a secret thought. Something in the house? Yes—there was something. There was the press in his father's bedroom, the keys of which were always in old Ready-money's possession. There were gold cups and silver cups in it; plate of all kinds; jewellery and diamonds; and there was, he knew, at least one bag of gold. Something in the house? He looked fixedly at Lafleur without answering.

Lafleur lighted another cigarette; and crossing his legs with an easy smile, asked casually—

"Is it money, Dick?"

Dick's face flushed, and his eyebrows contracted. Somehow, he had got out of sympathy with the old kind of life.

"I don't know for certain. I think there is money. Gold and silver things, diamonds and pearls. No one knows the existence of the bureau but myself. But I will not do it, Lafleur. I cannot do it. The risk is too great."

"Then you shall not do it, my partner. *I* will do it."

He went to his desk, and took out a little bottle, which he placed in Dick's hands.

"I suppose," he said, holding it lovingly up to the light, "that you are not ignorant of the admirable and useful properties of morphia. This delightful fluid—which contains no alcohol, like laudanum—will send your aged parent into so profound a slumber, that his son may safely abstract his keys for an hour or so, and give them to me. I should only borrow the gold, for the rest would be dangerous. The risk of the affair, if properly conducted, would be simply nothing. Or, another method, as the cookery books say. Let us get an impression of the keys in wax. That you can do easily. I know a locksmith—a gentle and amiable German, in Soho—whose only desires are to live blamelessly—and to drink the blood of kings. He will make me a key. You will then, on a certain night, make all arrangements for my getting into the house."

"Is that stuff harmless?"

"Perfectly. I will take some myself to-night, if you like."

"Lafleur, I will have no violence."

"Did you ever see me hurt any one?"

"No, by gad!" cried Dick, with a laugh. "But you've sometimes stood by, and seen me hurt people."

It had indeed been Dick's lot to get all the fighting, though it was hardly delicate to remind his partner of the fact.

"It is true," he said, with a slight flush. "There are many gentlemen in the United States and elsewhere who bear about them the marks of your skill. I will not harm your father, Dick. As for the money, it will be all yours some day, you know. And he can't spend it."

"I don't want to hear arguments about taking it," said Dick. "I want it, and you want it, and that's enough. But I will not run any risk, if I can help it. Good heavens, man! think of letting half a million slip through your fingers for want of a little patience."

"My dear Dick, I will manage perfectly for you. Make me a plan of the house. Get me a bed, because I am a commercial traveller. Let me have a map of the roads between the station and the house."

"There are two stations. You can arrive at nine-thirty, despatch your business, and take the night train by the other station to Crewe, at eleven-thirty."

"Better and better. Now for the plan."

With pen and paper, Dick proceeded to construct a plan and sketch of his father's house. The bedroom was one of three rooms on the first floor, the other two being empty. At the back of the house was a window opening on the garden. Old Hester slept in a garret at the top; Dick himself in Aunt Susan's room, on the second floor. Neither was likely to hear any little noise below.

"My father never locks his door, in case of fire," said Dick, completing his plans. "All you will have to do is to walk in, and open the press which stands here, where I mark it in black lines. You cannot make a mistake about the door, because the other rooms are locked. And don't take out a single thing except the money. When shall it be?"

"As soon as we can get the key made."

"Good! I'll administer the morphia, and get the key for

an impression. To-night is the first: we had better say in about a fortnight."

"Say this day fortnight, unless you write anything to the contrary—the fifteenth."

The pair, sitting at the table, with pencil and paper, arranged their plans quickly enough. In half an hour, Lafleur put the papers in his pocket, and slapped his partner on the back. Dick, however, was gloomy. He was planning to rob his father the second time, and he remembered that the first had not been lucky. Like all gamblers, he was superstitious.

While his son was preparing to rob him, Mr. Mortiboy, senior, was lying sleepless in his bed, with a new determination in his head keeping him awake.

"I'll do it," he said to himself—"I'll do it. Battiscombe and Ghrimes may say whatever they like, and Lyddy may think what she likes. Dick is the proper person to have my property. He won't waste and squander. He won't be got over by sharks. He knows how to improve and take care of it. I can trust Dick.

In this world, to be believed in is to be successful; and old Mr. Mortiboy believed in Dick.

"What a son," he said, "to be proud of: what a fine son! Thank God for My Son Dick!"

CHAPTER THE SEVENTEENTH.

NO need of morphia to get at the keys; for, the very next night, Mr. Mortiboy dropped them out of his pocket as he rose to go to bed. They lay on the chair, and his son, after dutifully escorting his sire to the foot of the stairs, went back, and took an impression of them. The operation took him three minutes and a half; and he then mounted to his father's bedroom, and gave back the bunch.

"A very dangerous thing," said Mr. Mortiboy; "a most dangerous thing; a thing I have never done before. A blessed chance, Dick, that it was you who picked them up. A Providence—quite."

A Providence—perhaps: because dispensations of all sorts happen. It is not fair to lay all the good things at the feet of Providence, and none of the bad. Dick put his wax impressions in a cough-lozenge box, and sent them to Lafleur, who briefly acknowledged their receipt.

His spirits began to rise again as the time for the exploit approached. He went about the house, surveying it with a critical eye—estimating the probability of Hester hearing anything—wondering if Lafleur would do it cleverly—making calm and careful preparations. He prised out two rails in the front garden at night; because the gate was always locked, and gentlemen do not like to be seen clambering over rails. He placed the ladder in readiness behind the water-butt, where it could easily be found. He rubbed candle-grease on the window, to make it open noiselessly. He put oil into the lock of the press, when his father was at the bank. He ascertained that there was no moon on the fifteenth. He found out from a book on medicine what amount of morphia would send a man to sleep.

"And now," he said to himself, "I can't do any more. The old man shall have his draught. Lafleur shall do the trick. I will remove the ladder, and destroy the evidence; and next day there will be the devil's own row! Ho! ho! ho!"

Dick shook his sides with silent laughter as he thought of his father's rage and despair at having been robbed.

"What if I rush to the rescue? Suppose I hear a noise, run downstairs with nothing on, but a pistol in my hand, fire at Lafleur just as he gets out of window, and rush to my father's assistance! What a funk Lafleur would be in!"

But he abandoned the idea, though extremely brilliant, as too dangerous. The report of the pistol might attract a policeman.

It was impossible to tell from his behaviour that anything was in the wind. Careless and jovial by nature, he played his part without any acting. He had little anxiety about the robbery, because things were planned so well. As for misgivings and scruples of conscience, they had vanished. In place of them, he daily had before his eyes the picture of his father tearing his hair at the discovery; his own activity in the work of detection; and the imaginary searching of the house, including his own room, " by particular desire."

After all his experience of life, Dick was still only a boy, with the absence of moral principle which belongs to that time of life, all a boy's mischief, and all his fun. One of the best fellows in the world if he had his own way—one of the worst if anything came in his way. He was big, handsome, black-bearded. He had a soft and mellow voice. He had gentle ways. He petted children. When he had the power, he helped people in distress. He laughed all day. He sang when he was not laughing. He fraternized with everybody. Men have been canonized for virtues fewer than these.

"I'll do it," said Mr. Mortiboy at night. He repeated it in the morning as he dressed. He stared very hard at Dick during breakfast. He sent for lawyer Battiscombe after breakfast, and repeated it to him.

"I'll do it at once," said the rich man.

"I have dissuaded you to the utmost of my power," said his lawyer. "It is a most irregular thing, Mr. Mortiboy. Think of King Lear."

"Mr. Battiscombe, do not insult my family," old Readymoney cried, in great wrath. "It is thirty years since I saw 'King Lear' at the theatre, but I suppose it isn't much altered now. And may I ask if you mean to compare my son, my son Dick, with those—those—brazen hussies?"

"Well—well—of course not. I say no more. The instrument, sir, will be ready in a day or two, and you shall sign whenever you please."

"The sooner the better, Battiscombe. Let us be ready on the fifteenth; that is Dick's birthday. He will be three and thirty. Three and thirty! What a beautiful age! Ah! Battiscombe, what a man I was at three and thirty!"

He was, indeed, a man; one who denied himself all but the barest necessaries of life, and was already beginning to break his young wife's heart by neglect and meanness.

This was on the fifth of the month. There yet wanted ten days to the completion of Mr. Mortiboy's design. He spent the interval in constant talk with Dick, who could not understand what it all meant.

"Let us walk in the garden, my son," said his father. "I want to talk to you."

The days were warm and sunny, and the garden had a south aspect. The old man, with his arms behind him, stooping and bent, with his eyes on the ground, paced to and fro on the gravel; while Dick, with his hands in his pockets and a pipe in his mouth, lounged beside him. A strange contrast, not of age only, but of disposition. As the mother, so the son. Dick's light and careless nature, and his love for spending rather than saving, came from poor Emily Melliship.

"I want to tell you, my boy," said the old man—"because I know you are careful and saving, and have just ideas of Property—how my great estate has been built up ; how I have got Money."

He told him. A long story—it took many days to tell—a story of hardness, of mean artifice, of grinding the poor man's face, and taking advantage of the credulous man's weakness ; a story which made the son look down upon his father, as he shuffled beside him, with contempt and disgust.

"We're a charming family," Dick said to Lafleur one day —"a delightful family, my partner. I think, on the whole, that Roaring Dick is the best of the whole crew. Damn it all, Lafleur, I'd rather hang about gambling booths in Mexico; I'd rather loaf round a camp in California, and lay by for horses to steal ; I'd rather live cheating those who would else cheat you, shooting those who would else shoot you, than live as my respected father and grandfather have lived. Why, man, there isn't an old woman in Market Basing who does not prophecy a bad end to money got in their way, and wonder why the bad end does not come."

"All very well," said Lafleur. "But I should like to have half a million of money."

"Criminals !" growled Dick, pulling his beard. "They'd call me a criminal, I suppose, if they knew everything. Why don't they make laws for other kinds of criminals ? "

"My friend," his partner softly sighed, "do not, I implore you, begin your remembrances. Life is short, and ought not to be troubled with a memory at all."

"Perhaps it's as well as it is. By gad, we should all be in Chokee ; and the virtuous ones, if there are any, would have an infernally disagreeable time of it, trying and sentencing. I should plead Insufficiency of income, and an Enormous appetite. What should you say ? "

On the morning of the fifteenth of May, Dick received a note from Lafleur, informing him of his intention to execute their little design that evening. He twisted up the note and put it in the fire, with a chuckle of considerable enjoyment, thinking of his father's misery when he should find it out.

Mr. Mortiboy was particularly lively that morning. He chattered incessantly, running from one subject to another in a nervous, excited way.

"Be in the house at three to-day, Dick," he said, solemnly.

"A most important business is to be transacted, in which you are concerned. Mr. Ghrimes is coming."

"Very odd coincidence," thought Dick. "There's an important business coming off to night at ten, in which *you* are concerned." However, he only nodded, and said he would remember.

He spent his morning in completing the arrangements for the evening, so far as anything remained to be done. Then he went to the bank, as was his custom, and talked with the people who called on business. They all knew him by this time; and, when they had fought out their business with Ghrimes, liked to have ten minutes' talk with the great traveller who dispensed his stories with so liberal a tongue.

At three o'clock, Mr. Ghrimes—punctual and methodical—arrived from the bank, and Mr. Battiscombe, with a blue bag, from his office. Mr. Mortiboy heard them, and led his son by the arm to the state-room—the parlour, which had not been used since the day of the funeral. Once more, as for an occasion of ceremony, the wine and biscuits were set out.

Mr. Mortiboy shook hands with all three, and stood on the hearth-rug, as he had stood when last they met together in that place. But this time his hand was on his son's shoulder, and his eyes turned from time to time upon him with a senile fondness.

"I am anxious," said Ghrimes, with a red face, "that you"—here he looked at Dick—"should know that I have done my best to dissuade Mr. Mortiboy from this step. I think it foolish and wrong. And I have told him so."

"You have, George Ghrimes—you have," said the old man.

"There is yet time, Mr. Mortiboy," urged his manager.

"Nonsense, nonsense."

Mr. Mortiboy made a sign to the lawyer, who produced a parchment from his bag, and handed it to him.

"George Ghrimes," he began, "when my son Dick was supposed to be dead, John and Lydia Heathcote were my apparent heirs. Between them and their daughters—for, of course, *I* should not have fooled it away in memorial windows, and hospitals, and peacockery—would have been divided all my Property. I can understand their disappointment. But they must also feel for the joy of a father when he receives back a long-lost son—a son like Dick, rich, prosperous, careful, and with a proper sense of Money. My son Dick has been home for three months. During that time I have watched him, because

I do not trust any man hastily. My son Dick has proved all that I could wish, and more. He has saved me hundreds."

"He saved the bank," interrupted Ghrimes.

"He did. He has saved me thousands. He has no vices —none whatever. No careless ways, no prodigality, no desire to destroy what I have been building up. What he is now to me I cannot tell you, my friends—I cannot tell you."

He stopped to hide his emotion. The poor old man was more moved than he had ever been before, even when his wife died. Dick stared at his father in sheer amazement. What on earth was coming next?

"And there is another thing. I am getting old. My nerve is not what it was. If it were not for my son Dick, and—and, yes, I must say that—for Ghrimes, I should be robbed right and left by designing sharks, I should lose all chances of getting money. My property is too great a burden to me. I cannot bear to see it suffer from my fault. I am going to put it into abler hands than mine. My son Dick shall manage it—it shall be called his. Dick, my son"—here he fairly burst into tears—"take all—take all—I freely give it you. Be witness, both of you, that I do this thing in a sound state of mind and body, not moved by any desire to evade the law and save money on that Awful probate duty; but solely out of the unbounded confidence I have in my son Dick." He paused again. "And now my friends, the work of my life is finished. I hope I shall be spared for some few years to see the prosperity of my boy, to mark the growth of the Property, to congratulate him when he gets Money."

Yes—all was Dick's! Old Ready-money had signed a Deed of Gift, passing away all his vast wealth to his son with a few strokes of his pen. The lawyer explained, while Dick was stupefied with astonishment, that he was the sole owner and holder of all the Mortiboy property. As he explained, Mr. Mortiboy sat back in his easy chair, drumming with his fingers on the arm, with a smile of intense satisfaction. Dick held the paper in his hand, and received the congratulations of the lawyer with a feeling that he was in a dream.

They went away. Mr. Mortiboy, left alone with his son, felt awkward and ill at ease. His effusion spent, and the deed done, he felt a kind of shame—as undemonstrative people always do after they have bared their hearts. He felt cold, too,—stripped, as it were.

"It will make no difference, Dick," he said in a hesitating way.

Dick only nodded.

"We shall be exactly the same as before, Dick."

He nodded again.

"I shall go out, father, and recover myself a bit. I feel knocked over by this business."

"Don't lose the deeds, Dick—give them to me to keep."

But Dick had stuffed them in his pockets, and was gone

CHAPTER THE EIGHTEENTH.

AFTER paying a tribute to his father's extravagant generosity by washing his throat with a wine-glass of Cognac in the pantry on his way out, Dick Mortiboy strode into the garden. He felt the want of light, and space, and air to appreciate his father's act.

In the close parlour, where old Ready-money had in one great gift beggared himself and made his son a millionaire, he could not think.

This rover of the seas went out into the air to realize his position; and then he did not do it in a moment. What a change a few up-and-down strokes of a pen can make! It seemed impossible. An hour before, Dick Mortiboy would have sworn that he had lived too long in a world of surprises to be surprised by anything. But the sudden transformation of Laflour's partner into the richest man in Market Basing was almost too much even for his adamantine nerves. The sensation of being respectable was too new. He was a little staggered: strode fast along the gravel paths of the old-fashioned garden—now pale, now slightly flushed; and, intense realist as he was, had a dim notion of something unreal in his great stroke of fortune. This feeling floated across his brain once or twice in the first few seconds only. He felt the stiff parchment crumple in the grasp of his sinewy fingers. This put dreams to flight: here was reality!

He held possession in his hand.

He stood in his father's shoes, he hardly knew how many years before he had expected to put them on.

From the moment he had made up his mind to stay with his father, he had played his cards well. But the end of the game had come almost too soon. Life thus lost one fertile source of amusement for Dick Mortiboy. And then the old man had outwitted him after all. Closely as he had watched him, he had never dreamed what was in the wind. He had seen the effect Mr. Melliship's death had had on his father, and had marked with interested eye the signs of his mental decay. But the idea of Ready-money Mortiboy making a transfer of everything to him had never entered his mind.

The man who would have grudged him a coin, gave him his hoards. Yet, in his heart, Dick had not one spark of gratitude towards his father.

"I've had a good many facers in my life," he said to himself, "but this is the most wonderful of any. Twelve years' knocking about ought to make a man equal to most accidents, but I don't suppose that any accident ever happened that could hold a candle to this. Fatherly affection must be a very strong sentiment with some people. I don't feel any such yearning after little Bill as the governor must have had for me. Wonder if he repents his ways, and is trying to make atonement? Can't be that. No, he thinks he has saved the probate duty, and made a nominal transfer to his affectionate, his clever, steady, honest son, Richard. Wonder if he thinks I'm going to let him have his own way? Can't be such a fool as that. Wonder if he believes all he says? Must. Most extraordinary old chap, the governor! What are we to do now? Shall we live in Market Basing, and 'see the Property grow?' I don't think we can. Shall we undeceive the old man?"

His face grew dark.

"He treated me like a dog. He gave me the wages of a porter. He starved me and bullied me. He turned me into the streets with a ten-pound note. When I come home and pretend that I am rich, he fawns upon me and licks my hand. 'Honour your father.' Now, I ask an enlightened General Board of Worldly Affairs—if there is such a thing—how the devil I can be expected to honour Mr. Mortiboy, senior? Ready-money Mortiboy, is he? Good. He shall have ready money for the future, and not too much of it. What he gave me, I will give him. I've been a forger, have I? I've been a gambler, and an adventurer—I've lived by tricks and cunning for twelve years, have I? I've been a bye-word in towns where men are *not* particular as to their morals, have I? I've done the fighting for Lafleur, and the lying for both of us, have I? I've been Roaring Dick, with my life in my hand, and my pistol in my pocket, sometimes with a fistful of money, sometimes without a dollar, have I? And whose fault?"

He shook his fist at the house.

"And now I'm master of everything. My affectionate father, your affection comes too late. I am what you made me—an unnatural son."

He was gesticulating a little in his anger, like Lafleur did when he was excited. He had picked up the trick from his partner. And he was speaking out in a loud tone of voice, and shaking his fist at the bottom of the garden, near the old door he had found locked on the Sunday morning when he first met Polly after his return. And the door had a very large keyhole, and there was an eye at it watching him with considerable interest.

Polly was there.

"D-I-C-K," she whispered through the keyhole.

He heard it, swore, and thought the place was haunted. His back was turned to the door.

"Dick," she called again, in a louder tone.

This time he knew the voice, and soon discovered where it came from.

"Good gad—Polly!"

He did not look pleased.

He put his foot on the pump, and looked over. She was dirty, and her clothes were very untidy.

"Dick, what were you going on like that for? I saw you when you were up at the other end of the garden, shaking your fist at your father's bed-room window. What's he been doing of, Dick?"

"What do you want here at this time of the day?" was the only answer she got to her queries.

She did not dare to repeat them. She was afraid of the man's anger.

"Dick," she said, "I want some money. Little Bill's been

took bad, and I've got nothing to send him. Scarlet fever he's got."

"Polly, my girl"—he was still on his own side of the wall —"you've had fifty pounds out of me in three months. Bill can't cost all that, you know. You'd better not try on any humbug, because I'm not going to stand it."

"Now, who was? And he's had every farden of it—except a pound or two I kep' for clothes myself. But he wants it, Dick."

"Then *I'll* take it to him."

The woman's expression grew obstinate and stubborn.

"You take me to your father, and say, 'Here's my wife,' and you shall have his address: not before, my fine Dick."

"Then," said Dick, "you may go to the devil!" And marched away.

Polly waited a few minutes, to see if he would come back; and then she too walked off.

The evening was a silent and dismal one. Mr. Mortiboy proposed a bottle of port to drink the occasion. Dick suggested brandy instead; and the old man drank three tumblers of brandy and water. In his excited state, the drink produced no effect upon him; and he went off to bed at half-past nine without the usual symptoms of partial inebriation. Then Dick relapsed into a gloomy meditation by the kitchen fire. He was aroused by the clock striking ten, and leaped to his feet as if he had been shot.

"Good Lord!" he ejaculated—"the very time for Lafleur. I had forgotten about him."

He kicked off his boots, and crept silently along the passage and up the stairs. A light came through the door of Mr. Mortiboy's bedroom, which was left ajar. He heard the sound of money.

"Cunning old fox," thought Dick; "hiding my money, is he?"

Then he crouched down in the dark passage, and waited.

The situation presently struck him as being intensely comic. Here was the old man counting his money in the bedroom, while Lafleur was probably getting up the ladder. Instead of sleeping off a dose of morphia, Mr. Mortiboy was in a lively state of wakefulness. Instead of robbing the father, Lafleur would be robbing him. He chuckled at the thought, leaning against the wall, till the floor shook.

In five minutes or so, he saw a black form against the window.

"There he is," thought Dick.

The real fun was about to begin.

Lafleur opened the window noiselessly, and stepped into the passage. He moved with silent steps, feeling his way till he came to the old man's door. Then he looked in, and stood still, irresolute—for the light was streaming out, and Mr. Mortiboy was not even in bed,

Dick crept along the passage, and laid a heavy hand upon his shoulder. Lafleur started, but he knew the pressure of that hand: it could only be Dick.

They peeped together through the half-opened door. Mr. Mortiboy had opened the doors of his great press, and brought out all the contents. They were scattered on the table. Gold and silver plate, forks, spoons, cups, épergnes—all lay piled in a heap. In the centre a great pile of sovereigns, bright and new-looking. The old man stood over them with outstretched arms, as if to confer his blessing. Then he laid his cheek fondly on the gold. Then he dabbled his hands in it, took it up, and dropped the coins through his fingers. Then he polished a gold cup with his sleeve, and murmured—

"Dick knows nothing of this—Dick knows nothing of this."

And then Dick gently led Lafleur away, and brought him silently to the kitchen, where with both doors shut, he sat down, and laughed till his sides ached.

"Pardon me," said Lafleur, whose face was white with rage and disappointment, "I don't see the joke. Pray was this designed as a special amusement for me?"

"I must laugh," cried Dick. "It's the finest thing I ever came across."

And he laughed again till the tears ran down his cheeks.

Lafleur sat down doggedly and waited.

"And now," said Dick at last, "let us talk. It's all right partner, and you can have your five thousand whenever you like."

"Now?" asked Lafleur.

"Well, not now. In a few days. Hang it, man! you can't get a big lump like that paid down at a moment's warning."

"Tell me all about it."

Dick told him in as few words as possible.

"It is all yours, Dick?"

"All mine."

"You are rich at last. Good." He was considering how

he might get his share of the plunder. "Let me have a few hundreds to-night, Dick. I lost a lot yesterday, and promised to pay to-morrow evening."

"How can I? To-morrow I can give you five hundred from the bank, if you like."

"Too late. If it is all yours, the money upstairs is yours. Let me have some of that."

Dick hesitated. Void of affection as he was to his father, he yet felt a touch of compunction at undeceiving him so soon.

"I meant to have an explanation in a few days. But if you cannot wait——"

"I really cannot, my dearest Richard. It is life and death to me. I must start from this respectable place to-night with money in my pocket."

"Then we must have our row to-night. It seems hard that the old man should not have a single night's rest in his delusion. However, it can't be helped. Give me your duplicate keys."

He put on his boots, took a candle, and went upstairs to his father's room. Mr. Mortiboy was in bed by this time and asleep, for the explanation of things had taken nearly an hour. Dick opened the press, took out a couple of bags, such as those used at the bank, containing a hundred pounds each, and threw them with a crash upon the table. The noise woke his father.

He started up with a shriek.

"Thieves!—murder!—Dick!—Dick!—thieves!—Dick!"

"It *is* Dick. Don't be alarmed, father. I am helping myself to a little of my own property. That is all."

The old man gasped, but could not speak. He thought it was another of the dreadful dreams which disturbed his night's rest.

Dick sat on the edge of his bed, with the candlestick in his hand, and looked him in the face, pulling his beard meditatively, as he always did when he was going to say a grave thing.

"It is quite as well, father, that we should understand one another. All your property is now mine. I can do what I like with it—consequently, what I like with you. I shall not be hard on you. What you gave me when I was nineteen, I will give you now that you are getting on towards seventy. An old man does not want so much as a boy, so the bargain is a good one for you. A pound a week shall be paid to you regularly, with your board and lodging, and as much drink as you like to put away. The pound begins to-morrow."

His father put his hand to his forehead, and looked at him curiously. He still thought it was a nightmare.

"It is not your fault that your estimate of my character was not quite correct, is it? You see, you never gave yourself any trouble to find out what I was like as a young man. That is an excuse for you, and accounts for your being so easily taken in by my stories. I wanted your money, which was natural enough. I knew very well that if I came snivelling home like a beggar, a beggar I should remain. So I came home like a rich man; flourished the little money I had in your face; bragged about my estates and my mines, and all the rest of it. Estates and mines were all lies. I've got nothing. I never had anything. I've lived by gambling and my wits. This very night, if it were not for the deed of gift you have made, I should have robbed you, and you would never have found out who did it."

The old man's face was ghastly. Beads of perspiration stood upon his forehead. His eyes stared fixedly at his son, but he made no sign.

"You see, my dodge succeeded. Dodges generally do, if one has the pluck and coolness to carry them through. Now I'm worth half a million of money. No more screwing hard-earned coins out of poor people. No more drudging and grinding for the firm of Mortiboy. The property, sir, shall be spent, used, made the most of—for my own enjoyment."

Still his father neither moved nor spoke.

"I've lived, since you kicked me out into the world, as I could—as a gambler lives. You have told me, in the last few days, how you have lived. Father, *my life has not been so bad as yours*. I've held my own among lawless men, and fought for my own hand, in my own defence. No one curses the name of Roaring Dick—not even the men whose money I have taken from their pockets; for they would only have done as much by me if they could. But you? In every street, in every house, yours will be a memory of hatred. I never robbed a poor man. You have spent your life in robbing poor men. There, I have had my say, and shall never say it again.' As for these things" kicking the door of the press— "they will be all sold. To-night I only want the money. Go to sleep now, and thank Heaven that you have got a son who will take care of your latter days."

He took his bags and left the room. His father threw out his arms after him in a gesture of wild despair, and then fell heavily back, without a sigh or a groan.

Lafleur returned to London by the night train with the money; and Dick went quietly to bed, where he slept like a top.

In the morning, Mr. Mortiboy did not appear at breakfast. Dick sent Hester up. His door was wide open. The press was open, the gold and silver plate lying about on the floor, as Dick had left it. But the late owner of all was lying motionless on the bed. He was stricken with paralysis. His power of speech and of moving were gone; and save for his breathing, you would have called him dead. Dick, with great thoughtfulness, had him removed downstairs to his old study, where he installed Hester as nurse and attendant, telling her to get another woman for the house. He had all the doctors in the place to attend his father, and expressed, with dry eyes, much sorrow at the hopeless character of the malady. Market Basing was greatly exercised in spirit at the event, which it considered as a " judgment," though no especial reason was alleged for the visitation. And all men began to praise Dick's filial piety, and to congratulate Mr. Mortiboy, or rather his memory, on having a son—*tali ingenio præditum*—gifted with such a remarkable sweetness of disposition, and so singular an affection for his father.

CHAPTER THE NINETEENTH.

HE duties of a son being performed, and his father formally placed under the charge of old Hester, Dick put the keys of office in his pocket, and walked over to the bank, where the news of old Ready-money's paralysis had already been received. Ghrimes and the lawyer were the only persons who knew of the deed of gift.

"Don't he look solemn?" asked the old women of each other, as the afflicted son went down the street.

"Such a son as he was, too! Ah, better than old Ready-money deserved."

Ghrimes, in the manager's office, was looking over papers.

"So," said Dick, shaking hands with him, and sitting on

the table, "you didn't approve of the deed of gift, eh? Never mind; quite right, and just like you to say so. However, that's all over. You've heard of the old man's stroke, I suppose? Doctor thinks some shock must have accelerated the final break-up. Shock of yesterday, I suppose. He couldn't bear to see the money go."

This was strictly and literally true. Mr. Mortiboy, though from his bed and not from his parlour, could not bear to see the money going.

"However, it's all over now, and things are changed. As for us two, Ghrimes, you have served my father so well that I hope you will go on serving me."

"I desire nothing better."

"Things will be different, I dare say, because I am going to manage matters after another fashion; but we shall pull together; never fear that. I pull with everybody."

"I've been in the bank, man and boy, for sixteen years. I should be sorry to leave it now," said Ghrimes, half to himself.

"Of course you will not leave it. You will go on managing. I'm not going to sit with my hands in my pockets, but I am not a meddler."

"And your estates in Mexico? How shall you manage about them?" asked Ghrimes, in perfect good faith.

"My partner has gone out," replied Dick, with unmoved face, "to superintend them. I shall not trouble about them."

"Indeed, you need not," said his manager, "for there is work enough here for three men. Here, for instance, is a case—one of those cases which your poor father would always decide for himself."

"Well, then, for once I will decide for myself. What is it?"

And here Dick began that course of social reform which has made him immortal in Market Basing.

"It's the case of Tweedy, the builder. What are we to do with him? Your father always declared that he would advance him no more money. His bill is due to-day. He can't meet it, I know."

"Tell me all about him in a few words."

"Furniture dealer—cabinet-maker. Took to building. As fast as he built got into difficulties, Mr. Mortiboy advanced him money; got his houses. Always in difficulties; will smash if we don't prevent it; pays his workmen by discounting small bills at the bank; is getting deeper every day."

"What have we got out of him?"

"About a dozen houses. That villa on the other side of the river in Derngate, among others. All profit, of course."

"That beats California. Send for him, and let us see him."

The man came; a man with a craze for designing and building; born to be an architect, but without an education; might have designed a cathedral, but expended his energies on Gothic villas, which he persuaded himself would make his fortune. Old Mortiboy had been getting money out of him for years.

"So you're Tweedy, are you?" said Dick, looking down at the nervous little man, from six feet one to five feet three. "I remember you when you had your shop. Where is it now?"

"I wish I had it now, sir," said the man.

"You *would* try to make your fortune, you know. And you were conceited enough to think you could. And what are you worth now?"

"Nothing, sir."

"Nothing—and a bill of two hundred pounds to meet. Now, Tweedy, suppose you go back to the furniture shop. Don't look scared, man. I'll give you a lift. That little villa that you put up behind Derngate—a good house, is it? very well—I'm going to live in it. Go up to town, and furnish it for me. Furnish it well—well, mind. Pay trade price, and charge yourself a fair profit. Get me good things; no gimcracks. Have everything ready in three days. The bill may stand over. If you don't like this, say so."

The man began a flood of gratitude, which Dick stopped by pushing him out of the door.

"He deserves something for building me a dozen houses for nothing," he said, coolly; "and I must get the place furnished. I made up my mind to live there this morning."

"One of your clerks, I am sorry to say, has embezzled some money. I found it out last night—though he does not know it yet."

"How much is it?"

"Five pounds."

Dick winced. It was the exact amount of his own forgery.

"What is his name, and what is his salary?"

"Sullivan; he draws sixty pounds a year."

Dick put his head out of the door, and shouted to the office generally—

"Send Sullivan here."

A pale-faced lad of twenty-two, with a weak and nervous mouth, and a hesitating manner, came in and shut the door, trembling.

"Well, Mr. Sullivan, and how about this five pounds?"

Mr. Sullivan burst into tears.

"The last clerk who embezzled money in this bank," said Mr. Ghrimes, solemnly, "was tried for the offence, and underwent a sentence of imprisonment for it."

"There, you see," said Dick.

Mr. Sullivan sobbed louder.

"You draw sixty pounds a year; a princely salary," continued his new master. "Do you drink, or play billiards, or what, to get rid of so much money?"

"Nothing, sir."

"My young friend, you had better make a clean breast of it to Mr. Ghrimes and me, or it will certainly be a case of the man in blue, and chokee. Now, think for a few minutes, and then answer."

The boy—he seemed little more—sat down, and laid his head in his hands.

"I cannot tell," he moaned. "I cannot tell you both."

Dick's face grew soft. The man who had not hesitated to tell his father the bitter truth, who had planned to rob him, who was devoid of scruples, or of restraint, or of fear, had yet a heart that could be touched. He could not bear the sight of misery.

"Leave us for two minutes, Ghrimes. Now, my boy, what did you do it for?"

"I had to find five pounds for her; and I borrowed the money."

"Who is *her*? And why did she want five pounds?"

Then the story came out; how he wanted to marry a girl, the daughter of a small tradesman; how he was forbidden to speak to her; how they took secret walks together; how the old, old tale was repeated; how it became necessary for her to leave home, and he had taken the money to help her to go. And then more sobs, and more softening of Dick's heart.

"Go away now," said Dick, "and go on with your work. I am not going to prosecute you. Bring her with you this evening, at nine o'clock, to Derngate."

The delinquent despatched, Dick proceeded to ask for the salaries book. The cheapness with which banking is conducted, as evidenced by the salaries of the clerks, struck him as very remarkable. Mr. Ghrimes, who managed a business worth many thousands a year, received the magnificent stipend of £200. The other employés from £120 to £50.

"Banking," said Dick, "seems about the easiest and cheapest way of getting money ever hit upon."

"When you've got your connection, it is," said his manager.

"Would you mind calling in the clerks? Gentlemen, I have no doubt," he said, addressing them in a body, in his best book English, "that my father's intention was to do just exactly what I am about to do. It must often have occurred to him, that to ensure zeal, punctuality, and diligence, as well as honesty"—here Sullivan trembled exceedingly—"it is necessary to pay those gentlemen whose services you secure as highly as is compatible with your own interests." Here the clerks nudged each other. "I am now acting as his representative. You used to call him 'Ready-money' Mortiboy. He will still more deserve the title when I inform you that all your salaries are raised twenty-five per cent. from this moment." They all stared at one another. "But if you get into money difficulties, and don't tell me, you'll find yourselves in the wrong box. Now, don't make a row, but go back to your work"—for the clerks were preparing to make a demonstration of gratitude.

"And, Sullivan," said Mr. Ghrimes, "don't let us have any more of that unpunctuality which I reproved you for just now"—for the clerk's eyes were still wet with tears, and his fellows had been questioning him.

"Kindly said, Ghrimes," said Dick. "Now for yourself."

That night Mr. Ghrimes went to bed with his salary trebled, and a cheque for a thousand pounds.

The clerk Sullivan appeared as the clock struck nine at the house in Derngate, accompanied by a young woman. The pair looked very young and very forlorn. Dick opened the door himself, and led them to his own room—that which had been the parlour, where a few alterations had been hastily made to suit his own tastes, previous to his removal.

He made them sit down, and stood with his back to the fire looking at one and the other.

"You are a pretty pair of fools," he said.

The girl began to cry. Her lover had spirit enough to answer for her.

"She is not to blame. I am the only one."

"Do you want to marry him?" asked Dick bluntly of the girl

She only cried the more.

"Well, then, do *you* want to marry her?"

"I do—of course I do."

"Which would you rather do, my dear—run away with him and be married in London, or be married here and go up to London afterwards on my business?"

"Oh, here—here, Mr. Mortiboy. But they won't let us."

"They will when I have seen your father. And I will see him to-night. Now, have a glass of wine. What is your name, child?"

"Alice."

"Then, Alice, here's a glass of port for you. Sullivan, if you ill-treat your wife, look out for yourself. You will hear from me to-morrow morning. Good-bye, Alice, my dear. Give me a kiss."

He went to the young lady's parent, and had an interview with him; the result of his arguments being that a wedding took place the following week.

Dick improved the occasion with his manager, pointing out to him the folly of putting young fellows in positions of trust without a salary sufficient to keep them from temptation; and he talked with so much wisdom that Ghrimes began to regard him as the foremost of living philosophers. Certain reflections, in the course of his life, Dick had certainly made. And he now began to act upon them.

In two or three days the furniture arrived, and the house beyond the river was rendered habitable, under the superintendence of Mrs. Heathcote. It was a small place, but big enough for a bachelor. And then, as Mrs. Heathcote observed, it was always easy to move, and of course he was not going to remain a bachelor always. Dick permitted the observation, in the presence of Polly—who had been brought by Mrs. Heathcote to help arrange and set to rights—to pass unanswered.

At first he announced his intention of having no servants in the house at all; but gave way at the remonstrances of Mrs. Heathcote, who felt here the family respectability was in danger.

"I will send you a nice old woman that I know, Dick," she said—"one that I can recommend."

The nice old woman—who was not nice to look at—came. She had a very bad time indeed, so long as she remained. Dick had given special orders that she was not on any account to cross the threshold of his smoking-room, an apartment which he intended to keep sacred. He did not lock the door; and on the very first day the old woman, urged on by the fury of feminine curiosity, opened the door. The astute Richard had affixed a cord craftily, one end being attached to the top of the sideboard, and the other to the door. All the glasses and decanters on his sideboard were pulled off and broken. There went three months' wages.

Dick disliked locking things up. The old woman loved strong drinks. On the second day, she drank out of a brandy bottle in which her master had mixed a certain medicine. That night she was very ill.

On the third day she was in his bed-room, where Dick had slung a hammock, as being more comfortable than a regular bed. An open letter lay on the table. She put on her spectacles and began to read it, holding it out, as old people do, between her hands. Dick, who was coming up the stairs—the big man moved noiselessly when he pleased—drew his pistol and fired—at her, she declared. The bullet passed straight through the letter, within an inch of her two thumbs. She dropped the paper, and fell backwards with a terrific shriek. Spectacles broken this time, too.

After that she resigned, and spread awful reports about the house.

Then Dick was left servantless, and for a day or two used to cook his steaks for dinner himself.

Mrs. Heathcote again came to his assistance.

"I don't know what you've done, Dick, but no woman in the place will come here. If you fire pistols at people, and poison your brandy, and tie ropes round your glasses, how can you expect it?"

"I didn't fire at her. I only frightened her."

"Well, would you like Mary? She wants to leave me—I don't know why. Says she must live nearer her mother. Perhaps she'd come. She's not so old as you might wish; but she's a well-conducted, handy woman, and I really think would make you comfortable."

He hesitated. The plan offered a good many advantages, not the least being that he would not have Polly coming secretly to see him, which was dangerous.

Dick had made a step in civilization. He began to respect people's opinions.

On the other hand, it would be disagreeable to have the

woman always in the house. He chose at last to have a sort of day servant, one who should come with as many attendant ancillæ as might be judged necessary, at eight in the morning, and depart at seven in the evening. He would have no one sleep in the house. And to this decision, irregular and un-English as it appeared to Mrs. Heathcote, he adhered. Polly, however, left the service of Mrs. Heathcote, and came to Market Basing to live with her mother.

Of course, Market Basing could think of nothing but this fearful and wonderful man. What he had done last—what he was likely to do—whom he would visit—were the chief subjects of their conversation at this period. They used to go to Derngate, and walk along the towing-path in hopes of seeing him in the Californian dress which he affected in warm weather. He was to be seen smoking a cigar after breakfast or dinner, in long boots, leather breeches, with a crimson silk cummerbund, an embroidered shirt, a richly braided jacket, and a Panama hat.

If he met any of the girls, he would converse with them without the ceremony of introduction: notably in the case of Lawyer Battiscombe's daughters, who, Mrs. Heathcote said, threw themselves at his feet. If he fell in with a man who pleased him, he would take him into the villa, and there compound him some strange drink which would make the world for a brief space appear a very Paradise—until presently the magic of the dose departed, and the drinker would be left with hot coppers.

He never went to church, and refused to subscribe to the chapel. To the rector he was polite—offering him, when he called, a glass of a certain curious restorative; and when the worthy clergyman turned the conversation on things ecclesiastical, Dick listened with the reverence of a catechumen.

"What I like in the church," said Dick, "is the complete equality that reigns in the building. All alike, eh? No difference between rich and poor in the matter of cushions and pews."

The rector felt that he was on delicate ground.

"And as to preaching, now. I suppose you find the people getting a great deal better every year?"

"Well—well—we do our best."

"They used to get drunk on Saturday nights. Do they still?"

The rector was obliged to own that they did.

"Now, rector, let us have a bargain. You shall preach on any given thing you like for a whole year; and if, after that time, you find the town better, and the—the special sin removed, come down on me for your schools, or anything you like."

The rector hesitated.

"The grocer puts sand in his sugar and mixes his tea; and the publican puts 'foots' in his beer; the doctor humbugs us with his pills; the tobacconist waters the bird's-eye; the labourer drinks half his wages; the women are uncleanly and bad-tempered. Come, rector, there's a splendid field for you."

The rector was silent.

"I don't like unpractical things," continued Dick. "There was a township in California, sir, where they thought they ought to have a church. So they built one, and subscribed their dollars and got a bran-new preacher in black togs from New York. Down he came; and the first Sunday they thought, out of common politeness, they'd give him a turn. He had a regular benefit: house full—not even standing room. Next Sunday nobody went: stalls, boxes, and pit all empty. So the minister went to the principal bar to ask the reason why. The chief man there—judge he was afterwards—took him up sharp enough.

"'You've got a fine new church, haven't you?'

"'Yes.'

"'And a handsome salary?'

"'Yes.'

"'And didn't we all come to give you a start?'

"'Yes.'

"'Then what on airth do you want more?'

"That's it, you see, rector. You get your innings every Sunday, and the people go to hear you just out of politeness and habit, and go away again. And if there's anything on airth you want more, you'd better try and work it another way."

CHAPTER THE TWENTIETH.

Specimen of Restoring.

THE very top attic of a very high house, in a street near the Mansion House. The sun shining brightly in at the window, and baking the slates overhead. The windows shut close, nevertheless. A queer room: the roof ill-shapen, and the windows odd. The only furniture a bench or table of rough deal, running across the place just under the windows. The floor stained of a thousand hues; every inch of its surface is saturated with paints and varnishes upset over it. The walls plastered with the scrapings of thousands of palettes, dried on in parti-coloured patches, and decorated with half a dozen soiled and smoke-begrimed cardboard scrolls, on which are written, like so many texts—" The eleventh commandment : Mind your own business," " From witchcraft, priestcraft, and kingcraft, good Lord, deliver us," and such-like legends, the work of a former prisoner there. On the floor is a great stack of pictures, which have been taken out of their frames in order to undergo the process of cleaning; gallon cans of copal and mastic varnish stand by them, in readiness for the varnishing. At the bench stands a young man in his shirt sleeves, rubbing away as hard as he can at the resinous surface of an oil painting, rapidly getting the old varnish off with his finger ends, and working down to the artist's colours again. He works with a will, singing at his work in the finest tenor voice you ever heard outside the walls of the Covent Garden Opera House.

It is Frank Melliship. How he came here I will briefly explain.

When ruin comes upon a young gentleman of expensive tastes, who has received the very best, and consequently the least useful, education that his country has to boast of, it generally finds him in a helpless and very defenceless condition. This was, as we have seen, Frank Melliship's lot. He had no longer any money to spend, and he had not been taught how to get any. Poverty would not have frightened him

much, because he was young, and did not know what it
meant: what grinding years of self-sacrifice and denial, what
bitterness of struggle, and what humiliations. But there were
his mother and sister. To knock about for a year or two—no
young man thinks he is going to be poor after five-and-twenty
or so—would have had the charm of novelty. But for these
two—the delicately reared gentlewomen—the change from
the house at Market Basing to the miserable lodgings in
Fitzroy-street, off the Fulham-road, was indeed a plunge.
And though Kate did her best bravely to meet the inevitable,
their mother, a weak and watery creature, never attempted to
conceal the misery of her new position, and to lament the
glories, which she naturally exaggerated, of the past.

"What have we done," she would say at each fresh reminder
of the social fall—" what did *we* do to merit all this?"

Frank and Kate, with the sanguine enthusiasm which belonged to their father's blood as well as to their time of life,
tried to cheer her with pictures of the grand successes which
were to come; but in vain. The good lady would only relapse
into another of her weeping fits, and be taken to her room,
crying, "Oh! Francis—oh! my poor husband!" till the enthusiasm was damped, and the present brought back to the
brother and sister in all its nakedness.

Every day they took counsel together. Frank's bedroom,
metamorphosed by Kate's clever hands till it looked no more
like a bedroom than Mr. Swiveller's one apartment, served as
their studio. An inverted case—which once, in what lodging-house keepers call their "happier days," had contained Clicquot
or gooseberry—served as a platform, on which Frank stood
for a model to his sister. They called it their throne.

"Do—my dear good boy—do hold out your arm as I placed
it," says Mistress Kate, sketching in rapidly, while Frank
stands as motionless as he can before her in the best suit he
has left. "I have wasted I don't know how much time to-day
in getting up to put you right."

"My dear girl, can I stand—I put it to you—can I stand
like a semaphore for an hour at a time? Even a semaphore's
arms go up and down, you know."

"Yes, I know, Frank, it's dreadfully tiresome, as I found
when I sat for your Antigone. But see how patient I was."

The advantage was certainly on Frank's side, because Kate
would stand in the same position for half an hour at a time—
twice as long as a professional model.

"How far have you got, Kate?"

"Don't move now—a moment more—only five minutes, and I shall have finished the outline."

She is sketching on a boxwood block. It was the first order they had received; it was to illustrate a poem in a magazine, and the price was three guineas.

"If you go on at this rate," said Frank, " it will pay a great deal better than oils. Why, you can do a block a day—easily —working up your back-grounds by candle-light."

" Yes—if we can get the orders ; but you must not forget the trouble we had in getting the first."

"C'est le commencement," said Frank. "Et gai, gai—" he began to sing.

"Do *not* move just now. Please don't."

> "'Bergeronnette,
> Douce baisselette,
> Donnez-le moi, votre chapelet,'"

sang her model, with one of his happy laughs. "Don't you remember, Katie, when I sang that jolly old French song last at Parkside, when Grace played the accompaniment? Dearest Grace! When shall I see her again?"

"Let us talk seriously," said Kate. "I am sure mamma *must* go away into the country somewhere. We could live cheaper than we can in London, and I know she would get back her health at some quiet seaside place ; and I could fill my sketch-book with pretty bits, and work them up into landscapes, like those you sold—"

"For fifteen shillings each," Frank laughed.

His experience of picture selling had been rather disheartening. But still he hoped ; nor was it unnatural that he should do so. He had a strong taste for art. He could do what few young men can do—draw nicely. He had been famous for his pen-and-ink sketches at Cambridge ; but Kate was much more proficient with her pencil than he was.

Kate guided their course. She chose the lodgings near the Museum. She was bursar for the family, and did the marketing, often at night, in the Fulham-road ; for her mother would speedily have outrun the constable by a distance.

As it was, John Heathcote's gift was reduced to small dimensions.

Grace's hundred pounds Frank held sacred, proposing to use it for his mother.

Kate took the necessary steps to their painting at the public galleries. They went at first on Wednesdays, Thursdays, and Fridays to the Museum. Then Frank went on Thursdays and Fridays to the National Gallery, leaving Kate to go to the South Kensington Museum by herself. They wanted to learn Art. Now, Art is learned, they had been told, by copying. So they set to work to copy. Kate spent three days a week for four months at Dyckmans' "Blind Beggar." It is a pretty picture, but copying it teaches nothing. She found that out before it was half done; but she made a splendid copy of it on panel, like the original. Frank copied Sir Joshua's "Heads of Angels," at the National. In this work there was something to be learnt. The softness, the delicacy, the angelic expression of those little cherubs' heads, all painted from one tiny mortal face, showed the student of art what it is in the hands of a master. And Reynolds is a master for a very unartistic nation to be proud of. Frank had finished this picture when Kate's "Blind Beggar" was half done. The copy he made was very good. At the Gallery the old women praised it; and as they had often copied it themselves, they were judges. A dealer who came in one students' day called it "clever." He was a burly man, with a tremendously red nose that told its own tale of knock-outs. This professional opinion encouraged Frank. He had hoped to sell it to some of those connoisseurs of art who loiter round the students' easels on closed days; but there had been no bid.

He had it framed; it happened to be at the shop of the red-nosed man, whose name was Burls. He paid two pounds ten shillings for an appropriate Reynolds frame for it.

Then he put his picture into a cab, and tried the dealers all over the West-end with it.

"What! buy a copy of a picture in the National Gallery? Not unless we knew where we could place it!"

It was a knock-down blow for our innocent young artist; but it was the answer he got everywhere, from rough dealers and smooth, Hebrew and Gentile. So, at last, in despair, he left it at an auction room in Bond-street, where a fortnight afterwards, Kate and he attended, and bought it in at two pounds seven and sixpence—half a crown less than the frame that was on it had cost him: and he had five per cent. commission to pay, and the cost of taking it home. This opened his eyes to the trade value of copies of pictures that are known.

A young lady at the Museum made friends with Kate—they all make friends with one another—and exhorted her to try at working on wood. So with Frank and her mother for models, and a back-ground out of her sketch book, she made a pretty picture, and despatched Frank to lay siege to the editors.

He took a few water-colour sketches of his own with him, to show at one or two picture-shops where he had seen similar sketches displayed in the windows.

He tried two shops—one was near Piccadilly—in his walk towards the publishers' shops. He was not afraid of talking to the shopkeepers, but he did feel a little nervous at the prospect of bearding an editor in his den.

So he showed his sketches, with some success. The answer at both the shops was—

"Do me some with shorter petticoats, and I'll give you forty-two shillings a dozen for them."

The shops were kept by brothers, and Frank's sketches were pretty young ladies. He profited by this experience.

He spent that afternoon, and the next, and the next after that in calling at different places with the inquiry, "Is the editor of the So-and-so in?"

With one result. The editor never was in—to a young man who did not know his name. At night, after the third of these excursions, he felt embittered towards these gentlemen, and told Kate he thought they might as well put their block in the fire, it would warm them so.

The weather was as warm as Frank's temper. Kate reproved him, and gave him her royal commands to try again.

"And now, Frank," she said after their mother had gone to bed, "I have made up my mind to go away from London, and take mamma with me—to Wales, I think. Living is cheap there, and the scenery is beautiful. She *must* be taken out of London."

Frank felt rather glad at this. He thought his mother and sister would be better in the country for a few months. When they came back to him, he meant to have a home for them.

"And I'll tell you why, Frank. I shall finish my picture; but it is not easy to do that. There are three people at it now—such a vulgar man; and oh! two such vulgar women—and they race on a Wednesday morning to get up the stairs before me, and secure their seats for the week close to the picture. The man elbows roughly by me, and I can hardly get a look at the picture myself."

Frank began to fume—his fingers tingled.

"The authorities should make some proper rules, I think, for I began my copy before any of them. Of course, I can't race up the stairs with them, and tear through the rooms to be first at the picture; and, then, Frank—you'll promise me to do as I tell you?"

"I don't know, Kate. I think I shall be at the top of the stairs before that fellow some day soon—"

"There now, I have done if you do not give me your word."

"Well—there, then—go on."

"Well, Frank, an old man—nobleman, they say he is—has been very attentive."

Her brother gave an angry snort, and his eyes looked very mischievous.

"Don't be angry—he is too ridiculous—the funniest old object, with teeth, and a wig, and stays, and a gold-headed cane. He wants to buy the 'Blind Beggar,' and has given me advice I don't want about painting it; and to-day, Frank—"

"To-day, Kate?"

"He brought me a bouquet, which of course I declined to accept. But I thought it best to put away my picture, and leave the gallery."

"I shall be there to-morrow."

He was, nearly every day after till Kate had finished her picture.

But the Earl of —— only paid one more visit to the Museum during his stay in town that season.

In the afternoon of the day on which Frank had given his card to his sister's admirer, he determined to try his luck again with the block and the portfolio of sketches. At the first place he called at, the man he saw took his name up to the editor of the magazine, and to his great surprise, he was asked to walk upstairs.

He found himself in a dingy room, in the presence of a fatherly young man, with a grave but kind face.

Frank told him how surprised he was at having the opportunity of showing his specimens, and asking for work.

The editor of the "Universal Magazine" was a scholar and a gentleman. He drew the young man out, looked at his sketches, and gave him a few words of judicious praise.

"But I don't use any blocks. The 'Universal' is not an illustrated magazine."

Frank was disappointed.

"I really had not thought of that," he stammered out.

"But I am always ready to help anybody I can. Wait a minute, Mr. Melliship. Your sister's drawings are really clever, and the sort of thing that is wanted. I will give you a note to a friend of mine who uses a great many illustrations." He handed Frank the letter, adding, " I shall be glad to hear of your success some day when you are passing this way. Stay, I will give you something else."

He wrote rapidly for five or six minutes, and then handed Frank a list of all the illustrated magazines of standing and respectability, with the names of their editors.

"I have put a star to those where you may just mention my name."

Frank thanked his new friend very sincerely, and bowed himself out—to get an order for a block fifteen minutes after.

The editor of the "Universal" blew down a pipe at his desk. Whistle.

"Sir?"

"Look in the contributor's book, vol. xxvii. Who wrote the article on 'Commercial Morality'?"

After an interval of ten minutes, a whistle in the editor's room.

"Well?"

"Mr. Francis Melliship, banker, Market Basing, Holmshire."

"Ah, I thought I knew the name. If I am not mistaken, I shall be able to pay this young man what his father refused to receive, the honorarium for several articles he did for us."

He entered Frank's name in his note-book.

But Frank was not the sort of gentleman to be helped. He would not ask anybody for assistance. Dick Mortiboy would have helped him; John Heathcote would have helped him; and in London, a dozen men who had known his father would have taken him by the hand. But Frank was too proud. He would make his own way—to Grace. It was always Grace, this goal he was hastening to. He devoured her letter to Kate. He inspired Kate's epistles in reply.

"Burn the boy's nonsense," honest John Heathcote had said a dozen times. " If we could only get at him, we might do something for him. Painter! I would as soon see a boy of mine a fiddler."

But Mrs. Heathcote was rather pleased than not. "What in the world can he do without any money?" she said. "If his father had brought him up to something, he would have stood the same chance as other people."

As the summer advanced, Mrs. Melliship's health became worse, and it was decided that Kate and she should go away into Wales. Kate had sold her "Blind Beggar" for twenty pounds, and with this money they paid their few debts, and Frank saw them off.

The world was before him. He took a lodging in Islington, and went on with his painting. He still meant to be famous. One fine morning he had no money left except a five-pound note he had resolved never to break into. This brought him down from the clouds. He had not been successful in getting any work for the magazines, so he determined, at whatever sacrifice, to turn his "Angels' Heads" into money.

He took it first to Mr. Burls's shop, and told the picture-dealer he had tried hard to sell it before, but had been unable to dispose of it.

"It isn't in our way, sir."

"Is it in anybody's way?" asked Frank.

"I should think not. Copies aren't no good at all."

"Would you give me anything for it?" asked the young man.

"Well, you may leave it if you like. I've got a customer I don't mind showing it to."

Frank called again a few days after.

"I'll give you six pounds for it, and then I dare say I shall lose by it," said Mr. Burls.

He had sold it for eighteen guineas to a customer who collected Sir Joshuas, and bought copies when the originals were not likely to come into the market. But Frank did not know this. He accepted the six pounds eagerly.

"I'm a ready-money man, my lad—there's your coin."

"Thank you," said Frank, pocketing the six sovereigns. "You have a great many pictures, Mr. Burls."

And he might have added, "very great rubbish they are."

"There's seventeen hundred pictures in this house, from cellar to garrets, lad," said the dealer.

They stood in stacks, eight or ten thick, round the cellar, down the open trap of which Frank could see. They were piled everywhere. One canvas, thirty feet by ten, was screwed up to the ceiling. They were numberless pictures of every age and school, Titians and Tenierses, Snyderses and Watteaus : all the kings of England, from the Conqueror down to William IV. ; ancestors ready for hanging in the pseudo-baronial halls of the *nouveaux riches ;*—in a word, furniture pictures by the gross.

"If there was seventeen hundred before, yours makes the seventeenth hundred and oneth, don't it?"

The dealer was pleased to joke. His shopman laughed, and Frank did too. He had put his pride in his pocket, for Mr. Burls amused him.

"Now, this here Sir Joshua ought to be wet; and not to ask you to stand, suppose we torse."

Frank assented, lost, and paid for three glasses.

"Where's Critchett?—I haven't seen him to-day?" Mr. Burls asked of his man.

"He has not turned up. The old complaint, I expect."

"Well, you can tell him from me, when he does turn up, he's got to the end of his tether," said Mr. Burls, very angrily. "Be dashed if I employ such a vagabond any longer. There's this picture of Mr. Thingamy's for him to restore, and I promised it this week faithfully."

"He's often served you so before," said the man.

But this remark did not soothe the dealer. It made him only the more angry.

Now, Mr. Frank Melliship had got to the end of his tether, too, for he had only the six pounds he had just received, and no immediate prospect of being able to earn more.

Opportunity comes once in a way to every man. It had come to Frank, and he determined to make the most of it.

" Could I restore the picture for you ?"

It was a great ugly daub—a copy, a hundred years old probably, of some picture in a Dutch gallery—and stood on the floor by Frank. Doubtless it had a value in the eyes of its owner, who thought it worthy of restoration : but a viler, blacker tatterdemalion of a canvas you never saw.

At Frank's question, Mr. Burls opened his eyes very wide.

"Show us your hands," he said. "That's what they say to beggars as say they're innocent at the station. Ah ! I thought so—you ain't done any hard work. Now perhaps you're what I call a gingerbread gentleman. Are you?"

The colour mounted to Frank's cheeks.

"I want employment. I am a poor man."

" He aint no use to us—is he, Jack ? "

Jack, Mr. Burls's man, shook his head.

" I could repaint that picture where it wants it," said Frank.

"Did you ever restore a picture before ? Restoring's an art: it's a thing as isn't learnt in a moment, I can tell you. 'Pictures cleaned, lined, and restored by a method of our own invention, without injury, and at a moderate charge,'" said Mr. Burls, quoting an inscription in gilt letters over Frank's head. "Now, did you ever clean a picture ?"

" No," said Frank.

" Do you think you could do the painting part if I taught you how to clean and restore on the system I invented myself ? "

" I think I could," said Frank.

" But if I teach you the secrets of the trade, what are you going to give me ? "

" I'm afraid I can't afford to give you anything," said Frank, " except labour."

" It's worth fifty pounds to anybody to know. Critchett might have made a fortune at it. Look at me. I began as an errand boy. I'm not ashamed of it. A good restorer can always keep himself employed."

" Indeed," said Frank—who contemplated with admiration a man who had been the founder of his own fortune—" I should very much like to learn the art of restoring, as I have not been successful in getting a living as an artist."

" Well," said the dealer, " I'll see first what you're up to, and whether you can paint well enough for me if I was to teach you the restoring. You may come upstairs. Bring that picture up on your shoulder."

Frank hoisted the canvas aloft, and followed Mr. Burls up the stairs.

CHAPTER THE TWENTY-FIRST.

IT was not very easy for Frank to get the picture round the turns of the narrow staircase, which led from Mr. Burls's shop to the room above, which he called the gallery. In this room, Frank saw that there were a number of pictures hanging round the walls, and on several tall screens. They were of a better class than those in the shop. Mr. Burls led the way through the gallery to a narrow flight of stairs at the end. Mounting these, with the canvas on his shoulder, Frank found more rooms full of pictures, framed and unframed, in stacks that reached up to his chin.

On the floor above, a number of men were employed in gilding and repairing frames. Up one more flight of stairs, and they were on the attic floor, apparently the sanctum of Mr. Critchett, the restorer—for in a little back room were his easels and palettes, and his battered tubes of paint, and several short and very black clay pipes.

"I find the materials," said Mr. Burls. "I've paid for all the paints and brushes, so I suppose they're mine."

"Certainly," said Frank.

"Now you can set to work on that Teniers as you've carried upstairs; and then I shall see what you're up to, and whether you'll suit me. If you aint got all the paints you want, come to me."

With this remark, Mr. Burls left Frank; and, pulling off his coat, set to work himself in the front room, a short description of which I gave at the beginning of my last chapter.

Left to himself, Frank looked about him. There was a good light, to the north; but when he stood upright anywhere in the room, his head nearly touched the ceiling.

The prospect from his window was limited almost entirely to tiles and chimney pots.

Pasted to the walls were a number of prints of the most celebrated characters of English history, which—as Frank rightly guessed—were used in the production of the genuine antique portraits which were founded upon them. Mr. Critchett had left a Queen Elizabeth, in a great starched ruff and jewelled stomacher, in an unfinished state on his easel.

The furniture of his atelier was by no means luxurious. It consisted of a cane-seated chair, with three orthodox legs, and an old mahl-stick for a fourth. A high rush hassock, tied on this chair, led Frank to suppose that his predecessor had been a short man. There were, besides, three easels, a fireplace with a black kettle on the hob, and several canvases—some new, some old—in the corners; and this was all.

Having made this short tour of inspection, Frank settled down at once to his work.

He found it easy;—little patches of paint gone here and there all over the portrait; and he supplied these, carrying out, as well as he could interpret it, the design of the original painter.

Mr. Burls was constantly walking in and out of the room, and looking over his shoulder, and volunteering unnecessary pieces of advice.

At four o'clock he left off "chafing" his pictures, and looked in at Frank, smearing his coarse hands with spirits, to get off the dirt with which they were ditched.

"There," said he, "I've done for to-day. I've chafed fifteen pictures: that's fifteen pound earned. I shall charge them a quid a-piece for doing 'em. I don't work for nothing, and I don't know anybody in the picture trade that does."

At six, he came up to Frank again, and looked at his work. "That'll do, my lad—that'll do," and went away again.

This cheered Frank, and he worked as long as it was light, and walked home to his lodgings at Islington a happy man.

Next day he finished the job, and Mr. Burls passed judgment on his work It was favourable to him; and he was duly installed in the place of Critchett, kicked out.

Frank wrote and told his sister and mother, staying at Llan-y-Fyddloes, that he had got regular employment that suited him very well, and that his prospects were brightening.

He did this to cheer them, and to some extent he believed what he said.

"If," he wrote to Kate, "I can only earn enough to keep myself, and send something every week to you, by the work I am at, and still leave myself time for study and improvement, I am satisfied. Depend upon it, you shall see me in the catalogue at the Academy before long, No. 00001, 'Interior of a studio,' by—" drawing a very fair likeness of himself by way of signature to his letter.

He said nothing to Kate about the amount of money he could earn at his new work, nor did he tell her what it was exactly. His reason for the first was that he wrote his letter before he had settled terms with Mr. Burls; for the second, because he knew his mother would become hysterical at the bare idea of her son working for a living in any but the most gentlemanlike manner, such as society permits. Now, for his part, Frank saw nothing degrading in any honest labour, and was quite content to put up for a while with such humble occupation.

"Hang it," he thought, "I'd rather do it than sponge on somebody else."

But Kate guessed it was something rather beneath his dignity to do, he was so reserved.

His arrangement with the picture dealer was in these terms:—

Burls: "I'm fair and straight, I am. I should not have got on if I'd done as many chaps do."

Frank: "To be sure. I think I am tolerably straightforward, too, Mr. Burls. I hope so, at least."

Burls: "I don't know nothing about you, do I?"

Frank (reddening): "No."

Burls: "Well, I don't want to ask no questions, my lad."

The man's familiarity was disgusting. It was a fine lesson in self-command for Frank to make himself stomach it.

"You want work, and I'll give you some. You can work for me instead of old Critchett. I'm fair and straight with you. Some chaps would want you to work six months for nothing."

Frank: "I could not do that."

Burls, continuing: "I don't ask you. You shall have what Critchett had—that's a shillin' an hour; and handsome pay, too, I call it. I like to pay my chaps well. Regular work, too. You may work eight hours a day if you like, and then you'll take eight and forty shillin' a week, you know."

Mr. Burls appealed to his shopman to support his statement that Frank's predecessor often "took eight and forty a week."

The terms seemed fair; though the remuneration for restoring, which required artistic skill, seemed to Frank to bear no just proportion to the money to be got by cleaning—for

Mr. Burls earned fifteen pounds before dinner at that, Frank recollected.

However, he could hardly expect to get more than Critchett had received before him; so he agreed to take a shilling an hour, and work regularly for Mr. Burls.

Burls: "Done, then, and settled. We don't want any character, do we, Jack? Pictures aint easy things to carry out of the shop, are they?"

Frank (very angry): "Sir!"

Burls: "No offence. Don't get angry. It was only a hint that we should not trouble you for references to your last employment. Rec'lect what I said about those hands. You've been brought up a gentleman, I dare say, but you're right not to starve your belly to feed your pride. Don't be angry with me. I'm straight and fair, I am. You'll find me that."

I have now explained how Frank came to be in the top attic of Mr. Burls's house of business. He remained in his situation about three months. While there, he learned a great deal. Mr. Burls took a fancy to him, and soon came to stand a little in awe of him—for he was educated and honest, and, in addition, plainly a gentleman. The dealer was very ignorant, and, from any point of view but that of his own class of traders, very dishonest—that is, he looked upon the public, his customers, as fair game; and would tell any lie, and any sequence of lies, to sell a spurious picture for and at the price of a genuine picture. The morals of commerce, in the hands of the Burlses, find their lowest ebb.

But, to some extent, their customers make them what they are. If a man who has money to spend on his house will have pictures for his walls, why not prefer a new picture to an old one? Why not an honest print before a dishonest canvas?

But it is always the reverse. He has a hundred pounds to lay out, and he wants ten pictures for the money—bargains—speculative pictures, with famous names to them, which he can comment on and enlarge upon, and point out the beauties of to his friends, until he actually comes to believe the daub he gave ten guineas for is a Turner; and the dealers can find him hundreds.

Why, the old masters must have painted pictures faster than they could nowadays print them, if a quarter of the things that are sold in their names were their true works. There are probably more pictures ascribed to any one famous old master now for sale in the various capitals of Europe, than he could have produced had he painted a complete work every day, from the day he was born till the day he died—and lived to be seventy, too.

Burls could find his customers anything they asked for. No painter so rare, so sought after, or so obscure, but there were some works of his, a bargain, in the dealer's stock.

He told Frank his history:—

"My father wore a uniform: he was a park-keeper in Kensington Gardens. I went to school till I was thirteen, then I went out as an errand boy. My master was a dealer, in St. James's street. I got to learn the gilding and cleaning; and when I was six-and-twenty, I earned two pounds a week. Well, my father had an old friend, and he had had some money left him. He gave his son two hundred pounds, and we went into business. His son died before we'd been partners a year. I bought his share, and here I am. I shall die worth a hundred thousand pounds, Shipley"—(this was Frank's name at Mr. Burls's)—"and this business thrown in —mark my words."

This was his story, and it was true. Like all men who have risen from nothing, Mr. Burls was inordinately pleased with himself. He attributed to his great ability what really ought to have been put down to his great luck.

He would be a fine specimen for the "Self-Help" collection in Mr. Samuel Smiles's book.

"Mind you," he often said to Frank, "there aint a man in ten thousand that could have done what I've done."

Now, Burls's life, as I read it and as Frank read it, was simply an example of the power of luck. Serving under a kind master, who lets him learn his trade. Luck. Finding a man who wants to put his son into business, and is willing to trust him. Luck. Getting all to himself. Luck. His shop pulled down by the Board of Works, in order to widen a street. Compensation paid just when he wants money, at the end of his second year's trade. Luck. And so on. Look into every adventure he has made, luck crowned it with success. And how we all worship success that brings wealth! Why, weak Mrs. Melliship would rather have seen Frank succeed in making himself as rich as Dick Mortiboy, than that his name should have been handed down to endless centuries as the writer of a greater epic than Milton, or the painter of a greater picture than the greatest of Raphael's cartoons.

Frank, on the other hand, never told all his story to his employer; but he was constrained to explain why he was in a position so different to that in which he had been brought up. And he did it in a few words, and without any expression of complaint. Burls only knew that his father had lost money by rash speculation, and had died, leaving Frank without resources. He did not inquire further, but remarked—
"What aint in my business is in the three per cent. Consols. Your father's ought to have been there."

Soon there came a very busy time at cleaning pictures, and Burls asked Frank to help him.

He found it a mighty simple matter, though it rubbed the skin off his fingers at first.

"Lay the canvas down," said Burls, "and rub it. If the varnish comes off after a few rubs of your finger, it's mastic, and 'll all rub off clear down to the paint. If it won't chafe, it's copal, and you must get it off with spirits, and be careful not to take the paint away with it. I've seen that done often."

So Frank and Burls spent much of their time together, chafing the dirty varnish off old pictures. When they had rubbed it off, and got down to the paint, one or the other dipped a wide brush in mastic varnish, dabbed it on like whitewash on a ceiling, and then laid the canvas flat on the floor of the next room.

"It all dries down smooth enough," Burls said. "That's the beauty of it."

And this, gentle British public, is the art of cleaning old oil paintings on a system invented by ourselves, without the slightest injury or damage, advertised by Bartholomew Burls & Co., Church-street, City. Country orders carefully attended to. And you are charged for it entirely according to Mr. Burls's belief in your capacity to pay—sometimes ten shillings, sometimes ten pounds; but the process is always the same, and it takes a very slightly skilled labourer any time from fifteen minutes to sixty to complete the operation.

Sometimes the pictures wanted repainting in places: then Frank took them into his own room, and did what was required, before they were varnished off.

"Mind you, cleaning's an art, and I've taught it you," Mr. Burls would say.

For painting and painters he had a proper contempt. He bought their works so cheap, and they—at least, the specimens he saw—were always such poor devils. But gilding frames, cleaning and restoring pictures—these were profitable arts, and he respected them.

He told Frank many queer anecdotes of the trade, of his customers, and how he had imposed upon their credulity And how credulous customers are, only such men as Mr. Burls know.

He told him tales of the sales and knock-outs; and one day took him to one at a public-house in Pall-mall, where Frank formed an acquaintance with the habits, customs, and language of the trade, and saw all the lots they had bought at Christie's put up again, and resold among themselves at a good profit.

"Look at that," said Mr. Burls one day to Frank—"that's a seller, aint it? I lay you a new hat I don't have that here a fortnight, and I shall ask sixty guineas for it."

"Is it not the one that has been in the shop some time?" Frank asked.

"No, it aint; but it's the own brother to it, and here's two more of the family—only they aint done up yet," said the dealer, pulling down two other canvases from a rack.

Frank opened his eyes—wide.

The pictures were landscapes in the style of Claude. The first was cracked all over, respectably dirty, and looked certainly a hundred years old. The paint of the other two was scarcely dry.

"It would have deceived me, I believe," said Frank.

"Deceive anybody," said Mr. Burls. "Now, you wouldn't look at that picture and think it's only a month old, would you? That's all it is. It was like these here two a month ago. I've sold four or five of 'em."

"It would not do to sell them to intimate friends, would it?" said Frank.

"Trust me for that. I send 'em about the country. I've bought everything lately at an old maiden lady's at Bexley Heath, and described the place to the customers; but I think I've used it up about. Give us a good name, now, of a place for stuff to come from."

Frank thought a moment, and suggested Compton Green.

"Where's Compton Green?" asked Mr. Burls.

"It's five miles from Market Basing, in Holmshire," said Frank.

"Well, I'll try Compton Green. I've got a customer coming to look at some pictures to-day. I hope it'll be as lucky

o

as Bexley Heath has been. Jack and me's sold some hundreds now, I think, from there; so it's time we had a change."

"Do," said Frank. "It has one advantage, at all events, nobody will know it."

"Now I'm going to show my customer this Claude. I wish I'd got a dozen as good. It cost me fifteen pounds; and it wasn't painted half a mile from where we stand. I want some imitations. Couldn't you paint me some?"

Frank tried; and, after some time, succeeded, to Mr. Burls's entire satisfaction, in imitating Old Cuyp.

"That's right enough," said the dealer. "I'll give you ten pound a piece for a dozen as good as that."

Frank was delighted. Here was fortune come at last.

"I'm fair and straight, I am," said the dealer. "There aint much in painting 'em when you've been showed what's wanted. It's the doing 'em up. That's a secret as only a few of us have got. It cost me something to learn it, I can tell you. I paid for it, and it's paid me. This picture, when I've done with it, 'll be worth sixty, if it's worth a sovereign. But there's art, I can tell you, in doing what I do to 'em."

There always was, according to Mr. Burls's version of the case, art in doing anything to a picture but painting it.

Frank watched the processes his picture went through with interest. It went to be lined, and stretched on an old strainer. As it was to be an old picture, the supposed old canvas it was painted on must be concealed by a lining.

Then it received several coats of mastic varnish, in which red and yellow lake and other colours were mixed to tone it down, laid on with Burls's liberal hand. As the first coat dried, a second, and so on.

Then it was brushed over one night with a substance which we have all eaten times without number. In the morning, Frank's Old Cuyp was cracked all over.

He was astonished, and well he might be. The surface, hard and dry, was a network of very thin cracks. It was put into a real old frame of the period, the door-mat shaken over canvas and frame several days in succession, and the business was complete.

The picture looked old and mellow; the cracks bore witness to its genuineness; it had been lined to keep the rotting canvas from dropping to pieces as it stood; but the frame was the one it had always hung in, in the old manor-house at Compton Green.

"It's a simple thing when you know how to do it, aint it?" asked Mr. Burls of Frank.

"It is, indeed," said the artist, astonished at his own work in its altered guise. "It is simple."

But what that simple thing is I must not tell, or I shall have some of my younger readers trying the experiment of cracking their fathers' pictures; and it wants some practice to ensure success in making the cracks natural in appearance, and not having too many of them.

Frank set to work to make more of these imitations.

He made them to order, not being a party to any deception which his employer might practise. A copy, or an imitation, whichever Mr. Burls wanted. What the dealer chose to do with it when the order was executed, was nothing to Frank. At the same time he had a shrewd suspicion, though Burls said nothing, that his pictures were sold as originals. It must be stated that Burls did not always sell a copy as an original. The imitations brought Frank ten pounds each; but they lost him his employment. In this way.

One day, as he was going out to his tea, when he got as far as the staircase that connected the gallery with the shop, he observed Burls showing some pictures to two customers; one of these was his Old Cuyp.

"Compton Green, I assure you, they all came from," Burls was saying.

"Near Market Basing?" asked a clerical old gentleman, who was one of his two customers.

"That's the place, sir. I fetched 'em all away myself, I assure you."

"But there is nobody there who ever had any pictures. I live near the village myself."

Here was a facer for the dealer.

He saw Frank, and called him. Frank had given him the name. Frank must get him out of the scrape.

"Here, Shipley"—he winked hard—" you went down with me to fetch these pictures. Tell this gentleman the house we got 'em from. It's a genuine Cuyp as ever I sold, sir,"— Frank was coming up the shop, and the old gentleman's back was turned towards him—" and it's a cheap picture at sixty guineas. I would not take pounds for it."

By this time Frank was close to him.

"Tell this gentleman where we got these pictures from, every one of them. You went with me."

Burls made a great mistake in his man. Frank was not going to tell lies for him. Besides, he knew the customer.

The old gentleman turned round, and saw him before he could escape. He fell back a step or two, shaded his eyes with his hand, looked very hard at Frank, then exclaimed, cordially holding out his hand—

"God bless me! Young Mr. Melliship!"

"Dr. Perkins!" stammered Frank.

"My dear young gentleman, who ever would have thought of seeing you here?"

Frank was interrupted in a rambling apology by Mr. Burls.

"Very clever young man—invaluable to me. He'll tell you"—here he winked again at Frank—"all about the place we fetched them from."

"Well, I shall have some other things to talk about with him of more importance; but perhaps he will excuse me if, to settle this, I ask where possibly at Compton Green there could be pictures without me knowing it?"

"Ah!" said Burls, "he can tell you. I go into so many houses, I forget where they are almost."

"Nowhere," said Frank, looking Dr. Perkins—whom he knew was an old friend of his father's—full in the face. "I painted it myself."

And he was gone out of the shop. It was in vain the old clergyman and his son-in-law tried to overtake him. They soon lost sight of him in the crowded street.

CHAPTER THE TWENTY-SECOND.

"I MUST tell you," wrote Grace to Kate, "of the great day we had at Derngate. You know all the dreadful news, because Lucy has told you how Uncle Mortiboy, after he had given all his money to Dick, had a paralytic stroke, and is quite helpless now. He seems to know people, though he cannot speak. He gives a sort of a grunt for 'yes,' and frowns when he means 'no.' Though we feel sure he will never recover his faculties again, poor old man, he is not at all a pitiable object to look at. He has completely lost the use of one side, and partially that of the other. His face is drawn curiously out of shape, and it gives him a happy and pleasant

look he never used to have. He actually looks as if he were smiling all the while—a thing, as you know, he did not often do. They have taken him downstairs, and old Hester looks after him. Dick has moved into that little villa which stands across the river, the only house there. He has a boat to go across in. It seems a prosaic way of getting over a river for a man who knows all about California and Texas, doesn't it? I told him that we all expected him to strike out a new idea.

"But the moving was the great thing. He asked us all there to come down while he ransacked the old house. So down we went. We went in to see poor old Mr. Mortiboy, and he seemed to know us, and to want to speak; but it was no use. Then our voyage of discovery began. We had Mr. Tweedy, the builder, who went about with the house-steps and a hammer. He went first. Dick came next. We followed, pretending not to be at all curious; and old Hester brought up the rear.

"First, Aunt Susan's room. Then we opened all her drawers, boxes, and cupboards. There was nothing in one of them except old letters and things of no interest or value. 'The old man,' Dick said, 'has been here before us.' I don't think that it's nice of him to speak of his father in that way; though mamma declares that his voice always shakes as he does it. All poor aunt's dresses were hanging up just as she had left them. Dick gave every one to mamma, with her lace—you know what beautiful lace Aunt Susan had. There is not much, after all; for she never dressed very well, as you know. Mamma transferred the gowns to old Hester on the spot, and kept the lace, of course.

"Then we went downstairs to the first floor—Mr. Mortiboy's own floor. Here we had a surprise. In the room was a long press, which Dick opened. My dear Kate, it was full of gold and silver cups, and plate of all kinds.

"Dick tossed them all on the table with his usual careless manner.

"'Now, cousins,' he said, 'if you can find anything here with the Heathcote crest on it, take it.'

"I found an old cup, which must have been my great-grandfather's, which I took home to papa.

"'I am going to pick out the Mortiboy plate,' said Dick, 'and sell all the rest.'

"Oh, Kate! among the rest was a great deal of yours, which Uncle Mortiboy had bought up from the sale. I waited till mamma was not looking, and I begged him not to sell that. He did not know that it was yours, and promised. So that is all safe for the present. And then he produced Aunt Susan's jewels and trinkets, and divided them between Lucy and me. I shall have such splendours to show you when we meet again. It is old-fashioned, of course, but very good.

"Then he put all the things back again.

"'We're going to look for money,' he said. 'Hester says he used to hide it away.'

"Then we saw the use of the steps and the hammer. Mr. Tweedy went about hammering everywhere, to see if things were solid or hollow. In a window-seat which he forced open —it had been screwed down—we found a bag full of guineas. I have one of them now. Behind a panel of the wainscoting, which had a secret spring—I did not know there were any houses in Market Basing with secret springs and panels—we found—not a skeleton, my dear, with a dagger stuck in its ribs, as there ought to have been in a secret cupboard,—but another bag, with thirty old spade guineas in it. Wherever a hiding place could be made, Uncle Mortiboy had hidden away some money. There was quite a handsome sum in an old and well-darned stocking foot, and ever so many guineas under his bed. He seems to have had a great penchant for saving guineas. Hester says he thought they brought luck.

"How much is left to find, of course we cannot tell. It seems now that he was never quite easy in his mind about the things in his house. You know their queer, narrow old staircase? Well, he used always to take his after-dinner nap on the stairs, where nothing could pass him without awaking him; and he used to pay the policeman extra money for giving a special look at the house. How it was he was not robbed, I can't think.

"After all this, we went home, loaded with spoil. Mamma began again about Dick's 'intentions;' but that only annoys me a very little now.

"Dick has got old Mrs. Lumley, whom you know, to look after him. But he won't let her sleep in the house. He fired pistols at his first woman, and she ran away. But Mrs. Lumley is not afraid, and I haven't heard of any pistols being fired at her.

"When are you going to give me fresh news of Frank? Kate, dear, give him my love—my real and only·love—and tell him not to forget me, and to keep up his courage. If he would only be helped, all would be well. I am sure papa liked him better than anybody that came to Parkside. And, after all, papa—is papa."

It was a fine time this, for Polly. She had plenty of Dick's society. He was at home nearly every evening, and generally alone. Then she would sit with him while he drank, smoked, told her queer stories, and sang her jovial sea-songs. As for her, she always behaved as a lady, put on a silk dress every evening, and invariably had her bottle of port before her, carrying her adherence to the usages of polite society so far as very often to finish it.

Occasional wayfarers along the towing-path would hear sounds of merriment and singing. It was whispered that Dick Mortiboy even entertained the Evil One himself, and regaled him with cigars and brandy.

Sometimes they played at cards, games that Dick taught her. Sometimes they used to quarrel, but not often; because once, when she threatened her husband, he took her by the shoulders, and turned her out of doors.

Her venerable parent was a bedridden old lady, of prepossessing ugliness, who resided in a cottage, neither picturesque nor clean, in the outskirts of Market Basing. By the assistance of her daughter, she was able to rub along and get her small comforts. She was not a nice old lady to look at, nor was she eminently moral; being one of those who hold that lies cost nothing, and very often bring in a good deal.

"Get money out of him, Polly," she said. "Get as much as you can—it won't last, you know."

"And why shouldn't it last? What's to prevent it lasting, you old croaker?"

"The other will turn up some day, Polly. I know it—I'm certain of it. Make him give you money. Tell him it's for Bill."

"Mother, Dick's no fool. I've had fifty pounds out of him for little Bill in the last four months. I told him, only a fortnight ago, that Bill had got the scarlet fever! and he told me to go to the devil. He's deep, too. He doesn't say anything, but he's down on you all of a sudden. Mother, I lie awake at night, and tremble sometimes. I'm afraid of him, he is so masterful."

"But try, Polly, my dear—try. Tell him I want things at my time of life."

"I might do that. But it's no use pretending anything about Bill for a while. The other night he said Bill was played out. He wants to know where the boy is, too."

"Where is he, Polly? Tell your old mother, deary."

"Sha'n't," said Polly.

She made a long story about her mother that very night, and coaxed ten pounds out of Dick for her. The old woman clutched the gold, and put it away under her pillow, where she kept all the money that Polly got out of Dick.

It was odd that he could endure the woman at all. She was rough-handed, rough-tongued, coarse-minded, intriguing, and crafty—and he knew it. Her tastes were of the lowest kinds. She liked to eat and drink, and do little work. They had no topics in common. But he was lazy, and liked to "let things slide." She had all the faults that a woman can have; but she had a sort of cleverness which was not displeasing to him. Sometimes ne would hate her. This was generally after he had been spending an evening at Parkside—almost the only house he visited.

Here, under the influence of the two girls and their father, he became subdued and sobered. The subtle influence of the pure and sweet domestic life was strong enough to touch him: to move him, but not to bring him back.

The sins of youth are never forgiven or forgotten. Now, when all else went well with Dick, when things had turned out beyond his wildest hopes, this woman—whom he had married in a fit of calf love—stood in his way, and seemed to drag him down again when he would fain have risen above his own level. Other things had passed away and been forgotten. There was no fear that the old Palmiste business would be revived. Facts and reports, ugly enough, were safe across the Atlantic. Of the twelve years of Bohemian existence no one knew: they were lost to history as completely as the forty years' wandering of the Israelites. Only Lafleur, who was sure to keep silent for his own sake, knew. And this woman alone stood in the way, warning him back from the paths of respectability—an Apollyon whom it was impossible to pass.

But one evening, Polly, who had come in to see him, cried in a maudlin way over the love she had for the boy; and pulling her handkerchief out of her pocket to dry her eyes, dragged with it a letter, which Dick, who was sitting opposite her and not too far off, instantly covered with his foot. Ignorant of her loss, she went on crying till the fit passed; and then, finishing off the port, marched away in rather a corkscrew fashion. Dick, lifting his foot, picked up the letter and read it.

It was a very odd epistle, and was dated from some suburb of London of which he knew nothing, called "Paragon-place, Gray's Inn Road."

The orthography was that of a person imperfectly educated, and Dick deciphered it with some difficulty.

"MY DEER POLY"—it went—"escuse Me trubbling you butt im hard up, haveing six of themm Cussed babies to look after and methoosalem and Little bill do eat ther Heds of and what with methoosalem as wont wurk and bill as Wont Prig im most crasy with them you Owe me for six munths which six Pound ten and hope as youll send me the munney sharp as Else bill he cuts his lucky so as hes your own Son and not mine i dont see wy should kepe him any longer for Nuthink and remain dear poly your affeckshunit

"ANN MARIA KNEEBONE.

"P.s.—[This in another hand]—i see the old woman a ritin her letter wich it toke her hall day and the babies a starvin, so i had a P.s. to say as she is verry hard up and so am i and so his bill. "METHOOSALEM."

Dick read this precious epistle with a look of extreme bewilderment. Then he read it over again. Gradually arriving at a sense of its meaning, he looked again at the address and the name, so as not to forget them—he never forgot anything —and then he twisted it up and burned it in the candle. After that he went to bed, putting off meditation till the following morning. Dick was not going to spoil his night's rest because Polly had told him lies.

Little Bill—that was Polly's child; presumably, therefore, his as well. Therefore, little William Mortiboy—the heir-apparent to his father's fortunes.

"William Mortiboy's position," said Dick to himself next morning after breakfast, appears unsatisfactory. He lives with a lady named Kneebone, who has a lodging-house for babies. Wonder if the babies like the lodgings? William Mortiboy associates, apparently, with a gentleman called Methoosalem, who refuses to work. Is he one of the babies?

Wonder if he is! William Mortiboy is expected to prig That's a devilish bad beginning for William. William Mortiboy's companions are not, apparently, the heir to anything—not even what the man in the play calls a stainless name. Polly, I'm afraid you're a bad lot! . . . . Anyhow, you might have paid the five bob a week out of all the money you've had in the last four months. But we'll be even with you. Only wait a bit, my lady."

CHAPTER THE TWENTY-THIRD.

T was a godly and an ancient custom in Market Basing, that on a certain Sunday afternoon in the year, the children should have a "church parade" all to themselves, followed by a bun. Of late years, an addition had been made to this festival by setting apart a week-day in the summer for a school feast and treat. It was generally a dreary affair enough. The boys and girls were marshalled, and marched to some field not far off, where they were turned loose previous to the tea, and told to play. As the Market Basing boys saw no novelty in a field—unlike the Londoner, to whom a bird's nest is a new discovery, and a field-mouse the most remarkable of wild animals—these feasts, although preceded by cake and followed by tea, had no great charms. Perhaps they were overweighted by hymns.

Now, Dick, pursuing that career of social usefulness already hinted at, had succeeded, in a very few weeks, in alienating the affections of all the spiritual leaders of the town. The way was this. First, he refused to belong to the chapel any more, and declined to pay for a pew in the church, on the reasonable ground that he did not intend to go to either. They came to him—Market Basing was regularly whipped and driven to religion, if not to godliness—to give money to

their pet society, which, they said, called alike for the support
of church and chapel, for providing Humble Breakfasts and
flannel in winter for the Deserving Poor. This was explained
to mean, not the industrious poor nor the provident poor, nor
the sober poor, but the poor who attended some place of
worship. Dick said that not going to church did not of itself
prove a man to be irreligious, artfully instancing himself as a
case in point; and refused to help.

Then the secretaries of London societies, finding out that
there was another man who had money to give, and was shown
already to be of liberal disposition, sent him begging letters
through the curates. They all got much the same answer.
The missionary societies were dismissed because, as Dick told
them, he had seen missionaries with his own eyes. That noble
institution in Lincoln's Inn Fields, which exists for the double
purpose of maintaining a large staff and converting the Jews,
was refused on the ground of no results commensurable with
the expense. He offered, indeed, a large sum for a successful
mission among the professions—especially the bar—in England.
And he rashly proposed a very handsome prize—no
less than a thousand pounds—to anybody who would succeed
in converting *him*. Rev. Potiphar Demas, a needy vessel,
volunteered; but Dick declined to hear him, because he didn't
want to know what Mr. Demas had to say. Now, this seemed
discourteous to the reverend gentleman.

All this might have been counterbalanced by his many
virtues. For it was notorious that he had given a pension to
old Sanderson, the ruined cashier of Melliship's bank; also that
he had withdrawn the Mortiboy claims on the Melliship estate:
this was almost as if the Americans were to withdraw their
Alabama claims, because there was no knowing where they
might end. Besides which, it made an immediate difference
of four shillings in the pound. Further, sundry aged persons
who had spent a long life in cursing the name of Mortiboy,
took to praising it altogether, because Dick was helping them
all. And the liberality towards his clerks with which he
inaugurated his reign was almost enough of itself to make him
popular.

But then came that really dreadful business about the old
women. This, although he was gaining a golden name by
making restitution for his father's ill deeds—like Solomon repairing
the breaches which his father David had made—was
enough to make all religious and right-minded people tremble

in their shoes. Everybody knows that humility in the aged poor is the main virtue which they are expected to display. In the church at Market Basing was a broad middle aisle, down which was ranged a row of wooden benches, backless, cushionless, hard, and unpromising. On them sat, Sunday after Sunday, at these services, constant, never-flagging, all the old women in the parish. It was a gruesome assemblage: toothless, rheumatic, afflicted with divers pains and infirmities, they yet struggled, Sunday after Sunday, to the "free seats," so called by a bitter mockery, because those who sat in them had no other choice but to go.

On their regular attendance depended not so much their daily bread, which the workhouse might have given them, but their daily comforts; their tea and sugar; their wine if they were ill—and they always were ill; their blankets and their coals. Now, will it be believed that Dick, instigated by Ghrimes, who held the revolutionary maxim that religion, if it is to be real, ought not to be made a condition of charity, actually found out the names of these old trots, and made a weekly dole among them, without any conditions whatever? It was so. He really did it. After two or three Sundays the free seats were empty, all the old women having gone to different conventicles, where they got their religion hot and hot, as they liked it; where they sat in comfortable pews, like the rest of the folk; and where they were treated as if, in the house of God, all men are alike and equal. When the curates called, they were cheeky; when they threatened, the misguided old ladies laughed; when they blustered, these backsliders, relying on their Dick, cracked their aged fingers in the young men's faces.

"He is a very dreadful man," said the rector. "What shall we do with him?"

He called. He explained the danger which befell these ignorant though elderly persons in frequenting an uncovenanted place of worship; but he spoke to deaf ears. Dick understood him not.

It was the time of the annual school feast. Dick was sitting, in that exasperating Californian jacket, in the little bank parlour, consecrated to black cloth and respectability. His legs were on the window sill, his mouth had a cigar in it, his face was beaming with jollity, his heart was as light as a child's. All this was very bad.

Foiled in his first attempt, the rector made a second.

"There is another matter, Mr. Mortiboy, on which I would speak with you."

"Speak, Mr. Lightwood," said Dick. "Don't ask me for any money for the missionaries."

"I will not," said good old Mr. Lightwood, mournfully. "I fear it would be of little use."

Dick pulled his beard and grinned. Why this universal tendency of mankind to laugh when, from a position of strength, they are about to do something disagreeable?

"It is not about any of our societies, Mr. Mortiboy. But I would fain hope that you will not refuse a trifle to our children's school feast. We give them games, races, and so forth. With tea and cake. We are very short of funds."

"Do you?" cried Dick. "Look here, sir. What would you say if I offered to stand the whole thing—pay for the burst myself—grub, liquids, and prizes?"

The rector was dumbfounded. It had hitherto been one of his annual difficulties to raise the money for his little *fête*, for St. Giles's parish was very large, and the parishioners generally poor. And here was a man offering to pay for everything!

Then Dick, who could never be a wholly submissive son of the Church, must needs put in a condition which spoiled it.

"All the children, mind. None of your Church children only."

"It has always been confined to our own children, Mr. Mortiboy. The Dissenters have their—ahem! their—their—treat at another time."

"Very well, then. Here is my offer. I will pay for the supper, or dinner, or whatever you call it, to as many Market Basing children as like to come. I don't care whether they are Jews or Christians. That is their look-out, not mine. Take my offer, Mr. Lightwood. If you refuse, by Jove, I'll have a day of my own, and choose your day. We'll see who gets most youngsters. If you accept, you shall say grace, and do all the pious part yourself. Come, let us oblige each other. I am really sorry to refuse you so often; and here is a chance."

What was to be done with this dreadful man? If you crossed him, he was capable of ruining everything; and to yield to him was to give up half your dignity. But concession meant happiness to the children; and the good old clergyman, who could not possibly understand the attitude of mind of his

new parishioner—seeing only perversity where half was
experience and half ignorance—yielded at once and gracefully.
Dick immediately assumed the whole conduct of the affair.
Without making any reference to church or chapel, he issued
handbills stating that sports, to which all the children in the
place were invited, would be held on the following Wednesday,
in his own paddock at Derngate. Then followed a goodly
list of prizes to be run for, jumped for, wrestled for, and in
other ways offered to public competition. And it became
known that preparations were making on the most liberal
scale. There was to be a dinner at one, a tea at five, and a
supper at eight. There were to be fireworks. Above all, the
races and the prizes.

Dick had no notion of doing a thing by halves. He got an
itinerant circus from a neighbouring fair, a wild-beast show;
a Punch and Judy, swing-boats, a roundabout, and a performing monkey. Then he hired a magic lantern, and erected a
tent where it was to be seen all day. He hired donkeys for
races, got hundreds of coloured lamps from town, built an
enormous marquee where any number of children might sit
down to dinner, and sent out messengers to ascertain how
many guests might be expected.

This was the happiest period in Dick's life. The possessor
of a princely income, the owner of an enormous fortune, he
had but to lift his hand, and misery seemed to vanish.
Justice, the propagation of prudential motives, religion, natural
retribution for broken laws, all these are advanced ideas, of
which Dick had but small conception.

Grace Heathcote described the day in one of her letters to
Kate—those letters which were almost the only pleasure the
poor girl had at this time :—

" As for the day, my dear, it was wonderful. I felt inclined
to defend the climate of England at the point of the sword—
I mean the needle. Dick, of course, threw California in my
teeth. As we drove down the road in the waggonette, the
grand old trees in the park were rustling in their lovely July
foliage like a great lady in her court dress. The simile was
suggested to me by mamma, who wore her green silk. Lucy
and I were dressed alike—in white muslin. I had pink
ribbons, and she wore blue; and round my neck was the
locket with F.'s portrait in it, which you sent me—you good,
kind, thoughtful Kate! Mamma does not like to see it; but

you know my rebellious disposition. And papa took it in his fingers, and then pinched my cheek, as much as to say that he highly approved of my conduct. Oh! I know the dear old man's heart. I talk to him out in the fields, and find out all his little secrets. Men, my dear Kate, even if they are your own father, are all as simple as—what shall I say?—as Frank and papa.

"We got into Market Basing at twelve. The town was just exactly like market day, only without the smell of vegetables. It felt like Christmas Day in the summer. You know the paddock? It is not very big, but it was big enough. The front lawn of Derngate—poor old Uncle Mortiboy inside, not knowing what was going on!—was covered with a great marquee. The paddock had a racecourse marked round it, and a platform, and posts between, which were festooned with coloured lamps. All the children, in their Sunday best, were gathering about the place, waiting to be admitted.

"As we drove up, Dick came out, with a cigar between his teeth, of course, and the crowd gave a great cheer. Mamma said it seemed as if it was meant for us; and so we all got out of the waggonette, trying to look like princesses; and Dick helped us, and they all cheered again. Really, I felt *almost* like Royalty; which, my dear Kate, must be a state of life demanding a great strain upon the nerves, and a constant worry to know whether your bonnet is sitting properly.

"'Are we looking our best, Dick?' I asked, anxious to know.

"'Your very best,' he said. 'I take it as a compliment to my boys and girls.'

"I wish that woman Mary, our old servant, had not been standing close by. She gave me a look—such a look as I never had before—as if I was doing her some mortal injury; and then turned away, and I saw her no more all day. I declare there's always something. If ever I felt happy in my life—except one day when Frank told me he loved me—it was last Wednesday; and that woman really spoiled at least an hour of the day for me, because she made me feel so uncomfortable. I wish she would go away.

"As one o'clock struck, the band—did I tell you there was a band? A real band, Kate, the militia band from the Stores —struck up 'The Roast Beef of Old England,' and Dick in five minutes had all the boys and girls in to dinner.

"The rector, and his curates, and the Dissenting ministers—

and what the paper called 'a select company,' which means ourselves chiefly—were present. We all sat down; I next to Dick on his left hand, mamma on his right. The rector said grace. Dick whispered that we could not have too much Grace—his Californian way of expressing satisfaction at my personal appearance—and we began to eat and drink. Spare me the details.

"One p.m. to two p.m.; legs of mutton, and rounds of beef, and huge plum puddings.

"Two p.m. to three p.m.: the cherubs are all gorged, and lying about in lazy contentment, too happy to tease each other, and too lazy to do any mischief. Old Hester crying.

"'What for, Hester?'

"'Oh! miss, to think that Miss Susan never lived to see him come home again. And she so fond of him. And he so good and so kind.'

"Poor old Hester! She follows her boy, as she calls him, about with her eyes. I have even seen her stroke the tails of his coat when he wasn't looking. Do men ever know how fond women are of them? And Dick *is* kind and good. He really is, Kate.

"At three, the games. And here a most wonderful surprise. Who should drive up to the paddock but Lord Hunslope himself, and the countess—who always gives me a cold shiver—and Lord Launton? The earl marched straight up to us, and shook hands with papa.

"'Pray, Mr. Heathcote,' he said, in his lordliest way, 'introduce Mr. Mortiboy to me.'

"The Heathcotes had Parkside and Hunslope too before ever the Launtons had left their counters in the city; but of course we didn't insist on our superior rank at such a moment.

"Dick took off his hat with that curious pride of equality which comes, I suppose, of having estates in Mexico and being able to throw the lasso. The countess shook hands with everybody; and Lord Launton, blushing horribly, dropped his stick, and shook hands too, after he had picked it up. I am quite sure that if Lord Launton, when he becomes a peer, could only have the gas turned off before he begins to speak, he would be made Prime Minister in a week. As it is, poor young man——

"We all—I mean the aristocracy—stayed together the whole afternoon, bowing affably to our friends of a lower rank in life—the Battiscombe girls, and the Kerbys, and the rector's wife. I really do not know how I am to descend again. The earl made some most valuable remarks, which ought to be committed to writing for posterity. They may be found, though, scattered here and there about the pages of English literature. The curious may look for them. You see, 'Les esprits forts se rencontrent.'

"After the games, the earl gave away the prizes. I send you the local paper, giving an account of the proceedings. Little Stebbing, Mr. Battiscombe's clerk, was acting as reporter, and making an immense parade at a small table, which he brought himself. I never saw any one look so important. I spoke to him once.

"'Pray, miss,' he said, 'do not interrupt me. I represent the Press. The Fourth Estate, miss. I'm afraid I shan't have enough flimsy.'

"Those were his very words, Kate. By flimsy, I learn that he meant writing paper. Do our great poets—does my adored Tennyson—write on 'flimsy'? Then the Earl-ly party went away, and I made a pun, which you may guess; then we had tea; then we had dancing to the band on the platform—Dick waltzes like a German angel—and then we had supper. And then, O my dear Kate—alas! alas! such a disastrous termination to the evening—for Dick put his foot into all the proprieties. It was when they proposed his health. He hadn't fired pistols at anybody, or taken the name of the missionaries in vain, or worn a Panama hat, or done anything disgraceful at all. And now it was to come. My poor cousin Dick! How will he get over it?

"They proposed his health after supper. The children were simply intoxicated—not with beer, for they had none: only lemonade and sweet things—but with fun, fireworks, and fruit tart. They cheered till their dear little throats were hoarse. Even the ugliest, reddest-faced, turnedestup-nosed girl looked pretty when papa called on them to drink the health of the giver of the feast. My own heart swelled, and Lucy cried outright.

"Then Dick got up. My dear, he looked simply grand in the flicker of the gas jets stirred about by the wind. He stood up, tall and strong, high up above us all, and passed his left hand down his long black beard. His brown eyes are so soft sometimes, too. They were soft now; and his under-lip has a way of trembling when he is moved. He was moved now. I can't remember all his speech. He began by telling

P

the children that he was more happy to have them about him
than they to come. Then he began good advice. No one
knows how wise Dick is. He told them that what they wanted
was fresh air, plenty of grub—his word, Kate, not mine—and
not too many books. Here they all screamed, and the clergymen shook their precious heads. I said, 'Hear, hear,' and
mamma touched me on my arm. It is wrong, of course, in a
young lady to have any opinions at all which the male sex do
not first instil into her tender mind. Then he called their
attention to the fact that they were not always going to be
children; and that, if they wanted plenty to eat, they would
have to work hard for it. And then he said, impressively
shaking an enormous great fist at them—

"'And now, my boys and girls, remember this. Don't you
believe people who tell you to be contented with what you've
got. That's all nonsense. *You've got to be discontented.* The
world is full of good things for those who have the courage
to get up and seize them. Look round in your houses, and
see what you have : then look round in rich men's houses—
say mine and the rector's—and see what we've got. Then
be discontented with your own position till you're all rich
too.'

"Here the rector rose, with a very red face.

"'I cannot listen to this, Mr. Mortiboy—I must not listen
to it. You are undoing the Church's teaching.

"'I've got nothing to do with the Church.'

"'You are attacking the Church's Catechism.'

"'Does the Catechism teach boys to be contented?'

"'It does, in explicit terms.'

"'Then the Catechism is a most immoral book.'

"Dick wagged his head solemnly.

"'Boys and girls, chuck the Catechism into the fire, and
be discontented.'

"Here the rector solemnly left the tent, and everybody
looked serious. Dick took no notice, and went on.

"'I'll tell you a story. In an English town that I know,
there were two boys and two girls. They were all four poor,
like most of you. They grew up in their native place till
they were eighteen and twenty, and the boys fell in love with
the girls. One was a contented fellow. His father had been
a farm labourer, like some of your fathers. He would go on
being a farm labourer. The other read that the world was
full of ground that only waited for a man to dig it up; and

he went away. I saw him last year. He had been out for four years. He had a farm, my boys, stocked with cattle and horses, all his own. Think of that! And he had a wife, my girls; his old sweetheart, come out to marry him. Think of that! Then I came home. I saw the other boy, a farm labourer still! He was bent with rheumatism already, because he was a slave. He had no money: no home: no prospects. And the girl he was to have married—well, my girls, if your teachers are worth their salt, they'll tell you what became of that girl. Go out into the world, boys. Don't stick here, crowding out the place, and trying to be called gentlemen. What the devil do you want a black coat for till you have earned it? Go out into the beautiful places in the world, and learn what a man is really worth. And now I hope you've all enjoyed yourselves. And so, good night.'

"Oh! Kate, Kate!—here was a firebrand in our very midst And people are going about, saying that Dick is an infidel. But they can't shake his popularity, for the town loves his very name."

Grace's letter was all true. Dick actually said it. It was his solitary public oration. It had a profound effect. In the half-lighted marquee, as the big-bearded man stood towering over the children, with his right arm waving them out into the world—where? No matter where: somewhere away: somewhere into the good places of the world—not a boy's heart but was stirred within him: and the brave old English blood rose in them as he spoke, in his deep bass tones, of the worth of a single man in those far-off lands;—an oration destined to bear fruit in after-days, when the lads, who talk yet with bated breath of the speech and the speaker, shall grow to man's estate.

"Dangerous, Dick," said Farmer John. "What should I do without my labourers?"

"Don't be afraid," said Dick. "There are not ten per cent. have the pluck to go. Let us help them, and you shall keep the rest."

CHAPTER THE TWENTY-FOURTH.

HEN Frank left Mr. Burls's shop, he felt that he had left it for good. It was Monday evening at five o'clock. He had received the money due to him for painting and restoring on Saturday evening as usual; therefore, all that the dealer owed him for was one day's work. This sum he determined to make Mr. Burls a present of. It was better they should not meet—at least, for the present, Frank thought. For the sake of earning money, he had borne for three months the coarse vulgarity and purse-proud insolence of Burls. He had felt that he should not be able to bear it much longer. The time had come. He had spoken the truth. The penalty was dismissal in anything but polite terms. He had seen Burls kick a man out of his shop for an offence which, compared to what he had done, was a trifle light as air. He felt he could work for such a knave, but he could not condescend to fight with him. So he prudently resolved to keep away, and dismissed himself there and then.

It was not very likely that worthy old Dr. Perkins would be able to overtake Frank; for he was a stout gentleman of sixty, more accustomed to jog behind his cob along the white Holmshire roads, than to run full pelt down a London street. Nor was his son-in-law of much assistance in the matter; for losing sight of his impulsive relative after the first few strides, and not catching a glimpse of Frank, he prudently devoted himself to the task of finding out where Dr. Perkins had disappeared to, and three or four minutes after found him making the most profuse apologies to a buxom lady he had nearly upset in turning the corner of the street. They did not return to Mr. Burls's shop; but, calling a four-wheeler, drove to their hotel.

"I shall communicate at once with that young man's friends," said this excellent old clergyman, as soon as he had recovered his breath. "I am shocked and grieved to see him wandering about like a child of Ishmael in the wilderness of houses. It would kill me. Only think of a young fellow brought up as he was, being reduced to such a pass! Nobody blames his unfortunate father now. There are plenty to help him and his poor dear mother and sister, and he shall be put in a way of doing something for himself without a day's delay."

It was not to be surprised at, that Frank was not overtaken by the friends who pursued him, for he had turned up a court—entered by a low archway, with shops on each side of it—while they had shot past it, keeping on their way straight down the street. In this court, at a comfortable eating-house, Frank was in the habit of taking his meals. He had his pot of tea, bread and butter, and watercresses, read the evening paper as usual, and started to walk home to his lodgings at Islington, just as the two gentlemen, who would have given almost anything to know where he was, were sitting down to their dinner at the Tavistock in Covent-garden.

"It must have come to this very soon," he thought, as he walked homewards; but he felt rather down at being again a man without an employment. "I couldn't have stood his company much longer. But I am such an unlucky beggar: if it had happened a fortnight ago, or a week or two hence, I should not have owed that confounded landlady anything."

The truth was, ever since Frank had been in Mr. Burls's employment, he had sent as much money as he could possibly scrape together by post-office order to his mother and sister, living in a farmhouse in the romantic village of Llan-y-Fyddloes. Their little income of two pounds a week was quite enough for their modest wants there, Kate often told him, in her weekly letter—a chronicle of small beer Frank looked forward to on a Monday morning with a feverish longing; for did it not always contain a letter from Grace, his love, to her dear friend Kate, which Mistress Kate enclosed for him to read, but which he never, on one single occasion, sent back in his next, as Kate invariably desired him to do? But Frank knew, though the money would not be spent, it would cheer his mother—and, for the matter of that, Kate too. They would have the strongest possible proof that he was getting on in the world. He had more than he wanted for himself, and could contribute to their support; and he wrote very flourishing accounts of how he was selling his works, and Kate would perceive how necessary it was for him to see Hampstead, and Highgate, and Richmond, and other of those charming suburbs of London, to fill his sketch-book with pretty bits; so she was to consider him a gipsy student of art, now camping here, now there, not tied to any spot above a week or so, roaming at his royal pleasure in search of the Picturesque. And so letters to him, to avoid delays, had better be addressed to a certain post-office, for Francis Melliship, Esquire, till called for; and as he was in London very often, he would always call when he expected a letter from her or from his mother, and they were the only people he wrote to now.

Not one word of the drudgery in Burls's manufactory of the sham antique; not one word of the dingy lodging in the back street; not one word of the groans of the lover's heart at the hopeless distance that still lay between Frank Melliship and Grace Heathcote.

In his letters, all was rose-coloured.

"Do you know, I really think Frank will do well, Kate," Mrs. Melliship said. "It is plain he is getting on with his pictures. I wish he had not so much boyish pride."

"Mamma, Frank is independent. He relies on himself, as a man should. I admire him for it."

"Well, my dear, I never heard of an artist that was what I call well off who wasn't an R.A. Who was that R.A. your father used to invite to stay with us?—the man that used to stop the carriage while he sketched things—dear me, I know it quite well! And when Frank could be an R.A., if he could get on as fast as possible, I don't really quite know—though it must be some years, of course. But he is certainly doing well, for he has sent us ten pounds twice within a month. No, I am wrong—five weeks. He is a dear, good boy; and I feel our misfortune more for him, Kate, than for you and me. Oh, dear! they all know it wasn't your poor father's fault at all; and I'm sure John Heathcote, besides many others I could mention, would do anything in the world for Frank. I suppose, poor boy, he has set his heart on Grace?"

"Yes," said Kate, demurely.

"Well, I always loved Grace and Lucy very much, and I could treat her as a daughter, and I should like to see Frank married and happy. I've heard your poor father say very often that John Heathcote could settle a handsome sum on his daughters when they married; and Kate, my dear, I think we ought to know Frank's address in London, and give it to friends who want to help him, and are always writing to me about it. A letter left at a post-office always reminds me so of Florence, where I was so miserable, because my dear mother died there; and we did not always get the letters that we had no reasonable doubt were posted to us—long before I married your poor father, Kate."

"Yes, mamma," Kate said, mechanically.

Her mother would run on for an hour, from subject to subject; and Kate often was thinking of something else, and only spoke when her mother came to a stop. Mrs. Melliship proceeded—

"I certainly like this village, though the name, and, for the matter of that, the people are very outlandish; and I should not care to go back to Market Basing, Kate, unless I could have my carriage. We used to visit people such a distance in the country, and we could not well do it without a carriage."

"Oh, don't let us go back to Market Basing, mamma. I like Wales so much."

"Well, my dear, I shall live wherever you wish me to, for I may say I live now entirely for you and Frank."

Here the simple lady took out her handkerchief, and shed a few tears—a termination to her speeches more common than not.

Then the two women kissed and comforted each other; and Kate found a book to amuse her mother.

Frank was in the habit of working an hour or two by gaslight of an evening, with pencil or crayons; but he was rather disgusted with art that night, and looked round his little sitting-room in a gloomy mood.

"Ah!" he said, "if people who must have pictures for their houses would only buy an honest new picture instead of a spurious old one, artists might live. After all, the worst of our works are better than what they do buy: they are what they appear. Why not go to the exhibitions, and buy some of the unsold pictures there? Or come to a fellow's place? We're poor enough to be modest in our charges. But they will have real Old Masters at ten pounds apiece; and there the dealers beat us. Art! There is no feeling for art in England—no desire to encourage artists of any kind. They're only a lowish sort of fellows. And then the beggars must go to dealers to buy their ancestors!"

He laughed savagely, and stuck the end of his brush through a half-finished sketch on paper.

"I wonder who'll paint Burls's genuine old pictures now; and dodge up the rubbish from the sales, and clean, and tone, and line, and varnish, and crack? What humbug it all is!"

There was a knock at his door, and his landlady's grubby little daughter gave him a note written on a sheet of paper, and enclosed in an envelope she had ten minutes before sent the young lady out to purchase for a halfpenny at the shop round the corner.

The corner bore the family impress—a dirty finger and thumb they put on everything they touched.

Frank laughed. He never could be surly with a child in his life.

"Tell your mother I'll see her before I go out in the morning.".

He owed two pounds four and sixpence for rent and commodities supplied, and he had only sixteen and sixpence to pay it with; which, under all the circumstances of the case, was awkward.

What wonders a good night's rest will effect!

In the morning, Frank paid his landlady ten shillings on account, listened to her impertinence without a reply, and quietly told her to let his lodgings, and keep his portmanteau for security till he paid her. He should not come back again, except to fetch away his things.

He had dressed himself in a new suit of clothes he had ordered on the strength of his successful manufacture of Old Cuyps and other masters. Nothing could make Frank look other than a gentleman; but to-day he looked quite like his old self of six months ago. He was not at all miserable; on the contrary, he felt quite happy and cheerful.

To be sure, it was a bright day—not too warm—when merely to breathe is a pleasure, even if you are a convict in Portland. Besides, he was free from a drudgery at which his soul had always revolted.

"But what next?" he asked himself. "Anyhow, I've done with painting. No more oils for me."

Passing a pawnbroker's as he spoke, he went in, for the first time in his life, and asked how much the man would advance on his watch and chain. He thanked the man for his information, and left the shop with his watch in his pocket.

"By Jove!" he said, "here's a new source of wealth. I can pawn everything by degrees."

Then he strolled westwards.

The omnibuses had blue and white posters on them—"To Lord's Cricket Ground."

"Why, it's the Oxford and Cambridge match to-day."

Without stopping to think twice, he jumped on an omnibus. "Why shouldn't I go? I can stick myself somewhere out of sight. I wonder how many of our Eleven I know?"
He counted them on his fingers. He wanted to see and yet not be seen.

Just as he was getting off the seat he had occupied by the driver's side, a carriage passed by. Lord Launton was in it, with the countess and two other ladies.

Frank saw the danger he should run of seeing a number of old and inquisitive acquaintances.

He hesitated a moment in the dusty road.

"No—it's nothing to me. I've no interest in it now. I won't go in. Besides, it's half-a-crown, I think."

He took the footway, and set his face towards Regent's Park.

He had not walked a dozen steps when an immense hand and arm were linked in his. He felt a friendly pull towards some great figure; and, looking up, was astonished beyond measure to see himself arm-in-arm with his cousin, Dick Mortiboy.

"Frank, old man!" cried Dick, crushing Frank's hand in his cordial grasp, "I would have given fifty pounds to find you, and here you are. I saw you getting off the 'bus."

Frank was surprised, and a little annoyed.

"After all, I've got no quarrel with Dick," he thought; and his face cleared, and he returned his cousin's salute.

Dick Mortiboy was accompanied by a thin, palefaced man, slight and foreign-looking.

"Lafleur—my cousin Frank," said Dick, introducing him.

"Fool of an Englishman," thought Lafleur, staring at Frank's bright, handsome face. "I leave you with your cousin. The cricket is not a game I care to waste time over," said he, softly. "We shall meet to-morrow, Dick. You will let me go now."

"To-morrow, at eleven. My old partner, Frank. Many is the jovial day we have had together."

"I don't like his looks."

"Insular prejudice, my cousin. Why have you never sent me your address, as you promised? Do you not know what has happened? The governor has got a stroke, and I've got all the money. We've all been trying to find you out. And here you are. I shan't let you go again in a hurry, I promise you."

He looked Frank up and down.
"Dressed fit for Broadway. Come on in."
Dick paid for two at the gate, and they were on the ground.

Dick watched the match with great earnestness. He was a splendid hand at games of skill himself. He knew nobody, nobody knew him. But his height, his splendid beard and brown face, and his careless dress, attracted observation. He only wanted people to bet with on the match to make him happy.

Frank saw lots of old friends.

They asked him his address.

"Only in town for a few days," he said, with an airy laugh.

At length Dick got tired of it.

"Come on, old man. I've had enough, if you have. Let's go."

At the gates, as they went out, stood a man who had been Frank's greatest friend at college. They had rowed together, driven to Newmarket together, got plucked together, written to each other until the smash came.

"Frank, by gad!" cried the man, running down the steps. "Shake hands, old fellow. And how are you? And what are you doing? Tell me you've got over your troubles. I heard all about it."

It was like a burst of sunshine, after the wretched time of the last few months, to find men who were glad to shake hands with him.

Frank tried to laugh; but his mirth was rather a hollow thing.

"I'm well, you see, Evelyn. That is, I'm not starving yet. But there's no money, and I'm still in a parenthetical stage of life."

"You know my address, Frank—give me yours. Let me help you, for old times' sake."

"Thank you, my dear Evelyn. It's like you to make the offer. Good-bye. I'll give you an address—when I've got one."

He left him, and walked quickly away on Dick's arm. He could not bear to let anybody help him with money. And yet Evelyn was longing to give his old friend help.

What is there in this word money, that I may neither give it nor take it? Why should I be degraded if a man slips a sovereign in my hand? Sovereigns are not plentiful. I should like the money. I am not degraded if a man leaves me a legacy of many sovereigns.

"Come," said Dick Mortiboy to Frank, when they had got out of their Hansom in Piccadilly, "you are not engaged tonight. Come and dine with me. After dinner we will talk. I·hate talking before. Let us have a game at billiards first."

He led the way to a public room near Jermyn-street. There were two or three men idly knocking the balls about. Dick took up a cue and made a stroke, missing it.

"Will you play fifty or a hundred up, Frank?"

"I play very badly. I am quite out of practice."

"Well, let it be fifty then," said Dick.

The room was one of bad repute. It was frequented by sharpers. There were three in the room—of course perfect strangers to one another.

Dick Mortiboy didn't know the character of the room he was in, and didn't care. He could give an account of himself anywhere. For his part, Frank had not played a game at billiards since he left Market Basing.

He was not amusement for Dick, for he played like a man wholly out of practice.

The gentlemen in the room became interested ·in the first fifty up between Dick and Frank, and one bet another a wager of half-a-crown on the result.

Dick won, and the loser offered to bet again, if the tall gentleman gave the other points. Dick did give points. The man—whom the marker called "Captain"—then offered to bet Dick Mortiboy half-a-crown his friend beat him. Dick took the bet, won it, and pocketed the half-crown. He was going to play another game with Frank, but was stopped by the marker.

"This is a public table, sir. Two fifty games, or one hundred, between the same players; then another gentleman has the table, if he likes to take it."

Dick was a little annoyed, but gave way.

"Should you like to play a game, sir?" said the marker to the man he had called Captain.

The fellow was a seedy swell, in clothes that had been fast twelve months ago, but now were well worn. His hat and boots showed signs of poverty.

"I should: but I don't wish to prevent these gentlemen from playing, I'm sure. I'll give way; but, really, I can't stay many minutes."

"Well, perhaps the gentleman that won will play a game with you—if you don't mind playing the winner?" the marker said.

"All right," said Dick, and pulled off his coat.

The Captain played badly: so did Dick.

Both were playing dark.

"Twenty all" was called.

"Shall we have a crown on, sir, to 'liven the game?" said the stranger.

"I'll back myself for a sovereign," said Dick.

"I don't often play for a sovereign a game," said the Captain; "but I don't mind doing it for once."

When Spot (the stranger) was forty, Plain (Dick) was only thirty-five.

"Make it a hundred up, sir, and have another sov on," said Spot.

"Done," said Plain.

Dick had bets, too, with the other two strangers and the marker.

At the end of the game, he had four pounds five shillings to pay.

Frank spoke his suspicions, in a low tone, before this game was finished.

Dick only nodded: he had seen they were common sharpers from the moment he entered the room.

"I'll let them have it," he said.

They played another game—Frank watching Dick's play. Up to the time the marker cried "sixty—seventy-two," Dick was behind generally about a dozen. His bets amounted to nearly twenty pounds with the three men.

Up to sixty he had played in a slovenly manner. At that point he took up his cue, and scored out in two breaks.

His play was superb. He was within a few points in a hundred of the best professional form. One of the men was going to leave the room. Dick called him back, and promised to finish the game in three minutes, and did it.

He asked the Captain if he would like another game?

"Not with a professional sharp. Though who you are, I don't know."

"You'll pay up then, gentlemen?" asked Dick.

One of the other men whispered the Captain.

"My friend suggests that it would be well if you were to give your name, sir. It is not usual to see men play in your fashion. You have sharped us, sir—sharped us. Give us your name and address—we are not going to part."

"Now, Captain," said Dick, "you've been licked, and licked easy. You may take it fighting, or you may take it quiet. Which shall it be?"

"Come on, Tom, don't let him bustle us out of it," said the Captain; "I'll take it fighting."·

There were four altogether, with the marker. They made a rush on Dick. Frank, not unmindful of Eton days, took them in flank, while Dick received them in front.

They had not the ghost of a chance. It was a mere affair of fists—a sort of light skirmish, which warmed up Dick's blood, and made him rejoice once more, like a Berserker, in the battle. And, after three minutes, the four fell back, and the Cousins stood with their backs against the wall, laughing.

"And now," said Dick, "open the door, Frank."

He stepped forward, seized the marker, who was foremost, by the coat-collar, and bore him swiftly to the door—the others not interfering. There was a great crash of breaking banisters. The marker had been thrown down the stairs.

"Don't let us fight with servants," said Dick; "let us have it out like gentlemen. Now then, Captain, we're all ready again."

"Let us go," said the Captain, with a pale face, handing Dick the money. "You have sharped and bustled us, and you want to bully us."

"You shall go when you have apologized to me, Captain—not before. You other two, get out."

He looked so fierce, and was undoubtedly so heavy about the fist, that the other two, taking their hats, departed swiftly, with such dignity as their wounds allowed.

"Now, Captain, let us two have a little explanation. I like rooking the rooks. I go about doing it. Beg my pardon, sir, or I'll spoil your play too, for a month of Sundays."

He seized the poor billiard-player by the collar, and shook him as if he had been a child.

"You may do what you like," said the man. "You have got every farthing I have in the world, and my little child's ill; but I'm hanged if I beg your pardon."

"Dick, Dick," said Frank, "give him back his money."

But, at the sight of the man's misery, Dick's wrath had suddenly vanished.

"Poor devil!" he said. "I've had some bad times myself,

mate, out in the States. Look here—here's your money, and something for the little one. And I say, Captain, if you see me drawing the rooks anywhere else, don't blow on me Good-bye. Come, Frank, let us go and dine. What a good thing a scrimmage is to give one an appetite. I do like a regular British row," said Dick with a sigh; "and one so seldom gets one. Now, over the water, somebody always lets fly a Deringer or pulls out a bowie, and then the fun's spoiled. You've got a clean style, Frank—very clean and finished. I thought we were in for it when I saw the place; so I went on. I was determined you should enjoy yourself thoroughly, old boy."

They had dinner, and talked. Dick's talk was all the same thing. It said—

"Take my money. Let me help you. Let me give. I am rich. I like to give."

Frank, with a proud air put him off, and made him talk of anything but him and his affairs.

CHAPTER THE TWENTY-FIFTH.

STREET, as Frank stepped into it from Dick's hotel, was alive with people, for the night was warm and fine. He bade his rich cousin good night, in his easy pleasant way, never hinting at the sore straits to which he was reduced. Dick was rather inclined to believe, indeed, from what little information he was able to elicit from Frank, that Art paid; —that Frank got a living at it, at all events, he was too proud to be helped when he saw the chance of doing well without help. Now, Dick rather admired this phase of Frank's character—as who would not? Yet he resolved that, when he saw him the next day, he would compel him to disclose the state of his finances and his prospects. While one cousin thought this, the other hesitated a moment in front of

the hotel, remembering suddenly that he had no bed to go to.
It was a curious sensation, the most novel he had ever experienced. No bed. Nowhere to go to. No money, or next
to none, in his pocket. Nothing at all resembling a home.
Even a portable tent, or a Rob Roy canoe, would have been
something. He shook himself all over, like a dog. Then he
laughed, for he had had a capital day and a good dinner, and
he was only five-and-twenty.

"Hang it," he said, "a night in the open won't kill one, I
suppose. Dick Mortiboy must have had many in his travelling days."

Then he lit a cigar. Dick had forced a dozen upon him—
which, with that curious feeling that permits a man to take
anything except money from another, Frank accepted with
real gratitude. With his hands in his pockets, and his hat
well back on his head, as all old Eton boys wear it, he strolled
westward, turning things over in his mind in that resignedly
amused frame of mind which comes upon the most unhappy
wight after a bottle and a half of claret. Our ancestors, in
their kindly brutality, permitted condemned criminals to have
a long drink on the way to Tyburn. The punchbowl was
brought out somewhere near the site of the Marble Arch; and
the *condamné*, fortified and brightened up by the drink,
ascended the ladder with a jaunty air, and kicked off his
shoes before an admiring populace;—just as well, it seems to
me, as keeping the poor wretch low, and making him feel all
his misery up to the very last. Frank, having had his bowl
of punch, was about to embark upon that wild and hopeless
voyage of despair, which consists in sailing from port to port,
looking for employment and finding none. There are certain
ships to be met with in the different havens of the world,
which are from time to time to be found putting in, "seeking."
They never find. From Valparaiso they go to Rio; from
Pernambuco to Port Louis; from Calcutta to Kingston; from
Havana to Shanghai. They are always roving about the
ocean, always "seeking," and always in ballast. Who are
their owners; how the grizzled old skipper keeps his crew
together; how they pay for the pickled pork and rum in
which they delight; how they have credit for repairs to
rigging and sails; how the ship is docked, and scraped, and
kept afloat—all these things are a profound mystery. After a
time, as I have reason for believing, they disappear; but this
must be when there is no longer any credit possible, and all

the ports in the world are closed to them. Probably at this juncture the skipper calls together his men, makes the weather-beaten tars a speech, tells them that their long and happy voyages must now terminate, because there is no more pickled pork and no more rum, and discloses to them a long-hidden secret. They cheer feebly, set the sails once more, turn her head due North, and steer away to that warm, windless, iceless ocean at the North Pole, where all vagrom ships betake themselves at last, and live together in peace and harmony far from the storms of the world.

Which things are an allegory. Ships are but as men. The North Pole ocean is as that hidden deep where dwell the men who have "gone under." They "go under" every day, falling off at each reverse more and more from the paths of honesty. One of them called on me a week ago. I had met him once, and only once, at Oxford, years since. He shook hands with me as with his oldest and best friend; he sat down; he drank my sherry; he called me old fellow; and presently, when he thought my heart was open to the soft influence of pity, he told me his tale, and—borrowed thirty shillings. He went away. Of course, I found that his tale was all a lie. He is welcome to his thirty shillings, with which I have earned the right of shutting my door in the face of a man who has gone under.

Was Frank thinking of all this as he walked through the squares that clear, bright night, among the houses lit up for balls, and the carriages bearing their precious treasures of dainty women? I know not. The thoughts of a man who has but six and sixpence in his pocket, and no bed to go to, are like a child's. They are long, long thoughts. If it is cold and rainy, if he is hungry or ill, he despairs and blasphemes. If it is bright and warm, if he is well-fed and young, he laughs and sings, with a secret, half-felt sinking of the heart, and a looking forward to evil times close at hand.

Along the squares, outside the great houses where the rich, and therefore happy, were dancing and feasting, thinking little enough (why should they?) about the poor, and therefore miserable, outside—beggars came up to Frank. One old man, who looked as if he had been a gentleman, stood in front of him suddenly.

"Give me something," he said, bringing his clenched fists down at his sides in a gesture of despair. "Give me something. I am desperately poor."

Frank put sixpence into his hand and passed on.
"Only six shillings left now," he thought.
Women—those dreadful women, all alike, who belong to certain districts of London, and appear only late at night—begged of him. These women apparently form a class peculiar to themselves. They are neither old nor young. They carry a baby. They are dressed in rusty black. They bear in one hand three boxes of cigar lights. They address you as "good gentleman," and claim to have six starving babies at home, and nothing to put in their mouths. Then the boys with cigar lights ran after him; and then more sturdy beggars, more women, and more boys.

He walked on. It struck ten. Frank's cigar was finished. Just then he passed—it was in one of those dingy, characterless streets, near the great squares—a low-browed, retiring-looking public house. From its doors issued the refrain of a song, the clinking of glasses, and stamping of feet. Frank stopped.

"I've got exactly six shillings," he said. "I may surely have a glass of beer out of that."

He went in and drank his glass. As he drank it, another song, horribly sung, began in the room behind the bar.

"Like to go in, sir?" asked the barmaid. "It's quite full. We hold it every Monday evening."

Frank thought he might as well sit down, and see what was going on—particularly as there appeared to be no charge for admission.

It was a long, low room at the back, filled with about thirty men, chiefly petty tradesmen of the neighbourhood. Every man was smoking a long clay pipe, and had a tumbler before him. Every man was perfectly sober, and wore an air of solemnity exceedingly comic. One of the men—the most solemn and the most comic—occupied the chair. By his right stood a piano, where a pale-faced boy of eighteen or so was playing accompaniments to the songs. A gentleman with a red face and white hair was sitting well back in his chair, holding his pipe straight out before him, chanting with tremendous emphasis and some difficulty—because he was short of breath. This, and not an imperfect education, caused him to accentuate his aspirates more strongly than was actually required:—

"Ho! the ma-hades of me-herry Hengle-land,
How be-hew-ti-ful hare they!"

Q

Somewhat apart from the rest, not at the table—as if he did not belong to them—sat a man of entirely different appearance. He was gorgeously attired in a brown velvet coat and white waistcoat, with a great profusion of gold chain and studs. He was about five-and-forty years of age. His features were highly Jewish, with the full lips and large nose of that Semitic race. His hair, thick and black, lay in massive rolls on an enormous great head—the biggest head, Frank thought, that he had ever seen. In his hand, big in proportion, was a tumbler of iced soda and brandy. He was smoking a cigar, and beating time impatiently on the arm of his chair.

Frank sat modestly beside him, and ordered another glass of beer.

"Know this place, sir?" asked the man with the big head, turning to him.

"Never saw it before," said Frank.

"No more did I. Queer crib, isn't it? I turned in by accident, because I was thirsty. They'll ask you to sing directly. Do, if you can."

The "Maids of Merry England" died away in the last bars which those who were behind time added to the original melody; and the chairman, taking up his tumbler, bowed to the singer, and said solemnly—

"Mr. Pipkin, sir, your health and song."

The company all did the same. Mr. Pipkin wiped his brow, and took a long pull at his gin and water.

"Now," said the chairman, persuasively, "who is going to oblige the company with the next song?"

Dead silence.

"Perhaps one of the visitors"—here he looked at Frank—"will oblige us?"

"If you can sing, do," growled Bighead.

"Really," said Frank, "I am afraid I hardly know any song that would please; but, if you like, I will sing a little thing I made myself once, words and music too."

"Hear, hear!" said the chair. "Silence, if you please, gentlemen, for the gentleman's song. Gentlemen, the gentleman written it himself."

Frank took the place of the pale-cheeked musician, and played his prelude. He was going to sing a song which he made at Cambridge, and used to sing at wines and suppers.

"It's only a very little thing," he said, addressing the

audience generally. "If you don't like it, pray stop me at the first verse. It never had a name."

"There was Kate, with an eye like a hawk;
There was Blanche, with an eye like a fawn;
There was Fanny, as fresh as the rose on its stalk;
And Annie, as bright as the dawn.
There were Polly, and Dolly, and Jessie, and Rose,
They were fair, they were dark, they were short, they were tall;
I changed like a weathercock when the wind blows,
For I loved them all—and I loved them all.

"Like the showers and sunshine of spring,
The quarrels and kisses I had;
Like a forest-bird fledgeling trying its wing,
Is the flight of the heart of a lad.
Oh! Annie and Fanny, and Jessie and Kate,
How love vows perish, and promises fall!
You were all pledged to me, and I wasn't your fate;
But I loved you all—and I loved you all.

"'Twas Annie I kissed in the wood,
And Fanny kissed me in the lane;
But Rosie held out, as a young maiden should,
Till she found I'd not ask her again.
Now they're married, and mothers, and all,
And 'tis Lucy clings close to my breast;
And we never tell her, what we never recall—
For I love my wife—how I loved the rest."

"Bravo!" growled the man with the big head. "Bravo! young fellow. Devilish well sung."

"Sir," said the chairman, "your health and song."

"Don't get up," said Bighead; "sing another. Look here, sing that. Mr. Chairman, the gentleman's going to sing another song."

It was "Adelaïde," that supreme tenor song—the song of songs—that the man handed to Frank. He took it from a portfolio which was standing beside him.

"Yes," he said, nodding, "I'm a sort of professional, and I know a good voice when I hear it. Can you play the accompaniment? If not, I will."

Frank yielded him the seat, and took the music. Yes, he could sing "Adelaïde." But how long since he sang it last! And—ah me!—in what altered circumstances!

But he sang. With all the sweetness and power of his voice he filled the room—laden with the air of so many pipes and reeking tumblers—with the yearnings of passion, which have never found such utterance as in this great song. The honest folk behind their pipes sat in amazement, half comprehending—but only half. The barmaid crept from behind the counter to the door, and listened: when the song was finished, she went back with tears in her eyes, and a throbbing heart. She was not too old to feel the yearning after love. The pale-faced young musician listened till his cheeks glowed and his eyes brightened: the poor boy had dreams beyond his miserable surroundings. The player—the big-headed man—as he played, wagged his head, and shook his curls, and let the tears roll down his great big nose, and drop upon the keys. For Frank, forgetting where he was, and remembering his love, and how he sang that song last to her, poured out his heart into the notes, and sang as one inspired.

"Come with me," said Bighead, seizing him by the arm as soon as he had finished. "Come away. Let us talk, you and I—let us talk."

He dragged him into the street. The clocks were striking twelve.

"Which is your way?"

"Which is yours?" said Frank.

The man moved his fat forefinger slowly round his head in a complete circle.

"All ways," he said. "Let me walk part of your way."

Frank turned to the left. It mattered nothing.

"Are you rich?—you are a gentleman, I see—but are you rich, happy, satisfied, contented, money in your pocket, money in the bank, therefore virtuous and respected?"

"No—I am none of these things."

"Then make yourself all these. Sing for money. Go on the stage. Good God, man!—Giuglini himself had not so sweet a voice. Give me your name and address." Frank hesitated. "Well, then, take mine." He gave him a card. "Will you come and see me? That can do you no harm, you know. Come."

"Candidly," said Frank, "I am looking for employment. But I would rather not sing for money."

"Rubbish! *I've* done it. *I've* sung second basso at the Italian Opera. Not sing for money! Why not? You'd write for money, I suppose? You'd paint for money? Why not sing? Now, come and pay me a visit, and talk it over."

"I must look about first. Are you really serious?"

"Quite. I don't care how it is you've got into a hole—

whether it's money, or what it is. On the boards, nobody cares much."

"You are quite welcome to know everything, so far as I am concerned," said Frank, proudly.

"So much the better. Then no offence. When will you come?"

"I will look for occupation to-morrow. If I don't get it, I will call on you in the afternoon.

"To-morrow. Good. Of course you won't get anything to do. How should you? Nobody ever gets anything to do. Good night, my dear sir. For heaven's sake, take care of your throat. Do wrap it up. Let me lend you a wrapper."

He took a clean red silk handkerchief out of his pocket, unfolded it, and wrapped it round Frank's throat, tenderly and softly. In the eyes of the big-headed man, Frank's voice was a fortune.

"Good heavens! if anything were to happen to an organ like that from exposure! Are you going to smoke again? Then take one of my cigars—they must be better than yours.'

"Mine are good enough, I think," said Frank, laughing, offering him one.

"Let me look—let me look. Yes, they're very fair. Don't smoke too much. And—and—" here he held out his hand—"Good-bye. Good-bye. Mind you come to see me. For heaven's sake, take care."

He strode away, leaving his red silk handkerchief round Frank's neck; and presently Frank heard him hail a Hansom in stentorian tones, and drive off. Then he was left alone, began to feel a little cold, as if the weather had suddenly changed.

CHAPTER THE TWENTY-SIXTH.

HALF-PAST twelve. The air of the streets is close and strifling. The Mall, St. James's Park, is still crowded. No wonder: for the air of the park is fresh, and the moonlight lies soft and bright on the trees. Frank slowly descends the steps at the Duke of York's column, and proceeds to search for a resting-place. All the seats—he counted them as he went along, forty—appear to be full, some of them occupied by men stretched at full length, others by women sitting two and three together. All the way to Buckingham Palace there is not a single chance even of sitting room.

"Very odd," said Frank, returning, "that the same idea should strike all these people as well as myself. What is to be done next?"

The problem solved itself as he came to the next seat, where a man was lying at full length. He suddenly rolled round, and came with a heavy thud on the gravel. Picking himself up, he staggered to where Frank was standing.

"I shay, old f'l'r—don't take that place, be-because it's going round."

Then he disappeared.

Frank sat down, and, stretching his legs on the wood, pulled his hat over his eyes, and tried to go to sleep.

It was of no use. Just as he was dropping off a cab would come by. People talked as they walked past. A breath of the night air touched his cheek, and reminded him, that he was not in bed. Besides, the bench was as hard as a third-class railway carriage. Even to an old campaigner, wood makes a poor substitute for a spring mattress.

"Hang these knots," said Frank, as the clock struck one. "I had no idea that knots were so much harder than common wood."

He shifted his position, and tried to persuade himself that he was getting sleepy.

"Adversity," he murmured, "makes one acquainted with strange beds. The advantage of the situation is, one is not afraid of fleas."

A caterpillar fell upon his nose.

He sat up in disgust.

"Alternative. We may have caterpillars if we lie under a tree, or we may be watered by the fresh dew from Heaven if we take a bench outside a tree. Which shall we do? Let us consider."

He lay back, and fell asleep.

Five minutes after he lost consciousness, he was awakened by something touching his feet. He started up from a dream of soft couches.

"I beg a thousand pardons," said a soft voice. "I thought there was room for two."

The speaker, as the half light of a summer night, not to speak of the gas, showed him, was a tall and rather handsome man of thirty or so, dressed in a frock coat. Frank noticed at once that the heels of his boots, as the lamp shone on them, were worn to the stumps. Further investigation showed that there were no signs of collar or shirt, and that his hat, as he took it off with a polite wave, was limp at the brim. By daylight, what appeared now as glossiness, would have shown as grease; but this it was impossible to tell by the moonlight.

"I dare say there's room for two," said Frank, "if we economize legs."

The stranger gravely took his place, and they divided the space so as to admit of four legs, all rather longer than the average.

"Do you a—often—use this place?" inquired the stranger.

"No," said Frank, with a laugh, half in bitterness. "This is the first time that I have tried the hotel. Perhaps it will not be the last. I find it draughty—exposed, perhaps, in situation. No doubt, extremely healthy."

"Ah!" said the other, with a ready sympathy. "You have, however, let me assure you, the very best bench, for a warm night, in the whole park. Are you sleepy, sir?"

"Not very. Who the devil can sleep here?"

"When you are used to it, it is really not bad for two or three months in the year. If I only had some tobacco, I should be quite comfortable."

"Take a cigar. I've got a few left."

He pulled out his case, and handed it to his newly-made acquaintance.

"A thousand thanks. When I was in the 4th Buffs—you've heard of that regiment?—I used to buy my cigars at Hudson's. I've got to smoke shag now, and can't always get that. A capital cigar. I'm *very* much obliged to you, sir—very—much—obliged—indeed. A very good cigar. If you were to keep them for a year in tea, you would find them ripen better, perhaps. But a very good cigar. I suppose you are——hard up?"

"Yes. Most of the visitors at this caravanserai are, I presume."

"In the service?"

"No."

"Ah! Excuse my impertinence. Well, I had my fling, and here I am. What does it matter to a philosopher?"

A slouching figure came by, apparently clad in the cast-off rags of some field scarecrow. He stopped before Frank's new friend.

"Night, Major."

"Good night to you, Jacob," said the other, with a patronizing air. "Things been going pretty well to-day?"

"No, dam bad. Here's your sixpence, Major."

He handed over the amount in coppers, lay down on the gravel, with his head on his arm, and in a moment was sound asleep, and snoring heavily.

"A humble retainer of mine," said the Major. "A follower, rather than a servant. Poor, as you see, but faithful. He does odd jobs for me, and I keep him going. Not a gentleman, you observe."

Frank laughed silently.

"It's a glorious thing, a good fling," said the Major. "Though it's ten years since I had mine, and it only lasted two years, I remember every day of it. You remember Kitty Nelaton, of the Adelphi?"

"No. Never had the pleasure of her acquaintance."

"A splendid woman. That, of course, was allowed. I took her, sir, from the Duke of Brentwood. His Grace nearly went mad with rage. Ah, I think I see myself now, tooling down to Richmond the loveliest pair of grays, I suppose, that ever were seen. But she was so devilish expensive. And I had a good year, too: got on the right thing for the Derby, landed at Ascot and Goodwood, and didn't do badly at Newmarket. Shall I tell you the story of my misfortunes?"

"Do," said Frank—"if it will not bore you."

"Not at all. It's a pleasure to talk to a gentleman; and besides, this is a capital cigar. It's ten years ago. Some of the other men have gone to grief, too; so that I'm not without companions. We meet sometimes, and have a talk over old times. Odd thing life is. If I could put all my experiences in a book, sir, by gad you'd be astonished. The revelations I could make about paper, for instance; the little transactions in horse-flesh—eh? and other kinds of——"

"I beg your pardon," said Frank, who had dropped off to sleep, and was awakened by his head nearly nodding him off the bench. "You were saying——"

"Let me begin at the beginning," said the Major, sucking his cigar, and beginning his story with the relish that "unfortunate" men always manifest in relating their misadventures "I was the second son of a Norfolk baronet. Of course, as the second son, I had not much to look for from the family estate. However, I entered the army, and at once became—I may say, deservedly—the most popular man in the regiment. This was owing partly, perhaps, to my personal good looks, partly to a certain superiority of breeding which my family was ever remarkable for. Then, I was the best actor, the best billiard-player, the best cricketer, the smartest officer in the whole garrison. This naturally led to certain successes which it would be sham modesty, at this lapse of time, to ignore. Do not you think so?"

"Humph—gr—umph," was Frank's reply.

He was sound asleep, and the rest of the Major's revelations were consequently not wanted. From the thrilling interest of the commencement, it may be conjectured that no greater misfortune could happen to the British public than Frank's collapse. But he was a very unlucky man at this juncture of his fortunes.

He slept two or three hours. He was awakened by a pressure at the chest.

He started up, and just had time to grip the wrist of the respectable Mr. Jacob as that worthy was abstracting his watch and chain. Frank was strong as well as young. Jacob was neither young nor strong. Consequently, in less time than it takes to write this line, the watch and chain were back in their owner's pocket, and the luckless Jacob was despatched with many kicks and a little strong language.

The Major was gone.

Frank rubbed his eyes, and sat down again. It was past four, broad daylight, and the sun had risen, as the gilded clock-tower plainly showed.

"Where's the Major?" thought Frank. "Did I dream? Was there a Major, or was it a nightmare? He began to tell me a story about somebody—Kitty somebody. I wonder if the six shillings are safe. Yes—here they are. What the deuce am I to do now?"

A lovely morning: a sweet, delicious air. London fresh and bright, as if night had cleaned it and swept it.

He got up, refreshed by his light sleep, and strolled down the silent avenue. On his right lay the sleepers upon the benches: poor bundles of rags, mostly; here and there, a woman with a baby: sometimes a girl, pale-faced and emaciated—perhaps a poor shirtmaker, starving in spite of virtue, because virtue, though it brings its own reward, does not always suffer that reward to take the form of a negotiable currency; sometimes a poor creature with cheeks that had once been fair, and had lately been painted—because vice though it sometimes brings sacks full of money with it, has a trick of running away with all of it in surprising and unexpected ways.

Frank stopped, and looked at one of them. She half opened her eyes. He listened. She murmured, "I shan't move on," and then went to sleep again. A few poor remains of finery were on her; a few tags of ribbon; a displaced chignon; a bonnet that had once been flaunting; little brodequins that had once been neat and pretty; a silk dress that had once not been discoloured and bespattered with street mud. Frank was touched with pity. He stooped over her, and spoke to her. She awoke, started up, and smiled—a horrid, ghastly smile, the memory of which haunted him afterwards.

"Why do you sleep here?" he asked, a foolish question, because there could be only one reason.

"Because I've got no money."

"What do you do in the day?"

"I hide. I come out at night, like the bats." She laughed discordantly. "Give me something, if you have anything."

"I've got six shillings. There are two for you."

"You're a good sort."

She pulled herself together, and got off the seat yawning.

"You had better finish your sleep."

"I have finished. I'm too hungry to sleep any longer. Now I shall go and buy something to eat. I must wake up my sister first, though."

She went and shook a figure in black stuff, without a chignon, who lay on the next bench. A woman about thirty—pale, thin, uncomely, long-suffering.

"Yes," said the first woman, "you see us both. Tilly was the good one. I'm the bad one. Good or bad, it makes no difference. We've got to starve all the same."

Frank shuddered. Is there nothing, then, in virtue? Can nothing ward off the evils of fate? Is there no power in self-denial, in bitter privation, to change remorseless circumstances, to stave off the miseries allotted by $ἀνάγκη$?

"Good or bad," she repeated, "it's all the same. Just as I told her ten years ago, when I was Kitty Nelaton, and she——"

"Good heavens! Am I dreaming?" said Frank, putting his hand to his head.

"Yes, Kitty Nelaton, of the Adelphi; and she was Tilly Jones the shirtmaker. And here we are, you see. Come Tilly, my dear."

"Stop," said Frank. "I've got four shillings more. Take two of them. I've got a watch and chain that I shall pawn by and by. Don't say there's no difference between good and bad. Don't, for God's sake, Kitty!"

The tears stood in his eyes.

"I told you so," said the other woman, in a dull, pathetic way. "I always told you so."

The enthusiasm of virtue had long since been crushed out of her by dire penury; but now that nothing else was possible, the habit of preaching virtue remained; and, like many preachers, who have small faith or none in their own creeds, she went on in the same old strain, repeating dead words to lifeless ears.

But they took the money, and went away. Frank noticed how they crawled like a pair of old women. But the elder to appearance, the younger in reality by five or six years, was the poor worn-out shirtmaker.

"Let me get out of this place," said Frank. "I should go mad if I came here another night."

It was at the time when the Embankment was building but not quite finished. Frank went down to the grand old river, which was at high tide, and saw—in the clear, bright air of early dawn, when the black pall of smoke over London lifts and is driven away, only to come back again when men rise from their beds—the towers and spires of the mighty city standing out against the blue sky of the morning.

He communed with himself. In that bright air, it was impossible to feel unhappy. At the age of five-and-twenty, it is impossible not to see hope in everything. Besides, there was literally nothing that he could reproach himself with. His life had been blameless. If we are to go by sins, Frank had none;—I speak as a layman. If we are to go by aims and hopes, Frank's were pure and lofty;—I speak as a layman. If to desire only what is good and right be in itself good and right, then was Frank, at this moment, one of the best of God's creatures. Perhaps I speak as a fool, but indeed I think he was. To few is it given to be so singlehearted and so pure. One sorrow he had, and one hope. That his father's name should be tarnished, was his sorrow. To wipe out the stain, and at the same time to win his love, was his hope.

But how?

He thought of the man with the big head, who wanted to employ him. This was clearly not the way to get large sums of money, or a great name. But yet—not yet. Two shillings in money—now that Kitty and Tilly were provided with the means of getting through the day—was all that he had in his pocket. Besides this, a silver watch and a chain, which might together fetch five pounds at a pawnbroker's.

It struck six.

"I'm hungry," said Frank, "and I'm dirty. Both are disagreeable things."

He left the Embankment, went up into the Strand, and had a cup of coffee and a piece of bread—giving twopence to the waiter, like a good Samaritan. The waiter had never had so much money presented to him, in the way of his calling, in all his life before. But instead of showing gratitude, he ran away to an inner apartment, for fear it might be a mistake.

Then he went to the old Roman bath, where he had a plunge in the coldest water in the world, south of the Arctic pole, and came out glowing and strong.

It was only half-past six, so he went back to the Embankment, and smoked a cigar, thinking what he should do next.

"Time goes very slowly for poor people," he reflected, "That, I suppose, is a compensation to them, because it flies so swiftly for the rich."

CHAPTER THE TWENTY-SEVENTH.

"PAVING-STONES come to feel hard after walking about on them for twenty-four hours or so, no doubt." Frank said to himself as he strolled along the Embankment, looking in vain for a seat. A policeman passed him. "Now, who would be a bobby?" he thought. "An awful time of it they must have. Yet I might put on the blue. I suppose I could procure a nomination. I might come down to that, and yet be—— No; a gentleman drives a Hansom, or he enlists as a soldier, but nobody ever heard of a gentleman in the police force. Officers, it is true; but even a metropolitan magistrate has never yet complimented them on their gentlemanlike demeanour in the box. Prejudices are queer things. I confess—though I haven't many left— I have an objection to the force. Francis Melliship you must really aim higher than the police force."

He pulled out his watch. It had stopped at half-past six. The key was at Islington. He looked up at the clock tower. It was a quarter to nine.

"A quarter to nine. I am getting hungry again. Remarkable thing. I do not remember being hungry before 9 a.m. since I left school. My appetite is becoming serious and embarrassing. 'The wind,' as the old French proverb very prettily says, though King David and Sterne generally get the credit of it, ' is tempered to the shorn lamb.' My experience is, that his appetite does not suit itself to his circumstances. Hang it, I must have some breakfast, and as well now as in an hour's time."

He walked through the Temple into Fleet-street. In the window of a modest-looking coffee-house, an impracticable china teapot, surrounded by freshly cut chops and rashers of ham, gave notice to hungry men that breakfast was to be had within.

Frank took a seat in a box near the door, and ordered his meal; ate it with the greatest relish, and wondered if Dick Mortiboy was up, and whether he would be surprised if his cousin failed to keep his appointment with him.

Then he took up that wonderful chronicle, the advertisement sheet of the *Times*. Order in disorder, if you happen to know where to look for things. Frank did not; so he looked at every page but the right before his eyes caught the columns of Wanteds and Want Places. He read the list—the contents of which everybody knows perfectly well, because it never alters—with the curiosity of one interested. He was struck, of course, with that coincidence of people advertising for a place in terms that exactly suit the apparent requirements of people advertising for a person. Everybody has noticed this peculiarity, and novelists have made the most of it.

"Why don't they read this paper, apply for the vacant places, and save their money?" was his reflection.

Any number of cooks and clerks were wanted by advertisers; any number of "gentlemen," possessed of every possible qualification, advertised for employment for time, capital, or both.

There was not in the list one advertisement which seemed to fit his case. Stay, there was one—a secretary was wanted for an established public company. "A knowledge of the Fine Arts absolutely requisite. Preference will be given to a graduate of Oxford or Cambridge." Frank wrote down the address in his pocket-book. It was an Agency; and Frank Melliship had neither heard nor read, nor learned from experience, that of all the humbugs in a city full of them, Agencies of all sorts are the greatest humbugs. And the very cream of these swindles are Agencies that rob those poor wretches who, having tried every other method of getting employment, as a last resource enter one of these spiders' dens. I will give an example of their common method of procedure, which is representative. I will take a Servants' Agency to serve my purpose.

Here is a copy of an advertisement from the *Times*. You may see one similarly catching any day and every day:—

GENERAL SERVANT. Is a good PLAIN COOK. Has no objection to undertake washing. Fond of children. Age 24. From the country. Clean, active, willing, and obliging. Waits well at table. 8½ years' excellent character. Wages £9.—"Mary," Mrs. ——,—— Street.

This advertisement appears in the *Times*, the *Telegraph*, and the *Standard* on the same day. The advertisements cost—say fourteen shillings altogether.

Now, how many poor innocent ladies do you think apply to Mrs. —— for that domestic treasure?—poor women who have large families and little means: who can only afford to keep one servant; and perhaps, ever since they were first married, have been wanting that clean, willing, country girl who will cook the dinner and nurse the children, and all well for nine pounds a year, and have never found her. How many? I should not like to say.

Do you think there ever was such a "Mary"?

Never.

Apply to the advertiser. You may write to her, or go and see her. If the latter, she will smile affably, and tell you—what she will tell you in a letter, if you write to her—that it is most unfortunate, because somebody else has just engaged that particular "Mary." On payment, however, of a fee of half a crown, your name may be placed on the books of the Agency, and you will, doubtless—say in a week or two—be rewarded by having just such another phœnix of domestic servants transferred to your own kitchen.

Transparent traps to catch half-crowns. The sun shines through ruses so clumsy. Very likely. But people won't see it. A proportion of the applicants—large enough to make the game at least remunerative—pay their half-crown in the certain assurance of getting a Mary exactly like the one who was so unfortunately ravished from their grasp. Of course, they never got her. Then the fool-trap is baited afresh.

Now, multiply Mrs.——'s humble half-crown by eight. That makes a sovereign. The fee is one sovereign. Divide the number of applicants by any numeral you think will give you the truth as the result of this sum in simple division, and you will know how much Mr.——, who flies at higher game, gets by his profession of not finding places for secretaries, clerks, ushers, and the rest, who want employment in this great city; always remembering that his most frequent quarry is the broken man who knows neither trade nor profession, but must have a gentlemanlike occupation: men who, like young Frank Melliship, are ruined; but who, unlike him, have no friend. Hundreds of these men have given a sovereign out of their 0 last two or three to the Agent, and received in return— 0.

To find these men who want work and can't get it, who deserve well—yet, asking bread, receive stones: here is a field for charity!

Now let us return to Frank Melliship.

I have not called him the hero of my story, because he has done nothing heroic—because he seems to stand in the way of his own success; and with that noble object he has in view, to be wasting precious time only to earn an indifferent living.

Why does he not apply to John Heathcote? Why will he not be helped by his superlatively rich cousin, Dick Mortiboy?

I will tell you why, for I want to paint him as he was. It was a point of pride: determination to show his independence of all those who, as he thought, ought to have saved his father from ruin, madness, and death.

"I will do without them. The world is wide. Energy overcomes all difficulties. 'Labor omnia vincit.'"

Boys' copybook rubbish. It does not. "Res omnia vincit." It is capital that conquers all things, from a kingdom up to a woman.

"To London and to Art." He had come to town something of an enthusiast. Where Art left him, we have seen. Was this the fault of Art? No.

He wanted long education and years of patient toil to paint even moderately well. This he did not know, and nobody but Kate had ever told him so.

Let us do him justice. He never thought himself a genius; but he believed in his energy, in his determination to succeed, and thought some way would be found by himself. He did not want to be shown the way, or to be helped by any friend of his prosperous days. His desire to be independent, and work his own way, was a sort of vanity; but it is not uncommon. I know a rich man who would rather *earn* a single guinea than that the goddess of Good Luck should shower a hundred into his pocket from the clouds. This was Frank's state of mind too.

He had made an entry of the address of the Agency in his pocket-book, and called the waiter to him; when the thought flashed across his mind that he had forgotten, when he ordered his breakfast, the emptiness of his pocket. He explained his predicament to the waiter, and offered to leave his watch with the proprietor. It was, he said, the only thing of value he had about him, except the guard.

The man saw he was a gentleman, and begged him not to trouble about the matter, but pay him any day when he was passing.

"It is the easiest thing in the world," thought Frank, "for a man who always has had money in his pocket, to walk into a shop and quite forget he has none."

He came to a pawnbroker's, and he thought he had better pawn his watch and chain at once. He must have some money.

There was a shop window full of plate and jewellery; in a side-street was an open door-way, revealing a row of little doors. Frank guessed what these cabinets were, but he was some few minutes before he could make up his mind to go in. He looked at the costly things in the window—he walked past the door-way; at last, looking cautiously up the street and down the street, as if he were about to commit a burglary, and was afraid of the policeman who might be round the corner, he plunged into one of the little boxes, falling over an old woman who was haggling with the shopman for sixpence more than she had got last time on a pair of sheets.

Frank flushed in his confusion, apologized, and tried the next cabinet. This was empty; and here, trying to look as if he had often done it before, he put down his watch and chain on the counter with the grace of a roué, and waited his turn.

The man examined his watch, asked if it was in going order, weighed his chain, and smiled as he leered at him through his spectacles.

Frank, despite his efforts, looked so completely innocent.

"How much?"

Frank hesitated before he answered.

"How much will you lend me?"

"Tell me how much you want?"

"Well, a fiver."

"All right. These aint been in before, young gentleman."

"How do you know?" asked Frank, blushing, and very much ashamed of the transaction he was engaged in.

"We've got a private mark in the trade we put on everything that comes in," said the man; and Frank believed him.

He began to write out the ticket.

"What name?"

"Must I give it?"

"Not unless you like. Any name 'll do. Mr. Smith, of Piccadilly, it generally is. Will that do?"

Frank nodded.

"Got fourpence? For the ticket, you know."

The poor boy blushed scarlet.

R

"All right, my lad: there you are. Four"—he dashed down the sovereigns—"nineteen, eight."

Frank put the money and the ticket in his pocket, and went back to pay for his breakfast.

Then he made his way to the Agency.

The proprietor had not come, but his clerk told Frank he had a very good list of appointments "suitable for any gentleman to take."

Frank was very glad to hear this, and asked for some particulars about the secretaryship advertised.

"Our fee for entering a name is a sovereign—over a hundred and fifty a year—half a sovereign under it. This secretaryship is three hundred. Fine Arts Company (Limited). The governor's in it, and it'll soon be got up."

To the credit of Frank Melliship's common sense, I record the fact that he did not pay the sovereign, but asked the fellow what they meant by their advertisement. He had a copy of it in his book, and he read it out.

The clerk was evidently of an irritable temperament. Perhaps they often had a row in the office. He was rude to Frank. He turned on his heel, and left the counter, with the words—

"P'raps you know gentlemen as hasn't got a sovereign. Coming here, wasting our time and kicking up a row!"

The being was too contemptible to thrash, but his remark opened Frank's eyes to the position of things. That such a little cad dared insult him!

He turned into a bye-street, and looked for a quiet corner where he could sit down and curse fate. There was none. So he cursed fate as he walked along.

After walking for half an hour or so, he began to pull himself together.

"Swearing will not help, at any rate. Something must be done, and that soon. I believe I am getting hungry again. What a misfortune to have such a twist. Poverty may be invigorating, but it's unpleasant. I don't think I'm strong enough to take the medicine. As for taking money from Dick, that, of course, is out of the question."

He was walking along a West-end street, and saw at a door a brass plate, with "University and Scholastic Agency" upon it.

"Let us try the schools. Perhaps they won't ask for a sovereign," he said, and went in.

They did not. The agent, a man of extremely affable and polished manners, invited Frank to sit down, and asked him what he could do.

"Tell me candidly. I've got plenty of places."

"I've taken a Poll degree at Cambridge. I know very little Latin or Greek, and no mathematics."

"Bad," said the agent. "Any French?"

"Oh, French—of course. And—and I can paint and draw."

"A good cricketer? Anything of an oar?"

"Yes—rowed five in the first college boat. Played in the college eleven."

"My dear sir, a public school will be delighted to have you. They don't care, you see, about their junior masters being great scholars, because they have found out that any one can teach the boys their Delectus. But they do want athletics. You'd be worth your weight in gold to a head master. Sit down at that table, and put down all you can do. First-class Poll, I think you said."

"No—last. I just scraped through."

"Well, never mind. Sit down and write."

"So"—he read over Frank's modest list of accomplishments —"I will find—it is now July the 10th—before the vacations are over, a really good opening for you."

"But I've had no experience in teaching."

"What does that matter? Look at your experience in the field and on the river. Give me your address."

"I must find one first. I am—I am looking for lodgings; but I will send it you as soon as possible."

He came out of the office with a lightened heart. Something would be got: something unpleasant, naturally—because the order of things allots all unpleasant things to poor men—but still, the means of life. In a few minutes he was perfectly happy in his new prospects—just as a drowning man is happy to find a plank even if he is in mid-ocean, with no ship in sight.

Then, a sudden reflection dashed his pleasure. He was to have his new post when the summer vacation was over. How was he to live till then? If on his wardrobe, there would be no possibility of presenting a respectable exterior; and his watch and chain would not go very far.

He put his hand into his empty pocket, and pulled out the card which he had taken from the Jewish gentleman the night before.

"By Jove! it's Bighead's card. I'll go and see him."

It bore the name of Mr. Emmanuel Leweson, and an address in Brunswick Square.

Thither Frank bent his steps, tired and fagged with the long walking about he had had. A cab, of course, was not to be thought of.

He sent in his card—Mr. Leweson was at home—and in a few minutes he found himself again in the presence of his acquaintance of the evening before.

Mr. Leweson looked more big-headed than ever, sitting over a late breakfast—it was half-past twelve—in a light dressing-gown. He had been breakfasting luxuriously. The table was covered with fruit and flowers. He was drinking Rhine wine from a long flask.

"Come in, Mr. Melliship—since that is your name. I am glad to see you—very glad. Take a glass of wine, and sit down. And now," he said, finishing his breakfast, and lighting a cigar, "let us talk business. Tell me as much as you like about yourself, Mr. Melliship. The more the better."

Frank told him as much as he thought advisable.

"So—no money; expensive tastes; habits of a gentleman; no special knowledge; art and music. Now, Mr. Melliship, do you know what I am?"

"No; something theatrical, I should say."

"That is because I wear a velvet coat, and breakfast off fruit and Rhine wine, I suppose? No. You are not far wrong, however. I am a musical composer by nature; the owner and manager of a London music hall by will of a malignant fate. Yes, young man—in me you see the manager of the North London Palace of Amusements."

He waved his hand as he spoke, as if deprecating the other's contempt.

"I know, I know. They sing, 'Rollicking Rams' and 'Champagne Charlie'—not a bad air, that last—and we are altogether a degraded and degrading place. But we must pay, dear sir, we must pay. I do more than the rest of them, because I always try to get something good. For instance, I've got you."

"I don't know that you have," said Frank, laughing. The big-headed man amused him tremendously.

"You will come and sing three songs every evening—allowing yourself to be encored for one only, because time is precious. You will thus gain confidence, as well as three guineas a week. I intend to push you, and we shall have you on the boards of the Royal Italian before many years. Then you will remember with gratitude that I brought you out."

"Do I understand you to offer me—"

"Do you want pen, ink and paper? Have I not said it? Ask the people at the music hall if Leweson's word is not as good as any other man's bond. Will you accept?"

"Don't ask me to sing under my own name."

"Sing in any name you like—only sing for me."

"Very well, then."

Mr. Leweson held out his hand, and shook Frank's by way of ratifying the bargain.

"And now come with me," he said, "and we will pay a visit to the Palace. A poor place, after all; but the people go there, the idiotic, stupid people. Would you believe that I brought out the music of my opera there, and they hissed it? Then I engaged the Inexpressible Jones, placarded all London, gave them, 'Rollicking Rams' and the rest of it, and the people all came back again. Dolts, asses, idiots, loonatics!"

He banged his head with his fist at every epithet, and then put on his hat—an enormous brigand's hat—with a scowl of revenge and hatred. Then he burst out laughing, and led the way out.

They took a Hansom from the stand.

"How I wish you could do trapeze business," said Mr. Leweson. "I suppose you can't, by any chance?"

"No—I'm afraid not."

"You could act so well with Giulia. The poor girl has only got her father and little Joe to fall back on. It would tell immensely if we could put you in. The talented Silvani family. Signor Pietro Silvani, Signor Francesco, and the Divine Giulia. A brilliant idea just occurred to me—a combination of three. The Signor at the bottom, with rings instead of a bar; you on his shoulders; Giulia on yours. Giulia is left at the first trapeze; you at the second; the undaunted head of the family goes on to the last. Bless you, Giulia wouldn't be afraid! She's afraid of nothing, that girl. But there, if you can't do it, you can't, of course. After all, it might spoil your career as a tenor. Don't let us think of it. Where do you live?"

Frank turned red.

"I'm looking for lodgings now."

"Oh! Well, then, the best thing I can do is to send you

to Mrs. Skimp's. She's cheap, and tolerably good. Here we are, sir, at the Palace, where every evening the British public may receive, at the ridiculous price of one shilling, the highest form of amusement compatible with their state of civilization. Here's the stage door. That is your door. I am busy to-day, and cannot give you any more time. Take my card, and show it to Mrs. Skimp. That will do for an introduction ; and for the present, at least, you can stay there. And come round here to morrow at one. Good-bye. Take care of your throat."

CHAPTER THE TWENTY-EIGHTH.

AFTER their dinner together at Dick Mortiboy's hotel, before he bade his cousin good-night, Frank promised to breakfast with him the next day.

The morning came. Breakfast was on the table, Dick was waiting; but no Frank arrived. So as young Ready-money—as the Market Basing people began to call him—never in his life had stood on much ceremony of any kind, he ate a very substantial breakfast without his guest; felt a little vexed that the cutlets were cold: wondered where Frank was, and why he did not come; and, finally, strolled into the smoking-room, and lighted his cigar.

He had scarcely drawn a dozen whiffs of smoke, when the waiter brought up a card on a silver tray.

"By Jove! here he is; but breakfast's done with." And without looking at the card, he said, "Show the gentleman up, and order some more breakfast."

But the card was not Frank's. It bore the name of Alcide Lafleur.

Let me say a word about Dick Mortiboy's partner.

All this time, what has Alcide Lafleur been doing ? What of the System, the infallible method of breaking banks, to follow up which was the primary object of the partners' return to the old country ? Dick, not unmindful of his pledge, very shortly after his accession to fortune, made over to Lafleur the five thousand he had promised him. He did not consider himself so bound by the terms of that old oath of his, which we have recorded, as to make an immediate division of his property into two halves, and to give Lafleur one; but he did consider himself bound, in a general way, to abide by him till their partnership was dissolved by mutual consent. Meantime, Lafleur seemed in no hurry to test his System: he stayed in London, drawing on Dick occasionally for small sums, and keeping the five thousand intact for the Hombourg expedition. Certain small dabblings he made at écarté, hazard, loo, and such games of chance as were to be found in London circles, just to keep his hand in; but his main business was to pore over his calculations, day after day, in order to reduce his method to a mathematical certainty. Lafleur, a cool, clear-headed man, studied, as soon as he found it likely to help him, the Science of Probabilities. It helped him to the extent of furnishing him with an inexhaustible supply of figures and calculations; and it strengthened, so far as he could see, the chances of the System he had perfected.

His System was to him what his model is to an inventor. It had grown up with years of steady play and unsteady fortunes. The idea of it came into his head when Dick and he were engaged in blockade running, and used to while away their leisure hours in a little game on the after-deck, while the crew were having their little games in the forecastle. It took root and grew slowly, taking form as it grew, till, to the inventor's eyes, it seemed absolutely perfect and consistent. No run of luck, he thought, would stand against it. With a capital of £5,000, so as to meet the very worst contingencies, it was so certain to win, that he could defy fortune. He had made one or two little ventures with it in America, before they came over, with perfect success; and then, having that kind of love for it which makes a man shrink from using his invention till the day of experiment comes, he postponed considerable operations till he could use it at the Hombourg tables. He was like an aëronaut with a new machine. He looked at it, examined it, admired it, ornamented it, boasted of it, but put off the day of its trial, which would be either his death or his glory. Dick provided him with money for his personal expenditure, so that the five thousand remained intact. For himself, Lafleur wanted comparatively little. He was not a man of expensive tastes. He drank, but apparently without great enjoyment, and never so as to produce any effect on his head. He smoked, but in great moderation, and only light cigarettes. He loved to dress well—but this was necessary for a gentleman in his line of life. And he liked to have the reputation of doing certain things well— with which object, he might have been seen practising with a pistol in a gallery, or fencing with a professional: this also with a view to certain contingencies.

He was so perfectly confident of his System—so thoroughly reliant on its power of breaking any bank ever started, however rich—that he did not, at this time, regard his old partner's altered position with either envy or distrust. Dick had kept his word by him honestly, as he always did—Dick's word being quite as good as any other man's oath. The money which he wanted for the System, on the possession of which he based all his calculations, was in his hands. So far, all was well. With this capital, he asked no more. Lafleur, at this time, was no vulgar and greedy adventurer, eager to get money anyhow. From this he was saved by belief in his System. All he wanted was the means of applying it. To get the means he was, of course, prepared—as we have already seen—to do anything, everything. Having the means, he desired only to bring his calculations to practical uses, and, after fleecing the bankers in a perfectly legitimate way, to settle down somewhere or other—say in Paris. He had not the delight in roving and wild scenes that his partner had. No coward, he shrank from that kind of life where personal conflicts are common. This dislike to rough-and-tumble fights —common enough among Frenchmen, was atoned for by his perfect readiness to fight with pistols or sword. Dick was ready, on the other hand, with either fist or weapon. The partnership between them had been at all times true, but at no time cordial—at least, on Lafleur's part. He admired the man who feared nothing and braved everything. He respected his pluck, his determination, his wilfulness, the way in which he forced his own way on people. What he disliked was a certain *brutalité* in his partner—a coarseness, he thought, of fibre—a want of delicacy in taste. He liked to dress carefully. Dick dressed anyhow—with a certain splendour when in funds. Lafleur liked to live fastidiously. Dick cared little what he ate and drank, provided the meat was in plenty, and the liquor strong, and in plenty too. A great beefsteak, and a pot of foaming stout—these represented to Lafleur his partner's tastes, to which he was himself so immensely superior. Dick, on the other hand, could not but feel some pity—a little mingled with contempt—for a man so slightly built, so singularly useless in a row. At the same time, he admired his dexterity at all games of chance, and the calm way in which he met the strokes of fortune.

A well-matched pair, so far as each supplemented certain deficiencies in the other: an ill-matched pair, because they had no kind of sympathy with each other: a partnership of a brace of penniless adventurers, determined to live on the world as best they might: a society which held together by the bonds of habit of long use, and the fact that each entirely trusted in the honesty of his companion—Dick because he was loyal, Lafleur because he was sagacious.

But now there was a feeling growing up in both men's minds that the partnership was to come to an end, and each be free to go his own way. How the separation was to take place, which of the two was to introduce the subject, neither knew. Dick, for his part—resolved Lafleur should no longer be associated with him in the new life he was to lead—was prepared to make almost any sacrifice to break off the connection. Lafleur, on the other hand, was equally ready to go, on no conditions whatever. He had the System, and the capital to start with.

They met, therefore, when Dick went up to town, on a new footing. Men have been divided into rooks and pigeons —borrowers and lenders—sharks, and prey for sharks. But there is a third and a very important class : the class of those who defend their own. As strong as the beasts and birds of prey, they are braver, because they are backed up by law and public opinion. It was to this class that Dick Mortiboy belonged now : Lafleur still to the camp which he had deserted. It is true that Dick half regretted the old days of excitement and peril, when they talked only to contrive new dodges, and went about to execute them. What he really missed, and would have recalled, was the wild freedom of the old life, not its antagonism to society. Conventionality, not mankind, was his enemy. This he hated, and it weighed upon him like a thick blanket on a summer's night.

Lafleur came into the room. Dick held out his hand.

His partner sat down. With the cold smile that always played about his pale face, he asked—

"When are we going to Hombourg ?"

"I don't know. I don't think I shall go at all."

"You were half engaged to go with me," said Lafleur, reproachfully. "But, of course, if you cannot come— Is your cousin with you still ?"

"No. I am waiting for him. You have been trying the System again ?"

"Dick, it is perfect." His face had a pallid enthusiasm when he spoke of his invention. "I have studied it so long that I know every combination the chances can take. I must win. I cannot help it. I am almost sorry I had so much money from you, because I really shall not want it all. My capital is too big."

"Still—still— You know, luck may go so as no mortal capital ever held can stand against it. Remember that night when we were cleaned out at St. Louis."

"It may—of course it may. But it never does. At whist, you *may* hold thirteen trumps, if you are dealing. But who ever does? No man in his senses ever contemplates a hand like that. The night at St. Louis was a bad one, I admit. It was before my System was completed, though, or else we should— No—no, we had no capital then. But I've counted every reasonable combination, Dick, everything I ever *saw* happen—and you'll admit that I've seen a good deal—I've played countless games on paper, and I've always won. Come over with me, and see me break the banks, one after the other. By heaven, Dick, I shall be far richer than you?"

"I should like to go. But, no—I think I had better not leave my own place just now. But there, you don't understand the position of things."

"I understand," said Lafleur, "that the position of Mr. Dick Mortiboy is considerably altered for the better. I suppose—But, Dick, really I did not think you would have been so quick in throwing over old friends."

"I have thrown over no old friends. Did I not honestly redeem my word, and hand you the capital you asked for?"

"You did. That is not quite all, though. Did we not discuss the System all the way across the Atlantic? Were you not as keen as I about it? Who but you thought of coming over to England? Why did we come? To get out of your father this very sum—not to hand over to me, Dick, but to enable us to go away together, and break the banks in our old partnership. And now, when all is gained, you care nothing about it. Is it what I expected from you, Dick? I counted on your seeing my victories as much as on making them."

This was true. He wanted Dick's admiration and praise. He wanted to feel a man's envy.

"Because, you see," answered his partner, "a good deal more is gained than we bargained for. I no longer care to gamble. What does it mean if you care nothing about winning or losing? Upon my word, Lafleur, I would almost as soon, if it were not for the habit of the thing, dance a waltz without any music as play at cards without caring to win. Life when you're rich is quite a different sort of thing to what we experienced in the old days. It's slower, to begin with. You find that everybody is your friend, in the second place. Then you discover that instead of looking about to do good to yourself, you've got to fuss and worry about doing good to other people."

"Fancy Dick Mortiboy doing good to anybody!"

"Queer, isn't it? But true. They tell me I'm doing good, so I suppose I am. Then, after all, you can't eat and drink more than a certain amount. You don't want to have more than a dogcart and a riding-horse. You can't be always giving dinners and things. What are you to do with your money? You've always got the missionaries left, to be sure; but you're an ass if you give them anything."

"By Jove—I should think so, indeed!" said Lafleur.

"Then what are you to do with yourself and your money? I make a few bets, but I don't care much about it. I play a game of billiards, but it doesn't matter whether I win or lose. Life's lost its excitements, Lafleur. The old days are gone."

"In England, you can always go on the turf. There is plenty of money to be lost there."

"I never cared much about horse-races, unless I was riding in them myself. I daresay I shall go on the turf, though, for a little excitement. I don't know what I shall do, Lafleur. When life becomes insupportable, I shall go across the water again, I think, and stay till I am tired of that, and want a change. But as for cards—why, what excitement is equal to that of playing for your very dinner, as we have done before now? How can one get up any pleasure in a game when it does not really signify how it ends?"

"You always think of the end. But think of the play, Dick. Think of working out your own plan, and going down with it, and fleecing everybody—eh? Is there no excitement there?"

"There would be if I wanted the money. Not now. I never cared to win from those who couldn't afford to lose, Lafleur."

"I know. You were always soft-hearted, Dick. Now, if a man plays with me, I play to win. It is his look-out whether he can afford to pay or not. I play to win. I've got no more feeling, Dick, over cards than the green table itself."

The candour of this admission of Lafleur's was equalled by its truth.

Dick sighed, and leaned his head upon his hand.

"By Jove, they were good times, some of them. Do you remember that very day, after the St. Louis cleaning out, how we woke up in the morning without a cent between us?"

Lafleur nodded. Some reminiscences of Dick's were unpleasant. But he seemed warming back to his old tone, and Lafleur wanted to take him over to Hombourg with him.

"You went to the billiard-rooms. I went to the Monty Saloon. And when we met again in the evening we had got six hundred dollars. That was the day when I fought the Peruvian. It was a near thing. I'll never fight a duel blindfolded again. I thought I heard his steps, and I let fly. He had it in the right arm—broke the bone. Then he fired with the left hand—being a blood-thirsty rascal—and hit Cæsar, the black waiter, in the calf. I remember how we laughed. Then we went on to Cairo. Upon my word, Lafleur, when I think of those days, my blood boils. All fair play, too. Every man trying to cheat his neighbour. Good, honest gambling, with a bowie knife ready at your neck."

"All fair play," echoed Lafleur, with the faintest smile on his lips.

"It was better than the blockade running, after all; though there were some very pretty days in that. It was better than —I say, after all, don't you think the best moment of our lives was when we stood on board the little schooner, dripping wet, after our swim from the reef of Palmiste?"

At another time, Lafleur would have resented this recollection of an extremely disagreeable episode in his life. Now he laughed.

"Yes," he said, "perhaps it was a moment 'of relief, after a *mauvais quart d'heure*. It was then that we swore our partnership."

"It was," said Dick. "We've kept to our terms ever since. Lafleur, the time has come for our separation. I can no longer lead the old life. All that is done with. We are adventurers no more. I have my fortune; you possess your capital and— your System."

"I shall soon be as rich as you with it," said Lafluer, confidently.

"We are partners no longer, then? It is dissolved, Lafleur. I've got the best of it; but don't say Dick Mortiboy ever turned his back upon a friend. If you have not money enough, let me know. Take more."

"I have plenty. I cannot fail. It is impossible. But I want you to come to Hombourg with me. See me succeed, Dick—see me triumph with my System. That is all I ask."

"I will see," said Dick. "I will not promise to go with you. Twelve years, Lafleur, we have fought our battles side by side. I remember the words of my oath to you as well as if I spoke them yesterday:—'If I can help you, I will help you. If I have any luck, you shall have half. If I ever have any money, you shall have half.' Was it not so? Yet you have only had five thousand pounds of all my money. It is because my father's money is not mine, really. I only hold it. I have it for certain purposes—I hardly know what yet. I could not keep my word in its literal sense."

"Dick, I don't ask you," said Lafleur. "I have told you I am satisfied."

"Then you give me back my word?" said Dick.

"I solemnly give it back, Dick," was the reply.

He held out his hand, which Dick grasped. He heaved a great sigh. Their partnership was dissolved. His oath had been heavy upon him, for Dick's word was sacred—the only sacred thing he knew. The vast fortune into which he had so unexpectedly fallen, with all its duties and responsibilities, which Dick was already beginning to realise, was so complicated an affair, that, in the most perfect honesty, he could not literally fulfil his promise. He did the next best thing. He gave Lafleur all he asked for. He was prepared to give him as much again—three times as much, if necessary. But he was glad to get back his word—returned to him like a paid cheque, or a duly honoured bill.

Is it not clear that Dick is progressing in civilization? He has recognised the voice of public opinion. He has remarked that the force of circumstances compels him, whether he will or no, to lead an outwardly decorous life. He has recognised, dimly as yet, that this vast property cannot be made ducks and drakes of, flung away, spent recklessly, as he fondly promised himself when he undeceived his father. He sees that it is like the root-work of some great trees, spreading out branches in all directions, small and great branches: to tear up and destroy them would be to change the fortunes of thousands, to ruin, to revolutionise, to devastate.

Things must be as they are. He is now free: he has got back his word, and is clear of Lafleur.

This is a great gain.

There is still, however, one link which holds him with the past.

It is————Polly!

CHAPTER THE TWENTY-NINTH.

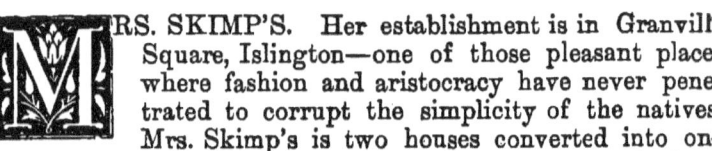RS. SKIMP'S. Her establishment is in Granville Square, Islington—one of those pleasant places where fashion and aristocracy have never penetrated to corrupt the simplicity of the natives.

Mrs. Skimp's is two houses converted into one by knocking a door through the partition wall on each floor. Everybody in the neighbourhood knows it, for Mrs. Skimp has been there a good many years. Frank asked the way to Granville Square at a baker's shop: it happened to be Mrs. Skimp's baker.

"This little b'y's just going there, sir," the woman behind the counter said, very civilly. "He will show you the way What number might you want, sir?"

"Thirty-three."

"Thirty-three and thirty-four. Mrs. Skimp's, sir," said the woman, her face brightening up at the prospect of three extra loaves a-week being wanted. "That's the house the little b'y's going to."

Frank followed the boy with his load of bread.

In three minutes they were in the square. It was an oblong really, and not so wide as Regent's Quadrant; and it had a badly kept strip of garden in the middle. The houses were plastered over; and with two or three exceptions, wanted a coat of paint as badly as houses could. Mrs. Skimp's was an exception. It was a house of three storeys, and attics in the roof. Over the doors were lamps slightly projecting from the pane of glass that lets light into the hall; and on these in huge gilt figures, 33 and 34 blazed in the sun. They were repeated again on the door.

The boy pulled the area bell, and pointed to the knocker and then to Frank, when a dirty servant came out at the basement door to take in the bread.

Frank's knock remained a minute unanswered: but he saw

the lace curtains of the window move, and caught sight of a face—apparently a young lady's—peeping at him over the blind.

Then the servant came and showed him into a room, evidently the dining-room.

Here he had to wait while Mrs. Skimp and her daughter "put themselves to rights."

Presently they came in together. Mrs. Skimp was tall, and of rather pleasing appearance. Her daughter was short and stout, and decidedly uninteresting.

"She takes after my lamented husband, the late Mr. Skimp," her mother often said. "She is quite unlike my family."

They both bowed very cordially to Frank. He bowed in return.

" I desire to—to—"

" Board and reside with a private family of good position. I quite understand, sir. Our circle is small and select. Terms from twenty-two-and-six, according to the room. Was it the *Telegraph* or the *Times*, sir?" asked this voluble personage.

"Neither, madam," said Frank. "Mr. Leweson recommended me to see you on the subject."

"Very kind, indeed, of Mr. Leweson. We know him quite well, my dear—do we not? A very agreeable gentleman, and quite the *artiste*. Such ears!"

Frank looked at her in surprise. He thought, at first, she alluded to the size of them, which was quite a natural, if not a polite thing, to say; but no, it was a tribute to his musical genius.

Mrs. Skimp, as the reader has already discovered, kept a cheap boarding-house. Like all of her profession, she persisted in calling it " a private family and a select circle."

She read Frank's name on Mr. Leweson's card, and showed him the bed-rooms then at her disposal, expatiating in glowing terms on the advantages of living in such a neighbourhood as Granville Square—and particularly with such a family as Mrs. Skimp's.

"We have the key of the square, for the use of the boarders, sir," she said.

Frank could not help contrasting in his own mind, the key of the square offered by Mrs. Skimp, with the key of the street so lately in his possession.

There certainly is some difference between the two.
His interview with Mrs. Skimp was short and satisfactory.
Anybody who came with Mr. Leweson's recommendation was
received by her with great pleasure. She was about forty-
five years of age, a widow with one daughter, Clara. She
was born to become fat and comfortable; but nature's intentions were so far frustrated by the hard conditions of life
that, while becoming fat, she by no means looked comfortable,
having an air of anxiety which came from an external effort
to bring her bills within the compass of her income. She was
short-winded, because the stairs, up and down which she ran
all day long, had made her so. She held her hand upon her
heart, not because she suffered from any palpitation, but from
a habit she had contracted after her husband's death. It indicated resignation and sorrow. Her hair was already streaked
with grey. Her eyes were sharp; but her mouth was soft.
That meant that she would have been kind-hearted, had it not
been her lot to contend with people who seemed all bent upon
cheating her.

She kept a cheap boarding-house. It was a place where
you received your dinner, breakfast, and bed-room for the
modest sum of twenty-five shillings a week—with the usual
extras, Mrs. Skimp would say, explaining that the gentlemen
paid for their own liquor, of which she always kept the very
best that could be got for money. They also paid extra for
washing. She took Frank over the house.

"This," she said, "is the dining-room."

It was a room with two pieces of furniture in it, a table and
a sideboard. The latter, a veneered piece of workmanship,
in an advanced state of decay, was covered with tumblers,
glasses, and bottles. Each bottle had a card tied round it,
with somebody's name on it. Round the red earthenware
water-bottle was tied a huge placard, on which was written,
in characters an inch long, "Mr. Eddrup." Mrs. Skimp took
it off with an air of annoyance, and tore it up. A dozen chairs
were ranged round the walls of the apartment. There was
very little besides: no pictures; dirty muslin curtains; no
carpet. It was the front room, and looked out into the
square, where half a dozen brown trees were making a miserable pretence of summer, and the children were tumbling over
each other on the pavement outside the rails.

"Yes, sir," said Mrs. Skimp, "it is a privilege of my
boarders to go into the garden, if they like, and smoke their

pipes there. And very beautiful it is, on a fine evening, when the flowers are out, I do assure you. Now, let me show you the billiard-room, sir."

At the back of the dining-room was a billiard table. Old it was certainly; the baize torn and patched, and torn again; the cushions dull and lumpy; the balls untrue from their long battering; the cues mostly without their tops;—but still a billiard table: undeniably, a billiard table.

"It is an extra, of course," said Mrs. Skimp, with pride. "We charge a shilling a-week for the privilege of coming into this room. Some of the gentlemen"—this with a deprecatory simper—"spend their Sunday mornings here instead of at church. But perhaps, sir, you've been better brought up."

She led the way to the drawing-room, ornamented with a round table in the middle, curtains, and two or three battered easy-chairs. In them were seated two men, smoking pipes. They looked up as Frank came in, but did not offer to remove their pipes from their mouths.

"This is the drawing-room, where the boarders sit after dinner, and play cards if they like, or amuse themselves," she whispered. "That is Cap'en Bowker, him with the red beard; and the other is Cap'en Hamilton, him with the moustache—both boarders, sir."

Frank gave half a look at them, and followed his guide to the bed-room. He got a small room—two of them had been made out of a big room by putting up a partition, and taking half the window—arranged to bring his portmanteau round at once, and went away.

"We dine at half-past five, Mr. Melliship—punctual. I do hope you won't keep us waiting, because the gentlemen use such dreadful language if the meat is overdone."

"I'll be punctual, Mrs. Skimp," said Frank, as he trudged off to his old lodgings, and brought away his luggage.

Then he strolled about the delightful neighbourhood of Islington—new to him—making acquaintance with the most remarkable monuments of the place; and then he found it was five o'clock, and he turned homewards to be in time for dinner.

"Not expected to dress at Skimp's, I suppose," he said.

The bell rang as he opened the dining-room door. The room was filled by about a dozen men of all ages. They greeted Frank with the stare of rude inquiry by which men of a certain class welcome a new comer.

S

"Swell down on his luck," murmured Captain Hamilton to the lad—a King's College medical student—who stood by him, leaning half out of window.

At the moment, a red-cheeked and bare-armed servant-maid brought in the dinner. She was followed by Mrs. Skimp, who had brushed her hair, and put on a clean cap for dinner, and now assumed the head of the table, rapping with the handle of her carving knife to summon her boarders.

They took their seats.

"You must take the bottom seat, Mr. Melliship," said the hostess, gracefully pointing with a fork. "No, not the end— that's Mr. Eddrup's. That's right: next to Cap'en Bowker. Jane, take the cover off."

Just then there glided into the room an old gentleman, dressed in black coat and gray trousers. He took his place at the end of the table. Nobody took the least notice of him— except Captain Bowker, who asked him, in a whisper, if he was better. Mr. Eddrup shook his head, and poured out a glass of water. This was a sort of signal; for there is no better opportunity of displaying wit than when you are waiting to be served, and no safer a method than that of chaffing an old man.

The medical student began. How delightful is the flow of spirits, unchecked by the ordinary restrictions of politeness, which distinguishes a certain class of medical students!

He burst into a horse laugh, and pointed at Mr. Eddrup.

"Ha, ha!—Ho, ho! There he goes again. Must cool his coppers."

"Where did you get tight last night, Mr. Eddrup?" cried Captain Hamilton, whom Frank set down at once as a leg of the most unmitigated description. He was one of those shady, suburban-race men who hang about at small meetings, living heaven knows how. At present, he was three or four weeks in debt at Skimp's, and was meditating flight, with the partial sacrifice of his wardrobe.

"I think I saw him at the Alhambra about eleven," said another, a City clerk. "He was winking at the ballet girls."

"Oh, Mr. Eddrup!—Oh, bad man!" was groaned all round the table; and then everybody laughed.

Mr. Eddrup took not the smallest notice of anybody, calmly sitting with his eyes fixed before him. The immobility of his features was very remarkable. He took no notice at all, either by look or gesture. He was a small, thin man, with a broad, high brow. His hair, which had not fallen off, and was still thick, lay in long, white masses—much longer than young men wear it—and gave him a singular, out-of-the-way appearance, not easily forgotten. But his face attracted Frank at once. It had a quite inexpressible charm of sweetness. The cheeks were pinched in; round the eyes were crows'-feet ; the lips were thin ; but in the sad smile that lived upon his mouth you could read the presence of some spirit of content which made the foolish gibes of the rest fall upon him unregarded. Who was he ? Why did he live at Skimp's ? Frank caught himself looking at him during the dinner with ever-increasing wonder. It must be poverty;—perhaps it was avarice. His clothes were worn and threadbare. He drank nothing but water with his dinner.

The dinner consisted of an enormous leg of mutton—the biggest ever seen, probably, and, Frank thought, perhaps the stringiest. He found that you could have beer, or even wine —only that luxury was hardly known at Mrs. Skimp's dinner table—by ordering it of the red-armed attendant. During the intervals of feeding, a running horse-play of wit went on at Mr. Eddrup's expense. His appetite was commented on— his personal appearance and habits. Stories, not the most delicately chosen, were told about his antecedents. To all this Mr. Eddrup was entirely callous. Captain Hamilton greatly distinguished himself in this feast of reason by a persistent disregard of a woman's presence, and a steady accumulation of insinuations against the morals of the old gentleman, which did him infinite credit.

"Does this sort of thing go on every evening ?" asked Frank of his neighbour, Captain Bowker, the only one who took no part in the conversation.

"Every morning and every evening. Breakfast and dinner. At two bells and the dog watch," replied Captain Bowker.

Frank hardly understood the last allusion, but let it pass.

Dinner concluded as it had begun, without the ceremony of grace, and the guests rose one by one, and strolled into the billiard-room.

Captain Hamilton and the three at the end of the table alone remained. He advanced to Frank with an easy grace, and tendered him his card.

"Let us know each other," he said, "as we are for the moment in the same hole."

Frank took the card: "Captain Hamilton." No regiment upon it.

"Ceylon Rifles," said the Captain.

"My name is Melliship," said Frank. He would not have another alias.

"Come and join our pool, Mr. Melliship."

"No, thank you. I never play at billiards, except—that is, I never do play."

"Come and look on. You can bet on the game, and smoke."

"I never bet, thank you," said Frank, coldly.

"Well, what do you do, then?" asked the Captain, rudely.

"What the devil, sir, is that to you?"

The blood rushed through Frank's veins again. He was getting combative against this thinly-disguised rook.

Captain Hamilton turned on his heel, and went away. A minute or two afterwards the click of the balls was heard, and an approving laugh at some anecdote of the gallant officer's—probably an account, from his own point of view, of his late interview with Frank.

Mr. Eddrup still sat at the end of the table—Captain Bowker beside him. They rose together as soon as the room was cleared.

"Young man," said Captain Bowker, "I am glad to hear that you don't bet—likewise that you don't play billiards. Come upstairs, and have a pipe in the drawing-room with me and Mr. Eddrup. We use this room pretty much to ourselves," said Captain Bowker, taking an easy-chair. "The others prefer the billiard-room. They go out, too, a good deal in the evenings. That's a great thing at Skimp's. A man *is* left alone if he likes."

The speaker was a man of about fifty-five or so—weather-beaten, rugged. He had fair hair and blue eyes, and had a habit of looking straight ahead at nothing, which comes of a dreamy nature. He was an old "ship captain"—*i.e.*, a merchant-service skipper.

It is a singular thing about skippers, that ashore they are all uniformly the most gentle, tractable creatures that walk about. They drink sometimes, which is their only vice. You may do what you like with them. A child can lead them with a thread. Afloat! Phew! Defend us from serving under the flag of a merchantman—British or Yankee. Language which belongs to the merchant-service alone; hard blows which belong peculiarly to the galleys, rough treatment, such as a Moorish prisoner used to look for—all these you may expect from the merchant captain.

But Captain Bowker was ashore now, and it was only from occasional hints in conversation that you got any gleams of light as to the other side of him.

Mr. Eddrup did not smoke. He sat at the window, and leaned his head on his hand.

"They're a wild set downstairs," said Captain Bowker. "They want a little discipline."

"They are all young," said Mr. Eddrup—"all young. We pardon everything to the young." He turned to Frank, smiling.

"I don't know," said Frank. "I should not be inclined to pardon everything to the young. I like men of my own age —I suppose I am young—to behave with some approach to good manners, as well as to be men of honour."

"Honourable. Yes—yes. The young must be always honourable. We can pardon anything but dishonesty. But good manners. Surely, sir, it is a very small matter."

"Well, yes—but a sufficiently important small matter, Mr. Eddrup. May I light a cigar?"

. He lit and smoked one of Dick's Havanas—Captain Bowker all the while puffing vigorously at a pipe with a long cherry stick, which held about an ounce or so of cut-up ship tobacco. No one came near them except Mrs. Skimp, who brought up tea. She gave Frank his cup, whispering in his ear as she did so—

"It's a shilling a-week extra. Only Mr. Eddrup and Cap'en Bowker has it."

Presently Mr. Eddrup got up, and stole out of the room. Frank saw him cross the square and disappear in one of the streets on the other side.

"He always goes out at eight, every night, and comes home at eleven," said Captain Bowker.

"What is he?"

Captain Bowker evaded the question.

"He's great company for me. If it warn't for him, Skimp's would be as dull as my old cabin in the Doldrums. I should go to live at Poplar, where I've got chums. You never went a long sea-voyage, I suppose?"

"No longer than from Newhaven to Dieppe."

"Ah! then you've got to find out what solitude means. Be

a skipper, sir, and you'll know. They look up to us, sir, and envy our position. It's natural they should." He spoke as if he was an admiral at least. "But it isn't all sailing with the sou'-west trade wind aft. Some of us drink. That's bad. Now, beyond my four or five goes of grog of a night, a pannikin or so of a morning, another about noon, and one or two after dinner, I never did drink. I'm not one of your everlasting nippers. And what's the consequence, sir? Here I am, sound in limb at fifty-five. Pensioned off by my noble firm after forty years service, and happy for the rest of my days."

He paused, and rang the bell.

"Bring the usual, Mary, and two tumblers. You shall have a glass of my rum to-night, Mr. Melliship. What was I a-saying?"

"You were saying that you were going to be happy for the rest of your days. So I suppose you are going to take a wife, Captain Bowker."

"A wife! The Lord forbid! No, sir, I did that once— fifteen years ago—once too often. Ah! well—she's dead; at least, I suppose so." He turned quite pale, and beads of perspiration stood on his forehead. "Well, let that pass. What kept me from drink was, that I had a resource which is given to few men. Do you compose, sir?"

"Compose? Music?"

"No—music—nonsense? Anybody can make music. Verses, sir,—immortal verses. That's what I used to spend my time in doing when I was below in the cabin. Now here"
—he pulled a folded and frayed piece of paper out of his pocket—"here is a copy I made in my last voyage home. Read it, and tell me candidly what you think of it."

Frank opened it. It began—

> "'Tis fearful, when the running gear is taut,
> And creaking davits yield a frail support."

"Hem! Rhyme rather halts here, doesn't it? Shall I read the rest at my leisure, Captain Bowker?"

"No, no—no time like the present. Give me hold, young man. Now, then—stand by—here's the rum. So, sit steady, and listen."

He read his composition. Frank listened as one in a dream. What next? To sing in a music hall, to live at Skimp's, to sit at the same table with Captain Hamilton, to hear Captain

Bowker read his verses: this was not encouraging. He would have to go to the Palace in the morning, to rehearsal. After all, it is necessary to live. At least, one would be able to pay one's way on three guineas a week.

"So, like the Doldrums' calm, his onward way
Is checked who dares thy laws to disobey."

It was the termination of Captain Bowker's poem. Frank woke up.

"Very good indeed, Captain Bowker. The last lines especially—very good. They remind me of Pope.

So, like the Doldrums' onward way, his calm
Is checked who dares to—'"

"Not quite right," said the divine bard, with a smile. "But you are not a sailor. Shall I read it again?"

"No, don't—pray don't."

"I won't. Let us talk."

That meant, " Let me talk."

Frank lay back in his easy chair, and dreamed of Grace, and the pleasant country-side. How was he to win her;— how to pay off those debts? It was not a hopeful reverie. There are times when the veil of illusion falls off. It is at best but a fog, most common in the morning of life, and extremely pretty when the sun shines upon it. It was fallen now. Frank measured the distance between himself and Grace, and saw that it was widening every day.

Captain Bowker recalled him. He was maundering on :—

"—when I commanded the *Merry Moonshine*, in the Chinese coolie trade, running to Trinidad. It was an anxious time, because we had four hundred of them aboard, and not too much rice. They used to murder each other—ten, a dozen or so—every night. That lessened the numbers."

"What did they do that for?"

"What do men always fight about? Then we had bad weather—terrible bad weather; got on the edge of a cyclone. We had the coolies battened down 'tween decks: and what with the noise of the storm, and the cries of them wild cats, and the mainmast going by the board, I do assure you it was as much as I could do to get that poem finished. As it was, it wasn't really finished till I got home—for there was a lot more unpleasantness. We put in at Allegoey Bay; and directly the coolies caught sight of land, I'm blest if forty or fifty didn't chuck themselves out of the ports and overboard, to swim ashore. 1

do not remember," he said, stroking his nose—" I do not remember hearing that any of them got there. There's sharks off that coast, you know. But think of the loss it was to me!"

CHAPTER THE THIRTIETH.

AFTER walking through a number of narrow and dark passages, Frank found himself at last in the North London Palace of Amusement and Aristocratic Lounge.

Dingy and dirty by daylight it appeared.

Plenty of light—to show the tawdry, gas and smoke-tarnished state of the decorations—came in through a lantern in the great domed roof; for the place had once been a daylight exhibition —a sort of superior Polytechnic, started at the same time as the mechanics' institutes, whither it was thought the people would eagerly flock to improve their minds. Mr. Leweson's company could therefore rehearse comfortably without the gas—except on very dark and foggy days.

The features of the building struck Frank as something familiar. His father and the flavour of Bath buns flashed upon him; for memory mixes incongruous elements as old recollections pour upon us. He had once been taken there as a little boy, when what was now a music hall had been the Lyceum. The place had now, however, tumbled down from its high estate, and in its fall had ruined half a dozen speculators before the genius of a Leweson made it pay.

Frank looked round. It was the same place—he was sure of that; though how changed was all about him!

He remembered the great, bare hall, with half a dozen dreary electric machines; the galleries, round which geological specimens were arranged; its side wings, where were displayed such objects as ancient British pottery, specimens of early type, botanical collections, and other dry and improving things. He remembered how he had been led round, wearily yawning, with a party of girls who began by yawning too, and ended by snapping at each other. All the time there had been the buzz of a lecturer's voice, as he addressed an audience consisting of an uncle and two miserable nephews, on the more recent improvements in machinery employed in the manufacture of cotton fabrics. And he remembered how his heart lightened up when they came to a refreshment stall, and everybody had a cake.

He rubbed his eyes, and looked round. Yes—it was the same place; but where the electric machines had stood was now a stage, where the geological collection had formerly been was now a row of private boxes. The apparatus had all disappeared: only the refreshment-room remained, and this was vastly increased and improved.

"Here we are," said Mr. Leweson. "This is where the loonatics come every night to stare, and listen, and drink. Amuse yourself by looking for half an hour or so."

"I have been here before," Frank began.

"Everybody comes here—it's one of the sights of London," said Mr. Leweson, interrupting him; "and the loonatics——"

It was Frank's turn to interrupt.

"I mean years ago, when it used to be called the Lyceum. I was a boy then."

"Phyoo!" the proprietor whistled. "Ah! quite another thing. It was a Limited Li Company. It would have smashed 'em all up instead of being smashed itself, if it hadn't been. It has been lots of things since then. Nobody made it pay till I took it in hand. Mark me," continued Mr. Leweson, with great gravity, and in his deepest voice—

"Well, sir."

"That'll be the end of that round place they're building at Kensington."

"What, the Albert Hall?" cried Frank.

"Yes; certain to come to it—only a question of time. Be a place just like this, and with the Horticultural Gardens at the back to walk out into and dance in the summer—Ranelagh, Vauxhall, and Cremorne thrown into one would be nothing to it. I'd give—I'd give—there, I don't know what I wouldn't give a year for that place, with the gardens thrown in; and pay the biggest dividend that ever was paid by anything in this world before."

"But, my dear sir," Frank began, shaking his head.

"Ah, you may laugh: and I may not, and I dare say I shall not, live to see it, but that is the future of those two places, as sure as eggs are eggs—take my word for it. But, there, I must leave you and attend to my business—they want me. Go anywhere you like, only not on the stage just yet—you'd be in the way. The new ballet is just coming on."

Mr. Leweson left Frank in front of the stage, and disappeared himself down a trap-door in the orchestra.

Frank took a seat in a box near the stage, and looked about him.

The scene was new to him, and, apart from the novelty, was interesting in itself.

The curtain was up. It revealed an immense stage, crowded with children, girls, and men. The wings and drops were representations of the foliage of a forest of palms. In the background was a vast gold fan, which at night unfolded and displayed Titania, Queen of the Fairies, reclining among her attendant sprites and fays.

In front, close to the wire fencing of the footlights, stood a little, mean table, covered with slips of manuscript. At the table sat the chief of the orchestra, making annotations on his score with a red chalk pencil, sometimes from the manuscripts, sometimes without reference to them. By the conductor's side stood an iron music-stand, three empty rush-bottomed chairs, and a fiddle in a case.

The rehearsal had not yet begun, and the girls were collected in little knots, always breaking up and re-forming; chattering together like so many grasshoppers, and laughing perpetually, at nothing at all, and just out of the irrepressible gaiety of their hearts. At the sides of the proscenium were two sheets of looking-glass. These were a great source of attraction, and never idle for a second. Constantly, one or two of the girls would leave the rest, and, going in front of the glass, execute a few choregic gyrations quite gravely, no one taking the least notice of them, nor they of any one else. It was quaint to see them staidly pirouetting, gyrating, and posturing before these great glasses, each one totally regardless of the rest. The private practice and self-examination before a woman's most faithful confessor accomplished, the young ladies would retire to their friends, and join in the never-ending chatter. Directly they left the mirrors, their places were seized by a lot of tiny children—girls—who, in ragged dresses, mere little children of the gutter, solemnly ambled up and down in front of the glass, put out their chubby little legs, and waved their little red arms. They never tired of looking at themselves. When their elder sisters came and turned them out, they fled like wasps from a honey pot. The moment the coast was clear, back they all came, tumbling over each other in their eagerness to be in the front, and began once more the children's imitation of their elders' vanities.

Frank looked on at this lively scene with great interest. He had never seen a rehearsal before. From what he had heard of the young ladies of the ballet, he had been accustomed to regard them as melancholy victims of mistaken art —persons who were compelled by want to sacrifice their self-respect, and go through a nightly course of public posturing for the admiration of a foolish crowd. Now he met them in flesh and blood, he found all his original ideas knocked on the head. So far from having no self-respect, they appeared to be full of it; so far from having any sense of humiliation, they evidently delighted in their calling. Of course, it will be seen that Frank was exceedingly inexperienced. At the same time, had he been the most hardened old *roué* that ever walked behind the scenes, he could not but be struck with the natural gaiety and light-heartedness of the girls. It was all real: no affectation or false semblance. They were all happy, all laughing, all chattering, all dancing, running, and capering about the stage.

The men and boys kept at the back. They were an exceedingly shady-looking lot. As it afterwards appeared, their business in the ballet was to come in and make gestures, to fill up the background, to stand in attitudes, and perform other easy and elementary parts which belong to dramatic representation.

The girls had nothing to say to them; and they, for their part, never spoke to the girls, but kept to themselves under Titania's great fan.

A little commotion among the crowd. It opened, and made a way for Mr. Leweson, the master of the ballet, and his two assistants. The three professors of the art of dancing were French—that was patent at half a glance. The same sallow, shaven cheeks, the same cropped black moustache, the same height, belonged to all. As Mrs. Partington would say, they might all three have been twins. And this natural resemblance was heightened by their all appearing in bluish pilot jackets, rather tight-fitting black trousers, and cloth boots.

Mr. Leweson signed to a pale man to open the fiddle case, and begin.

"We've got lots of work to get through, Mr. Sauerhäring"—the master of the ballet was an Alsatian by birth—"so let us get on. I want to see that ballet of butterflies perfect this afternoon."

"M'sieur, you shall see it."

"It's a very stiff job."

"Bah!—pooh!" dissented Sauerhäring. "It—is—noth—thing."

"Glad to hear it."

"Psha! You shall see it pairfect, while you say one, two." He looked at the fiddler. "Go on," he said.

His assistants vanished among the girls, when they were seen at intervals among the crowds of coryphées, setting good example. The fiddler struck up, and the ballet commenced. The girls were dressed in all kinds of costumes. Some had their plain walking-dresses of stuff or black silk, only with their bonnets and jackets off: some had the "bodies" of the dress—the skirts being removed—leaving them in soiled muslins; some wore a kind of short petticoat; one or two were in what theatrical critics call page dress, but what the girls call "shapes," such as they would appear in at night. They all wore silk stockings, some of them having on a kind of red gaiters, which Frank took to be elastic, and intended to strengthen the limb. He had noticed, previous to the rehearsal, one or two artistes more conscientious than the rest engaged in diligently rubbing their ankles and the circumjacent regions. At first he could not make out the reason of this manœuvre, but was at length reminded of Lillie Bridge and professional runners. Then he knew what it was meant for.

"Go an," said the ballet master, pronouncing the word as if he were an Irishman—"go an, lad-ees."

They went "an" in that vast hall, with one spectator—Frank—to the scraping of the solitary fiddle. It marked time: but for anything else, a battalion of Guards might as well have marched to the sounds of one penny whistle, or a cathedral choir have been accompanied by a jew's harp. They were learning the figures of the butterflies' ballet, and began the first with great vigour and energy.

But they were not right about it.

M. Sauerhäring threw out his arms, and trilled a prolonged guttural "Ah———h!"

"Bah!—pooh!—phit!—tush!—psha!" he cried in a string, and then gave a "klick," like a whole cab-rank starting in pursuit of a double fare.

The music stopped. The ladies laughed. The professor said—

"Stupeed! this is the step."

Then he capered solemnly in front of them.

"One, two; one, two—lal-lal-la, lal-lal-la; one, two; three, four."

Behind him, a long file of coryphées imitated his movements. To Frank, Sauerhäring's limbs seemed to be of india-rubber as he shook them from side to side.

"One, two—one, two. Now, again."

The odd thing being that they never once stopped chattering to each other and laughing.

They were admirably drilled. Not one but kept her eye fixed upon the master—that is, one eye, the other being given up to seeing how the other girls were getting on. It was wonderful to see them catching the combinations, and patiently working them out. As for patience, it was difficult to say whether the girls were more patient or the master more painstaking.

Presently the chief of the orchestra crossed the stage to M. Sauerhäring. Directly the master turned to speak to him, the girls began to romp about, one after the other darting from the ranks, and executing a pirouette on her own account in the centre of the stage, making believe to be for once a *première danseuse*. Then the master turned round, and order was re-established.

Presently came the children's turn. A ragged regiment they were by daylight; at night, butterflies and moths—all spangle and gauze. Now, with muddy stockings and shoes full of holes, giving M. Sauerhäring and his *aides de camp* a vast deal more trouble to teach them one figure than their elder sisters would do in learning a dozen. Their drilling lasted half an hour at least; and at least once in two minutes the indefatigable, and as it appeared, ubiquitous Sauerhäring stopped fiddle and children with his guttural, tremulant "Ah—h—h!" and reeled off the five expressions of discontent he had learned from a phrase book of the English tongue in the paternal orchard in his own Alsace—

"Bah!—pooh!—phit!—tush!—psha!"

To him they were a word in five syllables, and he ejaculated them to a sort of tune, as an angry vocalist might sound his "Do, re, mi, fa, sol."

Among the children, one little mite about six years attracted Frank's attention. She had been the most assiduous while she was on the stage in ambling up and down before the mirrors. Now she led off the train of children with a precision and solemnity that were most edifying, executing her simple steps most carefully and conscientiously. The moment she was free again, she ran off to the looking-glass, and practised them over again, with many curtseys and salutes, wonderful to see. That child will rise and be heard of in her profession, unless some unlucky accident cuts her off.

While this branch of the *corps de ballet* were practising figures and groupings, there came upon the scene one of the principal dancers, dressed as if for the evening, but without any flowers or jewels, just as she appears in the initial letter to this chapter. She walked across the front of the stage, regarding the lower members of the profession with that stare that sees nothing, common enough among the gentle daughters of England's aristocracy. A mere ballet girl, a troupe of ballet girls, what could they possibly be in the eyes of Mdlle. Goldoni, from the opera house of Milan? In her hand she bore a small watering-pot, with which she sprinkled the boards in front of the looking-glass on the left, took possession of it, and proceeded to practise by herself. First, she turned round on the left toe, with the right leg a foot and a half above her head; then she performed the same manœuvre with her right toe and left leg; then she placed her foot as high up on the gilded pillar of the proscenium as she could, and kept it there; then she began arching her feet before the glass; then she went over the whole performance again—never disturbed by the others, who took no manner of notice of her, and never herself taking the least notice of the rest;—all the while looking in the glass with a sort of curiosity, as if the legs belonged to somebody else. One or two other people, including a lady of immense proportions, in black velvet, came in, and sat on chairs in front of the stage. The little children romped round the house, and vaulted about over the backs of the seats. The unhappy-looking youths, in felt hats and greasy coats, at the back went through the semblance of what they were about to perform at night in spangles and hodden suits. The assistant ballet-masters capered and danced all over the stage. The girls went through their drill again and again. No one got tired. The melancholy fiddler, whose strains produced a profoundly saddening effect on Frank, played on with the pertinacity and monotony of an organ grinder. The conductor of the orchestra made his notes on the music; the big lady in black velvet gazed on unweariedly; the manager, Mr. Leweson, came and went, bringing his big head upon the stage and taking it off again at intervals.

At last he came round to Frank's box with a portfolio in his hand.

"Always a lot to do with the production of a new ballet. Now let us talk while they finish the rehearsal. You see, Mr. Melliship, the loonatics who come here like a ballet: not that they care, bless you, what it's like, or what it means, so long as there's plenty of short skirts on the stage. But it must be a Spectàrcle! Another thing the loonatics that frequent this miserable Palace of Humbug like is the sight of somebody running the risk of breaking their bones. So we've got a trapeze rigged up, as you see. But they must needs have a woman, so we've got the Divine Giulia—Giulia Silvani—to perform with her father. I daresay they'll be round presently. Comic songs of course they must have. We've got the Inexpressible Jones, and the Incomparable and Aristocratic Arthur De Vere. They only come at night, of course. Beautiful specimens of the aristocracy, both of them—but they go down with the loonatics."

He stopped, and began to look about in his portfolio.

He produced a manuscript.

"Now, with a singer like yourself, there are only two lines open. You must give up altogether the notion that the British loonatic wants music. He doesn't. He wants sentiment to make him cry, and patriotism to warm up his puny little heart. I'm ashamed of him, Mr. Melliship—I am, indeed. But what can I do? Here I am, after advertising you yesterday in all the papers, and sending sandwiches up and down the streets to-day——"

"Advertising me!"

"Yes. Look here: wonder you didn't see it as you came along."

He called one of the children, and sent her for a bill. She presently returned with a flaming poster.

NORTH LONDON PALACE OF AMUSEMENT AND ARISTOCRATIC LOUNGE.

IN ADDITION TO THE

GALAXY OF TALENT

Already engaged, the Manager has great pleasure in announcing that he has secured, for a short time only, the services of the

NEW AND GREAT ANGLO-ITALIAN TENOR,

SIGNOR CIPRIANO.

The Signor, who has never sung before in England, but who is well known to possess the finest Tenor Voice in the World, will Sing

TO-NIGHT,

AND UNTIL FURTHER NOTICE,

THREE BALLADS.

EVERY EVENING,

At Half-past Eight and Half-past Nine.

Across this announcement was a coloured strip, with "Tonight" upon it.

Frank read it with a mixed feeling of annoyance and amusement. After all it didn't matter. His new grand name was better, at any rate, than his own—if he must appear before a British audience.

"I suppose it's all right," he said, doubtfully, handing it back.

"Of course it is; but the thing is, what you're to sing. Now, I asked my man "—he meant a musical understrapper who composed songs for him, words and music, at a pound a-piece —" I asked my man to knock me off a little thing in imitation of the Christy's songs of domestic pathos—you know— like 'Slam the door loudly, for mother's asleep,' 'Touch the place softly, my pretty Louise,' 'Father, come home, for mother is tight';—charming songs, you know, with a chorus soft and whispered at the end, so as to bring the tears in the people's eyes. Now, what do you think he brought me this morning. Read that."

He looked at Frank curiously, while the latter read it and laughed.

It was a song based on one of the humblest and most ordinary topics of " domestic pathos," and ran thus :—

"He will catch it from his mother,
For the widow's heart is low,
And beneath the weeping willows
Still her wayward child will go,
O'er the river course the shadows—
He has spoiled his boots and hat—
While the sunset lights the meadows,
For his mother spank the brat."

"'Vulgar and coarse'? I knew you'd say so," said the Bighead. "It's a pity, too. My man told me it was written in direct imitation of the great original—with whispered chorus, and all. See what a capital effect it would have. You in the centre, head held down in attitude of listening—so ; voices behind—unseen, you know—'for his mother'—'for his mother'—'for his mother'—dying away, with a harp obbligato to follow."

"I'll sing it, if you like," said Frank. "What does it matter, if the people like it?"

"Ah, we must follow the loonatics, not lead 'em as I should wish," said Mr. Leweson, sighing. "Well, well, we'll have it ; though it's a shame—it's a shame to ask a man with your voice to sing such a song. Now for the second—'The Bay of Biscay.' It will suit you well. They'll encore that; or you may sing 'The Death of Nelson.' And now to try the room."

He led the way to the stage, had a piano wheeled in, sat down, and directed Frank where to stand—giving him, at the same time, a few hints on the art of bowing to an assemblage of British loonatics.

The acoustic properties of the place were splendid. Frank felt as if he had never sung in his life before, as he heard his own voice filling the great building and echoing in the roof.

"What do you think of that?" whispered Mr. Leweson to the conductor.

"How long have you got him for?"

"Two months' agreement first. I'm going to make him sign directly."

"How much?"

"Three guineas."

"Make it six months. You won't keep him a day beyond his time."

T

Frank finished.

"How was that, Mr. Leweson?"

"Very good—very good. A little softer at the finish: don't be afraid they won't hear you. I'll have the chorus all right for you by the time you come this evening. Now for 'The Death of Nelson.' You may make the glasses ring, if you like. Come in Patty, my dear. Where's your father?"

This was to a new comer—a singularly pretty, modest-looking girl. He did not wait for an answer to his question, but began at once.

Frank finished the song, and Mr. Leweson clapped his hands in applause.

"That'll bring the house down, if anything will. Bravo, Mr.—I mean, Signor Cipriano, you know. Now, look here—I'm not going to have you encored, and spoiling your voice, to please a lot of loonatics, so they needn't think it. To-night you may do it. I shall go on myself, and make a speech after it. You'll hear me. Patty, this is our new singer—a very different sort to the rest, as you'll find. Signor, this is the Divine Giulia Silvani—only at home we call her Patty Silver; and she's worth her weight in gold, I can tell you. Here's her father."

Frank took off his hat, and shook hands with the girl. Her hands were rough and hard, her fingers thick—he noticed that as she stood gloveless on the stage. But her face was wonderfully soft and delicate in expression: one of those faces—the features not too good, and perhaps commonplace in character—which one meets from time to time in the London streets;—not the face of a lady at all, but, at the same time, a lovable and good face. She was different to the ballet girls, somehow—had none of their restlessness, did not laugh, did not jump about before the glass; stood quietly beside the piano, and just listened and waited. She was the female trapezist, and with her father performed the Miraculous Flying Leap for Life every night. Her little brother completed the talented Silvani Family; and, though yet of tender years, was admitted to a trifling performance on a small trapeze of his own, from which he could not fall more than twenty or thirty feet or so—a mere trifle to a child of ten.

The family were special favourites of the manager, for some reason or other. His big head had a big heart connected with it, as more than one in the place had found out.

After singing his songs, and receiving the suggestions of his employer, Frank went with him to his private room. A paper was lying on the table.

"That's your agreement, Mr. Melliship. You pledge yourself to sing for me, and only me, for two months, at a fixed salary of three guineas a week, at least three ballads or songs every night. I introduce you to the public, and have my profit out of the small salary you will get. You see, Mr. Melliship, I'm a plain man. I like your voice. I like your appearance. I am making terms advantageous to myself, but not bad for you. And if you were to go to anybody in London, you wouldn't get better for a first engagement. My conductor advised me to nail you down for six months, but I keep to my original terms. Treat me well, Mr. Melliship, and I'll treat you well. So there we are; and, if you'll sign, a pint of champagne and a dry biscuit will help us along."

Frank drank the champagne, signed his name, and went away, free until eight.

He dined at Mrs. Skimp's where old Mr. Eddrup was, as usual, made the butt of "Captain" Hamilton's wit. After dinner he smoked a pipe in the garden of the square; and then, as the time was fast approaching, he dressed himself with considerable care, and walked to the Palace.

The place was crowded. Nearly every man had a glass before him, and a pipe or a cigar in his mouth. There were constant cries of "Waiter," constant popping of corks. The smell of tobacco was overpowering. The heat and the gas made the place almost intolerable. Frank stood at the sidewings while a ballet went on—not that which he had seen rehearsed, but a simpler one, intended to open the evening.

"After this, the Inexpressible Jones. After him, you," said Mr. Leweson. "That's to take him down a few pegs. He thinks he's got a tenor. With a voice like a cow."

The Inexpressible sang. He was encored. He sang again. They wanted to encore him a second time. It was a charming pastoral, relating how he, the I. J., had been walking one evening in the fields, with an umbrella, and had there met a young lady belonging to the same exalted rank among the aristocracy as himself; how he had held a conversation with her under his umbrella; how she had promised to meet him the next evening, provided he came with his umbrella; how he had kept his appointment, with his umbrella, and how she had not. It was a comic song, acted with an umbrella, so true to life that the "loonatics" shrieked with laughter.

When the laughter had quite subsided, it was Frank's turn to go on.

Mr. Leweson was below among the audience, contemplating his patrons with an air of undisguised contempt. He was the first person Frank saw in the mass of heads beneath and in front of him.

For a moment, he trembled and lost his nerve. Only for a moment. As the piano struck up, he managed to see the words that were swimming before him, and plunged at once into his ballad of the domestic affections.

The chorus was more than admirable—it was superb: an invisible chorus, in soft voices, murmuring the refrain like an echo—

"For his mother—for his mother—for his mother;"

till the people cried at the pathos.

"The loonatics," he heard the manager growling to himself.

The applause was tremendous. He retired amid a general yell of "'core—'core!" and reappeared a moment after with flushed cheeks—for even the approbation of "loonatics" is something—to sing "The Death of Nelson."

Frank went home that night satisfied, if not happy. He was a success at last—if only a success at three guineas a week. He prayed fervently that no old friends would come to detect him. If only he could preserve his incognito, all would be well

He reckoned only on old friends. He had forgotten new acquaintances.

The very next day, at dinner, after a general whispering at the upper end of the table, which Mr. Eddrup interpreted to mean an organized attack upon himself, Captain Hamilton turned to him, and openly congratulated him on his success the preceding evening at the North London Palace of Amusement.

"Of course," said the gallant officer, "it was an unexpected pleasure to see, in the person of Signor Cipriano, a gentleman who does us the favour to dine at our humble table."

Frank reddened, and could find nothing to say.

Mr. Eddrup answered for him. It was the first time the old man had ever been known to speak.

"I congratulate you," he said to Frank, "on the possession

of a talent which enables you to take honest work. Believe me, sir, all work is honest."

"Bravo, old Eddrup!" shouted the medical student. "We've made him speak at last. I always knew he was one of the most eloquent orators going."

Frank turned with flushing cheeks.

"At all events," he said, "it is better to sing at a public place than to—to—"

"To what, sir?" said the student.

"Singing cad!" escaped the Captain's lips, in tones very clearly audible.

Frank half rose from his seat, and turned towards the Captain.

"Better than loafing about in billiard-rooms, and on suburban racecourses, Captain Hamilton."

There was a dead silence.

"After dinner, sir," said Captain Hamilton, after a pause, "we must have a word together."

"And me, too," said the medical student, with disregard for grammar.

"Stick to 'em," whispered Captain Bowker. "Stick to 'em. They're only curs. I'll see fair play."

After dinner, Captain Hamilton, none of the rest leaving the room, came up to Frank as he stood in the window.

"Sir, you have insulted me."

"Probably."

It was said calmly, but Frank's lips were trembling.

"Sir, you must give me satisfaction."

"Take it, then," shouted the young man, striking out with his left arm.

The Captain fell—and did not get up again.

"Oh! gentlemen—gentlemen," cried Mrs. Skimp, running before Frank—"don't fight—oh! pray don't fight! He owes me for six weeks," she whispered.

"I said he was a loafer—a welcher. I know he is. I have seen him ducked in a horsepond before to-day," said Frank, who was recovering his calmness.

The others all burst out laughing, except the medical student, who thought that perhaps his turn was coming next.

The Captain rose slowly, but with dignity.

"This," he said, "will not end here. You will hear from me to-morrow."

He was leaving the room, the medical student going with him.

"Stop," said Frank. "There is something else to be said. Both yesterday and to-day—and, I believe, always—there has been made a series of attacks, personal, insulting, and caddish, on an old gentleman of perfectly inoffensive habits—Mr. Eddrup. The two principal offenders are you two—Captain Hamilton and you—whatever your name is"—he pointed to the medical student. "Now, as I, for one, decline to belong to those who wilfully insult an old man, I intend to take his quarrel upon myself. Who ever insults Mr. Eddrup henceforth, insults me. Now, Captain Hamilton, and you other, you may go to the devil."

They went out.

Mrs. Skimp was the only one who regretted the incident.

"Six weeks due from the Captain," she moaned, "and four from the other."

"Sir," said Captain Bowker, wringing Frank's hand, "I'm proud of you. You're a good fellow, sir—a good fellow. I wish I could do something for you."

Frank laughed.

"You can," he said. "You can come and hear me sing 'The Death of Nelson,' if you like."

"By the Lord, 1 will," said the Captain. "I haven't been to a place of amusement for ten years. I'll go to-night."

Mr. Eddrup said nothing. In his usual quiet and methodical manner, he stepped out of the room, and went upstairs.

In many cheap boarding-houses there is a Père Goriot, young or old. In very few is there a man to be found with courage to stand up and protect a butt from the assaults of his enemies.

That night, Captain Hamilton went out, and came back no more. His effects, when examined, were found to consist principally of one trunk, locked—filled with stones wrapped in newspapers.

CHAPTER THE THIRTY-FIRST.

AT an early hour on the morning after his "first appearance," Frank awoke with strangely mingled feelings of disgust and pride. Mr. Leweson's loonatics had cheered him to the skies: that was something. On the other hand, to have been cheered by loonatics was not in itself, after the first surprise, an exhilarating memory. He got up, cursing his fate.

He went down to the palace, after breakfast, in the gloomiest frame of mind. He found the same ballet rehearsal going on, only the second time it was not by any means so interesting, having lost its novelty. Ballet girls, he was able to remark, romantic as the profession appears to outsiders, possess much of the commonplace nature of the untutored feminine animal. He speculated on their probable ambition, on the subjects which occupied their minds, and exercised their intellects. Subsequent investigation, followed by discovery, taught him in time that they never do think at all, except about the means of getting dress, and have no intellects to exercise. Mr. Leweson was in his office, but too busy to see him, only sending out a note that the performance of last night might be repeated if he wished; if not, he only had to select his own songs.

Frank felt quite indifferent as to what songs he sang, and so was turning away to leave the place, when he saw the pretty girl to whom he had been introduced the day before—the Divine Giulia. She was with her father, superintending the arrangement of certain trapeze ropes for a new feat they were to perform that evening. Her dress was changed. She had on the singular costume which was invented, I suppose, when female gymnasts first came into fashion—something like the "page" dress of the stage. The Divine Giulia was attired in Turkish trousers—which disappeared at night—a crimson scarf, and what I have reason to believe is called a chemisette. Her hair—brown, full, and wavy—was gathered up at the back of her head in such rich masses that no chignon was necessary. Her father was also dressed in the uniform of his profession, but without the spangles which covered him in the evening. With them was a little boy, the youthful Joey, also attired in the family costume. Frank stayed to look.

"May I look on while you practise?" he asked, shaking hands with the acrobat and his daughter.

"Of course you may, Mr.—Signor."

"Signor Cipriano, father," said Patty.

"My name is Melliship," said Frank, reddening.

"You may help us, too," said the girl. "Set this mattress straight. So. Now lay this one along the tables. That is right. Ready, father?"

One of the men regularly employed stood at the bar, to set it swinging. They were to fly, one after the other—the girl first—across the house, swinging from one trapeze to the next, and landing on a little platform at the end: a common feat enough, complicated by what the playbills called a summersault in "mid-air" by the father.

Silvani, père, was a stout, strong-built man, about forty years of age, or a little over. The muscles showed through his tight fleshings like rope bands.

"Fancy having to assist your governor in turning summersaults," thought Frank.

It was a question whether the ropes should not be lengthened by a foot or so, which would naturally increase the distance to be traversed, but lessen the danger. Mr. Silver gave it against the longer length.

"But you may kill yourself," said Frank, "for want of that extra foot."

"I don't think so. After all, a man can only die once. Patty, my dear, you're not afraid?"

She shook her head merrily, and mounted the ladder. Frank trembled as she stood at the top—slight, graceful, slender—poising herself like a bird on the wing. Her father mounted after her, and took another pair of ropes, standing behind her.

She gave a sign: the man set the trapeze swinging, and Patty let herself go. The instant she touched the first bar, her father followed, catching it as it swung back when she left it. In a moment, they were standing side by side on a platform in front of the first circle.

"Not quite steady enough. We must do it again."

"No, don't," cried Frank—"don't. Surely once is enough."
The girl laughed, and climbed again. Frank was standing on the mattress at the far end of the house, nearly under the landing-place—that is to say, close under the dress circle. The feat looked a great deal more dangerous in an empty theatre, by daylight, than when the gas was lit, and the place crammed with spectators.

Now, whether his nervousness communicated itself to Patty, I know not; but when she left the two rings, and should have caught the first bar, she missed it. Frank rushed forward, and caught her by the shoulders, just as she would have fallen heavily on the mattresses.

The weight of a girl of eighteen, though she be a trapezist in full training, is no small matter—particularly when the velocity of her flight is taken into consideration. The momentum of a body in motion is represented, in applied mathematics, as a quantity composed of the mass multiplied by the velocity—which is, to the outer world, much as if one were to say pigs multiplied by candles. You will realize what is meant if anything heavy falls upon you. Frank fell back, with Patty upon him. She was up in an instant, unhurt.

Her father, seeing the accident as he flew through the air, kept tight hold of his rings, and swung backwards and forwards until he could safely alight.

"Why, Patty," he cried, "I've never known you do such a thing before."

The girl was up in a moment—shaken, but not hurt. Frank was not so fortunate. Her head butting full upon his nose, caused that member to bleed : a prosaic ending to a deed of some heroism and skill—for he caught her like a cricket ball, only with the softest and most delicate handling possible, just as if he had always been practising the art of catching trapeze girls so as not to hurt them.

Mr. Leweson, too, came running up. He was just in time to witness the accident.

"Are you hurt, Patty—are you hurt?"

"Not a bit—not a bit:" her lip was trembling in the effort to suppress an hysterical sob. "I should have been, if it had not been for Mr. Melliship, though. We ought to ask him if he is hurt."

Frank was holding his handkerchief to his nose, and only shook his head, to intimate that the damage done was such as could easily be repaired.

"Good heaven!" cried Mr. Leweson; "and you might have flown straight against the woodwork. Mr. Melliship, it was splendid—splendidly done, sir."

"Well," said Mr. Silver, "as nobody's hurt, and we've got to do it to-night, I suppose we'd better try it again, Patty."

"No—no," began Frank.

"Young gentleman," said Mr. Silver, "please don't interfere with our professional work."

"You are not too much shaken, Patty?" interposed the manager.

"Not shaken a bit. Now, father, we'll do it this time."

She ran up the ladder lightly with her rings, flew through the air from bar to bar, and arrived at the landing-stage with the precision of a bird, followed by her sire.

"Now, there," said Mr. Leweson, "is a splendid creature for you. Now you see why I wanted you to go on the trapeze with Giulia. Think of the Triple Act that I had in my mind—Signor Silvani holding the rings; three bars, each two feet lower than the other; on the Signor's shoulders you would stand, Giulia on yours. The flight through the air: the first bar for Giulia, the second for you, the third for the father of the family. The most magnificent idea in acrobatism ever conceived. But there, if it can't be, it can't, of course. Now, then, Patty, hoist up the boy, and get your practice done."

He walked aside, with his hand in Frank's arm, while the child went through his performances.

"Mr. Melliship," he said abruptly, "you are a gentleman, that is clear. I daresay an army man, now."

"No—I told you—I am a Cambridge man."

"Ah!—well. But there are different sorts of gentlemen, you see. Now, I think more goes to make a gentleman than knowing how to eat, and talk, and dress, and behave. I know the breed is rare; but there is a sort of gentleman in this country who does not run after every pretty face he meets, fancying that every pretty girl is his natural prey. I say there is that sort of gentleman in the world, and I should be very glad to think you belong to the kind, Mr. Melliship. That's a long preamble; but what I mean is this—excuse my plain speaking—but I don't want my little Patty humbugged, and I won't have it, sir, I say—I won't have it, by any one. There—there—I'm a fool."

"You can trust me," said Frank. "I am not likely either to fall in love with her, or she with me."

"Humph!" growled the man with the big head, looking curiously at him. "I don't know that. Well—well—I've said what I wanted to, and you are not angry; so it is all right. Come and have some fizz, Patty, my girl. After your shake, it will do you good."

They all went to the manager's room, when he produced a bottle of champagne, which they discussed together. If Mr. Leweson had a weakness, it was for champagne. Patty Silver shared it. Champagne was the one thing connected with the department of the interior which Patty cared for.

"Very odd," thought Frank. "Here's the manager giving champagne to a family of acrobats. Wonder if they always do it at music halls."

I believe, as a rule, that acrobats are not so well treated by managers.

In this particular case there were reasons why Mr. Leweson was especially kind to his talented Silvani Family. It is a story which hardly belongs to us. In the years gone by, there had been a forlorn little Israelite boy, whose father and mother died in a far-off land, leaving him alone to the care of strangers. None of his own people were in that American town. Then a Christian man, a blacksmith by trade, took him in, and housed him. The Christian man was Signor Silvani's father; the little Jew was Mr. Emmanuel Leweson. Years went on. The Jew became a musician, a singer, a composer; the Christians went down in the world; and the whirligig of time brought them all together again—Harry Silver an acrobat—Emmanuel Leweson the manager and part proprietor—principal shareholder—of the great North London Palace of Amusement.

All this is irrelevant, save that it explains why the manager produced his champagne, and why he gave his warnings to Frank in language so emphatic.

The family resumed the ordinary attire of humble British citizens, and Frank walked away with them. They lived in a small house, in one of those streets of gloomy small houses which abound in Islington. Patty nodded good-bye to him, and ran up the steps with her brother, opening the door with a latch key.

"Sir," said her father, when she had gone in, "you saved my daughter's life. What shall I say to thank you?"

"Nothing. Why do you let her do it?"

"We must live. There is nothing dishonest in it. There is not half the risk that you think about it. As for me, I feel almost as safe on the trapeze as you do on the pavement—and so does Patty, for that matter."

"But—but—" Frank hesitated.

"Immodest, you think it is. I don't know, sir—I don't know. There isn't a better girl than my girl in all London, and I defy you to find one. No, I had a great exercise of my conscience before I let her go—only her gifts were too strong. It was a-flying in the face of Providence not to let her take a way which was opened, so to speak, unto her. I laid the matter before my friend, Mr. Eddrup—"

"Eddrup! He that lives at Mrs. Skimp's in Granville-square?"

"There is only one Mr. Eddrup, young man. The Lord can't spare more than one at a time like him. Do you know him?"

"I live in the same house. Tell me about him."

"Ah, I think you had better find out about him. Well, I laid the matter before him, and he decided that if the girl liked, and I was always there to look after her, there would be no harm done. If you live in the same house as Mr. Eddrup, young gentleman, you try to talk to him. It was he that showed me the Light."

Frank stared.

"Before I knew Mr. Eddrup, I was clean gone astray, and out of the way altogether. Now, I'm a different man. So is Patty. Do you mean that Mr. Eddrup has never said a word in season to you?"

"Not yet. I've only been in the house two days."

"Then wait; or—if you are not one of those who go about scoffing and sneering at good men—come with me on Sunday evening. But you're a gentleman, Mr. Melliship. You go to the Establishment, I suppose."

Frank was too much astonished to find religion in an acrobat to answer.

"There is spiritual food of different kinds," Mr. Silver went on. "I can't get my nourishment in the Church of England. Mind you, I'm not saying a word against it. But I like freedom. I like to have my say if I've got anything to say, and when my heart is full."

"What denomination do you belong to?" asked Frank.

"To none, sir, at present. Why should I? Every man is a priest in his own house. I am of the religion of Abraham. First, I was a Plymouth Brethren; then I was a Primitive

Methodists, then I was a Particular Baptists. I've tried the Huntingdon Connection, and the Independents, and the Wesleyans; but I don't like them. I don't like any of them. So I stay at home and read the Book; or else I go and hear Mr. Eddrup on Sunday nights."

"Let me come and talk to you," said Frank. "You shall tell me more about yourself, if you will. I promise, at least, not to scoff and sneer at good things."

"I'm an illiterate man, sir, and you are a gentleman, with education, and all that, I dare say. But come when you like."

"Let me come next Sunday evening. You shall give me some tea," said Frank, in his lordly way, as if he were inviting himself to a man's rooms at college.

Mr. Silver looked after him with a puzzled expression, and went up the steps to dinner.

"A gentleman," he said to Patty, "who doesn't swear and use bad language: who doesn't look as if he got drunk; who doesn't go about with a big pipe in his mouth: who doesn't seem to mind talking about religious things. We don't get many such gentlemen at the Palace of Amusement, do us?"

"But, father," said Patty, laying the things out for dinner, "how does a gentleman come to be singing in the Palace? Gentlemen don't sing, do they, in public places for money?"

"I never heard of it. I will ask Mr. Eddrup. Here's dinner. Joey, say grace."

In these early days, Frank thought it best to go every morning to the Palace. This pleased Mr. Leweson, who had conceived an immense admiration for his new tenor. He showed this by solemnly presenting him with a tenor song of his own composing, which Frank sung, after the fourth night, in place of that song of the domestic affections already quoted. It was not so popular; but that, as Mr. Leweson remarked, was clear proof of its real worth. Had the loonatics applauded, he said he should have felt it his duty, as a musician, to put the song in the fire.

Sunday came, and Frank bethought him of his invitation to take tea with his new friends. Skimp's dined at four o'clock on Sundays. After dinner, Mrs. Skimp went to church, and her boarders chiefly amused themselves by playing at billiards. To the younger portion, the students, there was something particularly attractive in playing a forbidden game on Sunday; to the older ones, the chance of picking up a few stray sixpences at pool was quite enough of itself to make them prefer knocking the balls about to smoking pipes all the evening. Besides, they could unite the two amusements. Captain Bowker went to church, to smoothe out his ideas, he said—though no one understood in the least what he meant. I think he liked the quiet of church, where he could abstract his mind from all affairs—spiritual as well as worldly—and compose his verses. Mr. Eddrup, as usual, appeared at dinner, ate in silence what was set before him, and disappeared noiselessly.

Frank found his friends waiting for him—Patty with an extra riband. Her father was sitting with a Bible before him —his one book, which he read at all times. On Sundays, when he had a clear day before him, he used to read the Prophecies, applying them to modern times, and working out all problems of the present by their light. He had no books to help him, unless Swedenborg's "Heaven and Hell" be considered a help. Reading day after day, as he did, the words had come to have to him, as they have done to some theologians, a sort of threefold sense—the historic, the prophetic, and the hidden or inner sense. The pursuit of the last occupied all his thoughts.

The room was poorly furnished, for the family income was but small. Three or four chairs, a table, and a sideboard constituted the whole of it. No servant was apparent, and Patty and Joe were up and down the stairs, bringing up the tea things, laughing and chattering.

"I'm glad to see you, Mr. Melliship," said his host. "Now, I call this friendly. Patty, my dear, make haste up with the tea, because it's getting late."

"It's quite ready, father. We were only waiting for Mr. Melliship."

Watercresses, and bread and butter. Patty pouring out the tea. Her father with his finger on the Bible, enunciating things prophetic.

"I was reading what Ezekiel says about the world in our time, Mr. Melliship."

"Did Ezekiel write about our time?" asked Frank, thinking what a pity Patty's hands should be so spoiled by her acrobatic work.

"All time—every time. I can read, sir, the events of to-day and to-morrow in his pages, as plain as I can in a newspaper. I can tell you, if you like to listen, what is going to happen in the world before you die"

"Tell me," said Frank.

Mr. Silver held up his finger, and began. As he went on, in short jerky sentences, his eyes wandered from Frank's and fixed themselves in space—the gaze becoming deeper, and the expression as of one who reads things far off.

"A day of judgment and lamentation, when even the righteous shall be sifted. Afterwards the good time. A day of gathering of the nations upon the earth. The Great Battle—the Final Battle—shall be fought, after which there shall be no more wars. The Lord's battle will be fought on the Lord's battle-field, the Plain of Esdraelon: the battle of the people against the priests, and all their power. After it, the priests shall clothe themselves with trembling as with a garment. Know," he continued after a pause, stretching his hand across the table, and still with his eyes fixed in vacancy—"know that, from time long gone by, even from the days of the Chaldæan who first invented the accursed thing, the arm of the Lord has been against the priesthood. There is one nation the enemy of the human race—the nation of the priests. Whether they call themselves Catholic, or Anglican, or Dissenting, or Heathen, the spirit is alike. It is the spirit of darkness and tyranny."

"Mr. Melliship, is your tea to your liking?" whispered Patty.

"It is the spirit of pride and falsehood. Every dogma that blindfolds men's eyes is the invention of a priest; every accursed form of domination is the invention of the priests; every evil government has been maintained by the priests. They have made the world what it is; they have substituted fear for love; they keep the people ignorant, they darken counsel, and shut out light."

"Joey, run up and fetch my bonnet," said Patty.

"Then you want to abolish all priests?" said Frank, looking with wonder at the religious enthusiast.

"I am on the Lord's side," he replied, simply. "I would that I might live to fight in the Great Battle when it comes, and to fight against the priests. Priests! I am a priest. We are all priests;—every man in his own house, as the Patriarchs were before us. Remember, young man, that this is no light matter. It will be your place to take a side—and that before long. Russia is advancing south, as Ezekiel prophesied. Turkey is falling to pieces, and will soon be even as she who was once decked with ornaments—with bracelets on her hands and a chain upon her neck—who went astray and was confounded, as Ezekiel prophesied. All things came from Palestine: all things go back to Palestine. They are going to make a railway down the valley of the Euphrates: then they will rebuild the city of Babylon. In the time to come, that shall be the city of wealth and trade—when London will be deserted. The city of the Lord shall then be rebuilt, too: even the city of David, with a Temple which shall have no priests. It shall be the reign of peace. All nations shall come into the Church, and the millennium shall be begun. Even so, O Lord: Thy will be done!"

He folded his hands, as he concluded his speech, in a silent prayer.

"Drink your tea, father," said Patty; "it's getting cold—and it's late, besides."

"Where are we going, Miss Silver?" asked Frank.

"Miss Silver!" Patty laughed merrily. "I never was called Miss Silver in my life before. Call me Patty, Mr. Melliship."

"I will, if you will call me Frank."

"Indeed, I shall do nothing of the kind. You are a gentleman, and don't belong to our rank of life. Hush, don't move. Don't disturb father. He's often so, after talking about the Bible."

The enthusiast was bent forward, with his eyes fixed, gazing out of the window. He neither heard nor saw—he was in a trance. Frank looked at him anxiously. Then, moved by the impulse of his artistic nature, he took a book from the table. It was Patty's hymn-book—and on the fly-leaf began to sketch her father with his pencil. Patty looked over his shoulder in speechless admiration. In three minutes it was done—a rude, rough sketch, slightly idealized, so as to bring out the noble ruggedness of the man's brow, the wild depth of his eyes, the setting of his lips.

"Oh! it's wonderful," Patty whispered.

"Shall I draw you?" asked Frank, in a whisper. "Sit down, and I will try."

She sat down, blushing; but the next minute sprang up again, whispering—

"Not to-day—not while father is like that. Don't speak."

She took the Bible from him, and looked at the portrait with devouring eyes. Some subtle beauty the artist had put into the lines which she had never noticed before in her father's face, and saw it now for the first time.

They sat for two or three minutes more in silence, and then Mr. Silver threw his head back with a sigh, and looked round the room.

"It is late," he said. "Let us go."

"But where are we going?" asked Frank again.

"Why, to Mr. Eddrup's church, of course."

He followed in astonishment. Who and what was this Mr. Eddrup, that these people should so look up to him?

Patty and he walked together.

"I shall show the picture to father," she said—"but not to-night: not till the fit is off him. I suppose you were surprised to find us in such a nice house? We couldn't afford to rent it, you know; but it's Mr. Leweson's, and he gives it to us for nothing. We sometimes let lodgings, only I don't know—it is such a trouble."

"You had better again," said Frank. "I will be your lodger."

"Ah! I don't know. I should like it, you know," she replied, simply; "but father's particular. You might turn out bad, after all. And then see where we should be!"

"Well—I haven't turned out very good, so far," said Frank, with a sigh.

"Here we are at the church," said Patty, stopping at a door.

CHAPTER THE THIRTY-SECOND.

A STAIRCASE, steep as a ladder, led to a long low room, filled with people. It might have held about eighty, because audiences of all kinds, whether for religion or amusement, pack closely. The windows were open, because the night was close. The room was lighted by two or three gas-jets, and fitted up with benches for the body of the room, and a foot-high platform for the end. This was garnished with a rough hand-rail, not for any separation of the minister from the people, but for a leaning-place on which he might rest his hands. Two or three chairs were on the platform. One of these was empty. Mr. Silver, leaving Frank in the hands of his daughter, went to the end, and took the vacant seat with a slight but noticeable air of pride. The only arm chair was

U

occupied by Mr. Eddrup, who was leaning his head on his hands, motionless.

The people were the common people of the neighbourhood, rough, coarse men, and rough, coarse women. They all knew each other, and occasionally telegraphed salutes with friendly grins. A few carried babies; but there were very few children present, and those only so small as not to be able to take care of themselves. They whispered a good deal to each other, but in a hushed, serious way. Laughter and levity there were none.

The worshippers in this humble Ebenezer were called, as Frank afterwards discovered, the Primitive Blueskins, by the scoffers in the neighbourhood. The reason, as told to him was a queer story, which may or may not be true. It told how forty years ago, before Mr. Eddrup went to the place, there had been an attempt—a very little one—to promote in the court some form of Christian worship. This room, the same in which they always met, had been fixed upon as the only room available. It was old and shaky, and it was built over a dyeing establishment. One cold winter night, soon after they had formed themselves into a congregation, the reverend gentleman who conducted their exercises, whether driven by religious zeal or impelled by the severity of the weather, enforced his arguments by an unwonted physical activity, stamping, gesticulating, and even jumping. He calculated *nimium credulus*, on the strength of the floor. Alas! it gave way. The boards broke beneath the unaccustomed strain. The table, on which were two candles, was upset; and, amid the darkness, the little flock could hear only the groans of their pastor and the splashing of liquid. The last flash of the overturning lights had shown him vanishing through the flooring. They turned and fled. It was some time before they ventured to return. But they found their minister blue. He was dyed: he had fallen into the vat prepared for an indigo day. Besides this, he was half frozen. After this the congregation dispersed. Nor was it till Mr. Eddrup came that they reassembled; and when they did, the nickname stuck to them still.

Patty pulled Frank by the arm, and they humbly took the lowest places of all, the very last, with their backs against the wall.

"It's going to begin directly," whispered the girl. "You must look over my hymn-book. There's Mr. Eddrup."

As she spoke, the old man rose and advanced to the front of the platform, grasping the rail.

"If any have aught to say"—he spoke a kind of formula—"let him or her now say it."

A labouring man rose up, and incoherently delivered himself of a few short and unconnected sentences. Then he sat down, perspiring. He had an idea which he wanted to set forth, but language was too strong for him, and he had failed.

Mr. Eddrup looked round again. No one else spoke. Then he took a hymn-book, and gave out a number. They took their hymns, like their tea, sitting; but sang with none the less fervour,

Then their leader—for such Mr. Eddrup was—rose to address them, with his hands on the rail, his head held down, and his white hair falling forward in a long mass that almost hid his face.

"Into what queer world have I dropped?" thought Frank. "A religious trapeze family; a man who lives at Skimp's, and preaches to people; I myself, who sing at a music hall, and come here on Sundays. It all seems very irregular."

Mr. Eddrup, still looking on the ground, with his long, white hair hanging about him, began his discourse in a slow, hesitating way, as if he was feeling, not for ideas, but for fitting words to put them in. Presently he warmed a little with his subject, and lifting his head, spoke in clearer and fuller tones. His audience went with him, devouring every word he said. They were wise words. He spoke of the everyday life of a religious man, of the temptations that beset the poor, of the strength which comes of resistance. He had that native eloquence which comes of earnestness. He wished to say the right thing in the most forcible way. So, when he had found the right thing, he took the simplest words that lay to his hand, and the readiest illustration. Socrates did the same. A higher than Socrates did the same. He talked to them for two hours. During all that time, not a soul stirred. All eyes were fixed upon the speaker. There was no interruption, save now and again when a woman sobbed. It was not that he told them the hackneyed things that preachers love to dwell upon—the general phrases, the emotional doctrines; all these Mr. Eddrup passed by. He told them unpalatable things: little things: things which are a perpetual hindrance to the progress of the soul, which yet seem to have nothing to do with the soul. He laid down directions for them which showed that he knew exactly all their circumstances. He showed them how religion is a flower that grows upon all soils alike, nourished by the same sun which shines upon rich and poor. And, lastly—in a peroration which made the ears of those that heard it to tingle—he proclaimed the infinite love of the Creator. He stopped suddenly, sat down, and was silent.

They sang a hymn, and the people went away.

"Tell me the meaning of it," asked Frank of Patty. "Who and what is Mr. Eddrup?"

"Come away, and I will tell you. Father likes to have a chat with him of a Sunday night. Come Joey. He came here," said Patty, "forty years ago and more. He was a young man, I've been told, and strong; but he was always very sad and silent. He began by searching out—always in this court—the poor children, and getting them to school in the morning. He taught it himself, and gave them bread and tea for breakfast. People liked that, you know, and the children liked it. Then he got to having the men to evening school at eight o'clock. A few of them went. The court was the most awful place, I've been told, in all London. Mr. Eddrup was robbed a dozen times going away at night—beaten, too, and ill-treated. But he always came again next day, just as if nothing had happened. They do say that nothing would make him prosecute a thief. So when the boys found there was no danger and no fun in stealing his handkerchief or knocking him down, of course they left off. Well, so it went on, you see. Gradually the court got better. Mr. Eddrup got the houses into his own hands by degrees—because he's a very well-to-do man, you know—and made them clean. They were pigsties before. He never turned anybody out; never sold up their sticks for rent; always waited and waited—and, they say, he always gets paid."

"Has he turned the people into angels, then?"

"No. I don't say that. But they're better than the run of people. He has made them a religious lot which was the most dreadful lot in all London. Parsons come here now, and want the people to go to church. Not they. So long as Mr. Eddrup preaches in the little chapel, there they go."

"All this must cost him money as well as time."

"He spends all he's got, whatever that may be, Mr. Melliship, on the poor. I've been told that he never takes anything stronger than water, and has only one room to himself, all to have more for the poor people."

"Some of that is true, I know," said Frank.

"Oh! those flowers," cried Patty, as they passed a flower-girl. "How sweet they smell!"

"Let me give you some," said Frank.

Now, Patty had never had any flowers given her before. It was a new sensation that a man—or anybody, indeed—should pay her attentions. She went home with her present, and put the flowers in water. If Frank had been able to see how carefully those poor flowers were watered, and how long they lasted! It will be understood at once that Patty's stage career had been very different to that of most young ladies of her profession. Always with her father, taken by him to the theatre, brought home by him, she was as domestic a little bird as any in all this great wilderness of houses.

"Poor Patty!" thought Frank as he walked home. "A dreary life for her to risk her life every night for so many shillings or pounds a week; to have no lovers, like other girls; no pleasure but to go and hear Mr. Eddrup preach."

Mr. Eddrup had returned when he reached home, and was sitting, silent as usual, in the drawing-room with Captain Bowker—who had his long pipe alight, and his glass of rum and water before him.

"You were there to-night," said the old preacher. "The Silvers brought you."

"They did," said Frank. "Thank you very much."

Captain Bowker smoked on. He was in a meditative mood.

"I went once," he said, "myself. Should have gone again, but I saw one of my last old crew there. Couldn't go and sit on the same bench with him, you know. Stations must be observed. Mr. Melliship, it's just as well to say that Mr. Eddrup here doesn't care to have his Sunday evening's occupation known."

"Do good by stealth, and blush to find it fame," said Frank.

"No, Mr. Melliship—no," replied the old man, sadly. "There has never been a time when I have not been beset by temptation to be proud of a trifling piece of work like mine. I should like to be famous, if only in the smallest way. But I pray against it. I formed the resolution, very long ago, that there was only one course for me in life—to go through it as noiselessly as I could, to do as little mischief as possible, to resent no injury."

"But why?" asked Frank. "Why?"

"Some day I will tell you, perhaps. Not now. I am glad you came to hear me talk to my people, Mr. Melliship. It is a long time since we have had a—anybody but my own people. It does them good to see strangers. Let me look at your face, sir."

Frank held his face, smiling, to the light, while the old man walked feebly—Frank noticed how very feeble he was after his exertions in the chapel—to the chair where he sat, and looked at him steadily.

"There is the seal of innocence, and the seal of guilt. This is the seal of innocence. Keep it, young man. Look at mine. Do you see nothing?"

"Nothing," said Frank.

Mr. Eddrup sighed, and sat down again. A few minutes afterwards he stole out of the room, and slipped upstairs to bed.

"He's often like that," said Captain Bowker. "Something on his mind. I had a cook aboard the *Merry Moonshine* once, used to sit all day long, and never speak to a soul. Took a fancy to a Lascar, and would sometimes talk to him. No one else, mind. One day he up with the chopper, and buried it three inches in the Lascar's head. Then, before you could say Jack Robinson, over he went—ship going ten knots. Lascar dead in a minute. *Mr. Eddrup's took a fancy to you!*"

"That's a cheerful sort of story to tell. Do you think Mr. Eddrup may be tempted to do something rash with the carving-knife?"

"I can't say," said the Captain, solemnly. "No one can say what another man will do, or what terrible thing may happen to him. I've been married myself."

"Then you may be married again."

"Lord forbid! There's ghosts again. I suppose you never saw a ghost?"

"Never."

"Nor more did I. But I've *felt* one, young man. I've been beat black and blue by a ghost. Rum thing, that was."

"Tell it me."

"There it is, you see. You get making me sit up spinning my yarns when I ought to be in my berth. Sunday night, too. Well, I'll tell you this one. It was forty years ago. I was a midshipman aboard an East Indiaman. We'd had bad weather, and put into Port Louis to refit;—for the matter of that, we always put in there in the good old days. I was ashore with two or three more, drinking, as boys will, in the verandah of an hotel there. There was a chap, an Englishman, with a solemn face and a long nose, got talking to us. I remember his hatchet jaws now. Presently he whispers across the little table—

"'I want two or three plucky fellows. Will you come?'

"'What for?' we asked him.

"'Money,' says he. 'Treasure.'

"'Do you know where it is?' I said.

"'I do,' says he.

"'Then why don't you get it yourself?' says I.

"That seemed to fix him a bit. Then he says—

"'Because I can't do it alone, and I won't trust anybody but English sailors. It's money buried by the pirates up in the hillside over there. I know the exact spot. There is a story going about that the place is haunted; but we ain't afraid of ghosts, I *should* hope.'

"We agreed for next night, if we could get leave, and went aboard again. All that day and the next we were talking it over. The mate heard us. He came up to me laughing—

"'So you're not afraid of ghosts, are you?'

"However, we got our leave, and went ashore. The mate went too.

"It's dark in those latitudes between six and seven, and at that time we met our long-nosed friend. He had got pickaxes and a lantern, and led the way. There were four of us altogether. We had to pick our way, when we left the path, over stones and through bushes; and, what was very odd, I kept on thinking I heard steps behind us. Being only a slip of a boy, I begins to get nervous. Presently our guide stopped.

"'Here we are,' he says; and, pointing to a place under a tree, he hangs up the lantern, and takes off his coat and began to dig. 'Now boys,' he says, 'as quick as you can.'

"We fell to with a will. It was a precious hot night, and the ground was hard; but we made a hole in it after a bit, and then at it tooth and nail. Five minutes after we began, I looked up to straighten my back, and found the lantern gone.

"'Who's unshipped the light?' I says.

"We all looked round. There was a young moon to give us a little light, but no lantern. I, for one, felt queer. However, we all went on again without saying a word. We got a hole two foot deep, and were all in it. Then one of my mates wants to know how long the job's going to last.

"'Perhaps,' he says, 'the ghosts have sunk it fifty fathoms deep.'

"'Ghosts be d——d,' said lantern jaws. 'Dig away, boys.'

"Then we heard a laugh close by us.

"'Ho!—ho!—ho!'

"It was a curious place for echoes among the rocks, and the laugh went ringing round and round till you thought it was never going to stop. We all stopped for a bit.

"'Go on,' says our leader. 'They can't do more than laugh.'

"With that another laugh, louder than the first. However, we went on. Then I heard steps; and looking up, I saw three or four figures over the hole.

"'Lord!' I cried. 'Here's the ghosts.'

"Well, I hadn't hardly time to sing out, when whack, whack came half a dozen sticks on our heads and backs, and we all tumbled together. I suppose the sticks went at us for five minutes in all. When they stopped, I got up the first, grabbed my jacket, hanging on the tree, and legged it, tumbling over the rocks, and scratching myself in the bushes, as fast as ever mortal man ran in his life. The rest all came after me. What became of mealy face, I don't know. P'raps the ghosts finished him off.

"Half an hour after we got to the port, the mate came up with three friends. They were all laughing at some joke of theirs.

"'Well, my lads,' says he, 'did you see any ghosts?'

"No one answered, and they all laughed louder.

"The oddest thing of all, Mr. Melliship," concluded Captain Bowker, laying his pipe-stem impressively on Frank's hand, "was that next morning my cap, which I had left behind in the hole, was found in the boat. Now, *how did that get there?*"

CHAPTER THE THIRTY-THIRD.

A WORD about Parkside, where Grace Heathcote sat waiting and hoping. It is the way of things. A man works and hopes, and is sure to be disappointed. A woman waits and hopes, generally getting disappointed too.

Dull enough it was, and quiet, unless when Cousin Dick

was with them. The Heathcote girls were—by right of education—not of position—something better than the commonplace young ladies of the quiet market town. They saw little of them, and made few friends. Moreover, they were five miles away from Market Basing, so that they were practically thrown upon their own resources. That meant that they talked, and made each other unhappy. This, I believe, is not uncommon in English households—that sweet domesticity on which we pride ourselves covering an infinite amount of petty miseries, tiny bullyings, naggings, and prickings with tongues as sharp as needles. Sister against sister—mother against daughter. They love each other fondly, of course, because they are always supposed to love each other: domestic affection being as necessary in modern life as a shirt to one's back. Unfortunately, the love which reigns in the dear home life does not always bring with it that tenderness for each other's sensitive points which keeps out of the house ill-humours and sour tempers. The lower classes of England —I do not mean the very lowest—are much superior to the middle classes in this respect. I have found out the reason why. They don't sit at home so much. In London, they are always going to the theatre, which is almost the only amusement for the class who frequent the pit, and are not above the gallery. In the country, they go out and about as much as they can.

Now, Grace Heathcote had a large share not only of fidelity, but of obstinacy, which she inherited from her father. A woman's fidelity is very often like one of those plants which flourish best covered up and hidden. Grace's prospered best openly—in the sunshine—and was able to grow and flourish even against the east winds of her mother's opposition. To her, Frank was a hero. It seemed noble in him to go away into a sort of hiding—working, as she imagined, to pay off his father's liabilities, and hoping to come back after many months to claim her promised hand. This she thought, and this she said when, as happened not infrequently, her mother turned the talk upon Frank.

To Lydia Heathcote, Frank seemed as a fool. And she said so. For she was determined on one thing: her daughter should marry Dick Mortiboy. She saw that Grace attracted him. She was sure—for she meant well by her daughter—that he would make a good husband. She wanted to secure all that money of his for her own children. She was wise as well as determined. She knew that as the constant dropping of water wears away the hardest rock, so the constant insinuations of distrust and suspicion wear away the fondest woman's trust. Therefore she talked a good deal about Frank; repeated and reiterated her grief that he was doing so badly, as she assumed; pointed out how foolish it was to go away from his friends, and those who would help him to a decent position; hinted that it would be so much better if he were to emigrate, and follow the example of his cousin Dick; never failed to shed tears over the enumeration of dear Dick's many virtues, as contrasted with the failings and weaknesses of Frank; and always ended by reproachfully sighing over her daughter, as over one who trifles with a good man's love.

"But, mamma, Frank will get on, I'm sure. Kate said in her letter she knew he was doing well. He is very clever. He can paint beautifully; and it was only the other evening, at the rectory, that Mr. Nelson said artists were just as well off as any other professional men, and as well thought of. If he likes painting better than anything else, and sees his way to get on, why should he not be an artist?"

"Nonsense, child," was her mother's answer to Grace's special pleading. And then Mrs. Heathcote explained, for the hundredth time, the reasons why Frank could never, by any possibility, be in a position to marry. "Besides, if Kate knows he is doing very well in London, it is a strange thing they don't know where he lives. You know, your father would write to him if he knew where to find him. But we couldn't even give Dick his address before he went to town. Such a want of respectability about having no address! It's no use, Grace; I know perfectly well that the boy is doing no good for himself, else why not let his friends know his address?"

"I am not going to listen," said Grace, indignantly, "to things like that. You have no right to say such things of Frank."

"There—there, Grace, do be reasonable. It is all for your own good that I speak. If your own mother does not know the world, who should? Why, before I married your father, there were two or three people I fancied. Young Spriggs, the brewer, who failed for thirty thousand pounds, and cut his throat—I might have had him. Mr. Potterton, of Wyncote—he's got an asthma now: you can hear him a mile off, poor man. And old Mr. Humbledum, who died of drink last week—why, people used to talk about us. That was before I met your father. And look at Dick—poor Dick!—head over ears in love with you."

"To begin with, he is nothing of the sort. And if he were, it would be nothing to me."

"I can see it, girl," said Mrs. Heathcote, wisely nodding her head. "I've seen it for months now. I think it is—I suppose it doesn't matter what I think,—cruel of you never to give him the slightest civility. Poor fellow, you might be even polite to him when he comes."

Grace beat a tattoo on the carpet with her foot, but said nothing.

"I only hope he does not notice it so much as I do. I've no patience with your father; he's as easy as an old shoe about things. If he'd told you to give Frank up when they left—"

"Mamma!" cried Grace, her cheek reddening and her eye-flashing brightly. Mrs. Heathcote was a little afraid of her daughter when she looked like that. She saw she had gone a little too far—not for the first time. "Mamma, how dare you——"

The door opened and Mr. Heathcote came into the room. Grace fell into his arms, and with her head on his shoulder, sobbed like a child. She would not have broken out if they had remained alone.

"Lydia," said Mr. Heathcote angrily, "what have you been saying to Grace? Never mind, my child—never mind."

"Really, John," said his wife, "you and Grace together are enough to wear out the patience of Job," and she swept out of the room.

And so on. Scenes that happened not once, but often. And with each one Grace became obstinate, and her mother more irritating. Lucy was made unhappy. The farmer was made unhappy: that was nothing. Civil war raged in Parkside Farm, and the contest was maintained on terms of perfect equality, in which Grace, shielded by a stubborn resolution, received all her mother's blows, and only occasionally retaliated with words which had more of sharpness than of filial piety. Dick brought peace for the time, and there was renewed war when he was gone.

A truce was held on a tacit understanding, while Mrs. Heathcote tried to play off Lucy on Dick. This was, however, quite hopeless. First, Dick did not like women to be gentle and soft. He liked a girl with a fine high temper of her own, and a will, like Grace; and, secondly, Lucy did not like Dick so much as Grace did. From her constant visits to old Ready-money, she found out, by the old man's frowns when Dick came to see him, that there was something he had done. Of course, she knew nothing positive; but she had strong suspicions that all was not quite right between the father and the son. Her frequent absences in Derngate made matters even worse for Grace.

As for moving Farmer John out of his jog-trot ways, nothing could do that. He was quite ready to help Frank with money or counsel—for the Heathcotes were very well-to-do; but he was not going to put himself out of the way, and hunt him up. Let Frank come to him. Frank did not go to him: made no sign; and Grace's heart began to fail her.

Village affairs lost their interest. The rheumatics of the old women found her callous: their complaints fell on cold ears. She went through the daily routine of her small duties without interest. When her mother, the day's business finished, about ten or eleven—they breakfasted at eight—took her seat for the day, she tried to escape to her own room, or to the garden. She could sometimes—when Silly Billy could be spared to blow the organ—take refuge in the church. Her mother disliked music in the morning, so she could not play. Her pony was lame, and she could not ride. Mrs. Heathcote never drove out, except to town: like most country ladies, thinking very little of the lovely foliage and shady lanes of her own shire.

Sometimes one of the Battiscombe girls stayed with them —then they played croquet in the afternoon; Lord Launton very often finding something to say to Mr. Heathcote, which made it quite natural for him to stop and play with them till the dressing-bell rang at the Towers. It was curious that he found business which brought him to Parkside three or four times a week. He came in on any pretext, always about the same time—croquet time; stayed as long as he could, and almost forgot his shyness. Dick Mortiboy at first made him shrink into his shell; but he managed to creep out again gradually, and came to like him. Dick took a fancy to the shy young fellow: talked to him; told him stories—Dick always had the readiest perception of what kind of story would suit his listener: this was one great secret of his popularity—and pleased the viscount by not deferring to him in the slightest degree because he was a Lord.

So life went on;—Grace sad and unhappy; her mother angry and disappointed; all playing at cross-purposes—as we always do; all acting a part to the world—as we always do; all putting a good face on things—as of course we must. And do not quarrel with Grace when you read her letters to Kate, because they seem bright and happy. I knew a man once who wrote the brightest, gayest, happiest letter—full of mirth and fun, and good spirits—a quarter of an hour before he blew out his brains. Letters mean nothing, except that they are sometimes a natural relief to the heart, and the effort of pleasing a friend gives you good spirits in spite of yourself.

CHAPTER THE THIRTY-FOURTH.

MUST send you a piece of news, dearest Kate," wrote Grace, "before coming to what I have really to say;—that is, my letter is to be a woman's letter, with all the important part at the end. The news is, that Dick met Frank last week in London. The account of him is pretty good—for Dick, that is, who is a better story-teller than historian. That sounds like nonsense; but what I mean is, that he tells capital stories so long as he is allowed to draw upon the boundless fields of his own imagination, and keep to Texas; but when one wants exact descriptions of what really took place, one finds him sometimes a careless observer. This is a fault, perhaps, common with your great geniuses. For my own part, I never invented anything in all my life—and how people can write novels, goodness only knows!—but I can always manage to tell exactly what I saw. The feminine eye, my dear, has a remarkable power of taking in everything at a glance. I am sure you will own that no man ever yet was born—not even Robert Houdin—who could pass a woman in the street and be able to tell afterwards everything she had on, from top to toe, and what it cost. You and I can do it, easily. That was just what I wanted to know about Frank. 'Tell me,' I said, 'what he looked like, and how he was dressed.'

Well, you know, Dick was with him for eight long hours, and he can't tell me. He doesn't even know whether he wore gloves. He met Frank somewhere, and they went together to the University cricket match. After that they went and dined together of course—one cannot imagine men meeting without dining together. I begin to think that there must be some secret religious worship, a kind of stomachic Freemasonry, connected with dinners; or else that eating, with men, has a poetry about it which it fails to have for us. To-day, for instance, we had roast veal for dinner; but I am as prosaic after it as if it had been cold mutton. They dined together, Kate, and then they talked and smoked all the evening. Finally, Frank went away, half promising to call on Dick in the morning. *He never came.* All these details, I dare say, you know from Frank himself. What I wanted to learn exactly was how he looked, and if he was dressed properly; because I have often read in books that dress is a good rough test of prosperity, and if a man is doing well he always has a good pair of boots and a good coat. Don't be deceived by a bad hat, because the richest men sometimes have a bad hat. Poor Uncle Richard's hat was always really beyond everything. When a man begins to go downhill, it shows itself first in the heels of his boots, and next in his trousers. You would hardly believe that Dick—the man I believed so clever—never noticed Frank's boots at all. I made Lucy ask him the question, because I had asked after all the rest of his apparel, and Dick might have thought me inquisitive.

"'Boots?' asked Dick. 'I never looked at his boots.'

"And yet he calls himself an observant man!

"My dear Kate, I am so happy to have seen some one who has actually seen Frank, that I write all manner of nonsense. He was looking very well indeed, Dick declares. He was happy—had a pleasant day. Dick did hint at some sort of fight; but that must be an allegorical way of describing a pleasant day. Just like the Americans, when they go to see a great sight, say they are going to see the elephant, so my cousin, our cousin, Dick Mortiboy, when he wishes to convey the idea of perfect happiness, says he has had a fight. That is my theory, because I cannot believe that men can possibly feel any pleasure in banging each other about. Frank gave a happy and cheerful account of himself. Dick thinks that he is making money by art: or, at all events—because we hardly expect him to make money—that he is gradually getting work, and making a sucess for himself. The career of a man! Is it possible to be too ambitious? Lucy thinks that ambition means selfishness. She says that a man ought to follow what she calls the straight line of duty—look neither to right nor left, and be careless whether people praise him or not. I try to persuade her that all men are not clergymen. I like to have my clergyman really pious and disinterested—I suppose, because one never gets that kind of clergyman—just as I should like to have all sorts of impossible things in sealskin. A man—fancy, a Man!—came down here last winter with a long sealskin coat—real sealskin, mind—worth at least a hundred pounds. Now, that I call a wasting of good things. But about ambition. What I should like would be to see my husband distinguished: first in everything; people looking after him; pictures of him in the shop windows; a portrait of him in the *Illustrated;* biographies of him; cartoons, and even caricatures, of him. This is my ambition for myself. I should be plain Mrs.——; it's bad luck to write your married name before you are married—look after his house, see that his dinner was always exactly what he liked, and endeavour to find out what it is that men admire so much in different kinds of wine. Tell me you agree with me, Kate. But for a man not to be ambitious! If I had a husband not ambitious of doing something—of being first in his own circle, even—I would stick pins in him till he was. Would not you? But Lucy, the dear child, has no ideas that are not founded on what poor Aunt Susan used to tell her. Aunt Susan! What would she have thought of her nephew Dick? She was always talking to Lucy about him—always saying that she knew he was not dead—always praying for him—always telling of his good heart. How proud she would have been of him!

"Yes, Kate—Frank is well and happy. Of course he tells you he is; but it is really true—because Dick, who is unobservant about boots, would not be deceived in this. He laughs; he eats and drinks; he is well dressed; he is too proud to take any assistance; he is getting on in his profession; and, without telling Dick anything, he asked after me ten times. Ten times, Kate! Always my own Frank—with the same bright face, and the same cheery voice. And now I know this, I've got an answer always ready, in case of little domestic storms, which you may guess.

"And now for the real thing in my letter. Kate, you are

very wicked! You dare to make great successes, and to say nothing. You presume on our country ignorance. You knew that I should not go to town this season at all. You were afraid, perhaps, in your pride, that Dick would buy your picture: you were even too proud to have it exhibited in your own name. My dear, I am proud of you. Frank told Dick, who didn't think much about it—such is his Californian ignorance!—and casually told papa, who didn't think much about it, because his lines have not been cast much among picture galleries. He casually told me. I jumped—I did, indeed. A picture in the Royal Academy! Actually accepted, and hung in a good place, and sold! O Kate! how proud you ought to be! And never to have told me a word about it. Working away in your little Welsh village in silence, without a soul to speak to; sending up your picture in a name that prevented the committee from knowing whether it was a man or a woman! Of course, if they had known your sex, they would have rejected you with ignominy, in pursuance of their grand plan of keeping Us down. My dear Kate, it was sublime. Now the Academy is all over and done, and we have not even seen the picture. If we had known, of course we should have all gone to town—mamma, and Lucy, and myself, and Cousin Dick, to see it. Dear Kate, I am so glad, so very glad! It must be the best consolation you have had since your troubles. Write and tell me you are happy about it; and, *please*, don't keep secrets from me. I will guard your secrets so faithfully that not a soul shall known there is a secret. Tell me all your plans.

"Parkside is the same as ever. Somehow, we see more of Lord Launton than we used to. I wish he would not come in so often; for though he is very pleasant and all that, it is rather embarrassing if people come and find him there. We are partly his father's tenants, of course; but that is not a reason why he should come and play croquet with us. Then, we are not in a position to be invited to the Towers; and though he does not mean to be condescending, it is in some respects desirable, as mamma says, that he should not come. The worst of it is that we treat him, Lucy and I, as such an old friend, that we really do not take any notice of him, and quite ignore the fact that he is a real viscount. The other day, the Battiscombe girls were here. We had croquet, Cousin Dick, music, and a little dance. Lord Launton came in by chance, and stayed with us. They—I mean the girls—were immensely jealous of us; and, I have not the least doubt, hate us both for being intimate with him. I am reminded of our gardener—you know him? I saw him one day last autumn, standing for two hours together admiring his chrysanthemums. Then I went out to him, because I thought he might catch cold. He waved an admiring hand at the flowers.

"'Bless you miss,' he said in the grandest way, as if that was nothing to what he could do if he brought his mind to bear on it, 'I take no manner of pride in them.'

"That is what I say to Lucy about Lord Launton. Is it not rather humiliating to us that the earl allows him to come here so often? You see, he thinks that we are good, worthy people; and that papa, in whom he has the good sense to believe, is a most excellent person; and that we are all so deeply flattered by a visit from his son, that it is kindness to let him come as often as ever he likes. For my own part, I am going to take an early opportunity of speaking to Lord Launton seriously.

"I think Dick is recovering the ground he lost by his dreadful speech at the children's feast. The rector, good man, looks on him with eyes of suspicion, and so do the curates; but the people have taken his advice very much to heart; and, I believe, several *pères de famille* are seriously contemplating the desirability of sending their sons away. They go down, and consult Mr. Mortiboy at the bank. Dick gets a lot of maps, and points out where they can emigrate to, and what it will cost. He never fails to lecture them on the folly of trying to make their sons 'gentlemen,' as they call it—that is, to put them into banks and lawyers' offices, so that they may wear a black coat. He still continues his unrighteous practice of giving weekly doles to old women. I think Mr. Ghrimes instigates him to this. He tells us that he has dissolved partnership with his old friend, who has got all his Mexican estates. Those estates abroad do not seem to have weighed very much on his mind; and he confessed to me once that they were only valuable when a man of energy—meaning himself—was on the spot to superintend them. He showed me on the map where they were: put his thumb down—you know he has got an enormous thumb—and it covered a quarter of Mexico, about a hundred thousand square miles.

"'There,' he said—'my estates are exactly there.'

"'Thank you, Dick,' I said. 'I am very much wiser than I was before.'

"Then he laughed, and began to talk about something else.

"Whenever I write to you, I tell about Dick. I do not know how it is, except that he really does occupy our minds and our talk a good deal. What he did last, what he is going to do next, if he has committed any outrage on the church or conventionalities in general—this is chiefly what we talk about. I like him better every day. I think he is getting softened, and more companionable. He has left off the use of strange expressions in unknown languages. He has begun to dress more like an ordinary Christian. He falls in with our ways and habits of thought. In time, I hope we shall make him a steady, respectable member of society. What I try to teach him is, that we may be altogether wrong, but that we are all wrong together—only the division of a word, you see —and it is very disagreeable not to be like other people. We had a talk the other day about things.

"'You go to church because it is respectable,' he said.

"'Well, and what if we do? Going to church is good for people. If the well-to-do people did not go, the poor would not. And without church, they would have no weekly lesson in good manners, to say nothing of higher things.'

"'You subscribe a million a year to convert the niggers. You send out people you call missionaries, who live in comfortable houses, and bully and bribe the natives. I've seen them.'

"'Of course, if you've seen them bullying and bribing the natives, I can say nothing. There you have an advantage over us.'

"'All the time, you've got all your paupers at home starving, and going from bad to worse.'

"'What are we to do, Dick? People give because they think it is right. The missionaries may be bad men, but the object is good. The societies may be badly managed, but their aim is a good one.'

"'Your charities make the people paupers; your Church helps to make them hypocrites; your poor laws make them slaves; your trading interests grind them into the dust."

"'My dear cousin,' I said, 'don't say *your* in such a personal way. I really should be very glad if things were better. Tell me what I am to do. As for you—you have wealth; you, at least, can do something.'

"'I intend to,' he said. 'I am going to look about for a while, and then I shall start something.'

"Oh, Kate, that 'something'! When Dick appears in his character of social reformer, introducing his 'something,' I tremble for all our notions. His ideas of society are primitive and radical. Only, as he tells papa, he can't do any harm, because not five per cent. have got the pluck to think for themselves.

"I run on when I write to you, till I hardly know when to stop. I tell you everything. Don't you think people exchange their ideas and show their hearts better on paper than in words? I sit in my own room alone, after dinner, and write like this, till I have exhausted everything that was in my head. I wonder if you really like to read my letters. Then I sit back and read it all over again, and try to ascertain, by a calm, critical perusal, whether it is worth reading. Sometimes I say —'Kate will laugh at this;' 'This is well put, young woman;' and so on—like a friendly critic, just to encourage myself.

* * * * * *

"I have just read the whole letter through again. Kate, it is much too full of Cousin Dick. That is not my fault: it is the fault of his being always here. It is also much too full of myself. It is I, I, I—all *Is*, like the prophet's creature, that he saw in his vision. I must correct this fault in my next, and make it all U, U, U, in compensation, like a churchyard orchard. You know, Kate, I should like to make it all F, F, F—ective. Ah, me! if it were not for hope I should die. Suppose we go on for years and years and years. How would it be, do you think, when we are both past sixty, to fulfil our troth and marry? Dreadful thought! Love belongs to youth. If Frank cannot marry me when I am young, and when he can kiss me and fondle me for the sake of *mes beaux yeux*, let him not marry me at all. I would rather remain single *for his sake*. Would not you, Kate? Oh! to wait, and wait—his plighted word holding true—till my cheeks are withered and my beauty all gone, and there is nothing to remind him of the Grace he used to love: and then to feel that all the passion was dead, and nothing left but the smouldering ashes of duty! Let me marry my Frank when I am young and fair, or let me never marry at all. Farewell, dear Kate. Tell him from me—oh! what message can I send him? You are the kindest sister-in-law that ever poor girl was *going* to have. Tell him, in any guarded way that you like—not in so many words, because it is immodest and unwomanly, only it is true—that I love him

—I love him—I love him; and that there can never be more than one man in all the world to me. "Your own
"GRACE."

The foregoing very silly and young-ladyish effusion—over which I do hope my readers will not linger till they become critical—may be read by the light of the preceding chapter.

Those who are too captious about girls' letters will remark that there is no postscript at all in it.

CHAPTER THE THIRTY-FIFTH.

AFTER living three or four weeks at Mrs. Skimp's, Frank made up his mind to shift his quarters. Great joy, accordingly, fell upon the inmates of the boarding-house in Grenville-square, in whose opinion Mr. Melliship gave himself unbecoming airs—nobody except old Bowker and half-witted Eddrup, being good enough company for him.

"After all, what was he?" they asked scornfully. "A singer at a music hall!"

Captain Bowker, who had never before found such a listener as Frank, was most unfeignedly sorry to see the only person in the place with an ear for poetry depart. Besides, the old fellow liked Frank, and so begged him to come and spend Sunday evenings with him, when the others were generally out. This Frank promised to do when he could, to the Captain's great relief.

The first day after he left, one or two of Mrs. Skimp's gentlemen so far plucked up courage again as to begin their persecution of Mr. Eddrup as of old. But he had a friend in the old sailor, who, taught by Frank's example, confronted his assailants with so angry a visage, and language of such briny flavour, that they reluctantly gave up their fun.

So that at Mrs. Skimp's table Frank's memory was kept

green by the Captain, and the good he had effected in Mr. Eddrup's behalf was not allowed to perish.

As Mr. Leweson had sent him to Skimp's, when Frank made up his mind to leave there he mentioned the matter to him.

"You might lodge with the Silvers. They have room for somebody with them, I know," Mr. Leweson said—regretting next moment that he had suggested it, foreboding disturbance to Patty's peace of mind.

Frank offered to become the occupant of Mr. Silver's two vacant rooms, and was accepted without demur.

He was heartily glad to escape from the noise and coarseness of Skimp's to a room of his own, where, at least, he could be alone.

Patty Silver had furnished the first floor—left empty by their last tenant—for him, not magnificently, it is true, but as well as the slender funds of the family permitted. He had a bed; and, in his sitting-room, a carpet and a table, and as many chairs as he could expect for twelve shillings a-week.

Patty cooked his dinner for him; and before he went to the Palace, he took a cup of tea with the Silvani Family; then after he had sung his three songs, and borne the applause—which humiliated him more than singing the songs—he smoked a pipe in Mr. Silver's company before he went to bed; but as he smoked and listened, or replied in monosyllables to the prophetic discourse of the acrobat—who never talked on any subject but one—his thoughts were miles away in the past or in the future.

"The future!" he used to think, after his nightly purgatory. "How long shall I go on with it? And what next?"

He had the pleasure of sending something weekly to his mother and sister. He had the pleasure weekly of hearing of them and of Grace. But he could not continue to sing at the Palace after his engagement was over. It was but the shift of a penniless man. All day he lived in terror lest some old friend should see him, and proclaim his disgrace—as he thought it.

Night after night he searched the sea of faces for one he knew. He never saw one. The Palace is not a place where country cousins go. The "loonatics" who patronised Mr. Leweson were all of Islington blood; unmixed Cockneys; City clerks, dressed à la mode; young shopmen, making half-a-crown purchase nearly as much dissipation as a sovereign will buy in the west; with a good sprinkling of honest citizens, fond of an evening out, neither they nor their wives averse to the smell of tobacco and the taste of beer. But no face he knew. He was as safe from discovery, under the cover of Signor Cipriano, at the Palace as he would have been in San Francisco.

Still he resolved not to stay with Mr. Leweson after the two months' engagement had expired.

When he told him, Mr. Leweson sighed—

"I thought so—I always thought so. You are too good for my loonatics. Now I shall begin to advertise your last nights."

The posters came out. "Last Nights of Signor Cipriano!" in flaring capitals, stared Frank in the face from every hoarding round Islington. His fame went up by means of the bills to the breezy heights of Hampstead, to hilly Highgate, to the woods of Hornsey, and to far-off Finchley.

At his lodgings, Frank did not see very much of Patty. At tea and in the evening they met; but the girl hardly spoke. She left the talking to her father, who poured out a never-ending stream of commentary. Frank, as he listened, learned what strange shapes religion sometimes takes in a mind uneducated, but enthusiastic, simple, and imaginative.

Mr. Silver had but one desire—to spiritualise himself to the utmost. He cared nothing what he ate and drank; except that it must be sufficient to maintain his strength. He was indifferent to his calling, come failure or come success; save that he recognised the duty of doing his best in it. He had no fears for the future, either for himself or his children, in whom he thought he saw the "Light." A man indifferent to the world, utterly selfish, utterly *un-careful*. That his daughter should perform on the bars with himself seemed to him a matter so simple, after all the practice they had had together, that he never thought about it at all; and his own conscience being satisfied, he cared absolutely nothing about the opinion of the world.

It pleased him to have Frank with him. First, because he could talk. Talk with a man who disputes and argues is a great deal more refreshing than talk with one who accepts undoubtingly, as Patty and her brother used to do. Then Frank was cheery; he kept the children, as Mr. Silver called both Patty and Joe, alive and happy—told them stories, and made them laugh. The prophet, as Frank called him, had no objection to seeing people laugh—his religion was not a gloomy one.

I have shown how Frank sketched a portrait of Mr. Silver. But in three days after he moved into his new lodgings, he renewed his proposition to draw a portrait of Patty.

"Vanity," said the Prophet, with a smile.

"You were pleased with yours, father," urged his daughter.

"Draw her if you like, Mr. Melliship."

They had a sitting that very afternoon, in Frank's sitting-room. His easel, the table; his canvas, a large piece of rough drawing paper; his materials, chalks. He was going to draw her life-size. Mr. Silver thought there was going to be made a pencil sketch in a dozen touches, like that of himself.

Frank engaged the girl to silence, and worked away for a few mornings with a will. He only put in her head, as she refused to have her hands drawn. The poor girl was very sensitive about her disfigured hands. The likeness was perfect; but he permitted himself, with the licence of an artist, to add a few accessories. Her hair was dressed and crowned with flowers; jewels were round her neck. She was no longer Patty the acrobat, but a countess, a queen, dressed for conquest. The picture conquered Patty. Ever since Frank caught her in his arms, and saved her from death, the image of the fair-haired, sweet-spoken young man, the only gentleman she had ever spoken to, the only gentleman who had ever spoken to her, filled her foolish little brain. He came to tea with them; he came and lived with them; brought brightness into a house which had almost too much of Ezekiel about it. Then he brought flowers every day for her, because she liked flowers; he bought ribands for her, because she liked a little finery; and gloves, because her own pair were old and dirty. He paid her little attentions, meaning nothing, though she thought they meant a good deal. And so, like Margaret— type of every innocent and ignorant girl—she asked herself a dozen times a day, "He loves me—loves me not?" He loved her not; he hardly gave her a thought, save that she was nice, pleasant to look at, pleasant to talk to. But love!

Sometimes in the mornings, when there was no rehearsal, he went for walks with her, starting early, and going up to Highgate and beyond—where there are fields and wild flowers still to be had, though London is so near. The boy went with them; but Patty had the pleasure of talking to Frank, telling him all her little hopes; for the girl was as confiding as innocence could make her, save when her own secret was concerned.

The portrait was framed, and hung in the room where the family ate and drank and sat. This, in spite of protests from the father—who soon, however, got into the habit of looking at the portrait of his daughter. As he looked, he said, the likeness disappeared.

One day, after gazing steadily at the picture for a long time, he exclaimed—

"I have it now. It is no longer the portrait of my daughter—it is the picture of the daughter of Jephthah."

Frank looked at his handiwork. It was, in a sense, true. Patty's features; but somehow there was in her eyes, what he had never noticed before, a look of expectancy, as of suffering to come—the tale of lamentation and sacrifice foreshadowed in her gaze. It was wonderful. His hands had done it all unawares; but it was there.

"It might stand for the daughter of Jephthah," he murmured. "But Patty's face is too bright. See, Mr. Silver," he said, as Patty looked up from her work, "there is no sadness there. You don't see any sacrifice in Patty's eyes, do you?"

Patty blushed as her father looked first at her, and then at the picture.

"It is there; the expression is there—the look of Jephthah's daughter—as well as in the portrait."

He relapsed into one of his trances, becoming now more frequent, and was silent.

Patty's face, to an outsider, certainly offered as few indications of future sorrow as many girls'. The dimples in her cheeks showed how prone she was, by original sin, to lightheartedness and gaiety; the clearly defined arch of her eyebrows, her clustering chestnut hair, the deep brown of her eyes, the freshness of her cheeks, pointed her out as one destined to be loved. But to all this Frank was blind. He had only one love—only one idea of womanhood.

Blind! Blind!

For they were together during these weeks; and day after day, Patty was drinking new draughts of intoxication and of passion. She looked at herself in the glass more than she had ever done before; she put on the little bright bits of colour which Frank had bought her in the shape of ribands; she lamented over her hands; she began to be ashamed of her work. More than all, she began to be ashamed of her professional costume. She rejoiced that her performances began when

Frank's were finished, and that he did not see them; she thought little of the thousands of eyes that did. All these were nothing. What did it matter what she did before the stupid public who came to see her fly through the air, and perhaps kill herself?

"'He loves me—loves me not?' He is a gentleman, delicately nurtured. He cannot bear rough, coarse hands, pulled out of shape by hard, unwomanly work. He loves women with accomplishments, who can write without having to think how to spell the words. He loves women who can dress in silk and satin, and put on all manner of bravery. He has some one in that upper world to which he belongs—some one whom he loves."

Or she would awake, fresh and hopeful, and radiant as the rosy fingered dawn.

"He talked to me all day yesterday. He brought me flowers and fruit. He laughed at what I said, and called me silly. He admired my bonnet. He loves me! He loves me!"

So the little tragedy went on;—the girl trying to think that Frank loved her; the little heart beating with all the nameless hopes and fears; the eyes that watched for a sign, only the smallest sign, of love; the ears that listened for the least little vibration of passion; the cheeks that flushed when he drew near, and flushed again when he went away. And Frank and her father, callous to it all, ignorant of it, unsuspecting—each thinking of the thing that interested him most; Frank burning to get through his two months' engagement, the Prophet finding ever fresh food for his mystic imagination.

"Patty," said Frank, one morning, "one thing always astonishes me about you. Where are your lovers? What are all the young fellows thinking of?"

She flushed scarlet. Her lovers? Alas! she had but one, and he did not love her. And only this morning she had risen so full of hope and joy, because Frank had spoken to her the day before more kindly, as she thought, than usual.

"Lovers!" she echoed sharply. "I have none—I want none."

And went straightway to her own room, where she sobbed her eyes out.

Frank looked after her in some surprise. He had never known Patty in a temper before.

He went out to see Mr. Eddrup, knowing by this time where to find him in the morning.

Mr. Eddrup was in his court—the court which now, save one or two houses, belonged to him. It was his. In it he had organised a sort of parish, of which he was the sole minister and vicar in charge; for the parish had given it up in despair. Here he had a school; here was a chapel; here were a wash-house and baths; here, in itself complete, all the things that go to soften and ameliorate the lot of poverty. And here, for forty years, he had spent his days and nights; a long self-sacrifice, more complete than that of the hermits of the Thebaïd, perhaps with more suffering. Here he had spent every farthing that could be snatched from the expenses of his meagre life—the money that should have clothed him well, that might have procured him comfort, and even luxury—that might have given him a position in the world. And not the money only. That was nothing. But his youth, his pride, his ambition, his passion, his dreams of love and visions of fair women—all, all were merged and sunk in this little court of twenty houses, which he found a den of thieves, and had turned into a house of prayer. Seventy years of age now—an old man, bowed and bent, but full of zeal and energy—he went to and fro among his people. They were always sinning, and always being punished, because the poor get punished in this world more than the rich. They were always in distress, out of work, out of health, behind with everything; and they looked to him for everything— for help, advice, consolation. He gave them what he had. For money; he lent it, at no interest. They paid him back when they were able. Advice, consolation, experience, he gave them for nothing. It was his *metier* to give.

Not to give money: that was his rule. Not to pauperize the people. To avoid the mistakes of the Church; to make people provident; to help them in their efforts; to trust in their honesty, and to make them honest by trusting them. To teach especially the things that belong to poor people— the virtues, not of obedience and contentment, which are servile virtues, but of moderation, cleanliness, and good temper. This was his method. He neither wrote nor agitated; but found a little spot in this great London, and set himself to improve it. Presently, as it became improved, came the necessity for religion. Then he made himself their leader, and held services for prayer and praise, where every one might speak the thing that was in him. The people respected themselves; they respected their friend and teacher more.

Frank found him at the entrance of the court, preparing to slip away, in his noiseless and shy way, along the streets to Skimp's, in Granville-square. Frank offered him his arm, and walked with him. The old man was very silent, as usual. It was not by any means their first meeting in this way. Once or twice a week Frank came round to the court at three o'clock, the time when Mr. Eddrup's work was generally over, and walked home with him. They seldom talked much. But the old man's heart had warmed to Frank. He was the only one, for forty years, who had brought his youth and cheerfulness across his path; the only gentleman—and Mr. Eddrup's heart still warmed to gentlemen—who had crossed his weary path: always excepting Captain Hamilton and the medical students of Skimp's.

To-day, he said not a word till they reached the door of Skimp's.

"You asked me, some time since," he began, abruptly, pausing with the latch-key in his hand, " why I live this life. Come in, and I will tell you."

There was no one in the drawing room. Mr. Eddrup sat down at the open window, and passed his hand across his brow.

"Forty years," he murmured—"forty years. I am like the children of Israel in the wilderness. It is a long time. But it will soon be over. A few more months, or days, and my work will be done. Mr. Melliship, you have told me your story. It is a sad one—it is a very sad one. But you have one consideration—the greatest; it is not your fault that you are poor. You can look the world in the face and laugh at it, because you are innocent. I asked you to look at my forehead. Look again. Is there not the seal of guilt upon it? The mark of Cain? Look close. Do not think to spare me."

He threw back his long white locks with a gesture of despair.

"I see nothing," said Frank, "but the reverend white hairs of a good man."

Mr. Eddrup sighed.

"I will tell you. I knew I must tell it before I died," he said. " I don't ask you to keep my secret. All the world may know it again, as they did before. I shall some day— soon—tell my people: whenever I feel strong enough, I mean," he said, correcting himself hastily—" whenever I feel less cowardly, and able to do so. Mr. Melliship, I am nothing better than a convicted thief! You shrink—you shrink from me. See how quickly the veil of reputation drops off!"

"Mr. Eddrup, I did not shrink. What you have been matters not. The thing is, what you are."

"What I am—What I am!" he repeated. "What am I? A hypocrite, who wears a mask—a man who goes about the world under false pretences. See—see this—read it."

He took from his pocket-book part of a worn newspaper, yellow with age, ragged at the edges. An old *Times*, dated July the 8th, 1825. Frank half opened it, and then gave it back.

"I don't want to read it. Why should I? Mr. Eddrup, you who preach of faith and charity, have you forgotten hope?"

"It is more than forty years ago. I was poor. I was burning with zeal and ambition. I longed to distinguish myself. I had talents—not great talents, but some ability. But I was too poor to make myself known. I wanted to go into the world, and get friends. Then a terrible temptation assailed me. I was beset with it night and day. I had no rest. The voice of the tempter woke me at night, and kept me feverish all the day. It said, 'Use it, use it—no one will know. Presently you will have money, and you will replace it.' Trust money! I waited, and listened to the tempting voice. The years passed by. I was nearly thirty. I used it. It is forty years ago; but even now the memory of that day, and the misery I felt when my self-respect was gone, haunt me till I know not whether it is repentance or the gnawing of the worm that never dies. I used the money—for my own purposes."

Great beads stood upon his forehead as he made his confession. He was silent again for a space.

Frank held his breath.

"After a year they found it out. I had not yet been able to replace the money. They arrested me. It made some noise. They tried to get me off; but it was all too clear. I had six months' imprisonment, and came out into a world which was dark to me for the future. I was poor when I became a felon. I was rich when I came out of prison. One of my relatives had died, leaving me all his money—having forgotten, I believe, to alter his will. I paid back the money I had stolen. I hid myself for a year, in despair and misery, creeping out at night. What should I do with my life? I thought that I would bury myself in solitude, and try to do some secret good:

not in atonement, young man, remember—I never thought that. Nothing that man can do will ever atone. The evil remains. It is his misery sometimes to see the evil that he has begun work its steady way upward, like a tree that he has planted. Sometimes, if he does not see it, he *feels* it."

" Is repentance nothing ? Is a life of good works nothing?"

Mr. Eddrup shook his head.

" What I never shake off from myself is the feeling that one *never forgets*. I want an assurance of a river of Lethe. I want, not to be forgiven so much as to forget—not so much to escape punishment, as to hold up my head again. Punishment, pain, suffering—what does it mean ? Nothing, nothing. But self-respect. Can—will Heaven give back that ? Preachers tell us of sins forgiven: they say nothing of honour restored. A Heaven of Praise, with my brother sinners, because we have escaped punishment, would be no Heaven for me. I want more. It is the assurance of that perfect forgiveness which restores as well as pardons that I want. Young man, pray, night and morning, and all day long, that you may not be led into temptation."

He dropped his face into his hands; and Frank, meek and silent before this revelation and sorrow, slipped quietly away, and left him.

CHAPTER THE THIRTY-SIXTH.

HE summer passes into autumn: the woods of Hunslope Park are tinged with yellow. Dick Mortiboy, leaving Lafleur to work out the System alone, lingers at his villa. He has bought horses and traps ; he rides about the country ; he knows every village, and nearly every man in it, for miles round Market Basing; he gives dinners to his tenants; receives all his clients, from Lord Hunslope downwards, with the same affability; throws away his money—the Mortiboy money, gotten with so much labour and pains—with an easy prodigality endearing him to all that large class of mankind which admires generosity when it flows towards itself. But for one thing, his popularity would be perfect. Dick will go to no private parties. They lay traps for him; publicly invite him to dinner ; catch him by the button-hole, and try to inveigle him into an engagement; lead him to the doors of their

houses, and almost drag him in. But Dick won't go. One house alone he frequents: his cousins'—the Heathcotes'. Is he paying attention to one of the girls? A serious question to the ladies of Market Basing. If so, it must be Grace—that designing young girl who used to flirt with Frank Melliship, and threw him over when he was ruined. It can't be Lucy, who hasn't spirit enough even to look in the face of a man. He may be paying his attentions to one of the girls, but it is difficult to tell which.

And all this time, Dick is fighting a battle with himself. He went at first to Parkside because he liked to talk freely, and it was the only house, he thought, in his ignorance of the world, where people would not laugh at his rough speech. Fancy the world presuming to laugh at a man with half a million and more of money! He goes now—though he knows he ought not—because he likes to go there only too well. He has never dared—strong and brave as he is—to meet his thought face to face; but secretly there is growing up within him a passionate desire to be free: to shake off the yoke of Polly, and to seize for his own his cousin Grace. He is beginning to beat it down, this growing passion.

Grace, meantime, unsuspicious of his altered feelings, treats him with the same perfect freedom she might show to her own brother. But her mother was right—Dick Mortiboy loved her.

"I do wonder, Dick," she said sometimes, "how we should have managed to get on without you. What a good fellow you were to come home as you did, just at the time when you were most wanted, when we should have been left so lonely. I think we shall civilize you by degrees. Already you've left off some of your bad habits. Don't you think he's improved, Lucy? Women have some use in the world, Dick, however you may despise them."

"I don't despise them."

"They polish men and things. Jane, the housemaid, polishes the dining-room table; her mistresses polish their cousin Dick I don't know which is the pleasanter task."

They went out for drives in his dogcart—Grace in front, Lucy behind. Then he sat silent, and let Grace prattle to him. Or they went out for long rides with him, and were fain to confess that Dick rode better even than Frank.

"Are you girls happy?" he asked once, in an abrupt way.

"Why, Dick?"

"I can't make it out. You lead such quiet lives. You never go away anywhere. You see no strange faces—you have no excitement—you know nothing. I hardly call it life."

"Perhaps we like quiet lives, Dick," said Lucy.

"No, we don't Dick," said Grace. "What we are taught from our infancy is to be content with quiet lives, because we shall never get anything else. I should like to go about the world and see things. I should like to have a little peril—just a little, you know—to talk about afterwards. And I should like to see the beautiful places in the world that you talk about."

"I don't know," said Lucy; "I like being here best. I hope to stay here all my life. We are happy, are we not, Grace?" caressing her sister, whose temperament was so different from her own.

"Happy? Yes—I suppose so. Don't you know, Cousin Dick, that it is always prudent to confine your wishes within the probability of their accomplishment? That seems a very wise thing to say—but I saw it in a book the other day. The learned author went on to remark, that if you wisely wished for what was most likely to happen to you, and prayed night and morning for it to come, you would, in all probability, and provided you had faith enough, get what you prayed for."

"Grace, dear, don't."

But Grace went on.

"As for me, I am not so happy as I should like to be. Not because my life is dull; but—oh! quite another thing—because, you see, I am wishing and praying for what does not come. That is the only change I want. And, oh dear! it is a terrible great change to ask. Are you happy, Dick?"

"Pretty well. There are one or two things that bother me as I lie in my hammock at night."

"You would like poor Uncle Richard to get well again," said Lucy.

"No, that is not one of them. Of course I should, Lucy. But that is not one of them."

"Can we help you, Dick?" said Grace.

"No; I hardly think you can. But let me help you, if I may."

"Some day, Dick, I mean to ask you, perhaps."

She held out her hand frankly. At the touch of her slender fingers, the great, solid-looking man fairly trembled and shook. But Grace was gone, and he turned moodily away.

Was he paying attention? Was he in love with his cousin? Was he letting the thought of her dwell in his mind day after day, till it became a power almost too great to be resisted?

About two miles from Market Basing stands, on a small eminence, a cross—one of the crosses erected by Edward the First in honour of Queen Eleanor. It is placed at the side of the road, and, standing on its steps, you have a wide and very pretty view of Market Basing, and the surrounding meadows. On a platform of red sandstone, in seven steps, is the cross itself, about forty feet high. The lowest part is octagonal, bearing on its sides, much defaced, the arms of Castille and Leon, and Ponthieu in Picardy. Above this is another small tower of twelve feet. Every other side of this tower contains a crowned female figure, defaced, but not yet destroyed by time. This is surmounted by a small four-sided tower, on which is a marble cross, formerly gilt. It had been old Mr. Mortiboy's favourite drive. He would get down from John Heathcote's dogcart—for it was on the road to Parkside—and, leaving him standing in the road, would climb the steps, and contemplate the town and his property lying beneath him. When he was a younger man, he used to walk out and back.

Dick, one afternoon in September, was driving Grace Heathcote home in his dogcart. She had come to town with her father, who had business to detain him later.

As they passed the cross, Grace pointed it out to him.

"Your father used to be so fond of standing on the steps, and looking at the town, Dick, Let us get down and see the view. You can count your houses with your finger, as he used to do."

"I don't much care for views, and I don't want to count my houses," said Dick. "But you always have your own way."

"There is no use in being a woman unless you have it, is there?"

"Lead the horse to the top of the hill, walk him down, and wait for us, Bob."

They stood on the steps of the old cross: Grace on the top step, and Dick one or two steps lower.

"Look, Dick—look; is it not beautiful?"

A beautiful landscape of peace and plenty, lit up with an autumn sun, can make things beautiful. Dick turned for a moment to the scene, but his eyes went back to Grace. The girl touched him on the shoulder, and bade him look for his own house. A second time, at her touch, Dick trembled and shivered. For she had never looked so lovely.

"Don't, Grace," he said, in a constrained voice. He was exerting all his strength to prevent himself from taking the slight and delicate figure in his arms, and crushing it to his heart. "Don't, Grace. Don't touch me."

"Why not, Dick?"

"Because I love you, Grace. Because I cannot bear it any longer."

The girl shrank back in momentary dread. For his eyes were fixed on her, and had a hungry, yearning look—a wild look.

They heard no sound in the air, save the song of a lark above them, and the crunching of the gravel made by the horse's hoofs and the wheels of the dogcart. Another sound there was: but they were both deaf: the sound of voices—a woman's voice.

"Where's your master, Bob?"

"Nigh the cross, with Miss Grace."

Bob went on; and the woman, stepping on the grass by the wayside, noiselessly went on till she came to the cross. Then she slipped behind it, and listened.

"I love you, Grace," Dick went on. "I tell you that I have fought against it, because Lucy told me something—I half forget. There is another. What do I care about any other man? There is no man in the world I am afraid of."

"Do you think women are to be fought for, Dick? You are not in Texas now."

"Forgive me. I'm only a common and a rough man, Grace, my—my darling." She shrank farther back. The woman behind gave a little hiss, and clenched her fists. "I'm not fit to speak to a girl like you. If you knew all, you would say so yourself. But I can't help myself, Grace. I swear I can't help myself. Look here: if you touch me, I shake all over. Yet I am not happy except I am near you. If you speak to me, I tingle with pleasure. If you knew, Grace—if you only knew, what a wild beast is in me now, telling me to take you in my arms, and kiss, and kiss, and kiss you again, you would run away shrieking."

"I'm not afraid of you, Cousin Dick."

But she was.

"The devil and all of it is, you see, Grace," he went on after

Y

a pause, during which he was wrestling with and getting the better of his wild beast—" the devil of it is—I'm glad, after all, that I have told you, because now things will be easier—that I could not even ask you to marry me."

"You know, Dick, that it would be useless if you could."

"I know. The other—boy—Frank—Melliship—I know." He sat down on the lower step, and crunched his heel into the grass.

"If you knew all, I said—yes, if you knew all, I think you would—pity—me, Grace. If I could only find something to say that would make you love me! If I could only make you understand—only I can't talk as some men can—how I long for you, how I curse the—the cause that keeps me from hoping ever to marry you."

"Dick, I never—never could marry you."

"But I should have a chance—at least, I should think so—if it were not for her, Grace. He started to his feet, and stretched out his arms to her wildly. "Grace, what does all the world matter, and what they think or say? See, I love you, I will fight for you, and—and worship you all my life. I am rich, I will give you anything that you like to ask. The world over there is far more beautiful than here. Come away with me. We will build a house in California, in a spot I like well. The sun is always bright there. Grace, come with me. I am a man; I am not a puny stripling like Frank Melliship. Men know me, and are afraid of me. But *I*—I, my girl, am afraid of no man in the world—no man. Roaring Dick is king wherever he goes!"

He was mad with passion. His eyes were aglow with a strange fire, his voice was harsh and hoarse. He made a movement towards the shrinking and terrified girl, with outstretched arms. Grace shrieked, and fell back against the cross.

Then between them stepped the listening woman.

"No," she cried—" no, Grace Heathcote: leave me my husband, at least. Take his rings and his presents, hear his fine speeches—you may have them; but you shan't have *him*. Not that—not that. Leave him to me. He is mine—mine: my handsome Dick. You think you will get away from your Polly. Not you, my lad, not you. Not yet—not yet."

She had been drinking : her face was flushed and red; she wore a coarse country dress; she was frowsy and heated : her voice was thick. Good heavens! what a contrast to the sweet and delicate girl who stood above her on the steps, white and frightened.

"Pretty things for a wife to hear—very pretty things, upon my word. And as for you, you young minx—"

Here Dick laid his heavy hand on her shoulder, and swung her round. She looked up at him, in her rage and fury, with parted lips and flaming cheeks. Her husband was pale and calm, save for the trembling of his lips.

His eyes met hers.

You know how, in the Festin de St. Pierre, the statue of the Commandant lays his irresistible hand upon the shoulder of Don Juan. At its cold touch, the bravado and courage go out of the man. As it weighs him down, he sinks lower and lower till the earth closes over him.

At the first touch of Dick's hand, Polly trembled. When he turned her round, and she read, not wrath, but a cold pitiless determination in his face, her rage died out suddenly, and she became cold all over. She dropped her eyes. He looked at her steadily for a few moments, and then said, in a husky voice—

"Go away from this, Polly. Keep out of my way—you'd best—for the present."

The woman went on her way down the hill without a word.

Grace sat down, and buried her face in her hands. She forgot her own terror in her sorrow for Dick. Across his face had flashed, for a moment only, a look of misery and shame that cut her to the heart.

"Oh! Cousin Dick—Cousin Dick," she cried, bursting into tears—"I am so sorry."

"Forgive me, Grace," he said, quietly. "Forgive me. I get mad sometimes, you know. I was mad then. Tell me you forgive me."

She held out her hand. In truth, she had never caught the meaning of his words. How should she know what they meant?

He took her hand in his, and kept it.

"I was only nineteen when I married her. Even then there was no excuse for me. But she made me do it. I took her up to London, when my father sent me to work at our town agent's. We were married in St. Pancras Church. Then I left home, was turned out by my father—all my fault, Grace, not his, remember that—and I left her. Till the time I came home again, I never thought of her. Now I have to pay her to keep silence. Pity me, Grace."

"I do pity you, Dick—I pity you from my heart."

"I said what I ought not, my child. I said I loved you. That is true. You will always remember that I loved you, will you not? As long as I live, I shall love you. But you may trust me, Grace. I shall never offend you again. For I can never ask you to marry me."

"And, oh, Dick—oh, Cousin Dick, you won't try to do any harm to Frank?"

"Frank Melliship? I'm not the man, Grace. Marry whom you like. I will help you—that is, if I can."

She laid her hand in his once more. He looked down at her: the passion faded out of his deep black eyes—eyes now soft and tender as a woman's.

"Go, Grace. Keep my secret. I must stay here awhile, and think. Go home without me, my child."

"I am afraid—of her, Dick."

"She *dares* not touch you. By——!"—he clenched his fists—"But I will walk with you to the top of the hill, and see you safe with Bob."

"Good-bye, Dick. Don't do anything dreadful. Oh! I am so afraid you should." Then she added, almost in a whisper, "Don't be cruel to *her*."

They parted: she with a heart full of new and strange sympathies and sorrows; he subdued and heavy-laden.

He pulled out his cigar case, and smoked for above an hour, sitting on the steps of the old cross. Then the sun got low, and he got up and walked homewards.

At the foot of the rising ground on which the cross stands, runs the river which winds down the plain, and flows between his father's house in Derngate and his own little villa. He took the towing-path, and followed it moodily. It was a very lonely path: few people walked there by day, and none by night. The barges have all left it long since, and the deserted stream flows along broad and deep, between the trees which overhang it on either side.

Presently, before him in the path, he saw his wife. She had been drinking again, since he sent her away, to drown her fears; and now she stood in the way before him, facing him, with her arms akimbo, and a loud, defiant laugh.

"So you've done your fine talk with Grace Heathcote at last, and now you're coming to beg my pardon, I suppose."

Dick grew purple with passion. He seized her by the waist in his mighty arms, and, without saying a single word, raised her aloft, and threw her—heavy as she was—six feet and more into the river. With a shriek, the woman fell into the deepest part of the stream, and disappeared.

Dick's wrath, when there was no opposition to feed it, was as short-lived as a straw-fire. He looked at the rings of water widening round the spot where Polly had fallen in, with an expression which rapidly changed from extreme rage to one more like extreme vexation.

"Carambo!" he cried—"what if I've drowned her?"

But he might have spared himself his anxiety. The cold water sobered her in a moment; and rising from the mud at the bottom, into which her head had at first plunged, she came to the surface. Ten feet lower down, a fallen tree lay half across the stream. The current bore her on before she had time to sink again. She clutched the branches, which bent and ducked her again and again. But at last she landed herself, and clambering up the bank, wet and dripping, turned in fury upon her lord and master.

Dick was sitting on the grass, laughing as if it was the best joke he had ever known in his life.

"I told you how it would be, Polly, if you split. Now you see. Lord! if you could only get a sight of your own face!"

She had risen from the waves, like Venus Anadyomene. Encumbered as she was with her draggled clothes, she only resembled the goddess in that one fact. Besides the mud at the bottom, which was still in her hair and bonnet, she had collected a goodly quantity of duckweed on her way out of the water, which hung in graceful festoons upon her shoulders.

"You'd better go home to your mother and get dry, Polly."

"I'll cry all over Market Basing that I'm your wife. I'll have revenge, you black, murdering villain. I'll have my rights out of you, I will."

"Then, Polly, perhaps next time you go into the river, you will stay there."

Dick strode off alone, leaving his wife on the other side.

When he got home, he bolted the door, so that her key was of no use. About ten o'clock, a little gravel was thrown up at his window. It was Polly, crying.

"Dick, let me in—let me in, Dick. I'm very sorry, and I haven't told nobody—on my sacred word, I haven't. I said I'd been a blackberryin',' and fell in."

Dick poked an unrelenting head out of the window. At sight of it, his wife put her handkerchief to her face and sobbed loudly.

"Polly," said the inhuman Dick, "you may go to the devil."

Polly went home. She arose early next morning, and repaired again, trembling, to the house. But she might just as well have gone defiantly, for Dick Mortiboy was off to town by the six o'clock train.

CHAPTER THE THIRTY-SEVENTH.

AS the old novelists used to say, to Paragon-place, Gray's Inn-road. This pleasant retreat lies on the east side of the road, not very far from the lordly entrance to Gray's Inn. Paragon-place is a *cul de sac;* and as it consists only of six houses in all, it passes a peaceful and quiet existence, having but little intercourse with the outer world. It consists of a single row of five houses, with another at the end, looking down the court. They face a paved alley of ten feet in breadth. The northern side of Paragon-place is bounded by a brick wall, eight feet high, set about and garnished, for the better protection of the inhabitants, by a plentiful top-dressing of broken bottles. The wall may also serve as a protection to the printers' offices which lie beyond. At all events, it is a barrier insuperable between Paragon-place and the printers. Thus fashion separates itself from business: leisure and retirement from compulsory work.

I would that we might linger over Paragon-place and its inhabitants. About every house there hang half a dozen histories; from the tale of every dweller might be woven a romance of real life—that is, a tale of sin and suffering, of poverty and sorrow. We have to do with one only. It is the third tenement in the row. Like the rest, it consists of three main rooms, lighted, each "fore and aft"—the front window looking into the court, the back commanding a view of a small yard beyond, about six feet square, containing a water-butt and a heap of rubbish.

There is a staircase leading to two rooms, one over the other, above. On the left hand of the door, as you go in, is a sort of closet or small room, which may be used as a bedroom when the family overflows the rest of the house. It is lighted and ventilated by an aperture giving space for a single pane of glass.

The doors of the houses, which were once painted green, but long years since, stand open. Everything about the court is intolerably dirty. Odds and stray bits of vegetables, as cabbage stalks, potato peelings, and such small wreck and *débris*, lie about the stones; a gutter runs along the wall, down which is merrily flowing, at this moment, the bucket of soapsuds which No. 1 has just emptied into it. Two children, having hastily constructed a model ship out of a splinter of wood, have launched it upon this river, and are watching its progress down the tributary stream to the great Mississippi of Gray's Inn Road. They run out with it into the street, and stay there. Then the court is quiet again, except for the pulse of the steam press, which is never silent. The sun shines on the windows of the printers' office, and is reflected back on the doorstep of No. 3, where sits, basking in its warmth, a figure, muffled as if it were winter, and smoking a long clay pipe. He is apparently bent and doubled up, from the effects of age: his shoulders stoop, and his back is rounded. On his head is a soft felt hat, much too large for him, which flaps down on the side nearest the door, but is lifted up on the other side to catch the sun. A crutch is beside him. In his hand is a copy of the day before yesterday's *Daily Telegraph*; and he is reading aloud, slowly and painfully, making comments as he goes—not running so much as crawling—to his companion, a child of nine or ten, who is sitting on the stones, with his back against the wall, in the reflected sunlight. The boy's head is bare: his feet are bare. One sleeve of his jacket is quite gone, the other nearly. His trousers are all rents and tatters, his white legs gleaming through the holes. His shirt will no longer button, and shows signs of approaching dissolution. All this is a trifle, because the weather is warm; and rags are just as comfortable in warm weather as anything else. Besides, the boy has not been brought up in a school which teaches the cultivation of personal appearance by means of sartorial art. He was far more interested in the problem of how to satisfy that raging wolf which every day gnawed at his stomach, and instigated him to get food by any means.

"So you see, Bill," said the politician, in a thin, quavering voice, "the Guv'ment's gorn and done it agen, and the country's goin' to the devil. Now, if I was in the 'Ouse—" He stopped and folded his paper.

"Don't go into the 'Ouse, Thoozy," said the child.

"It's not the work'us, stoopid. It's the House of Parlyment Some day I think I shall go—to represent Finsbury. I wish there was the price of a half-pint in my pocket. Who's the swell coming up the court?"

The "swell," who was looking inquiringly up and down the court, seeing the pair outside the door, turned his steps in their direction.

"Can you tell me"—he spoke to the smoker, whose face was hidden by the flapping hat—"if a Mrs. Kneebone lives about here?"

He removed his pipe from his mouth, and his great hat from his head, and stood upright in the doorway, waving his hand with an air of authority.

Dick Mortiboy looked at him in astonishment. Behind the wrinkles and lines of age lay—not the colour, because the face was perfectly pale and colourless; nor the shape, because the cheeks were sunken and the features prominent; nor the comeliness, because the whole figure was starved and pinched; nor the redundant locks, because the scattered hairs, nearly white, lay sparse and thin about his temples—but an indescribable *look* of youth.

He was about four feet and a half in height: but then he stooped a good deal. He had on a long, coarse coat, made for a grown man. His legs were cased in winter trousers. He had a thick flannel shirt, and a wrapper round his neck. His chest was flattened in—his legs bowed—his body bent. Dick, standing before him on the stones, stared at him without speaking. He had never seen this kind of creature before.

"When you *think* you'll recognize me again," said the boy, sarcastically, "perhaps you'll let me know."

"It *is* a boy, by gad," said Dick.

The child previously addressed as Bill set up a yell of delight, clapping his hands and dancing round. It was as good fun as he ever assisted at. The other relaxed from his sternness of expression, conceding an aged smile to the frivolities of the situation.

"Are you a boy, or are you a man?" asked Dick. "What's your name? Tell me something about yourself."

"You can read, I suppose?" said the nondescript, with a patronizing air. "You *can* do that much, I presume. Young Bill, the writin' materials. Give the old man his bit o' whitin'."

Bill produced a piece of chalk from his trousers pocket.

"Here y'are, Thoozy. Hooray!"

Thoozy inspected the "materials" with care, and looked for a point. This—in what mathematicians would describe as a rough eikosihedron, or twenty-sided solid—was difficult to find; but selecting something which would suit, he marched gravely down the steps, and, turning the sleeve of his coat up to his elbow, while he supported his long tails under the left arm, raised his right hand to the brick wall. Then he stopped and turned round again.

"You *can* spell?" he said to Dick, looking at him sideways, as if with suspicion, but always with an eye on Bill.

Dick nodded.

"*And* read? Because I'm not going to take all this trouble for nothink, you know."

Little Bill screamed, and rolled himself over and over upon the cabbage stalks. Thoozy, with one eye on his young companion, proceeded slowly with his talk.

"Then," he said, stepping back and admiring the effect of the sunlight upon his strokes, "there's a C, and a OO, and a EK. If that don't spell Cook, that ain't my name, and Methoosalem ain't my nature."

"Oh, lord!" cried Bill, "ain't he a fizzer!"

Dick Mortiboy took the cigar out of his mouth, and contemplated the pair with an expression in which curiosity had the best part.

"So you're Mr. Methoosalem, are you? Pray, is this Bill —little Bill?"

"That *is* Bill, mister," said Thoozy, "and a very good little Bill he is. *I* educated that there boy. Bill, show the gentleman what you can do: the Catherine Wheel, my child."

He had resumed his commanding position on the doorstep, and issued his orders with a wave of the pipe, like the director of a circus using his whip.

The boy went through the graceful performance known

among his friends of the pavement as the Catherine Wheel. "Hoop-là!" he cried, bringing up his bare and dirty feet within an inch of Dick's waistcoat.

"*I* taught him the Wheel," said Thoozey. "I'm too old to do it myself. He learned the 'Hoop-là!' hisself the night we got hold of two gallery checks for the Gaiety Theatre. He learnt that there of a fine gal—a dooced fine gal, sir. If I was a younger man—" here he stopped and winked with a sigh. "Now Bill, the Inverted Column."

"Never mind the Inverted Column," said Dick. "Here's a shilling for you, Bill. Go and get something to eat."

"Half a pint will be enough for me, William," cried the other, grandly, relighting his pipe. "And get a penn'orth o' belly-ache for yourself first. Plums that is, sir," he explained to Dick.

"How old *are* you, may I ask" said Dick.

"Eighty-six I am—a great age. I was seventy when I was born, sixteen years ago. And I've been getting older ever since. My old woman in there is only seventy-five."

"Who is your old woman?"

"Here she is—Mrs. Kneebone, sir, herself: the lady you was axing after. Not my wife, you know, nor yet my mother, nor my grandmother. Come out, old woman. Here's a gentleman wants you to drink his health."

She was as withered and wrinkled as Methoosalem himself, but without his look of childhood. In her hand she held a wooden snuffbox, from which ever and anon she refreshed herself. She wore a dress of some kind of stuff, black in colour, and a bonnet on her head which might once have had some shape. At present it had none. An old woman who muttered as she went along: a creature who would have been burned as a witch in the merry old days: an evil-looking, miserable old woman.

She shaded her eyes from the sun, and peered up at the stranger.

"I don't know you, sir. I can't let you in. I never saw you before. You can't come in here."

"What are you talking about?" said Thoozy. "Who said the gentleman did know you? Who talked about comin' in? Yah! He wants to have five-minutes of your lively society, and he wants to look at you. You ain't none too pretty, neither."

"I want some information, for which I am willing to pay," said the stranger.

"About how long ago, sir?" asked the old woman, with a look of terror at the boy.

"About twelve years ago."

"What about twelve years ago?" She shook all over.

"That's when I begin to remember plain," said the boy. "Go ahead, sir—I can answer your questions. Old lady, cut it. Now go, d'yer hear?"

"Thoozy, my dear, be careful," she said, in a trembling voice. "Oh, be careful."

"Cut it, I say. Careful, indeed! Now then, sir. You can't have a more quieter and more genteeler spot than Paragon Place on a warm day in September, about two o'clock p.m., in the afternoon. The haristocracy is gone to the seaside, and there's no one to interrupt us. Fire away with your questions."

He put his hands in his pockets, and sat down on the doorstep again.

"First, then, that child. You said his name was Bill. Bill what?"

"Lord help you! He ain't got no other name. Now, sir, *do* you think—I asks you as a stranger—do you think it *can* be done for the money? Where's your profit? That's what I say. Where's your profit to come from out of five bob a-week?"

He stuck his thumbs in his arm-holes, and looked as sagacious as a publisher.

"Who brought him here? How old is he? Who does he belong to?"

"A-hem! As a proprietor of this yer hospital, and, I may say, the resident physician, I holds out my hand, and I says, says I, How much?"

"Isn't Mrs. Kneebone the proprietor?"

"On'y in the heyes of the bobby. If anything goes wrong, the coroner holds his inquidge round the corner, and Kneebone she goes before 'em and swears. I sits at home and smokes my pipe."

"Good. Tell me all about the boy. Here's a sovereign down, and five more if the inquiry leads me to anything I want."

"How do I know what you want?"

"That's just it. You don't know, and so you can't tell lies."

"Don't be too sharp, young feller, else you might fall down, though you are so big, and cut a hole in the pavin' stones.

Bill was brought here, a three-weeks' baby, just nine years and a half ago. There was the devil's own trouble to keep him goin'; and he wouldn't have been kep' goin' at all, only his mother come round herself every day."

"What was the name of his mother? Nine years and a half ago? Who was his mother?"

"Polly Tresler."

Dick gave a low whistle.

"You're sure of it? You would swear it? You are *certain* of the date?"

"Take my dick on all the Bibles in the jug. Ask the old woman. Here, mother, come out again!"

She hobbled out.

"Now then, old lady, tell the gentleman how old Bill is. Show him your book. She's got a book, sir, and puts 'em all down."

"I'll show him that page," said Mrs. Kneebone, looking suspicious, "but no more, for five shillings."

It was a sort of register she brought him, covering about twenty years. She turned over the pages slowly, and at last arrived at her date.

"There you are, sir. Read it, but don't look at no more."

Dick read—

"Nov. 5, 1860. Boy—three weeks old—to be called Bill. Eighteenpence a-week. Mother's name and address, Miss Tresler"—(here an old address had been scratched out, and a new one substituted)—"P. T., Post-office, Market Basing."

Dick's eye ran down the list on the page. There was about half a dozen in the year. To four of their names was written the word, "Dead." To one, "Taken away by his father." Bill made the sixth.

"And that boy, sir, he've been the apple of my eye. He have indeed."

Thoozy winked, and jerked his pipe, which he had resumed, over his left shoulder, to indicate that his partner, or Principal Nurse of the Hospital, was practising a little amiable deception. She went on without noticing.

"The clothes he's had o' me; the pocket money he's had o' me; the oranges and apples, and—and—and the tripe he's had: it's what you wouldn't believe, sir. A beautiful breakfast he got only this morning."

"Kinchined a kid and collared a bloater in the gutter," interposed Thoozy.

"Now, don't you tell no lies. A idle, good-for-nothin' vagabond, as won't work, and won't do nothin' but smoke and drink."—(Here Bill arrived with a cargo of plums and a pint of beer, which Thoozy tackled on the spot.)—"It's ten years, sir, if you'll believe me, and I wish-a-ma-die if it ain't gawspel, that that boy said he was gettin' too old to work, and hasn't done a stroke since, but eat up all he can lay his hands to."

"Ten years!" said Thoozy. "So it is. I was only seventy-six then. I made a curious discovery, mister"—here he winked sideways at the old woman—"a very curious discovery; and I thought I'd make the most of it. On the strength of that there discovery, I'm a-goin' to spend my old age in a honourable retirement, as they says in the papers."

The old woman moved her lips, but said nothing.

"About this boy, now?" said Dick, in reply. "Here he is. If you've given him clothes, old woman, he's worn 'em out; and if you've given him grub, it hasn't agreed with him. Here, let me come in, and I'll take down all you've got to say. Is there such a thing in the house as a table, and paper and pens? Don't be afraid, I'm not going to do you any harm."

He pushed by the woman, who tried to stop him, and passed in. The entrance to the house was like the entrance to Hades, as seen by Æneas, when, aided by the Sibyl, he undertook that perilous adventure of his—"for there were straightway heard cries, and wailing loud, and the spirits of infants weeping."

Dick pushed open a door, and looked in. There were lying on the floor, in sheets and flannels, four babies, from a few weeks to a year old; one or two clutching at life with strong and eager little fists; one or two meagre, thin, and emaciated. The old woman bustled by, and began to apply feeding bottles with great assiduity.

Dick looked at Thoozy with disgust.

"This is your precious hospital, is it, you little imp? Have you got another room?"

"There's my room and Bill's, up at the top—let's go there. Bill, run and fetch the gentleman a bit of paper, and a pen, and a penn'orth of ink. Upstairs, sir."

The stairs were horribly, fearfully dirty and noisome. Creeping things were on the walls. The bannisters were broken away; and on the top floor, where the boys slept, the planking of the stairs had been taken up to be burned for firewood.

There was no furniture in the room except a table, and a bed spread on the floor. Thoozy sat on the bed, and looked wistfully at his quiet guest.

"You don't want to do no harm to Bill, do you, sir?" speaking quite naturally, and like a boy. "You won't hurt he, will you? 'cos Bill's the only friend I got. The other boys laughs at me : says I'm too old to live long, and asks how long ago I was born, you see. But Bill, he was a right good sort, and we've slep' together ever since he left off pap. My boy, Bill is."

"I won't hurt him, but I shall take him away from here."

"If it's best for him, I shan't say nothink. Don't believe that 'ere old woman, sir. I would work if I could. But I can't. I'm too weak, and nobody won't have nothink to say to a baby-farm boy. I tried sellin' papers in the streets, and cigar lights; but the stronger boys pushed me about. I ain't strong, sir. Look at my legs." He pulled up his trousers, and showed a leg about half as big as Dick's wrist. "And I'll tell you something more about Polly, too, sir, if you'll be good to Bill. She was married lawful to Bill's father, 'cos I heard her tell the old woman so. He was a sailor, he was. And he went to sea. You ain't the man, are you, sir?"

Dick started. Here indeed was news worth having.

"You boy, find out that man's name, and keep a quiet tongue in your head, and I'll help you all round—except to find work, which is the only thing you can't get in this blessed old country."

"The old woman knows his name. I'll get it for you, never fear. She's afraid of me, she is, since I found her out. But she won't do it again, she won't."

"What is it you found out?"

"Here comes Bill," said Thoozy. "And the old woman, too——"

Dick pulled out five pounds, and laid them on the table.

"Now, Mrs. Kneebone, let us understand one another. This is for your information, provided it proves correct and true on subsequent investigation."

The old woman eyed the gold greedily.

She began her statement, which was in substance precisely the same as Thoozy had made; gave the dates exactly from her book; explained how the baby had been left with her at a charge of eighteen-pence a week, increased first to half-a-crown, and of late months to five shillings; swore that Bill was the child, and then held out her hand for the money.

"Not so fast," said Dick. "All that I knew before. This boy told me."

"You little devil!" cried Mrs. Kneebone, viciously to Thoozy, who nodded his head and laughed.

"I want more. I want to know about the boy's father. What was his name? and when was he married to Polly Tresler?"

"You want to know too much. Now, tell me, do you want to do Polly a bad turn?"

"I don't want to do her a good one, certainly. But I want to do a good turn to a friend of my own. And to get at the way of doing it, I want all the information I can lay my hands on."

"She's a bad lot, Polly is. I've knowed her for sixteen years and more. Ah me, I wasn't always in this poor place! But there—many's the good thing I've done for Polly. I introduced her to her first, down Poplar way—when I had as tidy a little tobacco shop as ever was. Ah! dear me."

"Her first?" Dick looked sharply at her. "Who was her first?"

"Oh, he was a mate—married at Lime'us Church. But they didn't get on. Polly used to beat him; and she got ashamed of a husband who couldn't beat her like the other men. A good quiet sort of body, too, and a first officer. Bowker his name was. So when he went away to sea, she went away from Poplar, too."

"There's two sovereigns for you. And now go on."

The woman looked thirstily at the rest of the money, and presently went on again.

"Now, I don't know very well. She took up with a young fellow down in the country—I'm not quite certain whether he married her or not—I only heard her story afterward. Then he ran away from her. She came up to London, and got married again."

"What, a third time?"

"Well, what was she to do? She'd run away from her first, and her second had run away from her, and so she took up with another. Well, he died. He was a sailor, too. Polly always liked sailors. Only this one used to whack her when he come home drunk, and I think Polly often enough regretted her first."

"About the first. Do you know if he is alive, and where to find him?"

"I do sir," said Mrs. Kneebone, "and Polly doesn't. At least, I know where to look for him: and he was alive when I was at Poplar last, because I heard about him from some old pals of his."

"What did you say his name is?"

"Don't you think I've earned the five pounds, sir?"

Dick pushed them across the table.

"Thank you kindly, sir. His name, sir, is Bowker: Cap'en Bowker—good gentleman. And I'll tell you where you can find all about him; and I'm sure you'll consider it an extra."

"Look here," said Dick, flushing—nothing in all his life ever gave him so much joy as the story of his wife's progress through life—"if all you say is true, this will be the best day's work you ever did. Now I'm going to pay you what Polly owes for the boy—five and thirty shillings. Here you are. Next, I'm going to take away little Bill."

She threw up her arms in an ecstasy of grief and lamentation.

"Take away my Bill? Take away my little boy Bill, that I raised with my own hands? Oh! sir, I couldn't let him go—I couldn't really; not under five pounds, sir."

"She never giv' me nothin', and she's allus whackin' me when Thoozy isn't by," said the object of the more than maternal solicitude.

Thoozy interrupted her, authoritatively bringing his crutch handle on the floor.

"You're a-goin' to let him go for nothink at all," he remarked, quietly—"so there ain't no more to be said. Hold your jaw. Bill, old chap, the big swell's a-goin' to take you away. He looks as if he was the sort to give you clothes, and make you respectable. Don't cry, because it's all for your own benefit; and he seems a good un, though he *is* so precious big."

"Come, Bill," said Dick, "will you come with me? Say good-bye to your friends, and come along. Old woman, you've had your money. Here, Thoozy, is your share."

"Don't cry, Bill," said Thoozy again, beginning to cry himself—"as it's all for the best. And what's for the best, you know, is got to be done, if it's physikin' the babbies, or a washin' of 'em."

Amid the tears of Thoozy and the lamentations of Mrs. Kneebone, Dick bore off his prize. Arrived at the foot of the stairs, they heard a curious noise above, as of heavy blows and wrestling.

"What are they doing, Bill?"

Here came thuds and groans.

"They're a givin' of it to one another. She wants to grab all the tin. Listen. Hooray! Thoozy's got his crutch. She was always a whackin' me awful, till he got the stick. Now she's a catchin' it. Oh, ain't Thoozy a good un, just!"

CHAPTER THE THIRTY-EIGHTH.

HEY went away, Dick holding the boy by the hand. He did not in the least know what to do with the child. He had taken him away by an impulse, thinking of the great fun it would be to carry Polly's own child down to Market Basing, and present him to his mother. But for the present, he found himself in a comparatively respectable part of London, with a ragged little unwashed *gamin* on his hands, not knowing what to do next. It was altogether an embarrassing position.

"As for the boy," he thought, looking down at the little mite holding his hand, I suppose he must be washed and dressed. But who's to do it? And as for Polly—upon my word, Polly, there's a heavy reckoning against you. I suppose I must go and find a lawyer. Bill, my boy, you're dirty, you know, and ragged—where shall we go to get you washed?"

"Dunno. Never was washed."

"Well, then, where can we go to get some new clothes?"

"Dunno. Never had no new clothes. I say, you go to the pawnbroker's—that's the place," said Bill, speaking from his own experience, and brightening up a little.

Dick stopped a policeman, who stared at the child with hungry eyes, apparently disappointed at finding that he was not to "run him in."

Bill howled dismally at the sight of the embodiment of civil power.

"I ain't done nothink," he cried, trying to escape.

"Comes of a bad lot, sir, I'm afraid; but he's never been in trouble yet."

z

"I want to get the boy washed and dressed. In fact," Dick explained, "I am going to take him away, and bring him up respectably."

The policeman's face brightened.

"Are you now, sir? I'm very glad to hear that, very glad indeed. They'll do what you want for you at a public-house I know, not far off. I'm just off my beat, and will go with you. So you're going to take him off the streets, are you? Well, now, that's good of you—that's real goodness and charity. The boy's got no belongings; living at an old woman's—ah, you know. If you can afford to spend the money—it is not much to rich people—take more than one. They're growing up here by hundreds. Take as many as you can afford, and put 'em to school. It'll cost money, because school ain't everything. Don't give to missionary societies and rubbish. They do tell me that three-quarters of a million a year is sent out to convert the blacks. Do you know, sir, how many boys and girls that would provide for? Fifty thousand, sir. Think of that. My son, who's a scholar, totted it up for me. Fifty thousand! If the rich people round London only knew what was inside it, they'd be frightened. I tell you what, sir, if things is going on like this, they'll have something to be frightened about, for the roughs are getting most too strong for us. There'll be an ugly rush some day, you'll see. But people won't do anything without societies. Well, sir, if you've got money, you get up a society for rich people taking children and bringing them up respectable—to be sailors and soldiers, and even—ah! ah! and why not?—even the police force, if they've got the brains."

"I will," said Dick, "if ever I do start a society—which isn't likely."

"None of your institutions, and refuges, and penitentiaries, and reformatories, and foolishness, sir. You go in for a society where the people are going to look after the children themselves, and not send them out into the world with a ticket all the rest of their lives. Who's going to get over being a reformatory boy? I hav'n't got patience with it. What I says to rich people is—don't talk about doing good, and don't belong to societies, but come down here. I'll talk to 'em; and pick out a boy and a girl, or half a dozen boys and girls, and have 'em taught, and washed, and kept respectable, and it'll be the best ticket to get into heaven that they'll find anywhere. Here's the place, sir. I'll go in with you."

The policeman led the way, and explained what was wanted. The boy was undressed, still crying, and put into a warm bath, Dick looking on—he was so horribly thin that every rib stuck out like a skeleton's—and for the first time in his life, thoroughly scrubbed and washed. Then, the policeman having brought an intelligent man from a second-hand shop, with a small bundle of all sorts, he was speedily dressed in a garb which astonished and delighted him beyond measure. For it was the garb of a "swell." He put his hands into his pockets, and left off crying. "Whacking" was not imminent, at any rate.

"Now," said Dick, "let us have a good look at him."

He put the boy on the table, and pulled his face back.

His eyes were blue, his nose was snub, his mouth thin and delicate, his chin sharp-pointed and clear, his hair so light as to be almost flaxen.

"Hum!" said Dick; "they can't say you are like me, anyhow. My hair's black, my nose is straight, my mouth is full, my chin is broad and square, like all the Mortiboys. And you're not too much like your mother either, except about the eyes."

Polly's eyes were a dark blue—an unusual colour, which this boy's had. For the rest, a mere shrimp of a boy—so small that you would not take him for more than seven; but a pretty, bright-faced child, now the dirt was taken off him, with the sharp expression that a London boy always has.

But somehow the boy, now he was dressed, had the look of a gentleman. There was no coarseness in his features or his expression; his eyes had a dreamy, far-off look, which is seldom seen in any but home-bred boys; his mouth was tremulous and sensitive. It was only when he spoke that his street education showed itself.

Dick paid for his accommodation at the public-house, thanked his friend the policeman, and took his prize away with him.

"How old are you, Bill?"

"Ten next January."

"Did you hear us talking about your mother just now?"

"Yes; but I never seen her."

"Would you like to see her?"

"Not if she's like Mother Kneebone. I'd rather stay with you."

"Suppose, Bill, you were to stay with me, and you were to see a woman called Polly Tresler?"

"That's her name?"

"Yes. And suppose she were to ask you questions, do you think you'd let out anything about Mother Kneebone?"

Bill looked up sharply.

"I'm fly," he said. "I won't let out nothink. Dam if I do."

"I say, young 'un, don't say *dam* again, because the swells never do that till they're grown up. It isn't wicked then, I suppose."

At his lodgings, Lafleur was waiting for him.

"What have you here, Dick—what new game is on?"

"Only a little game of euchre with a woman. And this is the Right Bower, though he don't look like it. I'm going to win it: the stakes are worth having, I can tell you."

"You always win everything, though he certainly does not look much like a winning card. Give him something to eat."

Dick rang the bell, and consigned the child to his landlady, with injunctions to give him plenty to eat and drink.

When he came home that night, at twelve, he found the boy curled up on the hearth-rug, sound asleep. He carried him into his bed-room, undressed him, and laid him in bed Bill opened his eyes for a moment; but not understanding the position of things, thought it was a queer dream, and went sound off to sleep again.

In the morning, Dick found him still asleep. He had curled his lean arms round Dick's neck, and laid his little cheeks in Dick's big beard, thinking he was in bed with Thoozy.

"Poor little cuss!" said Dick.

That morning he went to a lawyer, one whose name he had heard from Mr. Battiscombe at Market Basing. To him he confided the whole story of his marriage and Polly's wicked goings-on.

They had a long consultation, after which Dick strode away with a lightened countenance.

Bill was washed and dressed ready for him when he came back. The landlady was also ready with a representation. The boy was not in the agreement, and the trouble he gave was to be considered. Dick considered it. Then she begged to call Mr. Mortiboy's attention to the language in which he expressed his ideas—

"Which," she said, "is truly awful. If I had my boys home from school, they shouldn't stay in the same house with him, not for gold."

She shook her finger at Bill, who looked at his protector to see whether he was going to be "whacked." But Mr. Mortiboy only laughed.

"We shall cure him presently, I dare say. Bring him his dinner as soon as you can. Hungry, Bill?"

"I'm allus hungry," said the boy.

When his dinner came, which was also Dick's luncheon, Bill made a rush at the dish as soon as the cover was taken off. Chops! He seized one in his fingers, and ran to a corner of the room, where he fell to tearing it with his teeth, after the manner of a menagerie tiger. The landlady pointed out this conduct to her tenant.

"That's the way he had his supper last night, sir. A regular little savage."

Dick nodded, and laughed. The woman retired. As she shut the door, the urchin, encouraged by the approving smiles of his patron, as he thought, performed a Catherine Wheel all round the room, with the bone of his mutton-chop in his mouth, finishing off with a "Houp-là!" as he had done the day before. Then he went back to his corner, and gnawed the bone.

"Bill, take the bone out of your mouth, and sit down on that chair. Did you never sit down to table in your life?"

"Eh?"

"How did you get your dinner at Mrs. Kneebone's?"

"Never had no dinner. Morning, mother made tea for herself, and sometimes I got some if Thoozy was able to get up. When Thoozy had rheumatics dreadful bad, so that he couldn't get up, I only got a bit of bread. Went out all day on the cadge. If I got nothink, old Mother Kneebone giv' me a whackin' and another bit of bread. When Thoozy was all right, I got on first-rate. Thoozy used to help hisself and me too."

"Well, now you've got to learn manners."

Bill then received his first lesson in the usages of polite society—in teaching him which, as it was a novel occupation, Dick found the afternoon slip away pleasantly enough.

"Nobody ever taught you anything, I suppose?"

"Only Thoozy. He used to read to me. He's awful clever —knows everything. He promised to learn me to read as soon as he could find time. Once I was took up by a lady and put to school. It was a Sunday, because the bells were ringing, and the swells going to church. There was a bun and a cup of tea—jolly!—and then they taught us. I went lots of times on Sundays. They told me to say prayers and to sing hymns. I sang one at home they taught me, but old Mother Kneebone took a stick, and said she'd break every bone in my body if I didn't give over."

"They never taught you your duty, I suppose," said the moral Dick.

"What's that? There was a man in a straight black gownd said we was all going—Thoozy and me, and all the lot—to hell."

"That's good news to tell a child," said Dick.

"So I told Thoozy; and I asks him where it is, and what it's like when you've got there. He ups and says, 'If it ain't better than Paragon Place, it won't be very jolly for us, Bill. Let's hope there'll be plenty to eat, and no Mother Kneebone.' Then I thought I should like to go there. But Thoozy said school wasn't no good."

Presently, the boy, unaccustomed to a chop and half a glass of beer, fell into a profound slumber; and Dick smoked on, thinking what he was to do with him.

He stayed one week in town, having interviews with the lawyers, and making out his case against Polly. This was not, with the data they had to go upon, at all a difficult task. After a few days, the story ran much as Mrs. Kneebone had told him.

Polly, at the age of eighteen, had gone up to London into service. She made certain female friends who had belongings at Poplar, where she went on her "Sundays out." There she fell in with the mate of a sailing ship, a man twenty-five years older than herself, who was attracted by her rosy cheeks and bright eyes, and married her. According to Mrs. Kneebone—who ought to know something of feminine nature—the main cause of the conjugal unhappiness which ensued was that Polly despised a man who allowed his wife to beat him. No doubt there was a certain amount of truth in Mrs. Kneebone's remark: far be it from me to suggest suspicion as to any statement made by a woman in most respects so admirable. But this was not all the truth. When Captain Bowker went away, he left, in lieu of a monthly allowance from the shippers, which most merchant skippers' wives draw, a sum of money equivalent to it, calculated to last during the period of his absence. It must be observed that Polly was, if

I may coin the term, a pseudo-maniac: she lied habitually, and even causelessly. Had she been of a higher rank in life, she would have become, of course, a novelist, drawing from her imagination some of that superfluous energy which prompted her now to invent, whenever invention appeared not only profitable, but even amusing. She had, in obedience to this proclivity, lied about herself and her belongings to her husband. Bowker had been told by her that she came from Cumberland. Why from Cumberland? I don't know. Polly only knew that it was a long way off, so she said Cumberland; and as her husband had never been there, it answered as well as any other place.

When Captain Bowker had been away for about a year—that is, for more than half of his appointed time—Polly bethought herself that she ought to go to Market Basing, and pay a visit to her parents. She went; found her father dead, and her mother on the point of going to the workhouse; stayed there—promising at first for a few weeks only. But weeks passed into months; and when her husband returned —bringing a parcel of Chinese silks for his wife, and a parrot that knew how to cough and swear, having learned these accomplishments from a consumptive mariner—he found his house there, and "all standing," as he expressed it, but no Polly. Nor could he light upon any traces of his Polly. First, because he was a warm-hearted man, he shed tears, and wrung the neck of the parrot for swearing at him. Next, he thanked the Lord for being rid of a bad lot, sold the sticks, paid the rent, and went to sea again.

Then something happened to Polly. She met Dick Mortiboy: fell in with him in the fields as he was walking home from Parkside to Derngate; met him again—met him every night; saw that the boy was madly in love with her; encouraged him, but gave herself all the airs of a *vertu farouche;* received his presents; and then * * * *

Bigamy. It is an ugly word. Polly said it over and over to herself about this time. It means all sorts of unpleasantness: it conveys ideas of courts, policemen, prison, an unbecoming uniform, a diet rather plain than luxurious, compulsory early rising, a limited circle of friends, very few books to read. A very ugly word. But bigamy without the danger? to marry twice and not to be found out? to marry the son of the richest man in the town so that the sailor husband should never know? This seemed a prize worth risking something for. And what did she risk? Nothing. She asked her mother. Nothing, repeated the old lady. How could Bowker find out? He was bound to go to sea: He was always afloat: he was twenty years older than herself: he might get drowned—most likely he would get drowned—perhaps he was drowned already. And then she would have her new husband clear to herself.

And the son of the richest man in the town!

Young Dick pressed her. In his imagination, the fresh-cheeked, rosy village girl, who said she was eighteen when she was five-and-twenty, was an angel. Dick was a fool, of course: but many men have been fools at nineteen. He pressed her to promise to marry him. She promised. That meant nothing, because she could always break off. But his father sent him up to town to work for a time in a London bank, and—and—alas! for Polly's vow—it succumbed; and one fine morning she walked up the aisle of St. Pancras Church, and was married to Dick Mortiboy.

"Bigamy," said Dick, chuckling—"bigamy! That's a very pretty rod to hold over my Polly's head. And the worthy sailor still alive."

When Dick disappeared there were two courses open to his afflicted wife. She might go to Mr. Mortiboy, and proclaim herself his daughter-in-law; or she might go back to her Bowker. She reasoned out the matter with her mother; and, by her advice, elected to return to her first husband. The two reasons which the experienced matron, her mamma, urged were—first, that if Bowker found her out, it would lead to criminal proceedings and great unpleasantness; secondly, that if she told Mr. Mortiboy, he would infallibly, so angry would he be, refuse to afford her any assistance whatever. So she went to Poplar. Captain Bowker, her old friends told her, was gone to the China Seas in the country trade: would not be back for five years. Further, he had left a message that, if Polly came back, she was to be told that he was quit of her, and that she was henceforth no wife of his. That formula constitutes a nautical divorce. So Polly had to abandon hopes in that direction. Of course, she might, had she known, have gone to the shippers in whose employ her husband was, and demanded an allowance as his wife. She did not know their names. Then she fell in love for the first time. It was also with a sailor, one William Flint, ship's carpenter by profession, who so far overcame her scruples of conscience as to lead her to the altar a third time. Mr. Flint was the father of little Bill. He died before the birth of his son, after a short period of matrimonial happiness, during which he effectually taught Polly the beauty of submission by means of a thick stick. Mrs. Flint, thus bereft of two husbands and widowed of a third, left her child in care of Mrs. Kneebone, and lived in London for some years, still single, though not without admirers. When, like Horace's Lydia, she ceased to hear them knock at her door, she retired to Market Basing, where the rest of her history is known.

"The whole case," said the lawyer, after exposing the principal facts, "is as simple as possible. Bowker still lives, and has a pension from his employers. We can put our hands upon him whenever you please. The woman committed bigamy in marrying you. You may proceed against her if you like. Bowker may get a divorce if he pleases. The boy is no more yours than he is mine."

"Thank you," said Dick. "I'll wait a week or so, and think things over. I suppose I couldn't marry again without making any fuss about it?"

"You might, certainly; but you had better not just yet. Put yourself wholly in our hands, my dear sir."

Dick went away thoughtful. He was not altogether satisfied. Polly was a bad lot—a very bad lot. At the same time, it seemed mean to put her into prison, and bring her to utter shame and misery. He was always tender to criminals—not from any self-compunctions or prickings of conscience, but chiefly from the mental attitude of resistance to law into which his roving years had put him. Could not a compromise be effected? Suppose she were to go away, and be silent about it all? Suppose—but, in short, he would wait a little.

Then he thought of Grace. Free, free at last! The follies of his youth trampled down and forgotten! Love before him, and a peaceful life, such as he yearned after, away in some garden of pleasant England, hand in hand with Grace! Polly's chance was slender.

He went home to little Bill. It took some days to teach the child that mankind at large, though strangers, were not his mortal enemies. He learned the smaller lessons—those of propriety and the habits of civilization—easily enough, because he had nothing to unlearn, never having had any manners at all. He was a gentle child, too—submissive and docile. His worst difficulty, of course, was his language, which he readily perceived was not the same as that employed by his patron. He used to listen to what people said, and then go away and imitate them in a corner—gestures, and voice, and all. A perfectly wild boy: as untaught—save from the few lessons which he had got from Thoozy—as regards the outer world, as if he had been born in a desert and reared on the top of a mountain. A boy whose mind was like wax to receive impressions—a blank waxen tablet, for the stylus of Dick to work upon. Bad things he knew, after a fashion; but as they had never been called bad to him, of course it did not matter. As Euripides has explained, we only know what is bad by the canon of what is good. Good and bad were alike to little Bill.

In a day or two, the little animal was as fond of his patron and as entirely trustful in him as if he had been a dog. He ran about after him; he curled up at his feet if he sat down; he climbed upon his knees; he sat up solemnly, and stared at him; he listened to all he said, and repeated it to himself. And Dick gave him, in that week which was spent in completing the "case" against Polly, a whole volume of moral philosophy, and a complete sheaf of moral axioms.

Mindful of the untrustworthy character of the Church Catechism, from the evidence he had received of it—he had not read it since he was a boy—he composed a short one for himself, which he asked the boy daily.

"What is a boy's first duty, Bill?"

"Never steal, never tell lies, never swear, hold his jaw, do his work, go away from England, and get on."

He numbered his commandments off on his fingers, and went through them glibly enough.

"Right, boy. When I was your age, they used to teach me the Ten Commandments; but somehow they didn't seem to stick. I didn't want to worship graven images, so it was no good telling me not. Boys do prig, Bill, and don't get found out. They go on prigging, and then they do get found out. Then you know what happens.

"The thing to do is to persuade people to trust you. Show that you are able to get on, and you will. Whatever you do, Bill, put your back into it. I knew a poor creature in the States who was always having chances, and always failing, because he never had the pluck to take them. He had the fever last time I saw him, in a poor, mean sort of way. Hadn't the pluck to shake like other people.

"Here's another commandment for you, Bill. *Always be ready to fight.* It's the fighting men get the best of it. If a boy insults you, up with your fist. People are mostly cowards. If you make them afraid, they'll do anything. Remember that, Bill.

"Never you trust people that go round cracking you up to your face. If I wanted to get something out of you, I should say, 'Bill, you're a pretty boy, and a nice behaved boy.' As I want to do you good, I say, 'Bill, you're a thin, mealy-faced little devil, without enough strength to squeeze the life out of a mosquito.' You'll be no good till you're fat and strong, and know how to talk, and to behave, and to read. You remember that, Bill.

"You'll have to go to school soon, my boy. I'm not going to have you taught a lot of rubbish, on pretence of improving your intellect, because the masters don't know anything else. You'll learn to talk French and German; you'll learn music; you'll learn to ride, and to fence, and to box; and you'll learn all the science you can get stuffed into you. But no Latin, my boy, and no rubbish.

"Keep your eyes wide open, Bill, for shams and humbugs. Everybody in England, almost, is a humbug. You'll have to make money, and you can't do it, if you stay here, without pretending and telling lies. When you get big, old chap, you and I will go away to the West, and make a clearing, and grow our own crops. That's real, at any rate. Remember that, Bill.

"Don't be in a hurry to fall in love. Wait till you are five-and-twenty before you think about a girl at all. Then get married as soon as you can. When we get to Market Basing, I'll show you the kind of girl you may fall in love with. You remember that.

"Never be satisfied *till you've got all you want*. Rich people teach the poor to be humble and contented. That's because they want to keep what they've got. If you see a man humble, *kick him till he's proud*. And if you see a man contented, have him locked up in a lunatic asylum.

"I remember once, out there, we caught a man in the act of horse-stealing. Some were for hanging him. 'Don't do that,' I said. 'Let's tar and feather him.' So we did; and when the job was finished—he really looked beautiful—we made him dance a breakdown. The poor devil was frightened, and looked as miserable as if the rope was round his neck. So one of the crowd shouts out to him, 'Dance jolly,' he says— 'dance jolly; or, by the powers, we'll hang you.' That man instantly looked as jolly as if it was all fun and jokes—face wreathed with smiles, as the books say. I never saw a better breakdown. So, if you see a man humble, you kick him till he's proud. Remember that, Bill.

"One man's as good as another, Bill. Don't you be afraid of a man because he's got a carriage, and a different coat to yours. He's only better than you if he's stronger, and has got better brains.

"Never you take a thing on trust. A man on board the boat from America wanted to persuade me about his religious notions. Said they were Bishop somebody's. That's all he had to believe them by. Bill, it's a mighty poor way of knowing things, if you believe all they tell you. Some day I'll tell you what a priest in Mexico wanted me to believe.

"Manners, my boy. Get manners as soon as you can. They help a man more than anything else. Always be polite to everybody; but if you want anything, let them know it at starting. It saves a great deal of fighting. As I told you, if you have manners to start with, and pluck to back your demands, you'll get on."

The sermons, of which these are only notes, were not all delivered in a single day, or in a single week. They are inserted here to indicate the nature of the course of philosophy which Dick was putting his young pupil through. From time to time he examined him; added to the commandments which formed his catechism; illustrated his position by anecdotes; made a sort of running commentary on his teaching, or gave the boy an exercise on some knotty point.

All this excellent moral teaching we are fain to pass over, because space and time are limited. Anybody who wants to know more of Dick's teaching may purchase his aphorisms of me, on moderate terms, to be mutually agreed upon.

CHAPTER THE THIRTY-NINTH.

IT was in a very changed mood that Dick went back to Market Basing; one that boded little good to Polly. He went back rejoicing in his freedom. He could try once more for his cousin, Grace Heathcote. If she accepted he would—what would he do ?—write to his lawyers to get his marriage with Polly Tresler annulled in the quickest manner, and at any cost.

With him, of course, went little Bill. Dick had got him dressed in a fantastic garb of his own invention, consisting chiefly of brown velvet and gold lace, in which the child looked wonderfully beautiful. I said before that he had the look of a gentleman. It was more than this : he had that look of refinement and intelligence which might have been produced in a boy of extraordinary talent by a course of the most careful training, the highest kind of education. He was now almost presentable : he had ascertained most of the words which are *tapu:* he was convinced that his original theories as to the nature of women, based on his experience of Mrs. Knecbone, were erroneous, or at least not capable of general application; he did not take to his heels when he saw a policeman ; he ate and drank like a Christian. The only thing which made him sometimes troublesome was that he really did not know how, without using *tapu* words, to express his ideas. And he sometimes, by imitating exactly what he saw others do, provoked the observer's smile, or stimulated his curiosity.

Dick denied himself his cigar in the train, thinking that the smell of a smoking-carriage might be bad for the boy. Consequently there were ladies in the carriage ; two young ladies who whispered to each other, and shot telegraphic signals about nothing out of the corners of their eyes, and an old one. The old lady fell to admiring the boy. She looked at him for a long time, and could not resist the impulse to talk to him.

"Your son, may I ask, sir ?" she said to Dick.

"My ward, madam."

"Come to me, my dear. I've got a grandson something like him." She drew the child to her knee. Little Bill looked wistfully at Dick. "What is your name, my dear?"

"Bill."

"Y—e—s—William—a pretty name."

"'Taint William. It's Bill."

"Dear me!" thought the old lady; "this is a very vulgar child. Now talk to me, my dear," she said aloud.

This was a staggerer for little Bill. He was not anxious now to answer questions, being quite aware that his previous history, though not discreditable perhaps, had yet been unfortunate. He was silent for a little, and then, unfortunately recollecting exactly what he had seen his patron's landlady in London do one afternoon when she brought up the bill, he slipped off the old lady's knee, and, striking an attitude, half deprecating, half assertive, he coughed behind his hand, and murmured—

"It was not always thus with me. I have had happier days."

Then he placed his hand on his heart, and sighed deeply. Then he looked at Dick, to see if he had done anything wrong.

In a word the boy was a little monkey—just as imitative—just as quick and clever.

"God bless my soul!" cried the old lady; "what an extraordinary child!"

The two young ladies screamed. Dick laughed. And the boy, seeing their amusement, jumped up and down, laughing too.

"Pardon him, madam," said Dick. "By an unlucky series of accidents, my ward's education has been totally neglected. Sit here, my boy, and do not let us talk any more."

No one was in the villa to receive them. Dick took the boy by the hand, and led him into the house. All the magnificence bewildered him.

"Do you live here, Uncle Dick?"

"This is my house, Bill; and here you and I will live together as jolly as we can. Come upstairs. Now this, my boy, is to be your room. There isn't a bed in it at present, but I will get you one. It is your own room. We shall have you taught to read and write; and then you shall have books, if you take to books—as I expect you will. And now— I wish you could ride—we will have a little drive into the country together."

The groom brought round Dick's dog-cart, and they drove off.

First, to the bank. Bill trotted in after his protector, following him like a little dog.

"Who is this?" asked Ghrimes.

"This is little Bill—William Flint, by name, adopted ward of Mr. Dick Mortiboy. Don't look suspicious, Ghrimes."

"Indeed, I was not thinking anything of the sort."

Dick transacted his business, which did not take long, and went out. He took the road to Hunslope. People looked at the cart with astonishment. What new thing had happened? Young Mr. Mortiboy with a child beside him! Polly, standing at the door of her mother's cottage, saw him drive past. Saw the boy, too, and wondered. During this interval she had been full of fear, and uncertainty, and rage. It was not fear of "the other" turning up; it was bodily fear of being killed if she offended her husband. She resolved to go at least to the villa that very evening, and have it out. Not a thought of little Bill!

"Oh, what a pretty boy!" cried Grace. "Lucy come and look. Who is he, Dick?"

"He's my ward, now. A week ago he was anybody's ward, running about the streets. I've had him cleaned and new rigged, you see, and I don't think he looks amiss. Shake hands as I taught you, Bill. Grace, come and talk to me for five minutes in the garden. Lucy, take care of the boy, will you? Give him a lesson in good behaviour."

Grace saw that he had something of importance to say, and led the way to the garden without another word. It was one of those old-fashioned gardens, where you are sure of finding all the old flowers side by side with the best of the new—mignonette, wall-flower, sweet-William, Venus's looking-glass, polyanthus, London pride, and the rest. At the end lay a sort of little shrubbery, behind which again was an arbour.

"Come into the arbour, Grace," said Dick.

He was looking wonderfully serious and thoughtful,—his firm lips twitching with some anxieties, his eyes cast down.

He motioned to Grace to go in and sit down, but she remained standing outside.

They were behind the shrubbery, and hidden from the house.

"You remember the scene at the cross, Grace?"

"I have spoken to no one about it."

"I knew you would not. You found out then two secrets of my life, both of which I wanted to hide from you;—one, that I love you; the other that I am married already. Since that night, Grace, I have made a discovery."

"What is it, Dick?"

"That I can free myself, Grace—that I am free already. I can be divorced. The marriage was not a real one. I am certain of that. The obstacle exists no longer—or will exist no longer in a very short time. All that my money can do to further the separation of that woman from me shall be done. I have told the lawyers to spare no trouble to hunt up every atom and scrap of her life—to ferret out every secret she ever had. I shall hold myself up to ridicule in the papers, perhaps. What does that matter? Who cares for a day's notoriety? Free I *will* be—free I *must* be."

"I should like to congratulate you, Dick; but it seems all so dreadful. Are you quite sure? Oh, Dick, don't be cruel to—to an innocent woman."

"Am I sure? Grace, I could send her into court at once, to-day, with my evidence in my hands. But I will not: I will wait for more. How bad that woman is, you could never know, you could never even suspect. Bad wife of a bad husband. We were fitly mated then—we are not fitly mated now. And she must go." His face was stern and hard. Suddenly it lit up again, and he burst into one of those quaint, soft laughs of his which made every one else laugh too. His laugh was as infectious as another person's yawn. "I forgot to tell you, Grace. Such fun! After you went away, I met her again by the river. She had been drinking more, and said something or other which made me in a rage, I believe. At all events, I took her by the arms, and chucked her in."

"Dick!—you might have drowned her."

"Yes. I didn't think of that till she was at the bottom, and I saw the bubbles coming up—her bubbles! But there was no fear. Bless you, she came to the top, and floated like a cork. You should have seen her face when she came out!"

Dick told the story quite simply, as if it was the most natural thing in the world that he should throw his wife into the river. Grace looked at him with astonishment, and then began to laugh as well. It was impossible to treat Dick like an ordinary creature.

"Now look here, Grace, my dear," Dick went on. "I

offended you at the cross, and behaved like a—like a—mean Mexican, with my love, and my fury, and all the rest of it. I'm very sorry and ashamed. Tell me again I am forgiven."

"Of course you are forgiven, Dick."

"Yes; I was mad then because of Polly. But she's as good as gone now, and I am mad no more. And——the truth remains, Grace, that I love you more than all the world together. It is all exactly as I told you a fortnight ago."

"But you mustn't love me, Dick. I belong to somebody else."

"Must not love you, my dear? Why, Grace, you might as well tell me I must not eat or drink. Not love you when I see you, and talk to you, and take your hand in mine—this little hand"— he took it as he spoke, and held it in his, Grace only looking him straight in the face: "this little hand. Why, Grace, do you think I am made of stone?"

"Indeed, I am sure you are not, Dick. But do you think I am a woman to give her word one day, and recall it the next? Is that fair, Dick?"

"It would be if you loved me. I should not care unless you were to take away your word from me, Grace. All is fair in love."

"No; but I do not love you, Dick—I never can love you. Listen, and I will tell you all my secrets. I talk to you because you love me, as I can talk to no one else. And because I trust you, Dick, I tell you what I can hardly tell my own sister. Indeed she would not understand me." She laid her hand in his—it rested on the back of the garden seat. "Dick, do you remember what you told me—how you tremble when I touch you? It is all exactly the same with me. When I hear Frank's step—I never do now; but I say now, because I dream of it still—I tremble all over. When he comes near me, I feel all the blood rushing to my face. If he touches me, my pulses beat. If I see his handwriting, my hand shakes. If I awake at night, thinking of him, I do not want to sleep any more, and lie patiently, praying to God for him. When I pass their dear old house, I cannot keep my tears down. When I have nothing to do, I go to the lane—see there: you are tall, and can look over the hedge: it is in the lane beyond the next field—where he first told me he loved me, and sit down, and think it all over again. Oh, Dick, such a cold day it was!—and yet we were so warm: such a snowy, frosty, windy day in January, and yet I was so glad and happy! I

never knew that I loved him until he told me that he loved
me, and then I knew—oh, in a moment I knew, that there
could be no other man in all the world for me but Frank.
Dear Dick, I love you too, but not in this way. See—I can
give you my hand without trembling. I can see you coming
without my pulses beating faster. I read you all my heart:
more, more than I could ever, I think, tell to Frank. I tell
you to make you leave off loving me."

Dick shook his head. He was sitting down now, on the
garden seat, holding her hand in his. He stooped and kissed it.

"Dick—dear Dick!—don't be cruel to me. Mamma is unkind because she wants you to marry me, and says that I don't
encourage you."

Dick laughed ruefully.

"I don't want any encouragement, Grace."

"Everything seems somehow dark and gloomy. Don't be
cruel, Dick. Be my dear old Dick, like you were years ago,
before you went away, when I was a little thing, and you a
big boy. I can never love you, Dick. Let me say it again
and again, and over and over, so that you may believe me at
last. Then, if I were to marry you, how would it be with
you? How should you like your wife to be brooding over
her ruined lover, and trying to do a cold-hearted duty by her
husband? Dick it would be wicked. It would kill me—it
would drive you mad. Don't ask me—don't ask me, my
cousin, for I love my Frank."

She stopped now because she could not go on any longer,
and her voice broke down. Dick's head was bent above her
hand, and he said nothing. Presently a tear—only one—of
the largest size consistent with the laws which guide the
formation of drops, fell upon her hand. Grace had made her
lover weep. Since his mother died, he had shed no tear.
They stood so for some minutes.

Five minutes before this, Mrs. Heathcote, returning home,
found Lucy with the boy.

"It is Dick's new *protégé*," she explained. "Grace and he
are in the garden."

"*Protégé!*—stuff and nonsense!" said Mrs. Heathcote.
"What does Dick want with children?"

She went to the back of the house, and looked out into the
garden. No Grace there. Then she stepped softly across the
lawn, and heard voices behind the shrubbery. She stopped

and listened. She heard the words, "Don't ask me, my cousin. I love my Frank;" and, turning pale, hurried back to the house. She could not speak.

Presently Dick lifted his head with a smile. Grace knew then that she had won the battle.

"I give you up, Grace, dear. All the same, I love you still. But I will never again speak—of love to you. That, at least, I promise."

"You must promise me more, Cousin Dick."

"What more? I will promise you anything you like to ask, child Grace."

"Help Frank."

"Yes, my sister," answered Dick, humbly.

"Am I your sister? Then Frank is your brother, Dick. You must help your brother."

"Let me kiss you once, my dear. Let me have one kiss."

He took her head in his hands, and kissed her—solemnly, not passionately—on forehead and cheek. She disengaged herself, blushing and confused, with the tears in her eyes. What was she that this man—so good so kind—should love her so?

"There was a solemn oath in every kiss, Grace. You may trust me, for Frank and yourself, to the death. You are both mine. Tell me only what I am to do first."

"I will find his address from Kate, Dick, and then—oh, then we shall know what to do."

"I know what to do already," cried Dick, his face brightening up like a corn-field after a cloud has passed over it. "I know already what you would all like. We will make him a partner in the bank—Ghrimes and Frank together—and revive the old name. It shall be Melliship, Mortiboy & Co.— just as before. Eh, Grace? What a rage the old man would be in if he only knew it! Ho! ho!"

He laughed—with his jolly, mellow voice—as lightly as a boy, and with no sign of the emotion which had just possessed him, and left her. Mrs. Heathcote was gone to her own room. Lucy was sitting with the boy, who stared at her with great eyes, as a vision of another world. Taking him away, he drove back to Market Basing.

Mrs. Heathcote, too angry at first to speak, went back to the house and tried to think. Should she tell her husband? Should she remonstrate with Grace? What good would it do? They were both too obstinate to receive remonstrance with favour. She would only make things worse. Should she speak to Lucy? What use? So she had to keep it to herself, consoling herself with the thought that, after all, it was early days; perhaps Dick might propose again; perhaps Grace might not be always obdurate; perhaps Frank Melliship would "do something." Nevertheless, it was a cruel blow to overhear the rejection of half a million of money.

In the evening of the same day, Polly, not without a good deal of misgiving and consultation with her mother, went up to the villa, in order to have it out with her husband. She resolved for herself to assume an aggressive attitude, and meditated a line of action which she considered would prove most effective with Dick. First, she put on all her best things; then she stuck a pistol—it was only an old single-barrelled thing which she had by her—in her pocket; and under her shawl she carried the family carving-knife. Then she walked boldly over the bridge which arched the river half a mile above the villa, stepped across the fields, and knocked at Dick's door.

The proprietor of the house opened it.

"I thought you would turn up to-night. Pray come in, Polly. We will talk inside."

He spoke with so much politeness that Polly smelt mischief. But she followed without saying a word. He led the way to the smoking-room, where sat little Bill in his gorgeous attire.

"Who's that boy?" asked Polly.

"We'll come to him directly," said Dick. "Now, Polly, the game's played out, and you'd better throw up the cards."

"What do you mean, Dick? If you think I'm going to be murdered quietly, you're just mistaken; so see here!"

She took out her pistol and carving-knife, and standing with the table between them, brandished the weapons in his face with the air of a heroine at the Adelphi.

"Pretty toys—very pretty toys," said her husband. "No, Polly, I'm not going to murder you. As an old friend, I should perhaps advise you to make tracks. But, after all, you needn't do that, because you are quite certain to be followed."

She stared at him, wondering, with a sinking heart, what was to follow.

"Carry your memory back twelve years and three-quarters. Is it done?"

"It is. What little lark are you up to now, Dick?"

"What do you see?"

"I see you and me walking up the aisle of St. Pancras' Church."

"St. Pancras' Church. Very good indeed. Now carry your memory two years and three-quarters or so farther on. Where are we on a certain Monday about that time?"

She assumed a sulky and stubborn air. But she turned pale, notwithstanding.

"I don't know. How am I to remember so long ago?"

"You need not remember unless you like, you know, Well, let us have another question, and I have done. Carry your memory back to Limehouse Church, two years before the St. Pancras business."

This time she reeled as if she had been struck. For a space she did not answer.

Then she murmured, with dry lips—

"Prove it—prove it. You can't do it."

"Polly, the game's up. It's all come out. I'm trying now to find out the best way of getting rid of my marriage without, if you fall in with my views, bringing you before a court of law. Because you see, Polly, you've committed a very pretty bigamy. Bowker was alive when you married me, and you knew it. I can prove it. He's alive now!"

Polly let the pistol and carving-knife drop, and fell down on her knees moaning and crying.

"Oh! Dick—Dick. I married you because I loved you. I did indeed—I did indeed! And I married the other man because I thought you were dead. Believe me, Dick—oh, believe me and forgive me!"

She was serious in her grief at heart, because Dick represented money and ease to her. Besides, in her way—her coarse, rough way—she really loved the man.

"Forgive you?" said Dick. "I don't quite understand what you mean by forgiving. I'll forgive you fast enough as soon as we're divorced: not a moment before, if you pray on your knees from this till midnight. Get up, Polly, and don't be play-acting. Before your own son, too."

"My son!" She started up as if she had been shot. "My son! Oh, then, now I see who has done the mischief."

"Your son, Polly—Flint's son. Not mine at all, you know. Look at him, and tell me what you think of him."

She seized the boy, who was trembling with terror, and held him under the lamp to look at him

"Uncle Dick," he cried, "don't let her have me."

"He's my boy—he's my son. I shall take him away."

"No you don't, Polly. That's one of my conditions. Prisoners are not allowed, remember, to have their children in gaol with them. Now, listen to me. For the present, and until I have decided what to do, you go away from Market Basing. I don't care where you go to. My lawyers will give you a pound a week to live on: always understand that it is only for the present. You tell no one here anything: if you do, you go to gaol the next day. The boy remains with me. You write out to-morrow morning and give me a full confession, stating that you knew Bowker to be alive when you married me."

"I won't," cried the woman. "And I'll have my boy."

"That is what you will do," said Dick, unmoved. "If you break through any part of these conditions, you know the consequences. The whole story of your life is known to me. Your eight years in London, Polly—what do you think of that? Everything will be published in open court, and you will go off to gaol for a couple of years or ten years. And where will you be when you come out?"

"I'll kill Mother Kneebone," she hissed.

"That's as you please. Do anything you like with that old lady; but you will be hanged if you do, you know."

Polly wavered, and loosed her hold of the child, who instantly slipped behind Dick's legs for protection.

"Here is money to take you to London. Here is the address of the lawyers, to whom you will go for your weekly allowance. I shall write to them to-night. If you do not appear here before midday to-morrow to make your written confession, I shall write to them to take out the warrant that will send you to prison. Now go."

She took the paper and the money, and went away without a word or a sign.

CHAPTER THE FORTIETH.

OLLY went home to her mother. The dear old lady, in spite of Polly's assertion, had heard the truth about the ducking, and rejoiced, because it gave her daughter, as she thought, an opportunity of threatening reprisals.

Before she left on her errand of frightening Dick, her mother advised her—

"Don't you be afraid, Polly—he can't kill you. He calls hisself a gentleman, so I suppose he won't beat you. You stick up to him. Tell him you'll blare it all over the town. Threaten him, my gal. Don't never let out that you're afraid of him. If he won't come down with hush-money to keep it dark, tell him you're agoin' to git a warrant out against him for your own protection. That's the way, Polly. Give me my drops handy, against you come back."

Presently her daughter returned, but pale, startled, and faint.

"It's all up, mother," she murmured.

"What's all up, Poll? You ain't been such a fool as to let out that you was afraid, have you?"

"It's no use being afraid or not, now. It's all up, mother, I tell you. What you always prophesied has come. He has found out about the other two."

"Polly!—the other two? Both on 'em?"

"Both. Mother Kneebone told him. No one else could. No one else knew—unless he found out for himself. Oh, he's a devil—he's a devil!"

"Who's Mother Kneebone?"

"The woman as had the boy. Dick's got the boy now. Says he means to keep him. I don't want the brat, I'm sure."

"The woman who had the boy," snarled her mother. "The woman that had the secrets that you wouldn't tell your own mother. Serves you right, Polly—serves you right, for not telling me everything. Why did you let Mrs. Kneebone know about yourself at all?"

"She knew all along. It's no use singing out, mother. It's all up, I tell you. I shall go to London, and you must go to the union."

The old woman fell back moaning on her pillow. As her head touched it, there was a chink of money.

"My money!" cried Polly, brightening up. "My money! Let's see how much there is."

Her mother clutched the bag from under her head, and held it tight: not tight enough, however, in her old hands to save it from her daughter, who snatched it from her grasp after a brief and unequal contest.

It was a stocking, and in the toe lay all, or nearly all, the money she had got from Dick, except what she had spent in dress.

Polly counted it out. There were fifty-five pounds, all in sovereigns. She put back fifty into the stocking, which she carefully placed in her own pocket. Then she pulled out a purse, containing fourpence in coppers and a few shillings, put four of the sovereigns in it, and gave the remaining one back to her mother, who lay back in the bed, moaning and cursing—now loud, now soft—like a gale at sea.

"Oh! that ever I had a daughter," groaned the old woman. "Oh! I wish you'd never been born. To take and send me to the union. Oh! I'm sorry that ever I saw your face. Oh! I wish I'd drownded you when you was a baby, as I wanted to. To let her old mother go on the parish! I wish you was smothered! I wish you was dead! I wish you was transported! I wish you was hanged! I wish you was blind, and deaf, and dumb, and full of aches and pains! I do!"

She stopped, not for want of ejaculations, for her quiver was full of them, but for want of breath.

Polly, who was comparatively accustomed to these outbreaks, calmly proceeded to undress, with the design of going to bed. When her mother choked, she lifted her up, and patted her on the back to bring her round.

"You've had a good long spell out of the union, considering, mother, so you may as well make up your mind to go in quietly. Why, you must be past seventy now. It'll be good for you to have the chaplain coming round with his nice talk, and the services on Sunday. You've been a wicked old hussy, you know, and it may be the making of you, after all."

"I'm not so bad as you," cried the old woman, mad with rage. "You pepper and salt drab—you bag of wickedness—you, you—black, brazen, blaring, pitchfire, tom-cat."

Polly heeded not. She had let down her hair, and was looking at herself in her glass. Obedient to feminine instincts, the first use she had made of the money which Dick had given her was to buy a looking-glass. She saw a large coarse face—coarse through drink—with thick lips. Her nose, which had been straight and well formed, was puffy. This was through drink. Her forehead was swollen and red. Drink had left its mark. Her eyes alone remained—deep, large, limpid, dark blue.

"The boy has got my eyes," she murmured with a sigh, thinking of days when she had attractions enough to catch the calf-love of young Dick Mortiboy.

Then she went to bed, her mother pursuing her with execrations as she climbed the narrow stairs. They are not written down here, because they were unparliamentary, and unbecoming the general character of woman, from whose lips *nil nisi lene* ought to proceed.

Early in the morning she came down again, shook up the old woman—not unkindly—and began putting her things together.

"Look here mother—I must go to London, you know—because else I shall have to go to prison; so it can't be helped. You've got one sovereign already. I'll give you five more—come. That'll carry you on for a bit; and I'll tell Mrs. Smith's Ameliarann to come in and look after you. Let's part friends."

The old woman clutched the money, and Polly went away without those tender wishes and embraces which some parents lavish upon their departing children.

She was dressed in all her finery, to save the trouble of carrying the things, and had the rest of her belongings in a single bag, which she carried herself.

She went straight to the villa. Dick was already up, though it was only eight o'clock, and was waiting for her.

"Now then," she said cheerfully, "if I've got to write things down, I'd better begin. No; I won't write. I never can write decent. You shall write, Dick, and I will sign. Bless you, mother always said you'd find out some day."

Dick got the notes with which the lawyers had furnished him for reference, and sat down meekly to write at her dictation. Walking up and down, she began her narrative.

In a clear voice, in a free and easily flowing style, which would have done honour to me, the novelist, she recounted the events of her life, from her marriage with Mr. Bowker to her marriage with Mr. Flint. No motives assigned, no psychological doublings, no excuses offered, nor attempt to extenuate. Plain matter-of-fact statement. At the death of the dear departed saint, Mr. Flint, she stopped.

"I'm afraid, Mrs. Bowker," said Dick, "that we have not quite finished. There are still eight years."

"Two years I was at Market Basing, in service."

"That leaves six."

"I sha'nt tell you what I did in those six years."

"Perhaps you will let me write, and you can sign."

Dick took the notes, and rapidly wrote, in as few words as

possible, the story of those six years. Then Polly took the manuscript from his hands, and read it all through without blushing.

"Before I sign it, I want to put in something for myself."

"You are not in a position to make conditions."

"Then I want to ask a question. What are you going to do with this?"

"For the present, I am going to lock it up in my own safe."

"And not going to show it to any one? Oh! then it's all right. Hand me the pen, Dick. You're not the boy, my handsome Dick, to send an old friend to prison, because she loved you. There, Dick, you are free now. Shake hands with your old Polly."

Dick held out his hand. Polly threw her arms round his neck, and kissed him with a tear in her eye.

Then she went away. On the way to town, she formed a project. It was wild, perhaps, but bold: in the highest degree impudent and shameless; but it had the merit of possessing genius.

But first to Mrs. Kneebone's.

Paragon-place looked exactly as it had done when she had brought the baby ten years before, and left it to Mrs. Kneebone's fostering care. In the court, there were the children playing just as when she had been there last; the same squalor, the same dirt. At the entrance stood a figure she did not remember, with the shape of an old man, and the face of a boy, leaning on a crutch, looking up Gray's Inn-road. It was Thoozy, standing there on the chance of seeing little Bill pass by. For Thoozy's ideas of the outer world were limited. In spite of his occasional studies in the *Daily Telegraph*, he had never, by any experience of his own, arrived at a personal knowledge of any outer world except that of the heart of London. The world to him was a long succession of streets. Little Bill, taken from one Paragon-place, was in Thoozy's mind, transported to another: perhaps a finer and more wealthy street. On warm days he hobbled to the entrance of the court, and planted himself where, should his old friend by any lucky chance come by, he could not fail of seeing him.

Thoozy turned round to see where the lady in black silk— he knew the faces of the Church visitors: she was not a deaconess or a Sister of Mercy—was going to. She went straight to Mrs. Kneebone's. The door of the hospitable mansion stood open, as was its wont, and the lady walked in. Thoozy gave one more look up and down the road. No little Bill. Then he turned back, limped down the court—rheumatics being bad in this early autumn weather—and followed the visitor. She went into the nursery, where Mrs. Kneebone was employed among her tender charges. She shut the door. Thoozy limped in after her, and looked through the keyhole listening.

Mrs. Kneebone raised her head to see who was thus unceremoniously intruding on her privacy. In her first confusion, she dropped the baby which was on her knees. The child fell back upon its bed; and, as it instantly went sound asleep, was probably not much the worse for its fall. A special Providence looks after the lives of babies and young children, its interposition being nowhere so clearly marked as in baby farms and on board passenger ships.

"Lord bless my soul!" she exclaimed, rushing forward with effusion, and holding out her hands. "Why, it's Polly Tresler. Polly, my dear soul, and how are you, and what's got you all this time not to drop a line to your old—old friend?"

Thoozy, outside, laid down his crutch, and executed a short dance—more agile, perhaps, than might have been expected of one so decayed. Then he applied his eye to the keyhole again. The court was quiet, and the voices were shrill, so that he heard as well as saw.

"Now don't let's have none of your blarney, Mother Kneebone. So, drop it. Where's my boy?"

"Where's little Bill?" cried the old woman, in a tone of the deepest surprise. "Where's little Bill? Why, where should he be? Didn't you send for him yourself, but Tuesday was a fortnight? And, paid his bill and all?"

"I never sent for him."

"You never sent for him! Now, Polly, you always was one to crack a joke. A gentleman came himself to fetch the boy: said he was to pay for what there might be owing for him. You know, Polly, though I never would press you, I wrote you as there was five-and-thirty shillings due. So I told him, and he paid me honourable, and he gave me—what was it he gave me, now?—fifteen shillings besides. Two pound ten in all, because he said the boy looked so well-an'-'arty. And you know well, Polly—you know the soft heart of your old Kneebone, as couldn't abear to see the boy suffer, so many's the shillin' he cost me out of my pocket to keep him decent. Ax Thoozy if he didn't. Well, and the gentleman——"

"A tall, big man, with a black beard?"

"Tall and big he was, surely. And a black beard? Yes. With a leg. Oh, Polly, my dear, a beautiful leg of hese own. Which if he's your fourth, Polly, and not to deceive you, my dear, for worlds, it's a happy woman you ought to be."

Polly sat down on the only chair of the room, and stared.

"But what did you tell him about me?"

"Tell him? Now, Polly, do you think I'd tell him anything. Do you think I'd do it? Not for pounds, Polly. And how well and fine you're looking, to be sure. Most as young as you did ten years ago."

"He didn't ask no questions?"

"And he did, though. Asked if the boy was happy. Bill —oh, Polly, what a boy that is, and as like you as two peas, though a trifle thin in the face; 'cos, do what I would, he never did eat enough—he ups and he says that he won't leave his old mother. Reg'lar made me cry, he did, the dear. Then the gentleman—him with the leg—he says, 'Mrs. Kneebone, you're a good woman, and the Lord will reward you.'"

"That I swear he didn't," cried Polly, knowing that Dick was by no means likely to make any such pious remark.

"Well, then, he said somethink very much like it; and asked a lot more questions. Said he wondered why I kep' that idle, good-for-nothink vagabond, Thoozy, about the place. What a leg he have, to be sure!"

"Who's Thoozy?"

"A baby what I never got paid for. A boy growed up here who won't work. Ah, Polly, I've had a deal of trouble to keep little Bill from being led into bad ways by that Thoozy. But I've always had a soft heart, and I couldn't abide to send the poor boy adrift on the streets, and him on crutches and all. So you see I lets him stay on, bad as he is. And I do hope you won't find little Bill none the worse for his company."

"Oh!" whispered Thoozy. "I'll be even with you for this. Won't I!"

"Then you didn't tell him nothing at all?" said Polly, staggered.

"Not a syllable—not a word—not a thing, Polly, s'help me. And you haven't shook hands yet with your old friend as knowed you down at Poplar, when you married Bowker, and knows all your little buzzom secrets. Can't you trust your Kneebone, my dear?"

Polly got up, and shook out her skirts.

"He finds out everything," she murmured. "He knows it all. He's dreadful masterful. He's a devil—he's a devil!"

"Who knows everything, Polly?—not Bowker?"

"No. Nobody you know, Mother Kneebone. Well, I shall go. Good-bye."

"Don't go just yet, Polly. Stand a trifle for your old——"

"Oh, drat the old friend! Well, will half a crown be any good; because I ain't too rich? Here you are, then. Good-bye."

"Good-bye, deary; and give me news of my little Bill. If he sends his love to his old mother, be sure and let me have it. Ah! he *was* a boy, that boy—he *was* a boy!"

"I suppose he was," said Polly, "if he wasn't a girl. Good-bye, then."

She lingered, woman-like, to look at the babies; and Thoozy noiselessly crept out, and resumed his old place at the entrance of the court.

Presently Polly came out again.

"How d'ye do, Polly Tresler?" cried a squeaking voice in the passage.

She gathered up her skirts, and looked round.

"How d'ye do, Polly Tresler? Don't you remember me? I'm Thoozy. Lord bless me, I know you as well as if it was only yesterday. I remember your bringing little Bill to Mother Kneebone's."

This was, unhappily for Methusalem's credit as a truth-teller, a deliberate lie. He remembered nothing about it, though he did remember perfectly well having acted for a year or two as little Bill's dry nurse. For in early life the poor little wizenfaced cripple had developed a genius, almost ma-tronly, in the management of babics; and, on the strength of it, had been retained on the establishment in the capacity of nurse, until, by mere force of character and his fortunate discovery, he succeeded in promoting himself to the position of chief resident physician and real master of the hospital.

"Oh, you're Thoozy, are you? And what do you mean by speaking to a lady?" said Polly, looking at him with aston-ishment.

"Because you are a lady, a real lady, and nothin' but a

lady, silk stockin's and all. Oh, I knows a lady when I sees one. Sorry you didn't speak to me first, instead of Mother Kneebone, 'cos I suppose she has been a-gammoning of you."

Polly started.

"Look here, you boy—you little, withered-up imp—you miserable little rickety devil—if you tell me lies, I'll break every bone of your wretched little crooked body. Just you tell me right out all about it."

It will be seen that Polly was roused to wrath by Thoozy's suggestion of "gammon." Thoozy gave one look of rage and spite.

"I'll be even with both of 'em," he muttered. Then he smoothed out his face, and proceeded to reply.

A soft answer turneth away wrath.

"Don't be hard upon me, missus. I'll tell you all I know. Last Wednesday fortnight, a swell comes here when Bill and me was havin' our school in the court. I used to teach Bill, whenever the old woman gave him enough to eat. You can't teach a boy when he's starvin' for food—now, can you? That day, Bill picked up a bloater, and we had it between us for breakfast. In the afternoon the swell comes in.

"'Where's Mrs. Kneebone?' he says, as grand as you please.

"'She's in there,' says I.

"'Where's little Bill?' says he.

"'What little Bill?' says I.

"'Polly Tresler's little Bill,' says he.

"'Here he is,' says I.

"'Oh,' says he."

Polly's face became scarlet—a premonitory squall of a brewing storm.

Thoozy took breath, and went on.

"Then he goes in, and we goes in, after him. Offers Mother Kneebone five pounds for information. Kneebone, she pockets the dibs, and she begins.

"'Flint's the father of the boy,' says she. 'Flint was Polly's third. Polly's second I don't know, 'cos I never see him, and she wouldn't never tell me about him. And her first husband was Mr. Bowker, and he's livin' now; and I know where to put my 'ands upon him this very moment, if you please, for another five pound. Polly, she ran away from him because she——'"

"O—h—h!" It was as the roar of a tigress, and Polly turned from the boy, and rushed back to the house. Thoozy saw her go in, and looked up and down Gray's Inn-road—not for Bill this time, but for a policeman.

He saw one providentially fifty yards down the road, and hobbled to him as fast as his rheumatics would let him.

"Come up here," he cried, taking the man by the arm: "there'll be murder done if you don't come quick."

The policeman followed him.

They were not a bit too soon. Polly, with flaming eyes and scarlet cheeks, had the old woman by the throat on the floor. She was kneeling on her chest, beating her head upon the boards, mad with rage. In a few minutes more, the miserable old woman would have been done to death. The policeman dragged her off. He was a big, powerful man; but he had to use all his strength, and pinned her against the wall. Then he secured his prisoner by a dodge well known to London policemen: seized her wrist with his right hand, and twisted his left arm round it upon her shoulder. The prisoner may burst away if he likes, but will break his arm in the endeavour. Polly struggled furiously for a minute or two, and then gave in. She had still sense enough left to see that the battle had better be given over; and, for obvious reasons, she held her tongue.

Presently, the old woman began to revive. Thoozy fetched cold water, and threw it over her—a good lot at a time, because he knew how much she disliked that form of fluid. She sat up, and looked round.

"You've got to come up to Clerkenwell to-morrow. So mind that," said the policeman. "You boy, bring her along. And now, come away. If you'll promise to go quiet," he said, when they got into the open air, "I'll let your arm free."

"I'll go quiet," said Polly.

So, holding her gently by the wrist, the guardian of the peace led Polly away, and committed her to the custody of the law, followed by those of the population who had the shining hours idle on their hands, and were naturally anxious for amusement.

Polly had a bad and uncomfortable night. Mrs. Kneebone was left with a severe headache, and a shaking of the nerves so violent that it forced her to imbibe too much fortifying medicine, insomuch that she fell down among the babies, and slept there. Methoosalem administered the feeding bottles; took away the old woman's matches to prevent accidents with fire; and climbed to his own miserable bed, where he went to sleep, chuckling over the pious fraud by which, at one and the same time, he had paid off old and new scores. It may be remarked that his first thought had only been to reveal a portion of Mrs. Kneebone's *fourberies*, in order that shame, with perhaps a little personal chastisement, might fall upon her. But Polly's allusions to his own physical defects carried him a little betond the limits of a pure practical joke, and very nearly ended fatally for both Polly and his old woman.

In one or two of the papers there appeared, two days after, under the head of police news, a short account, headed " A Row in a Baby Farm," which described how a woman, calling herelf Mrs. Flint, a widow, of no occupation, was charged with violently assaulting an old woman named Kneebone, the keeper of a notorious baby farm. Evidence being heard, the worthy magistrate, without going into the antecedents of the prisoner, against whom the police had nothing to allege, remarked that it was clearly a very brutal assault upon an aged and infirm woman. He cautioned the prisoner very seriously on her ungovernable temper; remarked that it was well for her that the principal witness was able to appear that morning to give evidence; and sentenced her to a penalty of £5 fine, or a month's imprisonment, with hard labour. The money was paid on the spot.

Thoozy led home his old woman, not sympathizing much with her shaky condition, which he attributed more to the strong drink than the fright she had had.

" How did she go for to find it out ?" said Mrs. Kneebone. " You little devil, you told her."

" Never told her nothing. How should I know who she was ? Perhaps she met the big swell in the road. I thought I saw him pass," said the mendacious one.

CHAPTER THE FORTY-FIRST.

AFTER Mr. Eddrup's confession, Frank met him almost daily. The old man used to go to his court every morning at ten, and sit in his office—a single room— which was like the gate of an Eastern city, inasmuch as he sat there and administered justice. Haroun Al Raschid could not have been more just, Saladin was not more merciful. Thither came the women with their quarrels: "Forgive, forgive," he said. Thither the men out of work brought their tales of disappointment and privation: to these he lent money, or pointed the way to work. Here he received his rents, which amounted to a goodly sum, and devised means for the improvement of his dwellings. The court was a model. All the houses but two belonged to him. Gradually, by slow degrees, they had been pulled down and rebuilt in flats, with whatever improvements Mr. Eddrup and his builder could devise. The property paid him about two and a half per cent. Side by side with his stood the other two houses—squalid, mean, and decayed. They paid a good fifteen per cent. to the man—he was a leader at Exeter Hall, and knew nothing about his property except that it paid—to whom they belonged. Mr. Eddrup did what he could even here—persuaded the people to be clean, and made no difference between them and his own tenants.

One thing everybody knew: they might rob their landlord, refuse to pay his rent, maltreat him. All these, in the old times, they had done. He would never prosecute or use the law. He received his own by their good grace. Strange to say, he hardly ever lost by it. Old inhabitants of the court— especially one man, who had been the worst of the flock, and was shrewdly suspected of having personally robbed Mr. Eddrup, one dark night—protected his interests. Nobody was allowed to shoot the moon; public opinion was against it. Nobody told lies about back rents and the reasons for asking delay; public experience had proved it useless. Truth, when

B B

it does as much good, is much more pleasant to tell than a falsehood.

At one o'clock, Mr. Eddrup left his office, and generally went away home—that is, to Skimp's—where he sometimes sat in the dingy drawing-room, but oftener sat in his own single room, reading or writing, till dinner time. After dinner, he went back regularly to the court, when he lectured in the "chapel," as they called it, on some evenings, talking freely on all kinds of subjects connected with those branches of social science most useful and interesting to his flock; sometimes taught in a night school; sometimes paid visits among the people.

A scholar, a gentleman, wrecked in early life, he had the courage to make of his miserable fate a reason for a life of philanthropy and self-denial. What he might have been, had his power of resisting temptation always been as great, who can tell?

He talked freely at this time to Frank; told him of his hopes—they were all centred in that small row of houses where he spent most of his day; and of his fears—they were all for the future of his people when he should be gone.

"I might leave the property in trust; but in a few years the letter of the will would be executed, and the spirit neglected. A man can do no good after his death. Better let the money go, and trust that the work may go on. I have seen so much of charitable trusts, that I know the evil they produce; how they pauperize the people, and take away their self respect. I will have none of them. If only, Mr. Melliship, some men like you would take up the work."

"I cannot," said Frank. "I am one of those who only approve of good things, and stand idly by."

"There is Silver, the acrobat. He speaks well. But he would make the place a hot-bed of religious enthusiasm. Nevertheless, he has a burning spirit, and will some time or other become a preacher. I will speak to him about leaving his profession."

"Make him take his daughter away too, then. Patty has no business with that kind of work at all."

"Poor girl." said Mr. Eddrup. "When her father asked my advice, I had none to give him. Then she came herself. She said she knew nothing which she could do. The family kettle is very small, but it was hard to keep it going. I let her have her own way. But she is good and modest. Don't tell me she is not, Mr. Melliship, because I love the child. I have seen her grow up."

"I think you love all the people about you."

"I do," he said, simply; "God knows I do. I have been drawn to them by the thousand ties that struggle and endeavour engender. They were ignorant; I had knowledge. They are poor; I have money—enough, at least, to help them. They desired good things; I could show them the way to some good things. Never think that the poor are ungrateful; never think that they are forgetful: never believe that they are in any respect, whether of good feeling, of delicacy, of forbearance, inferior to yourself. Manners are but conventionalism. In my court there are men and women with as good manners, as far as consideration for others and unselfish labour go, as you will see in women and men of the highest culture in England. They are not better than the rich, I suppose; but they are as good. And remember, they are tempted tenfold as much. Tempted! Good God! When I think of myself, my miserable fall—when I see these people resist, I am fain to go away and weep by myself for shame, and cry for deliverance from the body of this death."

He was silent for awhile. They were walking in the garden of Granville Square, which they had all to themselves.

"Love them? Of course I love them. I know all their secrets. They bring me all their troubles. They tell me all their sins. They confess to me. St. Paul says it is good for men to confess to one another. He means not that priests have anything to do with it—the great-hearted preacher was too wise for that: but he knew that when the soul is burdened with sin and misgiving, the mere telling is a relief and a safeguard. We sin; we fall into temptation; we fall into evil; our minds are clouded. As prayer is a purification, so confession is an unburdening. In the darkness, evil visions rise and horrible forms dance before our eyes. We let in the light by confession—they vanish and die away. St. Paul knew what he was talking about. Mr. Melliship, my heart is full to-day. Come and hear me next Sunday evening. I have a thing to say to the people which must not longer be delayed."

Frank knew very well what the thing would be. He went, with Patty and her father, prudently silent as to what was to happen.

It was a crowded night. Every bench was full—the women and the men hushed with an expectancy of something about to happen. Patty and Frank, with the boy, took their seats, as usual, on the last bench. They were used to Frank by this time, and only supposed that he "kept company" with Patty, who was known to be a good girl, of eccentric habits of dress, which she gratified, with her father's sanction, at the music hall. In other words, her profession was no secret; and she was looked upon with considerable respect as a public character of unblemished reputation.

They had the usual hymn—one of those quiet old Wesleyan psalms, different fom the jubilant strains of modern Anglican hymns with which we nowadays proclaim a confidence and exultation we are very far from feeling. Not a triumphal song, not a meaningless rapture set to pretty music, not a vain and false celebration of an unreal New City; not a lying wish to behold beauties which would pall upon us in a week, just as much as the Crystal Palace; but a hymn in a minor key, attuned to the sadness that always fills the poor man's heart— one that they could sing with fervour, because it belonged so fully to themselves.

Then Mr. Eddrup rose, and, contrary to his usual practice, began to speak himself without asking if any had aught to say.

He commenced by reminding them that he had been among them for forty years. He told how his desire had been to communicate what little knowledge he had, and to do good, as best he might, with what little means he had. He reminded them of the duties of self-reliance and self-respect. He showed, for the thousandth time, how ignorance and sin are interwoven with all human suffering; how the former can be slowly removed, and the latter is generally a departure from the laws of nature. And then, with a great effort, he raised himself erect, threw back the long white hair off his face, and told them all his story.

Not with apologies; not with excuses; with no embellishments. The plain, black, ugly story: the story of violated trust and ruined honour, of disgrace, of prison. He hid nothing.

"Such I was," he said. "This is my history. I have always meant to tell it. I put it off half in cowardice, half because I thought I would wait until you learned to love me— till your hearts yearned towards me, even as mine does now to you. I think I have never till now won your perfect confidence. Only of late has it been impressed upon me that some of you look up to me with reverence and affection. To me—to a convicted thief! Therefore I could wait no longer. My children—I have seen most of you grow up; you have been in our schools; I have taught you: you are in very truth my children—you must respect me no longer. I am not worthy. I am meaner than the meanest—lower than the lowest. I am a convicted thief.

"Years ago I dreamed of this night. I pictured to myself how I should feel, standing before you all, with shamed face, telling you all that I am nothing better than a convicted thief.

"Respect me no longer. I have never been able to respect myself. Tell your little ones that the old man with white hair was not fit to sit among them; point your fingers out at him as he goes down the street, call after him, hoot him. He has been an impostor, a hypocrite, a deceiver. He pretended to be—

"No, my children, no— I am no hypocrite. I am a coward; because I should have told you all this long years ago. No hypocrite. Believe me, in this my solemn confession, that I repent and have repented. I have set myself to hide from the world, and work in this little corner, the servant of you all. To repent. Before you all, and in the face of GOD, in whose presence I stand, I say that I repent, and am heartily sorry. Shall I say more? Nay, for I would not that you think I should excuse myself. Let me have your pity—your pity, since I can no longer have your love. And pray for me—pray for me."

He sank upon his knees, his head in his hands, resting against the handrail; and, as he ceased, the women began to lament, and to cry aloud for sympathy and pity. Down the rugged cheeks of the men the great tears fell unchecked Some of them sobbed and choked. All looked bewildered at the spectacle of the poor old man, their benefactor, their patron, their saint—more to them than even Wesley was to his people —kneeling before them all, silent, bowed, abased. Frank wept unrestrainedly. Here was no acting. It was the truth, sublime and gracious. It was the final self-sacrifice of a man whose whole days had been a long sacrifice. He had LIVED THE LIFE. Truest Christian, noblest warrior in the army of God—he had won the last battle he would have to fight on earth before he was called away—

"Not in entire forgetfulness,
And not in utter nakedness,
But trailing clouds of glory shall he come
To Heaven, which is his home—"

to alter the words of the poet.

It was Mr. Silver who broke the silence.

"We have one thing to do," he said. "We are here a little congregation, the people of the Lord, met to pray and praise. One of us has told the story of his life, and of a great sin. Let us then pray that we be not led into temptation. Who shall cast a stone? Will you?—will you?—shall I? God forbid! Our respect for him remains. Our love remains. Friends all, I adjure you, lock up this thing in your hearts. Women, don't speak of it to each other: men, hide it away. Put the recollection of it out of your minds. Friend and father of us all, God has forgiven—we have forgotten."

From the voices of all there went up a mighty cry:

"We have forgotten—we have forgotten."

Silver tried to raise the old man. He had fainted. They brought water and sprinkled over him, as he revived. He sat, feeble and pale, while the women, in their tender way, busied about him. Then he signed to Patty to come to him.

"Go home for me," he said, "and bring down all I want—I will never leave the court again."

They took him to a vacant room in one of his own houses. They laid him in bed, and sent for a doctor. Nothing was wrong with him—only feebleness, only a sudden break-up. And from his little room, where he daily received his people, Mr. Eddrup was never to stir again. Frank went home with his friends, strangely agitated and moved. He had for once obtained a glimpse of the highest life—the courage which meets everything, which shrinks from no trial; the patience which endures to the end; the life before which all other lives appear so mean and paltry. Of the women in the room that night, all wept but one. Patty Silver sat with dry eyes. Her heart was full of questionings and doubts. She heard but half of what Mr. Eddrup said; for her eyes were bent furtively on Frank, and she was thinking if he loved her. "He loves me—loves me not." Surely when the Deluge came, and the whirling flood swept down the shrieking street, Marguerite, in her chamber, sat deaf and careless, thinking only, "He loves me—loves me not."

But that story which Mr. Eddrup told his friends lay buried in their hearts. They never spoke of it in his lifetime. They never speak of it now he is dead and gone to that silent Land where his honour, like the soldier's sword, has been restored to him.

CHAPTER THE FORTY-SECOND.

FRANK sitting in Mrs. Skimp's drawing-room with Captain Bowker. It is in the morning, but the master mariner is smoking his long cherrystick pipe. Time hangs somewhat heavily upon his hands since he has had nothing to do. Sometimes he takes the boat and goes down to the docks, where he picks up old friends, and spins old yarns. Sometimes he pays visits to ancient haunts at Poplar. Sometimes he makes a morning call upon his cousin, who lives close by, to please whom he has come to live at Skimp's. For the Captain has money—he got it in private ventures during his many voyages—besides the little pension which his late employers have given him It is not much; but it is enough to make it desirable to retain him near the family, for fear of foreign and malign influences. More often than anything else, the Captain spends his mornings at the table in Mrs. Skimp's drawing-room, with a sheet of paper and an inkstand, making innumerable blots as he corrects and adds to his poems. This work, indeed, constitutes the real pleasure of his life. To read his verses aloud, in the presence of a man who will listen without laughing, such as Frank Melliship, is pure and unmixed happiness. To get them printed is a dream which he just permits to himself. Some day, he thinks —some yet distant day—he will sacrifice the hundred pounds of capital needed to accomplish this object. He must pinch to make up for the loss of five pounds a year; but what is a little pinching in comparison with so great an object?

To-day he has been reading a remarkable poem, his *chef-d'œuvre*, on which he means to base his reputation. It is called "The Captain's Dream." In this work, imitating, unconsciously, the example of Dante and several other distinguished "makers," he has embodied in a vision the whole sum of his philosophy. Frank has been pretending to listen. The good-nature which prevents him from yawning in the honest Captain's face, also obliges him to come from time to time, and pay Mr. Bowker a visit, in order to give him pleasure. I, who yield to no man in the quality of good-nature, have ruthlessly cut out the whole of the Captain's poem, which is among the records from which this history is compiled, solely because it might bore my readers. I am far from saying the work is not remarkable in many ways : there is a flavour of the briny in it, a smell of pickled pork, occasional whiffs of rum, a taste of the pannikin, the breath of the ocean. Nautical metaphors alone are used—seafaring similes.

We are on board ship, and the wind is whistling through the shrouds. But—but—truth compels me to add that the poet's diction is commonplace, and his thoughts are not always exalted. Why do we not consider the varieties of the human mind in our estimate of poetry? There are gradations of intellect, like terraces. Instead of measuring a newly-fledged poet with a stupid, Procrustean bed of criticism, reducing all to one standard, why not make an effort to classify intellectual produce, as merchants classify colonial produce? I believe there are, in the single article of sugar alone, about twelve gradations from treacle to crystal. Suppose we made twelve grades or degrees in poetry? Our greatest poets would belong to the twelfth—the supreme degree which embraces all the rest. As every poet must have some brains, if only a thimbleful, it follows that he must have a very large mass of mankind beneath him. Martin F. Tupper, for instance, might be numbered one, or perhaps two, on account of some gleams of scholarship. Captain Bowker would belong to the first grade, without any possibility of promotion at all.

"So, Mr. Melliship, there's all my ideas for you. When I get more, I stick them in. As I go on living, the poem will go on growing—consequently improving."

"Do not your ideas change sometimes?"

"Never. When I get an idea, Mr. Melliship, it isn't a flash in the pan, like some people's. My ideas take me first of all unawares. They generally begin, like a toothache, when I least expect them. Perhaps when I feel a little buffy, in the morning; mayhap, after an extra go of grog the night before. Then one comes all of a sudden. I turn it over, and think it out. I'm rayther a slow thinker; but I'm an uncommon sure one, and I never let it go. I don't read much, except the newspaper; so that I've got a great advantage over most poets, all my ideas are my own. I don't steal them and alter them. I let 'em grow. It takes me a long time—perhaps months—

to work an idea into shape, but when I have got him, there he is, put into the poem neat and ship-shape, preserved for cure, like a bit of salt beef in a cask of brine. Woman, now—you remember the beautiful passage I read to you just now about woman?"

"Yes—yes—yes. Oh! don't take the trouble to read it again, Captain Bowker," cried Frank, hastily.

"A few lines to show my meaning," said the Captain, clearing his throat. "Here we are. Now listen:—

"'Woman is like a ship—new painted, gay,
Fresh holystoned and scraped, she sails away,
Manned by her captain. While the weather holds
The ship sails trim, the woman never scolds,
The dancing waves play on the starboard bow,
Her sails fill out, her pennants gaily flow;
The captain takes his thankful grog below.'

That's a good line, young man. That last is a very good line."

He read it over again, shaking his head slowly from side to side in admiration.

"'Look where ahead the black clouds rise, and see
How changed the lines of ocean; on the lee
The rocks rise threatening. Furl the mainsail, stow
All snug: here comes the tempest. Let her go.'

"I leave out the next fifty lines, where I follow up the comparison of a good woman to a good ship. She weathers the storm. Then I go on to talk of a bad woman; and I end thus:—

"'All lost—the ship obeys the helm no more.
She strikes—she sinks. Her voyages are o'er.'"

"Very fine," said Frank—"very fine indeed."

"Yes; I flatter myself that there is good stuff there. They've compared woman to all sorts of things. Look here. Here's a bit I cut out of an old play:—

"'A woman is like to—but stay—
What a woman is like, who can say?
She's like a rich dish
Of ven'son, or fish,
That cries from the table, "Come, eat me!"
But she'll plague you, and vex you,
Distract and perplex you,
False-hearted, and ranging,
Unsettled, and changing,
What, then, do you think she is like?
Like a sand? like a rock?
Like a wheel? like a clock?

"Now, you know, it's all very fine. That's not my notion of a simile. Don't hurry about from one to another to show your cleverness. Stick to one. Woman is like a ship, isn't she? Very well—there you are. Work it up, as I do. There's her hold, must be laden or in ballast; a woman without ballast is like a cork on the water. Her head is the captain's cabin—only room for one. The captain is the man at the helm. As for the rigging, some of it's ornamental, some of it's useful. You've got the bunting, and you've got the sails. The sails is her petticoats, without which, d'ye see, she can't sail out of port; the bunting is her ribbons, because they all, ships as well as women, sail better if they're proud of themselves. And as for her masts, her boats, her keel, her bowsprit, and her foksle, and all the rest of it—why, bless you, if I had time, I'd run through the whole and show you how the simile holds. Ah! it's a very delicate subject. Marriage, now. People will get married. Why? The Lord knows. I did myself once, and a pretty market I brought my pigs to. Ease and comfort? Quiet and tranquillity for composing? Not a bit of it. Morning, noon, and night went her tongue. It was, 'Jem, get this;' 'Jem, go there.' And if I didn't, squalls, I can tell you."

"Well, but you were the man at the helm," said Frank, with a smile.

"Man at the helm! I might as well have been in the bows; she stayed below all watches. She wouldn't answer the helm nohow. Never took no notice of the helm. Kept her own course. Never was such a craft. Neat to look at, too. Painted rosy red in the bows; full in the lines, but clean cut, down about the stern; always neat and tidy in the gear. But come to command her—phew!—then you found out what a deceptive, headstrong, cranky, difficult vessel she was. Ah, well; it's fifteen years ago since I saw her."

"Is she dead, then?"

"Hush!" said Captain Bowker; "don't speak so loud. If she ain't dead, where is she? She left me; went cruising on her own account; took in another skipper, may be. Anyhow, she went. We've gone away from each other. Dead? Well, she's as good as dead. Don't you every marry, Mr. Melliship. You're a young man, and the temptation will come strong over a young man at times. Fight it. St. Paul says himself it's better not to marry. I heard that in church last Sunday morning. Say to yourself, 'Which shall it be? Shall it be peace and repose; or shall it be nagging, and pecking, and boxing of ears? Shall it be your legs on the fender and your pipe in your mouth; or shall it be the legs of the chair about your head, and the pipe smashed? Shall it be fair weather, or shall it be foul?' There's more craft built for show than for use in these bad times. Don't trust any. Stick to yourself, and be happy. As for me, Mr. Melliship, I'm a fixture. Nothing can disturb me now. I'm in port. I defy the storms. To quote myself, I sing—

"'Laid up in dock, serene I shake my fist,
And fortune's storms may thunder as they list.'

Those are very fine lines, Mr. Melliship,—very forcible, strong lines indeed—

"'Laid up in dock, serene I shake my fist,
And fortune's storms—'"

"Please, Cap'n Bowker,"—it was the red-armed Mary Ann who interrupted him,—"there's a lady wants to see you."

"I suppose it's my cousin," growled the captain. "Why can't she wait for me to go and see her? It's my turn, too."

"No 'taint Mrs. Robins," said Jane, who knew the Captain's belongings; "this lady says she's your wife!"—grinning all over.

The captain's arms dropped, and his face turned an ashy white. Frank laughed at first; but the poor man's distress was so great that his sense of the ludicrous was lost in pity.

"Found me out, has she?" he murmured. "After fifteen years—'Laid up in dock, serene'—No; that won't do. Mr. Melliship, wait a moment. Don't go and leave me in this pinch. Can't nothing be done? See her. After fifteen years, to go back to prison! It's more than I looked for. Tell me what to do. Help me to ride out the gale."

"There is nothing to be done," said Frank. "But perhaps you had better see her. Suppose she is not your wife, after all?"

"Stay with me. Stand by an old shipmate. Don't desert me, Mr. Melliship."

"But I can't interfere between you and your wife. Be brave, man. You ought not to be afraid of a woman."

"As an ordinary rule," said Captain Bowker, clearing his throat, "there ain't a braver man going than me. Not another woman in the world I'm afraid of. But this one's an exception. You didn't know my Polly. I don't care for the rest of 'em, if they were all to come on together. But Polly's too much for any man."

There was a rustling of a dress on the stairs, and Frank waited for a moment.

A tall figure in black silk, with a thick veil, glided in. As Frank glanced at her, somehow he thought of Market Basing and Parkside.

"Don't sheer off," murmured the captain, in an ecstasy of terror.

But Frank stole softly out of the room, and closed the door, bringing the red-armed one down with him. She had followed Mrs. Bowker up the stairs, with intent to listen at the keyhole. Mrs. Skimp and her daughter were at the bottom, with the same laudable object.

"Now, Mrs. Skimp," said Frank; "no listening."

And he sat down on the bottom steps by way of precaution.

"O Jem!" cried Polly, falling on the Captain's unresisting neck, and kissing his grizzled forehead—"O Jem! to think I should find you, and after so many years, and your dreadful cruel conduct. Oh, this is a blessed day!"

"How did you find me, Polly?" asked her husband.

"Went to Leggatt & Browne's—your old firm. The clerks told me. This is a blessed day!"

"D—— the clerks," said the captain. "And why didn't you go before, if you wanted to find me?"

"Because I thought you were dead, Jem. I've wore black ever since in mourning for you. See here. They told me at Poplar that you was alive, and where to ask for you. Oh, what a joyful thing to find your husband after fifteen years!"

She pulled out her handkerchief, and began to weep; but not plentifully.

"Well, what's to be done now?" asked the captain.

"That's a pretty thing to say to your wife," she answered. "Done! What should be done? I've come to live with you."

"Oh!" groaned the captain.

"I'm not going to live in a boarding-house. How much money have you got?"

He named his modest income.

"That will do. We shall have lodgings. What's the name of the woman of the house?"

"Skimp."

She went to the head of the staircase, and called out—

"Mrs. Skimp! You Mrs. Skimp! Come up here at once."
Frank quietly went away.
"We're going to leave this to-day," said Polly. "A week's notice. Bring the bill in ten minutes. I'll pay it. And none of your extras for me."
"You don't stay in my house another hour," said the aggrieved Mrs. Skimp. "Cap'n Bowker, I'm ashamed of you. I pity you, I do. Paying attentions to my daughter, too."
"Eh!" said Polly. "What's that?"
"I never did," said the Captain, outraged and insulted. "They're all upon me, together. I never did. I'm—I'm—I'm DAMNED if I did! Mrs. Skimp, what do you mean by saying such things? And you a married woman yourself, and know the misery of being married. You ought to be ashamed of yourself. I never looked at your daughter, even. I never look at any woman."
"You won't pay her any more attentions, for you shall come out of this place in quick sticks," said Mrs. Bowker. "How long will it take you to pack your things up?"
"Well," said the unresisting seaman, fairly overstunned by the logic of facts, "I think to do it comfortable, you know, it might take a couple of hours."
"Very well," said the lady. "You pack everything up—mind you don't leave nothing behind you in a place like this—and I'll just go down to Poplar and let 'em know as I've found you, and I'll be back here before the two hours are up. This is a blessed day!"
She gave the Captain one chaste salute, shot a look of anger at Mrs. Skimp, and marched out of the room.

CHAPTER THE FORTY-THIRD.

NE fine morning at this time, Dick Mortiboy said to his ward, when they were out for a ride together—
"Bill, I do you the justice to believe that you don't care very much about your mother."
The boy shook his head.
"And you would not want to go away with her—to live with her, I mean?"
Little Bill's cheeks changed colour, and he turned his blue eyes appealingly at Uncle Dick.

"Very well, my boy, then never say anything about her."

The boy was mounted on an old pony that had been used occasionally to carry old Ready-money. It was very quiet and easy in its paces, and Dick had given his protégé a few lessons in horsemanship before they had ventured so far into the country together.

Of course, in a gossiping, tittle-tattling little place like Market Basing, there was an abundance of rumours rife concerning the parentage and history of little Bill. Widely as some of these reports differed from others in many particulars, they were all agreed as to one essential: it was that he was young Ready-money's son. I have never heard that anybody connected the boy with Polly.

Now, I do not say that Dick Mortiboy's argument concerning his ward was sound or just; but it was charitable. He argued thus:—"A few months ago I was told this was my son. I had not seen him. I did not love him. I was a poor man, and I contributed what I thought sufficient for his support. The boy had the reputation of being my son. Now I have seen him, and know that he isn't mine. I like him, and I'll take care that he gets some of the benefits he would have got if his mother's tale had been true."

It was rather from impulse than from reason that Dick Mortiboy had acted. He was big, and rough, and generous. He had taken the boy from Mrs. Kneebone's tender care, and brought him home with him. He had hardly thought of what he should do with him. He meant, after a time, to send him to school; for the boy was bright and sharp as a needle, and, till he talked, was quite a little gentleman in his new clothes.

As he looked down at the child's thin face and deep blue eyes, his heart grew soft. It seemed as if he had missed something all his life, which he was finding now. What he had missed were the influences of love: now they were upon him. He loved a woman. True, she did not love him; but she cared in a way for him. It was something to know that Grace loved him "as a brother"—as girls are fond of saying when they mean that they feel a friendly interest in a man, but would rather not have him making love to them.

Then came the boy. His love for Dick was wonderful. His loyalty and obedience to what Dick told him, the pains he took to do everything that Dick said was right, his confidence and trust—all this touched Dick, and moved him: it was the first step upwards—to something like repentance. Only as yet, the faintest glimmer, like the first grey streaks of light in the east.

So Dick Mortiboy rode along gently on the strip of grass by the side of the turnpike road, thinking of many things, when he became aware that his ward was calling out lustily—

"Mikey O'Grady! Mikey O'Grady!"

The boy was in the middle of the road, some twenty yards behind. He had reined in his pony, and was addressing by name a ragged, shoeless, dust-covered tramp. Dick stopped his horse.

"Mikey O'Grady," the boy called out again.

"Shure enough it's me name, your honour," said the man, hat in hand.

"Don't you remember me, Mike?"

The boy took off his cap, and shook his light hair over his eyes.

The Irishman gave a yell of delight.

"It's little Bill," he cried.

Dick listened to this colloquy, and said nothing.

"You're going to London, Mike, ain't you? Go to the old place, and find out Thoozy. You remember Thoozy, don't you? Well, then, give Thoozy my love—tell him I am very well, and very happy, and—and I wish he was."

Poor little Bill's eyes began to fill with tears.

"Give him the message, my man," said Dick. "Tell him, too, that when I come to town I shall go and see him. Perhaps I shall have something for him. And here's something to help you on your way."

The Irishman promised, and went on his way. Dick said nothing till bed-time came, when he patted his ward on the head, and said—

"Good boy, good boy. Another commandment, Bill. Never forget old friends. What is the whole duty of a boy?"

"Never steal—never tell lies—never swear—hold his jaw—do his work—go away from England—always be ready to fight—look out for shams—never be satisfied—never forget old friends. Ten of em' now, Uncle Dick."

"That's a curious coincidence," said Uncle Dick.

On the morning after his refusal by Grace Heathcote, Dick Mortiboy went down to the bank full of his new purpose. It was to make George Ghrimes and Frank Melliship his junior partners in the concern. The foundry and the brewery would still be managed by Ghrimes for Dick's sole benefit; but he had made up his mind to rehabilitate Frank's fortunes, and reward the honest and able services of Ghrimes, by doing what he thought was to both a simple act of justice.

Young Ready-money was not an adept in the art of speechifying, and did not know exactly how to begin. He set forth his intention to Ghrimes in a sort of preamble about Frank.

"Ghrimes," he said, "I've been thinking things over a goodish deal of late, and I've got a proposal I want you to consider. When I was a boy—before I went away from the governor—if I had a friend to say a word for me and give me a hand, besides John Heathcote, it was my uncle Melliship."

"He was a very good sort, poor man," said Ghrimes, guessing half of what was about to come from his employer.

"He was," Dick assented. "Well, Ghrimes," he went on, "they've got a sort of rough notion in those rough parts I lived in a good many years, that one good turn deserves another. The very roughest there act up to it. It is not a bad maxim, Ghrimes, anywhere. It seems to me that it is not affected by climate. My uncle Melliship did me many good turns. Now I am going to do his son one good turn: for I'm bound to help Frank. That's all clear, isn't it?"

Mr. Ghrimes nodded.

"Good. I knew you'd agree to all that. I've a word or two more to say before I've done. There's the man who greases the wheels—and there's a good many of 'em to grease —of my affairs, who keeps everything straight and square, and adds to the pile I've got already."

Mr. Ghrimes turned rather red.

"That's you, Ghrimes. You see it. Well, I think I'm bound to do something for you."

The manager of Dick Mortiboy's business looked at the pattern of the carpet, and said nothing. He had not had time to find words yet.

"What can we do best for all of us? The old bank was Melliship, Mortiboy, & Co. Why not revive the old title by taking Frank and you into partnership?—Mortiboy, Melliship & Ghrimes."

"Never alter the name of a bank," said Ghrimes. "The most unlucky thing that can be done. Remember Snow's bank, in the Strand."

"Well, we'll have it Melliship, Mortiboy & Co. I don't

quite know how these things are done; but I suppose there will be something to sign written in a big hand."

"A deed of partnership would have to be prepared, of course."

"Very well. You will do all that. Arrange it with Battiscombe."

Dick put on his hat.

"Stay, Mr. Mortiboy—this won't do."

"We're partners now, Ghrimes. Call me Dick."

"Well, then, Mr. Dick. I don't know how to thank you for myself. As for Frank, it is an act which I call noble. I say it is noble, Mr. Mortiboy—I mean, Mr. Dick."

"You wouldn't if you knew everything, perhaps," said Dick. " However, what is the hitch?"

"Why, this: we must arrange terms of partnership, proportions—all sorts of things."

"I will see Battiscombe, then, at once. We will have a deed drawn up on terms which shall be advantageous to yourselves, and consistent with my desire to do a mere act of justice. Ghrimes, my father was the real cause of Melliship's failure and suicide."

"To some extent, I am afraid he was," said Ghrimes. "If your father had been a different sort of man, poor Mr. Melliship would have had no scruples about asking a little accommodation from him: especially as he knew how easily he could give it. But your father always seemed to me to be trying to get him into his power. Not to break him, and ruin him; but to keep him in his power. Your father always loved to have people under his thumb."

"Just so, and my uncle Melliship's death was a protest against my father's way of dealing. We are doing simply an act of reparation. Go-to-meeting folks sometimes do acts of reparation, besides repenting of their sins, I hope, Ghrimes? That's their affair, not mine, however. I'm going to write to Frank and make him this offer. He'll accept it; and as soon as he comes down here we can all three sign Battiscombe's parchment, and enter into our partnership."

He went away. Bethinking him, however, that the letter should be written at once, he turned into his father's house in Derngate to do it.

He was very careful about this letter. He began by reminding Frank of their relationship; of the many kindnesses he had himself received from Frank's father; of the friendly and affec-

C C

tionate terms with which Mr. Melliship had received him on his return. And then he went on to enlarge upon the unhappy connection between his own father and the failure of Melliship, Mortiboy & Co. After this he proceeded to state his proposition.

"And now, Frank, having said so much, I have something to propose. I was yesterday talking about you to Grace Heathcote, and I have her authority for saying that she entirely approves of the proposition. What she approves of ought to be law to you. It is that you enter my bank as a partner, on equal terms with Ghrimes; that the name of Melliship be added to Mortiboy & Co.; that you come down here at once, and begin as soon as the deeds are drawn out. I hope you will see no obstacle to your accepting this proposition. Remember it comes from your first cousin, the man who owes a hundred debts of gratitude to your father; that Grace wishes it; that it will enable you to marry; in time, to pay off those debts with which your father's estate is encumbered; that it will do what is most desirable for your mother and Kate—bring them back to Market Basing; and bring you back, if this is anything, to all your old friends. Ghrimes is most eager that you will see your way to accept my proposal. He is as anxious as any one to see you back again, and in your right position."

He folded his letter, put it into an envelope, and took it to Lucy Heathcote, asking her to forward it to Kate Melliship, who in turn would send it to Frank.

Lucy was with her father—she was old Ready-money's constant nurse and attendant—and was walking by the side of the poor old paralytic, while Hester pushed his Bath chair along the gravel terrace at the back of his house.

The aspect was sunny, and every fine day the old man was twice wheeled out to take the air. His state of late had been a good deal improved, and Lucy was full of hope. At first he had been unable to move at all, and, besides, had been generally almost unconscious. Then as he got a little better, he had recovered the partial use of one arm, and his wits had brightened very much. He was so far recovered now that he knew everything that was said to him quite well—expressed acquiescence with a slight nod of his old head, and conveyed intelligence of refusal or dislike to anything by wrinkling his forehead into a frown.

When Dick came near him he puckered his face in a dozen ugly ways.

Probably, he only half recollected what had taken place on the night he had the stroke; but it was clear to his son there was some memory left of that night's doings. Young Readymoney did not trouble his father with much of his company. Lucy had got a porcelain tablet, and wrote with a blue pencil on it. This she held before the old man, and kept writing a fresh question, till she found out what he wanted. This process was often a very tedious one; but, with practice, Lucy Heathcote became very expert in understanding what was passing in her uncle's mind. His appetite was good; but as his faculty for tasting his food was gone, he had no disposition to quarrel with his cook. They gave him a little weak brandy and water to drink; and he spent his time between his bed, his sofa, and his Bath chair, happily enough. When Dick handed Lucy the letter for Frank, the old man frowned hard, as was his wont. The young man instructed his cousin as to the destination of the letter, asked after his father, and then strode away across the lawn, down the garden, and over the river towards his own little villa.

"Why does Uncle Richard always frown so desperately at Cousin Dick, whenever he comes here?" Lucy Heathcote asked herself.

She was frightened at Dick, and never had loved him much. She already had suspected there was something wrong—what she could not tell.

Nor did she set to work with slate and pencil to worm the secret out. But her uncle's conduct, when his idolized son approached him, left a disagreeable impression upon her mind she tried in vain to shake off.

Dick followed the river, passing the scene of his exploit with Polly, and the old cross where he had made known his love to Grace Heathcote. This was a sacred spot, and he sat musing under the shadow of the decaying stone for a good half-hour.

The river wound round the base of the hill on the top of which the cross stood, and presently struck across Hunslope Park.

Following the tow-path, Dick had not walked far before he saw the earl himself coming towards him. He shook hands with him very cordially.

"We are well met, Mr. Mortiboy. How do you do? I was thinking of calling upon you to-morrow at the bank. I want you to——"

"If it is about money matters, my lord, pray see Mr. Ghrimes. I may mention that he is, or will be in a few days, my junior partner in the bank."

"Indeed!" said his lordship, with surprise. "I was not aware that Mr. Ghrimes had any fortune, Mr. Mortiboy. I have known him for many years, of course. Very happy to hear it. Very obliging gentleman-like man."

"Glad to hear your lordship say so," said Dick. "All our customers like George Ghrimes, I think. But you were right about his having no fortune, my lord. The only capital that Mr. Ghrimes will put into my concern is incorruptible honesty, untiring zeal, and high capacity for business—unless I add to the credit account, my lord, my gratitude for fifteen years' faithful service in the firm of Mortiboy & Co."

It was rather a high-flown speech for Dick to make, and he felt it; but there is something very invigorating in talking to a lord, until you get quite used to them. And young Ready-money had only lately left a Republic behind him.

His lordship's business with Dick was to tell him he wished to overdraw his account to a greater extent than it usually was.

"I shall have to write a great many cheques, Mr. Mortiboy: and my steward will not pay in the bulk of the rents he has to receive for at least two months."

Dick replied—

"Of course, we shall do everything we can to fall in with your views."

".Thank you very much, Mr. Mortiboy. Pray, is that your son I have seen you riding with? I thought you were unmarried."

"So I am. That is my ward."

"We must marry you, Mr. Mortiboy—marry you, and put you into the House. You ought to sit for Market Basing."

"That's not my line, Lord Hunslope. I shall neither marry nor go into Parliament."

"Property has duties, Mr. Mortiboy. You have, if I am correctly informed, a very—very large stake in the country. In the interests of landed proprietors, we want men like yourself in the Lower House. Dangerous times like these demand the co-operation of all who have a stake in the country."

"No," said Dick. "I am only waiting here for a while, and I shall go away again, with the boy—to the West, probably, somewhere or other. As for the property, in course of time it will go to my cousins, the Heathcotes, just as if I had never come home at all."

Lord Hunslope stared curiously at the strange man who thought so little of a great property.

"You are a young man, Mr. Mortiboy. You will change your mind, and marry."

"I am not one of those who change their minds, Lord Hunslope. I shall never marry. A large part of my property, which my father made over to me, will go, I repeat, to my cousins. When they marry, they will have, as I intend to arrange before I go away, some portion of it as their marriage dowries. My cousins are very good girls, Lord Hunslope; and, so far as I can judge of young ladies, fit to take higher positions than that which farmers' daughters generally aim at. Not that I care much about position. You see, I am more of an American than an Englishman. In the States we don't ask many questions about a man's family."

"They are very—hum—very excellent young ladies. You know, Mr. Mortiboy, that Mr. Heathcote is a man for whom I have the highest respect."

"As your lordship is not a fool," said Dick, bluntly, "that goes without saying, as the French put it. You may add, if you like, that the Heathcotes are a very old family—had all this estate long before your ancestors got it."

"That, also, I know. The Heathcotes are a representative race," said Lord Hunslope, a little taken a back by Dick's plain speaking. "Call at the Towers sometimes, Mr. Mortiboy. The countess will be very glad to see you. Come now, and take luncheon with us."

Dick made an excuse, and turned his steps homeward. The earl looked at him, striding along, great and strong, with eyes of envy. He was young and rich. The peer was old and poor.

"He's only a great boy, after all," thought the earl. "He knows nothing about our English life—and cares nothing about it."

Then he bethought him about the Heathcote girls, and their prospects, and went home.

"Have you remarked," he asked the countess, "those two Heathcote girls?"

"Grace and Lucy Heathcote? Oh, yes. I know them very well. What about them? Their manners are quiet and simple, much above their station—very much above the manners of that very vulgar person, their mother."

"I think so myself. Those girls, Alethea, will have a fortune of half a million sterling. That is, that large property will be divided between them."

The countess looked up in amazement.

"Half a million? You must be joking."

"Not joking at all. I was never more in earnest. Young Mr. Mortiboy, whom you saw at the children's sports the other day, told me himself, this morning, that he should not marry. He intends to go back to America, with a boy he carries about, and settle there. The two girls will have his money."

"My dear, he is not five-and-thirty. He may live for ever. Above all, he is sure to marry."

"He may live a long time, but he will keep his word. I have heard that young Ready-money, as they call him, always keeps his word in the smallest particular—for the matter of that, his father always did the same. He told me this with the most perfect seriousness. Now, think."

The countess smiled.

"Mrs. Heathcote is a horribly vulgar woman."

"The father is not vulgar. John Heathcote is rough, but he is a gentleman in his way. There is no man I respect more than John Heathcote. A good old family, too. They had Hunslope long before we were heard of."

"Cadwallader founded my family," said her ladyship sweetly, who had only intermarried with the earls of Hunslope. "Certainly, with all that money, the girls would have a right to marry above their station, as things go."

"Ronald is so shy," said Lord Hunslope.

Yet this conversation was the beginning of Grace Heathcote's having a third wooer at her feet.

CHAPTER THE FORTY-FOURTH.

ONE more incident in the quiet life of Grace Heathcote. An event which was not calculated to add anything to the sum total of her happiness, grateful as conquest is to beauty.

The particularly fine evenings of that early autumn, coupled with the recollection that croquet is a game not to be played with comfort after the middle of October, did not tend to cause any diminution in the frequency of Lord Launton's visits to Parkside.

He always had some good excuse for coming, and he did not want much pressing to take a mallet and join the little party on the lawn when he was there; but out of mere shyness, he seemed on every occasion to pay more court to Lucy than to Grace.

It happened that, a very few days after Lord Hunslope's conversation with Dick Mortiboy, Mrs. Heathcote had Lawyer Battiscombe, his wife, and daughters, from Market Basing, spending the afternoon with her.

Mrs. Heathcote—who was very fond of showing her town friends the beauties and conveniences of country life, heartily loving to hear them praise everything that appertained to Parkside, and secretly rejoicing over their envy—had strolled with her friend as far as the little cottage where the poultry-woman lived, and where her turkeys and chickens were kept. The two ladies, with the skirts of their silks well bunched up in front of them, had hardly struggled through the ramshackle wicket into the poultry-yard, when Mrs. Battiscombe exclaimed,—

"Look, dear—there's a young gentleman coming to us. Why, isn't it Lord Launton?" she added, letting down the train of her dress, quite in a flutter.

Her friend was delighted. If there was one thing necessary to complete her triumph over the pretensions of the Battiscombe girls, it was to show off Lord Launton to their mother. She had been secretly hoping, ever since tea, that he would come. But she said, calmly enough,—

"Oh, yes, it's only Lord Launton. I dare say he wants to see me or John about something."

He came up, raised his hat to the ladies most politely, and began to stammer out his business to Mrs. Heathcote.

"I am a sort of deputation, Mrs. Heathcote."

"Yes, your lordship," said the lady, smiling very graciously.

"The boy's cricket ground in the park is spoilt now—we have so many things in one part, and in the other the ground is not level; and I am come to ask Mr. Heathcote to be good enough to let them play in his home field till the end of the season. It won't be long before it is over now."

The young man took a great deal of trouble to promote athletics among the Hunslope boys.

"I dare say he will, if they don't do any mischief," said Mrs. Heathcote; "but boys are so mischievous."

"You see, the field is close to the school; and they must have a cricket-ground close at hand, if we can get them one. May I go and look if the ground will do, if Mr. Heathcote says we may have it? I think the field is very level."

The home close was on the other side of the hedge.

"It is so close to my poultry-yard," said Mrs. Heathcote; "they all run in the field. I'm afraid the boys will pelt the guinea fowl and hens. We have often had one killed, haven't we, Mrs. Thompson?"

With the honest bluntness of speech, and stark insensibility to the claims of the peerage to complaisant treatment, which is characteristic of our peasantry when they happen to be somebody else's tenants, Mrs. Thompson replied,—

"That we have indeed, ma'am. There was the white speckly hen only last week; and a parcel of young tearbacons a-rommackin' all over the field, no poultry won't do no good—to say nothing of getting fat."

"I'll be answerable for the good conduct of the 'tearbacons,'" said Lord Launton.

"It is a good deal nearer my hencoops than I like, your lordship; but I've no doubt Mr. Heathcote will give the boys leave."

She meant to prevent him from doing it, though, all the same.

There was a pause in the conversation, broken at last by Lord Launton; who, feeling it a duty to say something, remarked, a little nervously,—

"What very fine turkeys you have, Mrs. Heathcote."

The woman who kept the poultry showed the visitors her collection of birds.

"Take that water away from the coop with the ducks in," said her mistress.

And then, turning to Lord Launton, she said,—

"They are two couples we're fattening, and I don't like to let 'em swill the barley-meal out as fast as they put it in."

The young man smiled.

"But, poor things, are they not thirsty this warm weather?"

"I don't know," replied the business-like lady—"they've got to get fat."

Lord Launton moralized to himself on the miseries of the

poultry-yard, until they were joined by Mr. Heathcote, who had come across his fields.

He gave his promise about the cricket-ground, much to his wife's chagrin. They strolled back to the house together, and joined the little party on the croquet lawn.

Sides were chosen afresh. John Heathcote, Grace, and Lord Launton played Lawyer Battiscombe, his two daughters, and Lucy.

Mrs. Battiscombe was charmed; but so was Mrs. Heathcote. The two dowagers sat under a great elm, on the rising ground at the top of the garden, where they had a view of the road and the village.

"Really, he's very affable," remarked Mrs. Battiscombe.

"He often comes over and plays at croquet. We like him very well."

"I hope he won't run away with one of the girls' hearts, my dear," said the lawyer's lady—as it were calling "check" to Lydia's king. She put her ring-bedizened hand affectionately on Mrs. Heathcote's arm.

"I never think of such things, Mary." They had been schoolfellows at Miss Prim's, and kept up the farce of Christian names, though neither had loved the other for ages. "He often comes to see us, and John likes him—that's all."

"Of course, we could never expect that he would be allowed—" Mrs. Battiscombe began; but her remark was stopped by hearing the sound of wheels. "A carriage and pair! Why, it is Lord Hunslope and the countess," she cried, craning out her neck among the boughs.

Now it was Lydia's turn to call "check."

"Lords are as common as blackberries about Hunslope, my dear. I'm sure we never take any more notice of them than of other folks."

But she stood up, with her best cap just over the laurel hedge, and when the countess bowed, and Lord Hunslope raised his hat, she gave a complacent, vulgar little nod.

Their son saw the carriage, and turned rather red; but when it stopped at John Heathcote's gate, and then came on slowly up the gravel drive, he became quite the colour of the poppies.

The earl got out, and shook hands with the Heathcotes, and bowed to the Battiscombes.

Lydia Heathcote took the visit as a matter of course. She left Mrs. Battiscombe under the tree, and strolled up to the carriage. She had never shaken hands with Lady Hunslope before in her life, and only some half-dozen times with his lordship—generally on such occasions as, riding round with his steward, he had called to solicit her husband's vote and interest for the Blues at the county election.

But Mrs. Heathcote did not see any good in letting the Battiscombes—and through them, all Market Basing—know this, and she shaped her course accordingly.

Lord Launton, recollecting that it was getting rather late, drove away in his father's carriage.

He expected to receive a sorrowing remonstrance from his mother; for the scion of the house founded by Cadwallader, had very clearly defined notions of the grades set out in the Table of Precedence—and sat, with his back to the horses, calmly awaiting it.

It did not come. All his mother said on the subject was comprised in a very few words : that Grace and Lucy Heathcote were very amiable girls, and had very good blood in their veins. William de Heathecoat, of Hunslope, was mentioned in Froissart.

Now you see the effect of Dick Mortiboy's candid confession to the earl. He had been deeply moved by the intelligence that a man so rich—so extraordinarily rich—was seriously promising not only to leave his very great fortune to his cousins, but also to endow them with a portion, when they should marry, fitting their future inheritance.

As for Mrs. Battiscombe, she went home with her maternal breast full of envy and uncharitable feeling, and spread the news all over Market Basing that Grace Heathcote had jilted poor Francis Melliship's son, as she always said she would, and was trying to catch Lord Launton, as if—etc.

Mrs. Heathcote, on the other hand, was in an ecstasy of delight. She got down "Burke's Landed Gentry" from the book-case, and read all about William de Heathecote, of Hunslope. She compared the Heathcote pedigree with the Smiths—only city bankers, and so, like her own family, the great Mortiboy stock after all.

From these authentic records she drew her own conclusions; and every day she talked of Lord Launton, praised his personal appearance—the youth was by no means ill-looking, having a certain air of nobleness which comes of good breeding, and a mind kept steadily at a certain elevation—commended his manners, which had whatever merit belongs to shyness and spoke in glowing terms of the happiness which would be the portion of that girl who might become his wife.

Now, all this fell upon the ears of Grace like the wind upon a fixed weathercock : it moved her not at all. She did not, to begin with, understand it. In the second place, she was too full of her own cares to think much about them. Least of all did she fancy that the heir of Hunslope Towers was about to propose to her.

"Really," she said, "I think, Lucy dear, that Lord Launton has—now, don't blush, my child, because it's quite possible, and you are very pretty—has fallen—fallen—fallen—shall I go on?"

"Grace, dear," said Lucy, blushing more than ever, "Don't —please don't."

"Then I won't, Lucy."

And the very next day, Lord Launton proposed to her.

Proposed in the garden, just where Dick had made the same offer of his hand and heart. Stammered and blushed— stammered till he could hardly speak; told her, in an infinite amount of reduplicated words and any number of consonants, how he loved her.

Grace, this time, was neither pained nor touched. She only laughed.

"Poor boy!" she said. "Do you know that I don't love you at all, and never could? And do you know that you are the future Earl of Hunslope, and I only the daughter of a *very* plain gentleman?"

"I know," said Lord Launton. "B—b—but I have my father's permission, and your father's p—p—"

"Prohibition, I should hope," said Grace. "No, Lord Launton. No—NO—NO! There, is that enough?"

The poor young fellow stooped his head to hide his hot face.

"Do I seem unkind?" Grace asked. "See, Lord Launton, I do not mean to be unkind. I like you very much. I cannot understand how your father could give you permission to speak to me, or my father either. But you may know that I am already engaged—to Frank Melliship, your old schoolfellow."

"I knew—that is, I ought to have known. G—G—G— Grace, is there no hope?—not the least hope?"

"Not the least spark. Not a glimmer, Lord Launton. And, besides, you have never paid me any attentions at all. I thought you liked Lucy better."

"That was b—b—because I loved you."

"I don't profess to understand the workings of a man's love; but I do know this, that when Frank Melliship loved me, he did not make pretence to my sister first. He came straight to me."

"I was wrong. Oh! Miss Heathcote, I'm a p—p—poor creature. I stammer, and am afraid almost to speak. Forgive my shyness."

"Indeed, there is nothing to forgive. But, pray, Lord Launton—no, I won't ask any more questions. Let all be as it was before. Come here as much as you like, and let us be friends. Shall it be so? Indeed, I am grateful for the honour—that is, I think I shall be, when I am an old woman. I shall remember that I had a chance of a coronet. But a woman can only love one man, and my love is promised—promised, Lord Launton."

She sighed wearily. Promised—and for how long?

Poor Lord Launton stood irresolute. His painful shyness interposed between himself and all his impulses. He beat it down, and said, with a mighty effort—

"Miss Heathcote, forget what I have said. I will endeavour to conquer my love for you. I am not a selfish egotist—that is, I will try not to be. If I can help your happiness, let me try to do so."

"You may help Frank, if you can. But alas! you cannot. Oh, Lord Launton, why have you brought this unlooked-for misery into the house?"

"What misery, my dear Miss Heathcote—what misery?"

"It is only that my poor dear mother will be dazzled by the chance that I have thrown away; and I shall have to endure her reproaches. Go, Lord Launton. If you must marry one of us, Lucy is a better match for you—not so stubborn, not so rebellious, not so self-willed; and oh, a great deal prettier, more gentle, more Christian. She would make a better wife. Go away, my dear boy. Why, you are only a month older than I am—you are only a boy yet, Lord Launton. And I am as tall as you, see—" She smiled through her tears. "And oh, it is such a pity, because I was so fond of you."

She took his beardless face in her hands—she was really as tall as her admirer, and looked taller, with her pile of hair—and drew it towards her, and kissed him on the forehead.

"There, Ronald, Lord Launton, that is a sister's kiss. It

would be hard to alter that. We have known each other as long as—oh, since we were little things, and used to meet you in the Pond Walk with your nurse. Be my friend— a great deal better for you, poor boy, than being my husband. Go, now, and come again just as usual."

It was a most ignominious dismissal. The heir of Hunslope Towers, conscious of having made himself an outrageous idiot, stole silently away. As he went through the house, he met Mrs. Heathcote. Truth to say, the poor lady had been to the highest rooms in the house, the servants' rooms, whose windows commanded a view of the heads of the performers in this garden act.

"Come in, Lord Launton, and talk to me," she said, graciously.

"No, Mrs. Heathcote," he stammered. "No—it's no use. She won't listen to me."

"Not listen to you? Nonsense! Not listen to you? Oh! give her time, Lord Launton. She's afraid of you."

"No—no—no. It is I who was af—f—fraid of her," he groaned. "It is no use, Mrs. Heathcote—I am refused."

Mrs. Heathcote went back to her parlour, and sat in a tumult of conflicting passions. Presently her husband came home. She said nothing. Lucy returned from choir practice. Grace came down from her own room, her eyes red with crying. She sat silent, with a book before her. Mr. Heathcote rang the bell for supper at the usual time. They sat down, Mrs. Heathcote sighing heavily.

"What's the matter, old lady?" asked John, with a misgiving that a family row was impending.

For all reply, she burst into tears, and sighed hysterically. The girls ran to her assistance.

"Go away," she said to Grace. "Go away, ungrateful girl! After all I've done for you."

"Eh? eh? eh?" asked John, looking from one to the other. "What is it, Grace?"

"Wicked girl," cried her mother. "Oh! John, John—a coronet thrown away! Half a million of money thrown away! Grace, I was in the garden and heard you refuse your cousin a week ago; and now you have refused Lord Launton. John Heathcote, your daughter Grace refuses to marry either Dick Mortiboy or the future heir of Hunslope, because she loves a pauper—a pauper and a painter."

Grace turned to her father.

"Papa, Dick asked me to marry him, and Lord Launton asked me to marry him. I was obliged to say 'No,' because I am engaged to Frank."

Mr. Heathcote sat down to the table, and cut himself deliberately a great slice of cold boiled beef, with a meditative air. Then he took some pickles; and then, having meanwhile turned the matter over in his mind, he said—

"Girls, sit down. Lydia, you're a fool. Grace shall marry anybody she likes. Come here, my dear, and kiss your father."

When John Heathcote put his foot down, which was very seldom, there was a general feeling in everybody's mind that the thing was definitely settled. Mrs. Heathcote said no more; but, heaving a profound sigh, she rang the bell for a candle, and retired to bed, taking the Bible with her, so that she might, at least, have the consolations of religion.

CHAPTER THE FORTY-FIFTH.

NO intelligence of Frank's whereabouts. "We only know that he receives our letters," wrote Kate, "because he answers them. They go to the post-office, Great Bedford-street. His own have for the last two or three weeks been more despondent, that is, less cheerful than ever before. They have not the true ring about them that they had. I think, though I dare not say so to mamma, that his good spirits are forced. I have written and told him about Dick's splendid offer. It is generous in the highest degree. It is more than generous. Tell him I think it is noble. I shall not write to him myself, till I have Frank's answer. Yes, Grace, my picture was accepted, hung and sold. I was at once glad to get the money, and sorry to let the picture go. I am doing another now, just a woodland scene— painted here in the mountains—with a single figure in it; a quiet picture, which I hope to succeed with. Only, when I have finished a picture I like, it goes to my heart to let it be sold. Frank keeps sending us money. It is such a pity, because we really do not want any. We have plenty. And we are happy again. Only nine months ago, Gracie, and what a difference!—what a difference!"

Thus far Kate Melliship. Grace showed the letter to Dick.

"There are two or three ways," he said, "of getting hold of Frank. A man can't hide himself altogether unless he cuts off communication by letter. Evidently he doesn't want at present to be hunted up. All the same, I will go up to London and find him for you, Gracie."

"But how, Dick? How can you find him?"

"Well, I shall go to the post-office where his letters are sent. I shall ask them who takes his letters, and how often they are sent for. If they won't tell me, I shall bribe them till they do. They are sure to do it for half a sovereign. After that, we have only to go on the day when he appears, and lie in wait to catch him beautifully. Once my hand is on his shoulder, Grace, you may be quite sure that I don't let him go again till I bring him back to you."

"When will you go, Dick?" she asked eagerly. "To-morrow? Go to-morrow, and make haste. I've got some foolish sort of nervous feeling, as if something was going to happen. I don't know what, or how. I've had it for a week. I suppose I'm not very well."

"Thunder in the air," said Dick. "If anything happens, it will be something good for you. So be ready to jump for joy."

That evening he told his little boy of his intention to go to London, and, still suspicious that Polly, of whom he knew nothing beyond the fact that she drew her pound a-week, might return in his absence and carry off the boy, he told him to be ready in the morning to go to town with him.

The fast train from Market Basing leaves at nine o'clock, and is at Euston at half-past ten. They started to walk to the station, for Dick hated luggage and always kept changes of raiment and fine linen at his chambers in Jermyn-street. Crossing the river, Dick bethought him that he had not seen his father for some days. So he passed through the garden into the house.

Mr. Mortiboy was in his bed. Hester was feeding him with a spoon; his breakfast consisting of bread and milk. He frowned at his son as usual, and then quietly took his milk a spoonful at a time until the basin was emptied. Dick sat by the side of his bed, and watched him eat. His appetite was very good; altogether there was a great change in him. The fixed smile had almost left his mouth, and the distortion of his face was much less noticeable. Then his eye was brighter, his memory better, the cloud seems to be gradually lifting from his mind. As his son sat by his bedside watching Hester feed the old man, and thinking of all that had happened, suddenly there flashed upon his memory an old, old day, so long ago that it had never once come back to him: a day more than a quarter of a century old: an autumn day like the present, when the golden tints were on the leaves; a morning when a child he walked hand-in-hand with his father, and asked him questions. He remembered how his father, lifting him in his arms, stroked his cheeks and kissed him; how he flung his own arms round his neck and kissed his father again. A simple childish caress: it might have occurred a thousand times to most children; to Dick it seemed only to have occurred once, because Mr. Mortiboy was an undemonstrative man, and with him such events were rare. As he remembered this, another thought came upon him: it was, that never once since that day, save when his own crime caused relapse, had his father's love ceased to burn in a steady flame. He knew it now: he recognised it even in the starved and pinched life he had been made to lead: even in the tyranny of his youth; even in the hard work and long hours to which his father subjected him—all this was to make him grow up like himself —and in the ready confidence and trust with which he received the prodigal returning home. He knew it all, in a single moment, and a sharp pain shot through him as he looked upon the wreck he had himself caused.

Dick was not one, however, to sit down and weep, throwing ashes upon his head and clothing himself with sackcloth. The thought came to him, as one which might often come again, a grave and saddening thought; his thoughts turned upon the boy whom he had adopted. Suppose little Bill should do something, should turn out somehow like himself. Then he cleared his throat, which was getting husky, and bent slightly over his father—Old Hester had left them alone together.

"Father," he said, "let us be friends again—I am sorry."

The old man moved his slow eyes upwards with a puzzled expression.

Dick looked at him, waiting, but no response came.

He joined the boy, and they set off together to walk to the station.

When Hester came back, she found Mr. Mortiboy looking troubled, and a tear or two had rolled down his withered cheeks.

"Bill," said Dick, in the train—he was quit accustomed to converse on all topics with the boy, who understood or not, as the case might be—"Bill, I wonder if we are going to have a collision and bust up."

"Why, Uncle Dick?"

"Because the Mexicans say that when a man is going to die he begins to think about the days when he was a child That's what I've been doing this morning. The only way you can be killed in this peaceful old country is by a railway accident."

"I saw a boy once, run over by a 'bus," said Bill, thoughtfully.

"Yes—there are other ways, I suppose. But a smash on a railway is the most likely thing. Perhaps, after all, the Mexicans are not always right."

There was no railway accident, at any rate.

At his chambers he found a letter, dated a fortnight and more back, from Lafleur.

"My dear Dick," it ran, "I am in want of money. Please send me a couple of hundred at once."

"In any case," said Dick, "it is too late now. Want of money? What has been done with the five thousand? The System has come to grief, I suppose, after all?"

It was not pleasant to think about. The man had been started actually with all the money he asked. The partnership was dissolved; the pair had separated, each agreed to go his own way, and yet, only two months after, came this letter. Dick crushed it in his fingers, looking stern and determined.

"It shall not be," he said, thinking aloud. "Polly is gone, and Lafleur shall go. I will have no witnesses left to remind me of the old days. I will live my own life now, with the boy to bring up. Lafleur shall not be with us to bring back what I would forget. No, M. Alcide Lafleur, it will not do. Your own secrets are as bad as mine, and worse. You dare not speak, at any rate. I will give you one more start, on condition that you go away to California, or somewhere over the water, and never come back again. You shall not stand in my way. I defy any man to stand in my way. My path is clear and certain. I will start Frank and Ghrimes. Then I will go

D D

away and stay away for ten years with the boy. And then I will come back, and put him out in life, and settle down. I shall be turned forty then. I shall never marry. I have said so. There will be other children then, Grace's children, to amuse me. I shall spend the rest of my life, thirty years and more, among the children."

He took no notice of the letter, and went on to the post-office, to find out Frank, if possible. It was a poor little post-office, kept by a bookseller in a small way, perhaps a man who should be described as one who sold small books. Specimens of his ware were in the window, cheap religious books mostly, and the doorway was filled with the *affiche* boards of daily papers.

Dick found a woman behind the counter, and stated his business.

"I—I—don't think it's hardly regular," she said. "People come and get their letters here, but I don't know that I ought to tell you anything about them."

"There's five shillings, now you will tell me."

It was blunt, but effective. The woman took the shillings, put them in her pocket, and went on at once.

"I don't know anything about the gentleman who has the letters addressed to him as Mr. Melliship. Sometimes he comes, a tall, fair-haired young man, quite the gentleman; sometimes it's a young person."

"A girl, you mean? A young lady?"

She smiled superior, and tossed her head.

"Not a lady, I should say, certainly. At least, I wouldn't compare her with myself. A young woman, sir."

"Pretty, as well as young?"

She bridled up. "That's a matter of opinion. I don't hold with a pink and rose face, and a bit of false hair."

"Is that all you can tell me?"

"That's all, sir, I'm sorry to say."

"Then you've taken five shillings out of me on false pretences," said Dick, pretending to be in a rage. "I've a great mind to report you to head quarters." The woman turned all colours. "Well, I won't this time, if you'll tell Mr. Melliship, or the young person, the next time the letters are asked for, that his cousin has been to see him, and wants him particularly. On what day does the young person come?"

"On Monday morning, always, sir, about eleven o'clock, unless he comes himself. Quite the gentleman, *he* is."

He was in the neighbourhood of Gray's Inn-road, and thought of Mrs. Kneebone's; he took his way down that thoroughfare with a view of finding out if Polly had been there, and what she had done.

Sitting at the entrance of the court was the boy Thoozy, looking wistfully down in the direction of Holborn. It was down the street that little Bill had gone with the swell; and he naturally expected that it was by that way he would return. Dick touched him on the shoulder.

He jumped up on his crutches, and grinned a perfect pæan of joy.

"Well, Thoozy," said Dick, "and how's things?"

"How's little Bill?" returned Thoozy.

"Well and strong. He sent you a message a little while ago by a tramp. Didn't you get it?"

"Never," said Thoozy. "Never. What was it?"

"Only to send his love, and you were not to forget him."

"I never forgets him," said the poor boy. "I got no one to talk to now he's gone; and the old woman's took on dreadful with drink ever since the day Polly Tresler came."

"Ah! what was that? Tell me all about it, boy. Come into the court and sit on your own step."

Mrs. Kneebone saw them coming up the road, and trembled. Was further information wanted, and should she expose herself to another assault, of an aggravated nature? She decided at once on her line of action, and, putting on her shawl, she took a jug, and a big key, so as to show that she meant business, and sallied down the steps.

"Me-thew-salem," she said, with great sweetness, "I'm obliged for to go out a little bit. Take care of them blessed children while I'm away. Good morning, sir. And it's hoping you found all that I told you c'rect."

Dick nodded his head, and she passed on, seeing no prospect of further coin. "Now, Thoozy," said Dick, "tell me all about it."

If Methusalem had been born in a somewhat higher sphere of life; if he had not been lame; if his flesh, which was weak, had been equal to his spirit, which was strong; if he had been educated for the stage; he might have made a low comedian of a very unusual kind. His talent was prodigious, but his training was defective.

With an instinctive feeling that a vivid picture of Mrs. Kneebone's discomfiture and Polly's subsequent disaster would be appreciated, Thoozy enacted the whole scene with a dramatic *verve* which set the tragedy vividly before his listener. The boy forgot his lameness and infirmity, mimicked their voices, alternately doing Mrs. Kneebone with her conciliatory hypocrisy, and Polly with her sulky disbelief. When he put in the finishing touch of Mrs. Kneebone's really illnatured remark about himself, Dick roared with laughter.

"Look here, boy," he said, "you are not very anxious, I suppose, to stay here all your life?"

"I'm an old man," said Thoozy, with a comical leer. "I'm getting very old, and past work. I used to think I'd stay on here all my days; but now little Bill is gone, and I get nobody to talk to, I think a change might do me good. My doctor did recommend," he added, waving his hand grandly, "that I should take six months' holiday, and go to one of our country seats. With port wine. Says I must drink port wine, three glasses a day. As the resident physician, I couldn't spare the time; but if you press me very hard, I might get away for a bit. I say, sir," he went on, in a changed voice, "let me see little Bill again. I won't do him no harm. I never did that I knows on. Let me have a talk with him once more, only once."

Dick hesitated. Why should he not take the boy away? With all his quaint affectations, his oddities, and infirmities, he could do no harm to his adopted son. Why not take him too? He took out a card case, and printed his address on a card in pencil.

"I live here. You can read that? Good. Jermyn-street, off Regent-street. Now be careful, and listen. Little Bill is with me there. You make your way at once to St. James's Park. Wait about the door of the Duke of York's Column. I will send Bill to you, or bring him if he doesn't know the way."

"Bill not know the way! He knows his way, like a ferret, all over London, even where he hasn't been. Bill wasn't along with me for nothing."

"Good. You two boys may spend the whole day together; bring him back to Jermyn-street at nine. As the clock strikes, mind."

"I will. Sharp at nine."

Dick considered a moment.

"Bill's got good clothes now, too," he said. "Would you like some decent things to put on?"

Thoozy looked at his old coat and his torn trousers, and sighed.

"Come, then. I know a man close by."

He took him to the same dealer who had refitted little Bill, and provided him with a suit of clothes, including stockings —quite unknown to Thoozy, except by hearsay, up to that time—better than he had ever dreamed of.

"Now you've plenty of time, go into Endell-street, and have a bath, brush your hair, and make yourself quite respectable."

He gave him a few shillings to complete his arrangements, and walked away.

Thoozy went back to the court, amid the jeers of the populace—who recognised him, in spite of his grandeur—just to see that the babies were not coming to any harm, rescuing an infant from imminent suffocation, by reason of a corner of the sheet, which it mistook, through want of experience, for the mouth of a feeding bottle. Thoozy shook them all up, and went his way.

It was one o'clock when Dick got back to Jermyn-street.

"There's a friend of yours wants to see you very much," he said to his ward.

"Thoozy! Thoozy!" cried the boy, with delight.

"That is the party. Are you hungry, Bill?"

"Very little, Uncle Dick."

"Got any money?"

Little Bill produced two and fourpence from his pocket.

"Go on, then. You can have your dinner with Methusalem, where you like. You know your way to the Duke of York's Column. Wait there till you see him."

Dick Mortiboy lunched in his own room, and then smoked the cigar of content and happiness. He embodied his discoveries at the Post Office in Great Bedford-street, in a short note to Grace Heathcote, and despatched it to the pillar box by the woman who was in charge. This was the purport of it:—"Frank calls for his letters, or has them called for by a young woman every Monday morning. We must wait till then. Next Monday I will be there."

It was about three o'clock that a man, all in rags and tatters, rang at the door bell. The old woman in charge—all the other lodgers were out of town—opened it and looked at him with suspicion.

"I want Mr. Mortiboy."

"Give me your name, and I'll see," she said.

"He knows me. Let me pass."

The man pushed by her, and mounted the stairs. Dick's sitting-room was at the back, second floor, a small room, but big enough for his purposes. He had, besides, a bedroom for himself, with a dressing-room, in which was a bed for the boy.

He was sitting over his third cigar. He never read books, having lost the habit of reading long since. Sometimes he looked at the newspaper, but not often. He was, therefore, like Captain Bowker in one respect, that all his ideas were his own. To-day he was more happy and contented than he had ever been before since his return. All was going well with him. Grace would not have him. Very good.

"If she be not fair to me,
What care I how fair she be?"

a quotation he certainly would have made, if he had known it. Unromantic as it may seem, Dick cured himself of his passion by the simple expedient of giving the girl up. He loved her no longer. Men only really love a girl—with that blind, passionate devotion which burns her image upon their hearts in indelible characters, like a tattoo on the arm—between the ages of twenty and thirty. After that—experience. Men past the sixth lustrum know womankind better. The know the other sex because they know their own. They know that no women are perfect, and they suspect their own passion. Now suspicion to passion is like the sunshine to a coal fire—puts it out. Dick gave up his love with a mighty effort, because it was very strong. But having given it up, he gave it up altogether. There is no half measures with Dick. Thorough at all times. If Grace had accepted him, no husband could have been more true and more faithful than he, more attentive, more thoughtful. Just as he had been a thorough rogue, just as he was going to be a thorough "respectable," just so he would have been a thorough lover. But it could not be; and therefore, as a philosopher, he acknowledged that it was better not to think of it. Now his plans were changed. To go away altogether, to take the boy with him he was now considering—even the thought of taking Thouzy, too, had crossed his mind—to come back after many years. This was his new programme. As he lay back in his easy chair, his handsome face breathed a sweet spirit of hope and cheerfulness, and with every fresh cloud of tobacco came another castle of contentment and repose.

His door opened. He looked round to see who it was, but started to his feet at sight of the miserable object before him. Alcide Lafleur stood in the doorway. Ragged, starving, pinched, and footsore, his old partner stood there in front of him, staring at him with haggard eyes.

"Good God! man," he said, "what is this?"

"Did you not get my letter, Dick?"

"To-day, this morning. What is this?"

"First give me money to get food and clothes. I am almost starving."

Dick thrust all the money in his pockets into Lafleur's hands. "Go quickly. Get things, and then come back. Take my latch-key, and return as soon as you can."

Lafleur took the money and the key, and crept away.

Dick lit another cigar. But the current of his thoughts was rudely disturbed. The clouds of tobacco were angry and threatening now, and filled with coloured pictures. He filled and drank three or four glasses of wine in succession. Then he sat down doggedly to wait, with his hands in his pockets. Presently the old woman came up.

"If you don't want me, sir," she said, "I've particular business, and should like to go out this afternoon."

She resented the appearance of lodgers in September, when everybody, including the landlady, was away; and she was not inclined to put herself about, to please anybody.

"Oh yes," said Dick; "you can go. I'm not likely to want anything. Be back by nine; the boy's coming in then, and will want some supper."

It was a little before six when the front door slammed and a footfall sounded on the stairs.

A moment afterwards, M. Alcide Lafleur, washed, shaven, trimmed, and dressed, darkened the threshold of his old partner's room. He was rehabilitated and, at least, externally restored to the semblance of his former state.

"*Sacré!*" he exclaimed, pinching up the sleeve of his new coat and turning it round. "What a climate!"

There were great rain spots on it. He wiped his new hat with his new cambric handkerchief.

"Never mind the rain," said Dick Mortiboy. "Now tell me all about it. How came you to get into such a mess?"

"Light your gas, first, my friend," said Lafleur; "it is cursedly dark in this little hole ——"

It was dark; the clouds were black: a thunderstorm had burst over London.

Dick put a match to his gas.

"Young Ready-money is the sobriquet the respectable citizens of your native village have conferred on their philanthropic millionaire," he continued, with that thin, sneering smile of his on his face. "I think if Alcide Lafleur had either the title or the money he would somewhere in London have found an apartment more distinguished than this is."

He looked round Dick's simple sitting-room and shrugged his shoulders. Gentlemen of his temperament soon recover themselves. Lafleur had already recovered. He was the same man that had got Dick Mortiboy out of the prison in Palmiste; that had traded with him, run the blockade with him, gambled, swindled, and lied with him. Lafleur was unchanged. But his partner was no longer Roaring Dick, and the company of his old companion was distasteful to him, his voice grated on his ear.

"The rooms do for me, Lafleur: nobody knows me, and if they did it would not matter."

"Always so careless, so rough. My dear Richard, if I had your money," he heaved a sigh: he thought of what he had given up in giving back Dick's word to him. "Ah! how unfortunate I have been—how lucky, you! and you are content with a hammock, a beefsteak, and a pot of beer!"

"Have you actually lost all?" asked Dick abruptly.

"My cursed luck," replied Lafleur, looking at the rain beating down the window. "How it pelts! *Ma foi!*"

"Never mind the rain; tell me all about it," said Dick a second time; and Lafleur told his story. It took him half an hour to tell it, but briefly it was the story of every man who ever went to Hombourg to break the bank—except that lucky thousandth one who breaks it. At first, luck was with Lafleur; night after night he went home with every pocket stuffed with gold pieces.

"Dick, if you had been with me I should have landed the grand *coup*—twice—instead of beggaring myself. You have pluck—dash—*élan*. You would have carried out the System and piled the money on. I was a coward; I hesitated. It came to putting down two thousand in one stake—the bank had been winning enormously, they would have covered any stake—the cards seemed bedevilled. And I dared not do it. Like a mad fool I left the table. Dick, the next time did it.

If I had only had pluck I should have landed myself with a profit of five thousand pounds on the run." He laughed— "As I always told you, the more the run was against you the more you must win—at the end. My System is perfect. I was the fool."

"Well," said Dick Mortiboy, "you had lost all?"

"Stay. Half—all my winning and half the money I took with me. Cool as I am, old hand as I am, my dear Richard, my nerve was gone—for the time. Not at the run against me. At my contemptible folly. I ran over to Wiesbaden and played a week at roulette. I won a five hundred there and then came back to Hombourg. The very same cursed luck attended me again. I had not pluck to put all my money down at one stake. I hesitated and was lost again. My head was gone. I deserted my System and played with the reckless folly of a madman——"

"And you were cleaned out?"

"Lost every farthing. But, Dick, you would have saved me. The System is perfect. Carry it out, and I defy you to lose—my want of pluck beat me."

"A cool player, Lafleur, but you always wanted courage."

"When all was gone I thought of you. I knew you would never turn your back on an old friend. I thought I would come back here to you for more money." Dick's face, as he heard this confession, grew hard. "I sold my clothes, and my rings, and watch; but I lost money on the way. I had only enough left to bring me to Newhaven. Dick, I have walked from Newhaven to London on tenpence, one franc, upon my honour. Of all my possessions, I have got nothing left but the six shooter you gave me ten years ago."

Dick got up and began to pace the room.

"Lafleur, let me say what I think, and then you shall speak. Our partnership is dissolved. You have given me back my word. You know that I never say things unless I mean them—when I sought that dissolution, I meant a complete severance of our connection. I meant that you should have no claim upon me—not the least—for the future. I belong to a different world henceforth. Go your way, and let me go mine. That is what I mean still. I am not surprised that the System has broken down—they always do. No man ever yet could invent, or will invent, a scheme to meet the chances of luck. When it isn't luck, it is skill. Now you know exactly what I mean, state exactly what you want me to do.'

Lafleur turned white. Tell an inventor that his model is worthless, the model over which he has grown grey: tell a poet that his poem is balderdash, the poem over which he has spent his life: tell a mathematician that his integrals are as useless as the mediæval scholasticism, those integrals on which he has sacrificed his youth—do all these things with impunity—you will only wound. But do not tell a gambler that his scheme is a mistake and a delusion. You will madden him.

He clutched the arm of his chair, but said nothing.

Dick went on.

"You know, Lafleur, in spite of our dissolution, that I cannot let an old friend come to grief without my trying to help him. Now I will do this for you—I will give you five hundred now, on condition that you go to America, and I will send you a thousand when I know you have arrived. Think it over."

"Go partners again with me, Dick, only in the System, you know. Come over to Hombourg, and play it yourself, with your own splendid luck. Dick, we must win, I am certain we must win. Bring ten thousand with you. I will be a half-partner, a quarter-partner, anything. Only let us try it once more."

"No."

Lafleur made no further effort. He knew his man.

"I accept," he said after a few minutes.

Dick took his cheque book and drew a cheque on his London agents for five hundred pounds.

"What is the day of the month? the twenty-third? I have filled it in with the twenty-second. Never mind, it will be all the same. Keep the condition, Lafleur, or I don't keep mine."

"Some men would threaten you, Dick," said Lafleur, pocketing the cheque. "I do not. I think you are treating me hardly, but I do not threaten."

"I should like to see the man who would threaten me," said Dick calmly.

Lafleur, whose whole bearing was changed, who had lost his ease and assurance, made no answer to this remark.

"Give me some brandy," he said after a pause; "I am a good deal shaken, I don't quite know what I am saying."

He drank a glass neat, and then had a tumbler of brandy and water mixed half-and-half fashion

"*Voilà*. I feel better," he said, putting on a little of his old style.

He walked to the windows and looked out. "How cursedly it pours down. What are we to do?"

"You can stay and smoke a cigar."

They smoked for some minutes in unbroken silence. The only sound in the room was the pelting of the rain against the window panes.

"Dick, may I propose half an hour at euchre:" he said this doubtingly, half afraid that Dick would refuse. "It is a long time since we played—we may never play again together —let us have a last game."

"I don't mind playing a game or two, Lafleur," he said. He took out his watch, "It is half-past seven now, I shan't play after nine; I shall leave off as the clock strikes. I've got an engagement then."

The first half-hour was over. The clock struck eight and the rain had ceased. The luck was all on Dick's side. He had won thirty pounds of Lafleur. It was scored down on a piece of paper.

"Shall we leave off? You're not in luck, and I don't want to win."

Lafleur begged him to go on. "Lend me ten again." Dick passed the money over the table, and made the score on the paper forty. At half-past eight the debt was a hundred.

"I won't take the money of you," said Dick.

"You shall take it," said Lafleur, tossing off another glass of brandy, "if you leave off a winner. Come on, deal the cards, we have only half-an-hour."

When half of that half-hour was gone, Dick Mortiboy sprang from his chair, leaned across the table, and brought his hand heavily upon the sleeve of his adversary's coat. In it was a knave, the best card at euchre, which Dick dragged forth.

"Swindler," he cried, "you would even cheat me." He pushed back his chair, turned over the table, and flung the cards in Lafleur's face. "Give me back my cheque," he said sternly, "I have done with you."

Without saying a word, the Frenchman flew at him like a tiger cat. Dick stepped lightly aside, and received him with his left. He fell heavily. He rose again, however, in a moment, and went at him again. A second time he fell.

This time he lay on the carpet with a livid face, and for a moment appeared not to move. But his white hand stole stealthily to his coat pocket. He half turned as if to rise, Dick watching him with flashing eyes, and then—then—the sharp crack of a pistol, a column of smoke, a heavy fall, and Dick Mortiboy lying flat on his face. Lafleur started to his feet. He had shot his adversary as he lay, without taking the pistol from his pocket. He leaned over Dick for a moment; he did not move; he turned him on his back; his eyes were closed: he breathed heavily. He unbuttoned the waistcoat: the bullet had entered his chest: he saw stains of blood upon his shirt. Then he went outside to the landing, and listened. Not a sound. He went to Dick's open desk. In it were about twelve sovereigns and some notes. He took ten pounds in gold, leaving the notes: put two of them in Dick's pocket. The keys were in the desk. He locked it, and placed them on the mantelpiece. He did this to prevent suspicion of robbery. Next he picked up the table, and hid the cards away, and put the furniture straight. Then he drank another glass of brandy.

One thing he had forgotten—the pistol—he laid it in the hand of the fallen man. As he placed it in Dick's hand, the fingers clutched over it.

And then he took his hat and glided out of the room.

He came back a moment after, and bent over Dick's face.

Dick neither moved nor spoke.

Enough. Lafleur stole gently away, down the stairs, out of the house, stepping softly through the door. He closed it after him, but the latch did not hold. The clock of St. James's church began to strike the hour of nine as he reached Piccadilly.

There was not a soul in the house. Jermyn-street, in September, is a howling wilderness. No one, save people at the back, heard the pistol shot. No one saw Lafleur enter or go away, and Dick Mortiboy lay supine, the wet beads of death clustering on his forehead, his life blood welling away from his wound.

CHAPTER THE FORTY-SIXTH.

HAT did he think of, as he lay there?—of his wild life, his lawlessness, his crimes?—of the singular chance which had landed him on the shores of respectability and fortune?—of his aims and hopes for the future? A man's thoughts when Death stares him in the face, are comprehensive. He thinks of all. In a dream, even of half a minute's duration, you may live through a lifetime. The Eastern monarch dipped his head into a tub of water, and straightway left his sultanship and became a wanderer for twenty years. At the end of that time he found himself lifting his head out of the water again. This adventure had taken him one minute to accomplish. A man told me that he slipped once in the Alps, and glided for two or three hundred feet, expecting instant death. He was pulled up, I forget how, and saved from death; but in that brief space he lived all his life over again. The dying thief upon the cross,—model and ensample of all who repent at the last moment,—at the close of his last hour, when suffering gave way to torpor, and physical pain, one would fain hope, became only a deadened misery, may so have lived in a moment through all his life, and seen clearly what might have been.

Who can tell what thoughts crowded into the brain of poor Dick Mortiboy, lying there alone and untended, stricken to death? I, for one, cannot. I only know that he was softened and changed of late weeks: that many things had quite suddenly become clear to him; that the old carelessness was changing into gravity; that he was beginning to recognise the evil of his ways; that life had changed its aspect. Wealth had done this for him; wealth that works in many ways, turning the unselfish man into the voluptuary; or the selfish man into one who lives and cares wholly for others. Wealth brings with it its curse or its blessing, just as its recipient is disposed. It is a means to make a Tiberius, or it may make its —— Here the law of libel interferes, or I might name one who has great wealth, a giant's strength, and owns it but as a trust for the improvement, as best he can, of his fellows, a single-hearted, honest man, a rich man, for whom the needle's eye is as easy to pass, as for the poorest pauper who breathes with resignation and dies with joy. So would it have been for my Dick Mortiboy. But at the moment when the tide was turned came the stroke of fate, and he who might have done so much, was forbidden to do anything. Ah! the pity of it—the pity of it.

At nine o'clock—before the old woman returned—came back the boys from their day's holiday. Laughing, radiant, happy, little Bill, followed by his limping companion, strangely diffident now, with his changed and glorified "young 'un," sprang up the steps of the house in Jermyn-street. They found the door open.

"Come in, Thoozy; come up with me. Uncle Dick said you was to come, you know."

Thoozy followed up the stairs, while Bill, running before with the impetuosity of a Peter, reached the door of Dick's chamber, and opened it.

The lamp was out. They stood in darkness. Only on the floor before them a black form.

Bill stopped and looked. A blank dread filled his soul. He trembled; he dared not speak. Behind him he heard Thoozy's crutch as he limped up the stairs. He waited.

"What's that, Thoozy?" he whispered, pointing to the floor.

Thoozy did not answer. The light on the staircase was in his eyes, and he could see nothing. The two boys, clinging to each other, stood shivering with fear, as in the doorway Thoozy made out, in the twilight, the figure of a man upon the floor.

"Go and get a light," he whispered. "Run, quick. Do you know where to find one?"

"They've always one on the stairs," replied the other. "Don't move, Thoozy; don't move?"

He disappeared. As soon as he was gone, Thoozy entered the room, and, kneeling down, felt the face of the man who lay so still. It was that of Uncle Dick. He knew it by the long silken beard. A whisper reached his ears.

"Go—fetch a doctor quick. Get a light—water, for God's sake."

Bill returned at the moment. Thoozy snatched the candle from him, and got a *carafe* from the bedroom, from which he poured a few drops into the dying man's mouth. He sprinkled his face. And then little Bill, who had watched him with pale face and trembling lips, fell headlong on the ground, weeping and sobbing, kissing the cheeks and lips of his patron, and crying in his agony—"Oh! Uncle Dick—Uncle Dick."

"Give him more water," said Thoozy; "I am going out for a doctor. Don't let him move till I come back."

Thoozy limped away, forgetting his crutch, and poor little Bill heard him descend step by step.

He was left alone with Dick. Terrors of every kind assailed his heart. He could not speak. All he could do was to lie along the floor, his cheek against Dick's to feel him breathing, to know that he was living. . . . Minutes that seemed hours passed slowly away. At last he heard footsteps again. Thoozy was returning, bringing some one with him. It was the doctor. Thoozy's good sense led him into Waterloo-place, where he knew there was a policeman; of him he got the address of the nearest surgeon. The policeman went with him, suspecting something wrong. The doctor was at home, and came at once.

He took the candle and began to examine his patient. A weak whisper greeted him.

"I have had an accident," Dick murmured feebly. "Half an hour ago—an old pistol—shot myself in the side—no one in the house to help me—left side—don't move me—I am bleeding to death."

"More light," said the doctor, "Boy, light that lamp."

It was a moderator, the mechanism of which was unknown to Thoozy.

The policeman lit it.

Then the doctor unbuttoned the waistcoat and looked for the wound. On the floor lay the pistol; he trod upon it. The policeman took it, and after carefully looking at it, placed it in his pocket.

"One chamber fired," he murmured. "Who is he?" he asked Thoozy.

"I don't know. He knows. Bill knows. He was a goin' to do something for me; he gave me these clothes to-day, and told me to come at nine," sobbed Thoozy.

"Who is it?" The policeman called to little Bill.

"Mr. Mortiboy," said Bill, as if all the world knew him.

"Does he live here always?"

"No: he lives at Market Basing," said Bill, trembling, in spite of the last few weeks' experience, at sight of a policeman. "He's my Uncle Dick."

"He isn't really his uncle," whispered Thoozy. "He took care o' little Bill. He's no relation at all—told me so hisself."

Meantime the doctor was at work. His face grew very

grave. Dick opened his eyes with an effort, and looked at him.

"How long?" he asked.

"It is a very serious accident," began the doctor.

"How long?" repeated Dick, in a hoarse whisper.

"Perhaps half an hour."

"Take paper, and let me make a statement to save trouble."

"Speak very low," whispered the doctor, "I can hear. Do not exert yourself more than you can possibly help."

Dick began in a faint voice—

"I—Richard—Melliship—Mortiboy—declare that I—have—accidentally shot myself, while preparing to clean my pistol."

You see, he was true to his old partner to the very last. Went out of the world with a lie on his lips, to save him.

The doctor wrote.

"Place the pen in my hand and guide me. I want to sign it, in presence of yourself and the policeman," said the dying man.

It was done. With faltering fingers Dick traced his name for the last time.

"Have you any testamentary depositions to make or alter?"

"Give me—water,—brandy,—something."

They held up his head—the forehead dank and cold, the cheeks pale, the eyes only opening from time to time with an effort—and the doctor gave him a spoonful of brandy. This revived him a little.

"Write," he said.

"Dearest Cousin Gracie, I am dying. You can find Frank easily. All my money will be yours and Lucy's. Let Frank and Ghrimes be partners. God bless you, my dear. If I had lived I would have—"

Here he stopped. Presently he went on again—

"Remember that I love you for all you have done for me, but that I give you up freely and entirely. Let the money go back to help the poor as much as may be."

He stopped again. Another spoonful of brandy.

"Tell my father—" Here he paused; a strange look of bewilderment crossed his face. "Ah!" he sighed, "it is no use now to tell him anything. I shall tell him myself."

The doctor thought he was wandering.

"Where is little Bill?" he whispered.

The doctor put the child's face to his.

"Oh, Uncle Dick! Don't die! Don't die, Uncle Dick!"

Dick kissed the tear-wet cheek that lay upon his cheek, and his head fell back.

"Poor little chap," he murmured.

They were his last words. A moment after, without a sigh or a groan, he turned his head to one side—they had brought a pillow from the bedroom—and opened his eyes no more. Dick was dead. Ah! the pity of it—the pity of it.

"Coroner's inquest," said the policeman. "Were you here, my boys?"

"No," said Thoozy. "We found him here. He told us to come at nine."

"Can we telegraph?" said the doctor.

"Who to? We may look in the desk. These boys can't help us. Go to bed, my lads," he said, in a kindly voice. "You can't do any good here."

They searched the desk. No sign of an address. There were no cards upon him, and no letters.

"We might," said the policeman, "we might send to the police office of Market Basing for information."

Thoozy followed little Bill to his bedroom. Both were crying and lamenting.

"Bill," said Thoozy, after a pause, "it's all over; he won't help you and me no more. He's dead, is Uncle Dick. Why couldn't I die? I'm no use in the world to nobody. I've got no money; I've only got rheumatiz. Why couldn't I die, and Uncle Dick live? Come, Bill, it's no use stopping here no longer. Let's go, you and me."

"Not back to Mother Kneebone's," said Bill.

"No, not back to Kneebone's. Let's go a long way off, miles away, where they won't find us, and live together. How much money have you got, Bill?"

"I've got a sovereign. He gave it me yesterday."

"I've got three shillin'. He gave it me to-day, and we've got our clothes. Let's go, Bill."

He took the child by the arm, and they stepped out stealthily upon the stairs, and crept down, Thoozy leaning on Bill.

When they got into the street, Thoozy led the way eastward. They passed through Covent-garden, and down Drury-lane. They walked up Fleet-street, Ludgate-hill, Cheapside,

E E

and so on to the Whitechapel-road. In fulness of time, after many stoppages—for they slept an hour on this doorstep, and an hour on that—they arrived, when day broke, somewhere in the East End of London, where there were masts of ships innumerable.

"It's the docks," said Thoozy. "Now we'll wait and look about us."

In the afternoon of that fatal day old Hester was pushing Mr. Mortiboy's Bath-chair slowly round the broad gravel paths, according to her wont, in front of the house in Derngate. Lucy Heathcote walked by her uncle's side, now and then saying a kind word to the old man, to rouse and cheer him. She had been more hopeful of his recovery of late days; the worst symptoms had improved; his eyes were brighter; he had begun to be interested in little things about him; and his features had gained back something of their old expression. In her hand was the Bible, from which she was reading favourite passages to her uncle. In health he never would be "read to," in his sickness he made no sign of dissent. Lucy's presence soothed him. He loved to have her near him. She knew he liked to hear her voice, though his poor palsied wits seemed to have neither memory nor understanding. So she read on.

She was stopped by a loud cry from Hester.

"Oh! Miss Lucy! look at your uncle, miss! Oh! what shall we do!"

Lucy dropped her Bible. The old man's face was suddenly distorted fearfully, and he lay back on his pillows breathing heavily and laboriously. He had had another stroke. The girl thought he would die there; Hester was helpless from fright.

"Run—run—for the nurse—then send for Dr. Kirby—don't lose a second," cried Lucy.

The nurse came from her tea with her mouth full of bread and butter. She was calm and unmoved in the young girl's grief and the old servant's terror. She was quite equal to the situation. It had been her business to see people die. She showed her superiority by giving her orders calmly.

Hester was despatched for the doctor.

"There's death in his face, miss. Let us take him in. He won't be with us many hours now."

Sobbing grievously, Lucy lent her hand to wheel the dying man into his bedroom. The window opened on to the lawn.

"Oh, how horrible it seems, nurse! Oh! let us try to get him out of his chair! Oh! poor Uncle Richard—my dear—my dear!"

He was a heavy weight—dead weight—for he could not move hand or foot—both sides were palsied now; but the arms of the nurse were as strong as a man's. With little help from Lucy she got him on to his bed.

The girl—sole one among his relatives who had ever *loved* old Ready-money Mortiboy—fell on her knees by the bedside and prayed to God.

The old man turned his eyes towards her. She saw he was still conscious.

"Oh! uncle," she implored, "try—try to pray—try to follow my words. Uncle Richard," she cried in an agony of grief, "oh! Uncle Richard—try to make your peace with God."

But Mr. Mortiboy was unconscious again.

The doctors came in a few minutes. Their language was plain; they did not try to disguise the truth. The period of the old man's life might be reckoned in minutes. They could do nothing—but they stayed to see the end.

Ghrimes was sent for. He alone knew Dick's London address. It was past eight o'clock before he came back from the country, where he had been on business. He came—touched his old master's powerless, helpless hand, and hurried away to the telegraph office to summon Dick from London. Vain errand!

For five hours from the time of his last stroke the old man lay on his bed like one dead. He breathed, but every moment with less strength. To Lucy Heathcote it seemed like five days. Her father and mother were there with her, but she thought only of him who lay dying with them all round his bed.

The death struggle came at nine o'clock. There was an inarticulate sound first from the old man's lips. Then he *spoke*. They all heard it.

He said—"My—son—Dick," and lay there dead.

"Dick ought to be here at half-past ten," John Heathcote whispered to his wife.

CHAPTER THE FORTY-SEVENTH.

DICK'S letter to Grace arrived at Parkside before the news of his death, which was brought by one of the bank clerks sent out by Ghrimes at eight o'clock. Grace was reading the letter which promised to find Frank in the course of a week, and had just passed it over to her father, who read it with much satisfaction. Mrs. Heathcote, too, read it, but with different feelings, which she was studying how to express with due effect, when the messenger of evil tidings from the bank arrived in Dick's own dog-cart.

The farmer was with him for five minutes. He came back with pale cheeks and quivering lips.

"Dick," he gasped, "Dick . . . he's gone . . . dead . . . he shot himself by accident last night, and died an hour afterwards. Poor Dick! poor Dick!" He recovered after a little. "Strange they both died at the same hour. A telegram came to the police office this morning at eight. They sent round to Ghrimes. Ghrimes has sent for me. Poor Dick! poor Dick!"

The presence of a tragic event like this melted for a moment the animosity of her mother to Grace. They fell into each other's arms, sobbing and crying. Dick was dead. Dick the generous: Dick the noble: Dick the true and brave. Dick was dead. Nor was it for a full half-hour that Mrs. Heathcote, recovering herself the first, was able dimly to realize the change that this event might cause to her. Dick was dead—alas! poor Dick! But then—but then—all the fortune—the half million of money—whose would this be? Whose should it be, she asked herself, but her own? And already beginning the imaginary reign of splendour over which she had brooded so many years, a dream interrupted by Dick's return, she held her handkerchief to her eyes, and in the intervals of weeping indulged in delicious visions of grandeur.

Mr. Heathcote found Market Basing literally in tears. The

people, nearly all tenants of the great Mortiboy estates, were gathered in knots, discussing the event. No news was come except by telegram, but there was scarcely any room for doubt. Dick Mortiboy was dead. The women wept aloud: the men in silence: all had lost a friend, the kindest hearted friend they ever had; the most ready to help, the most able to help. Not one to whom Dick, in his short reign of four months, had not done some kind action! not one who could not speak from experience of his soft heart and generous nature! As the farmer drove through the crowd that besieged the bank with inquiries, the fresh tears rose to his own eyes, and he got down at the door almost crying like a child.

No one cared about the old man now. Dead? Ready-Money dead? Well, he had been a long time dying. He had passed away, four months ago, from men's minds.

John Heathcote arrived at the bank, went through to the manager's office, where he found Ghrimes was there with Battiscombe, to whom Ghrimes had sent, after despatching his message to Parkside.

"Do you know of any will?" Mr. Battiscombe asked Ghrimes.

"None; I have the keys, I suppose we ought to look."

In Dick's private safe, business papers in plenty, but no will. Stay, a packet labelled "Private: to be opened after my death."

"Open it," said the lawyer.

Ghrimes opened and read it. It was short and concise. It was the confession of Polly Tresler. As he read it, his face assumed a puzzled expression. He handed it over to Mr. Battiscombe, who read it unmoved. Lawyers are seldom surprised at anything which appears abnormal to the rest of mankind. Ghrimes was shocked at the idea of Dick's secret marriage.

"That explains," he whispered, "the early quarrel between himself and his father. That is the reason why Dick ran away.'

"Perhaps. It is hard to say. No great crime for a young fellow to be beguiled by a woman into making a fool of himself," said the lawyer. "It is as pretty a confession of bigamy —trigamy, even—as ever I read. Names, dates, churches, all given. Upon my word, this woman is an exceedingly clever person. It is signed by her, and written by poor Mr. Mortiboy himself, dated too, only a fortnight ago. Mary Tresler— Mary Tresler—I know her, daughter of that drunken old gipsy woman who married my father's gardener, a long time ago. Ah! dear me!"

"What is to be done?"

"Clearly, we must first establish the truth of her statements. I think, Ghrimes, I had better go to town and see to this myself, to prevent complications. Meantime, say nothing to the Heathcotes—to anybody. There may, besides, be a will. To prevent raising hopes in their minds, tell them, what is quite true, that you don't know whether any will was made or not. You know, of course, that if there is no will, Mrs. Heathcote is the sole heiress—she inherits everything—everything.

Then Mr. Heathcote arrived.

"We must have a coroner's inquest," said Mr. Battiscombe, "there must be a funeral—there is everything to be done. Will you come to town with me?"

"No—yes—what shall I do, Ghrimes?"

"Go, by all means. The train starts in half an hour. I will send a message to Parkside. Go up to town and see the last of your poor cousin."

They went to London: down to Dick's chambers, where they found the doctor and the old woman in charge. The doctor was standing by the bedside, with his chin on his hands, thoughtfully gazing on the stark and stiff form which lay covered with a sheet. He gently took off the sheet from the face.

"You are his cousin?" he said. "I am taking a last look at the unfortunate man. It is a singularly handsome face; a face of wonderful sweetness and goodness—a good man, I should say. And the most splendidly built man I ever saw. How *could* he have done it?"

The lawyer was reading Dick's last words, his only will and testament. John Heathcote solemnly looked upon the features of him who had been almost his own son.

"He says he did it by accident," said Mr. Battiscombe.

"Yes—yes—but how? how? Look here," the doctor drew back the sheet and showed the spot where the wound had been inflicted. "You see the place. Very well, then; now take this pencil, hold it any way you like, and see if you could shoot yourself in the left side, so far back, if the pencil was a pistol. I defy you to do it. It is very odd, yet he said he did it."

Coroner's inquest that evening. Intelligent jury, after viewing the body, and reading the paper, Dick's last imposture—heard the doctor's doubts, and pooh-poohed them. Shot himself? of course he did. What did it matter how? As if a man would lie about such a thing as that. Verdict—" Accidental Death." The worthy coroner adding some severe strictures upon the frequency of gun accidents, and men's carelessness in the handling of weapons.

Dick was dead. The good that he had time to do lives still; the lives that he quickened, which were dead under the weight of grinding poverty and servitude, if they have relapsed to their old misery, which some may have done, have still the memory of better times, the knowledge of better things, and therefore nourish a healthy discontent. The stirring of the blood which his example and his words caused: his oration to the children which will never die out of their minds: his charity, for the first time in Market Basing, unconnected with religion and three sermons every Sunday: his sympathy with the fallen: his tenderness to the falling: his kind and rough wisdom: his unbookish maxims: his ready hand: his quick insight into humbug—all these things, and many more, make him to be remembered still. These live after him: the good that he did was a seed sown in fruitful soil, still growing up, destined to be in the after-years a goodly tree indeed. And the evil, does that still live? I know Palmiste pretty well, because I've lived in the island— he never did harm *there*, except to himself; well, you see, I haven't been to California, or to Texas, or to Mexico, so I do not know. If ever I do go to either or any of these places, I will inquire.

Poor old Ready-money was buried three days after his death in the family vault, unostentatiously, quietly. No one was present at his funeral but Ghrimes and Mr. Heathcote, with the lawyer. No one followed in token of respect. All his money had gone from him before he died. Therefore, all his respect. No property left; of course, he was no longer of any account.

It was felt that a public funeral was due to his son. Mr. Hopgood, the Mayor, had orders to prepare a simple funeral. But all Market Basing turned out to it. There was no mock mourning. It was no feeling of simple respect for property which brought all the women with the men to see the last of one who had been with them so brief a space, and had made himself so loved by all. Not one but had a kind word of his to remember him by: no poor man but had more than a kind word: no eye that was dry when the earth rattled upon his coffin, and the sublime service of the Church was read over his remains.

His pensioners, the old men and women, were there, loudly wailing. Those whom he had saved from starvation, like old. Mr. Sanderson, the cashier of Melliship's bank, were there; those whom he had saved from ruin, like little Tweedy, the builder; those whom he had saved from shame, like Sullivan, the clerk; those for whom he had ever found a word of rough sympathy, and a hand ready to help; above all, the children, awe-stricken and terrified, in whose memory he lived as the universal friend and benefactor. From highest to lowest, from Lord Hunslope to the beggarman, all came to shed tears over the untimely death of Dick Mortiboy. "Truly," said the rector, " charity covereth a multitude of sins."

It was all over now. His burly form was with them no more: the vault was closed; the service read; they would never again hear his ringing laugh, his soft and sympathetic voice. The women would no longer, if they were poor, go to him to pour out their tales of want; if they were well to do, look after him in the street, so handsome, so good, so softhearted, so strong. The men would no longer admire him for his skill and strength, or envy him for his prosperity. All was over. Dick Mortiboy was buried.

CHAPTER THE FORTY-EIGHTH.

F it was hard for Ghrimes, what, as the lawyer said, would it be for Frank?

He received the letter containing Dick Mortiboy's offer. It came on the Monday evening, the day before Dick's murder. He read it with an emotion which he thought he had almost conquered; for he read in it the signal to him to leave his uncongenial life, and go back to his own position. His heart beat high with joy. It was not only Dick's free and generous offer. It was Grace's command that he should take it. It was the recall of his sister and mother to the place where all their friends lived, and all their interests were centred. A letter of recall and pardon to an exile; the restoration of a prince to his own again.

"You've got good news, Mr. Melliship?' asked Patty, looking at his heightened colour, and flashing eyes.

"Good news? Yes, Patty, very good. The best possible. The best news that ever was brought to any poor, unlucky beggar."

But his pride. How was he to reconcile his pride to accepting help from the son of his father's enemy?

Pride—yes—he had some slight grounds for pride. In the first place he could be independent so long as his voice lasted. That great and splendid gift, a tenor voice, was his. It lay with him to accept Mr. Leweson's offer to go to Italy and study for a year or two, and then to return and make his fortune. It was certain that he could do so. But to return to the bank—to go back to the old life again!

He walked out to call on Mr. Eddrup.

The old man was dressed, and sitting on his chair, too feeble to move.

Frank told him the great offer which had been made him. Perfect confidence existed between the two, by this time. Frank had told him all his life, with its disappointments and misfortunes.

"Take it," said Mr. Eddrup. "I, too, have an offer to make you. I shall make it with all the more confidence, if I know that you are rich, and therefore can command the influence of wealth."

"What is it?"

"I have no children, no relations, except a few cousins, who are already wealthy, and who have lost sight of me for many, many years. I want to leave you all my money—in trust—in trust to find some one, if you can, to carry on the work which I have done. Would that you could carry it on yourself!"

"But how shall I find a man?"

"Silver is the man for you. He has enthusiasm; he has energy; he has the power of administration; he has sympathy. Let Silver be my successor."

"Then why not leave him the money in trust?"

"Because he would not quite understand; he would be trying to make it a means of forming a society with rules and creeds, and so crystallize and kill what I want to grow and develop. Remember, young man, faith is the fertilizer; creed is the destroyer. Further, I want you to bequeath the property, after your death, so that it may be used by your successor— whom you will have to find—in the same spirit. I will not lay down rules. I will not add another to the Charities which do already so much harm. I want my money to be used always in the most intelligent manner possible to the time:—never by a committee."

On Wednesday afternoon he sat down to write his letter. As he began—"My dear Dick," a boy came shouting down the street, with an early edition of the *Echo*.

Frank, moved by some impulse, opened the window and beckoned the boy. Then he left his letter-writing for a while, and leisurely began to read.

Presently, Patty knocked at the door. She found him staring vacantly before him, with the paper in his hands. The last two days had been a time of trial for the poor girl. She saw, by Frank's manner, on Monday, that something was going to happen—she knew not what—which would sever him from her. She had been striving herself, bitterly, but steadily, to look the truth in the face. Frank did not love her. In spite of his kind ways and little attentions, the sweeter to Patty because she had never known them before, and was never to know them again, he had never loved her. And she, poor girl, had given all her heart to him. For his sake she spent sleepless nights, devising things which would please him; and careful days watching to see if she had pleased him. All the little arts which she knew, few enough, she practised to catch his eye. For him she had learned to despise the calling in which she had once almost gloried, and herself for practising it.

She sat down before him, and waited, hands clasped, for him to speak.

"Patty," he said at last, seeing her beside him, "a dreadful thing has happened. Read that. He was my cousin—I was to have been his partner—and now he is dead. I was writing to him when I bought the paper—I am a beggar again!"

"Then you are just the same as you were last Sunday?" Her heart gave a little exultant bound.

"The same? No. Are you the same if, when you are thirsty, some one dashes the cup from your lips? You are thirsty still, you say. Yes, but you are more than thirsty. You are maddened. Patty, I have had the cup dashed from my lips. I cannot think of poor Dick Mortiboy. I can only think of myself. I am only selfish in my sorrow."

The final blow had fallen. Patty turned white, and bit her lips; for the blood left her cheeks, and she felt as if she would faint. Presently he made an effort to speak.

"How can I go to her now—to the girl I love? How can I say—take me—I am a beggar, and you an heiress—take me?" "If she loves you, what matter does it make? If I loved a man do you think it would matter to me that I had—oh! hundreds of pounds and he had nothing? Mr. Melliship, if she loves you, you must go to her. Perhaps I don't understand. I always thought that when people loved each other they don't care for money. Is it not so? I mean rich people; of course we poor people never think about it, because we never have any money to think about at all. That is a good thing for us, so far. Tell me more, Mr. Melliship. Does she know that you love her still? Have you promised each other?"

"Yes—too late! Yes—long ago—when I was rich."

"And—and—but I suppose I can't understand. Are you too proud to go to her? But she knows you have no money —there is nothing to hide. If you loved her before, of course you go on loving her now. Do all ladies' hearts change when they have money? What is her name?"

"Grace Heathcote."

"Grace Heathcote—a pretty name—Grace Heathcote. Does she live in the same town with your cousin who is dead?— what is it?" She looked at the paper again: "Market Basing?"

"Near it; ten miles out, at a place called Hunslope. At Parkside Farm."

"At Hunslope, ten miles out. At Parkside Farm," she repeated. Then she got up, with lips that quivered in spite of her courage, and went away.

On Saturday, after their early dinner, she plucked up courage to speak to her father.

"Father—I want to say something to you—two things—I can no longer go on at the Palace. Don't call me ungrateful, after the pains you've took, and all that—I'm not ungrateful, but I can't bear it any longer. I didn't know, till Mr. Melliship came and talked to me, that there was anything in it. I thought it was something to be proud of. But now I can't bear the dress, and I see the women in the place sneering, and the horrid men laughing, as I never saw them before—before Mr. Melliship came."

"Mr. Melliship? Mr. Melliship? Is he in love with you, Patty?"

"No, father," she answered, bursting into tears; "he never

loved me; he never said a word of love to me. But, I—oh! I'm only a silly girl—and I fancied he might take a fancy to me. Forgive me, father. It is all folly and wickedness. He loves another girl—a lady. What am I, that I should take the fancy of a gentleman? Only a poor trapeze girl; only a common thing. I can't write well; I can't dress well; I can't do anything—I don't know how—that he likes. I have tried—oh! how I have tried—and he so good. He never laughed at me. But I could see the difference that he felt. Let him go back to his own people, and let me be alone."

The prophet turned his eyes upon the portrait.

"Jephthah's daughter," he murmured. "Jephthah's daughter—I knew it all along."

"And I can't act any more," said Patty. "Tell Mr. Leweson so. He is very good to us. But I can't do it."

"I've told him, Patty. I've told him. For I had some news for you that I thought would keep till to-morrow. See, now. This is the last night of our performance. You and I and Joey act to-night for the last time. They've got another family—a poor sort, Patty, compared to you and me—but there they are. They begin on Monday. I meant to tell you to-morrow. But I can't keep it. I am to be Mr. Eddrup's clerk. His clerk, Patty, so long as he lives. Think of that. With a salary. I'm to preach every Sunday. And when Mr. Eddrup dies, Mr. Melliship is to have all his money, in trust for the poor people. For these, and all other mercies, God's holy name be praised."

Patty was silent for a moment.

"I've been very selfish and vain with my foolishness, father. Now the other thing I had to say: I want a whole sovereign, father, and I want to go away early to-morrow, and be away all day; perhaps all Sunday night and Monday morning. Let me go, and don't ask me the reason why. That is my secret. Give me the money and let me go. I must go. My heart is breaking till I go. Mr. Eddrup would say I am right. I know he would. Father, if you doubt me, I will go and ask him myself if I am not right."

"Nay; if he thinks you are right, I've got nothing to say. Does Mr. Melliship send you?"

"No——no———no———" she crimsoned violently. "Don't say a word to him about it. A secret, father, and not my own. Oh, don't say a word against it. Because I must do it. I must, indeed. It is somebody else's secret. And even he doesn't know."

"I suppose it is Mr. Melliship's, then?"
She turned scarlet.
"It is, father," she whispered, "and it is for his good. Give me the money and let me go."
"A great sum, Patty. But you're a good girl, and you shall have your own way. I wish it wasn't Sunday, because I'm going to tell the story, in the afternoon, of the Roman Catholic priests. I've been getting it out of Ezekiel; and you'd have liked to hear it, no doubt."

CHAPTER THE FORTY-NINTH.

MRS. HEATHCOTE is heiress to all. The gigantic estate of the Mortiboys, little impaired by Dick's lavish expenditure, is hers, to have and to hold. The fact has been communicated to her officially by Mr. Battiscombe. No will had been made. No frittering away of a great property by miserable bequests: nothing left to collateral branches of the family; Ghrimes and the Melliships out of it altogether. All Mrs. Heathcote's.

In the first stupor of delight she sat tranquil, scarcely able to face the fact that she was rich beyond her dreams. Then, and before poor Dick was buried, she began to make plans and settle how they were in future to live. She talked, the sealed fountain of her ambition once set moving again, perpetually on this one topic—what they should do, what changes they were to make in their style of living, how they were to astonish the world.

"We shall, of course," she said to her daughter, "go to London to live. Your father must give up his vulgar habits."

"My father has no vulgar habits," said Grace, always rebellious.

"Grace, don't contradict. Is it, or is it not, vulgar to smoke pipes after dinner?" No answer being given to this clincher she went on. "We shall dine at half-past seven; go into society; balls, I suppose, every night; we shall be presented at court, of course; your father will give up his poky farm, and we shall buy an estate somewhere. Ghrimes will go on managing the bank, though I must say the salary he draws seems ridiculous. Pictures again: I suppose we must patronize Art. My dear, it will be very hard work at first, but you may trust your mother to do the best for you; and when my girls do marry—if they marry with my approbation—" giving a glance at Grace, "they may depend upon my generosity."

"I am going to marry Frank Melliship," said Grace, quickly. Lucy said nothing. It was a constant trial to the poor girls to bear this grating upon their nerves; the more trying because they had to disguise it even from each other, and because it was so essentially different to that straightforward, honest simplicity, and even delicacy, of their father. There are some men without the slightest refinement in manner, not at all the men to be invited to dinner, who are yet the most perfect and absolute masters of good breeding, inasmuch as they never offend in their speech, and go delicately about among the tender corns of their friends. Such was John Heathcote. To him the doctor communicated the three or four lines which Dick had forced him to write. John took them to lawyer Battiscombe, in hopes that they would give his girls a claim to the estate which else his wife would have. What manner of life his would be if Lydia Heathcote got it all, he trembled to think. No use; the money was all his wife's. Battiscombe told him of Polly; he explained the law of the land as regards married women's property; and advised him as to the carrying out of Dick's intentions, in the spirit, if not in the letter.

Thus fortified, Farmer John felt himself strong enough to fight his battles, and began to put his foot down.

He let his wife run on till she was fairly exhausted, on the subject of improvements and changes, then he quietly asserted himself:—

"When you've done making your plans, Lydia, you may as well consult me, and ascertain what I am going to do."

"John Heathcote, who is the owner of the Mortiboy property?" asked Lydia with withering contempt.

"I am. Your husband is."

She gasped with astonishment.

"Do you mean to tell me, John Heathcote, that I am not the possessor of everything."

"Certainly not. All the personalty is mine absolutely.

All the realty is mine so long as you live. When you die, you may bequeath it to whom you will."

"Is that the law? Do you dare to assert that the law of England allows that? And they call this a Christian and a Protestant country."

"Let us understand one another, Lydia. We are plain people, and intend to remain so. You and I are old, and unfit for the society to which we were not brought up——"

"John—I unfit. Pray, do you forget that I was seven years at the best and most select boarding-school in Market Basing?"

"I dare say they finished you very well for a farmer's wife, such as you've been for five-and-twenty years. No, no; we are too old and too wise to change, Lyddy. No town life for us. I mean to go on exactly the same."

"You imagine, John, that I am going to consent to live like that, with all the money coming in? Do you call yourself a churchman, John? Do you know that it's your duty— your positive duty—to keep up your station? I, for one, shall not consent. So there."

"You need not, Lyddy," said her husband, quietly. "If you refuse, you must live elsewhere. And I don't know where you'll find the money. Don't be downcast, wife. A little extra finery you can have, if you like, and spend anything in reason, consistent with your position. I'm a farmer. The girls can spend the money when they marry. Another thing: whatever Dick intended to do, it is our duty to do. Now read that."

He put into his wife's hands Dick's last few words.

"Poor Dick! His last wishes. We must obey them."

"Papa," said Grace, eagerly, "you are really going to do all that Dick intended should be done?"

"All, Grace. Everything."

"Then consult George Ghrimes about another thing, papa. Ask him what Dick was going to do about him; and—ask, papa——"

"If there's secrets going on, I suppose I had better go," said her mother. "John Heathcote, when I married you, little did I think that I was marrying a man capable of sheltering himself behind the law, in order that he might continue in his low and grovelling position."

John Heathcote laughed. It was never his plan to argue with his wife, else the argument would have been perennial.

The next day, being three days after the funeral, Mrs. Heathcote thought she might as well make a visit to Derngate and the villa, and take possession of the things there, whatever there might be to have.

The garden door was open, and the front door was open.

She walked into the dining-doom—no one there—and into Dick's smoking-room.

In his easy chair, in deepest widow's weeds, with a handkerchief to her eyes, sat Polly.

It was her greatest *coup*, though it failed. She learned the death of Dick from the papers, and instantly made up her mind what to do. Without going through the formality of acquainting Captain Bowker with her intentions, she bought a widow's cap and crape, got into the train, and came to Market Basing. She would get her confession back first, and then, after laying hands on everything portable, would come to such terms as could, in a short space of time, and before the thing was found out, be obtained.

"Mary!" cried Mrs. Heathcote, "what is the meaning of this?"

"Mrs. Richard Mortiboy, Mrs. Heathcote, I should say Cousin Heathcote," said Polly, wiping her eyes again. "Oh, what a dreadful thing it is to lose your husband, and him but just returned from foreign parts and savages."

"Mary! woman! you are mad!"

She shook her head, and sobbed the faster.

"Poor Dick! I shall never see his like again. Mrs. Heathcote, won't you sit down? It's my house, and all Dick's money is mine; but we sha'n't fall out. Families ought to live peaceful. Sit down, young ladies."

Grace knew that she was speaking the truth, but silence was best. They remained standing. Polly still gave from time to time a convulsive heave, by which she meant to express the poignancy of her sorrow.

"Perhaps you will explain yourself, Mary Tresler," said her late mistress.

"Ho! there's no objection of explaining. None in the world, Mrs. Heathcote, Cousin Heathcote. I've been married to Dick Mortiboy for twelve years and more, married in London, at St. Pancridge's Church, where you may go yourself and look. And now I'm come to claim my rights, as in duty bound, and an honest woman should. Don't think I'm bearing any malice for old times, Mrs. Heathcote, though you always were a screw, and you know it. It isn't the place now nor the time, when I'm weeping over the last bier of my poor dear lost Dick, to throw your cold mutton and your broken victuals in your teeth; no, nor your eight pounds a year, paid to your cousin's lawful wife, nor your flannels at Christmas. No; let's be friends all round, I say. I only come up this morning, and here I'm going to stick. Perhaps, as you are here, you'll tell me where Dick's safe is, where he keeps his papers, because that's mine, that is, and there's something particular of my own that I want back again."

It was awkward for Polly, in the execution of her grand *coup*, that she had no conception where the safe was, in which she knew that her written confession lay, nor indeed what a safe was like when she saw one. She had a notion that it was a wooden box, kept probably in his bedroom, the breaking open of which would put her in possession of the dangerous document. But she could find no wooden box, though she had searched the whole house through, and she naturally began to feel uneasy. Where had Dick put it? Mrs. Heathcote was speechless. This, indeed, was a calamity far worse than the obstinacy of her husband. That the perfidious Dick should actually have had a wife, her own servant, and have said nothing to anybody, was a thing so utterly beyond the scope of her experience, that her brain seemed to be wandering. Her lips parted, but she said nothing.

"Oh, it's a dreadful thing," Polly went on, "to be a widow. And me so young; and such a good husband. I hope you may never experience it, Mrs. Heathcote; never, Cousin Heathcote. It's a dreadful thing, and money won't make up for it. What's money to the loss of my Dick?"

"Grace," said Mrs. Heathcote, "am I in my senses? Is this woman mad?"

"Woman!" cried the bereaved one, starting up in a violent rage. "No more woman than you are. How dare you call me woman? For two pins, Mrs. Heathcote, I'd scratch out your eyes. You and your cold mutton, indeed, and no followers allowed. But I'll comb you down yet, you see if I don't."

The door opened, and Mr. Ghrimes appeared. In his hand a bundle of papers.

"Oh," he said, coolly, seeing Polly, "Joe, the stable-boy, told me you were here. Now what may you be wanting in this house? No nonsense, you know, because it won't do with me."

"Mr. Ghrimes, my clerk," said Polly, "my servant and the

manager of my bank; don't be insolent, young man, or I'll give you warning, and send you about your business, sharp enough; so down on your knees, if *you* please. Other people can manage a bank as well as you." All the same, her heart misgave her at the sight of the calm cold man of business, who evidently knew exactly what he was saying, and was not a whit moved at her brave words.

"We will talk about discharging afterwards. At present, you had better go yourself. Yes; I mean that you must go, and that at once. Any insults to these ladies will be severely punished. Now go, or I will speak more plainly."

"I sha'n't go." Polly sat herself down in the armchair, and spread out her skirts in a very determined manner.

"You won't? Very well." Mr. Ghrimes stepped outside. Voices were heard, and steps in the passage, and Polly's cheek visibly blanched.

He came back. Behind him were Mr. Battiscombe, Farmer John, and a third person, a stranger to the rest, at sight of whom, Polly sprang up and sat down again, as if she had received a mortal blow. He was a middle aged man, with a red beard, and blue eyes, and a nervous hesitating manner, who came with the others half unwillingly; no other, in fact, than Captain Bowker.

"Now, madam," said Mr. Ghrimes, "who is this gentleman?"

"Oh," said Polly, "I'll take it out of you for this. Only you wait."

"Let me explain," said the lawyer. "We suspected your little game, you see, and we took our steps—had you watched, followed you to the station, found where you were going to, and brought Captain Bowker, *your husband*, down after you by the next train."

"Her husband!" cried Mrs. Heathcote. "You wicked, wicked woman! Mr. Battiscombe, what is the extreme penalty which the law exacts for this offence? Is it twenty years, or is it fifty? I forget at this moment. I know they used to hang for it in the good old days."

"What's more," said the captain in a husky voice, "they've told me your whole history, and I find I can be free whenever I like. So, Polly, you may go your own way. By the Lord, if you come near me again, I *will* be free, and you shall be in a prison. I'm going back to Skimp's. You shan't say I hid myself. There I stay—find me out there if you dare."

"You calf of a sea captain, do you think I want to come with you? I despise you too much," said Polly grandly.

"And her mother in the workhouse!" ejaculated Mrs. Heathcote, as if the fact had an important bearing on the case.
"Had you not better go now?" asked Ghrimes. "It will be well for you to go by the next train; it leaves in twenty minutes. I will drive you to the station."

Polly removed the white cap of widowhood, and laid it on the table.

"You may have it, Mrs. Heathcote, mum. Keep it for my sake, and be very careful about your cold pork. Go on locking up the key of the beer cellar, and don't let the maids have no followers, then you'll go on being as much beloved as you always have been much beloved, if you go on, that is, as you always have been a going on. Good-bye, young ladies. Miss Grace, I'd do you a good turn if I could, because you deserve it, and you know why: you was always the best of the bunch. Good-bye, Miss Lucy; eat and drink a bit more, and don't read too many tracts, and you'll be as pretty as your sister some day, but never so good. She knows how to hold her tongue, she does. One good thing," she concluded, looking at her husband with a gaze of concentrated hatred, which caused his knees to shake beneath him, "one good thing, one gracious good thing, I'm rid of a poor-spirited barrel of salt sea pork. I sha'n't see you no more. Ugh! you and your verses! If I get home first, I'll BURN 'em all."

"You can't, Polly," said her husband meekly; "I've got 'em in my coat-tail pocket, every one, with a new 'Ode to Resignation,' which I composed when you were asleep."

She passed out, holding her head high. Ghrimes followed her, and drove her to the station.

CHAPTER THE FIFTIETH.

T is Sunday, nearly a fortnight after Dick's death. The Heathcotes, returned from church, are on the lawn in front of the house. The noise of wheels on the private road leading to the farm is heard, an unusual thing, unless when poor Dick Mortiboy drove over on Sunday.

It was a town "fly,"—one of those delightful vehicles which are found at country stations, which have all the bad qualities of the London growler without any of its good ones, always supposing that it has good ones. It drove up to the door, and a girl got down and looked timidly at the group on the lawn. A pretty girl, a wonderfully pretty girl, pale faced, bright eyed, with regular if rather commonplace features, and a great mass of rich brown hair, neatly dressed in a coloured stuff frock, brown jacket, and a bundle of wild flowers in her hand. She could not resist the temptation of stopping the fly, to pick them from the hedge. She opened the gate, and walked in, colouring painfully.

Mr. Heathcote slowly walked down the gravel path to meet her.

"Mr. Heathcote?" she asked. "Oh! I don't want you — I want Miss Grace Heathcote. Which is Miss Grace Heathcote?"

"I am Grace Heathcote. Pray what can I do for you?"

Patty—it was Patty Silver—looked at her for a few minutes, and then, clasping her hands together, burst into tears.

For she contrasted herself with the girl who stood before her: herself, common, half educated, badly dressed, with this presence of a lady, glorious in her beauty and her grace.

The unconscious rival looked at her in wonder, but did not speak.

"Let me speak somewhere alone with you, Miss Heathcote," said Patty, "quite alone. I have something very important to tell you."

"Papa, I am going to take this young lady to the drawing-room. Do not wait dinner for me. Come with me, please."

She sailed across the lawn, taking poor little Patty after her, into the drawing-room, where Mrs. Heathcote heard the door shut and locked.

"John," she cried, putting her head out of the window, "pray who is that young woman?"

"I don't know," said John.

"John, if you were half a husband, to say nothing of a father, you would have known that it was your duty to bring her to me first. Secrets, indeed; I will have no secrets in my house, I can tell you. Grace, let me in this moment."

"Is that you, mamma?" answered her daughter, in the clear resolute tones which always made her mother quail and give way, "Is that you, mamma? Go on with dinner; do not wait for me; I shall be ready presently."

Mrs. Heathcote knocked once more at the door, but faintly, and finding no attention bestowed upon her, retreated again.

Dinner was served, but Grace did not return. So they sat

down without her, John Heathcote alone being able to take his meal with the usual Sabbath enjoyment.

"I believe, John," said his wife, "that you would go on eating if the world was on fire."

"Well, Lyddy, if my not eating could put out the fire, I would stop. If not, I dare say I should eat so long as I was hungry, unless the fire was burning my toes."

"John—you are blasphemous. On Sunday, too, and your daughter locked up with a stranger, talking secrets!"

"What if she is? Grace's secrets are not mine. There can't be any harm in Grace's secrets, poor girl, and she's welcome to a bushel of them. Something to do with Frank, I expect. That reminds me, Lydia. A week before his death, Dick had a deed of partnership drawn out, but not executed, between himself, Frank Melliship, and George Ghrimes."

"Not executed," said Lydia.

"No—but the intention was the same. I have had it drawn out again between myself, Frank Melliship, and George Ghrimes, on poor Dick's plan. I am going to take them both into partnership with me."

"John Heathcote," said his wife, "it is a dreadful thing, a really dreadful thing to see the way you are going on. If this partnership is carried into effect, I shall feel it my duty, as a wife and a mother—to—to——"

"What will you do, Lydia?"

"To call in London doctors, and have your brain examined for Softening. It *must* be Softening, John."

John put down his knife and fork, and laughed till the tears ran down his face. The idea of his brain softening was so novel, so unexpected, so good, that he laughed again and again. He was not in the least angry.

"You always would have your joke, Lyddy," he said, with a choke. "Softening. Ho! ho! ho! And you've always called me the hardest man you know. But I'm glad you approve of the partnership. Very glad. Because, though I *am* the administrator of all this money, I always feel that I'm doing it for you, Lyddy. It's well you are a good-hearted woman—very well. Some women would have made a fuss, and objected. Not you. That's what I like about you, wife. You never object when it's no good, and you're always ready to back me up when I'm doing what's right."

I have never been able to make up my mind, whether this speech of John's was stupid, or whether it was sarcastic. I fancy it was the latter, and that John was by no means so simple as his wife thought him.

"Now," said Grace, in the drawing-room, "sit down, and te'l me what you came to tell me."

She sat on the sofa and Patty on the easy chair by her side. The girl was lost in contemplating the length to which civilization can go in furnishing a room; the bright draperies and the dainty appointments. She looked up hesitatingly.

"Do all ladies have rooms like this?"

"Yes, I suppose so. Why? There is nothing very grand in this room, is there?"

Patty sighed. "You should see mine," she said, "and you would know what I mean.—Miss Heathcote, I came to-day from London. I come from Mr. Melliship."

"From Frank?"

"From Mr. Frank Melliship. He does not know I'm come. Let me tell my story from the beginning. He lives with father. So we know him, you see. Last Monday week I saw him reading a letter, and looking bright and happy. You know, miss, he'd been terribly pulled down and worried of late. He told me he had got good news—the best of news— and he went out, and up the street I saw him walking as if the ground was made of india-rubber. Then he came home, and sang all over the house like a lark. Next day, Tuesday that was, he said to me, ' Patty,'—he always calls me Patty, miss, because father does, I suppose,—' Patty, I sha'n't write my letter till to-morrow, because I'm waiting to find out how to answer the most generous man in the world.' And he pleased himself all day drawing pictures—such pictures—I've got them all. On Wednesday, I went in at half-past two. He had his writing-table before him, and he had the *Echo* in his hand. ' Patty,' he said, ' he's dead—and she is lost to me!'"

Grace turned colour. "Go on," she said.

"' She's lost to me!' Then he told me all about you, Miss Heathcote; how he loved you, and you loved him; and how Mr. Mortiboy was going to make him rich, so that you could marry, but he died and could not. And then he told me that he could never go to you now, because you were rich and he was a beggar. This was last Wednesday week. He told me with the tears running down his handsome face, where you lived, and all about it. . . . Well, Miss Heathcote, he's been getting lower and lower ever since; he doesn't eat, he doesn't sing, he never draws, he sits at the window with his head in his hands, and never speaks at all. I couldn't bear to see it; so I bought a railway guide, and found out the Sunday trains, and made father give me money to pay my return ticket, and came down here to tell you all about it. Miss Heathcote, it can't be that you're going to throw him over because you are rich? It can't be that you don't love him any more because he is poor? Don't tell me that—don't let him go on killing himself. Don't be proud. Ladies are mostly too proud, I think. And so are gentlemen. He will never come to you. Oh, Miss Heathcote, if I loved—if he loved me—and I was rich, I would go to him and kiss him, and say, Frank, what does it matter whether you have any money or not?—I am only a poor girl, Miss Heathcote, and no education, and get my living in a way I am almost ashamed to say—I'm a trapeze girl —but I should be too proud—oh, I should be too proud to let my love die when a word would save him."

"What is your name?" asked Grace, the tears running down her face.

"Patty Silver. I am only the girl that performs on the trapeze, at the Music Hall. I do it with my father, though."

"Patty Silver—you love Frank Melliship, yourself."

Patty covered her face with her hands.

"I do—I do—" she murmured. "Forgive me, Miss Heathcote. He never looked at me. I let myself love him without thinking. Who could help loving him? But he only loves you. He thinks of you. He draws your portrait always. Me? As if a gentleman like Mr. Melliship would think of me. But I loved him—oh! me—me—I loved him, and I love him always."

Grace knelt down, and took Patty's face in her hands, and looked at it.

"Poor Patty! Poor little girl! You will get over your love some day. Your trial is hard. What shall I do for you, for the joy and gladness you have brought me? I knew he would be faithful; but you know—girls are so—there were times when I doubted. Now wait a moment: you will see that I am not too proud, and not so cold a fine lady as you think me, perhaps. Wait here for one moment only."

She went into the dining-room, where her father was just opening a bottle of port.

"Papa, come into the other room with me."

"More secrets, of course," said Mrs. Heathcote.

John Heathcote, with a sigh, followed his daughter.

"Papa, this young lady comes to me, unknown to Frank, to tell me that he is ill and miserable. He got a letter from Dick the day before his death, offering him a partnership in the bank. Then he saw the death in the paper, and has been prostrated ever since. What ought we to do?"

"First thing, let him know that he is to be a partner. Make him a new offer."

"You must do that, yourself. What next?"

"Why, we must go and find him out as soon as we can, and bring him back here."

"What a good father it is!" said his daughter, wheedling him. "He always says the wisest things, and the kindest things. We must find him. Patty here will take us to him; you must tell him—you must go yourself; we must find him at once—we will go together—at once—to-day, by the afternoon train. We will go back with Patty—will we not?"

Here she gave way, and fell upon Patty's neck, crying and laughing. Lucy came running up stairs. Her mother stayed below.

"They may manage their own secrets themselves," she said, taking a glass of port with a bitter feeling.

"Lucy, my dear. My carpet bag with things for the night, and your sister's, too. Pack up quickly. Grace, take this young lady with you, and have some dinner, and give her some." He went down, and found his wife in a sour and crabbed frame.

"Lyddy, my dear," he said, with a cheerful smile, "I've got good news for you; we've found Frank Melliship. I'm going up to town with Grace to bring him back. He's all right. We'll marry them in a month, and you shall dance at their wedding, my girl. Give me a glass of wine."

He drank off hers, without an apology. "Oh! I forgot to tell you—keep this a great secret—I had a talk with Lord Hunslope yesterday about things. He hinted that though Grace would not have Lord Launton, perhaps his lordship would have better luck with Lucy. Eh! Lyddy, what do you think of a coronet for your girl?"

"Lucy, dear girl! she always was my own girl—took after my family and me," said Mrs. Heathcote, mollified. "Grace was always a Heathcote. Well, well, you must have your own way, I suppose. Come back to-morrow, John, if you can. Dear Lucy!—how she would become a coronet. After all, John, I hardly think poor dear Grace is quite the woman to be a countess. There's a little too much independence about her; too much of the Heathcote about her; not quite subdued enough in her manner. She will do admirably as a banker's wife, no doubt. Is the young person properly looked after?"

"Grace will do that."

"Then sit down, John, for five minutes and talk. Don't be racing up and down the stairs after dinner. At your time of life, too. You might get apoplexy, and go off suddenly, like poor Mr. Hawthorne, only three weeks ago. You think the earl means what he says?"

"The earl is straightforward enough, at any rate. He is poor and we are rich. Think on what we ought to give Lucy if it comes off. Don't say anything to the girl. She's as timid as a fawn, and would only run away and hide herself. But think what we ought to give, and tell me. The earl—whisper now—owes the bank fifty thousand pounds. There, wife; I've given you something to think over while I am gone."

Mrs. Heathcote kissed Grace with a really maternal affection again, whispering: "Bring him back, dear; you have your mother's approbation now. But you must forgive me for being a little disappointed before, you know. He was always my favourite, Frank, after poor Dick. As for Lord Launton, I forgive you. And no doubt it is all for the best. Give Frank my best love, dear—and bless you."

* * * * * *

Frank was sitting in his little room alone and miserable. Mr. Silver was gone off to chapel. There was nobody in the house. A cab came rumbling along the street, and stopped at the door. He did not hear it.

Patty opened the door with her latch-key, and led her guests upstairs. He looked up as they came into the room. It was Grace, with her father.

"Frank," whispered Grace, as he caught her in his arms, "you were too proud to come to us, so we have come to you."

"Not to let you go again, my boy," said her father, shaking him by the hand.

"Never again, Frank, never again. We part no more."

Love and joy in that little room. Upstairs, Patty lying on her bed, trying to stop the tears and sobs that shake her frame. The prophet was right. She was even as the daughter of Jephthah, doomed to lament her loneliness among the mountains all her days.

ENVOY.

THREE farewell tableaux. The first in Paris. It is at St. Cloud, when, close by the ruins of the château, in a small, close room, they are trying the Communist prisoners in the winter of last year. A long table, or a platform, behind which are sitting a dozen officers, whose cold, stern faces bode little mercy to the poor creatures brought before them. One by one they are brought up to receive their sentence. They are cowed by imprisonment and suffering; they are ragged, starved, miserable. Mostly, they receive their sentences, which are comparatively light, with a kind of gratitude, because they know the worst. There is one exception. He is a thin man, with keen, bright eyes. His cheeks and chin are covered with the ragged beard of three months' growth. His black hair is thick and matted; his clothes, such as they are, scarcely hold together upon him. He alone of the prisoners stands up before his judges with an air of defiance. Accused at first of being taken with arms in his hand, he is now, on further evidence, charged with complicity in the murder of the archbishop. He has neither boots nor shoes; a rag is round his neck; he shivers in the cold December air; but his hands are delicate, shapely, and white—the hands of a gentleman. He is asked his name and profession. He shrugs his shoulders and spreads out his hands.

"Bah! It is the hundredth time. I am tired of it. Let us finish. My name is Lafleur. I was in the ranks of the Commune. Did I love the cause of the Communist? No more than yourselves. Do I love your cause? Perhaps as much as you do. Did I assist at the execution of the archbishop? I did. Now, M. le Président your sentence."

It came swiftly enough.

In the cold grey of the morning, he stands against a wall with his hands in his pockets, a cigar in his mouth, and a mocking smile on his lips. No word of repentance? None. Of scoffing or blasphemy? None. The roll of the rifles for a moment, and the next, a dead man falls, face downward, on the ground. He could bear most things that fate had to bring; but the misery, the filth, the degradation, the starvation, the cold, rags, famine, evil companionship, to which the Versaillists have condemned their unhappy enemies, were too much for him. So he confessed—threw up the cards—and was sentenced.

Down at the docks there is a certain particularly dirty and muddy crossing, which requires in all weathers, so deeply rooted is its delight in mud, the constant attendance of a broom. It is wielded by a boy, small and thin, but strong and healthy. He answers to the name of Bill. On sunny days he is accompanied by a friend, older than himself, with a curiously wizened and lined countenance, like that of an old man. He does not work himself, but sits in the sunshine on the steps of a door which is never opened. Here the cold winds come not, and there is a southern aspect.

"Thoozy," says the boy, "it's more than a year since Uncle Dick died."

"So it is, old chap, so it is. Poor Uncle Dick! But we've done pretty well since then, haven't we, old chap? What's the whole duty of a boy, Bill, as he used to learn you?"

"Never prig, never tell lies—" he runs off Dick's ten commandments on his fingers, just as he had been taught.

"Right you are, Bill. Go away from England. Yes, we'll go some day, old chap, when we've saved a little money, and you've got stronger. Uncle Dick was a good sort, Bill, I can tell you. We shan't meet no more Uncle Dicks in the world. Let's remember all he used to say, and act on it, Bill, my boy."

Another scene. It is evening: three people are standing in the moonlight, in the square, place, or principal open street of Market Basing, before a newly-erected statue, unveiled that morning with much ceremony, bands of music, and many speeches. They are Frank and Grace, with them Patty Silver.

"I am glad it is like Dick," said Grace, with a sigh. "I couldn't bear that our noble Dick should look ugly and unlike. I'll tell you about him, Patty, some day, when we have it all to ourselves, and you want to learn a long story about a good and a great-hearted man. Let us go in now. I wanted to see it when all the people were gone, and have a little cry all to myself over it."

Patty is staying with them. She has given up her profession, and lives with her father; he preaches every evening, and will probably some day be reverenced as the founder of a new sect. Life is made easy for him by Mr. Edrupp, who lingers still, and by Grace Melliship, Frank's wife. Patty will never marry. To have loved a gentleman, not to have been loved by one, has been an education for the girl. She can never love one of her own class. But she is not unhappy, and among the poor people of her neighbourhood finds plenty to do in the way of help and advice. And sometimes Grace gets her to come down to Market Basing, and stay quietly with them till the roses come back to her cheeks, and she can return to her work, a life of unknown and unprofessional self-denial and toil.

Last time I was at Market Basing I made a curious discovery. Looking at Dick's statue, I read the inscription. The usual flourish of trumpets was on the front, setting forth his unblemished moral character, his philanthropy, his generosity, his great schemes for benefiting the human race. On one side was a passage in Greek:—

"Πολλῶν ἀνθρώπων ἴδεν ἄστεα καὶ νοὸν ἔγνω."

This was the rector's doing.

On the other side was a line of English:—

"Write me as one who loves his fellow-men."

This was Ghrimes's.

On the back, right in the corner, as if put there furtively, in quite small letters, "Rev. xiii. 4." I heard afterwards that Lucy Heathcote, or, to give her new name, Lady Launton, chose a text, which, not being approved of, she privately instructed the sculptor to insert where it could not be seen, anxious, good little soul, that religion should have some part. The sculptor put it in, but made a mistake as to the reference —a most unfortunate one, as I found on looking out the text to which attention is thus publicly called. By great good luck, nobody but Lady Launton and myself has found it out.

[May, 1883.

CHATTO & WINDUS'S
LIST OF BOOKS.

About.—The Fellah: An Egyptian Novel. By EDMOND ABOUT. Translated by Sir RANDAL ROBERTS. Post 8vo, illustrated boards, 2s.; cloth limp, 2s. 6d.

Adams (W. Davenport), Works by:
A Dictionary of the Drama. Being a comprehensive Guide to the Plays, Playwrights, Players, and Playhouses of the United Kingdom and America, from the Earliest to the Present Times. Crown 8vo, half-bound, 12s. 6d. [*In preparation.*

Latter-Day Lyrics. Edited by W. DAVENPORT ADAMS. Post 8vo, cloth limp, 2s. 6d.

Quips and Quiddities. Selected by W. DAVENPORT ADAMS. Post 8vo, cloth limp, 2s. 6d.

Advertising, A History of, from the Earliest Times. Illustrated by Anecdotes, Curious Specimens, and Notices of Successful Advertisers. By HENRY SAMPSON. Crown 8vo, with Coloured Frontispiece and Illustrations, cloth gilt, 7s. 6d.

Agony Column (The) of "The Times," from 1800 to 1870. Edited, with an Introduction, by ALICE CLAY. Post 8vo, cloth limp, 2s. 6d.

Aide (Hamilton), Works by:
Carr of Carrlyon. Post 8vo, illustrated boards, 2s.
Confidences. Post 8vo, illustrated boards, 2s.

Alexander (Mrs.).—Maid, Wife, or Widow? A Romance. By Mrs. ALEXANDER. Post 8vo, illustrated boards, 2s.; cr. 8vo, cloth extra, 3s. 6d.

Allen (Grant), Works by:
Colin Clout's Calendar. Crown 8vo, cloth extra, 6s.
The Evolutionist at Large. Crown 8vo, cloth extra, 6s.
Vignettes from Nature. Crown 8vo, cloth extra, 6s.

Architectural Styles, A Handbook of. Translated from the German of A. ROSENGARTEN, by W. COLLETT-SANDARS. Crown 8vo, cloth extra, with 639 Illustrations, 7s. 6d.

Art (The) of Amusing: A Collection of Graceful Arts, Games, Tricks, Puzzles, and Charades. By FRANK BELLEW. With 300 Illustrations. Cr. 8vo, cloth extra, 4s. 6d.

Artemus Ward:
Artemus Ward's Works: The Works of CHARLES FARRER BROWNE, better known as ARTEMUS WARD. With Portrait and Facsimile. Crown 8vo, cloth extra, 7s. 6d.
Artemus Ward's Lecture on the Mormons. With 32 Illustrations. Edited, with Preface, by EDWARD P. HINGSTON. Crown 8vo, 6d.
The Genial Showman: Life and Adventures of Artemus Ward. By EDWARD P. HINGSTON. With a Frontispiece. Crown 8vo, cloth extra, 3s. 6d.

BOOKS PUBLISHED BY

Ashton (John), Works by:
A History of the Chap-Books of the Eighteenth Century. With nearly 400 Illustrations, engraved in facsimile of the originals. Crown 8vo, cloth extra, 7s. 6d.

Social Life in the Reign of Queen Anne. Taken from Original Sources. With nearly One Hundred Illustrations. New and cheaper Edition, crown 8vo, cloth extra, 7s. 6d.

Humour, Wit, and Satire of the Seventeenth Century. With nearly 100 Illustrations. Crown 8vo, cloth extra, 7s. 6d. One Hundred large-paper copies (only seventy-five of them for sale) will be carefully printed on hand-made paper, crown 4to, parchment boards, price 42s. Early application must be made for these. [*In preparation.*

Ballad History (The) of England
By W. C. BENNETT. Post 8vo, cloth limp, 2s.

Balzac's "Comedie Humaine"
and its Author. With Translations by H. H. WALKER. Post 8vo, cloth limp, 2s. 6d.

Bankers, A Handbook of London; together with Lists of Bankers from 1677. By F. G. HILTON PRICE. Crown 8vo, cloth extra, 7s. 6d.

Bardsley (Rev. C.W.), Works by:
English Surnames: Their Sources and Significations. Crown 8vo, cloth extra, 7s. 6d.

Curiosities of Puritan Nomenclature. Crown 8vo, cloth extra, 7s. 6d.

Bartholomew Fair, Memoirs of. By HENRY MORLEY. A New Edition, with One Hundred Illustrations. Crown 8vo, cloth extra, 7s. 6d.

Beauchamp. — Grantley Grange: A Novel. By SHELSLEY BEAUCHAMP. Post 8vo, illustrated boards, 2s.

Beautiful Pictures by British Artists: A Gathering of Favourites from our Picture Galleries. In Two Series. All engraved on Steel in the highest style of Art. Edited, with Notices of the Artists, by SYDNEY ARMYTAGE, M.A. Imperial 4to, cloth extra, gilt and gilt edges, 21s. per Vol.

Bechstein. — As Pretty as Seven, and other German Stories. Collected by LUDWIG BECHSTEIN. With Additional Tales by the Brothers GRIMM, and 100 Illusts. by RICHTER. Small 4to, green and gold, 6s. 6d.; gilt edges, 7s. 6d.

Beerbohm. — Wanderings in Patagonia; or, Life among the Ostrich Hunters. By JULIUS BEERBOHM. With Illusts. Crown 8vo, cloth extra, 3s. 6d.

Belgravia for 1883. One Shilling Monthly, Illustrated.—"Maid of Athens," JUSTIN MCCARTHY'S New Serial Story, Illustrated by FRED. BARNARD, was begun in the JANUARY Number of BELGRAVIA, which Number contained also the First Portion of a Story in Three Parts, by OUIDA, entitled "Frescoes;" the continuation of WILKIE COLLINS's Novel, "Heart and Science;" a further instalment of Mrs. ALEXANDER'S Novel, "The Admiral's Ward;" and other Matters of Interest.
⁎ Now ready, the Volume for Nov. 1882 to FEBRUARY 1883 (*which includes* the BELGRAVIA ANNUAL), *cloth extra, gilt edges,* 7s. 6d.; *Cases for binding Volumes,* 2s. *each.*

Belgravia Holiday Number, written by the well-known Authors who have been so long associated with the Magazine, will be published as usual in July.

Besant (Walter) and James Rice, Novels by. Each in post 8vo, illustrated boards, 2s.; cloth limp, 2s. 6d.; or crown 8vo, cloth extra, 3s. 6d.

Ready-Money Mortiboy
With Harp and Crown.
This Son of Vulcan.
My Little Girl.
The Case of Mr. Lucraft.
The Golden Butterfly.
By Celia's Arbour.
The Monks of Thelema.
'Twas in Trafalgar's Bay.
The Seamy Side.
The Ten Years' Tenant.
The Chaplain of the Fleet.

Besant (Walter), Novels by:
All Sorts and Conditions of Men: An Impossible Story. With Illustrations by FRED. BARNARD. Crown 8vo, cloth extra, 3s. 6d.

The Captains' Room, &c. Three Vols., crown 8vo, 31s. 6d.

CHATTO & WINDUS, PICCADILLY. 3

Birthday Book.—The Starry Heavens: A Poetical Birthday Book. Square 8vo, handsomely bound in cloth, 3s. 6d. [*In preparation.*

Birthday Flowers: Their Language and Legends. By W. J. GORDON. Beautifully Illustrated in Colours by VIOLA BOUGHTON. In illuminated cover, crown 4to, 6s. [*Shortly.*

Blackburn's (Henry) Art Handbooks. Demy 8vo, Illustrated, uniform in size for binding.

Academy Notes, separate years, from 1875 to 1882, each 1s.

Academy Notes, 1883. With Illustrations. 1s.

Academy Notes, 1875-79. Complete in One Volume, with nearly 600 Illustrations in Facsimile. Demy 8vo, cloth limp, 6s.

Grosvenor Notes, 1877. 6d.

Grosvenor Notes, separate years, from 1878 to 1882, each 1s.

Grosvenor Notes, 1883. With Illustrations. 1s.

Grosvenor Notes, 1877-82. With upwards of 300 Illustrations. Demy 8vo, cloth limp, 6s.

Pictures at South Kensington. With 70 Illustrations. 1s.

The English Pictures at the National Gallery. 114 Illustrations. 1s.

The Old Masters at the National Gallery. 128 Illustrations. 1s. 6d.

A Complete Illustrated Catalogue to the National Gallery. With Notes by H. BLACKBURN, and 242 Illusts. Demy 8vo, cloth limp, 3s.

The Paris Salon, 1883. With 400 full-page Illustrations. Edited by F. G. DUMAS. (English Edition.) Demy 8vo, 3s.

At the Paris Salon. Sixteen large Plates, printed in facsimile of the Artists' Drawings, in two tints. Edited by F. G. DUMAS. Large folio, 1s. [*Immediately.*

The Art Annual. Edited by F. G. DUMAS. With 250 full-page Illusts. Demy 8vo, 3s. 6d.

Blake (William): Etchings from his Works. By W. B. SCOTT. With descriptive Text. Folio, half-bound boards, India Proofs, 21s.

Boccaccio's Decameron; or, Ten Days' Entertainment. Translated into English, with an Introduction by THOMAS WRIGHT, F.S.A. With Portrait, and STOTHARD's beautiful Copperplates. Cr. 8vo, cloth extra, gilt, 7s. 6d.

Bowers'(G.) Hunting Sketches: Canters in Crampshire. Oblong 4to, half-bound boards, 21s.

Leaves from a Hunting Journal. Coloured in facsimile of the originals. Oblong 4to, half-bound, 21s.

Boyle (Frederick), Works by:
Camp Notes: Stories of Sport and Adventure in Asia, Africa, and America. Crown 8vo, cloth extra, 3s. 6d.; post 8vo, illustrated bds., 2s.

Savage Life. Crown 8vo, cloth extra, 3s. 6d.; post 8vo, illustrated bds., 2s.

Brand's Observations on Popular Antiquities, chiefly Illustrating the Origin of our Vulgar Customs, Ceremonies, and Superstitions. With the Additions of Sir HENRY ELLIS. Crown 8vo, cloth extra, gilt, with numerous Illustrations, 7s. 6d.

Bret Harte, Works by:
Bret Harte's Collected Works. Arranged and Revised by the Author. Complete in Five Vols., crown 8vo, cloth extra, 6s. each.

Vol. I. COMPLETE POETICAL AND DRAMATIC WORKS. With Steel Plate Portrait, and an Introduction by the Author.

Vol. II. EARLIER PAPERS—LUCK OF ROARING CAMP, and other Sketches —BOHEMIAN PAPERS — SPANISH AND AMERICAN LEGENDS.

Vol. III. TALES OF THE ARGONAUTS —EASTERN SKETCHES.

Vol. IV. GABRIEL CONROY.

Vol. V. STORIES — CONDENSED NOVELS, &c.

The Select Works of Bret Harte, in Prose and Poetry. With Introductory Essay by J. M. BELLEW, Portrait of the Author, and 50 Illustrations. Crown 8vo, cloth extra, 7s. 6d.

Gabriel Conroy: A Novel. Post 8vo, illustrated boards, 2s.

An Heiress of Red Dog, and other Stories. Post 8vo, illustrated boards, 2s.; cloth limp, 2s. 6d.

The Twins of Table Mountain. Fcap. 8vo, picture cover, 1s.; crown 8vo, cloth extra, 3s. 6d.

The Luck of Roaring Camp, and other Sketches. Post 8vo, illustrated boards, 2s.

Jeff Briggs's Love Story. Fcap 8vo, picture cover, 1s.; cloth extra, 2s. 6d.

Flip. Post 8vo, illustrated boards, 2s.; cloth limp, 2s. 6d.

BOOKS PUBLISHED BY

Brewer (Rev. Dr.), Works by:
The Reader's Handbook of Allusions, References, Plots, and Stories. Third Edition, revised throughout, with a New Appendix, containing a COMPLETE ENGLISH BIBLIOGRAPHY. Crown 8vo, 1,400 pages, cloth extra, 7s. 6d.
A Dictionary of Miracles: Imitative, Realistic, and Dogmatic. Crown 8vo, cloth extra, 7s. 6d. [*In preparation.*

Buchanan's (Robert) Works:
Ballads of Life, Love, and Humour. With a Frontispiece by ARTHUR HUGHES. Crown 8vo, cloth extra, 6s.
Selected Poems of Robert Buchanan. With Frontispiece by T. DALZIEL. Crown 8vo, cloth extra, 6s.
Undertones. Crown 8vo, cloth extra, 6s.
London Poems. Crown 8vo, cloth extra, 6s.
The Book of Orm. Crown 8vo, cloth extra, 6s.
White Rose and Red: A Love Story. Crown 8vo, cloth extra, 6s.
Idylls and Legends of Inverburn. Crown 8vo, cloth extra, 6s.
St. Abe and his Seven Wives: A Tale of Salt Lake City. With a Frontispiece by A. B. HOUGHTON. Crown 8vo, cloth extra, 5s.
The Hebrid Isles: Wanderings in the Land of Lorne and the Outer Hebrides. With Frontispiece by W. SMALL. Crown 8vo, cloth extra, 6s.
Selections from the Prose Writings of Robert Buchanan. Crown 8vo, cloth extra, 6s. [*Shortly.*
Robert Buchanan's Complete Poetical Works. Crown 8vo, cloth extra, 7s. 6d. [*In preparation.*
The Shadow of the Sword: A Romance. Crown 8vo, cloth extra, 3s. 6d.; post 8vo, illust. boards, 2s.
A Child of Nature: A Romance. With a Frontispiece. Crown 8vo, cloth extra, 3s. 6d.; post 8vo, illustrated boards, 2s.
God and the Man: A Romance. With Illustrations by FRED. BARNARD. Crown 8vo, cloth extra, 3s. 6d.
The Martyrdom of Madeline: A Romance. With a Frontispiece by A. W. COOPER. Crown 8vo, cloth extra, 3s. 6d.
Love Me for Ever. With a Frontispiece by P. MACNAB. Crown 8vo, cloth extra, 3s. 6d.
Annan Water: A Romance. Three Vols., cr. 8vo, 31s. 6d. [*Immediately.*

Brewster (Sir David), Works by:
More Worlds than One: The Creed of the Philosopher and the Hope of the Christian. With Plates. Post 8vo, cloth extra, 4s. 6d.
The Martyrs of Science: Lives of GALILEO, TYCHO BRAHE, and KEPLER. With Portraits. Post 8vo, cloth extra, 4s. 6d.
Letters on Natural Magic. A New Edition, with numerous Illustrations, and Chapters on the Being and Faculties of Man, and Additional Phenomena of Natural Magic, by J. A. SMITH. Post 8vo, cloth extra, 4s. 6d.

Brillat-Savarin.—Gastronomy as a Fine Art. By BRILLAT-SAVARIN. Translated by R. E. ANDERSON, M.A. Post 8vo, cloth limp, 2s. 6d.

Burnett (Mrs.), Novels by:
Surly Tim, and other Stories. Post 8vo, illustrated boards, 2s.
Kathleen Mavourneen. Fcap. 8vo, picture cover, 1s.
Lindsay's Luck. Fcap. 8vo, picture cover, 1s.
Pretty Polly Pemberton. Fcap. 8vo, picture cover, 1s.

Burton (Robert):
The Anatomy of Melancholy. A New Edition, complete, corrected and enriched by Translations of the Classical Extracts. Demy 8vo, cloth extra, 7s. 6d.
Melancholy Anatomised: Being an Abridgment, for popular use, of BURTON'S ANATOMY OF MELANCHOLY. Post 8vo, cloth limp, 2s. 6d.

Burton (Captain), Works by:
To the Gold Coast for Gold: A Personal Narrative. By RICHARD F. BURTON and VERNEY LOVETT CAMERON. With Maps and Frontispiece. Two Vols., crown 8vo, cloth extra, 21s.
The Book of the Sword: Being a History of the Sword and its Use in all Countries, from the Earliest Times. By RICHARD F. BURTON. With over 400 Illustrations. Square 8vo, cloth extra, 25s. [*In preparation.*

Bunyan's Pilgrim's Progress. Edited by Rev. T. SCOTT. With 17 beautiful Steel Plates by STOTHARD, engraved by GOODALL; and numerous Woodcuts. Crown 8vo, cloth extra, gilt, 7s. 6d.

Byron (Lord):
Byron's Letters and Journals. With Notices of his Life. By THOMAS MOORE. A Reprint of the Original Edition, newly revised, with Twelve full-page Plates. Crown 8vo, cloth extra, gilt, 7s. 6d.

Byron's Don Juan. Complete in One Vol., post 8vo, cloth limp, 2s.

Cameron (Commander) and Captain Burton.—To the Gold Coast for Gold: A Personal Narrative. By RICHARD F. BURTON and VERNEY LOVETT CAMERON. With Frontispiece and Maps. Two Vols., crown 8vo, cloth extra, 21s.

Cameron (Mrs. H. Lovett), Novels by:
Juliet's Guardian. Post 8vo, illustrated boards, 2s.; crown 8vo, cloth extra, 3s. 6d.

Deceivers Ever. Post 8vo, illustrated boards, 2s.; crown 8vo, cloth extra, 3s. 6d.

Campbell.—White and Black: Travels in the United States. By Sir GEORGE CAMPBELL, M.P. Demy 8vo, cloth extra, 14s.

Carlyle (Thomas):
Thomas Carlyle: Letters and Recollections. By MONCURE D. CONWAY, M.A. Crown 8vo, cloth extra, with Illustrations, 6s.

On the Choice of Books. By THOMAS CARLYLE. With a Life of the Author by R. H. SHEPHERD. New and Revised Edition, post 8vo, cloth extra, Illustrated, 1s. 6d.

The Correspondence of Thomas Carlyle and Ralph Waldo Emerson, 1834 to 1872. Edited by CHARLES ELIOT NORTON. With Portraits. Two Vols., crown 8vo, cloth extra, 24s.

Century (A) of Dishonour: A Sketch of the United States Government's Dealings with some of the Indian Tribes. Crown 8vo, cloth extra, 7s. 6d.

Chapman's (George) Works: Vol. I. contains the Plays complete, including the doubtful ones. Vol. II., the Poems and Minor Translations, with an Introductory Essay by ALGERNON CHARLES SWINBURNE. Vol. III., the Translations of the Iliad and Odyssey. Three Vols., crown 8vo, cloth extra, 18s.; or separately, 6s. each.

Chatto & Jackson.—A Treatise on Wood Engraving, Historical and Practical. By WM. ANDREW CHATTO and JOHN JACKSON. With an Additional Chapter by HENRY G. BOHN; and 450 fine Illustrations. A Reprint of the last Revised Edition, Large 4to, half-bound, 28s.

Chaucer:
Chaucer for Children: A Golden Key. By Mrs. H. R. HAWEIS. With Eight Coloured Pictures and numerous Woodcuts by the Author. New Ed., small 4to, cloth extra, 6s.

Chaucer for Schools. By Mrs. H. R. HAWEIS. Demy 8vo, cloth limp, 2s.6d.

Cobban.—The Cure of Souls: A Story. By J. MACLAREN COBBAN. Post 8vo, illustrated boards, 2s.

Collins (C. Allston).—The Bar Sinister: A Story. By C. ALLSTON COLLINS. Post 8vo, illustrated boards, 2s.

Collins (Mortimer & Frances), Novels by:
Sweet and Twenty. Post 8vo, illustrated boards, 2s.

Frances. Post 8vo, illust. bds., 2s.

Blacksmith and Scholar. Post 8vo, illustrated boards, 2s.; crown 8vo, cloth extra, 3s. 6d.

The Village Comedy. Post 8vo, illust. boards, 2s.; cr. 8vo, cloth extra, 3s. 6d.

You Play Me False. Post 8vo, illust. boards, 2s.; cr. 8vo, cloth extra, 3s. 6d.

Collins (Mortimer), Novels by:
Sweet Anne Page. Post 8vo, illustrated boards, 2s.; crown 8vo, cloth extra, 3s. 6d.

Transmigration. Post 8vo, illustrated boards, 2s.; crown 8vo, cloth extra, 3s. 6d.

From Midnight to Midnight. Post 8vo, illustrated boards, 2s.; crown 8vo, cloth extra, 3s. 6d.

A Fight with Fortune. Post 8vo, illustrated boards, 2s.

Colman's Humorous Works. "Broad Grins," "My Nightgown and Slippers," and other Humorous Works, Prose and Poetical, of GEORGE COLMAN. With Life by G. B BUCKSTONE, and Frontispiece by HOGARTH. Crown 8vo, cloth extra, gilt, 7s. 6d.

BOOKS PUBLISHED BY

Collins (Wilkie), Novels by.
Each post 8vo, illustrated boards, 2s; cloth limp, 2s. 6d.; or crown 8vo, cloth extra, Illustrated, 3s. 6d.

Antonina. Illust. by A. CONCANEN.
Basil. Illustrated by Sir JOHN GILBERT and J. MAHONEY.
Hide and Seek. Illustrated by Sir JOHN GILBERT and J. MAHONEY.
The Dead Secret. Illustrated by Sir JOHN GILBERT and A. CONCANEN.
Queen of Hearts. Illustrated by Sir JOHN GILBERT and A. CONCANEN.
My Miscellanies. With Illustrations by A. CONCANEN, and a Steel-plate Portrait of WILKIE COLLINS.
The Woman in White. With Illustrations by Sir JOHN GILBERT and F. A. FRASER.
The Moonstone. With Illustrations by G. DU MAURIER and F. A. FRASER.
Man and Wife. Illust. by W. SMALL.
Poor Miss Finch. Illustrated by G. DU MAURIER and EDWARD HUGHES.
Miss or Mrs.? With Illustrations by S. L. FILDES and HENRY WOODS.
The New Magdalen. Illustrated by G. DU MAURIER and C. S. RANDS.
The Frozen Deep. Illustrated by G. DU MAURIER and J. MAHONEY.
The Law and the Lady. Illustrated by S. L. FILDES and SYDNEY HALL.
The Two Destinies.
The Haunted Hotel. Illustrated by ARTHUR HOPKINS.
The Fallen Leaves.
Jezebel's Daughter.
The Black Robe.

Heart and Science: A Story of the Present Time. Three Vols., crown 8vo, 31s. 6d.

Convalescent Cookery: A Family Handbook. By CATHERINE RYAN. Post 8vo, cloth limp, 2s. 6d.

Conway (Moncure D.), Works by:
Demonology and Devil-Lore. Two Vols., royal 8vo, with 65 Illusts., 28s.
A Necklace of Stories. Illustrated by W. J. HENNESSY. Square 8vo, cloth extra, 6s.
The Wandering Jew. Crown 8vo, cloth extra, 6s.
Thomas Carlyle: Letters and Recollections. With Illustrations. Crown 8vo, cloth extra, 6s.

Cook (Dutton), Works by:
Hours with the Players. With a Steel Plate Frontispiece. New and Cheaper Edit., cr. 8vo, cloth extra, 6s.
Nights at the Play: A View of the English Stage. Two Vols., crown 8vo, cloth extra, 21s.
Leo: A Novel. Post 8vo, illustrated boards, 2s.
Paul Foster's Daughter. Post 8vo, illustrated boards, 2s.; crown 8vo, cloth extra, 3s. 6d. [*Shortly.*

Copyright.—A Handbook of English and Foreign Copyright in Literary and Dramatic Works. By SIDNEY JERROLD, of the Middle Temple, Esq., Barrister-at-Law. Post 8vo, cloth limp, 2s. 6d.

Cornwall.—Popular Romances of the West of England; or, The Drolls, Traditions, and Superstitions of Old Cornwall. Collected and Edited by ROBERT HUNT, F.R.S. New and Revised Edition, with Additions, and Two Steel-plate Illustrations by GEORGE CRUIKSHANK. Crown 8vo, cloth extra, 7s. 6d.

Creasy.—Memoirs of Eminent Etonians: with Notices of the Early History of Eton College. By Sir EDWARD CREASY, Author of "The Fifteen Decisive Battles of the World." Crown 8vo, cloth extra, gilt, with 13 Portraits, 7s. 6d.

Cruikshank (George):
The Comic Almanack. Complete in Two SERIES: The FIRST from 1835 to 1843; the SECOND from 1844 to 1853. A Gathering of the BEST HUMOUR of THACKERAY, HOOD, MAYHEW, ALBERT SMITH, A'BECKETT, ROBERT BROUGH, &c. With 2,000 Woodcuts and Steel Engravings by CRUIKSHANK, HINE, LANDELLS, &c. Crown 8vo, cloth gilt, two very thick volumes, 7s. 6d. each.
The Life of George Cruikshank. By BLANCHARD JERROLD, Author of "The Life of Napoleon III.," &c. With 84 Illustrations. New and Cheaper Edition, enlarged, with Additional Plates, and a very carefully compiled Bibliography. Crown 8vo, cloth extra, 7s. 6d. [*Shortly.*
Robinson Crusoe. A choicely-printed Edition, with 37 Woodcuts and Two Steel Plates, by GEORGE CRUIKSHANK. Crown 8vo, cloth extra, 7s. 6d.
A few Large Paper copies, carefully printed on hand-made paper, with India proofs of the Illustrations, price 36s. [*In preparation.*

Crimes and Punishments. Including a New Translation of Beccaria's "De Delitti e delle Pene." By JAMES ANSON FARRER. Crown 8vo, cloth extra, 6s.

Cumming.—In the Hebrides. By C. F. GORDON CUMMING, Author of "At Home in Fiji." With Autotype Facsimile and Illustrations. Demy 8vo, cloth extra, 8s. 6d. [*Preparing.*

Cussans.—Handbook of Heraldry; with Instructions for Tracing Pedigrees and Deciphering Ancient MSS., &c. By JOHN E. CUSSANS. Entirely New and Revised Edition, illustrated with over 400 Woodcuts and Coloured Plates. Crown 8vo, cloth extra, 7s. 6d.

Cyples.—Hearts of Gold: A Novel. By WILLIAM CYPLES. Crown 8vo, cloth extra, 3s. 6d.

Daniel. — Merrie England in the Olden Time. By GEORGE DANIEL. With Illustrations by ROBT. CRUIKSHANK. Crown 8vo, cloth extra, 3s. 6d.

Daudet.—Port Salvation; or, The Evangelist. By ALPHONSE DAUDET. Translated by C. HARRY MELTZER. Two Vols., post 8vo, 12s.

Davenant. — What shall my Son be? Hints for Parents on the Choice of a Profession or Trade for their Sons. By FRANCIS DAVENANT, M.A. Post 8vo, cloth limp, 2s. 6d.

Davies' (Sir John) Complete Poetical Works, including Psalms I. to L. in Verse, and other hitherto Unpublished MSS., for the first time Collected and Edited, with Memorial-Introduction and Notes, by the Rev. A. B. GROSART, D.D. Two Vols., crown 8vo, cloth boards, 12s.

De Maistre.—A Journey Round My Room. By XAVIER DE MAISTRE. Translated by HENRY ATTWELL. Post 8vo, cloth limp, 2s. 6d.

Derwent (Leith), Novels by:
Our Lady of Tears. Crown 8vo, cloth extra, 3s. 6d.; post 8vo, illustrated boards, 2s. [*Shortly.*
Circe's Lovers. Three Vols., crown 8vo, 31s. 6d. [*Shortly.*

Dickens (Charles), Novels by:
Post 8vo, illustrated boards, 2s. each.
Sketches by Boz.
The Pickwick Papers.
Oliver Twist.
Nicholas Nickleby.

The Speeches of Charles Dickens. Post 8vo, cloth limp, 2s. 6d.

Charles Dickens's Speeches, Chronologically Arranged: with a New Life of the Author, and a Bibliographical List of his Published Writings in Prose and Verse, from 1833 to 1883. Crown 8vo, cloth extra, 6s. [*In preparation.*

About England with Dickens. By ALFRED RIMMER. With 57 Illustrations by C. A. VANDERHOOF, ALFRED RIMMER, and others. Sq. 8vo, cloth extra, 10s. 6d.

Dictionaries:
A Dictionary of Miracles: Imitative, Realistic, and Dogmatic. By the Rev. E. C. BREWER, LL.D. Crown 8vo, cloth extra, 7s. 6d. [*Preparing.*

A Dictionary of the Drama: Being a comprehensive Guide to the Plays, Playwrights, Players, and Playhouses of the United Kingdom and America, from the Earliest to the Present Times. By W. DAVENPORT ADAMS. A thick volume, crown 8vo, halfbound, 12s. 6d. [*In preparation.*

Familiar Allusions: A Handbook of Miscellaneous Information; including the Names of Celebrated Statues, Paintings, Palaces, Country Seats, Ruins, Churches, Ships, Streets, Clubs, Natural Curiosities, and the like. By WM. A. WHEELER and CHARLES G. WHEELER. Demy 8vo, cloth extra, 7s. 6d.

The Reader's Handbook of Allusions, References, Plots, and Stories. By the Rev. E. C. BREWER, LL.D. Third Edition, revised throughout, with a New Appendix, containing a Complete English Bibliography. Crown 8vo, 1,400 pages, cloth extra, 7s. 6d.

Short Sayings of Great Men. With Historical and Explanatory Notes. By SAMUEL A. BENT, M.A. Demy 8vo, cloth extra, 7s. 6d.

The Slang Dictionary: Etymological, Historical, and Anecdotal. Crown 8vo, cloth extra, 6s. 6d.

DICTIONARIES, *continued—*
Words, Facts, and Phrases: A Dictionary of Curious, Quaint, and Out-of-the-Way Matters. By ELIEZER EDWARDS. Crown 8vo, half-bound, 12s. 6d.

Dobson (W. T.), Works by:
Literary Frivolities, Fancies, Follies, and Frolics. Post 8vo, cloth limp, 2s. 6d.
Poetical Ingenuities and Eccentricities. Post 8vo, cloth limp, 2s. 6d.

Doran. — Memories of our Great Towns; with Anecdotic Gleanings concerning their Worthies and their Oddities. By Dr. JOHN DORAN, F.S.A. With 38 Illustrations. New and Cheaper Edition, crown 8vo, cloth extra, 7s. 6d.

Drama, A Dictionary of the. Being a comprehensive Guide to the Plays, Playwrights, Players, and Playhouses of the United Kingdom and America, from the Earliest to the Present Times. By W. DAVENPORT ADAMS. (Uniform with BREWER'S "Reader's Handbook.") Crown 8vo, half-bound, 12s. 6d. [*In preparation.*

Dramatists, The Old. Crown 8vo, cloth extra, with Vignette Portraits, 6s. per Vol.
Ben Jonson's Works. With Notes Critical and Explanatory, and a Biographical Memoir by WM. GIFFORD. Edited by Colonel CUNNINGHAM. Three Vols.
Chapman's Works. Complete in Three Vols. Vol. I. contains the Plays complete, including the doubtful ones; Vol. II., the Poems and Minor Translations, with an Introductory Essay by ALGERNON CHAS. SWINBURNE; Vol. III., the Translations of the Iliad and Odyssey.
Marlowe's Works. Including his Translations. Edited, with Notes and Introduction, by Col. CUNNINGHAM. One Vol.
Massinger's Plays. From the Text of WILLIAM GIFFORD. Edited by Col. CUNNINGHAM. One Vol.

Dyer. — The Folk-Lore of Plants. By T. F. THISELTON DYER, M.A. Crown 8vo, cloth extra, 6s. [*In preparation.*

Edwards, Betham-. — Felicia: A Novel. By M. BETHAM-EDWARDS. Post 8vo, illustrated boards, 2s.; crown 8vo, cloth extra, 3s. 6d.

Early English Poets. Edited, with Introductions and Annotations, by Rev. A. B. GROSART, D.D. Crown 8vo, cloth boards, 6s. per Volume.
Fletcher's (Giles, B.D.) Complete Poems. One Vol.
Davies' (Sir John) Complete Poetical Works. Two Vols.
Herrick's (Robert) Complete Collected Poems. Three Vols.
Sidney's (Sir Philip) Complete Poetical Works. Three Vols.

Edwardes (Mrs. Annie), Novels by:
A Point of Honour. Post 8vo, illustrated boards, 2s.
Archie Lovell. Post 8vo, illustrated boards, 2s.; crown 8vo, cloth extra, 3s. 6d.

Eggleston. — Roxy: A Novel. By EDWARD EGGLESTON. Post 8vo, illustrated boards, 2s.; crown 8vo, cloth extra, 3s. 6d.

Emanuel. — On Diamonds and Precious Stones: their History, Value, and Properties; with Simple Tests for ascertaining their Reality. By HARRY EMANUEL, F.R.G.S. With numerous Illustrations, tinted and plain. Crown 8vo, cloth extra, gilt, 6s.

Englishman's House, The: A Practical Guide to all interested in Selecting or Building a House, with full Estimates of Cost, Quantities, &c. By C. J. RICHARDSON. Third Edition. With nearly 600 Illustrations. Crown 8vo, cloth extra, 7s. 6d.

Ewald (Alex Charles, F.S.A.), Works by:
Stories from the State Papers. With an Autotype Facsimile. Crown 8vo, cloth extra, 6s.
The Life and Times of Prince Charles Stuart, Count of Albany, commonly called the Young Pretender. From the State Papers and other Sources. New and Cheaper Edition, with a Portrait, crown 8vo, cloth extra, 7s. 6d.

Fairholt. — Tobacco: Its History and Associations; with an Account of the Plant and its Manufacture, and its Modes of Use in all Ages and Countries. By F. W. FAIRHOLT, F.S.A. With Coloured Frontispiece and upwards of 100 Illustrations by the Author. Crown 8vo, cloth extra, 6s.

Familiar Allusions: A Handbook of Miscellaneous Information; including the Names of Celebrated Statues, Paintings, Palaces, Country Seats, Ruins, Churches, Ships, Streets, Clubs, Natural Curiosities, and the like. By WILLIAM A. WHEELER, Author of "Noted Names of Fiction;" and CHARLES G. WHEELER. Demy 8vo, cloth extra, 7s. 6d.

Faraday (Michael), Works by:
The Chemical History of a Candle: Lectures delivered before a Juvenile Audience at the Royal Institution. Edited by WILLIAM CROOKES, F.C.S. Post 8vo, cloth extra, with numerous Illustrations, 4s. 6d.

On the Various Forces of Nature, and their Relations to each other: Lectures delivered before a Juvenile Audience at the Royal Institution. Edited by WILLIAM CROOKES, F.C.S. Post 8vo, cloth extra, with numerous Illustrations, 4s. 6d.

Fin-Bec.—The Cupboard Papers: Observations on the Art of Living and Dining. By FIN-BEC. Post 8vo, cloth limp, 2s. 6d.

Fitzgerald (Percy), Works by:
The Recreations of a Literary Man; or, Does Writing Pay? With Recollections of some Literary Men, and a View of a Literary Man's Working Life. Crown 8vo, cloth extra, 6s.

The World Behind the Scenes. Crown 8vo, cloth extra, 3s. 6d.

Post 8vo, illustrated boards, 2s. each.
Bella Donna.
Never Forgotten.
The Second Mrs. Tillotson.
Polly.
Seventy-five Brooke Street.

Fletcher's (Giles, B.D.) Complete Poems: Christ's Victorie in Heaven, Christ's Victorie on Earth, Christ's Triumph over Death, and Minor Poems. With Memorial-Introduction and Notes, by the Rev. A. B. GROSART, D.D. Crown 8vo, cloth boards, 6s.

Fonblanque.—Filthy Lucre: A Novel. By ALBANY DE FONBLANQUE. Post 8vo, illustrated boards, 2s.

Francillon (R. E.), Novels by:
Crown 8vo, cloth extra, 3s. 6d. each; post 8vo, illust. boards, 2s. each.
Olympia.
Queen Cophetua.
One by One.

Esther's Glove. Fcap. 8vo, picture cover, 1s.

Frost (Thomas), Works by:
Crown 8vo, cloth extra, 3s. 6d. each.
Circus Life and Circus Celebrities.
The Lives of the Conjurers.
The Old Showmen and the Old London Fairs.

French Literature, History of. By HENRI VAN LAUN. Complete in Three Vols., demy 8vo, cl. bds., 22s. 6d.

Gardening Books:
A Year's Work in Garden and Greenhouse: Practical Advice to Amateur Gardeners as to the Management of the Flower, Fruit, and Frame Garden. By GEORGE GLENNY. Post 8vo, cloth limp, 2s. 6d.

Our Kitchen Garden: The Plants we Grow, and How we Cook Them. By TOM JERROLD, Author of "The Garden that Paid the Rent," &c. Post 8vo, cloth limp, 2s. 6d.

Household Horticulture: A Gossip about Flowers. By TOM and JANE JERROLD. Illustrated. Post 8vo, cloth limp, 2s. 6d.

The Garden that Paid the Rent. By TOM JERROLD. Fcap. 8vo, illustrated cover, 1s.; Cloth limp, 1s. 6d.

My Garden Wild, and What I Grew there. By FRANCIS GEORGE HEATH. Crown 8vo, cloth extra, 5s.; gilt edges, 6s.

Garrett.—The Capel Girls: A Novel. By EDWARD GARRETT. Post 8vo, illustrated boards, 2s.; crown 8vo, cloth extra, 3s. 6d.

Gentleman's Magazine (The) for 1883. One Shilling Monthly. "The New Abelard," ROBERT BUCHANAN's New Serial Story, was begun in the JANUARY Number of THE GENTLEMAN'S MAGAZINE. This Number contained many other interesting Articles, the continuation of JULIAN HAWTHORNE's Story, "Dust," and a further instalment of "Science Notes," by W. MATTIEU WILLIAMS, F.R.A.S.
. *Now ready, the Volume for* JULY *to* DECEMBER, 1882, *cloth extra, price* 8s. 6d.; *Cases for binding,* 2s. *each.*

German Popular Stories. Collected by the Brothers GRIMM, and Translated by EDGAR TAYLOR. Edited, with an Introduction, by JOHN RUSKIN. With 22 Illustrations on Steel by GEORGE CRUIKSHANK. Square 8vo, cloth extra, 6s. 6d.; gilt edges, 7s. 6d.

Gibbon (Charles), Novels by:
Each in crown 8vo, cloth extra, 3s. 6d.; or post 8vo, illustrated boards, 2s.
Robin Gray.
For Lack of Gold.
What will the World Say?
In Honour Bound.
In Love and War.
For the King.
Queen of the Meadow.
In Pastures Green.

Post 8vo, illustrated boards, 2s.
The Dead Heart.

Crown 8vo, cloth extra, 3s. 6d. each.
The Braes of Yarrow.
The Flower of the Forest.
A Heart's Problem.

Three Vols., crown 8vo, 31s. 6d. each.
The Golden Shaft.
Of High Degree.

Fancy-Free. Two vols., crown 8vo.
[*In the press.*

Gilbert (William), Novels by:
Post 8vo, illustrated boards, 2s. each.
Dr. Austin's Guests.
The Wizard of the Mountain.
James Duke, Costermonger.

Gilbert (W. S.), Original Plays by: In Two Series, each complete in itself, price 2s. 6d. each. FIRST SERIES contains The Wicked World—Pygmalion and Galatea — Charity — The Princess—The Palace of Truth—Trial by Jury. The SECOND SERIES contains Broken Hearts — Engaged — Sweethearts—Gretchen—Dan'l Druce —Tom Cobb—H.M.S. Pinafore—The Sorcerer—The Pirates of Penzance.

Glenny.—A Year's Work in Garden and Greenhouse: Practical Advice to Amateur Gardeners as to the Management of the Flower, Fruit, and Frame Garden. By GEORGE GLENNY. Post 8vo, cloth limp, 2s. 6d.

Godwin.—Lives of the Necromancers. By WILLIAM GODWIN. Post 8vo, cloth limp, 2s.

Golden Library, The:
Square 16mo (Tauchnitz size), cloth limp, 2s. per volume.
Ballad History of England. By W. C. BENNETT.
Bayard Taylor's Diversions of the Echo Club.
Byron's Don Juan.
Godwin's (William) Lives of the Necromancers.
Holmes's Autocrat of the Breakfast Table. With an Introduction by G. A. SALA.
Holmes's Professor at the Breakfast Table.
Hood's Whims and Oddities. Complete. With all the original Illustrations.
Irving's (Washington) Tales of a Traveller.
Irving's (Washington) Tales of the Alhambra.
Jesse's (Edward) Scenes and Occupations of a Country Life.
Lamb's Essays of Ella. Both Series Complete in One Vol.
Leigh Hunt's Essays: A Tale for a Chimney Corner, and other Pieces. With Portrait, and Introduction by EDMUND OLLIER.
Mallory's (Sir Thomas) Mort d'Arthur: The Stories of King Arthur and of the Knights of the Round Table. Edited by B. MONTGOMERIE RANKING.
Pascal's Provincial Letters. A New Translation, with Historical Introduction and Notes, by T. M'CRIE, D.D.
Pope's Poetical Works. Complete.
Rochefoucauld's Maxims and Moral Reflections. With Notes, and Introductory Essay by SAINTE-BEUVE.
St. Pierre's Paul and Virginia, and The Indian Cottage. Edited, with Life, by the Rev. E. CLARKE.
Shelley's Early Poems, and Queen Mab. With Essay by LEIGH HUNT.
Shelley's Later Poems: Laon and Cythna, &c.
Shelley's Posthumous Poems, the Shelley Papers, &c.
Shelley's Prose Works, including A Refutation of Deism, Zastrozzi, St. Irvyne, &c.
White's Natural History of Selborne. Edited, with Additions, by THOMAS BROWN, F.L.S.

Golden Treasury of Thought,
The: An ENCYCLOPÆDIA OF QUOTATIONS from Writers of all Times and Countries. Selected and Edited by THEODORE TAYLOR. Crown 8vo, cloth gilt and gilt edges, 7s. 6d.

Gordon Cumming.— In the Hebrides. By C. F. GORDON CUMMING, Author of "At Home in Fiji." With Autotype Facsimile and numerous full-page Illustrations. Demy 8vo, cloth extra, 8s. 6d. [*In preparation.*

Graham. — The Professor's Wife: A Story. By LEONARD GRAHAM. Fcap. 8vo, picture cover, 1s.; cloth extra, 2s. 6d.

Greeks and Romans, The Life of the, Described from Antique Monuments. By ERNST GUHL and W. KONER. Translated from the Third German Edition, and Edited by Dr. F. HUEFFER. With 545 Illustrations. New and Cheaper Edition, demy 8vo, cloth extra, 7s. 6d.

Greenwood (James), Works by:
The Wilds of London. Crown 8vo, cloth extra, 3s. 6d.
Low-Life Deeps: An Account of the Strange Fish to be Found There. Crown 8vo, cloth extra, 3s. 6d.
Dick Temple: A Novel. Post 8vo, illustrated boards, 2s.

Guyot.—The Earth and Man; or, Physical Geography in its relation to the History of Mankind. By ARNOLD GUYOT. With Additions by Professors AGASSIZ, PIERCE, and GRAY; 12 Maps and Engravings on Steel, some Coloured, and copious Index. Crown 8vo, cloth extra, gilt, 4s. 6d.

Hair (The): Its Treatment in Health, Weakness, and Disease. Translated from the German of Dr. J. PINCUS. Crown 8vo, 1s.; cloth, 1s. 6d.

Hake (Dr. Thomas Gordon), Poems by:
Maiden Ecstasy. Small 4to, cloth extra, 8s.
New Symbols. Crown 8vo, cloth extra, 6s.
Legends of the Morrow. Crown 8vo, cloth extra, 6s.
The Serpent Play. Crown 8vo, cloth extra, 6s.

Half-Hours with Foreign Novelists. With Notices of their Lives and Writings. By HELEN and ALICE ZIMMERN. A New Edition. Two Vols., crown 8vo, cloth extra, 12s.

Hall.—Sketches of Irish Character. By Mrs. S. C. HALL. With numerous Illustrations on Steel and Wood by MACLISE, GILBERT, HARVEY, and G. CRUIKSHANK. Medium 8vo, cloth extra, gilt, 7s. 6d.

Halliday.—Every-day Papers. By ANDREW HALLIDAY. Post 8vo, illustrated boards, 2s.

Handwriting, The Philosophy of. With over 100 Facsimiles and Explanatory Text. By DON FELIX DE SALAMANCA. Post 8vo, cloth limp, 2s. 6d.

Hanky-Panky: A Collection of Very EasyTricks,Very Difficult Tricks, White Magic, Sleight of Hand, &c. Edited by W. H. CREMER. With 200 Illustrations. Crown 8vo, cloth extra, 4s. 6d.

Hardy (Lady Duffus).— Paul Wynter's Sacrifice: A Story. By Lady DUFFUS HARDY. Post 8vo, illust. boards, 2s.

Hardy (Thomas).—Under the Greenwood Tree. By THOMAS HARDY, Author of "Far from the Madding Crowd." Crown 8vo, cloth extra, 3s. 6d.; post 8vo, illustrated boards, 2s.

Haweis (Mrs. H. R.), Works by:
The Art of Dress. With numerous Illustrations. Small 8vo, illustrated cover, 1s.; cloth limp, 1s. 6d.
The Art of Beauty. Square 8vo, cloth extra, gilt edges, with Coloured Frontispiece and nearly 100 Illustrations, 10s. 6d.
The Art of Decoration. Square 8vo, handsomely bound and profusely Illustrated, 10s. 6d.
Chaucer for Children: A Golden Key. With Eight Coloured Pictures and numerous Woodcuts. New Edition, small 4to, cloth extra, 6s.
Chaucer for Schools. Demy 8vo, cloth limp, 2s. 6d.

Haweis (Rev. H. R.).—American Humorists. Including WASHINGTON IRVING, OLIVER WENDELL HOLMES, JAMES RUSSELL LOWELL, ARTEMUS WARD, MARK TWAIN, and BRET HARTE. By the Rev. H. R. HAWEIS, M.A. Crown 8vo, cloth extra, 6s.

Hawthorne (Julian), Novels by.
Crown 8vo, cloth extra, 3s. 6d. each;
post 8vo, illustrated boards, 2s. each.
Garth.
Ellice Quentin.
Sebastian Strome.

Mrs. Gainsborough's Diamonds
Fcap. 8vo, illustrated cover, 1s.;
cloth extra, 2s. 6d.
Prince Saroni's Wife, &c. Crown 8vo,
cloth extra, 3s. 6d.
Dust: A Novel. Three Vols., crown
8vo, 31s. 6d.

Heath (F. G.). — My Garden
Wild, and What I Grew There. By
FRANCIS GEORGE HEATH, Author of
"The Fern World," &c. Crown 8vo,
cloth extra, 5s.; cloth gilt, and gilt
edges, 6s.

Helps (Sir Arthur), Works by:
Animals and their Masters. Post
8vo, cloth limp, 2s. 6d.
Ivan de Biron: A Novel. Crown 8vo,
cloth extra, 3s. 6d.; post 8vo, illustrated boards, 2s.

Heptalogia (The); or, The
Seven against Sense. A Cap with
Seven Bells. Crown 8vo, cloth extra,
6s.

Herbert.—The Poems of Lord
Herbert of Cherbury. Edited, with
an Introduction, by J. CHURTON
COLLINS. Crown 8vo, bound in parchment, 8s.; Large-Paper copies (only
50 printed), 15s.

Herrick's (Robert) Hesperides,
Noble Numbers, and Complete Collected Poems. With Memorial-Introduction and Notes by the Rev. A. B.
GROSART, D.D., Steel Portrait, Index
of First Lines, and Glossarial Index,
&c. Three Vols., crown 8vo, cloth
boards, 18s.

Hesse - Wartegg (Chevalier
Ernst von), Works by:
Tunis: The Land and the People.
With 22 Illustrations. Crown 8vo,
cloth extra, 3s. 6d.
The New South-West: Travelling
Sketches from Kansas, New Mexico,
Arizona, and Northern Mexico.
With 100 fine Illustrations and 3
Maps. Demy 8vo, cloth extra,
14s. [*In preparation.*

Hindley (Charles), Works by:
Crown 8vo, cloth extra, 3s. 6d. each.
Tavern Anecdotes and Sayings: Including the Origin of Signs, and
Reminiscences connected with
Taverns, Coffee Houses, Clubs, &c.
With Illustrations.
The Life and Adventures of a Cheap
Jack. By One of the Fraternity.
Edited by CHARLES HINDLEY.

Holmes (Oliver Wendell), Works
by:
The Autocrat of the Breakfast-
Table Illustrated by J. GORDON
THOMSON. Post 8vo, cloth limp,
2s. 6d.; another Edition in smaller
type, with an Introduction by G. A.
SALA. Post 8vo, cloth limp, 2s.
The Professor at the Breakfast-
Table; with the Story of Iris. Post
8vo, cloth limp, 2s.

Holmes. — The Science of
Voice Production and Voice Preservation: A Popular Manual for the
Use of Speakers and Singers. By
GORDON HOLMES, M.D. Crown 8vo,
cloth limp, with Illustrations, 2s. 6d.

Hood (Thomas):
Hood's Choice Works, in Prose and
Verse. Including the Cream of the
Comic Annuals. With Life of the
Author, Portrait, and 200 Illustrations. Crown 8vo, cloth extra, 7s. 6d.
Hood's Whims and Oddities. Complete. With all the original Illustrations. Post 8vo, cloth limp, 2s.

Hood (Tom), Works by:
From Nowhere to the North Pole:
A Noah's Arkæological Narrative.
With 25 Illustrations by W. BRUNTON and E. C. BARNES. Square
crown 8vo, cloth extra, gilt edges, 6s.
A Golden Heart: A Novel. Post 8vo,
illustrated boards, 2s.

Hook's (Theodore) Choice Hu-
morous Works, including his Ludicrous Adventures, Bons Mots, Puns and
Hoaxes. With a New Life of the
Author, Portraits, Facsimiles, and
Illustrations. Crown 8vo, cloth extra,
gilt, 7s. 6d.

Horne.—Orion : An Epic Poem,
in Three Books. By RICHARD HENGIST HORNE. With Photographic
Portrait from a Medallion by SUMMERS. Tenth Edition, crown 8vo,
cloth extra, 7s.

CHATTO & WINDUS, PICCADILLY. 13

Howell.—Conflicts of Capital and Labour, Historically and Economically considered: Being a History and Review of the Trade Unions of Great Britain, showing their Origin, Progress, Constitution, and Objects, in their Political, Social, Economical, and Industrial Aspects. By GEORGE HOWELL. Crown 8vo, cloth extra, 7s. 6d.

Hueffer.—The Troubadours: A History of Provençal Life and Literature in the Middle Ages. By FRANCIS HUEFFER. Demy 8vo, cloth extra, 12s. 6d.

Hugo. — The Hunchback of Notre Dame. By VICTOR HUGO. Post 8vo, illustrated boards, 2s.

Hunt.—Essays by Leigh Hunt. A Tale for a Chimney Corner, and other Pieces. With Portrait and Introduction by EDMUND OLLIER. Post 8vo, cloth limp, 2s.

Hunt (Mrs. Alfred), Novels by:
Thornicroft's Model. Crown 8vo, cloth extra, 3s. 6d.; post 8vo, illustrated boards, 2s.
The Leaden Casket. Crown 8vo, cloth extra, 3s. 6d.; post 8vo, illustrated boards, 2s.
Self-Condemned. Three Vols., crown 8vo, 31s. 6d.

Ingelow.—Fated to be Free: A Novel. By JEAN INGELOW. Crown 8vo, cloth extra, 3s. 6d.; post 8vo, illustrated boards, 2s.

Ireland under the Land Act: Letters to the *Standard* during the Crisis. Containing the most recent Information about the State of the Country, the Popular Leaders, the League, the Working of the Sub-Commissions, &c. With Leading Cases under the Act, giving the Evidence in full; Judicial Dicta, &c. By E. CANT-WALL. Crown 8vo, cloth extra, 6s.

Irving (Washington), Works by:
Post 8vo, cloth limp, 2s. each.
Tales of a Traveller.
Tales of the Alhambra.

James.—Confidence: A Novel. By HENRY JAMES, Jun. Crown 8vo, cloth extra, 3s. 6d.; post 8vo, illustrated boards, 2s.

Janvier.—Practical Keramics for Students. By CATHERINE A. JANVIER. Crown 8vo, cloth extra, 6s.

Jay (Harriett), Novels by. Each crown 8vo, cloth extra, 3s. 6d.; or post 8vo, illustrated boards, 2s.
The Dark Colleen.
The Queen of Connaught.

Jefferies.—Nature near London. By RICHARD JEFFERIES, Author of "The Gamekeeper at Home." Crown 8vo, cloth extra, 6s.

Jennings (H. J.).—Curiosities of Criticism. By HENRY J. JENNINGS. Post 8vo, cloth limp, 2s. 6d.

Jennings (Hargrave). — The Rosicrucians: Their Rites and Mysteries. With Chapters on the Ancient Fire and Serpent Worshippers. By HARGRAVE JENNINGS. With Five full-page Plates and upwards of 300 Illustrations. A New Edition, crown 8vo, cloth extra, 7s. 6d.

Jerrold (Tom), Works by:
The Garden that Paid the Rent. By TOM JERROLD. Fcap. 8vo, illustrated cover, 1s.; cloth limp, 1s. 6d.
Household Horticulture: A Gossip about Flowers. By TOM and JANE JERROLD. Illustrated. Post 8vo, cloth limp, 2s. 6d.
Our Kitchen Garden: The Plants we Grow, and How we Cook Them. By TOM JERROLD. Post 8vo, cloth limp, 2s. 6d.

Jesse.—Scenes and Occupations of a Country Life. By EDWARD JESSE. Post 8vo. cloth limp, 2s.

Jones (William, F.S.A.), Works by:
Finger-Ring Lore: Historical, Legendary, and Anecdotal. With over 200 Illustrations. Crown 8vo, cloth extra, 7s. 6d.
Credulities, Past and Present; including the Sea and Seamen, Miners, Talismans, Word and Letter Divination, Exorcising and Blessing of Animals, Birds, Eggs, Luck, &c. With an Etched Frontispiece. Crown 8vo, cloth extra, 7s. 6d.
Crowns and Coronations: A History of Regalia in all Times and Countries. With about 150 Illustrations, many full-page. Crown 8vo, cloth extra, 7s. 6d. [*In preparation.*

Jonson's (Ben) Works. With Notes Critical and Explanatory, and a Biographical Memoir by WILLIAM GIFFORD. Edited by Colonel CUNNINGHAM. Three Vols., crown 8vo, cloth extra, 18s.; or separately, 6s. per Volume.

Josephus, The Complete Works of. Translated by WHISTON. Containing both "The Antiquities of the Jews" and "The Wars of the Jews." Two Vols., 8vo, with 52 Illustrations and Maps, cloth extra, gilt, 14s.

Kavanagh.—The Pearl Fountain, and other Fairy Stories. By BRIDGET and JULIA KAVANAGH. Thirty Illustrations by J. MOYR SMITH. Small 8vo, cloth gilt, 6s.

Kempt.—Pencil and Palette: Chapters on Art and Artists. By ROBERT KEMPT. Post 8vo, cloth limp, 2s. 6d.

Kingsley (Henry), Novels by: Each crown 8vo, cloth extra, 3s. 6d.; or post 8vo, illustrated boards, 2s.
Oakshott Castle.
Number Seventeen.

Lace (Old Point), and How to Copy and Imitate it. By DAISY WATERHOUSE HAWKINS. With 17 Illustrations by the Author. Crown 8vo, illustrated boards, 2s. 6d.

Lamb (Charles):
Mary and Charles Lamb: Their Poems, Letters, and Remains. With Reminiscences and Notes by W. CAREW HAZLITT. With HANCOCK'S Portrait of the Essayist, Facsimiles of the Title-pages of the rare First Editions of Lamb's and Coleridge's Works, and numerous Illustrations. Crown 8vo, cloth extra, 10s. 6d.

Lamb's Complete Works, in Prose and Verse, reprinted from the Original Editions, with many Pieces hitherto unpublished. Edited, with Notes and Introduction, by R. H. SHEPHERD. With Two Portraits and Facsimile of a Page of the "Essay on Roast Pig." Crown 8vo, cloth extra, 7s. 6d.

The Essays of Elia. Complete Edition. Post 8vo, cloth extra, 2s.

Poetry for Children, and Prince Dorus. By CHARLES LAMB. Carefully Reprinted from unique copies. Small 8vo, cloth extra 5s.

Lane's Arabian Nights, &c.: The Thousand and One Nights: commonly called, in England, "THE ARABIAN NIGHTS' ENTERTAINMENTS." A New Translation from the Arabic, with copious Notes, by EDWARD WILLIAM LANE. Illustrated by many hundred Engravings on Wood, from Original Designs by WM. HARVEY. A New Edition, from a Copy annotated by the Translator, edited by his Nephew, EDWARD STANLEY POOLE. With a Preface by STANLEY LANE-POOLE. Three Vols., demy 8vo, cloth extra, 7s. 6d. each.

Arabian Society in the Middle Ages: Studies from "The Thousand and One Nights." By EDWARD WM. LANE, Author of "The Modern Egyptians," &c. Edited by STANLEY LANE-POOLE. Cr. 8vo, cloth extra, 6s.

Lares and Penates; or, The Background of Life. By FLORENCE CADDY. Crown 8vo, cloth extra, 6s.

Larwood (Jacob), Works by:
The Story of the London Parks. With Illustrations. Crown 8vo, cloth extra, 3s. 6d.
Clerical Anecdotes. Post 8vo, cloth limp, 2s. 6d.
Forensic Anecdotes. Post 8vo, cloth limp, 2s. 6d.
Theatrical Anecdotes. Post 8vo, cloth limp, 2s. 6d.

Leigh (Henry S.), Works by:
Carols of Cockayne. With numerous Illustrations. Post 8vo, cloth limp, 2s. 6d.
A Town Garland. Crown 8vo, cloth extra, 6s.
Jeux d'Esprit. Collected and Edited by HENRY S. LEIGH. Post 8vo, cloth limp, 2s. 6d.

Linton (E. Lynn), Works by:
Witch Stories. Post 8vo, cloth limp, 2s. 6d.
The True Story of Joshua Davidson. Post 8vo, cloth limp, 2s. 6d.

Crown 8vo, cloth extra, 3s. 6d each; post 8vo, illustrated boards, 2s.
Patricia Kemball.
The Atonement of Leam Dundas.
The World Well Lost.
Under which Lord?
With a Silken Thread.
The Rebel of the Family.
"My Love!"

CHATTO & WINDUS, PICCADILLY. 15

Life in London; or, The History of Jerry Hawthorn and Corinthian Tom. With the whole of CRUIKSHANK's Illustrations, in Colours, after the Originals. Crown 8vo, cloth extra, 7s. 6d.

Longfellow:
Longfellow's Complete Prose Works. Including "Outre Mer," "Hyperion," "Kavanagh," "The Poets and Poetry of Europe," and "Driftwood." With Portrait and Illustrations by VALENTINE BROMLEY. Crown 8vo, cloth extra, 7s. 6d.

Longfellow's Poetical Works. Carefully Reprinted from the Original Editions. With numerous fine Illustrations on Steel and Wood. Crown 8vo, cloth extra, 7s. 6d.

Lucy.—Gideon Fleyce: A Novel. By HENRY W. LUCY. Three Vols., crown 8vo, 31s. 6d.

Lunatic Asylum, My Experiences in a. By A· SANE PATIENT. Crown 8vo, cloth extra, 5s.

Lusiad (The) of Camoens. Translated into English Spenserian Verse by ROBERT FFRENCH DUFF. Demy 8vo, with Fourteen full-page Plates, cloth boards, 18s.

McCarthy (Justin, M.P.), Works by:
A History of Our Own Times, from the Accession of Queen Victoria to the General Election of 1880. Four Vols. demy 8vo, cloth extra, 12s. each.—Also a POPULAR EDITION, in Four Vols. crown 8vo, cloth extra, 6s. each.

A Short History of Our Own Times. One Volume, crown 8vo, cloth extra, 6s. [*In preparation.*

History of the Four Georges. Four Vols. demy 8vo, cloth extra, 12s. each. [*In preparation.*

Crown 8vo, cloth extra, 3s. 6d. each; post 8vo, illustrated boards, 2s. each.
Dear Lady Disdain.
The Waterdale Neighbours.
My Enemy's Daughter.
A Fair Saxon.
Linley Rochford.
Miss Misanthrope.
Donna Quixote.

The Comet of a Season. Crown 8vo, cloth extra, 3s. 0d.

McCarthy (Justin H.), Works by:
An Outline of the History of Ireland, from the Earliest Times to the Present Day. Crown 8vo, 1s.; cloth, 1s. 6d.

Serapion, and other Poems. Crown 8vo, cloth extra, 6s.

MacDonald (George, LL.D.), Works by:
The Princess and Curdie. With 11 Illustrations by JAMES ALLEN. Small crown 8vo, cloth extra, 5s.

Gutta-Percha Willie, the Working Genius. With 9 Illustrations by ARTHUR HUGHES. Square 8vo, cloth extra, 3s. 6d.

Paul Faber, Surgeon. With a Frontispiece by J. E. MILLAIS. Crown 8vo, cloth extra, 3s. 6d.; post 8vo, illustrated boards, 2s.

Thomas Wingfold, Curate. With a Frontispiece by C. J. STANILAND. Crown 8vo, cloth extra, 3s. 6d.; post 8vo, illustrated boards, 2s.

Macdonell.—Quaker Cousins: A Novel. By AGNES MACDONELL. Crown 8vo, cloth extra, 3s. 6d.; post 8vo, illustrated boards, 2s.

Macgregor. — Pastimes and Players. Notes on Popular Games. By ROBERT MACGREGOR. Post 8vo, cloth limp, 2s. 6d.

Macquoid (Mrs.), Works by:
In the Ardennes. With 50 fine Illustrations by THOMAS R. MACQUOID. Square 8vo, cloth extra, 10s. 6d.

Pictures and Legends from Normandy and Brittany. With numerous Illustrations by THOMAS R. MACQUOID. Square 8vo, cloth gilt, 10s. 6d.

Through Normandy. With 90 Illustrations by T. R. MACQUOID. Square 8vo, cloth extra, 7s. 6d.

Through Brittany. With numerous Illustrations by T. R. MACQUOID. Square 8vo, cloth extra, 7s. 6d.

About Yorkshire. With about 70 Illustrations by T. R. MACQUOID, Engraved by SWAIN. Square 8vo, cloth extra, 10s. 6d.

The Evil Eye, and other Stories. Crown 8vo, cloth extra, 3s. 6d.; post 8vo, illustrated boards, 2s.

Lost Rose, and other Stories. Crown 8vo, cloth extra, 3s. 6d.; post 8vo, illustrated boards, 2s.

BOOKS PUBLISHED BY

Maclise Portrait-Gallery (The) of Illustrious Literary Characters; with Memoirs—Biographical, Critical, Bibliographical, and Anecdotal—illustrative of the Literature of the former half of the Present Century. By WILLIAM BATES, B.A. With 85 Portraits printed on an India Tint. Crown 8vo, cloth extra, 7s. 6d. [*In the press.*

Magician's Own Book (The): Performances with Cups and Balls, Eggs, Hats, Handkerchiefs, &c. All from actual Experience. Edited by W. H. CREMER. With 200 Illustrations. Crown 8vo, cloth extra, 4s. 6d.

Magic No Mystery: Tricks with Cards, Dice, Balls, &c., with fully descriptive Directions; the Art of Secret Writing; Training of Performing Animals, &c. With Coloured Frontispiece and many Illustrations. Crown 8vo, cloth extra, 4s. 6d.

Magna Charta. An exact Facsimile of the Original in the British Museum, printed on fine plate paper, 3 feet by 2 feet, with Arms and Seals emblazoned in Gold and Colours. Price 5s.

Mallock (W. H.), Works by:

The New Republic; or, Culture, Faith and Philosophy in an English Country House. Post 8vo, cloth limp, 2s. 6d.; Cheap Edition, illustrated boards, 2s.

The New Paul and Virginia; or, Positivism on an Island. Post 8vo, cloth limp, 2s. 6d.

Poems. Small 4to, bound in parchment, 8s.

Is Life worth Living? Crown 8vo, cloth extra, 6s.

A Romance of the Nineteenth Century. Second Edition, with a Preface. Two Vols., crown 8vo, 21s.

Mallory's (Sir Thomas) Mort d'Arthur: The Stories of King Arthur and of the Knights of the Round Table. Edited by B. MONTGOMERIE RANKING. Post 8vo, cloth limp, 2s.

Marryat (Florence), Novels by:
Crown 8vo, cloth extra, 3s. 6d. each; or post 8vo, illustrated boards, 2s.
Open! Sesame!
Written in Fire.

Post 8vo, illustrated boards, 2s. each.
A Harvest of Wild Oats.
A Little Stepson.
Fighting the Air.

Marlowe's Works. Including his Translations. Edited, with Notes and Introduction, by Col. CUNNINGHAM. Crown 8vo, cloth extra, 6s.

Mark Twain, Works by:

The Choice Works of Mark Twain. Revised and Corrected throughout by the Author. With Life, Portrait, and numerous Illustrations. Crown 8vo, cloth extra, 7s. 6d.

The Adventures of Tom Sawyer. With 100 Illustrations. Small 8vo, cloth extra, 7s. 6d. CHEAP EDITION, illustrated boards, 2s.

An Idle Excursion, and other Sketches. Post 8vo, illustrated boards, 2s.

The Prince and the Pauper. With nearly 200 Illustrations. Crown 8vo, cloth extra, 7s. 6d.

The Innocents Abroad; or, The New Pilgrim's Progress: Being some Account of the Steamship "Quaker City's" Pleasure Excursion to Europe and the Holy Land. With 234 Illustrations. Crown 8vo, cloth extra, 7s. 6d. CHEAP EDITION (under the title of "MARK TWAIN'S PLEASURE TRIP"), post 8vo, illust. boards, 2s.

A Tramp Abroad. With 314 Illustrations. Crown 8vo, cloth extra, 7s. 6d.

The Stolen White Elephant, &c. Crown 8vo, cloth extra, 6s.

Life on the Mississippi. With about 300 Original Illustrations. Crown 8vo, cloth extra, 7s. 6d.

Massinger's Plays. From the Text of WILLIAM GIFFORD. Edited by Col. CUNNINGHAM. Crown 8vo, cloth extra, 6s.

Mayhew.—London Characters and the Humorous Side of London Life. By HENRY MAYHEW. With numerous Illustrations. Crown 8vo, cloth extra, 3s. 6d.

Mayfair Library, The:
Post 8vo, cloth limp, 2s. 6d. per Volume.

A Journey Round My Room. By XAVIER DE MAISTRE. Translated by HENRY ATTWELL.

Latter-Day Lyrics. Edited by W. DAVENPORT ADAMS.

Quips and Quiddities. Selected by W. DAVENPORT ADAMS.

The Agony Column of "The Times," from 1800 to 1870. Edited, with an Introduction, by ALICE CLAY.

Balzac's "Comedie Humaine" and its Author. With Translations by H. H. WALKER.

CHATTO & WINDUS, PICCADILLY. 17

MAYFAIR LIBRARY, continued—
Melancholy Anatomised: A Popular Abridgment of "Burton's Anatomy of Melancholy."
Gastronomy as a Fine Art. By BRILLAT-SAVARIN.
The Speeches of Charles Dickens.
Literary Frivolities, Fancies, Follies, and Frolics. By W. T. DOBSON.
Poetical Ingenuities and Eccentricities. Selected and Edited by W. T. DOBSON.
The Cupboard Papers. By FIN-BEC.
Original Plays by W. S. GILBERT. FIRST SERIES. Containing: The Wicked World — Pygmalion and Galatea — Charity — The Princess — The Palace of Truth — Trial by Jury.
Original Plays by W. S. GILBERT. SECOND SERIES. Containing: Broken Hearts — Engaged — Sweethearts — Gretchen — Dan'l Druce — Tom Cobb — H.M.S. Pinafore — The Sorcerer — The Pirates of Penzance.
Animals and their Masters. By Sir ARTHUR HELPS.
Curiosities of Criticism. By HENRY J. JENNINGS.
The Autocrat of the Breakfast-Table. By OLIVER WENDELL HOLMES. Illustrated by J. GORDON THOMSON.
Pencil and Palette. By ROBERT KEMPT.
Clerical Anecdotes. By JACOB LARWOOD.
Forensic Anecdotes; or, Humour and Curiosities of the Law and Men of Law. By JACOB LARWOOD.
Theatrical Anecdotes. By JACOB LARWOOD.
Carols of Cockayne. By HENRY S. LEIGH.
Jeux d'Esprit. Edited by HENRY S. LEIGH.
True History of Joshua Davidson. By E. LYNN LINTON.
Witch Stories. By E. LYNN LINTON.
Pastimes and Players. By ROBERT MACGREGOR.
The New Paul and Virginia. By W. H. MALLOCK.
The New Republic. By W. H. MALLOCK.
Muses of Mayfair. Edited by H. CHOLMONDELEY-PENNELL.
Thoreau: His Life and Aims. By H. A. PAGE.
Puck on Pegasus. By H. CHOLMONDELEY-PENNELL.
Puniana. By the Hon. HUGH ROWLEY.

MAYFAIR LIBRARY, continued—
More Puniana. By the Hon. HUGH ROWLEY.
The Philosophy of Handwriting. By DON FELIX DE SALAMANCA.
By Stream and Sea. By WILLIAM SENIOR.
Old Stories Re-told. By WALTER THORNBURY.
Leaves from a Naturalist's Note-Book. By Dr. ANDREW WILSON.

Merry Circle (The): A Book of New Intellectual Games and Amusements. By CLARA BELLEW. With numerous Illustrations. Crown 8vo, cloth extra, 4s. 6d.

Middlemass (Jean), Novels by:
Touch and Go. Crown 8vo, cloth extra, 3s. 6d.; post 8vo, illustrated boards, 2s.
Mr. Dorillion. Post 8vo, illustrated boards, 2s.

Miller. — Physiology for the Young; or, The House of Life: Human Physiology, with its application to the Preservation of Health. For use in Classes and Popular Reading. With numerous Illustrations. By Mrs. F. FENWICK MILLER. Small 8vo, cloth limp, 2s. 6d.

Milton (J. L.), Works by:
The Hygiene of the Skin. A Concise Set of Rules for the Management of the Skin; with Directions for Diet, Wines, Soaps, Baths, &c. Small 8vo, 1s.; cloth extra, 1s. 6d.
The Bath in Diseases of the Skin. Small 8vo, 1s.; cloth extra, 1s. 6d.
The Laws of Life, and their Relation to Diseases of the Skin. Small 8vo, 1s.; cloth extra, 1s. 6d.

Moncrieff. — The Abdication; or, Time Tries All. An Historical Drama. By W. D. SCOTT-MONCRIEFF. With Seven Etchings by JOHN PETTIE, R.A., W. Q. ORCHARDSON, R.A., J. MACWHIRTER, A.R.A., COLIN HUNTER, R. MACBETH, and TOM GRAHAM. Large 4to, bound in buckram, 21s.

Murray (D. Christie), Novels by:
A Life's Atonement. Crown 8vo, cloth extra, 3s. 6d.; post 8vo, illustrated boards, 2s.
Joseph's Coat. With Illustrations by F. BARNARD. Crown 8vo, cloth extra 3s 6d.

D. C. MURRAY'S NOVELS, continued—

Coals of Fire. With Illustrations by ARTHUR HOPKINS and others. Crown 8vo, cloth extra, 3s. 6d.

A Model Father, and other Stories. Crown 8vo, cloth extra, 3s. 6d.; post 8vo, illustrated boards, 2s. [July.

Val Strange: A Story of the Primrose Way. Three Vols., crown 8vo, 31s.6d.

Hearts. Three Vols., crown 8vo, 31s. 6d.

By the Gate of the Sea. Two Vols., post 8vo, 12s. [Shortly.

North Italian Folk. By Mrs. COMYNS CARR. Illustrated by RANDOLPH CALDECOTT. Square 8vo, cloth extra, 7s. 6d.

Number Nip (Stories about), the Spirit of the Giant Mountains. Retold for Children by WALTER GRAHAME. With Illustrations by J. MOYR SMITH. Post 8vo, cloth extra, 5s.

Oliphant. — Whiteladies: A Novel. With Illustrations by ARTHUR HOPKINS and HENRY WOODS. Crown 8vo, cloth extra, 3s. 6d.; post 8vo, illustrated boards, 2s.

O'Reilly.—Phœbe's Fortunes: A Novel. With Illustrations by HENRY TUCK. Post 8vo, illustrated boards, 2s.

O'Shaughnessy (Arth.), Works by:

Songs of a Worker. Fcap. 8vo, cloth extra, 7s. 6d.

Music and Moonlight. Fcap. 8vo, cloth extra, 7s. 6d.

Lays of France. Crown 8vo, cloth extra, 10s. 6d.

Ouida, Novels by. Crown 8vo, cloth extra, 5s. each; post 8vo, illustrated boards, 2s. each.

Held in Bondage.
Strathmore.
Chandos.
Under Two Flags.
Idalia.
Cecil Castlemaine's Gage.
Tricotrin.
Puck.
Folle Farine.
A Dog of Flanders.
Pascarel.
Two Little Wooden Shoes.

OUIDA'S NOVELS, continued—

Signa.
In a Winter City.
Ariadne.
Friendship.
Moths.
Pipistrello.
A Village Commune.

In Maremma. Crown 8vo, cloth extra, 5s.

Bimbi: Stories for Children. Square 8vo, cloth gilt, cinnamon edges,7s.6d.

Wanda: A Novel. Three Vols., crown 8vo, 31s. 6d.

Wisdom, Poetry, and Pathos, Selected from the Works of OUIDA. By F. S. MORRIS. Small crown 8vo, cloth extra, 5s. [In the press.

Page (H. A.), Works by:

Thoreau: His Life and Aims: A Study. With a Portrait. Post 8vo, cloth limp, 2s. 6d.

Lights on the Way: Some Tales within a Tale. By the late J. H. ALEXANDER, B.A. Edited by H. A. PAGE. Crown 8vo, cloth extra, 6s.

Pascal's Provincial Letters. A New Translation, with Historical Introduction and Notes, by T. M'CRIE, D.D. Post 8vo, cloth limp, 2s.

Paul Ferroll:

Post 8vo, illustrated boards, 2s. each.
Paul Ferroll: A Novel.
Why Paul Ferroll Killed His Wife.

Payn (James), Novels by:

Each crown 8vo, cloth extra, 3s. 6d.; or post 8vo, illustrated boards, 2s.

Lost Sir Massingberd.
The Best of Husbands.
Walter's Word.
Halves.
Fallen Fortunes.
What He Cost Her.
Less Black than We're Painted.
By Proxy.
Under One Roof.
High Spirits.
Carlyon's Year.
A Confidential Agent.
Some Private Views.
From Exile.

CHATTO & WINDUS, PICCADILLY. 19

JAMES PAYN'S NOVELS, *continued*—
Post 8vo, illustrated boards, 2s. each.
A Perfect Treasure.
Bentinck's Tutor.
Murphy's Master.
A County Family.
At Her Mercy.
A Woman's Vengeance.
Cecil's Tryst.
The Clyffards of Clyffe.
The Family Scapegrace.
The Foster Brothers.
Found Dead.
Gwendoline's Harvest.
Humorous Stories.
Like Father, Like Son.
A Marine Residence.
Married Beneath Him.
Mirk Abbey.
Not Wooed, but Won.
Two Hundred Pounds Reward.

A Grape from a Thorn. With Illustrations by W. SMALL. Crown 8vo, cloth extra, 3s. 6d.

For Cash Only. Crown 8vo, cloth extra, 3s. 6d.

Kit: A Memory. Three Vols., crown 8vo, 31s. 6d.

Pennell (H. Cholmondeley), Works by: Post 8vo, cloth limp, 2s. 6d. each.
Puck on Pegasus. With Illustrations.
The Muses of Mayfair. Vers de Société, Selected and Edited by H. C. PENNELL.

Pirkis.—Trooping with Crows: A Story. By CATHERINE PIRKIS. Fcap. 8vo, picture cover, 1s.

Planche (J. R.), Works by:
The Encyclopædia of Costume; or, A Dictionary of Dress—Regal, Ecclesiastical, Civil, and Military—from the Earliest Period in England to the Reign of George the Third. Including Notices of Contemporaneous Fashions on the Continent, and a General History of the Costumes of the Principal Countries of Europe. Two Vols., demy 4to, half morocco, profusely Illustrated with Coloured and Plain Plates and Woodcuts, £7 7s. The Volumes may also be had *separately* (each complete in itself) at £3 13s. 6d. each: Vol. I. THE DICTIONARY. Vol. II. A GENERAL HISTORY OF COSTUME IN EUROPE.

PLANCHE'S WORKS, *continued*—
The Pursuivant of Arms; or, Heraldry Founded upon Facts. With Coloured Frontispiece and 200 Illustrations. Crown 8vo, cloth extra, 7s. 6d.
Songs and Poems, from 1819 to 1879. Edited, with an Introduction, by his Daughter, Mrs. MACKARNESS. Crown 8vo, cloth extra, 6s.

Play-time: Sayings and Doings of Babyland. By EDWARD STANFORD. Large 4to, handsomely printed in Colours, 4s. 6d. [*Shortly*.

Plutarch's Lives of Illustrious Men. Translated from the Greek, with Notes Critical and Historical, and a Life of Plutarch, by JOHN and WILLIAM LANGHORNE. Two Vols., 8vo, cloth extra, with Portraits, 10s. 6d.

Poe (Edgar Allan):—
The Choice Works, in Prose and Poetry, of EDGAR ALLAN POE. With an Introductory Essay by CHARLES BAUDELAIRE, Portrait and Facsimiles. Crown 8vo, cloth extra, 7s. 6d.
The Mystery of Marie Roget, and other Stories. Post 8vo, illustrated boards, 2s.

Pope's Poetical Works. Complete in One Volume. Post 8vo, cloth limp, 2s.

Price.—Valentina: A Sketch. By E. C. PRICE. With a Frontispiece by HAL LUDLOW. Crown 8vo, cloth extra, 3s. 6d.; post 8vo, illustrated boards, 2s.

Proctor (Richd. A.), Works by:
Flowers of the Sky. With 55 Illustrations. Small crown 8vo, cloth extra, 4s. 6d.
Easy Star Lessons. With Star Maps for Every Night in the Year, Drawings of the Constellations, &c. Crown 8vo, cloth extra, 6s.
Familiar Science Studies. Crown 8vo, cloth extra, 7s. 6d.
Myths and Marvels of Astronomy. Crown 8vo, cloth extra, 6s.
Pleasant Ways in Science. Crown 8vo, cloth extra, 6s.
Rough Ways made Smooth: A Series of Familiar Essays on Scientific Subjects. Crown 8vo, cloth extra, 6s.

R. A. PROCTOR'S WORKS, continued—

Our Place among Infinities: A Series of Essays contrasting our Little Abode in Space and Time with the Infinities Around us. Crown 8vo, cloth extra, 6s.

The Expanse of Heaven: A Series of Essays on the Wonders of the Firmament. Cr. 8vo, cloth extra, 6s.

Saturn and its System. New and Revised Edition, with 13 Steel Plates. Demy 8vo, cloth extra, 10s. 6d.

The Great Pyramid: Observatory, Tomb, and Temple. With Illustrations. Crown 8vo, cloth extra, 6s.

Mysteries of Time and Space. With Illustrations. Crown 8vo, cloth extra, 7s. 6d.

Wages and Wants of Science Workers. Crown 8vo, 1s. 6d.

Pyrotechnist's Treasury (The); or, Complete Art of Making Fireworks. By THOMAS KENTISH. With numerous Illustrations. Crown 8vo, cloth extra, 4s. 6d.

Rabelais' Works. Faithfully Translated from the French, with variorum Notes, and numerous characteristic Illustrations by GUSTAVE DORE. Crown 8vo, cloth extra, 7s. 6d.

Rambosson.—Popular Astronomy. By J. RAMBOSSON, Laureate of the Institute of France. Translated by C. B. PITMAN. Crown 8vo, cloth gilt, with numerous Illustrations, and a beautifully executed Chart of Spectra, 7s. 6d.

Reader's Handbook (The) of Allusions, References, Plots, and Stories. By the Rev. Dr. BREWER. Third Edition, revised throughout, with a New Appendix, containing a COMPLETE ENGLISH BIBLIOGRAPHY. Crown 8vo, 1,400 pages, cloth extra, 7s. 6d.

Reade (Charles, D.C.L.), Novels by. Each post 8vo, illustrated boards, 2s.; or crown 8vo, cloth extra, Illustrated, 3s. 6d.

Peg Woffington. Illustrated by S. L. FILDES, A.R.A.

Christie Johnstone. Illustrated by WILLIAM SMALL.

It is Never Too Late to Mend. Illustrated by G. J. PINWELL.

The Course of True Love Never did run Smooth. Illustrated by HELEN PATERSON.

CHARLES READE'S NOVELS, continued—

The Autobiography of a Thief; Jack of all Trades; and James Lambert. Illustrated by MATT STRETCH.

Love me Little, Love me Long. Illustrated by M. ELLEN EDWARDS.

The Double Marriage. Illustrated by Sir JOHN GILBERT, R.A., and CHARLES KEENE.

The Cloister and the Hearth. Illustrated by CHARLES KEENE.

Hard Cash. Illustrated by F. W. LAWSON.

Griffith Gaunt. Illustrated by S. L. FILDES, A.R.A., and WM. SMALL.

Foul Play. Illustrated by GEORGE DU MAURIER.

Put Yourself in His Place. Illustrated by ROBERT BARNES.

A Terrible Temptation. Illustrated by EDWARD HUGHES and A. W. COOPER.

The Wandering Heir. Illustrated by HELEN PATERSON, S. L. FILDES, A.R.A., CHARLES GREEN, and HENRY WOODS, A.R.A.

A Simpleton. Illustrated by KATE CRAUFORD.

A Woman-Hater. Illustrated by THOS. COULDERY.

Readiana. With a Steel Plate Portrait of CHARLES READE.

A New Collection of Stories. In Three Vols., crown 8vo. [Preparing.

Richardson.— A Ministry of Health, and other Papers. By BENJAMIN WARD RICHARDSON, M.D., &c. Crown 8vo, cloth extra, 6s.

Riddell (Mrs. J. H.), Novels by: Her Mother's Darling. Crown 8vo, cloth extra, 3s. 6d.; post 8vo, illustrated boards, 2s.

The Prince of Wales's Garden Party, and other Stories. With a Frontispiece by M. ELLEN EDWARDS. Crown 8vo, cloth extra, 3s. 6d.

Rimmer (Alfred), Works by: Our Old Country Towns. By ALFRED RIMMER. With over 50 Illustrations by the Author. Square 8vo, cloth extra, gilt, 10s. 6d.

Rambles Round Eton and Harrow. By ALFRED RIMMER. With 50 Illustrations by the Author. Square 8vo, cloth gilt, 10s. 6d.

About England with Dickens. With 58 Illustrations by ALFRED RIMMER and C. A. VANDERHOOF. Square 8vo, cloth gilt, 10s. 6d.

Robinson (F. W.), Novels by:
Women are Strange, &c. Three Vols., crown 8vo, 31s. 6d.
The Hands of Justice. Three Vols., crown 8vo, 31s. 6d.

Robinson.—The Poets' Birds.
By PHIL ROBINSON, Author of "Noah's Ark," &c. Cr. 8vo, cloth extra, 7s. 6d.

Robinson Crusoe: A beautiful
reproduction of Major's Edition, with 37 Woodcuts and Two Steel Plates by GEORGE CRUIKSHANK, choicely printed. Crown 8vo, cloth extra, 7s. 6d. A few Large-Paper copies, printed on handmade paper, with India proofs of the Illustrations, price 36s. [*In preparation.*

Rochefoucauld's Maxims and
Moral Reflections. With Notes, and an Introductory Essay by SAINTE-BEUVE. Post 8vo, cloth limp, 2s.

Roll of Battle Abbey, The; or,
A List of the Principal Warriors who came over from Normandy with William the Conqueror, and Settled in this Country, A.D. 1066-7. With the principal Arms emblazoned in Gold and Colours. Handsomely printed, price 5s.

Ross.—Behind a Brass Knocker:
Some Grim Realities in Picture and Prose. By FRED. BARNARD and C. H. Ross. Demy 8vo, cloth extra, with 30 full-page Drawings, 10s. 6d.

Rowley (Hon. Hugh), Works by:
Post 8vo, cloth limp, 2s. 6d. each.
Puniana: Riddles and Jokes. With numerous Illustrations.
More Puniana. Profusely Illustrated.

Sala.—Gaslight and Daylight.
By GEORGE AUGUSTUS SALA. Post 8vo, illustrated boards, 2s.

Sanson.—Seven Generations
of Executioners: Memoirs of the Sanson Family (1688 to 1847). Edited by HENRY SANSON. Crown 8vo, cloth extra, 3s. 6d.

Saunders (John), Novels by:
Crown 8vo, cloth extra, 3s. 6d. each; or post 8vo, illustrated boards, 2s. each.
Bound to the Wheel.
One Against the World.
Guy Waterman.
The Lion in the Path.
The Two Dreamers.

Scott (Sir Walter).—The Lady
of the Lake. With 120 fine Illustrations. Small 4to, pine-wood binding, 16s.

"Secret Out" Series, The:
Crown 8vo, cloth extra, profusely Illustrated, 4s. 6d. each.
The Secret Out: One Thousand Tricks with Cards, and other Recreations; with Entertaining Experiments in Drawing-room or "White Magic." By W. H. CREMER. 300 Engravings.
The Pyrotechnist's Treasury; or, Complete Art of Making Fireworks. By THOMAS KENTISH. With numerous Illustrations.
The Art of Amusing: A Collection of Graceful Arts, Games, Tricks, Puzzles, and Charades. By FRANK BELLEW. With 300 Illustrations.
Hanky-Panky: Very Easy Tricks, Very Difficult Tricks, White Magic, Sleight of Hand. Edited by W. H. CREMER. With 200 Illustrations.
The Merry Circle: A Book of New Intellectual Games and Amusements. By CLARA BELLEW. Many Illusts.
Magician's Own Book: Performances with Cups and Balls, Eggs, Hats, Handkerchiefs, &c. All from actual Experience. Edited by W. H. CREMER. 200 Illustrations.
Magic No Mystery: Tricks with Cards, Dice, Balls, &c., with fully descriptive Directions; the Art of Secret Writing; Training of Performing Animals, &c. Coloured Frontispiece and many Illustrations.

Senior (William), Works by:
Travel and Trout in the Antipodes. Crown 8vo, cloth extra, 6s.
By Stream and Sea. Post 8vo, cloth limp, 2s. 6d.

Shakespeare:
The First Folio Shakespeare.—MR. WILLIAM SHAKESPEARE'S Comedies, Histories, and Tragedies. Published according to the true Originall Copies. London, Printed by ISAAC IAGGARD and ED. BLOUNT. 1623.—A Reproduction of the extremely rare original, in reduced facsimile, by a photographic process—ensuring the strictest accuracy in every detail. Small 8vo, half-Roxburghe, 7s. 6d.
The Lansdowne Shakespeare. Beautifully printed in red and black, in small but very clear type. With engraved facsimile of DROESHOUT'S Portrait. Post 8vo, cloth extra, 7s. 6d.

SHAKESPEARE, continued—

Shakespeare for Children: Tales from Shakespeare. By CHARLES and MARY LAMB. With numerous Illustrations, coloured and plain, by J. MOYR SMITH. Crown 4to, cloth gilt, 6s.

The Handbook of Shakespeare Music. Being an Account of 350 Pieces of Music, set to Words taken from the Plays and Poems of Shakespeare, the compositions ranging from the Elizabethan Age to the Present Time. By ALFRED ROFFE. 4to, half-Roxburghe, 7s.

A Study of Shakespeare. By ALGERNON CHARLES SWINBURNE. Crown 8vo, cloth extra, 8s.

Shelley's Complete Works, in Four Vols., post 8vo, cloth limp, 8s.; or separately, 2s. each. Vol. I. contains his Early Poems, Queen Mab, &c., with an Introduction by LEIGH HUNT; Vol. II., his Later Poems, Laon and Cythna, &c.; Vol. III., Posthumous Poems, the Shelley Papers, &c.; Vol. IV., his Prose Works, including A Refutation of Deism, Zastrozzi, St. Irvyne, &c.

Sheridan's Complete Works, with Life and Anecdotes. Including his Dramatic Writings, printed from the Original Editions, his Works in Prose and Poetry, Translations, Speeches, Jokes, Puns, &c. With a Collection of Sheridaniana. Crown 8vo, cloth extra, gilt, with 10 full-page Tinted Illustrations, 7s. 6d.

Short Sayings of Great Men. With Historical and Explanatory Notes by SAMUEL A. BENT, M.A. Demy 8vo, cloth extra, 7s. 6d.

Sidney's (Sir Philip) Complete Poetical Works, Including all those in "Arcadia." With Portrait, Memorial-Introduction, Essay on the Poetry of Sidney, and Notes, by the Rev. A. B. GROSART, D.D. Three Vols., crown 8vo, cloth boards, 18s.

Signboards: Their History. With Anecdotes of Famous Taverns and Remarkable Characters. By JACOB LARWOOD and JOHN CAMDEN HOTTEN. Crown 8vo, cloth extra, with 100 Illustrations, 7s. 6d.

Sketchley.—A Match in the Dark. By ARTHUR SKETCHLEY. Post 8vo, illustrated boards, 2s.

Slang Dictionary, The: Etymological, Historical, and Anecdotal. Crown 8vo, cloth extra, gilt, 6s. 6d.

Smith (J. Moyr), Works by:
The Prince of Argolis: A Story of the Old Greek Fairy Time. By J. MOYR SMITH. Small 8vo, cloth extra, with 130 Illustrations, 3s. 6d.
Tales of Old Thule. Collected and Illustrated by J. MOYR SMITH. Crown 8vo, cloth gilt, profusely Illustrated, 6s.
The Wooing of the Water Witch: A Northern Oddity. By EVAN DALDORNE. Illustrated by J. MOYR SMITH. Small 8vo, cloth extra, 6s.

South-West, The New: Travelling Sketches from Kansas, New Mexico, Arizona, and Northern Mexico. By ERNST VON HESSE-WARTEGG. With 100 fine Illustrations and 3 Maps. 8vo, cloth extra, 14s. [In preparation.

Spalding.-Elizabethan Demonology: An Essay in Illustration of the Belief in the Existence of Devils, and the Powers possessed by Them. By T. ALFRED SPALDING, LL.B. Crown 8vo, cloth extra, 5s.

Speight. — The Mysteries of Heron Dyke. By T. W. SPEIGHT. With a Frontispiece by M. ELLEN EDWARDS. Crown 8vo, cloth extra, 3s. 6d ; post 8vo, illustrated boards, 2s.

Spenser for Children. By M. H. TOWRY. With Illustrations by WALTER J MORGAN. Crown 4to, with Coloured Illustrations, cloth gilt, 6s.

Staunton.—Laws and Practice of Chess; Together with an Analysis of the Openings, and a Treatise on End Games. By HOWARD STAUNTON. Edited by ROBERT B. WORMALD. A New Edition, small crown 8vo, cloth extra, 5s.

Stedman. — Victorian Poets: Critical Essays. By EDMUND CLARENCE STEDMAN. Crown 8vo, cloth extra, 9s.

Sterndale.—The Afghan Knife: A Novel. By ROBERT ARMITAGE STERNDALE, F.R.G.S. Crown 8vo, cloth extra, 3s. 6d. ; post 8vo, illustrated boards, 2s. [Shortly.

CHATTO & WINDUS, PICCADILLY. 23

Stevenson (R. Louis), Works by:
Familiar Studies of Men and Books. Crown 8vo, cloth extra, 6s.
New Arabian Nights. New and Cheaper Edition. Crown 8vo, cloth extra, 6s.

St. John.—A Levantine Family. By BAYLE ST. JOHN. Post 8vo, illustrated boards, 2s.

Stoddard.—Summer Cruising in the South Seas. By CHARLES WARREN STODDARD. Illustrated by WALLIS MACKAY. Crown 8vo, cloth extra, 3s. 6d.

St. Pierre.—Paul and Virginia, and The Indian Cottage. By BERNARDIN DE ST. PIERRE. Edited, with Life, by the Rev. E. CLARKE. Post 8vo, cloth limp, 2s.

Strahan.—Twenty Years of a Publisher's Life. By ALEXANDER STRAHAN. Two Vols., crown 8vo, with numerous Portraits and Illustrations, 24s. [*In preparation.*

Strutt's Sports and Pastimes of the People of England; including the Rural and Domestic Recreations, May Games, Mummeries, Shows, Processions, Pageants, and Pompous Spectacles, from the Earliest Period to the Present Time. With 140 Illustrations. Edited by WILLIAM HONE. Crown 8vo, cloth extra, 7s. 6d.

Suburban Homes (The) of London: A Residential Guide to Favourite London Localities, their Society, Celebrities, and Associations. With Notes on their Rental, Rates, and House Accommodation. With a Map of Suburban London. Crown 8vo, cloth extra, 7s. 6d.

Swift's Choice Works, in Prose and Verse. With Memoir, Portrait, and Facsimiles of the Maps in the Original Edition of "Gulliver's Travels." Cr. 8vo, cloth extra, 7s. 6d.

Swinburne (Algernon C.), Works by:
The Queen Mother and Rosamond. Fcap. 8vo, 5s.
Atalanta in Calydon. Crown 8vo, 6s.
Chastelard. A Tragedy. Crown 8vo, 7s.

SWINBURNE'S WORKS, *continued*—
Poems and Ballads. FIRST SERIES. Fcap. 8vo, 9s. Also in crown 8vo, at same price.
Poems and Ballads. SECOND SERIES. Fcap. 8vo, 9s. Also in crown 8vo, at same price.
Notes on Poems and Reviews. 8vo, 1s.
William Blake: A Critical Essay. With Facsimile Paintings. Demy 8vo, 16s.
Songs before Sunrise. Crown 8vo, 10s. 6d.
Bothwell: A Tragedy. Crown 8vo, 12s. 6d.
George Chapman: An Essay. Crown 8vo, 7s.
Songs of Two Nations. Crown 8vo, 6s.
Essays and Studies. Crown 8vo, 12s.
Erechtheus: A Tragedy. Crown 8vo, 6s.
Note of an English Republican on the Muscovite Crusade. 8vo, 1s.
A Note on Charlotte Bronte. Crown 8vo, 6s.
A Study of Shakespeare. Crown 8vo, 8s.
Songs of the Springtides. Crown 8vo, 6s.
Studies in Song. Crown 8vo, 7s.
Mary Stuart: A Tragedy. Crown 8vo, 8s.
Tristram of Lyonesse, and other Poems. Crown 8vo, 9s.
A Century of Roundels. Small 4to, cloth extra, 8s. [*In preparation.*

Syntax's (Dr.) Three Tours: In Search of the Picturesque, in Search of Consolation, and in Search of a Wife. With the whole of ROWLANDSON'S droll page Illustrations in Colours and a Life of the Author by J. C. HOTTEN. Medium 8vo, cloth extra, 7s. 6d.

Taine's History of English Literature. Translated by HENRY VAN LAUN. Four Vols., small 8vo, cloth boards, 30s.—POPULAR EDITION, in Two Vols., crown 8vo, cloth extra, 15s.

Taylor's (Bayard) Diversions of the Echo Club: Burlesques of Modern Writers. Post 8vo, cloth limp, 2s.

Taylor's (Tom) Historical Dramas: "Clancarty," "Jeanne Darc," "'Twixt Axe and Crown," "The Fool's Revenge," "Arkwright's Wife," "Anne Boleyn," "Plot and Passion." One Vol., crown 8vo, cloth extra, 7s. 6d.

∗∗ The Plays may also be had separately, at 1s. each.

Thackerayana: Notes and Anecdotes. Illustrated by Hundreds of Sketches by WILLIAM MAKEPEACE THACKERAY, depicting Humorous Incidents in his School-life, and Favourite Characters in the books of his every-day reading. With Coloured Frontispiece. Crown 8vo, cloth extra, 7s. 6d.

Thomas (Bertha), Novels by:
Each crown 8vo, cloth extra, 3s. 6d.; or post 8vo, illustrated boards, 2s.
Cressida.
Proud Maisie.
The Violin-Player.

Thomson's Seasons and Castle of Indolence. With a Biographical and Critical Introduction by ALLAN CUNNINGHAM, and over 50 fine Illustrations on Steel and Wood. Crown 8vo, cloth extra, gilt edges, 7s. 6d.

Thornbury (Walter), Works by:
Haunted London. Edited by EDWARD WALFORD, M.A. With Illustrations by F. W. FAIRHOLT, F.S.A. Crown 8vo, cloth extra, 7s. 6d.
The Life and Correspondence of J. M. W. Turner. Founded upon Letters and Papers furnished by his Friends and fellow Academicians. With numerous Illustrations in Colours, facsimiled from Turner's Original Drawings. Crown 8vo, cloth extra, 7s. 6d.
Old Stories Re-told. Post 8vo, cloth limp, 2s. 6d.
Tales for the Marines. Post 8vo, illustrated boards, 2s.

Timbs (John), Works by:
The History of Clubs and Club Life in London. With Anecdotes of its Famous Coffee-houses, Hostelries, and Taverns. With numerous Illustrations. Crown 8vo, cloth extra, 7s. 6d.

TIMBS' WORKS, *continued*—
English Eccentrics and Eccentricities: Stories of Wealth and Fashion, Delusions, Impostures, and Fanatic Missions, Strange Sights and Sporting Scenes, Eccentric Artists, Theatrical Folks, Men of Letters, &c. With nearly 50 Illusts. Crown 8vo, cloth extra, 7s. 6d.

Torrens. — **The Marquess Wellesley,** Architect of Empire. An Historic Portrait. By W. M. TORRENS, M.P. Demy 8vo, cloth extra, 14s.

Trollope (Anthony), Novels by:
The Way We Live Now. With Illustrations. Crown 8vo, cloth extra, 3s. 6d.; post 8vo, illust. boards, 2s.
The American Senator. Crown 8vo, cloth extra, 3s. 6d.; post 8vo, illustrated boards, 2s.
Kept in the Dark. With a Frontispiece by J. E. MILLAIS, R.A. Two Vols., post 8vo, 12s.
Frau Frohmann, &c. With Frontispiece. Crown 8vo, cloth extra, 3s. 6d.
Marion Fay. Cr. 8vo, cl. extra, 3s. 6d.
Mr. Scarborough's Family. Three Vols., crown 8vo, 31s. 6d.

Trollope (T. A.).—Diamond Cut Diamond, and other Stories. By THOMAS ADOLPHUS TROLLOPE. Crown 8vo, cloth extra, 3s. 6d.; post 8vo, illustrated boards, 2s.

Turner's Rivers of England: Sixteen Drawings by J. M. W. TURNER, R.A., and Three by THOMAS GIRTIN, Mezzotinted by THOMAS LUPTON, CHARLES TURNER, and other Engravers. With Descriptions by Mrs. HOFLAND. A New Edition, reproduced by Heliograph. Edited by W. COSMO MONKHOUSE, Author of "The Life of Turner" in the "Great Artists" Series. Large folio, 31s. 6d. [*Shortly.*

Tytler (Sarah), Novels by:
What She Came Through. Crown 8vo, cloth extra, 3s. 6d.; post 8vo, illustrated boards, 2s.
The Bride's Pass. With a Frontispiece by P. MACNAB. Crown 8vo, cloth extra, 3s. 6d.

Van Laun.—History of French Literature. By HENRI VAN LAUN. Complete in Three Vols., demy 8vo, cloth boards, 22s. 6d.

Villari. — **A Double Bond:** A Story. By LINDA VILLARI. Fcap. 8vo, picture cover, 1s.

Walcott.— Church Work and Life in English Minsters; and the English Student's Monasticon. By the Rev. MACKENZIE E. C. WALCOTT, B.D. Two Vols., crown 8vo, cloth extra, with Map and Ground-Plans, 14s.

Walford.—The County Families of the United Kingdom. By EDWARD WALFORD, M.A. Containing Notices of the Descent, Birth, Marriage, Education, &c., of more than 12,000 distinguished Heads of Families, their Heirs Apparent or Presumptive, the Offices they hold or have held, their Town and Country Addresses, Clubs, &c. The Twenty-third Annual Edition, for 1883, cloth, full gilt, 50s.

Walton and Cotton's Complete Angler; or, The Contemplative Man's Recreation; being a Discourse of Rivers, Fishponds, Fish and Fishing, written by IZAAK WALTON; and Instructions how to Angle for a Trout or Grayling in a clear Stream, by CHARLES COTTON. With Original Memoirs and Notes by Sir HARRIS NICOLAS, and 61 Copperplate Illustrations. Large crown 8vo, cloth antique, 7s. 6d.

Wanderer's Library, The:

Crown 8vo, cloth extra, 3s. 6d. each.

Wanderings In Patagonia; or, Life among the Ostrich Hunters. By JULIUS BEERBOHM. Illustrated.
Camp Notes: Stories of Sport and Adventure in Asia, Africa, and America. By FREDERICK BOYLE.
Savage Life. By FREDERICK BOYLE.
Merrie England in the Olden Time. By GEORGE DANIEL. With Illustrations by ROBT. CRUIKSHANK.
Circus Life and Circus Celebrities. By THOMAS FROST.
The Lives of the Conjurers. By THOMAS FROST.
The Old Showmen and the Old London Fairs. By THOMAS FROST.
Low Life Deeps. An Account of the Strange Fish to be found there. By JAMES GREENWOOD
The Wilds of London. By JAMES GREENWOOD.
Tunis: The Land and the People. By the Chevalier de HESSE-WARTEGG. With 22 Illustrations.
The Life and Adventures of a Cheap Jack. By One of the Fraternity. Edited by CHARLES HINDLEY.

WANDERER'S LIBRARY, *continued*—
The World Behind the Scenes. By PERCY FITZGERALD.
Tavern Anecdotes and Sayings: Including the Origin of Signs, and Reminiscences connected with Taverns, Coffee Houses, Clubs, &c. By CHARLES HINDLEY. With Illustrations.
The Genial Showman: Life and Adventures of Artemus Ward. By E. P. HINGSTON. With a Frontispiece.
The Story of the London Parks. By JACOB LARWOOD. With Illusts.
London Characters. By HENRY MAYHEW. Illustrated.
Seven Generations of Executioners: Memoirs of the Sanson Family (1688 to 1847). Edited by HENRY SANSON.
Summer Cruising in the South Seas. By CHARLES WARREN STODDARD. Illust. by WALLIS MACKAY.

Warrants, &c. :—

Warrant to Execute Charles I. An exact Facsimile, with the Fifty-nine Signatures, and corresponding Seals. Carefully printed on paper to imitate the Original, 22 in. by 14 in. Price 2s.
Warrant to Execute Mary Queen of Scots. An exact Facsimile, including the Signature of Queen Elizabeth, and a Facsimile of the Great Seal. Beautifully printed on paper to imitate the Original MS. Price 2s.
Magna Charta. An Exact Facsimile of the Original Document in the British Museum, printed on fine plate paper, nearly 3 feet long by 2 feet wide, with the Arms and Seals emblazoned in Gold and Colours. Price 5s.
The Roll of Battle Abbey; or, A List of the Principal Warriors who came over from Normandy with William the Conqueror, and Settled in this Country, A.D. 1066-7. With the principal Arms emblazoned in Gold and Colours. Price 5s.

Westropp.—Handbook of Pottery and Porcelain; or, History of those Arts from the Earliest Period. By HODDER M. WESTROPP. With numerous Illustrations, and a List of Marks. Crown 8vo, cloth limp, 4s. 6d.

Whistler v. Ruskin: Art and Art Critics. By J. A. MACNEILL WHISTLER. Seventh Edition, square 8vo, 1s.

White's Natural History of Selborne. Edited, with Additions, by THOMAS BROWN, F.L.S. Post 8vo, cloth limp, 2s.

Williams (W. Mattieu, F.R.A.S.), Works by:
Science In Short Chapters. Crown 8vo, cloth extra, 7s. 6d.
A Simple Treatise on Heat. Crown 8vo, cloth limp, with Illustrations, 2s. 6d.

Wilson (C.E.).—Persian Wit and Humour: Being the Sixth Book of the Baharistan of Jami, Translated for the first time from the Original Persian into English Prose and Verse. With Notes by C. E. WILSON, M.R.A.S., Assistant Librarian Royal Academy of Arts. Crown 8vo, parchment binding, 4s.

Wilson (Dr. Andrew, F.R.S.E.), Works by:
Chapters on Evolution: A Popular History of the Darwinian and Allied Theories of Development. Second Edition. Crown 8vo, cloth extra, with 259 Illustrations, 7s. 6d.
Leaves from a Naturalist's Notebook. Post 8vo, cloth limp, 2s. 6d.
Leisure-Time Studies, chiefly Biological. Second Edition. Crown 8vo, cloth extra, with Illustrations, 6s.

Winter (J. S.), Stories by:
Cavalry Life. Crown 8vo, cloth extra,. 3s. 6d.
Regimental Legends. Three Vols.,. crown 8vo, 31s. 6d.

Wood.—Sabina: A Novel. By Lady WOOD. Post 8vo, illustrated boards, 2s.

Words, Facts, and Phrases: A Dictionary of Curious, Quaint, and Out-of-the-Way Matters. By ELIEZER EDWARDS. Crown 8vo, half-bound, 12s. 6d.

Wright (Thomas), Works by:
Caricature History of the Georges. (The House of Hanover.) With 400 Pictures, Caricatures, Squibs, Broadsides, Window Pictures, &c. Crown 8vo, cloth extra, 7s. 6d.
History of Caricature and of the Grotesque in Art, Literature, Sculpture, and Painting. Profusely Illustrated by F. W. FAIRHOLT, F.S.A. Large post 8vo, cloth extra, 7s. 6d.

Yates (Edmund), Novels by:
Post 8vo, illustrated boards, 2s. each.
Castaway.
The Forlorn Hope.
Land at Last.

NOVELS.

NEW NOVELS at every Library

Behind a Brass Knocker: Some Grim Realities in Picture and Prose. By FRED BARNARD and C. H. ROSS. Demy 8vo, cloth extra, with 30 full-page Drawings, 10s. 6d.
The Captains' Room, &c. By WALT. BESANT, Author of "All Sorts and Conditions of Men," &c. Three Vols.
Annan Water. By ROBERT BUCHANAN. Three Vols. [*Shortly*.
Heart and Science: A Story of the Present Day. By WILKIE COLLINS. Three Vols.
Port Salvation; or, The Evangelist. By ALPHONSE DAUDET. Translated by C. HARRY MELTZER. Two Vols., post 8vo, 12s.
Circe's Lovers. By J. LEITH DERWENT. Three Vols., cr. 8vo. [*Shortly*.
Of High Degree. By CHARLES GIBBON, Author of "Robin Gray," "The Golden Shaft," &c. Three Vols.
The Golden Shaft. By CHARLES GIBBON. Three Vols.
Fancy-Free. By CHARLES GIBBON. Two Vols., crown 8vo. [*Shortly*.
Dust: A Story. By JULIAN HAWTHORNE, Author of "Garth," "Sebastian Strome," &c. Three Vols.
Self-Condemned. By Mrs. ALFRED HUNT. Three Vols.
Gideon Fleyce. By HENRY W. LUCY. Three Vols.
Val Strange. By D. CHRISTIE MURRAY. Three Vols.
Hearts. By DAVID CHRISTIE MURRAY. Three Vols.
By the Gate of the Sea. By DAVID CHRISTIE MURRAY. Two Vols., post 8vo, 12s. [*Shortly*.
Wanda. By OUIDA. Three Vols., crown 8vo.
Kit: A Memory. By JAMES PAYN. Three Vols.
A New Collection of Stories by CHARLES READE is now in preparation, in Three Vols.
The Hands of Justice. By F. W. ROBINSON. Three Vols.
Women are Strange, &c. By F. W. ROBINSON. Three Vols.
Kept in the Dark. By ANTHONY TROLLOPE. Two Vols. 12s.
Mr. Scarborough's Family. By ANTHONY TROLLOPE. Three Vols.
Regimental Legends. By J. S. WINTER. Three Vols.

THE PICCADILLY NOVELS:
Popular Stories by the Best Authors. LIBRARY EDITIONS, many Illustrated, crown 8vo, cloth extra, 3s. 6d. each.

BY MRS. ALEXANDER.
Maid, Wife, or Widow?

BY W. BESANT & JAMES RICE.
Ready-Money Mortiboy.
My Little Girl.
The Case of Mr. Lucraft.
This Son of Vulcan.
With Harp and Crown.
The Golden Butterfly.
By Celia's Arbour.
The Monks of Thelema.
'Twas in Trafalgar's Bay.
The Seamy Side.
The Ten Years' Tenant.
The Chaplain of the Fleet.

BY WALTER BESANT.
All Sorts and Conditions of Men.

BY ROBERT BUCHANAN.
A Child of Nature.
God and the Man.
The Shadow of the Sword.
The Martyrdom of Madeline.
Love Me for Ever.

BY MRS. H. LOVETT CAMERON.
Deceivers Ever. | Juliet's Guardian.

BY MORTIMER COLLINS.
Sweet Anne Page.
Transmigration.
From Midnight to Midnight.

MORTIMER & FRANCES COLLINS.
Blacksmith and Scholar.
The Village Comedy.
You Play me False.

BY WILKIE COLLINS.
Antonina. | Miss or Mrs?
Basil. | New Magdalen.
Hide and Seek. | The Frozen Deep.
The Dead Secret. | The Law and the
Queen of Hearts. | Lady.
My Miscellanies. | The Two Destinies
Woman in White. | Haunted Hotel.
The Moonstone. | The Fallen Leaves
Man and Wife. | Jezebel's Daughter
Poor Miss Finch. | The Black Robe.

PICCADILLY NOVELS, continued—

BY DUTTON COOK.
Paul Foster's Daughter.

BY WILLIAM CYPLES.
Hearts of Gold.

BY J. LEITH DERWENT
Our Lady of Tears.

BY M. BETHAM-EDWARDS.
Felicia.

BY MRS. ANNIE EDWARDES.
Archie Lovell.

BY R. E. FRANCILLON.
Olympia.
Queen Cophetua.
One by One.

BY EDWARD GARRETT.
The Capel Girls.

BY CHARLES GIBBON.
Robin Gray.
For Lack of Gold.
In Love and War.
What will the World Say?
For the King.
In Honour Bound.
Queen of the Meadow.
In Pastures Green.
The Flower of the Forest.
A Heart's Problem.
The Braes of Yarrow.

BY THOMAS HARDY.
Under the Greenwood Tree.

BY JULIAN HAWTHORNE.
Garth.
Ellice Quentin.
Sebastian Strome.
Prince Saroni's Wife.

BY SIR A. HELPS.
Ivan de Biron.

BY MRS. ALFRED HUNT.
Thornicroft's Model.
The Leaden Casket.

BY JEAN INGELOW.
Fated to be Free.

BY HENRY JAMES, Jun.
Confidence.

BY HARRIETT JAY.
The Queen of Connaught.
The Dark Colleen.

PICCADILLY NOVELS, continued—

BY HENRY KINGSLEY.
Number Seventeen.
Oakshott Castle.

BY E. LYNN LINTON.
Patricia Kemball.
Atonement of Leam Dundas.
The World Well Lost.
Under which Lord?
With a Silken Thread.
The Rebel of the Family.
"My Love!"

BY JUSTIN McCARTHY, M.P.
The Waterdale Neighbours.
My Enemy's Daughter.
Linley Rochford.
A Fair Saxon.
Dear Lady Disdain.
Miss Misanthrope.
Donna Quixote.
The Comet of a Season.

BY GEORGE MACDONALD, LL.D
Paul Faber, Surgeon.
Thomas Wingfold, Curate.

BY KATHARINE S. MACQUOID.
Lost Rose
The Evil Eye.

BY FLORENCE MARRYAT.
Open! Sesame!
Written in Fire.

BY JEAN MIDDLEMASS.
Touch and Go.

BY D. CHRISTIE MURRAY.
A Life's Atonement.
Joseph's Coat.
Coals of Fire.
A Model Father.

BY MRS. OLIPHANT.
Whiteladies.

BY JAMES PAYN.
Lost Sir Massingberd.
Best of Husbands
Fallen Fortunes.
Halves.
Walter's Word.
What He Cost Her
Less Black than
We're Painted.
By Proxy.
High Spirits.
Under One Roof.
Carlyon's Year.
A Confidential Agent.
From Exile.
A Grape from a Thorn.
For Cash Only.

PICCADILLY NOVELS, continued—

BY E. C. PRICE.
Valentina.

BY CHARLES READE, D.C.L.
It is Never Too Late to Mend.
Hard Cash.
Peg Woffington.
Christie Johnstone.
Griffith Gaunt.
The Double Marriage.
Love Me Little, Love Me Long.
Foul Play.
A Simpleton.
The Cloister and the Hearth.
The Course of True Love.
The Autobiography of a Thief.
Put Yourself in His Place.
A Terrible Temptation.
The Wandering Heir.
A Woman-Hater.
Readiana.

BY MRS. J. H. RIDDELL.
Her Mother's Darling.
Prince of Wales's Garden Party.

BY JOHN SAUNDERS.
Bound to the Wheel.
Guy Waterman.
One Against the World.
The Lion in the Path.
The Two Dreamers.

BY T. W. SPEIGHT.
The Mysteries of Heron Dyke.

BY R. A. STERNDALE.
The Afghan Knife.

BY BERTHA THOMAS.
Proud Maisie. | Cressida.
The Violin-Player.

BY ANTHONY TROLLOPE.
The Way we Live Now.
The American Senator.
Frau Frohmann.
Marion Fay.

BY T. A. TROLLOPE.
Diamond Cut Diamond.

BY SARAH TYTLER.
What She Came Through.
The Bride's Pass.

BY J. S. WINTER.
Cavalry Life.

Cheap Editions of POPULAR NOVELS. Post 8vo, illustrated boards, 2s. each. [WILKIE COLLINS'S NOVELS and BESANT and RICE'S NOVELS may also be had in cloth limp at 2s. 6d. See, too, the PICCADILLY NOVELS, for Library Editions.]

BY EDMOND ABOUT.
The Fellah.

BY HAMILTON AÏDÉ.
Carr of Carrlyon.
Confidences.

BY MRS. ALEXANDER.
Maid, Wife, or Widow?

BY SHELSLEY BEAUCHAMP.
Grantley Grange.

BY W. BESANT & JAMES RICE
Ready-Money Mortiboy.
With Harp and Crown.
This Son of Vulcan.
My Little Girl.
The Case of Mr. Lucraft.
The Golden Butterfly.
By Celia's Arbour.
The Monks of Thelema.
'Twas in Trafalgar's Bay.
The Seamy Side.
The Ten Years' Tenant.
The Chaplain of the Fleet.

BY FREDERICK BOYLE.
Camp Notes.
Savage Life.

BY BRET HARTE
An Heiress of Red Dog.
Gabriel Conroy.
The Luck of Roaring Camp.
Flip.

BY ROBERT BUCHANAN.
The Shadow of the Sword.
A Child of Nature.

BY MRS. BURNETT.
Surly Tim.

BY MRS. LOVETT CAMERON.
Deceivers Ever.
Juliet's Guardian.

BY MACLAREN COBBAN.
The Cure of Souls.

BY C. ALLSTON COLLINS.
The Bar Sinister.

POPULAR NOVELS, *continued*—

BY WILKIE COLLINS.
Antonina.
Basil.
Hide and Seek.
The Dead Secret.
Queen of Hearts.
My Miscellanies.
The Woman in White.
The Moonstone.
Man and Wife.
Poor Miss Finch.
Miss or Mrs. ?
The New Magdalen.
The Frozen Deep.
The Law and the Lady.
The Two Destinies.
The Haunted Hotel.
The Fallen Leaves.
Jezebel's Daughter.
The Black Robe.

BY MORTIMER COLLINS.
Sweet Anne Page.
Transmigration.
From Midnight to Midnight.
A Fight with Fortune.

BY MORTIMER AND FRANCES COLLINS.
Sweet and Twenty.
Frances.
Blacksmith and Scholar.
The Village Comedy.
You Play me False.

BY DUTTON COOK.
Leo.
Paul Foster's Daughter.

BY J. LEITH DERWENT.
Our Lady of Tears.

BY CHARLES DICKENS.
Sketches by Boz.
The Pickwick Papers.
Oliver Twist.
Nicholas Nickleby.

BY MRS. ANNIE EDWARDES.
A Point of Honour.
Archie Lovell.

BY M. BETHAM-EDWARDS.
Felicia.

POPULAR NOVELS, *continued*—

BY EDWARD EGGLESTON.
Roxy.

BY PERCY FITZGERALD.
Bella Donna.
Never Forgotten.
The Second Mrs. Tillotson.
Polly.
Seventy-five Brooke Street.

BY ALBANY DE FONBLANQUE.
Filthy Lucre.

BY R. E. FRANCILLON.
Olympia.
Queen Cophetua.
One by One.

BY EDWARD GARRETT.
The Capel Girls.

BY CHARLES GIBBON.
Robin Gray.
For Lack of Gold.
What will the World Say?
In Honour Bound.
The Dead Heart.
In Love and War.
For the King.
Queen of the Meadow.
In Pastures Green.

BY WILLIAM GILBERT.
Dr. Austin's Guests.
The Wizard of the Mountain.
James Duke.

BY JAMES GREENWOOD.
Dick Temple.

BY ANDREW HALLIDAY.
Every-Day Papers.

BY LADY DUFFUS HARDY.
Paul Wynter's Sacrifice.

BY THOMAS HARDY.
Under the Greenwood Tree.

BY JULIAN HAWTHORNE.
Garth.
Ellice Quentin.
Sebastian Strome.

BY SIR ARTHUR HELPS.
Ivan de Biron.

BY TOM HOOD.
A Golden Heart.

POPULAR NOVELS, continued—

BY VICTOR HUGO.
The Hunchback of Notre Dame.

BY MRS. ALFRED HUNT.
Thornicroft's Model.
The Leaden Casket.

BY JEAN INGELOW.
Fated to be Free.

BY HENRY JAMES, Jun.
Confidence.

BY HARRIETT JAY.
The Dark Colleen.
The Queen of Connaught.

BY HENRY KINGSLEY.
Oakshott Castle.
Number Seventeen.

BY E. LYNN LINTON.
Patricia Kemball.
The Atonement of Leam Dundas.
The World Well Lost.
Under which Lord?
With a Silken Thread.
The Rebel of the Family.
"My Love!"

BY JUSTIN McCARTHY, M.P.
Dear Lady Disdain.
The Waterdale Neighbours.
My Enemy's Daughter.
A Fair Saxon.
Linley Rochford.
Miss Misanthrope.
Donna Quixote.

BY GEORGE MACDONALD.
Paul Faber, Surgeon.
Thomas Wingfold, Curate.

BY MRS. MACDONELL.
Quaker Cousins.

BY KATHARINE S. MACQUOID.
The Evil Eye.
Lost Rose.

BY W. H. MALLOCK.
The New Republic.

BY FLORENCE MARRYAT.
Open! Sesame!
A Harvest of Wild Oats.
A Little Stepson.
Fighting the Air.
Written in Fire.

POPULAR NOVELS, continued—

BY JEAN MIDDLEMASS.
Touch and Go.
Mr. Dorillion.

BY D. CHRISTIE MURRAY.
A Life's Atonement.
A Model Father.

BY MRS. OLIPHANT.
Whiteladies.

BY MRS. ROBERT O'REILLY.
Phœbe's Fortunes.

BY OUIDA.
LIBRARY EDITIONS of OUIDA'S NOVELS may be had in crown 8vo, cloth extra, at 5s. each.

Held in Bondage.	Pascarel.
Strathmore.	Two Little Wooden Shoes.
Chandos.	
Under Two Flags.	Signa.
Idalia.	In a Winter City.
Cecil Castlemaine.	Ariadne.
	Friendship.
Tricotrin.	Moths.
Puck.	Pipistrello.
Folle Farine.	A Village Commune.
A Dog of Flanders.	

BY JAMES PAYN.

Lost Sir Massingberd.	Gwendoline's Harvest.
A Perfect Treasure.	Like Father, Like Son.
Bentinck's Tutor.	A Marine Residence.
Murphy's Master.	
A County Family.	Married Beneath Him.
At Her Mercy.	
A Woman's Vengeance.	Mirk Abbey.
	Not Wooed, but Won.
Cecil's Tryst.	£200 Reward.
Clyffards of Clyffe	Less Black than We're Painted.
The Family Scapegrace.	
Foster Brothers.	By Proxy.
Found Dead.	Under One Roof.
Best of Husbands	High Spirits.
Walter's Word.	Carlyon's Year.
Halves.	A Confidential Agent.
Fallen Fortunes.	Some Private Views.
What He Cost Her	
Humorous Stories	From Exile.

BY EDGAR A. POE.
The Mystery of Marie Roget.

BOOKS PUBLISHED BY CHATTO & WINDUS.

POPULAR NOVELS, *continued*—

BY E. C. PRICE.
Valentina.

BY CHARLES READE.
It is Never Too Late to Mend.
Hard Cash.
Peg Woffington.
Christie Johnstone.
Griffith Gaunt.
Put Yourself in His Place.
The Double Marriage.
Love Me Little, Love Me Long.
Foul Play.
The Cloister and the Hearth.
The Course of True Love.
Autobiography of a Thief.
A Terrible Temptation.
The Wandering Heir.
A Simpleton.
A Woman-Hater.
Readiana.

BY MRS. RIDDELL.
Her Mother's Darling.

BY BAYLE ST. JOHN.
A Levantine Family.

BY GEORGE AUGUSTUS SALA.
Gaslight and Daylight.

BY JOHN SAUNDERS.
Bound to the Wheel.
One Against the World.
Guy Waterman.
The Lion in the Path.
The Two Dreamers.

BY ARTHUR SKETCHLEY.
A Match in the Dark.

BY T. W. SPEIGHT.
The Mysteries of Heron Dyke.

BY R. A. STERNDALE.
The Afghan Knife.

BY BERTHA THOMAS.
Cressida.
Proud Maisie.
The Violin-Player.

POPULAR NOVELS, *continued*—

BY WALTER THORNBURY.
Tales for the Marines.

BY T. ADOLPHUS TROLLOPE.
Diamond Cut Diamond.

BY ANTHONY TROLLOPE.
The Way We Live Now.
The American Senator.

BY MARK TWAIN.
Tom Sawyer.
An Idle Excursion.
A Pleasure Trip on the Continent of Europe.

BY SARAH TYTLER.
What She Came Through.

BY LADY WOOD.
Sabina.

BY EDMUND YATES.
Castaway.
The Forlorn Hope.
Land at Last.

ANONYMOUS.
Paul Ferroll.
Why Paul Ferroll Killed his Wife.

Fcap. 8vo, picture covers, 1s. each.

Jeff Briggs's Love Story. By BRET HARTE.
The Twins of Table Mountain. By BRET HARTE.
Mrs. Gainsborough's Diamonds. By JULIAN HAWTHORNE.
Kathleen Mavourneen. By Author of "That Lass o' Lowrie's."
Lindsay's Luck. By the Author of "That Lass o' Lowrie's."
Pretty Polly Pemberton. By the Author of "That Lass o' Lowrie's."
Trooping with Crows. By Mrs. PIRKIS.
The Professor's Wife. By LEONARD GRAHAM.
A Double Bond. By LINDA VILLARI.
Esther's Glove. By R. E. FRANCILLON.
The Garden that Paid the Rent. By TOM JERROLD.

J. OGDEN AND CO., PRINTERS, 172, ST. JOHN STREET, E.C.

www.ingramcontent.com/pod-product-compliance
Lightning Source LLC
Chambersburg PA
CBHW051854300426
44117CB00006B/393